103

527

ATE DUE

LEARNING, LANGUAGE, AND COGNITION

Theory, Research, and Method

for the Study of Human Behavior

and Its Development

LEARNING, LANGUAGE, AND COGNITION

Arthur W. Staats

University of Hawaii

HOLT, RINEHART AND WINSTON, INC.

New York   Chicago   San Francisco   Atlanta
Dallas   Montreal   Toronto   London

To Pavlov and Thorndike

Preface

THIS BOOK is offered as part of my conviction that a great deal of the importance of psychology as a science derives from what it can contribute to an understanding of human behavior in its complex forms and to the solution of the problems of human behavior. This by no means displaces the importance of basic experimental psychology, a realm of investigation that has significance in and of itself. Actually the book includes a new basic learning theory in summary form, as well as basic research and methodology. But I am convinced that the principles and methods of experimental psychology—especially those of the psychology of learning—are also the building blocks from which to construct a general conception of human behavior, a conception that is basic to the various behavioral and social sciences, to the professions that deal with human problems, and to man in general. The task of demonstrating this is one to which I dedicate my efforts, and the present book is a step in that direction.

To accomplish this task I wish to suggest that we need a new learning theory, and a new approach to theory construction in learning. None of the presently constituted classic theories of learning will serve in this capacity. As the present book will attempt to show, an adequate theory of learning for human behavior must abstract, interrelate and elaborate the "heavyweight" empirical principles of learning, cutting across traditional theoretical lines, and then further elaborate the basic principles to show how complex environmental and behavioral events can become functionally related, in specific stimulus-response terms. This basic theory must then be extended to various realms of actual complex human behaviors, in detail—which again means an S–R theory is required. In addition to the theoretical analyses, research must be conducted and procedures derived for actually working with the problems of the various areas of behavior.

I would also suggest that our traditional methods of experimentation in psychology require innovation if we are to begin dealing with significant human behaviors, and to begin developing means for dealing with the problems of human behavior. Our traditional experimental methodology, valuable as it is, nevertheless has harnessed us with restrictions that prevent our entrance into these areas of study.

The present book will elaborate these several suggestions in the context, primarily, of the study of language and intellectual development. I feel that this realm of human behavior is central to all human activity, and a detailed analysis of human behavior must commence here. Moreover, any theory of human behavior which attempts to inspire much confidence must be capable of treating language behavior in detail, providing both an understanding of the acquisition of language and its function, as well as analyses and procedures with which language learning can be produced, maintained, and changed. It should be noted that it is impossible to deal with human learning, even language learning, without consideration of motivation. Thus, the integrated learning theory and the detailed treatment of language herein allows the development of a more complete theory of human motivation. In return, the analysis of human motivation is necessary in developing a comprehensive theory of language learning and function.

The book is intended for general psychology students of learning, human learning, language, symbolic processes or cognition, and the like. And, as a general conception of child development with attendant experimentation, as well as a general strategy for child research, the book is appropriate for use in courses in child psychology. Often, students in these psychology courses will have had a course in learning. However, this is not necessary since the relevant learning principles are described herein, and the book is thus self-contained. I might add that although some of the research presented herein has been published in scientific journals, the principles that form the basis of the research, with few exceptions, are not complicated, and I have attempted to write with simplicity in discussing the principles as well as their extensions. For this reason the book is not intended only for the advanced student.

In addition to the above, the book is intended for students in educational psychology, both for introductory courses and for advanced students. That is, the book could be used to introduce such students to the study of the psychology of learning *within* a context that is of significance to them—and as such could be used as a text in the psychology of learning. The lack of appreciation that many students of education and educational psychology have for the psychology of learning stems largely from the use of books which survey antagonistic learning theories and divergent experimental findings neither of which are anchored in relevant areas of human behavior. Thus, the subject has remained highly academic, abstract, and nonfunctional even when the textbook writer has attempted to make it easy. I would suggest that a more effective strategy is to retain the rigor of the psychology of learning but to deal with matters of importance to the student, that is, to significant human behaviors.

In any event, the author has previously suggested that it is now possible to develop an experimental educational psychology based upon the use of a learning theory of human behavior and the research methods of experimental psychology when elaborated so that they are relevant to complex human learning. The present book will be of interest to the advanced student of educational psychology in demonstrating some of the possibilities for this development and in providing theory and methods with which to advance this development.

I would also suggest that professionals who work with human problems, adult and child—for example, clinical psychologists, child psychologists, psychiatrists, workers in special education, and so on—will find herein an understanding of a central type of human behavior that will prove useful in dealing with many types of problems. Furthermore, the basic learning theory and analyses of complex behavior are presented, and methods are described, that can be used in the treatment of a number of types of human problems and in doing research on these problems. Thus, much of the material is relevant to the area of experimental-clinical psychology (especially behavior modification and behavior therapy).

Finally, I also feel that the present conception will be useful to investigators in the area of anthropology, sociology, and social psychology who are concerned with language and cognition. The present account treats the *function* of language as well as its development. It also deals with the various aspects of language in a more comprehensive manner than has yet been attempted. As such, it provides the basis for dealing with individual, group, and cross-cultural differences in language. As the title indicates, moreover, the Whorfian concern with the relationship of language and cognition is dealt with, and the learning analysis permits specification of the mechanisms involved.

In the past twelve years of work on this learning conception of human behavior I have had the able assistance of a number of individuals—students and colleagues. Thus, although I have formulated the rationale and the experimental methods of each of my works, and have written the publication that ensued, a number of individuals assisted in the conduct of some of the research projects, including some of those to be reported herein. For these contributions I am very grateful. My wife Carolyn helped on a number of my early projects, performing various functions: she was responsible for some of the methods of statistical analysis, she helped in the conduct and supervision of several of the studies and critically read my resulting papers, she contributed material or suggestions to several chapters in my first book, including one co-authored chapter, and she assumed for some years most of the administrative responsibilities connected with the conduct of a research program supported by several governmental agencies. Karl A. Minke, Judson R. Finley, and William G. Heard also helped in the conduct of some of my experiments, in the construction of some of the apparatus, and also assumed general administrative responsibilities in the research projects. Other individuals—Montrose Wolf, Richard E. Schutz, Lloyd O. Brooks, Larry P. Nims, John Mabry, Hugh L. Crawford, J. Grayson Osborne, William Quinn, William Butterfield, Adrian VanMondfrans, Joan Jacobson, Michelle Minnis, and Judith McBurney—contributed to one or more studies. In each case, the help was greatly appreciated as will be noted at appropriate places herein. The agencies supporting this research were the Office of Naval Research and the National Institute of Mental Health through Arizona State University, and the Office of Education through grants at Arizona State University and in the year 1965–1966 at the Research and Development Center for Learning and Re-Education at the University of Wisconsin.

I am indebted in writing the present manuscript to several individuals and institutions. First, Wendell Jeffrey and Dale Harris initially read the manuscript in its original form and their suggestions led to very helpful revisions in several cases, and in general contributed greatly to the final product. I wish also to express appreciation to the institutions with which I was connected during the several years I worked on the manuscript: the University of California at Berkeley, the University of Wisconsin, and presently the University of Hawaii. Mrs. Jan Rabidou, Mrs. Victoria Chang, Mrs. Alice Inada and Miss Linda Chang aided in the final preparation of the manuscript; I am grateful to them for helping smooth this arduous task.

HONOLULU, HAWAII   A. W. S.
NOVEMBER 1967

Contents

LEARNING, LANGUAGE, AND COGNITION

part
1

*Classical
conditioning
and
word meaning*

1

Introduction

In various areas of social and behavioral sciences it is generally conceded that human behavior is largely learned. Anthropologists, sociologists, psychologists, educators, and most individuals systematically interested in complex human behavior, agree that as one goes up the phylogenic scale the experience of the organism assumes more importance in contrast to the behaviors that are laid down by the biological structure of the organism. At the very least, everyone would agree that important aspects of human behavior are learned.

In view of this, one would have to expect that the experimental science of learning in the field of psychology would be a basic science to the social and behavioral sciences. This has not been the case in the past, and the task of bringing this about can only now be begun with confidence. The newness of this opportunity is reflected in the fact that many people in the field of the psychology of learning itself, not to mention other areas of study, are still unaware of the potential of the development. At any rate, the discrepancy between the relevance of and the actual application of the psychology of learning to understanding human behavior calls for some explanation, as well as suggestions for accelerating what, even on face value, should be a very productive approach.

It is illuminating to indicate to some extent why the principles and methods of the psychology of learning have not played a more significant role in the study of actual problems of human learning, as well as in the treatment of these problems. Two major reasons may be cited here. One of them is simply natural to the development of a laboratory science. In order to establish the basic principles of learning, that is, the way that the environment (experience) affects the individual's behavior, it is the strategy of a laboratory science to artificially simplify the events with which it deals. Thus, the laboratory investigator of learning does not in the beginning take a sample of the complex environments seen in everyday life. He takes a very simple sample of the environment, a simple stimulus that he can readily observe and manipulate. Nor does the laboratory investigator in the beginning take a sample of complex human behavior. Rather, he deals with a simple sample that can be objectively observed. Furthermore, he cannot when looking for the basic principles deal with an organism that has such a complex history that it would be impossible to tell if the experimental manipulation of the simple stimulus had any systematic effect on even a simple response. So, laboratory research was at first also restricted to work with simple organisms. Since these samples in their simplicity will differ a great deal from the complex events that occur in everyday life, basic study will appear to have little value in understanding the practical problems of human behavior.

However, in looking at the progress of the experimental science of learning we can now select from among the various findings and chart a course of progress. That is, it may be suggested that the first step was to discover the basic principles using simple samples of the environment: a light, a bell, or the like; simple samples of behavior; salivation, a bar press, and the like; and simple samples of living organisms; rats, dogs, pigeons, and the like. Later, after discovery of the basic principles, the principles and methods could then be applied to humans and more representative samples of environmental events as well as more representative samples of behavior.

In following this interpretation, it is suggested that one of the main lines of development of the field of learning theory must be devoted to the experimental and theoretical analysis of complex human behavior, as well as to the creation of findings with which to deal with actual human problems. It is suggested that perhaps the central feature of the development of a learning theory will be the incorporation of more and more aspects of human behavior within the framework of the principles from one learning theory. This has not been self-consciously seen as a major line of progress of the science by its most influential members—which is another reason why the principles and methods of learning have not had a greater impact upon the social and behavioral sciences.

Theory in the new science of learning has been restricted primarily to gaining the appearance and general character of the physical sciences in the statement of its principles—and thus largely restricted to the findings of the basic laboratory. The prestige of this type of theory has been enhanced to the degree to which it resembled these sciences in the use of mathematics and formal logical methods. It would not be remiss to suggest that research and theory that concerned actual human problems was accorded much less status.

In following this path, the psychology of learning, as well as psychology in general, became very separatistic. A major part of the field was broken into warring factions that proceeded to develop separate research procedures, separate philosophies of science, and separate terminologies (theories). For a long time the matters of greatest importance in the field involved the contests between the major approaches. This still continues. Thus, in the field of language learning there have been very distinct and very separate approaches. Individuals concerned with the learning of word meaning have largely not concerned themselves with the principle of reinforcement (reward) as it pertains to the learning of speech, and the converse is largely true. As another example, the large number of investigators interested in the learning of word associations and other verbal learning experiments have been largely ignored by the other two, and vice versa.

Thus, although the restriction of the psychology of learning to simple behaviors, simple situations, and simple organisms, was a part of the growth of the science, the separatism that has been described in the field, at least as the field pertains to human behavior, can now be seen as an anachronistic obstacle to the creation of a general theory of human behavior. And, this obstacle has had serious disadvantages. For one thing, the separatistic approaches to learning have individually been inadequate to deal with complex human behavior. In the field of language learning, for example, the isolated and fragmented approaches have been open to criticism (Chomsky, 1959; Miller, 1965; Weinreich, 1958) because each by itself is unable to handle the scope of this aspect of human behavior.

Furthermore, the various approaches and controversies in the field of learning have presented a picture of confusion to the scholars of other fields who were interested in human behavior. Thus, we find that educational psychologists, clinical psychologists, child and social psychologists, as well as sociologists, anthropologists, and other behavioral scientists, when they have attempted to organize the field of learning to focus on the problems in their area of study, have found the field to be of relatively little use. Either they have accepted one or the other approach to learning and found the approach inadequate, or they have used a potpourri of the various learning theories and their findings. Such a survey is academic in the pejorative sense of the word, is difficult to understand, even in its own context, and has little to offer to an understanding of human behavior.

It is suggested, however, that learning in its role as a theory of human behavior has to be approached differently. The field has a great deal to offer as a general conception, but not as a tangle of competing theories, or through the study of single areas of the field, or indeed by summarizing the various experimental findings and theories in the field.

To serve as a theory of human behavior it is necessary to abstract the major empirical principles of learning from the confusion of the experimental and theoretical controversies. These must be the heavyweight, important, basic, principles of learning. In many areas the major research has gone past the major principles to deal with details that cannot readily be applied to human behavior. Inclusion of all the minor findings and controversies has yielded a body of principles too cumbersome to apply to more complex realms of events. In selecting the major principles it is necessary to cut across theoretical lines, thus producing a set of principles that are interpreted within one set of theoretical terms.

In addition, traditional learning theories were not constructed to serve as a basic conception for complex human behavior—but rather to systematize the results of the animal laboratory. There are basic principles, however, that do not readily emerge from animal research but which are important in human circumstances and activities. As one example, the *interactions* between the major principles of learning have been largely overlooked. Thus, the development of even the basic learning theory must be guided by the goal: that of providing a learning conception of human behavior.

In addition to the major principles, it is necessary to outline the ways that the principles can combine to produce complex interactions of environmental events (stimuli) and behaviors (responses). Thus, although single responses may be studied in the laboratory, and the principles thus derived corroborated with humans, we are rarely interested in single responses when we are concerned with human problems. Although the basic principles of learning may be the same from animals to man, human learning is fantastically complex. For example, we must be concerned with how many, many, S–R (stimulus–response) processes are acquired if we are interested in cognitive learning. Furthermore, rather than single responses, human behavior may involve complex sequences of responses. And one stimulus can come in the child's experience to elicit many different responses, depending upon other conditions. Conversely, many different stimuli may affect the occurrence of a single response. In addition, different types of responses may be intertwined—in fact most important human behaviors are of this type. That is, as an example, environmental stimuli may first elicit verbal responses in the individual, and these responses may in turn elicit emotional responses, and the emotional responses will in turn determine what the individual actually does. Again, although the principles may be simple, learning occurs at each level, with each type of response, and the overall acquisition of the behavior may be exceedingly complex.

Thus, in summary, a very important aspect of a learning theory of human behavior must involve the selection, integration, and derivation of a comprehensive set of heavyweight learning principles from among the confusing mass of experimental findings and theoretical controversies that are presently available, as well as from naturalistic observations and concepts. These principles must then be elaborated to show how various *combinations* of stimulus and response events can occur, including motor, emotional, and verbal responses.

Furthermore, it is necessary to take the principles and methods of this integrated learning theory and to begin to study various human behaviors and to actually deal with those behaviors. Although at the beginning it was necessary to sample simple behaviors and situations, ultimately it is necessary to conduct research with human beings involved in learning complex behaviors, or behaviors that are more unique to man. The full status of the field of learning as a science will come when its principles and methods have been shown to be relevant for the consideration of various aspects of complex human behavior.

This brief statement is a summary of the present approach which will be elaborated by the contents of the book. The author has called the approach an *integrated-functional learning theory* of complex human behavior (Staats, 1966), to characterize the two main themes of (1) abstracting, interrelating, and deriving the heavyweight learning principles, and (2) extending the principles and results to *functional* human behaviors significant to individual and group adjustment. The author has presented his position as it applies to *various* areas of human behavior on a more general level (Staats, 1964a, 1966; Staats and Staats, 1963).

It is suggested that this approach produces a conception of man's behavior that is central to the various social and behavioral sciences— as well as the various areas of psychology. In the present case, for example, it is suggested that linguists and psycholinguists who are concerned with language acquisition and the language-cognition relationship will find the theory, methods, and findings to be relevant to their interests. As the title indicates, a central theme of the book is that language learning underlies, or *is*, much of what we consider to be man's intellectual or cognitive nature, including the differences we see among individuals and cultural groups.

The present book will include findings from over a decade of the author's experimental, theoretical, and methodological research in the area of learning, language and cognition—and will thereby characterize and extend the learning theory as well as the understanding of human behavior.

It should be noted that the basic learning theory and the theory construction philosophy, as well as the analyses of various aspects of human behavior are intended to be applicable to additional areas and types of human behavior. The term integrated was selected to characterize the approach in part because it is felt that areas in psychology ordinarily considered as diverse can be unified through the use of the learning theory. This is demonstrated herein largely within the area of focal concern— language—in dealing with topics as diverse as word meaning, communication, concept learning, propaganda, imagery, linguistic relativity, grammatical speech, originality, language as theory, as well as reading acquisition and function, writing, and number concept learning. The latter topics, usually assigned to applied psychology, are dealt with not only because of the intrinsic importance of these cognitive repertoires but also to illustrate the need for development of the *functional* aspect of learning theory within the scientific concerns of the field.

The unified nature of human behavior, and thus the need for a unified theoretical foundation, is also shown in the present book by treatment of such nonlanguage topics as human motivation, imitation, and child development (especially cognitive development). Full conceptions in these areas are presented. The major point here is that the divisions we have had in the study of human behavior are artificial and have prevented us from gaining a general theory—a topic that will be exemplified and discussed further on.

Although other learning approaches to aspects of language have been presented previously, some of which are in the background of the present book, no general learning theory of language has been offered, nor one that includes extensive research support. The present effort attempts to combine both experimental and naturalistic observations in producing a comprehensive learning theory.

The book will examine and develop major learning principles as they relate to language learning. Classical conditioning and instrumental (or operant) conditioning principles are considered to be the basic laws. Since the purpose of the book is to present a learning theory of language, the principles of learning themselves will not be treated extensively, although a basic learning theory is included. Thus, the subprinciples— for example, extinction, stimulus generalization, and the like—will be omitted or only briefly mentioned. The author has made a more complete treatment of learning principles (Staats and Staats, 1963). However, the present account covers additional progress in developing the basic principles as well as their interrelations and extensions—including a new terminological convention for the description of the basic principles and S–R processes (see also Staats, 1966).

The first part of the book will be concerned with elaborating the importance of the principle of classical conditioning in understanding an important type of word meaning. The second part of the book will involve an explication of the principles of instrumental conditioning in the learning of vocal behavior and its function. The third part will describe the ways that classical and instrumental conditioning interact in human learning. This part will indicate also the pluralistic nature of the conception, as well as describe some of the complex stimulus-response mechanisms acquired on the basis of the principles.

The fourth part of the book will indicate how a learning theory of language can be extended into considerations of functional language repertoires; preliminary analyses will be given of writing and number concept learning, as well as of reading acquisition. Laboratory research will be presented that tests the main principles of the three cognitive analyses and research methods will be described with which to study complex cognitive learning and problems of learning. Part 5 then presents a theory of child development, especially in cognition, and a detailed analysis of reading as an important aspect of cognition. In Part 6 the implications of the integrated-functional learning theory for further research are summarized, and in a final chapter the implications of the research as a general method are discussed and the present approach to psychological theory construction is outlined in general terms.

2

Classical conditioning and emotional (attitudinal) word meaning

There are apparently many environmental events (stimuli) that when presented will elicit a response in the normal human. That is, when one of these stimuli occurs it will be followed by the particular response it customarily elicits. There are a number of responses lawfully related in this way to the presentation of stimuli. Loud sounds, tactual stimuli, electric shock, food, visual stimuli, and so on will elicit various responses. Many of the responses involved are ones that would ordinarily be called reflexes; various internal responses such as changes in the flow of gastric juices, the rate of the heart beat, the blood volume in various internal organs, the adjustment in size of the pupil, the activity of the sweat glands, and the like. Some motor responses are also elicited in this manner, for example, the blink of the eye to corneal stimulation, the knee-jerk to stimulation of the patellar tendon, and so on.

When first observed this type of finding was quite momentous. The demonstration that responses of organisms resulted from external stimulation began to indicate that at least certain aspects of behavior occurred according to natural forces. Prior to demonstrations that responses could be lawfully caused, the prevailing belief was that behavior was a function of internal, supernatural, and unknowable forces.

The power of the demonstration that some responses are a result of the preceding presentation of a stimulus was very considerably extended

10

by the findings of Pavlov. He demonstrated that stimuli that did not have the power to elicit a particular response, as did other stimuli, could gain that power. That is, a stimulus that does not elicit a response can come to do so if it is paired with a stimulus that does elicit that response. As one example, food powder in the mouth is a stimulus that reliably elicits the response of the salivary gland, resulting in the rapid excretion of saliva into the mouth. If a stimulus that does not elicit this response is paired with the food powder, this stimulus will after a number of pairings also come to elicit the response. This process is depicted in Figure 2.1.

The stimulus that originally elicits the response is called the unconditioned stimulus. This type of stimulus will be indicated in the notation system by ^{uc}S. In the example, this stimulus is the food powder. The stimulus that does not at first elicit the response but will come to do so if it is paired with the unconditioned stimulus is to be called the ^cS. The response will be abbreviated by R. It should be pointed out that not all of the total response (or responses) elicited by the ^{uc}S will ordinarily be conditioned to the ^cS. Thus, a food stimulus elicits movements of the tongue, lips, and jaws, which may not be stably conditioned to the ^cS, although part of the total response, the salivary response, may be.

FIGURE 2.1.   Classical conditioning (first order).

One further point should be added here. If, after the conditioning, the ^cS is presented many times by itself, without the ^{uc}S being presented also, the response to the ^cS will begin to weaken. This process is called extinction. Thus pairing the ^{uc}S with the ^cS will condition the response to the ^cS, but presentations of the ^cS by itself a number of times will result in extinction of the response. It should be indicated, however, that the response to the ^cS can be maintained if it is only intermittently paired with the ^{uc}S, and conditioning can also in this way become very resistant to extinction. Furthermore, responses can be so strongly conditioned in real life, with intermittent conditioning trials continuing to occur, so that to all intents and purposes, the conditioning is permanent—and the ^cS

can continue to be presented by itself many times and still elicit the response.

The discovery of the principle of classical conditioning suggested that behavior is even more affected by the environment than had been previously thought. Not only are behaviors caused by the occurrence of environmental events, but environmental events that were formerly ineffective could acquire the power to also elicit responses. This suggested that perhaps broad aspects of human behavior were so acquired. There were early attempts to interpret human behavior in general in terms of these conditioning principles (Watson, 1924). Although such attempts contained some truth, they were far from presenting a complete conception of human behavior. Some of the important principles of learning were not yet clearly known, nor was there abundant experimental evidence to indicate how the principles applied to human behavior. Thus, early learning accounts of human behavior were less than convincing.

Derivations from the Theory

The principle of classical conditioning cannot serve as a theory with which to consider complex human behavior in general. However, there are certain aspects of human behavior that do appear to be acquired according to the principle. For example, Watson and Rayner (1920) showed very early that a child can acquire an emotional response to an object according to the principle. In providing this demonstration of the relevance of the principle for human behavior, they used an infant as the subject, presenting a white rabbit as the ^cS and a loud noise as the ^{uc}S. The noise elicited a crying response as well as escape responses of various kinds. After pairing the two stimuli several times, the child came to make the responses to the white rabbit by itself. Formerly, the child had responded positively to the animal.

Although this was not explicated in this early study, this experimental test may be seen as a theoretical extension of the basic learning principle. That is, an important aspect of any set of higher-level principles (a theory) is the derivation of lower-level hypotheses or empirical propositions. A theoretical principle is general and important to the extent that lower-level hypotheses can be derived from it that refer to many different observable events.

In the present case, the higher-level theoretical principle used was that of classical conditioning. The principle had been found in experimentation with dogs. In the study of Watson and Rayner, a derivation was made from the principle. The derivation may be described as follows. Emotions are responses. As such they should follow the principle of classical conditioning. If an emotion inducing stimulus (^{U}CS) is paired with a neutral stimulus (^{C}S), the neutral stimulus will come to elicit the emotional response. The specific experimental hypothesis, of course, was that the rabbit as a stimulus, when paired with the loud noise, would come to elicit the fear response—which occurred.

This description of the experiment in terms of its significance for psychological theory is summarized here because it illustrates the general strategy to be followed throughout. The various learning principles to be presented may be considered to constitute the set of higher-level theoretical principles, that is, the basic theory. These principles will be extended to the consideration of various aspects of behavior and in many cases experimental hypotheses will be derived from the extensions and tested. The first type of language learning to be considered in terms of the principle of classical conditioning will be that of affective or emotional word meaning.

PRIMARY CLASSICAL CONDITIONING OF EMOTIONAL WORD MEANING

An important type of response to stimuli consists of what would be described in common sense terms as emotional. The effects of emotional responding upon other behaviors of the individual will not be mentioned at this point. It will suffice to say that stimuli that we ordinarily think of as inducing positive emotions elicit certain internal physiological responses. Stimuli that we consider to induce negative emotions elicit certain internal physiological responses also. Furthermore, we may also state loosely at this point that positive emotional stimuli are ones we ordinarily approach, and negative emotional stimuli are ones that we escape and avoid.

In the present context it is important to indicate that language stimuli occur contiguously with emotion-causing stimuli in our learning experiences, and this gives certain important properties to language. That is, in our language-learning experience, certain words are systematically paired with a particular emotional stimuli. Even on the basis of naturalistic circumstances we can see that words like *joy, happy, play, dinner, pretty, sweet, good,* and the like are systematically paired with certain types of "emotional" stimuli. On the other hand, words like *angry, hurt, dirty, awful, sick, sad, ugly,* and the like, are systematically paired with other types of "emotional" stimuli.

Using the theoretical principle that has been introduced so far, and these naturalistic observations, we should be able to explain certain aspects of the effects of language. Emotional stimuli may be considered to be ^{U}CS that elicit emotional responses. If a word stimulus is systematically paired with such a ^{U}CS, the word should become a ^{C}S and also elicit the emotional responses. This is the lower-order theoretical principle that this chapter will be concerned with; empirical hypotheses will be derived from this lower-order principle which can be experimentally tested.

Experimental-Naturalistic Research

An immediate empirical derivation from this analysis is that one could establish word meaning by manipulating classical conditioning procedures. The author first explored this possibility in informal conditions presented in a usual life situation. However, the procedures which were used were systematically derived and applied. The organism used was a cat named Max, accessible as a family cat. The informal research was conducted in 1953 while the author was still a graduate student and was part of his early work in extending learning principles to a consideration of the ways that actual behaviors are acquired.

The conditioning process was introduced as part of the animal's toilet training, a necessary feature of every well-bred cat's experience. One time-honored strategy is to catch the animal in the undesirable act and to apply a mildly aversive stimulus. In this case a spanking with a rolled-up piece of newspaper was used and this was followed by ejection from the premises.

Since this type of training was necessary, with the opportunity for many training trials, it was available as the unconditioned stimulus for testing the experimental hypothesis. The only thing still necessary was to present the word to be used as the conditioned stimulus each time that Max was "stimulated" with the paper roll.

The "spanking stimulus" would be expected to elicit internal responses of various kinds in addition to the observable escape responses made by Max. The word NO was paired with the ^{U}CS and would be expected to become a ^{C}S and elicit at least part of those responses. And that is what occurred. After a number of these trials Max very reliably responded appropriately to the word NO. If she began to claw the sofa, for example, it was only necessary to say the word NO and she would stop what she was doing and scamper a few feet away from the spot. If she jumped on the kitchen table it was only necessary to say NO and she would jump off. This was very efficacious to both Max and to the author as well —for control of Max's behavior no longer required leaving one's chair. (Of course, reconditioning training was necessary from time to time.)

In common sense terms it would be said that Max had learned the meaning of the word. If cats were able to talk as we do, Max would undoubtedly have said that the word NO had an unpleasant meaning, that she did not like the word and so on. This type of "awareness" is not available to cats, however, but she did give adequate indication by her overt behavior of the effect of the conditioning. The learning of this type of word meaning is schematized in Figure 2.2. The unconditioned stimulus is the spanking, the conditioned stimulus is the word NO. The emotional and escape responses elicited by the spanking become conditioned to the word.

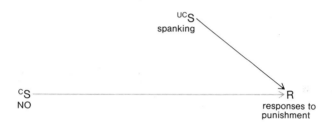

FIGURE 2.2.   Classically conditioning an emotional response to the word "No."

The experimental hypothesis that a response could be classically conditioned to the word NO in this procedure was tested with three additional animals at a later time. That is, when Max reached adulthood she had two kittens, and they served as subjects in two replication experiments. Even later on the author became the owner of a beagle pup and she was also given the same type of language training. In each case the results were the same. It was possible to classically condition the animals to respond meaningfully to the word NO.

While the hypothesis and the theory from which it derived held up very well in this experimental-naturalistic type of study, most journals will not publish this type of evidence. It was thus desirable to extend the results to an assessment of the hypothesis in a more formal manner. Furthermore, the research had been conducted with lower organisms and the next step was to verify the findings with human subjects.

The experiment to be summarized is very analogous to the exploratory experiment with Max, with the addition that one of the physiological responses elicited by the ^{uc}S was recorded. Furthermore, since human subjects were used it was also possible to have them indicate verbally how they felt about the ^{c}S word.

First-Order Conditioning of Meaning and the
Parallel Conditioning of a GSR

One of the ways of making the results with the animals more formal would have consisted of having some means of measuring some of the internal, "emotional," responses that should have been conditioned. It is not difficult to select such a response that is observable and can be classically conditioned. For the present study the response of the sweat glands in the palm of the hands (called the galvanic skin response, or GSR) was selected to assess the possibility that with human subjects emotional responses may be conditioned to words.

However, an indication that the GSR had been conditioned to a word would be only part of the test of the classical conditioning theory of word meaning. An equally important aspect of the preliminary study with Max was that the word came to control appropriate, meaningful, behavior of the animal. In the present study, in addition to the measurement of conditioned "emotional" responses, the possibility was tested that the process of classical conditioning would produce effects in the subject that were more obviously what we refer to as word meaning.

That is, it has been found that word meaning may be reliably judged by individuals using seven-point rating scales. Using factor analytic methods Osgood and associates (Osgood, *et al.*, 1957; Triandis and Osgood, 1958) have shown that what is called evaluative or emotional meaning is a widespread type of word meaning both in terms of the number of words with such meaning as well as in the fact that this type of word meaning occurs similarly in different language cultures. Moreover, inspection of words that are strong in evaluative meaning lends support to the conditioning analysis. That is, words that have positive evaluative meaning (for example, *good, beautiful, sweet, tasty, fragrant, dinner, happy, dollar, swim,* and the like) customarily occur when "positive" types of environmental events are present. On the other hand, words that have negative evaluative meaning (like *ugly, sour, dirty, awful, foul, sick, pain, cry, hurt,* and so on) are more customarily paired with aversive stimulus events. An example of a seven-point scale for the measurement of word meaning may be given by the following.

SUFFER
pleasant:__:__:__:__:__:__:__:unpleasant

Subjects in English-speaking countries would rate this word as having a negative or unpleasant meaning. It may be suggested that this would occur because in our language community the word is paired with stimuli that produce negative emotional responses and these responses are conditioned to the word.

At any rate, following the theory, pairing aversive stimuli with a word should condition a negative emotional (physiological) meaning response to the word. In addition, as a result of the same conditioning process, the meaning of the word should move toward the negative evaluative pole of an appropriate rating scale. These were the experimental hypotheses tested in the present study to more fully validate the author's analysis.

The study was published (first in technical report form in 1958) with Carolyn K. Staats, who aided in the construction of the experimental apparatus and selected the method of statistical analysis of the data, and with Hugh L. Crawford, who ran the subjects and tabulated and analyzed the data.[1]

Method

SUBJECTS The Ss were 47 students from introductory psychology courses at Arizona State University, randomly selected and assigned to one of two groups. Participation in an experiment was a course requirement.

APPARATUS Galvanic measures were made from a modified Stoelting psychogalvanoscope in conjunction with a Varian G-10 recorder. Verbal stimulus materials were presented to the Ss orally by E. The two ^{uc}S were a loud raucous noise delivered through an earphone and an electric shock delivered to the right forearm. The shock source was a Grass stimulator and the shock level was adjusted for each S so that it was "uncomfortable" but not "painful"—this was also done for the sound.

The verbal stimuli were *radio, these, chair, lake, box, large, five, paper, in, glass, book, key, sofa, cup, car, up, pen, with, room, big, cord, clock, twelve, letter, fork.* The word used as the ^cS was *large.* The verbal stimuli were arranged in a series of 77 words. The ^cS was presented 14 times, the others varying numbers of times. The occurrence of the ^cS-word in the list was randomized.

[1] For the complete study, see Arthur W. Staats, Carolyn K. Staats, and Hugh L. Crawford. First-order conditioning of meaning and the parallel conditioning of a GSR. *J. gen Psychol.*, 1962, **67**, 159–167.

PROCEDURE   The general procedure followed Mednick (1957). Ss in both groups received the same conditioning procedure. The experiment was conducted in a virtually soundproof room. Each S was seated in a comfortable chair. The apparatus for recording the GSR was located in an outside room. The S was instructed that the experiment concerned the effect of shock and noise as distractors in a learning task. The level of shock to be used was then adjusted. The S was told he should learn as many of the words in the series as possible. A short period of relaxation followed these instructions and then the conditioning procedure commenced.

For the experimental group, one of the ^{uc}S followed the ^cS (the interval was approximately 1 second) on nine of the 14 occasions it was presented. Of the nine trials five used shock as ^{uc}S, four used sound. This was done to prevent adaptation to the stimuli. For the control group, the ^{uc}S were presented nine times, each time after one of the filler words. For this group, the word *large* never immediately preceded or followed a filler word which was paired with the ^{uc}S. For both groups the order of the word was the same. The time between presentation of words varied from 8 to 12 seconds in order to allow time for return of the S's response to basal level.

Following the presentation of the list, the electrodes and earphones were removed. The S was then told that the way people learn words may be affected by the way they feel about the words. For this reason it was necessary to find out how he felt about some of the words he had just attempted to learn. Instructions were given on rating the evaluative meaning of words using a semantic differential scale of *pleasant–unpleasant*. Each S was given a small booklet with a word on each page and the seven-point *pleasant–unpleasant* scale beneath it. The six words used were listed in the following order: *chair, large, loyal, room, big,* and *tie*. The S scored the meaning of each word and indicated whether or not each of the words was one of those just presented in the learning task.

Results

Using the method suggested by Lacey and Siegel (1949) raw ohms resistance data were transformed into conductance units, micromhos (M), by use of the formula $M = 10^6 \, (1/r)$ [1].

For each S, the GSR elicited by one of the neutral words (*with*)—a word which had never been preceded or followed by the noxious stimuli—was subtracted from the GSR elicited by the last presentation of the word *large*. The difference score was obtained to control for individual differences in responsivity. This procedure resulted in difference scores for both the experimental and control groups. These difference scores were essentially normal in distribution. Two *t*s were computed. The mean of the difference scores (*large* minus *with*) for the E group exceeded that for the C group ($t = 3.67$, significant at the .01 level).

A comparable analysis was conducted on the semantic differential data. For each S the combined mean of the scores for the neutral words included in the test booklet was calculated, i.e., the mean for the scores of *chair, loyal, room,* and *tie.* For each S, this mean was subtracted from the semantic differential score of *large.* This procedure controlled for individual tendencies to mark words "pleasant" or "unpleasant." Groups E and C were compared on the differences. The difference between the groups on the *large* minus the neutral words was significant at the .0005 level ($t = 10.15$) with the word *large* scored more unpleasant in meaning for the E group.

Of the 28 Ss in Group E, 21 were aware that *large* was often followed by noxious stimuli, but only two of these saw any connection between this and the semantic differential measurement of the words.

An additional analysis was conducted to test a possible relationship between the intensity of the conditioned meaning response and the intensity of the conditioned GSR. Since individual variation in GSR level and in meaning response level could obfuscate any real relationship, the difference scores already explained were used. The GSR difference scores (*large* minus *with*) were correlated with evaluative meaning difference scores (*large* minus the neutral words). The Pearson *r* on the 28 pairs of scores was .39, which is significant at the .05 level. Thus, there was a significant tendency for Ss with more extreme conditioned GSR scores to the word *large* also to display more intensive negative evaluative meaning scores for the word.

Discussion

Thus, when subjects had the experience in which a word was systematically paired with aversive environmental stimuli, the word gained a negative evaluative meaning as measured by the two indices used in the present study. That is, the word came to elicit one of the easily measurable emotional responses elicited by the aversive stimuli, the galvanic skin response, and the subjects later on also rated the word as having an unpleasant affective meaning. These results substantiated the theory that a word may gain its meaning according to the principles of classical conditioning. The manner in which this process of conditioning word meaning may be thought to have taken place, and the processes involved in the conditioning, are schematized in Figure 2.3.

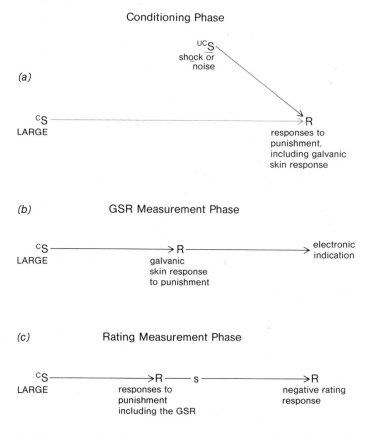

FIGURE 2.3. (*a*) The classical conditioning of the GSR to the word; (*b*) the measurement of the GSR conditioning through presentation of the word; (c) presentation of the ^cS elicits the conditioned emotional response which in turn mediates the "unpleasant" rating of the word.

The top part of the figure shows that the unconditioned stimuli of shock or the loud noise each elicited a total response. This total response included the GSR, but it must also be concluded that many other internal responses also occurred, for example, a change in heart rate, changes in circulatory responses, glandular responses, and also responses in the central nervous system. As a consequence of the systematic pairing of the word and the unconditioned stimuli, the word should come to elicit some of the components of this total emotional response. This possibility is later tested in the GSR measurement part of the figure by presenting the word without the ^{UC}S to see if the word by itself would now elicit the GSR. As the results showed, the GSR response was conditioned to the word, as was expected.

In addition, the subjects were asked to rate the meaning of the word and it was found that the subjects who had been conditioned rated the meaning of *large* as unpleasant. This may be conceptualized as follows. The total response elicited by the ^{UC}S (or at least parts of it) was conditioned to the word. When the word was presented in the rating procedure, the word elicited those conditioned emotional responses. These responses elicited by the word then resulted in (mediated) the negative affective rating of the word. That is, the word elicited the emotional responses, and these responses then elicited the rating response.

The fact that the intensity of the rating of the meaning of the word and the magnitude of the galvanic skin response, were significantly related gives further support to the analysis. That is, this finding suggests that the two indices were part of the same process. The more strongly the individual subject was conditioned to make an emotional physiological response to the word the more strongly he felt about and rated the meaning of the word.

These findings may be considered to be very well verified. That is, very recently this entire experiment has been replicated by Maltzman, *et al.* (1965). Using the same type of experimental setup they obtained the same findings in every respect. Emotional meaning (GSR) and rated meanings were conditioned to the word. Moreover, the stronger the conditioning, which was manipulated by varying the intensity of the aversive ^{UC}S, the stronger was the GSR conditioning as well as the word meaning conditioning.

At this point it would seem appropriate to suggest some of the implications of the classical conditioning analysis of word meaning and its empirical verification. First, it may be suggested the analysis and results explain the emotional effects of language. That is, it may be commonly observed that an individual may be told something and respond with the same emotion as he would if the actual events themselves had occurred. As an example, an individual told by a physician that he has cancer will customarily respond emotionally as he would to the consequences of the disease—whether or not he actually is ill. Many such examples can be given, involving both the elicitation of positive as well as negative emotional meaning responses. These naturalistic observations can be accounted for by the higher-level principle of classical conditioning and the derived principles of the learning of word meaning.

Furthermore, the analysis may be extended to the more specific consideration of an important aspect of language learning in children. This analysis yields directives concerning how to arrange training circumstances if we wish the child to respond appropriately to language. That is, it is important for the child's adjustment that words come to control his behavior in certain ways. For example, it is important that the word *no* elicit avoidance responses, if the child is to respond appropriately in many situations. We want the words *hurt, dangerous, awful, bad,* and others to elicit certain negative emotional responses. And we want words like *home, country, family, good, kind, joy,* and many others to elicit positive emotional responses. Although the manner in which these aspects of language are acquired cannot be fully accounted for on the basis of the analysis given so far, it may be suggested that at a very basic level some words in our language must be paired with positive stimuli and others with aversive stimuli in the language training of the child. Without this training it would be expected that the child would not be able to profit as expected from language interactions with other people, or in fact from his own language behaviors. More will be said of these matters later on.

Summary

A GSR was conditioned to the word *large* by pairing the word with aversive ^{UC}S in a classical conditioning procedure. Subsequent to this conditioning procedure, the evaluative meaning of *large* was measured using an appropriate semantic measurement scale. Negative evaluative meaning had also been conditioned to *large* by the procedure. It was found, in addition, that the intensity of the conditioned GSR was significantly correlated with the intensity of the conditioned meaning response. The results support the theory that emotional word meaning consists of responses that are classically conditioned to a word through the systematic pairing of the word with particular aspects of the environment in the natural language experience we receive.

LANGUAGE CONDITIONING OF MEANING
FROM WORD TO WORD

It has been suggested that an important understanding of behavior was gained by the demonstration that certain environmental stimuli could lawfully elicit responses in various organisms. The implications of this finding were markedly extended in generality and importance when Pavlov found that the ability of a stimulus to elicit a response could be *acquired.* Another basic principle of learning, which is one of the higher-level principles in the theory, is called higher-order classical conditioning. This principle, which is also based upon laboratory experimentation, states that a stimulus not only acquires the power to elicit a response, but once having done so the stimulus can then "pass" the response on to yet a new stimulus. Thus, a third stimulus can come to elicit a response without ever having to be paired with the original environmental stimulus that elicits the response.

Let us refer for the moment back to Figure 2.1. This illustrated what is called first-order classical conditioning. A stimulus, the bell, which does not elicit the salivary response is paired with the food powder, which does elicit the response. After a sufficient number of pairings, the bell also comes to elicit the response. Thus, the bell has acquired the power of eliciting the response.

In addition, however, if the bell is now paired with another stimulus that does not elicit the response, the new stimulus also will come to do so. Let us say that a light would be turned on in front of the dog and this stimulus was shortly followed by the ringing of the bell. After a few trials of the pairing of these two stimuli the light stimulus would now come to elicit the salivary response by itself—without the bell being presented. Thus, the power to elicit the response, which had been acquired by the bell stimulus, would also be transferred to any other stimulus with which the bell was paired. This process is schematized in Figure 2.4. In this procedure the bell is now used as the unconditioned stimulus, that is, it is the stimulus that reliably elicits the response. The light is the ^{c}S. When the two stimuli are paired, the light comes to elicit the conditioned salivary response.

FIGURE 2.4. Higher-order classical conditioning. The bell was itself a ^{c}S in an earlier process (see Figure 2.1).

This process would be called second-order conditioning, a form of higher-order conditioning. If the light was paired with a new stimulus and further conditioning occurred, this would be a case of third-order conditioning, and so on. Each case after the first-order conditioning is a case of higher-order conditioning. It is difficult in the laboratory to get very high orders of conditioning when working with physiological responses, although Zimmerman (1957) has shown that some characteristics of conditioned stimuli may be stably established. At any rate, in actual life where the number of conditioning trials may be very large, with intermittent pairing of the ^cS and ^{uc}S, higher-order conditioning of great magnitude appears to be possible. It is also the case that first-order conditioning can continue to take place from time to time in the everyday situation and so maintain the strength of the ^cS.

Now, the major principle of classical conditioning was tested in the context of language learning with both animal and human subjects and was found to be relevant. That is, it appeared that word meaning could be acquired according to the principles of classical conditioning. This verification of the major principle of the theory gives support to the validity of the other principles of the theory in the same context of language learning. That is, it has been suggested that a word can become meaningful when it has been paired as a ^cS with an aspect of the environment that elicits an emotional response. The word will then come to elicit the response, or part of it, and thus acquire a meaning.

That support, however, raises the possibility that higher-order conditioning of word meaning also occurs. That is, if one word which has come to elicit a response is paired with another word which has no meaning, the latter word should thereby acquire a meaning.

Something akin to this was seen with Max the cat. After the word NO had become a ^cS for her, when the word was presented it would elicit a withdrawal response. The author observed, in addition, that after using the word several times when she began to claw the drapes, for example, Max stayed away from the drapes. This would be expected on the basis of higher-order conditioning. That is, the word NO would elicit the withdrawal response while the animal was looking at the drapes, the conditioned stimulus. After a few trials, the drapes as a visual stimulus should come to elicit the withdrawal response.

This is very analogous to telling a child that a type of food tastes bitter. If the child has been conditioned to respond to the word with withdrawal (and other conditioned emotional responses), he will "withdraw" from the food that has been paired with the word. Furthermore, it would be possible on the basis of higher-order conditioning to establish the meaning of new words.

Let us say, using another example, that a child has through first-order conditioning of the type already described acquired a meaning to the word BAD. That is, the child has received aversive stimulation in contiguity with the presentation of the word stimulus. Let us also say that the child later on reads a new word *evil*—a word that he has never seen before, thus, to him a nonsense syllable. He is then told by a parent or teacher that EVIL MEANS BAD and he repeats this to himself several times. These experiences would constitute conditioning trials in which the word BAD would serve as the ^{UC}S and the word EVIL as the ^{C}S. Through this conditioning the new word, EVIL, would come to elicit the same meaning response as the word BAD. It would not be necessary that the word EVIL ever be paired with an unlearned aversive stimulus.

Meaning Established by Classical Conditioning

The first-order conditioning experiment already described formalized the observations of everyday life and the results of the manipulation of conditioning variables in the author's study with the cat. The methods of experimentation used in the experiments now to be described were developed by the author in a similar fashion. The hypothesis derived from the basic theory was that a word can elicit an emotional meaning response. If this word is paired a number of times with a neutral stimulus, like a nonsense syllable, the meaningless word will in the process come to elicit the meaning response. It will thus acquire meaning itself. Then, if the person so conditioned rated the nonsense syllable, the rating should be a function of the conditioned meaning response. In exploring this possibility the author first showed the nonsense syllable to subjects and following this pronounced a word with a particular meaning. Later the subjects rated the meaning of the nonsense syllable. Two syllables were actually used in the procedure, one paired with a positive evaluative meaning word and another syllable with a negative evaluative meaning word.

The expected conditioning effect appeared to occur. This informally supported the hypothesis that a nonsense syllable paired with a meaningful word would be conditioned to elicit the meaning response already elicited by the word. This simple procedure needed improvement, however. For one thing, if the same word was paired many times with the nonsense syllable, the fact that the syllable came to elicit the word's meaning response could be accounted for on the basis of a direct association between the syllable and the word itself. That is, if the word was *pleasant*, for example, and the rating scale was *pleasant–unpleasant* then the syllable would elicit the word response *pleasant* and that response could mediate the scoring of the rating scale as *pleasant*.

The direct association between the nonsense syllable and the word it was paired with could be eliminated, however, even with multiple syllable-word pairings. This would be possible by pairing the syllable on each trial with a different word, all of the words having, however, an identical component of emotional meaning. These words would not have to be synonyms if a word may be considered to have been conditioned to elicit more than one meaning response. That is, when the word CANDY is paired with the presentation of a piece of candy, more than one response is conditioned to the word. The visual stimulus of the candy might elicit sensory responses that were conditioned to the word, in part forming the meaning of the word. In addition, however, the piece of candy in the mouth elicits a salivary response as well as further sensory responses that would be conditioned to the word and in part becoming its meaning. The word CANDY, as a result of the conditioning comes to elicit a positive emotional response and other responses as well.

Thus, in the present procedure it should be possible to select words that elicit one type of similar meaning response even though their other components of meaning differ. For example, the words PRETTY, SWEET, and HEALTHY have in common a positive evaluative meaning, and yet are quite different in meaning otherwise. By using such words on each conditioning trial the nonsense syllable could be paired with a different word and yet the same component of the meaning response would be evoked by each word and associated to the syllable. If the nonsense syllable was never paired with the same word more than once, a stable association between the syllable and the word itself would not be made. The association would be between nonsense syllable and meaning response.

After making this analysis, the author conducted additional informal explorations with adult subjects. Again the results suggested that the higher-order conditioning of meaning occurred. However, there were many uncontrolled conditions in the procedure. For example, the different prior experiences of the subjects would lead them to give different meanings to the nonsense syllables even before the experimental procedures. Thus, the experimental effect did not appear to be large enough to be reliably evident with every subject. Although the pilot studies were encouraging they indicated the need for a more formal experimental test involving a group of subjects.

The author then designed and conducted a formal experiment to test the hypothesis that the higher-order conditioning of emotional (or evaluative) meaning from a word to a new word can take place. The expected conditioning occurred and validated the author's theoretical rationale. Following this verification, two replication studies were conducted as a doctoral dissertation by Carolyn K. Staats employing two additional types of word meaning. The three experiments were then published in the *Journal of Experimental Psychology* (1957).[2]

Method

SUBJECTS The Ss were 86 students in elementary psychology at Arizona State College. They participated in the study to fulfill a course requirement. For 32 Ss the ^{uc}S's were words with high loading on the evaluative factor (Experiment I); 24 Ss had activity words as ^{uc}S's (Experiment II); and 30 Ss were conditioned with words with a high loading on the potency factor (Experiment III).

EXPERIMENT I The Ss were run in groups. There were two groups with one-half of the Ss in each group. Two types of stimuli were used: nonsense syllables which were presented visually by slide projection on a screen, and words which were presented orally by E, with Ss required to repeat the word aloud immediately after E had pronounced it.

The Ss were first seated in a room so they could all see the screen and not see each other's papers. They were told that they were to be Ss in an experiment concerned with studying two different types of learning—to see the effectiveness of each. One learning task was to concern non-sense syllables, and the other words.

Two tasks were presented to train Ss in the procedure and to orient them properly for the next phase of the experiment where the hypothesis was tested. The Ss were then told that the primary purpose of the experiment was to study "how both of these types of learning take place together—the effect that one has upon the other, and so on. Six new syllables were used: YOF, LAJ, XEH, WUH, GIW, and QUG. The syllables were presented in the same way. Approximately 1 second after the syllable appeared on the screen E pronounced a word aloud. The intervals between presentations of syllables were again less than 1 second. The Ss were told they could learn the syllables by just looking at them, but that they should simultaneously concentrate on pronouncing the words aloud and to themselves since there would be many words, presented only once.

The nonsense syllables were presented in random order, though never more than twice in succession, so that no systematic associations were formed between them. Each nonsense syllable was presented 18 times, and each time it was paired with a different word, that is, there were 18

[2] For the complete study, see Carolyn K. Staats, and Arthur W. Staats. Meaning established by classical conditioning. J. *exp. Psychol.*, 1957, **54**, 74–80.

conditioning trials. A nonsense syllable was never paired with a word more than once, so that stable associations were not formed between a nonsense syllable and any word. Thus, 108 different words were used. Two of the syllables were always paired with words which had high loadings on evaluative meaning. Most of the relevant meaningful words were taken from Osgood and Suci (1955). When appropriate words with high loadings could not be found in this way, a thesaurus supplied them. The other four syllables were paired with words which had no systematic meaning.

[The positive emotional meaning words were *beauty, win, gift, sweet, honest, smart, rich, sacred, friend, valuable, steak, happy, pretty, healthy, success, money, vacation, love*. The negative emotional meaning words used as the unconditioned stimuli were *thief, bitter, ugly, sad, worthless, sour, enemy, cruel, dirty, evil, sick, stupid, failure, disgusting, agony, fear, insane, poison*.] For Group 1, XEH was paired with different words which had a negative evaluative meaning, and YOF was paired with words with a positive evaluative meaning. For Group 2, XEH was paired with the positive meaning words, and YOF with the negative meaning words, word order remaining constant.

When the conditioning phase was completed, Ss were told that E first wished to find out how many syllables they remembered. At the same time, they were told it would be necessary to find out how they felt about the syllables since that might have affected how the syllables were learned. Each S was given a small booklet in which there were six pages. On each page was printed one of the nonsense syllables and a semantic rating scale. The scale was the seven-point scale which Osgood and Suci describe [9], with the continuum from pleasant to unpleasant. An example is as follows:

> QUG
> pleasant:__:__:__:__:__:__:__:unpleasant

In the booklet, QUG was on the first page and the other syllables on the following pages: XEH, LAJ, WUH, YOF, and GIW, in that order. The Ss were told how to mark the scale and to indicate at the bottom of the page whether or not the syllable was one that had been presented.

The Ss were then tested on the words. Finally they were asked to write down anything they had thought about the experiment, especially the purpose of it, and so on, or anything they had thought of *during the experiment*. It was explained that this might have affected the way they had learned the task.

EXPERIMENT II The procedure was exactly repeated for these Ss except that the words used to condition meaning to XEH and YOF had high loadings on the activity factor. The "active" words used are as follows: *fast, ferocious, tense, energetic, hot, brisk, agitate, speed, eager, sharp, quick, haste, fidgets, excited, young, hustle, frisky, spry.* The "passive" words used are as follows: *slumber, cool, listless, drowsy, loafing, dull, lazy, calm, old, slow, relaxed, sleep, resting, peaceful, inert, sluggish, lag, lifeless.* Since all other conditions were identical to Experiment I, it is not necessary to completely list the syllable-word pairs.

The Ss were again divided equally into a Group 1 and a Group 2. For Group 1, YOF was paired with passive meaning words and XEH with active meaning words. This was reversed for Group 2. The semantic measurement booklet was also the same except the syllables were judged on an active–passive dimension.

EXPERIMENT III The procedure was again the same, except that words with high loadings on potency meaning were used. The words used are listed as follows with "strong" words first and "weak" words second: *powerful, athletic, sturdy, masculine, robust, healthy, heavy, rugged, brave, active, hard, loud, deep, sharp, rich, wide, thick, large; crippled, feeble, soft, frail, narrow, poor, dull, thin, cowardly, feminine, lame, fragile, delicate, sick, quiet, passive, small, shallow.* The syllables were later judged on a strong–weak dimension. Group 1 had YOF paired with strong words, XEH paired with weak words; Group 2 had this reversed.

Design

The data for the three experiments were treated in the same manner. Three variables were involved in the design: conditioned meaning (pleasant and unpleasant, active and passive, or strong and weak, depending upon the experiment); syllables (XEH and YOF); and Groups (1 and 2). The scores on the semantic differential given to each of the two conditioned syllables were analyzed in a 2×2 latin square as described by Lindquist (1953, p. 278) for his Type II design.

Results

All Ss had been questioned about the purpose of the experiments. Of the 86 Ss, indicated awareness of a relationship between certain words and syllables. For these Ss it could be suggested that any meaning which the syllables had acquired was due to this awareness. For this reason, the data were analyzed without the scores of the "aware" Ss. In order to maintain a counterbalanced design when these Ss were excluded, it was necessary to randomly eliminate three additional Ss from the data. The result-ing Ns were as follows: 30 in Experiment I, 20 in Experiment II, and 24 in Experiment III. The results of the analysis indicate that the hypothe-sized conditioning effect occurred. In Experiment I the F for the condi-tioned evaluative meaning variable was significant at better than the .001 level. None of the other variables were significant.

In Experiment II the F for conditioned activity meaning was significant at better than the .05 level. None of the other variables were significant. In Experiment III the F for conditioned potency meaning was significant at better than the .06 level. The df in this case was only 1 and 22. None of the other variables were significant.

Discussion

In the three experiments the common components of the total meaning responses of the words were conditioned to contiguously pre-sented nonsense syllables. This conception is schematized in Figure 2.5,

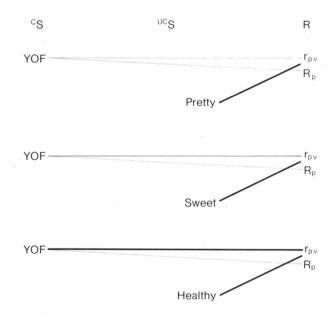

FIGURE 2.5.   The higher-order classical conditioning of meaning.

and in so doing, the way the conditioning in this study was thought to have taken place is shown more specifically. The nonsense syllable YOF, in this example, is presented prior to the word PRETTY. PRETTY elicits a meaning response. This is schematized in the figure as two component responses: an emotional response r_{PV} (in this example, the words have a positive value), and the other distinctive responses that characterize the meaning of the word, R_P. The pairing of YOF and PRETTY results in associations between YOF and r_{PV}, and YOF and R_P. In the following presentations of YOF and the words SWEET and HEALTHY the association between YOF and r_{PV} is further strengthened. This is not the case with associations R_P, R_S, and R_H, since they occur only once and are followed by other associations which are inhibitory. The direct associations indicated in the figure between the nonsense syllable and the individual words would in this way be inhibited.

It may be added that since this study was published, a number of studies have been conducted that replicate the results (see Cohen, 1964; Das and Nanda, 1963; Di Vesta and Stover, 1962; Paivio, 1964; and Pollio, 1963). The findings show in general that the meaning of a word will be conditioned to other words with which it is paired. Pollio has shown that in the procedure, in addition to the conditioning of the meaning response to the nonsense syllable, the nonsense syllable also comes to elicit some of the words with which it is paired. In Cohen's experiment a larger percentage of the subjects than in the present study became aware that the nonsense syllables were paired with certain types of words. However, although Cohen's article does not stipulate this clearly the subject's were asked a more leading question following the experiment than was asked in the original procedure—which would be expected to increase their reports of awareness.

Summary

Three experiments were conducted to test the hypothesis that meaning responses elicited by a word can be conditioned to a contiguously presented neutral stimulus, a nonsense syllable. The study assumed that total word meaning is composed of response components which can be separately conditioned. A nonsense syllable was visually presented 18 times, each time paired with the auditory presentation of a different word. While these words were different, they all had an identical meaning component. In Experiment I, one nonsense syllable was paired with positive evaluative meaning and another was paired with negative evaluative meaning; in Experiment II "active" meaning and "passive" meaning responses were conditioned; and in Experiment III, "strong" and "weak" meaning responses were conditioned. In each experiment there was significant evidence that meaning responses had been conditioned to the nonsense syllables.

ATTITUDES ESTABLISHED BY CLASSICAL CONDITIONING

The preceding analysis and the experimental results (see also Staats, *et al.*, 1959, 1963) have suggested that "emotional" word meaning is acquired according to the principle of classical conditioning. It turns out, however, that similar occurrences are usually described in common sense terms as well as in technical language as attitudes. That is, the terms negative emotional response, and negative emotional stimuli, as examples, have been employed in the previous discussions. The same events could as well be described by the terms negative attitudinal response or negative attitudinal stimuli. The same is true for positive attitudes.

It may be suggested that the process by which attitudes are formed is the same as the process by which emotional or evaluative or affective meaning is formed—that is the process of classical conditioning. The only difference that appears to occur, when the different terms are used, is in the nature of the stimulus involved. If the stimulus is a social stimulus object then in common sense usage we tend to use the term attitudes. This is also true with verbal stimuli. If the verbal stimulus concerns people, political slogans, and so on, we tend to speak of one's response to the stimulus as an attitude. We do not as readily state that we have an attitude toward the stimulus object of a dinner, or the word DINNER. However, the process by which the word DINNER comes to elicit a positive emotional response is the same by which the terms AMERICAN, DEMOCRACY, FREEDOM, and so on, come to elicit positive emotional responses.

It may be suggested that this analysis applies to other types of stimuli which we call by various names. Thus, the term *values* in social psychology and sociology, *needs* and *interests* in personality theory, *drives* and *motivations* in experimental psychology, *fetishes* and *urges* and *cathected objects* in abnormal psychology, to mention a few examples, all refer to stimuli that have come to elicit emotional responses in the individual according to the principles of primary classical conditioning or higher-order classical conditioning.

It is the author's contention that one of the powerful aspects of language is that words that have come to elicit those types of responses, that is, that have positive or negative emotional meaning (attitudes), may transfer this type of meaning to other environmental stimuli with which they are paired. It is suggested that the process by which this is done is also one of classical conditioning. This is of special importance when the stimuli with which the words are paired are social stimuli, that is the stimuli of other human beings, or the stimuli that are associated with or represent other human beings.

These suggestions were tested in part using the author's methods that have just been described. That is, the study extended the original experiments on the conditioning of meaning by studying the formation of attitudes (emotional meaning) to socially significant verbal stimuli through classical conditioning. The socially significant verbal stimuli were national names and familiar masculine names. Both of these types of stimuli, unlike nonsense syllables, would be expected to evoke attitudinal responses on the basis of the pre-experimental conditioning experiences of the individuals involved as subjects. Thus, the purpose of the study was to test the hypothesis that attitudes already elicited by socially significant verbal stimuli could be changed through the procedures of higher-order classical conditioning, using other words as the unconditioned stimuli.

The results showed that subjects' attitudes toward the national names DUTCH and SWEDISH could be conditioned in either a positive or negative direction. The same was true of the names TOM and BILL. Thus, a group of subjects could be conditioned to a statistically significant extent to have positive or negative attitudes towards other groups of people. This could be accomplished in a very brief procedure in which words were simply paired with the name of the group. The individuals who were so conditioned were not even aware of the purpose of the conditioning experience to which they had been subjected (Staats and Staats, 1958).

It should be added that it was not a rating response that was conditioned in this procedure but rather an implicit attitudinal response which mediated the behavior of scoring the semantic rating scale. The rating scale may be considered to be analogous to an item on an attitude testing device. The same conditioned attitudinal response could have been measured in various ways and would be expected to elicit or mediate many different types of overt responses, depending upon the other conditions in the situation.

It is possible with this conception to interpret two studies by Razran (1938, 1940) which concern the conditioning of ratings. Razran found that ratings of ethnically labeled pictures of girls and sociopolitical slogans could be changed by showing these stimuli while subjects were consuming a free lunch and, in the case of the slogans, while the subjects were presented with unpleasant olfactory stimulation. The change in ratings could be thought to be due to the conditioning of an implicit emotional (attitudinal) response, to the stimuli by means of the lunch or the unpleasant odors. That is, part of the total emotional response elicited by the food, for example, was conditioned to the pictures or slogans and became the response process which in turn elicited the positive rating.

HIGHER-ORDER CONDITIONING
OF MEANING AND COMMUNICATION

Thus, these and the preceding results corroborate the experimental hypothesis that when a word that elicits an emotional meaning response is paired with a stimulus that does not elicit that response, the stimulus will come to elicit the meaning response. The principle of higher-order classical conditioning was supported in the context of language learning.

This has several significant implications. First, this suggests that much language learning may take place on the basis of the principle. That is, once the individual has acquired meaning responses to word stimuli, he is prepared to expand his repertoire of meaningful words through additional verbal experience. An individual without a basic repertoire of meaningful words will not acquire an expanded meaningful word repertoire when he is faced with the new verbal experience. That is, for a child who has already been conditioned to respond appropriately to the word GOOD, further language learning will be produced when he is told EDUCATION IS GOOD. The same sentence will not produce a positive meaning for EDUCATION in the child who has not previously been conditioned to respond to GOOD.

Furthermore, when the individual has such a repertoire of meaningful words, he can learn new responses to *aspects of the environment,* as well as to other words, purely on a verbal basis. Thus, for a nonverbal child in this sense, it might be necessary that he receive direct aversive experience while in the street before he would be conditioned to avoid the street. With the child who already has a negative emotional meaning for HURT, however, it will only be necessary to provide the higher-order language conditioning stimuli such as IF YOU GO IN THE STREET YOU WILL GET HURT.

To illustrate the whole process more fully, let us say that a child has been given training in which the word HURT is paired with various aversive stimuli. That is, the child will inevitably receive various bruises and abrasions in his everyday activities. Accidents that produce these painful stimuli may be employed as the ^{uc}S in conditioning procedures in which the child is trained to the customary meaning of the word HURT. This can be done by pronouncing the word shortly after the accident, while he is being cared for, but is still in pain.

As a consequence of systematically pairing the word with various aversive stimuli in this manner, the word would be expected to come to elicit part of the responses elicited by the aversive stimuli. The word would come to be a conditioned stimulus and the conditioned emotional response would give the word its meaning. This process of the first-order conditioning of meaning is schematized in Figure 2.6a.

Following with the same example, let us say that later on the child engages in a precarious activity and is told, THAT IS DANGEROUS, YOU WILL GET HURT. This and similar instances of higher-order conditioning would be expected to condition the emotional response to HURT to the new word DANGEROUS. This conditioning is schematized in Figure 2.6b.

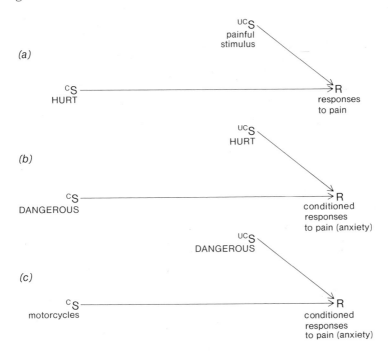

FIGURE 2.6. (a) The original conditioning of a negative emotional meaning to the word HURT; (b) the conditioning of the negative meaning of HURT to the word DANGEROUS; and (c) the conditioning of the negative meaning of DANGEROUS to a motorcycle.

After this type of learning has occurred, the word DANGEROUS may be paired with various other stimuli and these new stimuli will come to elicit the same conditioned response. The same youngster later on in life may be told by an anxious mother THEY ARE DANGEROUS as he looks at a motorcycle. Through this type of experience, without ever having had firsthand experience with motorcycles, the child would be conditioned to respond to them as if he *had* such aversive experiences, as in Figure 2.6c.

Actually, it would not even be necessary that the child be told DANGEROUS at the time he is looking at the motorcycle. It would be effective to simply tell him, MOTORCYCLES ARE DANGEROUS. The sentence would condition the meaning responses of DANGEROUS to the word MOTORCYCLE. When the child later saw the stimulus object, it would elicit a naming response and the word stimulus produced would elicit the emotional meaning response. (The process whereby stimulus objects come to elicit naming responses will be discussed in Part 2.)

It would thus be expected that through verbal experience of these types the individual may be conditioned to respond as though he had had direct experience with the environmental stimulus object involved. Because of this process, and other learning mechanisms yet to be described, the human individual does not need to directly contact various environmental situations and problems. He may acquire appropriate responses to situations he has never experienced, purely on a verbal level. These types of higher-order conditioning of meaning are some of the language learning processes that are commonly called communication. Related accounts of communication have been given by Mowrer (1960*b*) and Osgood (1953). A more complete analysis has been made by Staats (see Staats, 1964*a*; Staats and Staats, 1963) and this topic will be expanded in a later chapter.

At any rate, it may be suggested that one of the reasons that man has such great learning powers can be accounted for on the basis of these aspects of language. It may also be suggested that deficits in one's meaningful word repertoire can be one of the reasons underlying certain learning difficulties. Retarded children can be seen as one example. Another example that probably heavily involves a deficit in the repertoire of emotional meaning words may be seen in the behavior of psychopaths who do not, for example, profit from verbal warnings, remonstrations, and the like, as do other people. It would be expected in general that a child who does not have a meaningful word repertoire in the sense discussed would not be able to learn from the customary presentation of verbal stimuli.

This is not to say, however, that all verbal conditioning of this kind provides the individual with responses that are adjustive to him and to other people in his society. Taking the experiment on the conditioning of attitudes as an example, an individual can be conditioned to respond to words, and thus to the objects named by the words, in a manner quite unlike the responses he would have learned if he had had direct experience with the objects. Let us say, to follow the example, that in the short experimental conditioning process the subject had been conditioned to have a very negative meaning response to the word DUTCH. Later on, if the individual was introduced to a person who said he was DUTCH, the subject would have a negative response to the person. The negative attitude would be a function of the language conditioning procedure, which might actually be quite the reverse of the direct conditioning that would occur with direct experience with the person himself.

When language conditioning produces learning that is different than would be produced by direct experience with the stimulus objects (social or physical) themselves, then it can be said that the language conditioning was not serving its role as a "surrogate teacher." It would also be expected that the conditioning that occurred would be maladjustive. Continuing with the example, let us say that the individual who has learned a negative attitude toward the word DUTCH would avoid interaction with Dutch people. If he would actually derive rewards from such interaction, then the verbal conditioning that prevented the interaction would not be adjustive.

This is only a very mild example, however. It can be suggested that many of the social problems that occur between groups of people are heavily contributed to by the language conditioning individuals in each group have. Not only do people avoid one another socially on the basis of negative attudinal conditionings, but they may respond in other ways that are undesirable as well; this may include cruel behavior, derisive or insulting comments, obstructionistic behavior, antagonistic responses, oppositional voting, refusing to serve or hire, as well as servile, cringing, afraid behavior, and so on. When such behaviors occur on the basis of language conditioning, and in a direction opposite that which would be produced by direct contact with the members of a particular group, this may be seen as quite maladjustive. The same type of "unrealistic" attitudinal response could also occur in a positive direction, for example, unrealistically positive attitudes towards a leader.

Actually, in the preceding study of attitude formation, the language conditioning procedure lasted for only a few minutes and involved but a few conditioning trials. It would be expected that the conditioning produced would be only slight and would not last. However, if in the few minutes of conditioning the group of subjects could be affected to a statistically significant extent, one can readily guess what could be done with this type of conditioning over a period of years.

That is what happens, of course, in many cases in everyday life. That is, individuals may be raised in certain circumstances where they experience continually the pairing of certain types of words with certain social stimuli such as national, group, or ethnic names. The child raised in the southern part of the United States will ordinarily have language experiences in which the name NEGRO, or other variations of the name, will be systematically paired with words that elicit negative attitude responses, for example, *poor, stupid, immoral, dirty, undependable, improvident,* and so on. Many of these words would elicit even more intense negative meaning responses. It is to be expected that after years of such continuous conditioning, negro people would elicit negative attitude responses in the usual white person in the South, even if the white person has had no personal contact with negro people.

This is a hypothetical example. The white person in the South would actually also have had *direct* experience with black persons which, because of the social organization, would produce negative conditioning likely to support the immense amount of conditioning that he would have been subjected to on a verbal level. Other examples can be cited that show more purely the effect of this type of language conditioning, without the interference of direct experience.

Thus, many people in World War II had no direct experience with Japanese individuals. During the war, however, they had a great deal of language experience from various mass media that conditioned them negatively to the name JAPAN, JAPANESE, and so on. It would be expected that this conditioning would have drastically changed the responses of the members of the audience to the names and to individual people who would elicit this name. After the war, on the other hand, language conditioning occurred through the same media that tended to reverse or re-condition the attitudes of the audience. As a consequence, the usual attitudinal response to a Japanese person, or to the name JAPANESE, would now be expected to be more like it was prior to the war.

It should be emphasized that these three levels of negative attitude toward the members of a group of people were formed in many cases with no direct conditioning experiences. When this has been the case, it is quite possible for the attitudes formed to be entirely unjustified and maladjustive.

Of course, it is more customary that the language conditioning that we are subjected to is in agreement with the actual happenings, which if we had experienced them directly would have conditioned us in the same manner as did our language experiences. It is because of this that language is overall very, very adjustive for us. It is well to keep in mind, however, that language experience may not be veridical in this sense.

In that case our language experience will condition us to respond in ways that do not agree with reality.

Language conditioning occurs in our ordinary verbal interactions with people. Many times the individual providing the language conditioning for someone else is not aware of this fact. In many cases, however, the individual who provides the language stimuli does so with the awareness that he wishes to manipulate the behavior of his audience.

Advertising is in many cases a deliberate attempt to "condition" us (even though the advertiser may not use the same terminology). The advertiser, for example, pairs the name or picture of his product with words, and other pictures, that will elicit positive attitude responses in his audience. In doing this he conditions the positive response to the product in the same manner as if the members of the audience have had direct experience with the product.

The political editorialist or propagandist also does the same thing. Thus, social security may be discussed as SOCIAL SECURITY IS SO-CIALISTIC. The major effect of this verbal stimulus would be to condition the negative attitudinal response elicited by SOCIALISM to the word SOCIAL SECURITY. Completion of such conditioning would help insure a vote against a measure for social security, or a candidate who stood for the measure. The propagandist in this manner may condition his audience to respond to the names and labels of the things in which he is interested. In doing so he insures that his audience, or a substantial portion of it, will respond in the manner he desires. This can be done whether or not the attitude so conditioned is realistic, that is, would be like the attitude produced through direct contact with the event which is of concern. For this reason, individuals when responding to a message should always note the source of the message and ask whether some benefit (reward) will be derived by the source if the message is effective in producing language conditioning. If so this may be the determinant of the message, rather than the events to which the message is supposed to refer.

Before concluding this section, one qualification should be made to account for the seeming inconsistencies in response to language stimuli that seem to occur. For one thing, conditioning does not occur the same to individuals who have learned different meanings to words. Furthermore, language conditioning occurs in the context of other conditioning experiences. That is, if the individual has had many conditioning trials (either from direct or language experience), a few conditioning trials of the opposite sort will not change his response a great deal. Thus, the propagandist may not change certain members of his audience to any great extent, if they have been conditioned strongly in the opposite direction. It is also true that because of the person's past training he may respond to the efforts of the propagandist by saying to himself WHAT THIS MAN IS SAYING IS NOT TRUE, SUCH AND SUCH IS REALLY A GOOD PROGRAM (or person). In such a case the individual's past training will result in verbal behavior that actually counters the conditioning provided by the communication source.

All of the types of language learning involved in the above example have not yet been described. Thus, it is not possible at this point to consider in detail the various possible outcomes of such a message. However, it may be said in general that although a message may affect individuals differently, these differences may be accounted for when a full set of learning principles are applied in a detailed analysis. It should also be realized that although the present account will give independent descriptions of the various S–R mechanisms that are learned, the everyday life situation involves the interaction of many such mechanisms.

It may be additionally noted in this case of language behavior, and in every case to follow, that *the same conditioning results from language stimuli whether the stimuli are produced by someone else, or by oneself.* Thus, when the individual says *to himself,* as in the above example, that such and such IS REALLY A GOOD PROGRAM, the positive attitudinal response to GOOD PROGRAM is conditioned to the name of the program. It is in part by showing that our own language (behavior) affects our later behavior that a rapprochement between learning theory and cognitive theory (and other naturalistic conceptions of man) may be achieved. By such means we can begin to understand how it *appears* that we determine our own behavior by our thoughts and decisions (behaviors), and yet still consider human behavior within a scientific determinism—as lawfully caused rather than spontaneous.

One additional point which will be elaborated later should be stressed here. Emotional word meaning (as well as other language functions yet to be treated) was said to be learned. This has implications for considering the cognitive development and behavioral adjustment of the child, as well as for methods of accelerating or improving the child's development. Thus, to illustrate the use of classical conditioning procedures the author systematically produced many meaningful words (emotional *and* denotative) with his own young daughter. This has many implications for child training practices.

3

Denotative meaning: images in language

It has been suggested that many words are systematically paired with an aspect of the environment—with a particular stimulus. According to the principle of classical conditioning, any response that the stimulus elicits should be conditioned to the word involved. The preceding discussion has suggested that many stimuli elicit emotional responses, and thus that many words come to elicit this type of meaning response. However, there are many stimuli that we are "sensitive" to that do not elicit such responses. We *see* these stimuli, *hear* them, *feel* (touch) them, and so on, but these stimuli have no effect in eliciting emotional responses.

Nevertheless, even in these cases, naturalistic observation suggests that the process of classical conditioning—of pairing a word with one of these types of stimuli—does affect the word involved. For example, the word BLUE which is systematically paired with blue light acquires different qualities than does the word SQUEAK which is systematically paired with a certain type of auditory stimulation. If we assumed that such sensory stimuli also elicit responses—sensory responses—the manner in which words acquire *denotative* meaning would also be suggested from our knowledge of classical conditioning.

That is, it can be suggested that seeing a visual stimulus is actually *responding* to the stimulus, hearing a sound stimulus is responding to the stimulus, touching a tactile stimulus is responding to the stimulus, and so on. Furthermore it can be suggested that *part* of the sensory response elicited by a sensory stimulus can be conditioned to another stimulus with which it is paired. When this has occurred the new stimulus will come to elicit the conditioned part of the sensory response, which we commonly call an image. Finally, it may be suggested that many *words* are stimuli that in this manner come to elicit conditioned sensory responses (images) in the individual who has been so conditioned.

These suggestions have been couched in terms that suggest speculation. However, in addition to the theory of classical conditioning, the foregoing analysis, and supporting naturalistic observations, there are experimental results that actually lead to these statements as conclusions. Thus, Leuba (1940) has shown that a neutral stimulus paired with a sensory stimulus as the ^{UC}S will become a ^{C}S that elicits what is described in everyday life as an image. For example, while a subject was hypnotized Leuba paired a buzzer as the ^{C}S with a pinprick as the ^{UC}S. It was found that the subject would later report a painful sensation on his hand simply on the presentation of the buzzer. Ellson (1941) has also shown that a light as the ^{C}S when paired with a tone as the ^{UC}S will come to elicit the faint hearing of the tone before the tone has been presented. He called these hallucinations, produced by sensory conditioning. Ellson cites other evidence in the literature for the conditioning of sensations.

These are examples of the direct conditioning of sensory responses. In addition, however, there are a number of other experimental results that support the same analysis. Some of these experiments have generally been given the term sensory preconditioning. Brogden (1939) originally paired a bell and a light for a number of trials, using dogs as subjects. Then he later used one of these two stimuli as the ^{C}S in another phase of the experiment and conditioned a response to it. It was then found that the response when conditioned to the bell sound, for example, would also be elicited by the light—even though the response had never been conditioned to the light. Thus, as a result of being presented together a number of times, light and the bell had become functionally the same. What happened to one of the stimuli would result in (or generalize to) the same type of conditioning to the other stimulus. This type of result has been shown to occur with human subjects (see, for example, Brogden, 1947).

These results would be expected on the basis of the following analysis. If each sensory stimulus, the light and the bell, elicits a sensory response that can be conditioned, then the pairing of the stimuli would result in two types of conditioning. The sensory response to the light, the seeing of the light, would be conditioned (at least in part) to the bell sound.

When this result is considered, the bell is the ^cS and the light which elicits the seeing response is the ^{uc}S. The process is shown in Figure 3.1. The seeing response, r in the figure, is printed in lower-case letters to indicate that it is not directly observed in the experiment. The seeing response is also depicted as having stimulus properties also, that is as r–s. (In general, although not always diagrammed, every response is assumed to produce stimulus events, so the present case is no exception.)

In addition, the same process should also occur with the sensory response to the bell. That is the bell as a ^{uc}S results in the response of hearing the bell, which according to the same rationale should be conditioned to the light. This process is exactly the same, except that the roles of the ^cS and the ^{uc}S are filled by the light and the bell respectively rather than the reverse.

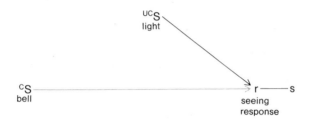

FIGURE 3.1. Classical conditioning of a sensory (seeing) response to another stimulus.

Thus, as a result of the pairing of the two stimuli, each comes to elicit the sensory response elicited by the other. Because of this it would be expected that the two stimuli, the bell and the light, would now have become functionally the same—even though before this process they had not been. That is, now if one of the stimuli is involved in an additional conditioning process, the resulting conditioning will affect the other stimulus in the same way for the subject involved.

The rationale for this expectation is shown in Figure 3.2. Let us say that in addition to the first conditioning, the subject who had previously been presented with the bell and the light is put into another conditioning procedure. In this one the light is again presented, this time paired with an electric shock as the ^{uc}S. Now electric shock elicits as a response a change in the rate at which the subject's heart is beating. This response, among other occurrences, will be conditioned to the *stimulus produced by the seeing response elicited by the light.* That is, the light as a stimulus elicits the seeing sensory response r–s and the heart rate response will be conditioned to the stimulus part of this sensory response. The stimulus part of the sensory response thus would become a $^c s$ for the heart rate response (see Figure 3.2a).

Now it can be seen why the conditioning of the heart rate response to the light will have the same effect upon (will generalize to) the bell, even though the bell has never been paired with the shock. The bell, because of previous pairing with the light, also elicits the seeing response on a conditioned basis and this conditioned sensory response will elicit the heart rate response, as shown in Figure 3.2b.

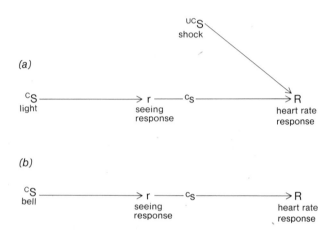

FIGURE 3.2.   (a) The light is paired with the shock as the ^{uc}S. The light elicits a seeing response and the stimuli produced by this sensory response function as the $^c s$ and come to elicit the heart rate response.   (b) Later, the bell stimulus is presented. It elicits the seeing response also—because of prior pairing with the light—and the seeing response elicits the heart rate response. The bell, it should be remembered, has never been paired with the shock.

This is a complicated analysis. However, it does suggest that sensations have response characteristics which can be conditioned to new stimuli. There are additional experimental results that anchor these findings and the resulting analysis more firmly in the area of language learning. This type of study has been considered under the label of semantic generalization.

In one type of semantic generalization study a response of the subject is conditioned to a word and then the stimulus object the word "denotes" is later presented to the subject. It has been found that the object, never itself conditioned to elicit the response, will do so, if the word has first been conditioned to elicit the response. That is, the two stimuli—the word stimulus and the object stimulus—are functionally equivalent. Something that happens to the word generalizes to the object. The converse is also true. If the response is conditioned to the stimulus object, the word will as a result also elicit the response.

The following may be used as an example. Let us say that the word BLUE has been used as the ^cS in a classical conditioning procedure, being paired with an electric shock as the stimulus. After some trials the word BLUE will come to elicit a conditioned heart rate response. At a later time if the subject involved is shown a blue light it will be found that the blue light will also elicit the conditioned heart rate response.

This equivalence of function reminds us of the equivalence already described which occurred between the two sensory stimuli after they had been paired together. Actually, the same analysis may be used to account for the facts of semantic generalization. That is, the reason this word to object generalization will take place may be thought to involve previous conditioning like that in the sensory preconditioning. That is, in our language culture we have all had a past history when the word BLUE as a stimulus had been paired with blue light on multitudinous occasions. For example, we have all had experience when the word BLUE is spoken by ourselves or someone else at the same time that we are looking at a blue object. This "preconditioning" experience would be expected to perform the type of conditioning shown in Figure 3.3.

As shown in the Figure 3.3a when the word BLUE is paired with the blue light, the blue light elicits its sensory response. The sensory response is conditioned to the word BLUE which then comes, as a ^cS, to elicit the conditionable parts of the blue sensory response. At this point, for this subject, both the blue light stimulus and the word BLUE elicit the same, or similar, response.

At a later time, in the semantic generalization experiment, the word BLUE is paired with the electric shock as is shown in Figure 3.3b Each time the word BLUE is presented it elicits the blue sensory response previously conditioned to it. The shock elicits the heart rate response, and this response is conditioned to the blue sensory response (or, rather, the stimulus components of this response). Thus, as a result of *this* conditioning the blue sensory response comes to elicit the heart rate response.

This then establishes the circumstances for the blue light also to elicit the heart rate response, even though this light has never been paired with the shock. This is shown in Figure 3.3c. That is, the presentation of the blue light results in the elicitation of the blue sensory response, and the stimulus of the blue sensory response is a ^cS for the heart rate response.

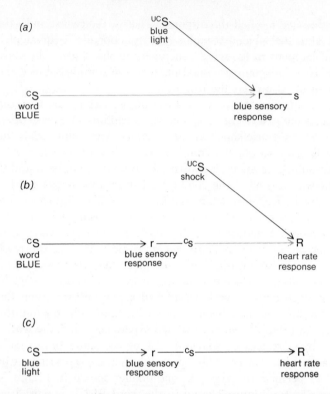

FIGURE 3.3.   (a) Pairing of the word BLUE and the blue light conditions the blue sensory response to the word.   (b) In further work with the subject shock is paired with the word BLUE, thus conditioning the heart rate response to the conditioned blue sensory response.   (c) The blue light now also elicits the heart rate response since it elicits the blue sensory response (on an unconditioned basis).

Thus, the original pairing of the blue light and the word BLUE made them functionally the same. It would also be expected that conditioning involving a blue light would generalize back to the word BLUE on the basis of the same rationale. In addition, it would be expected that if there was another word that had been paired with blue light many times in the past, as the word AZURE may have been for someone in our culture, the same functional equivalence would also apply to this word. That is, if a response was conditioned to blue light it would generalize to the word AZURE since it too would elicit the same sensory response as the light.

In addition, however, the two words BLUE and AZURE would also be functionally equivalent. Any experience that the individual had with one word would generalize to the other. This would be expected since each would elicit the same conditioned blue sensory response. It is suggested that this is one basis for synonymity. If two words are paired with the same, or similar, stimuli they will come to elicit the same or similar conditioned meaning response. Then anything that happens to one word stimulus, which conditions a new response to the word's conditioned meaning response, will generalize to the other word. (Synonyms would, of course, also be functionally equivalent in the type of communication already described.)

For a summary of the experimental evidence of these various types of semantic generalization see Cofer and Foley (1942) and Osgood (1953). Phillips (1958) has also more recently performed an experiment that illustrates very nicely the various processes involved. These various experiments support the author's theory that sensory stimuli actually elicit sensory responses in the individual and that these sensory responses can be conditioned in part to other stimuli. The results also suggest that such conditioned sensory responses, or images, can be conditioned to word stimuli, forming the meaning of the word. If this analysis is true then it should be possible to derive testable hypotheses from the analysis that will be verified in the laboratory in the context of conditioning and word meaning.

The author derived such an hypothesis and tested it (Staats, *et al.*, 1959) using the same language conditioning procedure that has already been described in which meaningful words were used as the ^{uc}S and a nonsense syllable was used as the ^{c}S. The rationale in the hypothesis may be stated in the following manner. When a word elicits an *emotional* meaning response, if that word is paired with another word, the second word will also come to elicit the emotional meaning response. If it is true that words also come to elicit sensory meaning responses in the same manner as they come to elicit emotional meaning responses, then the same expectation should hold. That is, when a word eliciting a sensory meaning response is paired with another word, the second word should also come to elicit that sensory meaning response.

In the study, following the procedure already described, a nonsense syllable was paired once each time with a number of different words— all of the words, however, elicited the same sensory meaning response. Thus, twelve words with angular sensory meaning—*square, box, roof, triangle, steeple, diamond, window, hallway, zigzag, book, pyramid, wedge* —were paired with a nonsense syllable for one group of subjects. Twelve words with another sensory meaning—*coil, globe, hub, barrel, bulb, target, wheel, marbles, knob, hoop, pearl, ball*—were paired with another nonsense syllable. For another group of subjects the nonsense syllable in each case was paired with the words having the other type of meaning. It should also be added that although these two groups of words differed in the sensory meaning responses they elicited, they were chosen not to be different in the emotional meaning they elicited. Thus, any result in the conditioning of meaning would be the effect of the conditioning of the sensory response meaning.

The results showed that the conditioning of the sensory response meaning did indeed occur. When a nonsense syllable was paired with words that elicited angular sensory responses (images) the nonsense syllable was later rated as having an angular meaning. When a nonsense syllable was paired with words that elicited round sensory responses (images) the nonsense syllable was later rated as having a round meaning.

It may be concluded that denotative meaning (or conditioned sensory responses) may be conditioned to new meaningless words. Moreover, the principles of classical conditioning appear to be involved, as is the case with affective word meaning responses. Other studies (such as, Leuba, 1940; Ellson, 1941; and Phillips, 1958) provide evidence that sensory responses can be conditioned in first-order classical conditioning procedures. The same process appears to occur with words in higher-order conditioning.

Thus, it is suggested that some words elicit conditioned sensory responses, or images. On the basis of this analysis, it may also be suggested that the principles of classical conditioning will account for what we call word imagery. That is, when an individual hears or reads a descriptive passage that contains an account of sensory stimuli, it is frequently said that the individual experiences imagery that is like the actual events being described. The individual would in a sense be seeing or hearing, or whatever, something like that which the actual stimuli would arouse.

This vicarious sensory experience through words may be considered to be one of the powerful functions of language. Through words the individual can have experiences that provide learning similar to that which the actual events would have provided. The individual can thus acquire new sensory experience without ever having had contact with the objects themselves. For example, many people have never had contact with a jellyfish. If they were told, however, that a jellyfish is "mottled purple, pink and white," is "gelatinous in its flexibility," comes in "various sizes around eighteen inches across," and gives a "stinging sensation on contact," these words would elicit grossly appropriate sensory responses. Even in this simple example, the individual so conditioned by these verbal means will acquire a constellation of sensory responses that approximates to some extent the sensations he would receive if he had direct contact with the organism. Furthermore, other behaviors that he might learn under the control of the organism itself as a stimulus could also be learned to the conditioned sensory responses. That is, if told to avoid touching the organism, although he had never seen such an animal, he would avoid one on the very first direct contact.

There are several points implicit in this discussion that should be elaborated. First, it is suggested that we acquire a repertoire of words that elicit general sensory responses. That is, white light is a stimulus that is part of many different stimuli. When the word stimulus white is paired with many different objects which reflect that type of light the word comes to elicit a "white conditioned sensory response." That is, pairing the word with a white ball, a white dress, a white car, a white house, and so on, will condition the sensory response elicited by white stimuli to the word. This word may then be used (as a "concept") in combination with many different words that elicit sensory responses to produce new combinations of sensory responses.

Take this example. *It was bright white, rotund, with short legs and hooves, and a very long neck, with bright black stripes around it. It had a thick, flat head with wide jaws, and long yellow teeth, and the animal growled loudly.* All of the words in this example have acquired their meaning through being paired with various sensory stimuli and have come through this to. elicit a particular conditioned sensory response. Such words have been called concepts; in the present terms such concepts are words that have come to elicit one or more conditioned sensory responses in the manner described.

The above example also illustrates more clearly that when words, each of which elicits a sensory response, are combined, a larger, combined, sensory response may result. It would then be expected that if a new word was paired with this combined sensory response, the new word would become capable of eliciting the total sensory response. Thus, the individual would have acquired a new, complex image, which would be elicited whenever the word occurred. Thus, if the word GLOX was paired with the sensory words in the above example—as in the statement A GLOX IS BRIGHT WHITE, ROTUND, WITH SHORT LEGS, and so on—GLOX would come to elicit the combined sensory response.

This is a powerful form of human learning. The individual may think with these new images, formed on the basis of language conditioning. The words which elicit the new combined images could also be combined with other words to form new conditionings and thus new images. *Moreover, this analysis allows a rapprochement between cognitive ap-*

proaches to human behavior, and a stimulus-response approach. The
processes of this type that are seen as cognitive events may be considered
in terms of stimuli, responses, and the principles of classical conditioning.

It should be remembered that the ability of the individual to learn in
the ways that have been described depends upon previous training that
had conditioned the sensory responses to the words. This type of training
may be considered to yield a basic behavioral repertoire—which will
enable the individual to learn further from words in a variety of experiences. If the individual does not have this basic behavioral repertoire, he will be unable to profit in the same manner as others do from
the multitude of language experiences to which he is subjected. More
will be said later of other constituents in the basic behavioral repertoire
of the individual which are necessary for complex cognitive development
of this type. Learning such repertoires may be manipulated.

One final point is important here. Words that elicit conditioned sensory responses may be combined in ways that yield a composite sensory
response that has no real counterpart in experience. The example of the
GLOX above was such a case. It is also true that no one has ever experienced referents for GOD, DEVILS, FLYING SAUCERS, and many
other current terms. Yet for many people these words elicit vivid sensory
responses. Good examples may be drawn from history. For example, in
the middle ages people accepted as real the existence of various forms
of witches, hobgoblins, elves, dragons, spirits, and so on.

> . . . [T]he basilisk kills serpents by his breath and men by his glance. . . .
> "As to the ant-lion, his father hath the shape of a lion, his mother that of an
> ant . . . these bring forth the ant-lion, a compound of both and in part like
> to either. . . ." [T]he "cockatrice" of scripture . . . "drieth and burneth leaves
> with his touch, and he is of so great venom and perilous that he slayeth and
> wasteth him that nigheth him without tarrying. . . ." (White, 1899, pp. 899–
> 900)

There are, of course, no such actual stimulus objects, so man's sensory
responses to this and other such words must have been acquired through
language conditioning.

Thus, it may be concluded that we can learn sensory responses that
could not arise from contact with actual events—which do not exist. It
may be added that sensory conditioning from language can in this sense
produce images that are not adjustive for the individual. When an individual responds to a "nonexistent image" with behavior that is maladjusted, we may speak of this as an hallucination.

part
2

*Instrumental
conditioning
and speech*

4

Speech
as a
stimulus

INSTRUMENTAL CONDITIONING

The importance of the principles of classical conditioning for understanding human behavior, especially aspects of language behavior, has been suggested. However, even though it is recognized that the types of responses conditioned to words (including both sensory responses as well as affective or attitudinal responses) are very important, this by no means covers the types of human behaviors in which we are interested. There are complex overt motor behaviors and skills that do not seem to be elicited by stimuli in the manner of classically conditioned responses. That is, there are complex motor behaviors for which we could find no unconditioned stimulus. Thus, if we wanted to train such a behavior, we could not do so by finding an unconditioned stimulus that would elicit the response. While there are a number of responses that are reflexly elicited by stimuli, many of our most important behavioral skills are not acquired in that manner.

As has been described, the basic principle of classical conditioning was first systematically investigated in the laboratory by Pavlov. In an analogous way, it was E. L. Thorndike who discovered the other type of conditioning that provides higher-level statements in the present theory. Thorndike found that the stimulus consequences of a certain type that *follow* a motor behavior will affect the frequency of the *future* occurrence of that behavior. The principle as it is used herein may be stated as follows. If, in the presence of a particular situation (stimulus complex), the organism responds and this is followed by a certain type of stimulus the response will later tend to occur more frequently in the presence of that situation. When the consequence of a response is another type of stimulus, the principle is that the response will later occur less frequently in that situation.

The types of stimuli that will have the effect of strengthening (making more frequent) responses they follow are usually referred to as rewards. Consequences that have the opposite effect, that is weaken responses they follow, are called punishments in everyday life. The principle involved was called the law of effect. Later investigators (for example, Clark L. Hull) came to call it the principle of reinforcement. However, the principle was the same, namely that the rewarding and punishing effects, or consequences, of responses will influence the *future* occurrence of the responses.

An important part of the field of experimental psychology, especially in the United States, has been devoted to the exploration of the principle of reinforcement. Various types of experimental apparatus have been devised for this purpose, and the details and corollaries of the principle have been specified in laboratory research. One of the most prominent pieces of apparatus developed was the maze. Thus, an animal might be reinforced for traversing a runway, or turning in one direction rather than another direction, and the effect of the reinforcement on its behavior could be objectively ascertained.

More recently, Skinner (1938; Ferster and Skinner, 1957) has devised an apparatus for the investigation of the principle of reinforcement which has good reliability and which has been used successfully with various organisms. Some of the detailed characteristics of the principle of reinforcement have been better specified through the use of this apparatus. The principle of reinforcement will now be described more fully in the context of this type of experimental situation.

Let us say that a rat is placed in a box in which there is a lever. The lever is connected to a mechanism such that whenever the lever is depressed, the mechanism will deliver a pellet of food into a dish that is available to the animal. In the example, our rat has been deprived of food and each of the food pellets thus constitutes the type of stimulus that has been termed a reward or, technically, a positive reinforcer, or positive reinforcing stimulus. The convention for depicting such a stimulus is ^{R+}S.

Now, let us say that the rat has not been placed in this apparatus before. In his first such experience, he will thus respond in various ways. He will wander over the box, smell the various parts, paw them, and so on, in addition to performing other behaviors such as grooming. Eventually, however, in the conduct of these behaviors, he will depress the lever. If the animal is provided with a pellet following each bar press response the principle would state that this response would increase in frequency of occurrence. This principle has been found to hold for various responses and for various species.

Let us say that a recording mechanism was attached to the lever. That is, there is a mechanism that contains a moving sheet of paper on which a pen traces from left to right. The line drawn by the pen is a measure of time since the paper is moving at a constant speed. In addition, however, the pen takes a small step upward each time the lever is depressed. The resulting record is depicted in Figure 4.1. The baseline of the

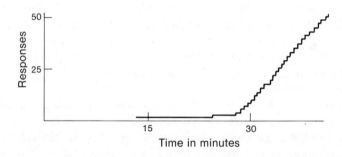

FIGURE 4.1. The cumulative record of the instrumental conditioning of a bar-press response. (Adapted from *The Behavior of Organisms* by B. F. Skinner. Copyright, 1938, by D. Appleton-Century Company, Inc. Reproduced by permission of Appleton-Century-Crofts.)

record indicates the length of time involved. The vertical axis of the record indicates the number of responses the animal has made. At first the responses occur infrequently, so the slope of the line is almost horizontal. When the response increases in frequency, the line rises more steeply. The steepness of the slope of the line indicates how rapidly the animal is responding. If the record were to continue until the animal was surfeited with food pellets, the responses would occur less frequently and the line would again become horizontal. However, the response would have been strongly learned by this experience, for if the animal was removed from the apparatus and not fed for a time, upon being replaced in the box it would immediately begin to press the bar at a high rate.

As already mentioned, there are environmental consequences that have just the opposite effect upon the strength of the behavior they follow. These types of stimuli, which are commonly called "punishments," are technically termed negative reinforcers, or negative reinforcing stimuli ($^R\text{-}S$). Thus, if we took the rat that had been conditioned to press the bar and each time the response occurred then presented a very loud noise, it would be observed that the response would decrease in frequency. If the noise was painfully intense, the response would decrease to a very low frequency of occurrence with only a few trials.

Whether or not a stimulus is rewarding (a positive reinforcer) or punishing (a negative reinforcer) is defined by the effect that it has upon the strength of a response. Some stimuli have one or the other effect upon behavior. It should be pointed out, however, that many stimuli do not have this effect upon behavior at all. There are many stimuli which if presented contingent upon a response will have no later effect upon the strength of the behavior. If we wished to ascertain for an organism what stimuli would not strengthen or weaken behavior, and what stimuli would either strengthen or weaken behavior, in the total absence of any information on the organism we would have to test the organism with the various stimuli.

However, there is no circularity in the term *reinforcing stimulus*, for *the experimental finding that a stimulus will strengthen a response is not restricted to the situation in which this finding was established, or to the specific response or the specific organism treated.* That is, if it is found that a stimulus will strengthen a response for a particular organism, then that stimulus will strengthen other motor responses of that organism if presented following those other responses. Furthermore, a stimulus that has reinforcing value with one member of a species that has not been subjected to specific training with that stimulus will generally also have reinforcing value for other intact members of that species. Thus, the finding that a stimulus has reinforcing value can be used to predict further effects upon different behaviors of the same organism, as well as to predict effects upon the behavior of similar organisms.

Many times, indeed, *types* of stimuli that have reinforcing effect for one species will also have the same reinforcing effect for other species. Examples of such general reinforcers are food (which may differ from species to species), sexual contact, warmth, water, air, and so on. In each case, in order for the stimulus to be reinforcing the organism has to have first been deprived of the stimulus. Thus, sexual contact is reinforcing to the sexually deprived, to a much less extent to the sexually satiated.

As has been mentioned, many environmental stimuli have little or no reinforcement value. Presented contingent upon a behavior, such stimuli will not result in future strengthening of that behavior. An important corollary of the principle of reinforcement is that such neutral stimuli can become reinforcing stimuli. That is, if a neutral stimulus is paired a number of times with a reinforcing stimulus, the neutral stimulus will also become a reinforcer. In such a case, the stimulus is then called a learned, or more commonly, a conditioned reinforcer. It is called a conditioned reinforcer because experience is necessary for the stimulus to acquire reinforcing value. This is a most important principle, as will be discussed further on in the present book, because so much of human behavior is acquired through the action of conditioned reinforcers.

It has been stated that a reinforcing stimulus has its effect when the organism has been deprived of the stimulus. In general, that seems to hold for both conditioned reinforcers as well as for the primary (unlearned) reinforcers.

It has been said that there are stimuli which when they follow a response will increase the strength of the response; these are positive reinforcers. Conversely, some stimuli applied in this manner will weaken a response; these are negative reinforcers. The operation involved here is the presentation of the stimulus following a response. It may be added that the opposite operation, taking away the stimulus following a response, will also have a reinforcing function—but in the direction opposite to that of the presentation of the stimulus. That is, if the organism has a positive reinforcer which is taken away following a response, the response will occur less frequently in the future. The same principle holds for negative reinforcers also. That is, if a negative reinforcer has been presented—let us say that the organism is being given electric shock—but when the organism makes a particular response the negative reinforcer is withdrawn, the response will be increased or maintained in strength.

As with classical conditioning, unlearning of a response, or extinction, can also take place. That is, as one example, a response that has occurred and has been followed by a positive reinforcer a number of times will increase in frequency and be maintained at the higher level of frequency. However, if conditions change and the response is no longer followed by the positive reinforcer, the response will weaken. After a number of such unreinforced responses has occurred, the response will return to about its preconditioning strength, occurring at about the same frequency as before.

In addition to the major principles of operant conditioning, there are a number of secondary principles that specify in detail the manner in which reinforcers affect behavior. Many of these principles have to be considered when dealing with various aspects of human behavior. However, the purpose of the present book is to present a very simple account of the two major types of learning, operant and classical conditioning, and to show the importance of these principles in the study and manipulation of language behavior. Only those secondary principles that are directly relevant to the present account are being introduced—although it is true that all of the secondary principles should be relevant for various other features of human behavior, including aspects of language. The author has presented a more complete description of the various learning principles important to complex human behavior (Staats and Staats, 1963). A more advanced version of the basic theory using an improved notation system will be given in the beginning of Chapter 6 in very brief form.

One point should be emphasized here because it corrects prevalent misconceptions. A reinforcer has its effect upon the *future* strength of a response—it cannot be considered to strengthen the response that it follows—causation in science moves in a forward direction. The author (Staats, 1963; Staats and Staats, 1963, pp. 46–47) has discussed such points because of their bearing upon purposive (teleological) conceptions of human and animal behavior. By the same token a goal (reinforcer) which has not yet occurred cannot affect a response that occurs at a prior time. That is, it is many times suggested that the goal determines (or attracts) the behavior of the individual. However, to say that is inconsistent with notions of scientific causality. The future goal cannot affect a behavior that precedes it in time—unless in some way the goal is brought into the presence of the behaving organism. As the author has indicated (Staats, 1963; Staats and Staats, 1963) stimulus-response mechanisms, especially verbal mechanisms, may serve to bridge the gap. Such mechanisms, which will be among those described herein, only make it appear as though a future event can determine human behavior.

In concluding this section, the principle of instrumental conditioning will be stated in summary fashion, as follows, using positive reinforcement as the example. If in the presence of a particular situation (stimulus, or stimulus complex), the organism responds and this is followed by a reinforcing stimulus, the response will be increased in strength (or maintained if already strong) on future occasions when the organism is again in that situation or a similar one. Thus, it should be remembered that the operation of reinforcement actually strengthens the response in the presence of the stimuli that are present. When the stimuli, or some of them, occur again they will be likely to bring on the response. For example, when the rat was reinforced for pressing the lever in the box it was stated that he would come to press the lever more frequently.

However, the animal would not make the lever response more frequently when he was not in the presence of the lever. The fact that the stimulus situation is gaining control over the response that is reinforced in its presence is frequently ignored because that is a constant in many experiments. The behavior of the animal is only studied when he is in the experimental chamber. Nevertheless, it may be suggested that a reinforced response is strengthened in the presence of the particular stimulus situation.

As will be described later on, various component features of the complex stimulus situation may also come to control the response, if the response is only reinforced when these stimuli are present. Thus, the stimulus control of a response through instrumental conditioning can come to be very specific and precise. The stimulus controlling an instrumentally conditioned response is called a *discriminative stimulus*.

SPEECH AS A STIMULUS

One aspect of the field of learning, or behaviorism, has been an interest shown by some workers in extending the principles of learning to consideration of human behavior. Watson, for example, attempted to provide a general conception of human behavior, including speech, on the basis of conditioning principles. His conditioning principles were not precisely stated, however, seeming at times to mix together both classical conditioning and instrumental conditioning principles.

Clark L. Hull followed in the tradition of extending the basic principles of learning to the consideration of human behaviors, including some symbolic behaviors. Hull invested his major efforts into systemizing the laboratory findings of conditioning into a general theory, the merits of much of which are open to question at this time. Unrelated to these aspects of his theory, however, his extensions of learning principles to consideration of more complex behaviors generated many important conceptions of aspects of human behavior. This interest in the extension of learning principles to aspects of human behavior has been continued by a number of theorists such as Miller and Dollard (1941), Dollard and Miller (1950), Mowrer (1950, 1960a, 1960b), Osgood (1953), Skinner (1953, 1957), and Staats (1955, 1961, 1964a, 1966; Staats and Staats, 1963).

It was on the basis of Hull's analyses of the principles of learning and the general suggestion of his work that learning principles could be extended to human behavior that the present author began his investigation of language learning as part of the general study of complex human behavior. This included dealing both (1) with language as a stimulus which affects motor responses of various kinds, as well as (2) with language as a motor response itself. Actually, language is frequently both. That is, the person speaks, which is a response. But his speech response produces an auditory stimulus that can affect both his own and other people's motor behaviors. These aspects of language may be separated, however, for purposes of analysis and experimentation. In doing this language will first be considered in its role as a stimulus that controls other behavior.

As in the study of the classical conditioning of word meaning, the author began the study of the principle of instrumental conditioning with a lower organism, in what has been termed experimental-naturalistic research. The same animal was used, and the training was conducted at the same time the animal was being classically conditioned to respond appropriately to the word NO.

The principle that forms the basic theory in the present extension to the consideration of language is that of instrumental conditioning. In the extension of this basic theoretical principle, the author assumed that words, in auditory form, are stimuli and as such can become discriminative stimuli that will control motor behaviors. Naturalistic observation supports this hypothesis; there seem to be many verbal stimuli which separately and in combinations will control a response.

Following this theoretical analysis, the procedure used was that of instrumental conditioning; where one waits for a response to occur (or arranges circumstances so that it does occur) and then follows the response by presenting a reinforcing stimulus. The complex behavior of walking, the one involved in the training to be described, cannot be considered to be a reflex. For example, it is not possible, as in classical conditioning, to simply present some stimulus to an animal that has never walked with the stimulus eliciting walking behavior in a reflex manner. There is no stimulus that elicits walking in this manner.

Most complex motor behaviors are of this type. They are acquired behaviors—there are no ^{uc}S that can be presented that will elicit them. When the organism has such a complex behavior in its repertoire, however, the behavior can be conditioned in the sense that it can be made to occur more frequently in the presence of *new* stimuli. This can be done according to the principles of instrumental conditioning, where the behavior is reinforced in the presence of the stimulus.

At any rate, the goal of the proposed training was to bring the previously acquired walking (or approach) response of the kitten under the control of a language stimulus—the kitten's name, MAX. This was done in the following manner. The author first kneeled several feet away from the animal and extended a morsel of food. (This was done prior to feeding time to insure that the animal was deprived of food.) Then the kitten's name was called. This was done until the kitten looked at the food and then walked to the author and obtained the food. (A complete analysis of this training would have to indicate why the sight of the food controlled the approach response. That will be accepted here as a given, although it may be briefly suggested that the same principles were involved in the sight of the food becoming a controlling stimulus as are involved in the language training being described.)

This procedure fulfills the requirements involved in instrumental conditioning. That is, a response was reinforced in the presence of a stimulus situation. It would be expected that the stimulus situation would come to control the response. And that is what occurred. After several conditioning trials of this type, when the author kneeled and said MAX and extended a bit of food, the cat would approach and take the food.

At this point, however, the training which aimed to make the verbal stimulus of the cat's name constitute a stimulus that would bring on approach responses was not complete. While the verbal stimulus was part of the total stimulus that would control approaching, the other stimuli—especially the sight of the food—were still more effective in this respect. The author then began conditioning procedures to gradually bring the cat's approach response under control of the verbal stimulus by itself. First, this training procedure consisted of conditioning trials conducted when the author was progressively further and further away from the cat.

Under this circumstance the cat soon came to any part of the room when the author kneeled, called MAX, and extended the food. Then the author began to make the food stimulus less conspicuous, and finally kept the food hidden in his hand. At this point the controlling stimuli for the kitten's approach response was the sight of the author kneeling and the verbal stimulus MAX.

The next step was to remove the sight of the author as a controlling stimulus. This was also done in steps. First the author positioned himself so that he was only partly visible behind a door leading to another room in the house. Then trials were conducted where he was not visible, but was out of sight in that room. At this point the verbal stimulus MAX had come to control the approach response. The completion of the training then only involved making the verbal stimulus a controlling stimulus no matter where it emanated from. Thus, the author would then place himself in various places in the house in a kind of "hide-and-seek" training. The conditioning was the same: the kitten's name MAX would be called—several times as the animal "attempted to locate the source of the sound." After success inside the house, this training was elaborated to include the outdoors.

The training extended over a period of time, with only a few trials being conducted each day. After the first few trials the kitten's response became quite active and when the name was presented the animal moved with alacrity. The analysis of this type of language learning and the experimental procedure itself were confirmed in replications involving the two additional cats and the beagle dog already mentioned. In each case, after the animal involved came to respond to its name stimulus, further training was conducted to bring the approach response under the control of the author's whistle—since this is a more effective stimulus for application out-of-doors.

This training was conducted simply by calling the animal's name, when the author was out of sight, and then following this by a whistle. The stimuli were alternated until the animal responded correctly. The verbal stimulus would control the approach insuring that the response occurred in the presence of the whistle which was to become a discriminative stimulus. After several trials, the verbal stimulus was removed; approaching the whistle alone then occurred and was reinforced. Repetitions of this experience brought the response under the control of the whistle. It should be indicated that this training was actually a type of communication. That is, the verbal cue MAX which had come as a discriminative stimulus to control a motor response could "transfer" the control to another stimulus. This type of communnciation will be described more fully later on.

In the case of the beagle dog, this training was extended an additional step in a procedure conducted to insure that the dog stayed near the house. Beagles tend to be wanderers and, after losing the animal for a week the following training was conducted. The animal would be left out-of-doors and allowed to wander a short distance away. Then the author would whistle and, when the dog came running, would reinforce the behavior with a bit of food.

Gradually, longer and longer periods of time were allowed to lapse before the training trials were presented. The training insured, however, that many times during the day the animal would be reinforced for responding to the whistle and running back to the house. The result was that the dog stayed in the proximity of the house, and responded to the author's whistle with precision and exuberant alacrity.

The principle of learning involved in this study will be dealt with extensively further on, both theoretically as well as experimentally. It may be stated here, however, that the type of conditioning involved in these experimental-naturalistic demonstrations constitutes a very important part of human language learning. For example, at a very basic level of cognitive development it is very important that speech stimuli come to generally control motor behavior of the child. Children differ in the extent to which verbal stimuli gain this control and their ability to learn from verbal stimuli is affected. Thus, in the present example it was easy for the cat to learn to respond to the whistle, based on the fact that she already had learned to respond to the word MAX. Because of the language learning, the long drawn out original training could be short-circuited.

In general, a child who more quickly comes under the control of a wide variety of verbal stimuli will be in position to learn things more quickly, and will not require more cumbersome, and some times punitive, treatment. A child who responds appropriately when the adult says COME TO ME, for example, will be treated differently than the child who does not respond at all, or only responds with a long delay. As will be discussed in greater detail later, a child who makes the appropriate motor responses to the verbal stimuli LOOK AT SUCH AND SUCH will receive learning experiences that will not occur if his motor behavior is not appropriately controlled. There are many, many such examples.

Initial procedures for training the child, so that verbal stimuli control his motor responses, can be derived directly from the preceding analysis. An example may be taken from another experimental-naturalistic demonstration, this time with the author's preverbal daughter (aged in the vicinity of 7 months). The same procedures were used. The verbal stimuli were COME TO DADDY. The stimulus that originally controlled the approach (crawling) response would be an attractive toy or object (jingling keys, for example). Later, reinforcement consisted of affection, play, or edible stimuli. Through this type of training the child came to respond to the verbal stimuli. At an even earlier stage the parent can make his verbal stimuli control attentional responses—another type of experimental-naturalistic finding that will be discussed further on.

From these beginning steps in bringing the child's motor behaviors generally under the control of verbal stimuli, extensive learning experiences of the individual ordinarily result in a vast repertoire of verbal stimuli-motor response associations. Thus, the child may bring a house visitor an object like an ashtray. When this motor behavior is reinforced as is customary, it may be observed that the child's general "bringing" behavior is strengthened under the control of the visitor, and the child will bring various items. This behavior will finally not be reinforced. Over a period of time the child will receive reinforcement for bringing things only when a preceding verbal stimulus has been presented, for example, BRING ME SUCH AND SUCH.

It is because we are reinforced for doing things in the presence of verbal stimuli that they become discriminative stimuli capable of controlling our behaviors. We pass the salt in the presence of the verbal stimuli PASS THE SALT PLEASE, as another example. Actually, during the course of the child's training a large repertoire of responses is learned in this way. In the presence of such verbal stimuli as OPEN YOUR EYE, EXTEND YOUR TONGUE, BEND YOUR LEG, PUT YOUR RIGHT FOOT FORWARD, LOOK AT THIS CURVE, PRESS WITH YOUR INDEX FINGER, and so on, the person is reinforced for making the correct response. It should be emphasized that a very extensive repertoire of verbally controlled behaviors must be acquired. Such a repertoire is crucial in the individual's intrapersonal (as in reasoning) and interpersonal adjustment. Severe deficits in this repertoire may lead to inappropriate behaviors in many life situations, as will be discussed later.

It should be pointed out that the individual will ordinarily also learn in the same manner to respond to the verbal stimuli he himself produces. A child will customarily be reinforced when he does what he says he will do. When a child says he will mow the lawn, the motor behavior that is controlled is followed by reinforcement. If the child says he is going to raise his arm he is reinforced for the appropriate motor responses, not some other response. When the individual's actions are not appropriate for what he has said he will frequently be punished, not only just not reinforced.

The importance of language as a vast quantity of stimuli that control various types of human motor behavior cannot be underestimated since it is one of the most powerful functions of language, accounting for a good proportion of the efficacy of human behavior. As will be described later on, the individual may, for example, acquire new sequences of motor skills by responding individually to series of verbal stimuli. At any rate, for almost every individual, training is given in which verbal stimuli (produced by others or by oneself) come to control motor responses. The extent to which one will acquire such a repertoire will of course vary as a function of one's training. Thus, the dancer will acquire skilled motor behaviors under the control of verbal stimuli in a manner that the ordinary person will not. It is suggested that because of these individual differences in conditioning experiences, people will differ widely in the extent and quality of the development of this repertoire. These differences will affect the individual's performance and learning in many situations.

One more point should be made. It has been suggested that a speech response may serve as a conditioned stimulus (^CS) and elicit an emotional response (or a conditioned image). It has also been suggested that speech may serve as a discriminative stimulus (^DS) and control instrumental behaviors. Later it will also be shown that speech may have an additional stimulus function—it may serve as a reinforcing stimulus which can strengthen other behaviors according to instrumental conditioning principles. Moreover, as we will see, *these three functions of stimuli are interrelated.* Although this was not noted in each case, it is extremely important to stress again that the individual's own speech may serve all of these stimulus functions for himself (as well as for others). *This suggests that the individual's own speech will contribute to the control of his other behaviors in the same manner as someone else's speech. And the individual will also condition himself through his own speech in the various ways possible through language.* We can control someone's behavior by what we get them to say—which is why communication, propaganda, and so on, are so significant as determinants of human behavior.

5

Speech as a response

In the preceding section the theoretical extension of the principle of instrumental conditioning was that verbal stimuli can become discriminative stimuli which will control motor responses. Naturalistic observation suggests that an important part of language involves such control by verbal stimuli. The principle of instrumental conditioning, however, also extends to language in another way since speech itself is a motor response.

This is not a new suggestion. Watson (1924), for example, suggested that vocalizations are responses, subject to the principles of conditioning. This may be considered to be a theoretical extension of the basic principles. In the case to be dealt with, the hypothesis involved is that vocalizations are motor responses which are acquired according to instrumental conditioning principles. This hypothesis, as will be described, has been involved in the work of a number of investigators (see Krasner, 1958; Rheingold, *et al.*, 1959; Skinner, 1957; Salzinger, 1959; Staats, 1955, 1957*a*, 1957*b*, 1961, 1963, 1964*a*; Weisberg, 1963). Skinner (1957) and Staats (Staats, 1961, 1964*a*, 1964*b*, 1964*c*, 1964*d*, 1966; Staats and Staats, 1963) have developed general learning analyses of language in which these principles play an important role.

The manner in which the hypothesis that vocalizations are responses that are instrumentally conditioned has been experimentally verified may be briefly mentioned at this point. Rheingold, *et al.* (1959) performed a very original and important study in which they demonstrated that the vocalizations of 3-month-old infants could be increased in strength by presenting reinforcers contingent upon this type of response. The procedure was a simple one. An experimenter stationed himself by the infant's crib and whenever a vocal response was emitted the experimenter smiled, clucked, and lightly squeezed the child's abdomen—in the traditional manner of parents. Under this type of conditioning, the frequency of vocal responses was increased. When the reinforcement for the vocal responses was no longer presented, extinction ensued as would be expected. These results have been replicated with more precise experimental control by Weisberg (1963).

Speech responses have also been shown to function according to operant conditioning principles by Salzinger, *et al.* (1962). These investigators arranged a situation in which when the child spoke for a certain period of time this was counted as a response and reinforcement was presented. It was found that the rate of speech responding could in this way be increased through reinforcement, and that withdrawal of reinforcement resulted in extinction of the strength of the response.

In addition, a number of studies have been conducted with adults which involve making a reinforcement contingent upon speech responses (see Krasner, 1958; and Salzinger, 1959, for summaries), then assessing whether the speech responses increase in frequency. In a typical experiment of this type, the subject may simply be told to say different single words, not sentences. The experimenter will reinforce a particular class of speech responses and measure the relative frequency of the class in the total vocal responses emitted by the subject. Let us say that the experimenter is reinforcing animal words. Whenever the subject says an animal word the experimenter will present the reinforcer. Common reinforcers used have been other words such as *good, fine, very good,* and the like, or points which the subject has been told he should accrue to the greatest extent possible.

The results have generally shown that when individual members of a class of speech responses are reinforced, the other members of the class of responses also increase in strength. Although these experiments are deficient in not indicating why words like *good* function as reinforcers, and why reinforcing one word will strengthen others, in general the results support the operant conditioning interpretation of speech responses. (These two aspects of these studies will be discussed further in later chapters.)

SPEECH ACQUISITION

The author has analyzed the original acquisition of speech by the infant in more detail (Staats and Staats, 1963), and the process will only be summarized here. (This analysis is based partly on derivations from the basic learning theory and naturalistic observations, but primarily upon experimental-naturalistic research on the speech training of the author's daughter.) In infancy it is likely that speech sounds are simply neutral stimuli, having no reinforcing properties. However, it is customary for the parents to speak in the presence of the infant frequently, many times at the same time that the parent is engaged in caring for the child. By caring for the child is meant the act of providing the child with positive reinforcers (food, water, warmth, tactual stimulation, and the like) as well as the removal of negative reinforcers (wet, dirty, and chafing diapers, painful stimuli of various kinds, and so on). As a consequence, the speech sounds of the parent, as well as the other stimulus aspects of the parent, become positive learned (or conditioned) reinforcers. The precise principles will be described later, but the important fact that the parents' voices become reinforcers should be well understood.

The reason that this is so important in the early development of speech is that the child's voice is similar to the speech sounds of the parents. The more similar the child's speech sound is, the more reinforcing it will be. Following this analysis, it would be expected that when the child made a vocal response that produced a sound like that in the speech of the parents, the vocal response would be more heavily reinforced than when the child produced a sound very unlike the speech sounds of the parents. Thus, because certain of the infant's speech sounds are more reinforcing (more like those of the parents) the infant should through instrumental conditioning come to make those responses more frequently. Moreover, the reinforcement should have the effect of molding the child's specific vocal responses to more and more resemble the speech sounds of the parents. (The technical term for this type of learning is differentiation.) There are many, many opportunities for such conditioning trials. As would be expected on the basis of this analysis, observations of infant's speech shows that it gradually comes to include syllables that occur in the parents' speech (Irwin, 1948, 1952).

Based upon this analysis, the author in the experimental-naturalistic study of his daughter's speech development systematically paired his voice with stimuli that were positive reinforcers for the child. Thus, before entering the child's room in the morning the author would first say

"Daddy," "Daddy." This would be expected to make the auditory stimulus a positive reinforcer since the parent is a positive reinforcer, especially after an absence. In addition, whenever presenting a reinforcing object or event to the child, the name of the stimulus was spoken. Systematic attempts were also made to speak when the child was eating or otherwise experiencing positive reinforcement. This is done by some parents simply because of their own training. However, as in the present example, systematic attention to the opportunities for producing the conditioning should accelerate the process. It is worth noting that the present child began speaking clear words at the age of 9 months.

In short, it is suggested that these are generally the principles involved in the original acquisition of speech sounds. Some of the child's speech sounds become especially reinforcing. This has the effect of differentially strengthening those vocal responses that produce the reinforcing sounds. There are large opportunities for making the parents' vocal sounds (and thus the child's) into strong positive reinforcers. On the other hand, a training environment may be deficient in that it fails to provide the correct conditions for learning. It is no wonder, then, that there are children who are greatly accelerated in this type of behavior development, and on the other hand children who are very retarded or who do not develop the behavior at all.

After this gradual acquisition of a repertoire of imitative vocal responses through differential "self-reinforcement," a response (or a few responses) will become so like the speech sounds of the parents that they will consider it a recognizable word. At this point the parents can begin to directly reinforce the speech response of the child. When the child makes the response the parents can provide some reinforcing stimulus and the word response will rapidly become more frequent in the child's vocal repertoire. Thus, when the child says "Mommy" or "Daddy" the parent will ordinarily respond immediately with attention, affection, and so on. When the child says BREAD he is reinforced with that stimulus. When he says LOOK he is reinforced by the parent looking at him. Of course, the first responses of this type are not perfect and only will gradually become so because the more perfect responses produce more reinforcing sounds (more like the parents) and because the parents, and others, will respond more quickly to such sounds, and thus provide more immediate reinforcement for the vocal response. Of course, even at this early level of language development, different parents will vary in the extent to which they are good and sensitive "trainers." Some will be sensitive to the child's behavior and respond (reinforce) appropriately. Parents who do not do so when the first good word responses occur will not have children who speak as early as would be possible. Parents who do not gradually reinforce better speech responses in their children will not have children who acquire a precise vocal repertoire as rapidly as would be possible. This applies to each of the other types of training in which the parents participate.

THE STIMULUS CONTROL OF SPEECH

In the preceding section, vocalizations were discussed in their role as responses, and it was indicated that vocal responses that are reinforced increase in frequency. That is, the responses that receive reinforcement become more dominant in contrast to responses that do not occur in that language community and thus are not reinforced.

In the differential "self-reinforcement" process of acquiring the original parent-like speech response, the stimulus situation in which the response occurs is not likely to be very important, except in a more general way. That is, the child might tend to vocalize more in his crib when he is alone, or in various parts of the house during certain types of activities. However, a very important aspect of speech development involves the fact that specific vocal response will come under the control of specific stimuli. It is not only necessary that the child acquire the motor skills involved in sounding a word, but in addition particular stimuli must come to bring on the response. Ordinarily, the conditioning experience necessary to establish the stimulus control of vocal responses begins as soon as the people begin to reinforce the child for speaking.

That is, the vocal responses of the child are customarily reinforced only when the response occurs in the appropriate stimulus circumstances. This was implicit in the discussion presented in the preceding section. For example, the child is reinforced, when he says LOOK, by the parent's response—but the parent must be present before this can occur. So such verbal responses must come under the control of people as discriminative stimuli. As another example, the child is reinforced for saying CAT when he is looking at a cat—not when he is looking at a baby. This is generally the case with many noun verbal responses such as DADDY, MOMMY, CAR, DOG, and so on.

This treatment of course fulfills the general requirements for instrumental conditioning which states that a response which is reinforced in the presence of a stimulus will come to be controlled by that stimulus. When the child is reinforced for saying DADDY while looking at his father, it is to be expected that his father as a stimulus will come to control that response. It will thus be more likely that the child will say DADDY when his father is present.

It is quite easy to show in the laboratory that fine discriminative stimulus control may be established through instrumental reinforcement. Let us say that we have operantly conditioned a rat to press the lever frequently. Then we introduce a new condition, sometimes a light bulb is turned on outside of the conditioning apparatus, sometimes it is off, and the two are alternated. However, when the light is off if the rat presses the bar he is reinforced with a food pellet. When the light is on, on the other hand, his responses are not followed by reinforcement. Under this circumstance the response will extinguish in the stimulus condition with the light. The light stimulus situation will come to control no-responding. On the other hand the reinforcement will strengthen the bar-press response in the presence of the stimulus situation when there is no light.

It should be seen that when the light is turned off the rat will immediately begin responding. When the light goes on, however, this stimulus condition will result in cessation of bar pressing. Thus, the two events will come to *control* the animal's behavior. The stimulus (the absence of light) that controls the responding is called the discriminative stimulus. The other stimulus (the presence of light) is also a discriminative stimulus ($^D S$). However, in this case it comes to control not making the response.

There have been many demonstrations that coming to say a vocal response under the control of a stimulus follows instrumental learning principles. For example, many studies of paired associate and serial verbal learning have shown that subjects can learn to make a particular vocal response in the presence of a verbal stimulus. While his account of language is subject to many criticisms (see Chomsky 1959; Miller, 1965), Skinner (1957) has productively suggested that vocal responses come under the control of various broad categories of stimuli in everyday life. The suggestion lends itself to a general consideration of the manner in which instrumental conditioning principles are involved in naturalistic language learning. One of the important categories of controlling stimuli consists of environmental stimuli. The present author (see Staats, 1964a; Staats and Staats, 1963) has extended the principle of instrumental discrimination to consideration of various aspects of language development and function. Additional extensions will be added in the following summary.

Word Responses under Environmental Stimulus Control: Labeling

When the child first says DADDY, or some approximation, the child's parents reinforce the response, let us say. However, if this is done, as may be the case, whether or not the father is present or the child is looking at the father, the response will be strengthened in the presence of various stimuli. Since the stimulus control is not specific the child may say DADDY when the father is not present, while he looks at other people, and so on. Ordinarily, however, the parents will come to selectively reinforce the response so that reinforcement occurs only when the father *is* present. Thus, when the father is present he may go to the child, look at the child, and so on; but when the father is absent no such consequence takes place. The person present is likely to simply correct the child.

At this point, because of this differential reinforcement, a certain amount of precise stimulus control will be established, but the process will not be complete. Thus, it may be seen that the child will say DADDY in the presence of males similar to the father, although he would not do so to females and children. Since the response will only be reinforced when he calls the father DADDY, further discrimination training will result in precise stimulus control of this response.

The author has tested the possibility of producing language development in this way many times in experimental-naturalistic research. For example, it is possible to quickly develop stimulus controlled speech responses by noting word responses (babbling) that resemble an adult's labeling response for an object. Thus, the author's daughter would say DA frequently. It was relatively simple to show her a toy dog on one of those instances, and provide her with social reinforcement (and also repeat the word DA, and by this means increase the frequency of saying "da" in the presence of the toy dog. A "game" can easily arise here where the dog is presented when the child says DA, thus providing further opportunity for reinforcing the speech response in the presence of the object. (As will be described later this type of training also produces imitative speech responses in the child.) Systematic training procedures of this type can quickly produce a small stimulus-controlled speech repertoire in the child before he is a year old.

Although the first verbal responses under environmental stimulus control come about through this type of instrumental discrimination training, after the child has learned a repertoire of imitative vocal responses learning will become more rapid. That is, the parent may hold up a ball and say BALL, CAN YOU SAY BALL? When the child imitates the word while looking at the ball, the parent may hug the child, compliment him, or present some other conditioned reinforcer. Later when the child is trying to get a ball that is out of reach the parent may say WHAT IS THIS? and when the child says the word (or reasonable facsimile) reinforce him by giving him the ball. Each of these are instrumental conditioning trials which will bring the child's response BALL under the control of the ball as a discriminative stimulus.

This vocal response, however, would be expected to also occur to similar stimulus objects as a consequence of the preceding conditioning. However, if the word response BALL is reinforced *only* in the presence of balls—not in the presence of apples, oranges, and other round objects— only ball stimuli will come to precisely control the vocal responses.

It is suggested that these types of conditioning experiences are very important to the child's language development—and numerous experiences of this kind appear to occur for most children. When the child goes on an automobile ride with his parents, for a walk to the store, and so on, there are many occasions upon which the child looks at an object or event at the same time as the appropriate word is presented. The child is asked to repeat the word, and the response is reinforced. Thus, the child acquires naming vocal responses to a variety of environmental events.

For example, in the presence of a moving automobile the child might be told that it is moving. When the child says MOVING in the presence of something moving, the response is reinforced. A moving object thus becomes the discriminative stimulus for that speech response. If an automobile is also a discriminative stimulus for the response AUTOMOBILE, then in the presence of a moving automobile, the child will tend to emit the response AUTOMOBILE MOVING, or some such statement. Through this training the child may be thought to learn both simple and complex speech responses to many events.

The child may also learn to name various actions of other organisms in a similar manner. In the presence of certain visual and auditory stimuli occurring when father is angry, such as scowling facial expressions or a loud voice, the child may be told DADDY IS ANGRY, and reinforcement follows if he repeats ANGRY. In this way the child would be instrumentally conditioned to make the appropriate speech response in this particular stimulus situation. Other verbal responses will ordinarily be conditioned in this manner to other stimulus situations that involve various postures and movements of people and animals.

This learning seems also to be carried on in great detail in ordinary language training. Although at first reinforcement may follow upon saying AUTOMOBILE in the presence of the total stimulus object, eventually reinforcement may be made contingent upon emitting the appropriate speech responses with various parts of the object serving as the discriminative stimuli. In other words, the child may be put through very detailed discrimination training in the presence of subaspects of the total stimulus. The acquisition of each new speech response involves the same principles.

The quality, extent, and precision of the individual's speech repertoire with respect to labeling objects and events is of great importance in his cognitive development. Such training is important for the scientist, for example. Before he can respond differentially to complex stimuli and to slight differences in such stimuli, the individual must have undergone complex discrimination training. The responses involved in this type of training are usually verbal. Thus, one aspect of becoming expert in a particular field is the acquisition of appropriate vocal responses to the objects and events with which that field is concerned. The botanist acquires his special repertoire of speech responses to certain objects, as does the biologist or physicist, or the physician or lawyer.

Again great differences occur in the extent to which the parent is a good "trainer" of a labeling repertoire in his child. Deficits, or idiosyncrasies in the parent's repertoire—or lack of training skills—will incapacitate the parent in this role. It is also to be expected that a parent or teacher who himself has been trained to respond discriminatively to fine details of his environment will be able to apply finely detailed discrimination training to the child. The child on a hike with the ordinary parent, for example, will receive verbal discrimination training in the presence of trees, bushes, flowers, and so on. The child of the parent whose verbal responses are in addition under the control of different types of trees, and the like, as well as various parts and functions of these stimulus objects (as would be the case with a botanist), will undergo a greatly expanded form of discrimination training. This child will consequently emerge with a much finer set of verbal discriminations.

The importance of the labeling repertoire in cognitive development and function has not been adequately studied. It is also important to develop specific procedures for producing this repertoire quickly and in the form that is desired. Later studies will illustrate experimentally these possibilites.

Word Responses under the Control
of Internal Stimuli: Self-labeling

It has been suggested (Skinner, 1957) that the operation of deprivation comes to control verbal responses, without specifying what the controlling stimuli might be. This suggestion may be elaborated by indicating that deprivation produces internal stimuli. Furthermore, there are many other types of internal stimuli that must come to serve as controlling discriminative stimuli for various speech responses.

Let us first take an example involving drive stimuli. An individual who has not had liquids for some time will experience dryness in his mouth and throat. This may be considered to be a stimulus, which can assume any of the functions of a stimulus, including that of becoming a discriminative stimulus which controls some vocal response. The way this can come about appears to be relatively simple. Let us say that a child has gone without fluids for some time. This will produce various aversive internal stimuli, including those mentioned above. As a consequence the child will display irritable and restless behavior. The parent who has observed the deprivation of fluids and the irritable behavior can then say DO YOU WANT WATER? Let us also say that the child has learned to repeat the word WATER, and does so here. If the parent then gives the child water, which will constitute a reinforcing stimulus, then the procedures for instrumental conditioning will be complete. That is, in the presence of the internal stimulus of the dry mouth and throat, and so on, the child will have been reinforced for saying WATER. These stimuli would thus become discriminative stimuli which would later control the vocal responses of saying WATER.

There is an analogous process for more easily seen aversive drive stimuli. The presentation of aversive stimuli may come to control verbal responses because the verbal behavior has in the past been reinforced by the removal of the aversive stimulation. We learn to say WOULD YOU PLEASE TURN THE RADIO DOWN because in the presence of the aversive auditory stimulation this speech response has been followed by the reinforcement of the diminution of the stimulus. Toilet training of a child appropriately involves the same principle. In the presence of a distended bladder or rectum, which produces aversive stimulation, the child can be prompted to say "potty" and then be helped to reduce that stimulation. This training makes the internal stimulation into a discriminative stimulus controlling the vocal response. When these internal stimuli come to control the child's verbal and overt behavior, then the child is toilet-trained.

A similar type of training seems to be involved in the development of another type of very important verbal response, "the ability to report internal conditions." Unlike adults, young children, prior to the requisite training, are not able to "tell you what is wrong with them." A young child may cry and fret and in general give the impression that something is wrong, but make no specific speech response. Until the appropriate training has occurred, the many internal stimuli which for an adult control certain verbal responses will not control the child's verbal behavior in that way.

Eliminating crying as a verbal response, an example of a first speech response which seems to come under the control of painful stimuli, especially as the result of an accident, can be the word HURT. In the same manner as described, this single response to a constellation of stimuli will be elaborated into a large vocabulary of speech responses under the control of internal stimuli. When the child comes to the mother and says HURT, the parent can respond WHERE? Although the child has an earache, these stimuli will only elicit the response HURT even though the child may have the speech response EAR in his repertoire. The parent may notice, however, that the child is rubbing an ear and ask, DOES IT HURT IN YOUR EAR? When the child nods, the parent should say, YOU HAVE AN EARACHE. When the child repeats EAR-ACHE this vocal response will come under the control of the specific painful stimulus. (As will be indicated later, it is not necessary to present reinforcement to complete the conditioning after the child's language repertoire has progressed sufficiently.)

Each child normally receives this type of training in the presence of a multitude of internal stimuli. When the child's verbal responses come under the control of specific aversive internal stimuli, it is often possible to reduce this aversive stimulation (which means to positively reinforce the child). Again, the more detailed the child's ability to respond discriminatively to these stimuli, the more appropriate the possible treatment. Ordinarily, fine discrimination will occur to different types of internal aversive stimuli such that discriminated verbal responses as IT BURNS, IT THROBS, IT IS A DULL ACHE, IT IS A SHARP PAIN, and so on, will be formed.

There are many other internal stimuli besides those produced by responses to injury or illness to which the child may be trained to respond discriminatively with different speech responses. In the presence of the stimuli resulting from deprivation, the child will learn to say I WANT SUCH AND SUCH. In the presence of the same stimuli, but also in the presence of the failure to obtain the object, the individual will learn to emit such speech responses as I AM FRUSTRATED BECAUSE I CAN'T GET SUCH AND SUCH, and so on. The individual seems to receive training through which the verbal responses, I AM HAPPY, I HATE TO WORK, I LOVE YOU, I AM JEALOUS, I DESIRE THIS, I'M IMPA-TIENT, and so on, come under the control of the appropriate internal stimulation. In all probability this discussion oversimplifies the complex learning involved here. It is suggested, however, that this type of learning is involved in the child's acquisition of verbal statements made to his own body sensations.

Another situation in which verbal behavior should come under the control of internal stimuli according to the principles of instrumental discrimination learning involves the formation of verbal discriminations to one's own overt behaviors. In the same manner that a child may learn to label an event, he may learn to label the event of his own behavior— again, on the basis of the stimuli it produces. For example, the child may be prompted to echo the word RUNNING while looking at a boy running and be reinforced when he says the word. After this, the child would be likely to emit the speech response RUNNING in the presence of the visual stimulus of a running boy. In the same manner, the child may be prompted to emit the response running in the presence of the stimuli produced by his own running, and the verbal response would thus come under the control of these stimuli. The stimuli would include the internal stimuli produced by the rapid muscular and tendon movements, as well as external stimuli such as visual stimuli.

The child will normally learn verbal discriminations to many of his movements; for example, in the presence of the stimuli produced by his lifted arm, he will have some tendency to say I LIFTED MY ARM. Such discriminations may be formed far past the point usually required under average circumstances, although normally this requires a specially trained parent, coach, or teacher. We would find, for example, that an expert diver, ballet dancer, boxer, or violinist would have a repertoire of discriminated speech responses to different movements that are much more finely detailed in certain ways than are the responses of people in general; these discriminations would also differ from one of these experts to another. These discriminations may be very important in the further learning of the individual and constitute a basic and general skill.

The developing child will learn such speech responses not only to the stimuli produced by specific movements, but also to the complex stimuli of various kinds produced by certain of his own complex acts. For example, if a child strikes another and the other child cries, an adult may respond with YOU SHOULDN'T DO THAT and prompt the child to repeat the phrase I WAS MEAN, I SHOULDN'T DO THAT, reinforcing the child upon the emission of that response. In this way a child seems to learn speech responses to his own behavior and its effects upon others. That is, the stimuli produced by his own behavior and the behavior of those he effects will come to control certain speech responses. The individual thus learns a whole repertoire of verbal responses descriptive of his own behavior and the responses of others to his behavior. In various situations the child learns to say I WAS MEAN, I WAS KIND, I WAS AMUSING, I WAS SUCCESSFUL, I BEHAVED LIKE AN IDIOT, I WAS SOCIABLE, and so on. As the author has indicated, the verbal responses he learns to his own stimuli—internal, external, and behavior produced—are heavily involved in what is called the *self-concept* (Staats and Staats, 1963).

These are only examples of the types of stimuli that are thought to come to control particular speech responses of the individual according to learning principles. These verbal responses enter significantly into other behaviors of the individual and help determine the individual's adjustment. In order to understand how language functions in this manner it is necessary to understand thoroughly the development of the specific behaviors involved.

A Symbolic Function of Images:
Control of Speech and Other Instrumental Behaviors

An important aspect of a theory of language involves explication of its function as well as its acquisition. In the preceding part it was indicated that some environmental stimuli elicit sensory responses in the individual. These sensory responses, or images, can be conditioned to various stimuli including verbal stimuli (words). The conditioned sensory responses constitute a type of word meaning, some of the functions of which will be described now.

As has been indicated, conditioned sensory responses have stimulus properties. For example, visual conditioned sensory responses have visual stimulus properties. (These properties are reduced versions of those that occur when the full sensory response is elicited by the actual stimulus object—rather than the conditioned sensory response that occurs when the object is not present.) To continue, however, since conditioned sensory responses have stimulus properties (which are the images) they can come to control other responses. Instrumental responses of various kinds can come under the control of such images.

For example, the child who has been instrumentally conditioned to cry at the sight of an actual dog will cry or whimper in reduced form at the image of dog as it occurs in a dream, or as the image is evoked by words in a story. This is a complex S–R process which will not be detailed here. The process, however, involves the elicitation of the conditioned sensory response by some stimulus, which could be a preceding image in a sequence. The image produced by the sensory response then controls the instrumental response.

One of the important types of instrumental behaviors that comes to be controlled by images is that of speech (including such forms as writing). A more detailed analysis of this mechanism will be made later on in the description of verbal habit-families. At this point, however, it should be indicated that labeling speech responses that describe objects come under the control of the sensory responses made to those objects. When these sensory responses in conditioned form occur later on, in the absence of the object, the stimuli they produce (the images) may control the speech responses as though the relevant object were present. Thus, an individual may have certain primary sensory experiences that produce a sequence or constellation of sensory responses. Later on, when the conditioned sensory responses (resulting from this experience) are elicited by some other stimulus, they may control the speech responses. The result is a description of the original sensory experience. That is, a person, let us say, takes a sight seeing trip during which time a sequence of environmental stimuli elicit in him a sequence of sensory responses. Through classical conditioning the first sensory responses comes to elicit the next conditioned sensory response, this comes to elicit the next conditioned sensory response, and so on. The result is a sequence of conditioned sensory responses. Later on when asked what he has seen, the sequence of conditioned sensory responses are elicited and the images that are produced serve to mediate the individual's description of the actual events.

As will be described in the analysis of verbal habit-families, since the words elicit the same conditioned sensory responses in the listener, the listener too may have a sequence of images that is like the events seen by the speaker. Thus, these processes serve a symbolic function for the person who has the direct experience as well as for anyone else whom he stimulates through his written or spoken speech.

The function of conditioned sensory responses in controlling other instrumental behaviors constitutes an extremely important aspect of cognitive behavior. It is this mechanism that enables many of the symbolic aspects of language to occur. It should be noted that the parent may hasten this type of cognitive development by providing his young child with experiences in which verbal stimuli are paired with the appropriate stimulus object or event.

A Symbolic Function of Emotions: Control of Speech and Other Behaviors

It may be added here that the same analysis applies also to conditioned emotional responses. There are stimulus components to emotional responses; and other responses, including speech responses, can come to be controlled by these stimulus components. This mechanism will be elaborated later on. It may merely be stated here that positive emotional (reinforcing) responses come to control a large class of verbal and non-verbal "approach" responses and negative emotional (aversive) responses come to control a large class of verbal and non-verbal "avoidance" responses. To give an example of this type of language control, let us say that a child has been to the doctor's office where he received a painful shot. The negative emotional response elicited would be conditioned to the sensory responses of the doctor and his office, and so on. On being asked later about doctors, or his visit, the negative emotional response would be elicited. This emotional response would produce stimuli that would control verbal responses such as I HATE DOCTORS, I DON'T WANT TO GO TO THE HOSPITAL, and so on. The child would also physically avoid the actual stimuli, if possible.

Vocal Imitation (Word Matching)

When the child has come to emit a vocal response which is like a word used in the speech community (for example, the family) and when the stimulus produced by the vocal response is a reinforcing stimulus, then the stage is set for the child to learn an imitative vocal response. Let us say that the child emits a vocal response that produces a word stimulus that is reinforcing. If that is so, the reinforcement will result in the response occurring again, in a repetitive fashion. This will mean that the auditory word stimulus will be followed by a vocal response which produces a reinforcing word stimulus. Thus, the word stimulus will occur both before as well as after the vocal response.

When the word stimulus precedes the vocal response, and since the vocal response is followed by reinforcement, it would be expected that the word stimulus would become a discriminative stimulus which would bring on the vocal response. This indicates the process by which the child can first learn to "repeat" word sounds. It is suggested, in a manner similar to that suggested by others (Allport, 1924), that babbling which involves repetitions of syllables and words may be considered to involve this imitation learning. In the present case, moreover, it is possible to describe this process in terms of instrumental conditioning principles.

However, the child does not train *himself* to an imitative repertoire. The parents ordinarily come into the process when the child begins to emit vocal responses that are like words. The following example, which occurred to the author in training his daughter, may be used to illustrate the process.

Upon first hearing the child say BEEBEE the author reinforced the child by smiling, attention, and so on, and at the same time said himself BAYBEE, VERY GOOD, BAYBEE. This would be expected to increase the strength of the child's response and it would be likely that the child would repeat the word response, as happened. This then constituted another conditioning trial in which the vocal response BEEBEE was reinforced in the presence of the stimulus *baybee*.

Taking the example a step further, however, let us say that the parent gets a doll and shows it to the child and says "baybee," and the child repeats his response by saying BEEBEE. When this is followed by reinforcement two types of conditioning result. The child's response BEEBEE will come under the control of the doll as a discriminative stimulus. And, the discriminative stimulus control of the parent's speech stimulus "baybee" for the child's speech response BEEBEE will be further strengthened.

The latter type of learning is the subject of attention here, and the illustration can be considered to be one example of how the child acquires repertoire of imitative vocal responses. It seems that children normally learn to match their speech responses to the speech responses of others in an analogous manner. When the parent states, "Say water," a response which produces a sound like that made by the parent is reinforced immediately. If a different sound is emitted, however, the request is repeated and reinforcement delayed. In other words, in the presence of matched imitated sounds, one of which he has produced himself, the child receives reinforcement—but no reinforcement is forthcoming in the absence of matched sounds. It is suggested that the child thus comes to discriminate matched from unmatched sounds.

Word Responses Controlled by (the Stimuli Produced by)
Preceding Word Responses

Concern with "mental" associations, like an interest in word meaning, predates the development of scientific psychology by several centuries. Not, however, until the latter part of the nineteenth century did experimental work on word associations commence. Prior to that time, philosophical contributions to knowledge were based largely upon introspection of their own experiences. And, the philosophers were interested primarily in associations as a source of information about the nature of the "mind." They were not concerned with establishing relationships between independent variables and the consequent behavior they produce.

Since the beginning of the experimental study of the variables that affect word associations, however, innumerable laboratory studies have been conducted to show how one word response (or the stimulus it produces) can come to control a following word response. While laboratory studies have been quite successful in isolating in considerable detail those variables involved in the acquisition and maintenance of word associations, there has been little systematic effort to analyze the ways that word associations are formed in everyday language experience, and to relate the function of word associations to other complex cognitive behaviors. The functional significance of word associations will be discussed later. At this point the process by which word associations are established will be described.

The study of the formation of word associations has been studied under the label of *serial verbal learning* and *paired associate learning*. In the latter method the learning procedure involves the presentation of the verbal stimuli in pairs. The subject's task is to respond to each verbal stimulus that is presented. Thus, if the stimuli are printed he will make the verbal response under the control of the first stimulus—that is, read the stimulus—and then he will make the verbal response under the control of the second stimulus. This process may be depicted as follows.

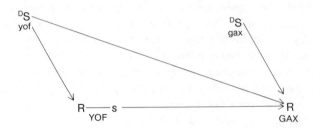

FIGURE 5.1.   The learning of a word association sequence.

That is, let us say that the first printed word, as a discriminative stimulus, elicits the first vocal response. This vocal response will produce the word stimulus. Then the subject looks at the second word stimulus and this elicits the second word response. As a consequence of this process, two types of conditioning would be expected to result. First, the second word response should come under the control of the stimulus produced by the first word response. That is, this word stimulus should become a discriminative stimulus and tend to elicit the second word response. This, then, is an example of a word association. In the figure, the first word response was YOF and this response (actually, the stimulus it produces, the auditory sound *yof*) now has tendencies to elicit the second word response GAX.

In addition, however, since the word response GAX has also occurred following the printed word stimulus *yof*, it would be expected that the printed word stimulus *yof* would also become a discriminative stimulus which would tend to elicit the word response GAX. Thus, as a result of this conditioning experience, and in addition to the above, it would be expected later on that if the subject was presented with the printed word *yof* and asked to say the first word that came to mind, he would tend to say GAX. Or if someone else were to pronounce the word *yof* and ask the subject what word this made him think of, he would tend to respond with GAX. These are ways that word associations are assessed.

One point may be touched upon here to indicate what may seem to be a discrepancy between the usual procedure for paired associate learning and the paradigm for instrumental conditioning. That is, in the paired associate learning procedure the subject is given no reinforcement although instrumental conditioning has been described to include reinforcement following the S–R occurrences. This seeming paradox will be elaborated upon later. At this time it will merely be said that instrumental conditioning can take place without reinforcement in the case where there is already a strong discriminative stimulus that controls the response. Then the discriminative stimulus may be used to bring on the response, and the response will come under the control of any stimulus that is present—simply on the basis of contiguity. Thus, a principle of higher-order instrumental conditioning is suggested.

Procedures analogous to those producing word associates seem to take place in everyday life, it may be briefly noted. It is not a complicated matter to see how the child acquires two word responses in sequence in the same manner as one response is acquired. Let us say, for example, that the child is at first reinforced when he simply says MILK. After a time, however, his parents may instruct him, PLEASE, SAY PLEASE, and withhold the milk reinforcement until the child says MILK PLEASE. This training would be expected to produce a word association between the first word response and the second in this and similar stimulus circumstances.

In addition to the laboratory experiments which have explored the principles involved in the acquisition of word associations, there have been a number of studies that have surveyed the associations which people acquire to words in our language (see Bousfield, *et al.*, 1961; Deese, 1959; Kent and Rosanoff, 1910; Russell and Jenkins, 1954). A method for ascertaining the word responses that a verbal stimulus will elicit is to present a series of words, one at a time, to a large group of subjects, and have them write down in each case the first word they "think of" (the first word response they make). These responses can then be tabulated over the group of subjects, and the word associates of each stimulus word for various people can be determined. Ordinarily, it will be found that many different subjects respond with the same associate, fewer subjects respond with another associate, fewer yet with a third, and so on. For example, when the first word response to the stimulus TABLE was obtained from 1008 college students, 840 gave CHAIR, 41 FOOD, 21 DESK, 15 TOP, 11 LEG, 9 EAT, 8 CLOTH, 7 DISH, 6 WOOD, and so on (Russell and Jenkins, 1954).

There are many other very strong associations that can be observed to occur in the speech customs of everyday life, and there are many weaker associations that, although not as obvious, nevertheless determine what our next response will be following a particular word response. These are topics, however, that will be treated more fully later on.

This completes the summary of the instrumental conditioning prin ciples and indicates some of the ways in which the principles are relevant to certain aspects of language behavior. It should be realized that there are many, many, categories of simple instrumental speech responses, only a few of which have been categorized here. It should also be indicated that category names such as labeling, self-labeling, imitation or echoing, and so on are simply descriptive terms for certain speech responses. In every case the speech response is an instrumental response, and no explanatory implication resides in the category name—which is why it is preferable to use common sense names rather than technical names. The common sense category names applied to different speech responses delineate the responses only by the type of stimulus that controls the speech response. For example, labeling responses are under the control of environmental stimulus objects and events—many nouns, and verbs, adjectives, and adverbs are in this category. Self-labeling responses are controlled largely by various internal stimuli, including emotions and images. Imitational speech is controlled by the speech stimuli of other individuals, and so on.

As some of the preceding analyses have implicitly indicated, the principles of classical conditioning and the principles of instrumental conditioning interact in the realm of human behavior—including language behavior. The next section will further elaborate the basic learning theory, additionally describing classical and instrumental conditioning principles in an integrated manner, and showing their interrelationships in language and cognitive development. Furthermore, the next section will indicate some of the complex ways that stimuli and responses can be joined together through learning, to form complex constellations, or complex S–R mechanisms. In addition to showing how learning principles apply to the acquisition of relatively simple stimulus and response mechanisms, it is important to indicate how more complex repertoires are acquired and function in the individual's adjustment. Thus, the next part elaborates and extends in summary form the conditioning principles; shows their interrelationships (which do not emerge from the animal laboratory) utilizing a new notational system; illustrates some forms of complex S–R mechanisms; and employs this basic, integrated learning theory in treating language and cognitive behavior.

Integrated learning theory and complex language interactions

6

*Basic learning principles
and their interaction,
the notational system,
and derived S–R mechanisms*

As has been described, the field of the experimental psychology of learning has largely been a morass of theoretical controversy and unorganized experimentation—from the standpoint of the person who is interested in understanding significant human behaviors. Competing theorists have developed separate terminologies. Multitudes of experiments have stemmed from each approach. And, as in any science, much experimentation produces results which will not be in the future mainstream of later theory development.

The systematist's task in such a case is to abstract the parts of this morass of knowledge which are relevant to the events in which he is interested. In doing this he must cut across the different terminologies in which the experimental results are couched—to pull together, elaborate, and derive principles that form an integral theoretical whole. Later, of course, the resulting theory and related procedures must be tested for what they yield in further experimental and theoretical efforts.

Without this type of effort the field of basic learning is not of great use in providing a general conception of human behavior, as well as in providing procedures for doing something about the problems of human behavior. As has been suggested, the field of the experimental psychology of learning has not been utilized by areas in the behavioral and social sciences because its principles and methods cannot easily be seen to form a general conception of human behavior.

Part of the task of systematizing the principles of learning into a theoretical form relevant to human behavior involves couching the terms so that classical conditioning and instrumental conditioning may be interrelated. One of the basic splits in the area of learning involves the fact that investigators tend to work either with instrumental or classical conditioning. Perhaps as a consequence, separate conventions have developed for the depiction of the S–R principles involved in each type of conditioning—with little indication of the points of overlap.

In several of the discussions to be presented, the manner in which the principles of classical and instrumental conditioning are related will be indicated. And, in this chapter summarizing the principles of an integrated learning theory, a terminological convention will be presented that reflects this integration. In addition, even at the level of stating the basic principles, the theorist must also elaborate and extend the basic principles in cases where they have not yet been treated in the laboratory. Thus, as one example, it has been suggested herein that higher-order instrumental conditioning occurs—where the discriminative control of a stimulus is transferred to a neutral stimulus with which the former is contiguously paired. This principle is a derivation that is supported by naturalistic observations and experimental-naturalistic data.

These matters concern the first level of the development of a learning conception of human behavior, the statement of the basic principles. The next lower-level theoretical statements must show how the basic principles can form complex stimulus response (S–R) constellations or mechanisms. The study of the basic, more general, principles attempts to isolate the principles in circumstances involving the simplest stimulus and response conditions. However, human behavior involves very complex stimulus-response configurations, which have been acquired over a long history of conditioning. The way these more complex S–R mechanisms are formed in terms of (or are derived from) the basic principles must be understood. While this cannot be expanded here, it is suggested that in developing a basic learning theory to be applied to human behavior, the theory must be elaborated with the goal in mind. Thus, the basic principles must be elaborated, with their interactions derived on the basis of naturalistic observations of human behavior, as well as on the basis of the findings of the basic laboratory.

The first chapter will set forth in summary form the basic learning theory. For a more complete but less advanced outline of the basic learning principles, and some of the derived S–R mechanisms, see Staats and Staats, 1963. Furthermore, the new notational system will be used and samples of complex S–R mechanisms will be described. Later chapters in the present part will deal with some of the complex aspects of language and cognition which demand analysis by such an integrated learning theory.

It is felt that a theory that organizes various results and areas within the field of learning, put into a consistent terminological convention, offers a more powerful conception of human behavior which has great generality. The discussions to be presented were formulated to show that the various simplistic learning approaches to language behavior are inadequate by themselves, but that an integrated learning theory including an elaboration of complex S–R mechanisms, constitutes a more adequate approach to language learning and cognitive development.

THE PRINCIPLES, THEIR INTERACTION, AND THE NOTATIONAL SYSTEM

The principles that form the basis of the present approach to complex human behavior, the higher-order (most general) principles, are those of classical conditioning and instrumental conditioning. From these few, relatively simple, learning principles the various more complex stimulus-response constellations can be derived. This body of basic principles and complex S–R mechanisms then constitutes a framework from which hypotheses concerning various aspects of human behavior can be further elaborated.

This is not to say that the basic principles are so firmly established that they are beyond further consideration; that all their interrelationships have been elaborated; that on these levels there is an absence of controversy; that additional research is not necessary; or that further theoretical clarification may not occur. Future research may well require revisions even in certain aspects of the basic level of the theory. However, the basic principles of classical and instrumental conditioning in general may be considered to be relatively well substantiated in laboratory research and their interrelationships may be straightforwardly derived and tested.

As has been stated, the study of instrumental and classical conditioning have tended to be separate—and separate statements of principles and terminological conventions have arisen that do not indicate the ways in which the two sets of principles interact. Thus, a separate symbolic convention has traditionally been used for operant conditioning consisting of the term S^D to stand for discriminative stimulus, S^R to stand for unlearned reinforcing stimulus, and S^r to stand for learned, or conditioned reinforcing stimulus. This convention has remained separate from the symbols which depict classical conditioning, that is, ^{uc}S for unconditioned stimuli, and ^cS for conditioned stimuli. The separate terminology for the two types of learning fails to indicate the overlap in principles which occurs between instrumental and classical conditioning. While the responses involved in the two types of conditioning are largely separate (motor responses in instrumental conditioning, versus visceral responses in classical conditioning) there is overlap in the *functions* that an S can have.

A stimulus can have multiple functions both within one of the types of conditioning as well as between them. That is, one stimulus can be both a discriminative stimulus as well as a conditioned reinforcer. It is also the case that one stimulus can be a conditioned stimulus, a conditioned reinforcer, as well as a discriminative stimulus, as another example. Perhaps the most important point is that these stimulus functions are related; as a stimulus becomes a conditioned stimulus it may as a consequence become a reinforcing stimulus, and this will increase its discriminative stimulus value. Thus, at a very basic level instrumental and classical conditioning appear to be related, and the symbolic convention should reflect this. In general, when conditioning principles are applied to other areas of complex human behavior, a notation system that shows the relationship of the reinforcing, eliciting, and controlling (discriminative) functions of stimuli is very advantageous. These are the symbols with which an S–R theorist does his thinking when creating a learning conception of human behavior.

Thus, all stimuli regardless of function should be depicted by an S. The functions of the stimulus, if it has any, should be depicted by super-prefixes, a more convenient method for S–R diagrams than the more commonly used suffixes. It should be noted that a stimulus, a physical event in the internal or external environment of the organism, may have no functions. Physical events (stimuli) that have a function for one organism may not have that function for another organism, even within the same species when the function is learned. Thus, a sound stimulus may have a function for one individual, yet have no function for another individual. The functions that a stimulus can have for an organism will be outlined and in doing so the basic principles of learning will be summarized, the interactions among the principles exemplified, and the various symbols listed.

(1) There are stimuli that elicit a response when the organism has had no prior training with the stimuli. Such a stimulus is called an unconditioned stimulus, or ^{uc}S. The responses involved are ordinarily

those that would be called reflexes, including the response of internal organs and glands, but would also include sensory responses elicited by sensory stimuli. (Thus, all stimuli to which the organism is sensitive are $^{u c}$S in this sense.) Emotional responses are also among those that may be elicited in this manner.

(2) An S that will not elicit such a response will come to do so, will become a ^{c}S, when contiguously paired with a $^{u c}$S. This is called first-order classical conditioning. The principle also has several corollaries that will be mentioned. First, when a ^{c}S has come to elicit a response in the process of classical conditioning, other stimuli that are physically similar to (are on the same physical dimension as) the ^{c}S will also elicit the response—even though they have not been involved in the conditioning process. This is called the principle of primary stimulus generalization —conditioning to one stimulus generalizes to similar stimuli. However, if the stimuli similar to the ^{c}S are presented to the subject of the conditioning a number of times, without being paired with the $^{u c}$S, the response to these similar stimuli will weaken. This weakening may occur even though the response to the actual ^{c}S is maintained in good strength by conditioning trials in which the ^{c}S *is* paired with the $^{u c}$S. Through this process a discrimination may be formed such that the response is elicited by the ^{c}S but not by other stimuli, even those closely similar to ^{c}S.

The process of weakening described above, that is where a stimulus that elicits a response through a prior conditioning process will no longer do so because it is presented without the $^{u c}$S, is the process called extinction. This is a corollary of the major principle of classical conditioning, and it also applies to the ^{c}S itself. That is, if the ^{c}S is presented repeatedly without the $^{u c}$S it will lose its eliciting function for the conditioned response.

Several additional corollaries to the principle of extinction may be listed here, also. The stronger the conditioning (like shorter ^{c}S–$^{u c}$S intervals, larger numbers of conditioning trials), the more resistant to extinction the ^{c}S will be. Furthermore, a ^{c}S will be more resistant to extinction if in the conditioning process there have been occasions when the ^{c}S has been presented without the $^{u c}$S—that is, after the ^{c}S has been presented a number of times with the $^{u c}$S, the introduction of some trials without the $^{u c}$S will increase resistance to extinction.

(3) Once a stimulus has strongly become a ^{c}S it can be paired with a new S in what is called higher-order classical conditioning and the S will also become a ^{c}S. The new stimulus will in this process thus come to elicit the response without ever having been paired with the $^{u c}$S. This

is a very important extension of the power of the principle of classical conditioning. A ^cS not only comes to elicit the response, but it will "transfer" this function to any new stimulus with which it is paired.

(4) Some ^{uc}S also have an additional function besides that of eliciting a response. When they are presented following a motor response they will later have a strengthening or weakening effect upon the response. When such an unconditioned stimulus is used in this manner to strengthen instrumental behaviors it functions as a reinforcer. One type of this stimulus is called a positive unconditioned reinforcing stimulus, or $^{uc \cdot R}+S$. When one of these stimuli is presented following a response, the response will occur more frequently—or if the response is already strong, it will be maintained in good strength by being followed by such a stimulus. When this type of stimulus is withdrawn following a response, on the other hand, the response will occur less frequently in the future. This type of stimulus is called a reward in common sense terms.

There are stimuli, usually termed punishing or aversive, in everyday life, that have the opposite effect upon the strength of motor behaviors when they are presented or withdrawn following the behavior. These unconditioned negative reinforcing stimuli, or $^{uc \cdot R}-S$, when withdrawn after the occurrence of a response, will increase the frequency of the response in the future. And, when such a stimulus is presented following a response, future occurrences of the response will decrease.

The principle involved here is called the principle of reinforcement or the principle of instrumental conditioning. There are several corollaries to this principle. If the strength of a response has been increased through reinforcement, the strength of response will diminish if the response occurs repeatedly and is no longer reinforced. This process is called extinction for this type of conditioning also. Resistance to this extinction process is increased if in the conditioning process the organism has had a greater number of conditioning trials or has had experience where the response has sometimes been reinforced and sometimes not. The value of the reinforcing stimulus and the time intervening before presentation are again important conditions that will determine the strength of the response. Stronger reinforcers, presented immediately after the response, will produce stronger conditioning. It should also be noted that the frequency or rate of the response can be altered by the proportion of responses reinforced (schedule of reinforcement). Moreover, the form and intensity of a response may be altered by selective reinforcement of responses that have a particular characteristic.

It should be remembered, however, that unlearned reinforcing stimuli are also ^{uc}S. That is, reinforcers are also stimuli that elicit responses in a classical conditioning sense. This is a basic area in which there is overlap in the principles of classical and instrumental conditioning—which when recognized has important implications, which will be described more fully in points number 7, 8, and 9.

(5) Although this is not usually mentioned, the principle of reinforcement actually applies to the response *in the stimulus situation in which it has been reinforced*. Thus, when a motor response is reinforced in the presence of a particular stimulus situation, the response will become more frequent *in that situation*. In addition, according to the principle of primary stimulus generalization, the response will also become more frequent in *similar* stimulus situations. Actually, the stimulus in the presence of which a response is reinforced thus gains the power to elicit that response. The stimulus that acquires this power is called a ^DS, or discriminative stimulus. When a response is weakened in the presence of a stimulus, either through extinction or punishment, the stimulus will also come to be a ^DS, but in this case the stimulus will control "not-making-the-response."

It has been stated that stimulus generalization applies in instrumental conditioning, and it may be added that discrimination can be produced by training that is very fine. That is, an organism that has been reinforced for a response in the presence of a light of a certain intensity will be more likely to make the response when that light is presented. In addition, however, lights of somewhat different intensities will also control the response according to the principle of stimulus generalization. However, if the response is reinforced only in the presence of a light of that particular intensity the control of the other lights will weaken (through extinction) and the particular light will be the only ^DS that brings on the response, the other lights will not.

(6) A process analogous to higher order conditioning appears to occur also with instrumental conditioning. That is, when a new stimulus is simply paired with a ^DS, whether or not the response elicited by the ^DS is reinforced, the new stimulus will also become a ^DS, for that response. Thus, a ^DS can "transfer" its function simply by being paired with another stimulus. This principle, which needs further exploration, is novel to traditional learning theories, as are some of the other principles.

(7) It has been stated that some stimuli have two functions. That is, for example, a $^{UC \cdot R}S$ will elicit a response in the manner of a reflex. In addition, such a stimulus can also be used to strengthen any motor response that it follows. Food is such a stimulus. It will elicit a salivary response as an unconditioned stimulus. In addition, however, if food is presented to an organism after the organism has made a motor response, the motor response will be strengthened. Thus, food as a $^{UC \cdot R}S$ has two functions. The important point here is that any new stimulus that is

paired with such a $^{UC \cdot R}S$ in a classical conditioning process will acquire both of these functions. The new S will become a ^{C}S and elicit the same response as the $^{UC \cdot R}S$ (in the example, the salivary response). Presumably because of this acquired eliciting function, the stimulus will also become a $^{C \cdot R}S$, a conditioned positive reinforcing stimulus that is capable of effecting the strength of any motor behavior that it follows. The importance of this principle will be indicated later as it applies to the dual functions that some words have; that is by becoming a ^{C}S in a classical conditioning process, they also become a $^{C \cdot R}S$ (conditioned reinforcing stimulus).

(8) It should be pointed out that the process of instrumental conditioning will also make the ^{D}S a ^{C}S and $^{C \cdot R}S$, since in the process of discrimination training the stimulus involved is paired with a $^{UC \cdot R}S$ or a $^{C \cdot R}S$. Thus, as an example, when a rat is reinforced with food in a white light when he makes a bar press response, the white light will become a ^{D}S and tend to bring on that response. In addition, this process will produce other conditioning results. The process will also have included the paired presentation of the stimulus of the light and the food stimulus. The food stimulus is a ^{UC}S for the salivary response as well as a $^{UC \cdot R}S$ for any motor response. As a result of the paired presentation, the light stimulus would be expected to become a ^{C}S for the salivary response and also a $^{C \cdot R}S$, capable of affecting the strength of motor responses when applied in a response contingent manner.

(9) Higher-order conditioning also applies to the conditioning of the reinforcement function. That is when a $^{C \cdot R}S$, that has gained its reinforcement value from being paired with a $^{UC \cdot R}S$ in a classical conditioning procedure, is itself paired with a new stimulus, the new stimulus will also come to be a $^{C \cdot R}S$. Thus, a stimulus can acquire the reinforcement function, and when it has this function, it can transfer the function to yet another stimulus. This principle is of great importance in the realm of language, as are so many of the other principles.

(10) In the naturalistic situation the child also has experience that produces another interaction of classical and instrumental conditioning that is very important and will be involved in later analyses. Through a process to be described in more detail later the reinforcement value of a stimulus (acquired through classical conditioning) becomes related to its discriminative stimulus value. That is, a stimulus that is positively reinforcing will yield reinforcement to an approach response that obtains the stimulus. That means the response was reinforced in the presence of that stimulus; thus, the stimulus will gain discriminative control over that response. The child will have much learning experience in which various stimuli which are positive reinforcers will come to control a large class

of "striving for" behaviors. Moreover, as will be described more fully in the context of human motivation, the reinforcement value of a stimulus becomes related to its discriminative stimulus value. As a result, increasing the positive reinforcement value of the stimulus (through classical conditioning) will increase the extent to which it (as a discriminative stimulus) will control "striving for" behaviors.

The converse is also true. Increasing the negative reinforcing value of a stimulus will increase the extent to which the stimulus controls a large class of "striving away from" behaviors.

It is thus suggested that (1) conditioned stimulus value underlies conditioned reinforcement value, (2) that reinforcement value comes to produce discriminative stimulus control, and (3) thus that classical conditioning is related to both reinforcement value and the discriminative control of instrumental behavior.

(11) Finally, it may be concluded that any particular stimulus may have all the functions mentioned. A stimulus could be a ^{UC}S for one response and a ^{C}S for another classically conditioned response, which could also make the stimulus a $^{C \cdot R}S$. If the latter conditioning took place in an instrumental discrimination task, the stimulus would also become a ^{D}S for a motor response. One stimulus would thus be a $^{UC \cdot C \cdot R \cdot D}S$.

The author has found this set of principles and notational system to be effective pedagogically, helping clarify the confusion that arises when instrumental conditioning principles and classical conditioning principles are discussed with different notational conventions. Difficulties occur, for example, when in describing classical conditioning in conventional terminology food is mentioned as a ^{UC}S and later in the context of instrumental conditioning as an S^{R+}. Further complications occur when it is stated that the stimulus paired with food becomes a ^{C}S, and in a later description, in the context of operant conditioning, the same stimulus is said to become an S^{r+} through the same process of being paired with food. Not withstanding, the usual statement of learning principles and the usual notation system does not acknowledge the relationship of the two stimulus functions.

More importantly, however, the present principles and notation system have heuristic value and aid one's thinking in elaborating the basic principles and extending the theory to the area of complex human behavior. As one example, as has been described, words have been shown to be conditioned stimuli (^{C}S) which elicit emotional response. The above type of analysis suggests, furthermore, that such words may also be expected to be reinforcing stimuli, or $^{C \cdot R}S$. This suggestion will be elaborated in the next chapter and later discussions will deal with other examples of the interacting principles briefly described here.

It should be emphasized that this is only a very brief summary, which does not include all of the basic principles that should be dealt with in the learning theory—only those of special relevance to the present subject matter. (See also Staats, 1964*a;* Staats and Staats, 1963.) One point should be made at this time, however, which deals with motivation. The strength of a positive reinforcer is affected by the length of time the organism has been deprived of the reinforcer. The strength of the reinforcer will be low when the organism has had unlimited access to such reinforcers. Thus, a stimulus may have a great deal of reinforcing value to the organism when he has not had access to such reinforcers, but have little or no reinforcing value when the organism is surfeited. This principle seems also to apply to conditioned reinforcers ($^{C \cdot R}S$) as well.

It is interesting to note, again, that the deprivation-satiation condition also effects the functions of a stimulus that are important in classical conditioning. That is, as an example, food as a ^{UC}S will not elicit the salivary response in a food satiated organism, nor will a ^{C}S that has come to elicit the salivary response. The same variables affect both principles.

COMPLEX S–R MECHANISMS

The basic principles (but not their interactions) were primarily discoveries of the laboratory, found by means of simplifying the events being studied to the greatest possible extent. In trying to find the basic, analytic, principles of behavior, laboratory control demands that a single simple stimulus be manipulated and the effect upon a single simple response be observed. Thus, the principles are usually based upon the study of simple stimulus-response (S–R) mechanisms.

Human behavior in naturalistic circumstances, however, rarely involves such simple constellations. Ordinarily, the individual learns complex combinations of stimulus and response events. Most human acts involve several principles, as well as many stimuli, controlling many responses.

For this reason, an important part of a learning theory of human behavior must include specification of the ways that the principles of learning can operate to produce more complex S–R mechanisms. Critics are quite correct when they say that human behavior cannot be adequately described in terms of single S–R events. To serve as a model of various human behaviors a learning theory must sketch out some of the general ways that complex S–R mechanisms can be formed. With these mechanisms it is then possible to consider complex human behaviors.

Examples of such mechanisms have been explored in basic experiments. Others were abstracted from naturalistic observations. Actually, however, all of the combinations of S–R events could be derived from the basic principles in a purely deductive manner as some were. Thus, the basic learning principles themselves constitute the higher-order postulates of a learning theory of human behavior. The ways in which the basic principles can produce complex S–R mechanisms constitute lower-order, derived, principles.

It may be added that although the conditioning principles themselves are simple, the S–R mechanisms that are formed in real life consist of exceedingly complex arrays and constellations. The first elaboration to be made is that single S–R events may be combined into *sequences* on the basis of conditioning principles. That is, responses can be thought to have stimulus properties. Muscular responses activate nerve cells in the muscles and tendons. Vocal responses produce auditory stimuli. Many visceral responses have sensory qualities, and so on. Thus, a response can be conditioned to the stimulus produced by a preceding response. When this occurs a sequence of responses is formed like that depicted in Figure 6.1. Such sequences may be of great length and contain many members. Language behavior is replete with such examples. Simple word associations have been described already. In addition, however, long sequences of word responses (that is, sequences of word associations) can be formed through instrumental conditioning. The responses in a sequence, or in the other S–R mechanisms to be described, may be either classically conditioned responses or instrumentally conditioned responses.

$$R_1 \text{——} S_1 \text{————} R_2 \text{——} S_2 \text{————} R_3 \text{——} S_3 \text{————} R_4 \text{——} S_4$$

FIGURE 6.1. A response sequence exists when the stimulus produced by one response tends to elicit another response. Sequences can involve various numbers of responses (All figures in this section are from Staats' chapter in B. Kleinmuntz, Ed., *Problem Solving*. New York: Wiley, 1966 by permission of the publisher.)

Furthermore, however, more than one response may come under the control of a particular stimulus, as Hull (1943) showed with rats. The extent to which the stimulus will elicit each response will depend upon the strength of the conditioning (the number of conditioning trials, the time between the ^cS and the ^{uc}S, or the response and the reinforcer, as the case may be, the intensity of the ^{uc}S or reinforcer, and so on). Thus, when the stimulus occurs it will tend to elicit the various responses that have been conditioned to it. These responses may be competitive, that is only one or the other can occur. When this is so, the particular response that occurs may also depend upon the other stimuli present in the situation that tend to elicit one or the other response. A man hurrying toward his office when passing an acquaintance will tend to (1) stop and talk, (2) hurry by, (3) greet the individual but state he must be on, (4) nod and continue walking. Which of the responses under the control of the social stimulus will actually be emitted will depend upon other stimuli, such as whether the acqaintance looks at him, looks down, what the clock on the building states, and so on. (Thus, it should be realized in all the S–R diagrams that a stimulus has only a tendency to—a probability of—eliciting a particular response.) This type of mechanism is depicted in Figure 6.2.

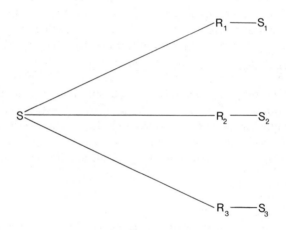

FIGURE 6.2.   An S–R mechanism in which one stimulus has come to elicit several different responses.

Conversely, different stimuli may come to elicit the same response, as Hull (1943) has also suggested. Different words as stimuli, as one example, may all elicit the same word responses. Thus, the Russell and Jenkins norms (1954) indicate that the words BED, DREAM, COMFORT, and DEEP as stimuli tend to elicit the word associate SLEEP. This type of mechanism is depicted in Figure 6.3.

Moreover, these mechanisms may combine into even more complex mechanisms. Thus, a sequence of responses may actually be a sequence in which the stimulus produced by one response controls more than one following response, with more than one such stimulus controlling any particular following response. Thus, in our language culture the stimuli

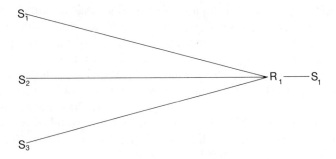

FIGURE 6.3. An S–R mechanism in which several stimuli have come to elicit the same response.

of the word response GIVE will be followed in the child's experience by the personal pronouns HIM, HER, and ME and acquire tendencies to elicit those responses, among others. This will also be true of the word responses THROW and PUSH. A relatively simple sequence of these multiple stimulus-response mechanisms which everyone in our language culture would have acquired through his language experience is depicted in Figure 6.4.

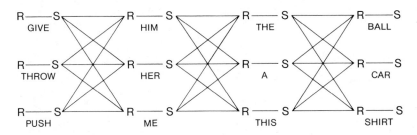

FIGURE 6.4. A complex S–R mechanism consisting of a sequence of convergent stimulus mechanisms and response hierarchy mechanisms.

Mediated generalization studies have also discovered an important type of S–R mechanism. The studies indicate, in general terms, that two different stimuli will become functionally the same if the stimuli each come to elicit the same response. That is, two "dissimilar" stimuli are those which are not functionally the same in terms of primary stimulus generalization. A response conditioned to one will not be elicited by (generalize to) the other—which is the index of similarity. However, if two such stimuli are first made to elicit the same response, then any further experience (conditioning) the individual has with one *will* generalize to the other. As an example, let us say that two people, a man and a woman, are dissimilar stimuli. Let us say, however, that the child is trained to call each of them DOCTOR. In addition, however, the child is later taken to one of them over a period of time and is given a series of painful shots. Each such experience would condition negative responses to the word DOCTOR. This conditioning would then generalize to the other person, and in fact to all people called DOCTOR. This general process is schematized in Figure 6.5.

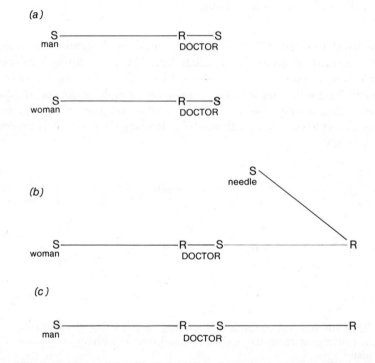

FIGURE 6.5.   (*a*) The child has previously been trained to call the man and woman (otherwise "dissimilar" stimuli) by the common response DOCTOR.   (*b*) When the child has unpleasant treatment from the woman, another response, R_2, is conditioned to the response DOCTOR.   (*c*) Since the man also elicits the response DOCTOR, the response R_2 learned to the woman will generalize to the man.

Thus, this type of mechanism, response mediated generalization, has additional implications, as has been described. Words come through conditioning to also be functionally the same as the environmental stimuli with which they are paired. That is, if a word is systematically paired with a certain aspect of the environment it will come to elicit the same responses as does the environmental stimulus with which it is paired (see Staats, 1961). Since the word and the environmental stimulus both elicit the same response, further experience with one will generalize to the other. When this mechanism has been formed experience the individual has with the word will generalize to the environmental stimulus. Direct experience with the environmental stimulus is then not necessary for the individual to learn further how to respond to the environmental stimulus. This, of course, is one of the powerful types of human learning. The human need not have direct experience, words perform the same function—and an S–R account can handle this type of phenomena.

Another similar aspect of cognitive behavior may be considered in terms of verbal responses (or the stimuli they produce) coming to control motor responses. It has been suggested that the individual through instrumental discrimination training acquires a very large repertoire of motor responses and motor skills under the control of verbal stimuli. Because of this training, when the verbal stimulus is presented it controls the appropriate motor response. An individual with such a verbal-motor response repertoire can then acquire new motor skills simply on the basis of contact with verbal stimuli. This process may short-circuit what may have taken centuries for the motor skill to develop. Many years, for example, have gone into the development of the present day motor skill of high jumping. However, the young athlete today does not have to go through the various steps involved in this development. A coach presents instructions (verbal stimuli) that control the appropriate behaviors. Much perfection of the final motor skill by the athlete is still necessary. However, the main skill can be imparted on a verbal level. This process requires, of course, that the verbal stimuli have come to control the correct responses. Thus, an important S–R mechanism that accounts for much human behavior involves series of verbal stimuli that when presented individually control motor responses. Although at first the motor responses may depend upon the verbal stimuli for elicitation, if the motor responses occur in sequence a number of times through the verbal control, the motor responses will be conditioned in a sequence and will occur under their own control! At this point the verbal instructions are no longer necessary. Such a mechanism is depicted in Figure 6.6.

It is also true, as already mentioned, that verbal responses (or the stimuli they produce) can also elicit emotional (reinforcing) responses, either of a positive or negative kind. This has a good deal of significance for understanding certain aspects of human reasoning, including social

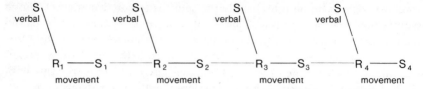

FIGURE 6.6.   When a series of verbal stimuli are presented, each
of which controls a particular movement, and this process is repeated, the stimuli produced by each movement will come to control
the next movement. In this way a new complex movement sequence
can be established by language means.

reasoning. Sequences of verbal behavior are many times elicited that are
relevant to future events. The student is asked to accompany a friend to
a show and this and other stimulus circumstances elicit a long sequence
of verbal responses. He says, let us say, IT IS A VERY FUNNY PIC-
TURE. HOWEVER, I HAVE NOT STUDIED FOR MY EXAM TO-
MORROW AND IF I DO NOT I WILL FAIL THE COURSE. The
word stimuli VERY FUNNY are positive conditioned reinforcers, for the
individual with the appropriate conditioning history, and would tend
to control the approach behaviors of attending the movie. The word
stimuli FAIL THE COURSE, on the other hand, will control conditioned
negative emotional responses in the individual with the appropriate conditioning history, and these emotional (reinforcing) responses will in
turn control behaviors that avoid the proposed activity.

What the individual does in this problem situation will be influenced
by his sequence of verbal behaviors and their reinforcement value. An
oversimplified depiction of verbal behaviors controlling emotional responses that in turn control motor responses is depicted in Figure 6.7.

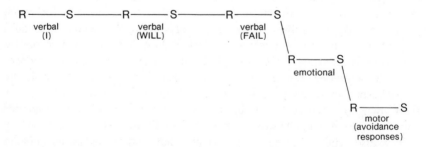

FIGURE 6.7.   A sequence of verbal responses elicits an emotional
response which in turn elicits a motor avoidance or withdrawal
response.

One further point should be made in the context of the present examples of complex S–R mechanisms. As is commonly recognized, and has been experimentally shown many times, responses may occur covertly—that is, responses can occur but not be accessible to naturalistic observation. Many times these covert responses may be quite complex, and show themselves by the effects they have on other overt behaviors of the individual. Thus, the individual may make a series of covert thinking (verbal) responses, and these covert responses may then result in the individual doing something.

It may be suggested at this point that the various S–R mechanisms that have been described may take place entirely or partly on a covert level. This is especially true in the realm of language behavior. Much of the complex sequences of hierarchies of word responses, for example, take place covertly—and are called thinking. In addition, however, emotional responses, sensory responses, and many implicit motor responses are not directly observable. As the author has indicated (Staats and Staats, 1963) covert responses can be specified by indirect observational methods using various devices—thus the concept of the covert response is an empirical one.

In concluding this section it may be suggested that learning theory, certainly in the area of complex human learning, now requires an integration of empirical conditioning principles in concert with an elaboration of the various interactions between the conditioning principles as well as an elaboration of the various types of S–R mechanisms. The present section thus outlines an integrated learning theory based upon a notation system for integrating instrumental and classical conditioning principles. Part of the theoretical body for dealing with complex human behavior also includes the manner in which more complex S–R combinations develop on the basis of the higher-order (more general), basic principles. It is suggested that these S–R mechanisms, including their pictorial representation, constitute an important part of a learning theory of complex human behavior. The other, more basic, part of the theory consists of the various principles involved in the study of classical and instrumental conditioning and their interactions.

It is also suggested that although the basic principles are simple, their possible combination into constellations of multiple stimuli and multiple responses of various kinds provides a theory that includes all the potential flexibility and discovery that we see in complex human behavior. *Moreover, because the theory is based upon empirical principles, an analysis of human cognitive behavior in the terms of this theory will suggest empirical hypotheses for research as well as hypotheses for dealing with problems of human behavior.*

It should be stressed that the preceding section does not attempt to elaborate in its potential fullness the complex S–R mechanisms that must be included in a complete learning theory of human behavior. Rather, the section attempts to illustrate the general conception as well as to describe several of the complex S–R mechanisms that will be important in later parts of the book.

The chapters that follow in the present part of the book will illustrate some of the complex S–R mechanisms that are important to cognitive behavior. Actually, a start has already been made in this task through the experiments and analyses already discussed, but further elaboration is needed. In addition, the papers that follow will demonstrate some of the ways that instrumental and classical conditioning principles are interrelated in the context of human behavior.

7

The instrumental function
of attitudes:
an interaction
of basic principles

One of the disadvantages of the traditional learning theories has been that the overlap and interaction between the two types of basic principles has not been explicated. As a consequence it was impossible to see some of the most powerful implications of learning theory for understanding human behavior. As has been suggested, one of the reasons the traditional learning theories fell short in this area was because of the nature of the task presented to the theorist. Theory construction in learning has traditionally meant the systematization of the empirical principles found in the basic animal laboratory. This work is predicated upon disassembling complex interactions and isolating the principles, and the major assumption has been that the responsibility of the learning theory was to "explain" the empirical principles. On the other hand, when the task is seen as one of providing a theory by which to account for human behavior, one gains a new perspective, including impetus for discovering the interactions that occur in the major principles.

The various inadequacies of the traditional learning theories cannot be dealt with here. However, it may be noted that Hull (1943) did not differentiate between the basic principles of classical and instrumental conditioning—which prevented the elaboration and differentiation of each. While in certain respects his theory nevertheless began to indicate one of the relationships of the two principles, later approaches, although better distinguishing the principles, in other respects produced an even less effective understanding of the interrelationships of classical and instrumental conditioning and thus a less effective learning theory for understanding human behavior. Thus, Skinnerian theory is nominally a two-factor learning approach. It distinguishes the principles of classical and instrumental conditioning—in fact the sharp separation of the major principles has been very carefully set forth and emphasized. Moreover, the separate terminology given to the principles—where quite different symbols have been used for classical and instrumental conditioning—has helped prevent others from recognizing the interrelationships of the principles (Staats, 1964a, 1966, in press a, 1967b; Staats and Staats, 1963). In any case, classical conditioning has been underplayed in the basic theory and research of the operant conditioning approach. As a matter of fact, in the only indication of an interrelationship between classical and operant conditioning principles, Keller and Schoenfield (1950) attempted to make classical conditioning secondary by accounting for conditioned reinforcement in terms of instrumental discrimination learning. Furthermore, operant conditioning theory has failed almost completely to extend the principle of classical conditioning to complex human behavior. In operation, then, Skinner's approach has been a one-factor learning theory in the realm of complex human behavior—a crucial weakness.

It may be added here that Skinner's rejection of the theoretical endeavors of Hull and others, although correct in part in the context of that period, has had the effect of generally suppressing theoretical endeavors in learning. This also has prevented elaboration on a theoretical level of the basic learning principles and their interrelationships. Skinner's approach has also rejected detailed stimulus-response theorizing, a crucial drawback which, again, has retarded detailed theoretical analysis of complex human behavior. (An example of the theoretical sterility which the methodology or philosophy engenders may be seen in most of the work in the field of programmed instruction, a topic to be mentioned further on. The field has through its atheoretical, nonanalytic, approach become almost entirely concerned with curriculum development and the innovation of apparatus. While these may be productive, they are piecemeal and applied, and have not led to a general conception of cognitive development—which should be the real source from which to derive applications.) The present discussion cannot deal generally with these topics. However, they will be reflected in analyses to follow.

The principles to be described now—the interrelationship of classical conditioning and instrumental conditioning in the realm of the establishment of conditioned or learned reinforcers—actually provide a substantial part of the basis of a theory of human motivation. This area will be dealt with in a later section and the present chapter will be concerned with experimental verification of the analysis in the context of several important aspects of language learning as well as the affects of language on other behavior and further learning. It may be suggested, however, in beginning the account that many aspects of human motivation can be understood when it is seen that it is through classical conditioning that the learned reinforcers that are effective for the individual are learned— but it is through the principles of instrumental conditioning that these stimuli have their affects. It may also be suggested that various areas of the study of human motivation can be integrated by the present analysis. For this reason the present discussion of reinforcers should be understood to apply to what we also designate in the various behavioral and social sciences by the terms attitudes, emotions, interests, needs, urges, cathexes, group cohesiveness, motivations, utility (economics), evaluative meaning, and so on. It should also be noted that in the present case the reinforcing stimuli involved will be words, but the same principles would hold for all varieties of motivational (attitudinal) stimuli, for example, various stimulus objects, events, activities, people and their behaviors and roles, and so on.

More specifically, it has already been suggested that words can be conditioned stimuli. When they are paired with a stimulus that elicits a response, the word will come to do so also. An important type of stimulus consists of those that elicit positive or negative emotional (or attitudinal) responses, for these responses will also condition to words (or other stimuli). The first part of the book dealt with this aspect of language learning. The attitude or emotional conditioning was measured by rating scales as well as by physiological measurements of the galvanic skin response.

In the preceding chapter which described the interactions of classical and instrumental conditioning it was suggested that stimuli that elicit emotional responses will also function as reinforcers. Moreover, it was hypothesized that a neutral stimulus paired with another stimulus that elicited an emotional response would acquire both functions: (1) the neutral stimulus would become a ^cS and elicit the emotional response and (2) as a consequence the stimulus would function as a reinforcer ($^{c \cdot R}S$) for any instrumental behavior.

In the present context it would thus be expected that words that had come to elicit emotional responses as measured by rating scales would also function as reinforcing stimuli. The experiment to be described in the present chapter will test that hypothesis.

At this point it is worthwhile to indicate some of the important implications of this analysis. First, there are many different kinds and instances of stimuli in our life experience that have rewarding or punishing power (elicit positive or negative emotional responses). In the language experience of the child, for example, many of these stimuli are each paired with a particular word or small group of words. These words should then come to elicit emotional responses *and also serve as conditioned reinforcing stimuli.* Moreover, there would be many of these words.

If that is the case then much human behavior can be understood in terms of the powerful "motivating" functions of language. Thus, it may be suggested that one person can reinforce the behavior of another when he says certain words which elicit positive emotional responses and are thus positive reinforcers. Studies (see Krasner, 1958; Salzinger, 1959) have shown that words like *good* and *fine* will serve as reinforcers. It may be suggested that they do so because they have become $^{C \cdot R}S$ words and elicit an emotional response. It should be noted, however, that *good* and *fine* are usual rewarding or praising words. The present analysis would suggest that *any* positive meaning word would serve the same function. Words like *food, happy, vacation, travel, America, honest,* and so on, since they are paired with positive reinforcing stimulus objects, events, and activities should also become reinforcers and be potential stimuli for conditioning behavior. It is hypothesized that such words, delivered by other people, contingent upon our behaviors, mold our behaviors according to the principles of reinforcement—in powerful ways that are subtle and obscure to naturalistic observation.

The examples have used only positive reinforcing words. It would be expected, of course, that there would be a very large class of words that had become negative reinforcers through being paired with aversive stimulus circumstances. Such words should serve the role of negative reinforcers. For example, if a child has performed a behavior that the parent does not like (does not find reinforcing) the parent may say "You should not do that because it is . . . " and then use suitable words such as *dangerous, unlucky, sinful, unhealthy, unattractive, unlikeable,* and many others. Many subtle forms of negative reinforcing words may be worked into conversation which is made contingent upon some undesired behavior of someone else—and this can be expected to mold the behavior of the person so treated. The behavior would be expected to decrease in frequency as a function of the treatment—provided the words actually are negative reinforcers.

Moreover, not only would words of other people mold our behavior; our own speech responses should perform the same function. One of the reasons a learning conception of human behavior meets resistance from people is that it suggests that human behavior is molded only from external sources, whereas the common human experience is that we manipulate and control our own behavior. The paradox is in part accounted for in terms of the present principles (as well as others to be described later). That is, although the individual's language repertoire is learned from without, the language repertoire functions itself to mold future behaviors of the individual. The individual may perform an action and then say out loud or to himself that what he has done is *dangerous, unworthy, silly, degenerate, illegal,* and so on, and thereby punish and decrease the strength of that behavior. Or conversely he may say words which positively reinforce and strengthen future occurrences of the behavior. A significant aspect of human motivation may be found in this analysis.

It is also interesting to consider the implications of this analysis for explaining how the individual appears to be affected by future events, like goals or anything else which the individual appears to strive for or away from. That is, while the future event that has not yet happened cannot affect a behavior that occurs before it in time, what the individual *says* about the future event can indeed alter his behavior by strengthening or weakening it (and by other learned S–R mechanisms). That is, the person can talk to himself about future events and in this way reward or punish behavior that is relevant to that possible future event. The student, as he returns home late on a study night, can say to himself "If I keep staying out late every night I will not pass my final exam." This self applied punishment would be expected to decrease the strength of the behavior—if the words "not pass" are strong negative reinforcers. (Of course, what the student actually does will be functions of other events also.)

At any rate, this type of analysis should remove the criticism of learning theories which do not account for the 'goal-directed' nature of human behavior. Human behavior appears to be, and in a sense is, goal-directed because the individual brings future events into the present—largely via language. The words he says regarding the supposed future event serve as reinforcers which affect his behavior before the event occurs. Later, when the discriminative function of reinforcing words is discussed, an additional mechanism will be added that can be used to explain goal-directed behavior.

Since an important aspect of the individual's motivational system consists of the word stimuli that are affective reinforcers and punishers for him, understanding of this aspect of language learning and function is important to various areas of the study of man. A few cursory examples may serve to illustrate some of the areas of application of the learning analysis. In the area of clinical psychology, for example, classical conditioning techniques (see Eysenck, 1960) have been used for some time in behavior therapy. However, the work must be fitted into an appropriate conceptual framework. To illustrate, in aversion therapy for alcoholics, the alcohol as a ^CS may be paired with electric shock. Although the procedure is classical conditioning, it is the change in reinforcing ($^{C \cdot R}S$) value of the stimulus that is important, that turns the patient's "approach" response to one of "escape." Explicit realization of the two principles involved might be expected to yield more precise knowledge of the procedures and their effects. (The author has recently elaborated this analysis [Staats, 1967b].)

In addition, verbal psychotherapy can be seen, in the light of the preceding discussion, to involve classical conditioning procedures in which words as ^CS are used to change the reinforcing value of other words and objects important in the patient's life. The change in reinforcing value then effects the patient's behavior. Abnormal behavior has been considered by the present author (Staats, 1967b; Staats and Staats, 1963) in terms of the unusual development of such conditioned reinforcers.

In social psychology, attitude formation can be considered to involve the development and function of conditioned reinforcers. And the study of group cohesiveness may be considered the study of the classical conditioning principles by which people in a group as stimuli for each other acquire reinforcement value by verbal and nonverbal conditioning, as well as the study of the instrumental conditioning principles by which group member behavior is affected. (See Staats, 1967c, in press b, for a detailed analysis of attitude formation and function in this context.)

Moreover, the concerns of other behavioral scientists such as anthropologists, sociologists, and economists heavily involve descriptions of reinforcers for individuals and groups. To illustrate this, the author (Staats, in press b) has suggested as one example that a learning analysis of the reinforcer system is basic to cross-cultural research. And the description of the reinforcer system of a group would include a description of word reinforcers.

In educational psychology, a primary concern of education with the motivation of children may be considered within the principles that have been presented. For example, the stimuli produced by learning itself must become a reinforcer if the pupil's attention and studying behavior is to be maintained in the classroom situation. Other important sources of verbal conditioned reinforcers are the approval of the teacher, parents, siblings, and schoolmates (see Staats and Staats, 1963). Understanding the principles by which reinforcers are formed and by which they effect pupil's behavior is central to the treatment of many educational problems —as will be treated further on.

Thus, it is suggested that the present analysis is very relevant for consideration of individual and group differences in various areas of study. It is worthwhile noting also that the analysis is important in considering psychological measurement of human motivation. That is, interest tests, attitude tests, tests of values, and other personality tests, may in many instances be considered to provide measurements of the reinforcing properties of words—in the same manner as the rating scales will be used in the experiment to be described. Actually, the present analysis may be used as a conceptual framework within which to consider (and develop) verbal tests of motivation. It may be suggested in a preliminary fashion that analyses of learning principles extended to the problems of clinical, educational, and social psychology, as examples, will help bring together basic psychology and the various applied fields—and the present area of study should prove a fertile one in this rapprochement (Staats, 1967*b*, in press *b*.)

Perhaps this analysis suggests some of the immense power of language in affecting behavior. Actually, as later discussions will indicate, there are many other ways that language determines human behavior of various types—emotional, cognitive, social, sensory-motor, and so on. The present account of one of the powerful motivational aspects of language is considerably extended, for example, by referring to the classical conditioning procedures described in the first part of the book. That is, it has been suggested that when a stimulus is a ^{C}S and also a $^{C \cdot R}S$ it will transfer both functions to any stimulus it is paired with. The previous studies showed this to be the case with the transfer or conditioning of positive and negative emotional or attitudinal responses. A strong hypothesis must be, especially in view of the results of the study to be reported, that the higher-order classical conditioning process would also transfer reinforcement value. That is, if a nonsense syllable or any other neutral stimulus object, event, activity, person, and what have you, was paired with words such as *bitter, poison, ugly, dirty, disgusting,* and so on, the neutral stimulus would be expected (as was shown) to come to elicit a negative emotional response. As a consequence, in addition, the neutral stimulus would be expected to become a *reinforcing stimulus* capable of molding the behavior of the individual according to the principles of instrumental conditioning.

Thus, it is suggested that the whole motivational system of reinforcers that functions for an individual (or group) can be expected to be heavily built on classical conditioning procedures involving language. (Actually, a quicker process for creating new reinforcers is also possible. That is, just attaching a name or label or descriptive adjective to a stimulus would bring the process to bear. For example, if *enemy* is a word that elicits a negative emotional response, and is thus a negative reinforcer, getting a person to name someone *enemy* will make him respond to the person so named as a strong negative reinforcer. All forms of address—titles, names, physical and behavioral descriptions, and so on—should exert this affect.) Language thus has an enormous affect upon human behavior in these ways and others that have not yet been touched upon. The study that follows has implications for beginning broad research on the motivational aspects of language.[1]

Evaluative Meaning (Attitude) Words
as Reinforcing Stimuli

As has been described, the first two functions of classical conditioning procedures have been shown in a number of studies (Staats, 1961). For example, the above experiment of Staats, *et al.* (1962), showed that a word paired with aversive ^{UC}S would (1) as a ^{C}S come to elicit the relevant GSR response and (2) would also be rated as having negative evaluative meaning. The third expectation would be that the word would also have become a negative reinforcer (Staats, 1964*d*).

The present study tests the third possibility; that words that have acquired evaluative or affective meaning for a subject will serve as reinforcers in the instrumental conditioning of a motor behavior. This hypothesis was first tested in a preliminary fashion with three groups of children; with one group a positive evaluative word was presented whenever the child made one of the two motor responses, for another group a negative evaluative word was presented in that manner, and for a third group a neutral word was presented. The words had previously been rated by the children. The experimental hypothesis was verified; the positive evaluative meaning word acted as a positive reinforcer, the negative evaluative word as a negative reinforcer; the neutral meaning word had an intermediate effect.

The same procedures were followed in the present experiment, except that a number of different word reinforcers were used with each subject, one time each, none of which are commonly used to evaluate performance. Furthermore, the affective meaning ratings on the words were obtained from different subjects than were used in the instrumental conditioning.

---

[1] For the complete study, done as a doctoral dissertation under the direction of the second author, see Judson R. Finley, and Arthur W. Staats. Evaluative meaning words as reinforcing stimuli. *J. verb. learning verb. Behav.*, 1967, 6, 193–197.

Method

FACILITIES   The experiment was conducted at the Gililland Junior High School, Tempe, Arizona, in a small, partially soundproofed room which contained a metal desk and two chairs.

SUBJECTS   Forty sixth grade children drawn from four different classes constituted the group on whom the words to be used in the conditioning experiment were standardized. The word rating was done in a school-room in eight groups of either six or seven Ss. Thirty-seven children from two previously unused sixth grade classes served individually in the conditioning procedures.

SELECTION OF THE EVALUATIVE MEANING WORDS   Two hundred and fifteen A or AA Thorndike-Lorge (1944) words were obtained, composed equally of positive, negative, and neutral evaluative meaning words. These were randomly arranged with no two consecutive words from the same evaluative group. The words were arranged into 8 columns, and each group of Ss began with a different column (that is, ABCDEFGH, BCDEFGHA, CDEFGHAB, and so on). The words were presented orally to the Ss spoken in a monotone in the manner used later in the instrumental conditioning. The S's task was to give a number in response to each word spoken by E, depending on whether the word seemed very pleasant (1), quite pleasant (2), slightly pleasant (3), not particularly one way or the other (4), slightly unpleasant (5), quite unpleasant (6), or very unpleasant (7).

From this collection of word ratings were selected a group of positive evaluative words (mean rating 1.72), a group of negative meaning words (6.08), and a group of neutral words (3.86). The positive meaning words included *cheerful, famous, fun, holiday, enjoy, brave, family, swim, laughter, surprise, christmas, smile, honest, blossom, joy, favorite, dollar, happiness, sunshine, america, gift, home, hero, angel,* and so on. Examples of negative evaluative meaning words are: *guilty, afraid, spoil, ugly, pain, bitter, die, sad, starving, foolish, hate, fat, blame, thief, sick, hunger, fell, harm, ashamed, lost, shock, hurt, worry, poison,* and so on. Some neutral words used were: *trunk, every, terms, stem, cover, pack, report, bridge, spread, next, bone, enter, page, brick, those, section, moment,* and so on.

INSTRUMENTAL CONDITIONING APPARATUS   The conditioning apparatus, which consisted of several separate pieces of equipment, was collapsible and portable for ease of handling and storage. The vertical partition was an 18 by 26 inch piece of fibreboard painted flat black. On the E's side of the partition was the electrical operating equipment (three ac relays) and the response monitoring equipment (two signal lights which corresponded to the S's two response buttons).

A white stimulus light (Christmas tree bulb) was encased in a metal mounting and suspended over the top of the partition in front of the subject in the conditioning phase. The E controlled the onset of the stimulus light by a switch.

The S held upon his lap an 11 by 14 inch black response panel on which were centered two buttons approximately 7 inches apart. The buttons operated separate microswitches in such a manner that a single press of either button could terminate the white stimulus light, as well as activate the appropriate signal light indicating which button the subject had pressed.

INSTRUMENTAL CONDITIONING PROCEDURE   S was handed the response panel, asked to rest it comfortably on his lap, and was instructed to watch for the light to come on and then turn it off by pressing either one of the two buttons. S was also told that speed was not important and to relax.

Following the instructions, the experimenter moved behind the partition and presented a series of 60 trials. Each trial for S was initiated by the onset of the white stimulus light. The 60 trials were considered in terms of 6 blocks of 10 trials each. For the first 10 trials no words were presented. This constituted an operant level block, or a measure of the distribution of responses prior to the introduction of the verbal reinforcers. Five blocks of conditioning trials were then presented in which a word was spoken by the experimenter each time the subject turned off the light with a *left-side* button press response. Words were presented in a forceful, monotone voice for all three word groups so as to hold constant the possible variable of vocal intonation. A word was spoken the instant the signal light indicated that the subject had used the left-side button on a trial. Right-side presses also turned off the light, but did not result in the presentation of verbal stimuli.

The interval between the S's response on one trial and the onset of the stimulus light for the following trial was governed by the time required for E to react to the signal lights (indicating the button used on the trial), present a word (if required on the trial), record the response data, and activate the switch for the next trial. Each word in the list to be used was typed on a 2-1/2 by 3 inch card. E simply read the top card in the appropriate stack. Ss who scored 10 out of 10 responses on any one button during the preconditioning block were to be eliminated from the study.

Results and Conclusions

Seven Ss were eliminated from the study for initial perseverative responding. Thus, 10 Ss, 5 of each sex, served in each of the three groups.

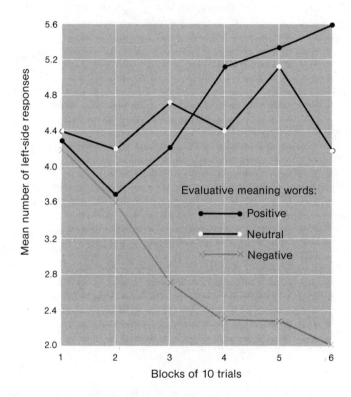

FIGURE 7.1.   The mean number of left-side responses emitted by the subjects in three word meaning groups. Reprinted from Staats' chapter in B. Kleinmuntz, Ed., *Problem Solving,* New York: Wiley, 1966 by permission of the publisher.

The mean number of left-side button press responses emitted in each block of 10 trials by each group is depicted in Figure 7.1. Examination of the figure shows that, although the groups displayed similar pre-conditioning responding, the Positive Evaluative Word Group's left-side responses increased across conditioning trials, the Negative Evaluative Word Group responses decreased, and the Neutral Word Group responses showed an intermediate pattern.

An analysis of variance (Edwards, 1960) of left-side button press scores was conducted to evaluate the possible effect of the other variables in the study: Word Meaning Groups (positive, neutral, negative meaning); Sex (boys, girls); and Trials (six blocks of ten trials each). The analysis showed significant F-ratios only for the Word Groups variable (P < .01), and for the Groups × Trials interaction (P < .005). The remaining comparisons were not significant.

The central test of the data concerned the question of whether the strength of the left-side response changed over the conditioning trials as a result of the type of words that were presented contingent upon the response. Thus, a trend analysis (Edwards, 1960) of the trial totals for the three groups was computed. The results indicated that the Groups × Trials linear component figure was statistically significant (P < .005).

Furthermore, in theory positive evaluative words should be stronger positive reinforcers than neutral words. And the negative evaluative words should have a stronger negative reinforcing function than the neutral words. To test these possibilities comparisons were made between the relevant conditions. The trend analysis for the positive versus neutral meaning words indicated the Groups × Trials linear components were significantly different (P < .05). The trend analysis for the negative versus neutral meaning words indicated the Groups × Trials linear components were also significantly different (P < .005).

The combined data for the 30 Ss showed that in the operant level block a mean of 5.7 right-side responses occurred as compared to 5.0 expected by chance. However, the slight initial preference for the right-side button was easily modified by the conditioning procedure.

Discussion

The results support the hypothesized relationship between the evaluative meaning of certain words and the reinforcement value of these words. In both experiments words of positive evaluative meaning served as positive reinforcers or rewards, words with negative evaluative meaning served as negative reinforcers or punishments, and neutral words were shown to have no reinforcing function.

These findings appear to have general implications. There is a large number of words with either positive or negative evaluative meaning in our language as well as in other languages (Osgood, *et al.*, 1957; Triandis and Osgood, 1958). The samples of these classes of words appeared in the present study to have reinforcing properties. It was thus possible to produce new learning of a motor response based upon the response-contingent presentation of words from these classes. It may be suggested that because of the large number of words that exist in each class, and the extent to which they occur in everyday life, they must have a very general effect upon human learning. The nature of this effect should be further studied.

In the classical conditioning of word meaning (see Staats, 1961), it has been possible to use group norms to assess the type and intensity of meaning which words have for individuals. The same appears to be true of the reinforcing value of these types of words. Thus, the function of evaluative meaning words for the individual appears to have considerable cultural determination. Words that are reinforcing for one individual tend to be reinforcing for other individuals. It would be expected, of course, that individuals would differ in this respect, in ways that should have important effects upon the individual's behavior, it might be added. In addition, it would also be expected that different subgroupings of a society as well as different societies would also show differences in this important area.

The findings of the present study also have several other interrelated implications. First, in concert with previous theoretical analyses of word meaning as a classically conditioned response (Mowrer, 1960b; Staats, 1961), the present results support the hypothesis that stimuli that become ^{c}Ss will, at least in certain cases, also as a consequence become reinforcers. This is important support for a learning theory which integrates the principles of instrumental and classical conditioning (see Staats, 1964d, 1966).

The results also support the contention that rating scales such as used herein do indeed measure the meaning [or attitudinal] response elicited by a word, not just the word associations elicited by a word. That is, there is no reason to expect a word association per se to have reinforcing value. As described in the introduction, however, there is reason to expect the classical conditioning of an affective (emotional) meaning response to confer reinforcement properties on the ^{c}S-word. The results thus contribute support to the interpretations of the language conditioning of meaning previously given by Staats (1961). In addition, by itself, the fact that rating scales can be used to assess the reinforcing value of a stimulus has significance. It is important in research many times to identify effective reinforcers prior to their use in laboratory experimentation (see Witryol and Fischer, 1960; Schutz and Naumoff, 1964), [and prior to their use in clinical and educational practice]. It is suggested that the type of single rating scale used in the present experiment could offer a more practical method for identifying reinforcers than some of the elaborate procedures currently employed (see Heber, 1959; and Patterson, 1967). [It may be suggested that a good deal of additional research should be conducted to investigate the three interrelated functions of words as conditioned stimuli, reinforcing stimuli, and discriminative stimuli (see Staats, 1967b, in press b).]

Data concerning awareness of the Ss were not taken in the present study, by intent, for several reasons. It is not clear that when subjects are aware and also condition that the former determines the latter; the reverse is an equally likely interpretation. As has been shown (Staats and Staats, 1959a) subjects do not become aware until conditioning trials are sufficient to produce conditioning, and it is the highly conditioned subject who becomes aware. In any event, the task of both a learning position as well as a cognitive position is to find the determinants of the behaviors in which they are interested. Delay of this effort in a controversy concerning learning without awareness will lead only to another "nature versus nurture" or "latent learning" cul-de-sac, and this is to be avoided by the experimentalist interested in investigating a particular set of principles and developing a particular theory. It should be remembered that many important findings in science are and have been interpretable in more than one theory; the theory that ultimately wins out is the one that incorporates the most findings, generates the most research, and has principles and procedures that have the most general value in the solution of various problems.

Summary

An experiment was conducted to test the possibility that evaluative (affective) meaning words will serve as reinforcing stimuli. Words previously rated by other Ss as having either positive, neutral, or negative evaluative (emotional) meaning were presented contingent upon a motor response. Response-contingent positive evaluative meaning words strengthened the motor response, negative evaluative meaning words decreased the strength of the response, and neutral words had an intermediate effect.

8

Communication:
a pluralistic learning conception

There is an implicit characteristic of psychology which has its origins in the history of psychology, but which continues to function. The characteristic has an unfortunate effect upon contemporary research and theory. That is, psychology has been strongly affected by what may be called a classificatory approach. One way of organizing a field is to group similar events into categories. While classification has many uses in science, it may also have drawbacks, which are apparent in psychology. Thus, human behavior has traditionally been divided into categories such as intelligence, perception, problem solving, concept formation, reasoning, attitude formation, creativity, and so on. Unfortunately, there is also a strong tendency to infer in each area some common process which when discovered will account for the various occurrences in that area. Thus, we find investigators who offer monolithic conceptions of what problem solving is, suggesting one unitary underlying mechanism to generally account for all problem solving. We see individuals who talk in the same way about some inferred process that is supposed to account for creativity, intelligence, concept formation, and so on.

The whole position of the present approach is that we have been misled by our classificatory schemes. There are no underlying unitary processes in the various areas. There are rather different types of behaviors, different types of stimuli, involving different learning principles and different S–R mechanisms. A search for the one process underlying communication, for example, is a search for the holy grail. An explanation of communication will come from outlining the various acts in which we are interested and specifying the relevant stimulus events and the behavioral events. The various learning principles involved require specification as do the various complex S–R mechanisms.

It is interesting to note that the traditional classificatory approach to human behavior has dictated even what the learning oriented theorist and experimenter will do. That is, the learning person on becoming interested in human behavior has customarily accepted the previous, nonlearning, classification system. Thus, for example, if he is interested in problem solving he will accept the unitary process conception and attempt to define this process in terms of one learning mechanism. He will set up one problem solving task, assuming that the process shown in this task will apply to problem solving in general. This approach has tended to keep learning approaches simplistic and, it might be added, inadequate.

The present chapter will be concerned with a very brief discussion of some of the various learning principles and S–R mechanisms involved in the interactions that are usually termed communication. This account will thus indicate, as an exemplification, how human behavior requires a pluralistic application of learning principles and S–R mechanisms, rather than the traditional consideration of human behavior in broad classes, expecting unitary processes to be found within each category.

Mowrer (1954) in a very productive paper suggested that communication consisted of the higher-order classical conditioning of the meaning of the predicate word (or words) of a sentence to the subject of the sentence. While this analysis concerned an important aspect of communication, it was only a small portion of a complete analysis of the various occurrences which we call communication. The principle of classical conditioning applies to communication in additional ways, other than those stated by Mowrer. Furthermore, many other S–R mechanisms are involved in communication as well as learning principles other than classical conditioning. To present a convincing learning theory of communication it is necessary to present a larger sample of the acts involved, analyzed in terms of their stimulus and response events.

Communication may be considered to involve various diverse circumstances in which stimuli confront the individual which affect his behavior —the effects depending upon his past learning. Thus, communication will be considered as the functioning of previously acquired S–R mechanisms which involve verbal stimuli or verbal responses. Sometimes the significant effect of the communication stimulus is the behavior, that is, the effect is on performance rather than in producing new learning. Sometimes it is the new learning produced—the new S–R mechanisms—that is important. Sometimes both are involved, that is, the communication stimulus may produce new S–R mechanisms whose importance lies in the other behavior they will later bring on when the individual is in appropriate circumstances. The examples of communication to be described, some of which have previously been described by the author (Staats, 1961, 1964a; Staats and Staats, 1963), will illustrate these possibilities. These discussions will be limited to cases in which the communication stimulus is verbal or where the response produced is verbal.

The first type of communication interaction to be described is very simple. When one individual says something to another individual, eliciting an appropriate response in the second, we would say the first individual has communicated. Communication has occurred when the mother asks the child to go to the store and get a loaf of bread and the child does so. The mechanism has previously been described as instrumental discrimination learning in which the verbal stimulus becomes the discriminative stimulus that controls the motor responses.

It is interesting to note that lower animals in a rudimentary way are capable of this type of language communication when they have been appropriately trained by a human. Thus, the previously described process whereby the verbal stimulus of the cat's name was made into a discriminative stimulus that would control the cat's approach behavior is an example. Ordinarily, however, lower organisms create very few of such S–R mechanisms on their own. It should be indicated that the same process may involve other instrumental responses than motor responses. Thus, the response may be verbal—the communicator may say to the child, "That's a cow, can you say cow?" When the child makes a verbal response controlled by the stimulus an act of communication has been completed. The communication act may also involve a series of responses, as in the teacher's request to add several numbers and the child's motor and verbal responses in doing so.

The same mechanism based upon classical conditioning can be involved in a communication interaction. That is, words as conditioned stimuli can elicit responses that complete a communication act. Let us say that because of the individual's past training the word stimuli "You have cancer" when presented by a physician elicit a strong negative emotional response in the individual. This would constitute an act of communication in the same sense as the above. Many aspects of literature consist of the presentation of verbal stimuli that will elicit emotional responses, and the communication act is complete when this has been done.

Again, as has already been described, lower animals in a rudimentary fashion can be trained to S–R mechanisms that allow such communication. It is of interest to point this out in view of the great surprise and interest that has been aroused because dolphins have been shown to be able to imitate human speech sounds. It should be realized, however, that various animals are capable of acquiring certain aspects of language in rudimentary form, but not the various aspects, in the complexity necessary to produce true language, and not on their own.

These examples have involved primarily performance, that is, the way that previously learned S–R mechanisms can function—where the communicator presents the stimulus and the communicatee responds. There are many examples of communication, however, where the communication stimulus has an additional function, that of producing new S–R mechanisms in the communicatee. Thus, as one example, the communicator may present a sequence of verbal stimuli to the communicatee each of which elicits a matching verbal response. It is to be expected in such a case, especially with repetition, that the communicatee's verbal responses will be formed into a sequence also—where the stimulus produced by each of his verbal responses elicits the next verbal response.

A specific example may be seen in the case of the child who is first told to repeat "Now I lay," until he says the sequence smoothly. Then he is told to repeat, "Now I lay me down to sleep," and so on, until the full verbal response sequence has been formed in good strength. This type of learning through communication may also take place where the verbal responses of the communicatee are subvocal, as in the case where the communicatee learns the words to a song through repeated presentations of the song stimuli, but without overtly singing the words.

Although some verbal behaviors are significant in and of themselves, such as those involved in rendering a poem, or learning a fact of history. Others are important, however, for the motor behaviors which they will control (mediate) in the individual. Thus, the verbal sequences that are acquired by the engineer, many through the above process, are important for the motor behaviors that they will control in the individual, or in some other individual, in the act of constructing something. Let us take a more mundane case as an example. That is, the new communicatee is told "Go 4 blocks to Randolph Street, turn left and go 2 more blocks to a white gas station, take the first street past that to the right, and look for number 5304." After several prompted repetitions of the communication stimulus by the communicatee he will acquire the verbal response sequence. This newly acquired verbal S–R mechanism will then control a sequence of motor behaviors when the external stimulus conditions are appropriate.

Because verbal stimuli come to control motor responses, when the individual acquires new sequences of verbal responses his overt behavior may be altered. This type of mechanism is very important in communication and may be seen in many aspects of human behavior, from the most complex cases of intellectual learning, to everyday functioning in life's tasks. It is this mechanism that may also bridge the gap between the time when the communication is presented, and the time when the appropriate overt motor behavior is elicited. That is, in certain cases the communication stimulus produces the verbal responses in the communicatee, but the verbal stimuli are only effective at a later time when other stimuli in the situation also contribute to bringing out the overt behavior.

The examples given consist of three levels of occurrence: the communication stimulus, the verbal response sequence formed on the basis of the communication, and the motor behavior controlled by the verbal stimuli produced by the verbal responses. It should be realized that in many cases there may be many possible levels of learning and elicitation here. The overt motor responses elicited in the third stage may produce results that control additional verbal responses that in turn control new motor responses and so on. Furthermore, the communication may involve more than two people. The original verbal stimulus may create the verbal sequence in one individual and he in turn may provide verbal stimuli for another, the latter's overt motor responses being the culmination of the communication interaction. These are examples of complex social interactions based upon learning principles.

In Chapter 7 an S–R mechanism was described in which a sequence of verbal stimuli is presented each of which elicits a motor response. When this is repeated the motor responses (through the stimuli they produce) come to elicit one another in sequence. This may be considered to be a type of communication in which new motor skills are produced through the presentation of verbal stimuli which constitute the communication stimuli. This is an exceedingly important learning mechanism, accounting for the development of many motor skills.

There is also the case, previously described, where the significant aspect of the communication is that the response elicited by one word stimulus is brought under the control of another word stimulus. Thus, using Mowrer's example, the word *thief* elicits a meaning response (negative emotional response). When the sentence "Tom is a thief" is presented to the individual the word thief acts in the role of a ^{uc}S. The word elicits the meaning response which is then conditioned to the word *Tom* which serves the role of the ^cS. Later, for the person presented with the communication stimuli, the word *Tom* will elicit the same meaning response as the word *thief*.

It must be realized, of course, that although the principle involved here is valid, as the experimentation described in the first part of the present book demonstrated, a number of other principles must be added before the conception becomes believable—even in considering only the transfer of emotional meaning from word to word. Thus, for example, it must be realized that a word is a stimulus that may serve as a component of various compound stimulus complexes. Although the word *thief* alone may elicit a negative meaning response, when it occurs along with other stimuli it may not do so to the same extent. When the word is presented with the words *not a* as in "Tom is not a thief," it will not elicit the same response and thus the same conditioning will not occur. The term *not a thief* does not come to elicit the same response as *thief* alone because of our conditioning histories.

Furthermore, the communication stimulus "Tom is an old horse thief," presented with a smile and a chuckle will not elicit the same response as the word *thief* alone, and thus not result in the same conditioning effect. These points are added because the conception of this type of communication has been challenged by critics who point out that the principle of classical conditioning cannot be applied because it does not function in all cases. However, it is the critics who are at fault for not applying the principle in the detail necessary. The naturalistic example used to illustrate the principle is subject to various qualifications. However, the experimental demonstration of the principle of the higher-order conditioning of the meaning response of one word to another word is quite clear cut.

It should be emphasized again, however, that this principle accounts for only one type of communication. The other examples have indicated other types of communication. Several additional types will be presented now, beginning with one that is related to the higher-order conditioning of meaning responses.

Basically, it has been said for classically conditioned meaning responses that when a word elicits a meaning response it will be conditioned to other words with which the word is paired. It is suggested that this principle holds also for instrumentally conditioned responses as well as for classically conditioned responses—although a new learning principle must be invoked to make this suggestion. That is, the author generally suggests that when a discriminative stimulus that controls a response is paired with a stimulus that does not control that response, the latter stimulus will also come as a new discriminative stimulus to control the response—simply on the basis of contiguity, in the same manner as for classical conditioning.

As an example, let us say that the word *close* has become a discriminative stimulus for the child such that it controls a "closing" motor response. When presented with the verbal stimulus "Close the door," the child will make the appropriate response.

Let us say that the word *shut* has never before been presented to the child and is, in essence, a nonsense syllable. It is suggested that if the child was told "Shut means close" that *shut* would come to control the response which *close* already controls. In the future if the child is told "Shut the door," evidence of the higher-order conditioning of an instrumental response will be seen by the fact that the child will perform the response of closing the door. This process is diagrammed in Figure 8.1 because the process constitutes an important type of communication and an important basic learning principle.

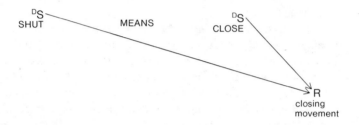

FIGURE 8.1. When a word ^DS which controls a motor response is paired in a sentence with a meaningless word, in this sense, the meaningless word becomes a ^DS for that response. In the example, the new word SHUT becomes a ^DS for the closing response through being paired with CLOSE in the sentence SHUT MEANS CLOSE.

It may be indicated that while the hypothesis under discussion was rationally derived from the basic principles, the author has subjected the hypothesis to experimental-naturalistic test. That is, employing his 4-year old daughter as subject, the author told the child "Wug means close." This was repeated several times. Then she was told "Wug the door," and she promptly got up and closed the door. This analysis suggests that the contiguous pairing of the two words resulted in the communication process. That is, the word *close* already elicited the motor response. When *close* was paired with the new word *Wug* the new word also came to control the response. The miniature study consisted of an informal test of the hypothesis that higher-order instrumental conditioning is possible and when verbal stimuli are involved constitutes a type of communication. It should be noted that additional research in the animal laboratory should be conducted to test the basic principle, and additional research should be conducted to test the significance of the principle in various areas of human learning, including communication.

One further point should be made here. In the case of responses classically conditioned to words, the response is usually not directly observable by naturalistic means. Whether the response is a sensory response or an emotional response, customarily it takes place internal to the individual subject involved. In the case of instrumental responses that have been conditioned to words, the response may be either overt or covert. Thus, in the above example, although the child was tested for the communication by asking her to "Wug the door," the effect of the communication must have been covert. That is, the word *close* must have elicited an implicit motor response (or perhaps the response was a process of the central nervous system). The implicit motor response could be considered then to be conditioned to the new discriminative stimulus, the word *Wug*.

Two additional communication acts will be mentioned here. First, it has been suggested that words may function as reinforcing stimuli when applied in a response contingent manner. It may be suggested that this constitutes verbal communication also. That is, when the individual performs some response and this is followed by a verbal reinforcing stimulus, the effect is to increase the strength of that response in the presence of the situation. Later, the same situation will be more likely to control the response. The experiment in the preceding chapter is analogous to a commonly occurring extended communication act in which *many* words and *many* conditioning trials are employed in strengthening or weakening another person's behavior.

In everyday life more dramatic effects of this type of communication may be seen—examples that do not require multiple conditioning trials before an effect is demonstrated. In beginning to explain this it should be noted that it is possible in the basic laboratory to create an organism that requires only one reinforcement in order for a response to be increased to high strength. Take, for example, a rat that is reinforced for a while for a response until it becomes strong and is then subject to no reinforcement until the response decreases in strength so that it rarely occurs. Let us say that these conditions are alternated a number of times, that is, the animal receives long sequences of continuous reinforcement interspersed with long periods of no reinforcement. It will be observed that the conditioning and extinction processes begin to occur more rapidly. Ultimately, the first nonreinforcement trial, following a number of reinforced responses, will immediately result in drastically weakening the response. Then the first reinforced response, following a period where the infrequently given responses have not been reinforced, will result in immediately strengthening the response.

The human is subjected to analogous training and he is conditioned so that one reinforced response in the presence of a stimulus situation will bring the response strongly under the control of the situation. When this is the case the presentation of a verbal reinforcer following a behavior may quickly bring the response under the control of the stimulus situation. Let us say, for example, that the employee has said "I don't care much for liquor," in the presence of his employer and the latter has presented verbal reinforcement contingent upon the response. The efficacy of the communication could be observed by the fact that that type of verbal behavior, in one conditioning trial, would strongly come under the control of the employer as a stimulus. The employee would be likely to repeat his dislike for liquor in various ways, and also to emit other behaviors—such as the avoidance of drinking—under the control of the presence of his boss. This type of communication is also very prevalent and a very important function of language.

We can see another example which can be observed readily with children. When children are young, having been reinforced for requesting things, they will continue to make requests even after the mild punishing stimulus, the verbal stimulus of the word, *no,* has been presented. The child will ask for the desired object many times before the punishment (or extinction) is effective. If, however, the child is never reinforced for begging after the verbal negative reinforcer (the word *no*) is given the word will become after many trials effective on one presentation. Then the communication stimulus may be seen to have an immediate effect. The child asks for something, this is followed by the verbal negative reinforcer, and the asking behavior is immediately weakened to zero.

The last type of language communication to be used as an example deals with the learning of new verbal responses, on the basis of nonverbal stimulus presentations. It has already been stated that various nonverbal stimuli come to control vocal responses through instrumental conditioning. The child, for example, learns to label various environmental stimuli through this type of training—he learns to say "cow" when looking at a cow. This will ordinarily include training in which complex stimulus events come to control complex responses. Thus, the visual stimulus of a boy pulling a girl's hair will come as a discriminative stimulus to control the appropriate verbal response sequence of the observing child, "He pulled her hair."

The example may be considered to be a form of communication. Its importance may be seen more clearly by indicating that it is possible

to establish new sequences of verbal responses in a communication interaction by presenting a series of environmental objects to the individual.
A silent film would be an example of a situation in which a sequence of
nonverbal environmental stimuli each of which controlled verbal responses could result in a new complex verbal response sequence—which
in this case would more or less accurately parallel the story of the movie.
This may also be considered as communication: the process depends
upon previously acquired S–R mechanisms and produces new verbal
S–R mechanisms.

The generality of this type of formation of new verbal response
sequence can be seen by pointing out that the various environmental
stimuli experienced by an individual in his life circumstances would be
expected to produce characteristic verbal response sequences. These
aspects of an individual's language are thus produced by nonverbal
stimuli, and in this sense the environment, both social and physical,
"communicates" with the individual. As will be discussed more fully in
Chapter 10, when the environmental stimuli are novel, they may produce novel or original verbal responses—based upon the individual's
already acquired language repertoire.

In conclusion, it has not been the intention of the author in this short
article to present an exhaustive or detailed discussion of the learning
mechanisms whose operations are popularly termed communication. The
article is intended to indicate that the term communication applies to various verbal interactions that involve diverse learning principles and verbal
mechanisms. Perhaps, also, the discussion indicates how instrumentally
learned language mechanisms can function both in controlling appropriate behavior and in producing new learning for the individual. These
functions are important products of the individual's language repertoire.
Perhaps, also, the discussion indicates that when the empirical principles of classical and instrumental conditioning are integrated and some
of the S–R mechanisms described, the resulting theory forms a more
powerful conception with which to consider human behavior—in this
case certain aspects of language function.

Before concluding this section there is a qualification that should be
made for the benefit of the reader who is skeptical of the utility of the
learning analysis of human behavior. A traditional criticism of an S–R
approach to human behavior goes grossly as follows. An S–R approach
states that human behavior is a function of learning laws. Thus, it is to be
expected that the presentation of certain stimuli will produce lawful
results. However, as one example, we find that the presentation of a
communication stimulus will produce diverse effects in the audience. This
type of evidence is used widely to conclude that human behavior cannot

be accounted for in terms of general laws, and that human behavior contains an element of spontaneity or freedom. A believable learning theory thus must indicate how individuals may all be behaving according to the same laws, yet the same stimulus circumstance will differently affect them.

Actually, the reasons are quite simple and some of them will be summarized here. This will be done in the context of communication but the discussion has general implications for the questions concerning spontaneity or freedom in human behavior. One important item in this account is that people will respond differently to a communication stimulus depending upon the nature of their past experience. Let us say that two children have had the following experience. The adults within one child's experience have habitually given the child some positive reinforcement when they have said "Come to me," and the child has made an approach response. Let us say, however, that the other child has had frequent experience where when an adult has said "Come to me," the child has responded appropriately. However, let us say that this has been followed by mildly aversive stimulation, such as being restrained too long or too vigorously, or being pinched affectionately but painfully. Under such circumstances we will see that the two children will behave quite differently to the same communication stimulus. What appears to be a difference in their personal choice is actually a function of their conditioning. Thus, although there is considerable similarity within a culture in the responses that verbal stimuli will come to control, there are considerable individual differences also. When the individual diverges in his language conditioning experience quite largely from other individuals in his group, we will see that he responds to communication stimuli in an abnormal manner. It may be suggested that many cases of pathological behavior involve such atypical language conditioning histories.

This principle of individual differences in learned responding may involve very complex examples and the operation of complex S–R mechanisms. For example, it must be understood that the individual's own verbal behavior may produce all the results which communication stimuli from other people produce, and the individual's own verbal behavior, which is many times covert, may enhance or countermand the affects of a communication stimulus from some other source.

Take, for example, the communication stimulus "Tom is a thief." Let us say that person A has said this to person B. Ordinarily, the negative response to the word *thief* would be conditioned to the word *Tom,* for person B. Let us say, however, that person B has seen person A in interaction with the person named Tom. Let us also say, as a consequence of this observation, that person B has concluded that person A dislikes Tom, and so on. Later, when the communication stimulus is presented to him, and because of his previous learning, he might say to himself "Person A says that Tom is a thief because he does not like him and wishes to do Tom harm. In my experience Tom has always been scrupulously honest. I believe that person A is lying." If this did occur the communication stimulus would not have its intended effect. Person B's own verbal behavior would provide conditioning that would countermand the conditioning provided by the communication stimulus. Furthermore, his verbal behavior would condition him negatively toward the communicator, person A.

Thus, although learning principles would have been operating quite lawfully, the result of the communication as far as naturalistic observations are concerned would be quite opposite of that which might be expected on the basis of a simplistic analysis. A learning theory which is capable of dealing with human behavior must deal with the complex events that can affect behavior—including the individual's own language behavior. What the individual says out loud or to himself may be a very important determinant of his behavior, even though his own language behavior is determined strictly according to learning principles.

The fact that the individual's own verbal behavior may act in a manner that countermands other determining events that are observable is one of the things that gives the impression that human behavior is spontaneous or free. It is this deficit in accounting for the "self-determination" of human behavior in traditional learning theories that offends many critics, and keeps learning and cognitive theoretical approaches divided. However, it is possible to suggest a learning theory that is strictly deterministic in terms of learning principles, but which also provides that the individual's own behaviors, especially language behaviors, act as determining events for other things that he will do. As such the individual's language becomes a determinant of his behavior along with other social and environmental events that we can more readily observe.

This appearance of spontaneity or self-determination in human behavior is enhanced because the individual's past learning, in conjunction with new present stimulus conditions, can produce *novel* verbal behaviors. When novel verbal behavior occurs and the verbal behavior then controls overt behaviors that are novel or unexpected, there is a stronger suggestion that there must be spontaneous, creative, processes within us. Some mechanisms by which novel verbal behaviors can arise will be described in Chapter 10. This account plus the present one will indicate how the individual's behavior may spring lawfully from environmental circumstances but may also enable behaviors that go beyond the circumstances.

The examples of communication presented which involved verbal stimuli have concerned vocal communication stimuli. It may be noted here that the same types of communication may in most instances also take place on the basis of written or printed verbal stimuli—through the act of reading. These important aspects of communication will be described in a later section concerned with the functions of a reading repertoire.

9

Complex verbal S–R mechanisms and concept learning

This article summarizes one of the author's early integrations of learning principles in the context of language. The analysis indicates that the principles of classical and instrumental conditioning are not incompatible and seem to be simultaneously involved in the development and function of various aspects of language behavior.

The article makes additional pluralistic analyses, showing for example the simultaneous operation of both of the learning principles in the language training of the child. Thus, when the mother prompts the child to say BALL in the presence of the object, the child receives training which will bring the vocal response under the control of the stimulus object. In addition, however, since the word and the object are contiguous, the meaning (sensory) response elicited by the object will be conditioned to the word.

The article is also important in showing that the application of learning principles to human behavior requires not only the description of the two types of learning principles as they apply to simple S–R associations. A prominent aspect of a learning theory of human behavior must also include an elaboration of the complex S–R mechanisms that function in significant human behaviors. The verbal habit-family is an example of a very complex S–R mechanism.

The present analysis was first presented as an Office of Naval Research

Technical Report (#10) in 1959, in somewhat longer form. In 1961 it was published in the *Psychological Review*.

VERBAL HABIT-FAMILIES, CONCEPTS
AND THE INSTRUMENTAL
CONDITIONING OF
WORD CLASSES

In several papers Hull (1934*a*, 1934*b*) has described the concept of the habit-family which he felt would "prove to have an extremely wide application as an explanatory principle in many subtle and otherwise inexplicable forms of behavior at present usually designated indiscriminately as intelligence" (1934*b*, p. 147). The concept has already been applied by Hull and others and this paper falls into the category of additionally, or more specifically, making applications to certain complex human behaviors. Before discussing the applications, it would seem useful to give a short summary of the concept of habit-families.

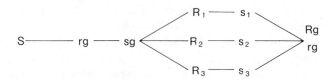

FIGURE 9.1. A habit-family. (Direct associations between S and the instrumental responses are not depicted in this and the next figure.) From A. W. Staats, Verbal habit-families, concepts, and the operant conditioning of word classes. *Psychological Review*, 1961, **68**, 190–204 by permission of the publisher.

Figure 9.1 schematizes a habit-family, in a somewhat simplified way. In the figure a part of a response which originally was elicited by the final stimuli in a sequence becomes elicitable by earlier stimuli in the sequence. This partial response is called the fractional anticipatory goal response, rg. Since rg may be elicited by the stimulus at the beginning of a sequence this rg may precede other, instrumental, responses elicited by the stimulus. When this occurs the rg and the stimuli it produces are contiguous with the instrumental responses and these stimuli will come to elicit the instrumental responses R_1, R_2, and R_3 in a divergent mechanism. The stimuli produced by these three responses will be associated with the goal response, R_g, and tend to elicit the goal response (including the portion which becomes the rg) in a convergent mechanism. Thus, a simple habit-family could be summarized as a stimulus which has tendencies to elicit an anticipatory goal response which in turn has tendencies to elicit a hierarchy of responses, each of which tends to elicit a common final response, part of which is the anticipatory response. This summary ignores the direct associations between the original stimulus and the instrumental responses.

Mediated generalization would occur from one instrumental response to the others (because of the common response that is associated to each of the other responses, that is the common rg).

Verbal Habit-Families

CLASSICAL CONDITIONING OF WORD MEANING   The first part of the present book was devoted to a theoretical and experimental analysis which suggested that responses are conditioned to words through classical conditioning. It was suggested that these conditioned responses account in part for what is called word meaning in everyday life.

This concept of word meaning can be considered to be analogous to what Hull called an rg fractional anticipatory goal response. The habit-family concept may thus be altered to take a more general form which is included in the theory of language. That is, classically conditioned responses elicited by words can enter into the formation and function of the more complex stimulus-response constellations that will be called verbal habit-families. It may be stated again that such conditioned (meaning) responses may be of an affective (emotional) or sensory (image) nature.

Following the conception that sensory responses may be conditioned, the pairing of the auditory presentation of the word BALL and the visual presentation of the object ball, as an example, would be expected to condition the child to respond to the auditory verbal stimulus with part of the visual responses elicited by the ball itself. The word stimulus would now be meaningful. Additionally, the child's own speech response BALL can be considered to be equivalent to the word as a stimulus since it produces the same type of sound. Thus, after the conditioning experience, both the presentation of the word by some other person or the saying of it himself would elicit the meaning response.

INSTRUMENTAL CONDITIONING OF WORD RESPONSES   As has been described, in addition to the learning of word meaning responses, the individual learns through instrumental conditioning to emit vocal responses. And these vocal responses will through additional instrumental conditioning experiences come under the precise control of various types of stimuli: internal stimuli, environmental stimuli, printed and written verbal stimuli, and so on.

MEANING AS AN ANTICIPATORY RESPONSE   According to the conventions
of this paper the conditionable sensory component elicited by the object
ball may be conditioned to the stimulus word BALL. In addition, if the
child is reinforced after saying BALL while responding to the object, as
occurs in the instrumental conditioning of verbal behavior, an association is established between the stimuli produced by the sensory responses
to the ball and the speech response. The formation of both of these associations is depicted in Figure 9.2. Thus, through classical conditioning, the

(a)

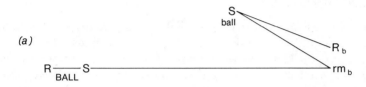

(b)

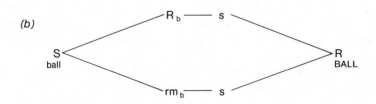

FIGURE 9.2. $a.$The conditioning of a meaning response to the stimuli produced by a word response. (When the mother says BALL,
$R_{\overline{BALL}}S$, and presents the ball S_{ball}, part of the sensory responses
elicited by the object, rm_b, are conditioned to the auditory stimuli.
Part of the responses elicited by the ball, R_b, are not conditionable.)
[The figures in the present article do not include prefixes to indicate
the type of stimulus function involved.] $b.$The conditioning of a
word response to the stimuli produced by the conditionable sensory
response components. (When the child is reinforced for saying BALL
in the presence of the ball, the speech response, R_{BALL}, comes under
the control of the stimuli produced by the conditionable sensory response components, rm_b–sm.) From A. W. Staats, Verbal habit-
families, concepts, and the operant conditioning of word classes.
$Psychological\ Review$, 1961, 68, 190–204 by permission of the publisher.

conditionable sensory responses elicited by the ball, $rm_{\overline{b}}$s, are conditioned to the word response BALL, $R_{\overline{BALL}}S$. In addition, when the child
is reinforced for saying BALL while looking at the ball, the verbal re-

sponse is conditioned to the same sensory responses, $rm_{\overline{b}}$s. Thus, the word response $R_{\overline{BALL}}$S tends to elicit $rm_{\overline{b}}$s, but $rm_{\overline{b}}$s also tends to elicit the word response.

When the meaning response (conditionable sensory response) which has been conditioned to a word response has also become anticipatory to the word response, the meaning response is analogous to Hull's rg. That is, an rg is conditioned to the stimuli produced by preceding instrumental responses, but also comes to elicit those instrumental responses.

Divergent Mechanism

It will be remembered that Hull's habit-family consisted of a stimulus which would elicit an anticipatory response which had tendencies to elicit a divergent hierarchy of responses, each of these responses having tendencies to elicit the same goal response, part of which was the anticipatory goal response. To continue with the example, not only will the naming response BALL be reinforced in the presence of the stimulus object ball (and similar stimulus objects), but in addition a number of other word responses will receive the same treatment, such as, ROUND, CIRCULAR, SPHERICAL. That is, in the presence of the ball, the child will be reinforced if he says, "It is round, it is spherical, etc." Because of this experience, the sensory responses produced by the object (actually a class of similar objects) will come to tend to elicit each of these speech responses in a divergent hierarchy of responses. Thus, the sensory responses elicited by an object, including the portion which is conditionable, come to control more than one naming response.

Convergent Mechanism

In addition, each of these stimulus words (or word responses, through the stimuli they produce) will have been conditioned to elicit the same end response component, their common meaning. This forms a convergent hierarchy. Each of the set of words or word responses of the individual comes to elicit the common meaning in the manner previously described as the first-order conditioning of meaning, for example, through being paired with the object ball when someone says, "This is round," in the presence of the object.

The Mechanisms as a Verbal Habit-Family

These divergent and convergent hierarchies (including both meaning and word responses) actually compose a habit-family, united by the common meaning response component. That is, an "anticipatory" response ($rm_{\overline{r}}$s in Figure 9.3) has been formed which when elicited by a stimulus will tend to elicit a class of responses (R_{ROUND}, $R_{CIRCULAR}$,

R$_\text{SPHERICAL}$, R$_\text{BALL}$, and R$_\text{ORANGE}$) all of which (through the stimuli they produce) culminate in the elicitation of the common response. In terms of the language responses, a verbal habit-family exists when an anticipatory meaning response component elicited by a stimulus has tendencies to elicit a class of word responses and each of these word responses has tendencies to elicit the same common meaning response component. The verbal habit-family in the example is depicted in Figure 9.3.

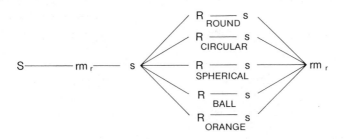

FIGURE 9.3.   The verbal habit-family for "roundness." From A. W. Staats, Verbal habit-families, concepts, and the operant conditioning of word classes. *Psychological Review,* 1961, **68**, 190–204 by permission of the publisher.

Many different stimuli could tend to arouse the verbal habit-family through eliciting the anticipatory meaning response, that is, verbal and nonverbal stimuli conditioned to elicit the anticipatory meaning response, the objects involved in the original conditioning since they elicit the conditionable sensory components, and objects which elicit similar sensory components. Thus, there could well be a hierarchy of stimulus situations with varying strengths for eliciting the anticipatory meaning response and, thus the verbal habit-family. This would be analogous to Maltzman's (1955) compound habit-family. Any variable which strengthened the association of the anticipatory meaning response to a stimulus (where this is appropriate) would strengthen each of the individual word responses in the verbal habit-family, mediated by the anticipatory meaning.

To further complicate the situation, since meaning is composed of independent response components, a word response could be in more than one verbal habit-family. And a stimulus situation (or stimulus word) could elicit more than one unconditioned or conditioned anticipatory meaning component, and thus have tendencies to elicit more than one verbal habit-family.

Concepts

Hull (1920) originally posited that concepts are developed by abstracting the common stimulus elements in a series of stimulus objects. In his experimental demonstration of this approach he used as stimulus objects groups of Chinese characters. For each group there was a common component imbedded in each individual character. The subjects' task was to respond with a particular nonsense syllable to a group of characters. It was found that the subjects improved in anticipating correctly the syllable name of a new character, after having experience with other characters containing the same element. That is, they were able to "abstract" the common elements.

Osgood (1953), however, feels that consideration of concept formation as the abstraction of identical stimulus elements would not distinguish the process from all learning, making the term useless. He states that even most lower animals could learn to do what Hull showed in his experiment.

> Fields . . . showed that rats could learn to jump toward a triangular form. . . . Yet, should we conclude that the rat can understand the *abstract* concept of triangularity? Would the rat respond positively to three dots in a triangular arrangement versus four dots arranged in a square? Or react positively to three people, three places on a map, a three-cornered block, as "triangles." . . . It would seem that the only *essential* condition for concept formation is the learning of a common mediating response (which is the meaning of the concept) for a group of objects or situations, identical elements and common perceptual relations merely facilitating the establishment of such mediators. (pp. 667–668)

Osgood, while rejecting the notion that concepts are based upon identical stimulus elements, does not adequately specify how the objects come to elicit a common response or what the common response is. If the three dots, for example, do not elicit a response like that elicited by a triangle on an unconditioned basis, how do they come to do so? How is the power of abstraction gained? The processes involved must be specified to a much greater extent before concepts can be accounted for in S–R terms.

Kendler and associates (Kendler and D'Amato, 1955; Kendler and Karasik, 1958; Kendler and Mayzner, 1956; Kendler and Vineberg, 1954) have also considered concept formation to be the acquisition of a common implicit response to different stimuli. In addition, Kendler and Karasik (1958) have extended this to verbal concept formation which they assume occurs "when S learns to respond to a set of different words with the same implicit response" (p. 278). The conceptualization that words which elicit a common implicit response are involved in a verbal concept begins to focus on the verbal aspect of concepts in the "two-stage" S–R framework. However, further specification as to the processes of the development and function of verbal concepts is necessary, since the common meaning response to the words used by Kendler and Karasik had been acquired by the subjects prior to the experiment.

The following discussion will attempt the necessary elaborations. One type of concept may be regarded as a verbal habit-family formed usually on the basis of a class of stimulus objects having identical elements. Take, for example, the "animal" concept. The individual words in the concept will gain their meaning through classical conditioning where the word is paired with the appropriate stimulus objects (actually a number of stimulus objects having closely common characteristics). DOG is paired with dogs, COW with cows, and so on, and the conditionable sensory components elicited by the stimulus object are conditioned to the word involved.

Now each of the stimulus objects in the class has certain identical elements (such as legs, head, spontaneous movement, furry, and so forth) and the objects in the class will thus elicit sensory response components which also have identical elements. Conseqently, part of the meaning response component conditioned to the word DOG will be identical to those which, in the same manner, are conditioned to the words COW, HORSE, and PIG, and so forth. This common response could be called the *animal* meaning response component, rm_a in Figure 9.4.

In addition, however, each stimulus object elicits conditionable sensory response components which the other objects in the class do not. Since these conditionable sensory responses are characteristically elicited only by the specific animal, they are only conditioned to the specific animal word with which the object contiguously occurs. Thus, each of the animal words comes to elicit an animal meaning response component shared by the others, and also a specific meaning response component which none of the others elicit, rm_d, rm_c, rm_h, or rm_p in the figure.

Now, each of the stimulus objects will also occur in the presence of the word ANIMAL. For example, in the presence of each animal the child will be told, "That is an animal." In this process the common conditionable sensory response component elicited by all the animals, the animal component, will be strongly conditioned to the word ANIMAL, and each of the specific conditionable response components elicited by only one of the animals will be weakly conditioned to the word ANIMAL.

The meaning responses which are conditioned to the words will also become anticipatory to the words through the labeling process which has been described. Thus, the animal meaning response and the animal word responses form a verbal habit-family as Figure 9.4 indicates.

The associations depicted in Figure 9.4 indicate why, in the presence of a particular stimulus object in the class, the individual is likely to specifically "label" the stimulus object rather than to say ANIMAL, or one of the other words. For example, the stimulus object cow would elicit the sensory response component, rm_a, which in turn would equally tend to elicit all of the animal word responses, including COW and ANIMAL. Thus, all of the words would have an equal probability of occurring simply on the basis of this association. The stimulus object cow would elicit in addition, however, the characteristic sensory response, rm_c, which in turn would strongly tend to elicit the word response COW and, also, though not so strongly, the word response ANIMAL—but none of the other word responses. Thus in the presence of the stimulus object cow there are two strong associations for the elicitation of the word response COW, one strong and one weak association for the word response ANIMAL, and only one strong association for the elicitation of any other word in the concept class.

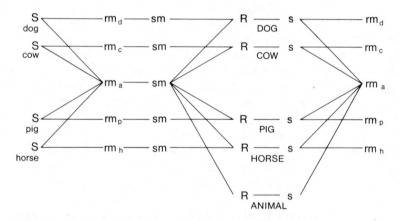

FIGURE 9.4. The "animal" concept. From A. W. Staats, Verbal habit-families, concepts, and the operant conditioning of word classes. *Psychological Review*, 1961, **68**, 190–204 by permission of the publisher.

But this does not yet account for abstraction, that is, how the individual comes to respond in the same manner to a new object which does not have identical stimulus elements with the other objects in the class and so does not elicit the common response,—how one responds to three dots as a triangle. It would seem that abstraction first comes from the verbal family hierarchy. To realize the explanatory value of the verbal habit-family, one of the principles of communication which have been presented must first be summarized.

Using a conception of meaning such as had been described herein, that is, an implicit mediating response, it has been suggested that a sentence is a conditioning device and that communication takes place when the meaning response which has been elicited by the predicate is conditioned to the subject of the sentence. In addition, since the subject of the sentence will also elicit a meaning response which has stimulus properties, the meaning response elicited by the predicate will be conditioned to the stimuli produced by the meaning response elicited by the subject of the sentence. That a meaning response may be conditioned to the stimuli produced by another meaning response has already been shown (Staats, Staats, and Heard, 1959a). Using Mowrer's (1954) example, Figure 9.5 demonstrates this process and the resulting associations and mediated generalization.

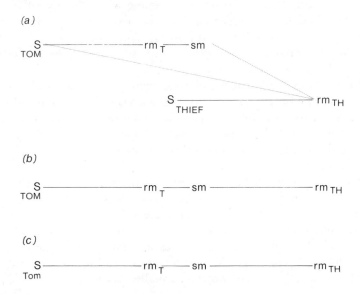

FIGURE 9.5. Mowrer's conception of communication. (a) As a result of the sentence, the meaning of THIEF, rm_{TH}, is conditioned to the word TOM and also to the stimuli produced by the meaning response elicited TOM, rm_r–sm. (b) The word TOM, S_{TOM}, now elicits the meaning of the THIEF, mediated by rm_r–sm. (c) The same is true for the person himself, S_{TOM}, since he also elicits rm_r–sm on an unconditioned basis. From A. W. Staats, Verbal habit-families, concepts, and the operant conditioning of word classes. *Psychological Review*, 1961, **68**, 190–204 by permission of the publisher.

The function of the verbal habit-family in making abstraction possible may now be described, that is, how stimulus objects get into the concept class when they do not have identical stimulus elements and so do not elicit responses common to the objects which are in the class. Returning to the animal concept example, the individual having learned a meaning response to the word ANIMAL will be conditioned to make this same response to the word WORM if told, "a worm is an animal." When the animal meaning response has become anticipatory to the word WORM in the manner already described, the word would be fully in the concept verbal habit-family.

Following the conception the sentence would also condition the meaning of ANIMAL to the meaning of WORM, that is, form an $rm \overline{} sm - rm_a$ association. Thus, the object worm (and any object eliciting rm_w, such as caterpillar) would now elicit the animal meaning response and so be in the animal class of objects.

It is also likely that backward conditioning would broaden the animal concept through the same sentence by conditioning the meaning of worm to the word ANIMAL and its meaning. This would generalize to the other animal words. Dostálek (1959) discusses the importance of backward conditioning in verbal learning.

Whether or not this backward conditioning takes place, the concept animal could be further broadened on the basis of language conditioning. For example, the sentence, "animals consume oxygen," would condition the responses elicited by the predicate of the sentence to the meaning response elicited by the word ANIMALS, with the expected generalizations occurring.[1]

Thus, with continued verbal experience, the verbal habit-family (concept) grows in terms of the objects and words which elicit the concept meaning. In addition, the concept meaning is broadened to include parts of the response made to new objects and words.

On the basis of verbal habit-families and language conditioning and generalization, learning which is originally derived from experience with a relatively small class of objects, usually having identical elements,

---

[1] It is also true that the concept word (ANIMAL) in a concept could gain its meaning on a language basis rather than through being paired with the various objects in the original stimulus class. That is, it should be possible for the concept word to gain its meaning through being paired with subordinate words in the verbal habit-family which had already been conditioned to their meanings. Or the concept word could be presented in sentences with appropriate adjectives and the meanings of the adjectives conditioned in this manner to the concept word. These processes would be higher-order conditioning.

may be transferred to many new situations and tasks.[2] The child first learns the "triangle" verbal habit-family on the basis of direct experience with a few stimulus objects, that is on the basis of the common stimulus elements and the common responses they elicit. Later, however, he is told that three dots, or three people, are a TRIANGLE; and through the meaning which has previously been conditioned to the word TRI-ANGLE, the concept meaning, the new objects, and other objects which are similar to *them* enter the concept class. It is suggested that these are some of the processes which underlie the progression from concrete to abstract thinking which has frequently been said to occur in child development (Brown, 1958), and which are involved in "understanding" a concept.

Osgood was correct in stating that a rat cannot understand a concept —not, however, because it cannot form a common response to a class of stimulus objects. This part of concept learning the animal would be capable of. However, the rat is not capable of acquiring verbal habit-families to correspond to such concept mechanisms and the power of abstraction is thus lost to the animal. The process of concept formation is seen as one which involves complicated principles of learning, communication, and mediated generalization. The relationships between the language processes and the environmental process are complex. The language processes arise from response to the environment but then in turn effect response to other aspects of the environment.

Actually, concepts would not usually be as simple as portrayed. Figure 9.6 makes one elaboration of the animal concept to include a sub-concept, the "dog" concept. Although all of the stimulus objects in the general concept elicit the common animal meaning component, rm_a, three of the objects (the dogs) also elicit a meaning component (rm_d) common to them but not the other stimulus objects. This component comes to elicit the dog word responses, including the concept word DOG itself, and is conditioned also to each of the dog word responses and becomes part of the meaning of each of these word responses. Each of these dog stimulus objects, in addition to the rm_a and rm_d conditionable sensory response components, would also elicit a specific response component which is common to none of the other dog stimulus objects. This would also be true of the other stimulus objects. The figure is simplified by not showing these associations.

[2] The class of stimulus objects in a concept usually has identical elements, but the same process could start with just one object and through conditioning meaning to meaning as in Mowrer's communication paradigm, grow to a class of objects which elicit a common meaning response and a class of words, etc.

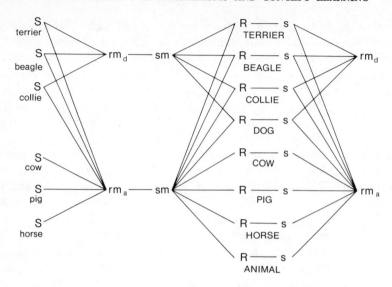

FIGURE 9.6.   This diagram depicts a concept ("dog") which is included in a larger concept ("animal"). From A. W. Staats, Verbal habit-families, concepts, and the operant conditioning of word classes. *Psychological Review,* 1961, **68,** 190–204 by permission of the publisher.

It would be expected that the greater the extent of overlap in meaning response components between any two habit-families, or any two words, the greater the amount of generalization that would occur. Thus, following Figure 9.6, if one said "Animals are dangerous," the meaning of DANGEROUS would be conditioned to the meaning of the word ANIMAL, and consequently equally to all of the words and objects in the figure. If, however, one said, "Dogs are dangerous," there would be greater generalization to the dog objects and words than to the other animal objects and words. In a semantic generalization paradigm, a response conditioned to the ^{c}S DOG should generalize more to TERRIER than it would to ANIMAL since the two dog words share two strongly conditioned meaning components, rm_a and rm_d as shown in Figure 9.5. This has been shown by Razran (1949).

Instrumental Conditioning of Word Classes

A number of recent experiments as summarized by Krasner (1958) and Salzinger (1959) have shown that reinforcement of individual words emitted by individuals will result in the strengthening of a class of words containing the individual words. There are some questions which seem unresolved in these studies—and there is little articulation of these studies to the principles and studies concerning the semantic properties of language. Primarily, there is not adequate rationale concerning the instrumental conditioning of classes of responses which are as diverse as the classes of verbal response which have been conditioned, such as, travel words (Wilson and Verplanck, 1956), living thing words (Wilson and Verplanck, 1956), animal words (Ball, 1952), action words (Wickes, 1956). In his article on the conditioning of verbal behavior, Salzinger (1959) seems to recognize the need for such a rationale in discussing the definition of verbal response classes, stating that responses in a class may be substituted for one another, are followed by the same reinforcement, or are emitted in the presence of the same discriminative stimulus.

It is not the case, however, that a word in one of the verbal response classes which has been conditioned may be substituted for any other word in the class. In language usage individual words of a word class are not functionally equivalent as are the rat's bar press responses. Substitution of class words into a sentence could make the sentence meaningless. Nor can it be said that all words in the classes which have been instrumentally conditioned are followed by the same reinforcement in language usage. Most words, regardless of what class they are in, are followed by the same reinforcers, for example, naming living objects with living thing words is reinforced by the same generalized reinforcers as is naming transportation objects. Nor can it be said that the words in a class are emitted in the presence of the same discriminative stimulus. For example, one is reinforced for saying the specific, living thing word in the presence of the specific living thing, not for saying *any* living thing word. On closer examination, the conclusions made by Salzinger are thus untenable. Salzinger, however, is quite correct in recognizing the need to explain why verbal response classes are strengthened when individual members are reinforced. The paradox is that as responses these words in the word classes may be very discrepant, and cannot be considered as functionally equivalent, yet response induction occurs nevertheless.

As would be expected from the above analysis, it is not possible to predict what words will operantly condition as a class from an operant conditioning rationale, as Salzinger (1959) admits: "Generally, investigators have had to rely upon their common sense knowledge of verbal behavior to decide upon the constitution of response classes." (p. 70) He continues to suggest that studies of semantic generalization or measurements of the connotative meaning of words may be used to discover response classes. Thus, in both cases, this implicitly recognizes that the commonality of words in the classes which have been instrumentally conditioned concerns the semantic properties of the words. Notwithstanding this, the account of verbal behavior offered by Skinner eschews the concept of meaning and his example appears to be followed by other investigators interested in the application of operant conditioning principles to language behavior. At any rate, it does not seem to be defensible to exclude the concept of meaning in accounting for the operant conditionability of classes of word responses, and then suggest that meaning properties be used to choose classes of words which *will* condition. In conclusion, this suggests that a combination of operant principles of conditioning along with the semantic properties of words such as has been offered herein, will offer a more complete explanation of language behavior.

In short, it is suggested that word response classes which will condition are verbal habit-family hierarchies. Subjects in the verbal conditioning studies are reinforced when they utter a word from a certain class of words. The verbal habit-family (that is, concept) depicted in Figure 9.6 will be used as an example. In this example, if the subject spoke an animal word the rm_a meaning response would be elicited. If a social reinforcer was then presented, it would be expected that the rm_a meaning response as well as the verbal response itself would be conditioned to the cues of the situation. The strengthening of the individual speech response would not generalize to different topological speech responses even though they were in the same class of words. However, if only animal words are reinforced, the strongest meaning association to the situation will become that of the animal meaning response component. Since the animal meaning response component is also the anticipatory response for the class of animal words, it would be expected that the whole class of animal words would be strengthened, that is, the frequency of their occurrence would be heightened. It is the strengthening of the common anticipatory meaning response in the verbal habit-family that mediates the generalized strengthening.

In Figure 9.6, which is used as the example, some of the words are in subconcept classes, which actually have aspects of separate verbal habit-families. Reinforcing a word in one of the subclasses would strengthen all the meaning responses elicited by the word. In the case of the word TERRIER, for example, both rm_a and rm_d would be strengthened. Because of this there would be a greater tendency for another word in the subconcept to be emitted than one only in the general concept. This might lead to the strengthening of classes of words other than those the experimenter had intended to strengthen, and this apparently occurs, according to Salzinger (1959):

The problem which arises here is the discrepancy between the experimenter's definition of the response class and the response class which is actually being affected by the experimental manipulations. In one study . . . for example, the experimenter tried to condition plural nouns but actually caused an increase in a subset, i.e., names of tribes. (p. 68)

This result is accounted for by the present model, that is, the experimenter strengthened all the meaning response components elicited by the word responses he reinforced. A few reinforcements of the names of tribes could so strengthen *all* the meaning components so that only these types of responses would be elicited.

One implication involved in this discussion is that if classes of words can be instrumentally conditioned, then they are members of a verbal habit-family, and therefore have a common meaning response component. Thus, semantic generalization should be possible between individual members of the words in a class which can be operantly conditioned, as Salzinger has implied. And, on the other hand, any concept, or verbal habit-family, should be capable of being instrumentally conditioned. Thus, for example, each of the concept classes of words found by Underwood and Richardson (1956) should be capable of instrumentally conditioning as a class since each group of words shares a common meaning response component.

The many variables concerned with the strength of the concept meaning response, the extent to which the response produces distinctive cues, the dominance of the concept meaning response in the total meaning elicited by the words in the class, and so on, should be factors in the ease of the operant conditioning of the word class. . . .

Experimental Verification

The foregoing article suggests that any set of words that elicits a common meaning response should instrumentally condition as a word class. The analysis, thus, suggests that a set of words eliciting a common meaning response, with the meaning response also tending to elicit each of the words, is a verbal concept. Reinforcement of one word in the verbal concept should have the effect of strengthening the other words in the concept.

This analysis was tested in the following way. A group of 40 words was selected (Staats, 1963) each of which elicited the common meaning response of positive evaluative meaning. That is, subjects rated the meaning of each of the 40 words as highly *pleasant* on a seven-point scale ranging from *pleasant* to *unpleasant*. Thus, although each of the words elicited other meaning responses that were quite different, they all elicited a positive evaluative meaning response. Examples of the positive meaning words are *beauty, happy, devoted, loveable.*

Each of these words was presented on a card with three other words of unsystematic meaning. Examples are *with, article, various,* and *rather.*

Randomization procedures were followed with respect to the position of the words on the cards, as well as the order of the cards. The subjects in the experimental group were presented with each card, were directed to select one of the four words, and were socially reinforced by the experimenter upon selecting one of the positive meaning words. Control group subjects were treated similarly except that they were not reinforced after they had selected the word.

The results showed that the group of subjects that were reinforced for saying the positive evaluative meaning words began to select this type of word more frequently. It should be remembered that a word was presented only one time during the procedure. Thus, being reinforced for saying one positive meaning word increased the strength of other members of this class of word responses. The subjects were significantly conditioned to say words with positive evaluative meaning.

Furthermore, it was possible to replicate the study (Staats, 1963) using negative evaluative words rather than the positive meaning words. Examples of these words are *agony, abortion, failure,* and *hate.*

The results thus support the suggestion that some verbal concepts consist of sets of words that elicit a common response, and that reinforcement of one of the words in the set will strengthen other words in the set. In doing so the study shows how an integration of learning approaches yields a more powerful conception of language. That is, the analysis integrates the instrumental conditioning conception of speech behavior with the classical conditioning conception of word meaning. The integration of the two conceptions enables the construction of the conception of the verbal habit family mechanism which has implications for understanding what verbal concepts are as well as why it is possible to instrumentally condition such concepts.

Additional S–R Mechanisms as Concepts

The preceding analysis suggests several ways that the basic principles can interact in producing complex stimulus-response mechanisms. Not only can a word come through classical conditioning to elicit a particular meaning response, but additional words may also come to elicit the same meaning response. When this is the case the words will function similarly, as was described in the discussion of semantic generalization in the first part of the book.

Furthermore, when the meaning response has come to elicit each of the words, the words will acquire additional similarities of function. The reinforcement of one in a stimulus situation will strengthen all of the responses. Or, if the stimulus situation has tendencies to elicit one of the words in a stimulus situation it will tend to elicit all of the words in the concept class (verbal habit-family). These are some of the characteristics, it may be suggested, that identify one type of what is commonly called a concept.

It should be pointed out, however, that the term *concept* as commonly used is applied to many different functions of words. Much of the language learning discussed in the first two parts of the book would be termed concepts. For example, when the cat had been classically conditioned to respond appropriately to the word *no,* we could say that the cat had formed the concept of the word. Thus, it is suggested that there are no unitary entities or processes for the term *concepts.* There are only complex stimulus-response mechanisms that the individual acquires—most centrally verbal S–R mechanisms. Thus, a pluralistic conception is also necessary in the study of concepts.

Various numbers and types of principles and various numbers and types of responses may be involved. As in the preceding case the verbal habit-family as a concept mechanism involved both classically conditioned and instrumentally conditioned responses. The verbal habit-family may be considered to be one type of complex S–R mechanism that would be called a concept. This does not limit the field to word responses connected by a classically conditioned meaning response, however. A number of other possibilities for the formation of complex S–R mechanisms (concepts) is possible. Several examples will be briefly described.

Word Association Verbal Habit-Families

Further consideration of the verbal habit-family mechanism indicates that it has more generality than indicated. That is, words which are in the same habit-family on the basis of sharing a common classically conditioned meaning response should demonstrate the characteristics of a word class. But, in addition, any group of words each of which elicit a common response, if that response also tends to elicit each of the word responses, should condition as a class. The common response could be a word associate, for example. An illustration of a case in the English language of a word associational S–R mechanism that is analogous to the verbal habit-family may be found in the word association norms of

Russell and Jenkins (1954). The word SLEEP elicits BED, DREAM, COMFORT, and DEEP, as associates to varying degrees. BED, DREAM, COMFORT, and DEEP, in turn, also elicit SLEEP as a word associate response.

This type of S–R mechanism should function as a concept. For example, the reinforcement of one of the words in this class should have the effect of strengthening other words in the class, because of the one word associate response that is common to all of the words. Thus, it would be expected that if an individual with such a word association structure emitted the response BED, the stimuli produced by this response would elicit the implicit response SLEEP. If a reinforcer was then presented the response SLEEP would be strengthened to the situational stimuli. Since the response SLEEP (or its stimuli) tend to elicit the words DREAM, COMFORT, and DEEP, the situational stimuli would now tend to elicit those word responses.

The same thing would occur if any of the other words were reinforced in the situation—each would also elicit the response SLEEP and it would be conditioned to the situational stimuli. And, of course, the more strongly the response SLEEP was conditioned to the situation the more strongly would its associates tend to be elicited.

Word Associational Sequences as Concept Mechanisms

There are additional possibilities for demonstrating the advantage of an integrated learning approach in accounting for the instrumental conditioning of word classes and in making a detailed analysis of verbal concepts. It has been shown that the implicit word associates of a stimulus word are elicited when the stimulus word is presented, and that these implicit word responses may have a learning function (Russell and Storms, 1955). That is, subjects were able to acquire more easily an A–D association, where A–B, B–C, and C–D associations already existed. Thus, when a verbal response sequence has been formed, the occurrence of the first word in the sequence will implicitly elicit the second, the second will elicit the third, and so on.

On the basis of implicit sequences of verbal responses, it would be expected that any serial chain of word associates, that is, word responses, would demonstrate concept characteristics in the instrumental conditioning situation. That is, if the first response in a sequence was emitted, its word associates, the next several responses, would be elicited implicitly. The occurrence of reinforcement would then strengthen the tendency for all of the implicit responses to be elicited by the situation. If the next response in the chain occurred, the same process would be repeated and would make it even more likely that the third response in the sequence would be elicited. Each succeeding word response in the sequence, when it occurred, would further increase the likelihood that the next response would be elicited.

It would also be expected that a serial chain of responses would constitute a word class in an instrumental conditioning situation even when not emitted in the serial order. That is, when a series of word responses are chained in a serial learning task, associations are formed between words other than those that are directly contiguous. Nevertheless, the closer the order to that in the serial learning task, the stronger the associations would be and the greater the extent of the operant conditioning expected.

The author and associates (Staats, et al., 1966) tested these expectations in the following study. The subjects first learned two separate serial lists (two separate word response sequences) by the paired-associate method of anticipation. The items on the lists were nonsense words such as HUFOD, TEBAM, and SOZOG. Later, the first words from each of the lists was placed upon a card, the second word of each list on another card, and so on. Then, in the serial order, the cards were individually presented to the subject with instructions to select one word. The word responses in one of the lists (the list opposite to that which was chosen on the first card) were then reinforced. Of the three subjects so treated each selected 9 or more words from that list out of the possible 11— a statistically significant performance in each individual case—for a mean of 9.67.

This procedure was replicated for six additional subjects with one change. The order of the presentation of the words in the instrumental conditioning was 1-3-5-7-9-11-2-4-6-8-10-12. The mean number of words from the reinforced list was 7.50. Another group of subjects was presented with the pairs of words on the cards in which the cards were randomly selected. The mean for this group was 6.67. And finally, for a control group where the word response sequences were not established in the subjects at all, the mean number of responses selected from the reinforced list was 5.67. Chance selection of the words would result in selection of 5.50 words from either list.

Thus, the extent of instrumental conditioning of the groups was greatest for subjects presented the word selections in the serial order in which they were learned, next greatest for subjects presented the words in the somewhat different alternate order, next for subjects given the markedly different random order, and least for the control subjects for whom there were no associations between the words. A regression analysis of the treatment conditions indicated a linear trend significant at the .005 level. That is, the conditionability of the concept class of word responses was dependent upon the strength of associations between the words. The effect of the concept class depended upon the strength of associations of the words in the verbal response sequence.

The study thus illustrates another type of verbal concept, and another type of S–R mechanism. The S–R mechanism concerns the formation of sequences of verbal responses. The author has suggested that many of our adjustive behaviors are based upon having acquired many such mechanisms (Staats, 1964a, 1966; Staats and Staats, 1963), for example, problem solving may depend upon such verbal response sequences.

Word Association Clusters as Concept Mechanisms

In addition to the preceding types of S–R mechanisms that appear to constitute what would be called concepts in everyday life as well as in laboratory research, there is one other example that will be described. Any words that occur frequently in contiguity with each other in our language experience should come to be associated with each other as a "word associational cluster," and therefore function as a class.

Take, for example, the word associates to a stimulus word in word-association norms. Many of them are interassociated, presumably because they occur in contiguity with each other in various circumstances. For example, in the word association responses to MUSIC there are SWEET and SOFT, but SWEET and SOFT also elicit MUSIC. In addition, the word LOUD, although not elicited by MUSIC, is elicited by SOFT. Thus, LOUD would tend to occur as a response to MUSIC, since it is mediated by the response SOFT. Now LOUD as a stimulus word has as its associates a number of responses which are also direct associates to MUSIC, as well as the word MUSIC itself. If complete word-association norms were available for these words, additional inter-associations would be seen.

Based upon the previous analysis, such a group of words should also form a verbal concept and instrumentally condition as a class. This was tested (Staats, 1963) using the methods of instrumental conditioning already described, for the word associates to MUSIC. That is, 25 associates to the word MUSIC were taken from Russell and Jenkins (1954), and each was presented with two nonmusic words on a card to two groups of subjects. All subjects were instructed to select one of the three words. In the experimental group selection of a music word was followed by reinforcement, but no responses were reinforced in the control group. The results indicated that the number of MUSIC word responses significantly increased for the experimental group relative to the control group in a linear fashion significant at the .01 level.

This study thus illustrates another type of S–R mechanism, or in other terms another type of concept. Thus, it is suggested that there are a number of different types of S–R mechanisms that the individual acquires and which function in his adjustive behaviors. Many of these mechanisms are commonly called concepts, especially when verbal responses are involved. This analysis thus suggests that there are also many different types of S–R mechanisms that would be called concepts. The preceding studies contain an additional suggestion concerning the *function* of concept classes. Concept formation tasks can be solved on the basis of verbal concept classes. And it has been shown that generalization will take place among words in a concept. The present results showed that concept words will also instrumentally condition as a class.

Furthermore, the preceding studies made a deeper analysis of the determinants of word classes based upon an integration of learning principles from various areas of study. The research also involved the same type of integration of experimental methods—instrumental conditioning procedures, serial learning methods, semantic measurements, as well as word association norms. The present analysis has been included in part to indicate the great complexity of human behavior to be expected when detailed S–R analyses are made and the interactions of the learning principles are indicated. It may be expected that such detailed analyses are necessary to deal specifically with many behaviors. While it is appropriate to commence the study of human behavior using simple samples, one line of progress will involve advancement to more complicated repertoires. As will be shown later, one way of making feasible the study of complex repertoires is to work with young children still in the beginning stages of the acquisition of the repertoire.

10

Language learning and linguistics and additional aspects of language and thought

In 1959 the linguist Chomsky wrote a critique of Skinner's account of verbal behavior (1957), which has never been answered. Following this successful challenge of Skinner's operant conditioning interpretation of certain aspects of language, there has been a tendency to disqualify all learning approaches to language, as if they had been tarred with the same brush. It is apparently felt by psycholinguists at any rate that criticizing one learning theory is criticizing them all (see also Bever, *et al.*, 1965, for an example).

As has been indicated, however, the various learning approaches to language have been separatistic and by themselves have been incapable of dealing comprehensively with language. Furthermore, the major learning interpretations of aspects of language (such as Skinner's) have not included supporting experimental evidence.

It is suggested, however, that an integrated learning theory of language provides a more comprehensive interpretation of language learning and function, including experimental evidence, than is otherwise available. (This is thus the major answer to criticisms of the importance of learning to language development.) Although it is not possible herein to completely discuss the linguistic and psycholinguistic challenge to learning theory (see Staats, in press *a* for a more complete discussion), the following discussions will deal with topics that are relevant to this topic. In addition, a few words may be in order here concerning some of the misconceptions that have been put forth in criticism of the idea that language is learned.

First, it is well to clarify the nature of the learning theorist's task in approaching the study of language, as contrasted to the linguist's task. To do this it is necessary to sketch out in brief what constitute explanatory principles in dealing with human behavior and what constitute only predictive principles. To begin, explanation in psychology may be considered to be obtained when one can state the conditions that give rise to the behavior involved. These conditions could be of a biological nature; genetic, anatomical, or physiological. Or the conditions that give rise to the behavior may be those of experience, that is, learning. When either type of principle has been discovered one can predict the behavior from a knowledge of the "causative" condition. When the causative condition can be manipulated the behavior can be produced or prevented from occurring.

Although it is very important simply to observe behavior in systematic detail, and to present these observations in formal clarity, observations of behavior alone do not yield explanatory statements in the sense described above. Sometimes it is possible from a simple description of behavior to get prediction, however. For example, children who have more complex behavioral skills at an early age are likely to have more complex behavioral skills at a later age, at least the relationship generally holds true when a large group of children is involved. Thus, it is possible to predict the later behavior from knowledge of the earlier behavior and this may be a very useful principle.

But such response-response (R–R) principles are not explanatory in the sense described. That is, one still does not know the conditions that have given rise to the development of either the earlier or the later behavior. R–R principles do not tell you what to do if you wish to produce a behavior, or to prevent a behavior from developing. For this type of knowledge one must have contact with the biological or learning events—for these are the determinants of behavior.

This has been briefly stated because the fact is that the realm of linguistics does not include the study of explanatory events of either the biological or learning kind. Thus, while linguistic theory may make very significant observations and descriptions of language behavior, and also construct R–R laws by which one type of language behavior may be predicted from a knowledge of another type of language behavior, *linguistic theory cannot make explanatory statements*. The linguist has no contact with the determining conditions, only with the behavior (language) itself.

This limitation of linguistic theory has not always been clear to the individuals interested in this approach such as Bever, *et al.* (1965), Mc-Neil (in press), as well as Chomsky. That is, various psycholinguistic theorists have assumed, following Chomsky, that the linguistic rules which describe in a formal manner the utterances of people are explanatory concepts. They assume that there are cognitive structures or processes that correspond to these rules. Thus, the utterance, the verbal behavior, is thought to be caused by the cognitive structure (linguistic rule). Remember, however, that the linguistic rule was derived from observations of language behavior. The linguistic rule is the representation of the language behavior, albeit in very abstract, symbolic, form. This being the case, no matter how abstract the linguistic rule appears to be, it is a description of the language behavior, and cannot be thought to explain the language behavior. As stated, for explanation one must have contact with the events that "cause" the language behavior.

Furthermore, it is not possible for the cognitive structure (psycholinguistic) theory of language to be proven by showing that learning theories are inadequate. Such criticisms may indicate the limitations of the learning theory involved. But in no way does this support the conception of a cognitive structure interpretation of language. The individual who wishes to develop a cognitive structure explanation of language must have observations of such cognitive structures or processes; which means observations in the biological realm. There are no such observations available. Thus, this type of psycholinguistic theory is at present a weak hypothesis—not an explanatory theory.

This is not said with malice, but to prevent a continuing controversy that will absorb time, energy, and journal space—to no effect. We have had in the history of psychology issues that correspond to the present learning versus psycholinguistic controversy, with relatively little lasting worth for the effort expended. For example, there was at one time a great controversy concerning whether the development of behavior seen in children was due to an inferred maturational process that was related to biological conditions, or whether behavior development was due to learning.

Early child developmentalists had made many significant observations of behavioral development. They saw that behavior development had a lawful appearance. The child did certain things before he did other things. Since there was a great generality in these lawful developments, it was thought that there must be certain underlying processes that determined the course of behavior development. The child developmentalists thought that they could advance their interpretation by studies showing that child behavior was not learned. But even if they could have shown that learning theories were not adequate to account for the events of behavioral development, their theory would not have been much advanced. No explanatory theory of behavior can be founded only upon observations of the behavior itself, as has been suggested. The developmentalists would have had to make observations of the determining biological events, if there are such, and have related these events to behavior development.

The psycholinguistic position is actually analogous to that of the maturational theorists. The psycholinguists have almost no contact with the determining events for language development and can thus make no positive statements in this arena. Their efforts at criticism cannot lend credence to their "cognitive structure" type of theory. As the present effort is attempting to show, on the other hand, a learning approach does have the capability of making explanatory statements, and also the capability for generating studies that deal with causative conditions, including procedures for doing something about the development of language behavior and of treating problems in this area. There are no comparable linguistic or psycholinguistic findings, that is, studies in which variables are manipulated and language behaviors are produced.

It may also be noted that some of the psycholinguistic assertions that language is not learned have been quite wide of the mark. For example, Fodor (1965) has stated that verbal responses are not controlled or elicited by external stimuli. Even naturalistic observation demonstrates beyond a doubt that much language behavior is stimulus controlled. All the naming or describing activities are under environmental control—not to mention ordinary conversation in which people respond in large part under the control of the partner's utterances as well as his facial expressions, and so on. (Many cases of stimulus control are quite complex, but many are simple and easy to demonstrate or observe.) With only naturalistic observations at hand one might have denied that learning principles underlie the establishment of the stimulus control, but not that such control exists. However, the experimental evidence in the present volume, and also elsewhere, shows very reliably again and again that learning principles do account for wide aspects of language.

In conclusion, let me say that the work of linguists and psycholinguists is extremely important in its own realm. For example, in having linguistic descriptions of a language we will know that most people in the language community will say some things but not others. We can also compare languages in ways that we could not without the precise descriptions, and grammatical rules are helpful in learning a second language. We have a better way of talking about (a theory of) languages. From a precise description of the language, moreover, we may get much useful information concerning what it is the child has to learn. Based upon this information we may better devise materials for training the child. This concerns the "descriptive" aspect of language.

However, on the basis of linguistic theory we can do nothing about the language development of the child. When a child does not develop language as expected, or in any case of language pathology, we must look to the learning conditions involved (and in some cases to the biological conditions). If we wish to *produce* the language development we must manipulate learning conditions. The cognitive structure concepts, and the linguistic rules upon which they are based, are not explanatory and cannot help in these tasks. Thus, another aspect of the study of language concerns the learning principles involved in its acquisition.

Finally, a comprehensive theory of language must also tell us how language functions. For we are crucially interested in the ways that differences in one's language repertoires will determine important aspects of complex human behavior. It is interesting to note that the major hypothesis of the linguist Benjamin Whorf was that the nature of one's language determined one's cognitive processes. Linguistics and the experimental psychology of language have largely not concerned themselves with these crucial adjustive functions of language. However, the integrated learning theory is fully capable of indicating in a credible and useful manner how language behaviors mediate such cognitive behaviors as reasoning, problem solving, intelligence, perception, and so on.

Several items of relevance to the "linguistic-versus-learning controversy" will be presented in this chapter—in elaborating some of the S–R mechanisms in language. The first excerpt is adapted from the present author's chapters on language development and function (Staats and Staats, 1963, pp. 169–178.)[1] Jenkins and Palermo (1964) have since presented a similar analysis of certain aspects of grammatical word classes.

Following the learning analysis of the several aspects of language, a discussion will be made to suggest that people may emit original behaviors, behaviors on which they have received no training, and yet their original behaviors will be a result of learning conditions. Several other topics of concern to a comprehensive analysis of language will then be briefly discussed in the present chapter.

---

[1] See *Complex Human Behavior* by Arthur W. Staats with contributions by Carolyn K. Staats. Copyright © 1963 by Holt, Rinehart and Winston, Inc.

LEARNING AND GRAMMATICAL HABITS

It is suggested that because of an individual's history of conditioning, S–R mechanisms, (primarily word associations) are formed which determine the way in which sentences are generated—that is, the order in which word sequences are produced. Grammatical usages may be considered to reflect such acquired verbal mechanisms. It would seem for example that certain word responses come to follow other word responses because in the spoken and written customs of a language community those words as stimuli occur in that order. The listener thus responds in the same order when stimulated by the language. Moreover, in the language development of the child when he emits word responses in the "proper" order he is reinforced; when he does not he is likely to have to repeat the behavior, which means the delay of reinforcement and the expenditure of additional energy.

The following is an explicit example of grammatical habits.

> Wilson Taylor . . . using his "cloz" procedure in which the subject fills in the gaps in mutilated messages, finds that with both sides of the gap given as in his method structural determinism is almost perfect (for example, in filling in "the old man _____ along the road," all subjects will fill in a verb form even though they vary semantically in what verb they choose). Miller and Selfridge . . . and others have demonstrated that ease of learning and retention of meaningful materials varies with the degree of approximation to English structure. Along similar lines . . . (Swanson) compared the ease of learning nonsense sequences that retained the structure of the English sentences from which they were derived, for example,
> The maff vlems oothly um the glox nerfs
> with matched materials in which the grammatical cues had been eliminated, for example,
> maff vlem ooth um glox nerf.
> Despite the greater absolute amount of material in the structured forms, they were learned significantly more easily than the matched strings of nonsense items. (Osgood, 1957, p. 88)

Even this naturalistic evidence suggests that grammatical usage in speech is acquired according to the principles of learning and that the product is an extremely complex repertoire of verbal habits. If that is indeed the case, it would seem that a better understanding of grammatical usage would result from a more detailed S–R analysis of the topic.

Acquisition of Simple Grammatical Habits

Although it is not possible herein to attempt a complete analysis of complex grammatical language behaviors, several studies may be described in terms of behavior principles to suggest that such an analysis would be productive.

The work of Brown and Fraser (1961) and Brown and Berko (1960) constitutes a most important step in bringing together the methodology and principles of the linguist with some of the experimental methods of psychology. For example, in discussing an analysis of parts of speech, Brown and Berko make the following point.

> The linguistic scientist defines the part-of-speech in purely syntactic or formal terms. He has shown that the English teacher's semantic definitions (e.g., "a noun is the name of a person, place, or thing") are imprecise approximations to the underlying but less obvious syntactic facts. The noun, in descriptive linguistics, is a class of words having similar "privileges of occurrence." Nouns are words that can follow articles and can occur in subject and object positions and, in this respect, are distinct from such other classes of words as the verb, adjective, and adverb. (1960, p. 2)

As an example, Brown and Fraser show how "count nouns" may be defined in the following description.

> Hearing car as a new word in the sentence: "See the car" a child could use this context as a basis for listing car with count nouns and so be prepared to hear and say such additional sentences as: "I own a car"; "The car is new"; "This car is mine." And a multitude of others. Of course the particular sentence uttered on a given occasion would depend on semantic and motivational factors, but the population of sentences from which the particular could be drawn would be established by the syntactic kinship linking car with house, barn, table, and fence. (1961, pp. 7–8)

This type of analysis seems to provide an excellent systematic description of certain language behavior that can serve as the basis for an investigation in terms of learning principles. For example, the term "privileges of occurrence" seems to refer to the fact that certain groups of words occur in certain circumstances, or rather, in a certain relationship to other words. That is, what a child reads and hears and what he is reinforced for saying will be of a certain form. Extrapolating from the previously presented learning theory, including the S–R mechanisms, it could be said in general that such experiences should produce a systematic set of language habits or verbal S–R mechanisms.

If that is the case it should be possible to discover the principles and the particular controlling variables underlying the formation of these classes Brown and Fraser describe. The following fairly complicated set of S–R mechanisms is offered to explain the finding that having heard SEE THE CAR, a child can then emit the response CAR in other syntactically appropriate sentences, such as I OWN A CAR, THE CAR IS NEW, and THIS CAR IS MINE.

First, let us say that the responses THE, A, and THIS, among others, have each come to have extensive associations with many words. For example, the child has heard, read, and been reinforced for saying THE HORSE, THE HOUSE, THE DOG, THE TABLE, and so on. The stimuli provided by the vocal response THE should come as a consequence (according to the principles of conditioning) to tend to elicit many word responses.

In turn, however, one could expect THE to be elicited by the stimuli produced by many other word responses. SEE, OWN, WHAT, for example, should all come to elicit THE through being in contiguity with THE in sentences such as SEE THE BLANK, I OWN THE BLANK, DO YOU KNOW WHAT THE BLANK IS?, and so on.

Thus, let us say, the word THE is elicited by certain types of words and tends to elicit certain types of many other words. This is depicted in Figure 10.1. The term "privileges of occurrence" may be thought to refer to the learning conditions that produce such hierarchies of responses. It is suggested that as a consequence of these associations, formed through conditioning during one's extensive language experience, an individual will say such things as SEE THE HORSE but not HORSE THE SEE.

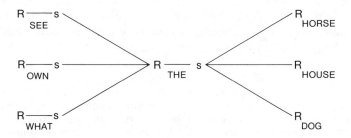

FIGURE 10.1.   In the individual's experience the responses SEE, OWN, and WHAT, among others, are paired with the response THE and come to elicit this response. In the same manner the response THE comes to elicit HORSE, HOUSE, DOG, and so on. From *Complex Human Behavior* by Arthur W. Staats with contributions by Carolyn K. Staats. Copyright © 1963 by Holt, Rinehart and Winston, Inc. Reprinted by permission of Holt, Rinehart and Winston, Inc.

The generality of word usage Brown and Fraser describe would be expected to occur according to this interpretation, on the basis of such S–R mechanisms. That is, a new word, through being paired with THE, would become associated with THE. In other words, THE would tend to elicit the new word. The sentence SEE THE CAR, for example, would establish the sequence THE CAR. As a consequence, the response CAR would tend to occur in all situations that elicited THE—for example, I OWN THE CAR, I LIKE THE CAR, and so on. The key to the syntactically appropriate emission of CAR would depend upon the association $R_{\overline{THE}}s\text{————}R_{CAR}$. Any time THE would be elicited, one of the words it would tend to elicit would now be CAR.

However, let us say that in addition to these associations, the child also forms in his early learning associations between THE, A, and THIS, among others.[2] As a consequence, any one of these word responses would have a tendency to elicit either of the other two. With these associations added, Figure 10.1 would be much more complicated.

Moreover, there would be even greater generality of usage due to this training, produced by the associations between THE, THIS, and A. It would be expected that when CAR is associated to THE it would also become associated with THIS and A, among other words. Thus, any time THIS or A is elicited in the individual, CAR would also tend to occur.

These, of course, would constitute the syntactic associations. In the emission of any particular sequence of verbal responses (such as a sentence) the specific words emitted would be under the control of the particular stimulus objects and stimulus events that were acting at the moment.

With these concepts in hand, the important experimental results of Brown and Berko can be described in terms of behavior principles. They discuss the research in the following manner.

> The general plan of this test is to introduce to S a new word (actually a pronounceable nonsense syllable) by using it in two sentences. The two sentences are adequate to place the word in one of six parts-of-speech: the count noun, mass noun, transitive verb, intransitive verb, adjective, or adverb. After this introduction to the word, S was asked to use it in sentences of his own creation, and these were scored as correct if the new word was used as it ought to be in view of the part-of-speech implied by the introductory sentences.
>
> As "new words" 12 nonsense syllables were used. . . . There were 12 problems in all with two syllables assigned to each of the six parts-of-speech. . . .
>
> For each problem, S was shown a colorful picture of either a girl, a boy, a man, a woman, a cat, or a dog, and E read text of the following kind: "Do you know what a *wug* is? This is a picture of a little girl thinking about a

---

[2] A more complete analysis of this would involve the implicit elicitation of all three of these responses by stimuli like SEE, OWN, and WHAT. As a consequence of this implicit elicitation, the words THE, A, and THIS are contiguous and become associated.

wug. Can you make up what that might mean?" This was the presentation identifying *wug* as a count noun. Where *wug* was to be identified as an intransitive verb, *E* would say: "Do you know what it means to *wug?* This is a picture of a little boy who wants to *wug.*" With *wug* as a mass noun there would be such sentences as: "This is a cat thinking about some *wug.*" With *wug* as a transitive verb such a sentence as this was used: "This is a woman who wants to *wug* something." Where *wug* was to be identified as an adverb *E* spoke of a dog thinking of doing something *wuggily.* (1960, p. 6)

Actually, all these cases may be considered in terms of S–R mechanisms that are very similar to the one already described. The analysis of the first case, concerning the count noun, seems to be precisely the same. WUG is conditioned to A, let us say, and the type of generalization already described should take place. The same is true of the mass noun. When WUG is conditioned to SOME, any set of verbal stimuli that will elicit SOME should now tend also to elicit WUG. It would be expected that the child, after being told THIS IS A CAT THINKING ABOUT SOME WUG, would say such things as I WOULD LIKE SOME WUG, WHEN DO I GET SOME WUG, EVERYONE ENJOYS SOME WUG, and so on. The same is true of the intransitive verb. The sentences should produce in the child the response sequence $R_{\overline{TO}}$—s———R_{WUG}. Thus, whenever a set of verbal stimuli that will elicit TO is presented, it will tend also to elicit WUG. After having heard such sentences, the child would be likely to say, I LIKE TO WUG, MY SISTER TRIES TO WUG, WHERE DO YOU GO TO WUG? As the reader will be able to see by this time, a similar analysis can be made for the transitive verb, the adverb, and the adjective.

This interpretation may also be used to consider the additional important result of Brown and Berko's experiment that children showed an ability, increasing with age, to construct grammatically correct sentences using new words. This finding would be expected on the basis of the behavioral analysis. Since the S–R mechanisms involved seem quite complex, it would be expected that many conditioning trials would be required to establish all the associations involved. Ordinarily, the older the child, the more such trials he would have an opportunity to experience.

Development of Syntactical Habits

The relationship of age to syntactical usage—that is, to the learning of syntactical habits—should be considered in somewhat greater detail. Such consideration should help specify the results of the process of "privileges of occurrence."

For example, on the basis of the foregoing analysis, certain systematic changes would be expected in word-association norms as a function of age. Thus, responses given to a stimulus word should change as new verbal associations were formed. It has long been known that children's associations differ in a systematic manner from those of adults (Woodrow and Lowell, 1916). And Ervin (1957) has shown that there are changes in word responses as a function of children's ages. Moreover, she found that the grammatical nature of the responses differed systematically— that is, older children tended to give as a word response the same part of speech as the stimulus word.

Brown and Fraser (1961) have also systematically observed and described the natural speech habits of children between the ages of 24 and 36 months of age. They found that the number of word responses included in each separate sentence (complete sequence of verbal responses) increased as the children grew older. In addition, they noticed that the speech of these young children was systematically abbreviated, and the extent of abbreviation was related to the number of word responses they produced in their average utterance. Children who produced a low average number of word responses per complete utterance tended to say I GOING TO TOWN rather than the complete I AM GOING TO TOWN.

These investigators further studied the abbreviation effect by having the children match, or echo, sentences produced by the experimenter. They found that with increasing age the match made by the child included more of the individual words presented by the experimenter. In addition, when words were excluded, they tended to be the less essential words: "words that occur in intermediate positions in the sentence, words that are not reference-making forms, words that belong to such small-sized grammatical categories as the articles, modal auxiliaries, and inflections; words that are relatively predictable from context and so carry little information, and words that receive the weaker stresses in ordinary English pronunciation." (pp. 37–38) This led the authors to describe the speech of the children as "telegraphic English" and to attribute the increased ability to match sentences to an increase in "memory span."

Although these authors interpret their findings in these other terms, an analysis of children's speech development in terms of behavior principles suggests the determinants of the "telegraphic English," as well as the development of the increased ability to repeat sentences ("memory span").

As an example, let us say that a young child has just been conditioned to say the single word BALL as in naming, requesting, or repeating. The child, of course, will not be able to repeat the sentence GIVE ME THE

RED BALL solely on the basis of this training. In time, however, the child should, by the same type of training, be able to make the response sequence RED BALL. Each time he does this the tendency for the first response to elicit the second would be strengthened. In time the child will also, through conditioning, come to make the response GIVE and thus to be able to emit the sequence GIVE RED BALL. In further training the child will be prompted to repeat THE RED BALL instead of the simpler phrase, and when he makes the complete response he is more heavily reinforced. Finally, articles and pronouns would be expected to be habitually included in such verbal response sequences, and the child comes to say GIVE ME THE RED BALL. These various word response sequences are depicted in Figure 10.2 part A.

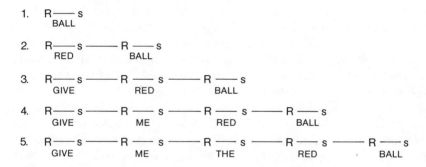

FIGURE 10.2. The step-by-step acquisition of a verbal response sequence. The simple response is established first, and later, with more conditioning trials more complicated sequences are established. Line 5 indicates a five-link verbal response sequence. From *Complex Human Behavior* by Arthur W. Staats with contributions by Carolyn K. Staats. Copyright © 1963 by Holt, Rinehart and Winston, Inc. Reprinted by permission of Holt, Rinehart and Winston, Inc.

This training seems to take place over a period of years, starting from the conditioning of simple responses up to the formation of the complex response sequence. At the same time, other responses also would be reinforced in combination with each other and would acquire tendencies to elicit each other in certain orders. That is, not only would GIVE come to elicit ME, but so would other responses—THROW, PUSH, and so on. In addition, not only would ME come to be elicited by those verbs, but so would HIM and HER, etc. It is suggested that at each point in the response sequence there would be a hierarchy of responses which would tend to be elicited, and these hierarchies would in many cases be extremely large. It can be seen that the possible combinations for even this simple sentence on the basis of the existing associations would be extremely numerous. These sequences of hierarchies of responses are depicted in Figure 6.4.

After such hierarchies of responses had been formed the child would find no difficulty in repeating a sentence that was composed of any of these alternatives; the associations would already be there. This would be true even though the new sequence of responses (the new sentence) had never occurred before in that particular combination. As long as GIVE tended to elicit HER and HER elicited THIS and THIS elicited SMALL and SMALL elicited SHIRT, the sentence GIVE HER THIS SMALL SHIRT could be readily emitted, controlled either by environmental or verbal stimuli, even though the child had never heard or repeated such a sentence before.

It is thus suggested that the source of the child's "memory span" for words consists of the skilled vocal responses and the various associations between (sequences of) these responses. In the same way an adult's "memory span" for MAFF VLEM OOTH UM GLOX NERFS would also be expected to be very poor. Even though the skilled vocal responses are in the adult's repertoire, there are no associations between the responses, and the adult would consequently not be able to repeat the material. Moreover, as will be described in the discussion of originality, previously established "grammatical" word associations will enable the individual to perform well in many situations, for example, in answering an achievement test in grammar.

Another example of syntactic training seems to reveal another S–R mechanism that functions to produce grammatical verbal response sequences. It has already been suggested that the child, in the course of his language training, will go through a large number of similar experiences involving word-response sequences which are in part the same and in part different—THE GIRL IS FAT, THE DOG IS RUNNING, THE CAR IS BIG.

As a consequence of this type of experience, the word response IS should, in part, come to be elicited by the stimuli produced by the response THE—but not *solely* by these stimuli. That is, in the presence of the stimuli produced by THE, plus the stimuli produced by another word response following THE, the word response IS would be reinforced. However, in the presence of THE and the absence of another word response, the response IS would not be reinforced. The controlling stimuli for IS, in this case, would thus come to be those produced by the response THE *plus* another word response, such as THE BALL, THE GIRL, or THE HOUSE. The combined stimuli would have strong tendencies to elicit IS, whereas THE alone would not. In making this analysis it is necessary to see that the effective stimulus may be a compound which takes many forms. Contemporary concepts of the events which constitute stimuli must be expanded theoretically and experimentally to reflect what apparently occurs in naturalistic human behaviors.

It would be expected on the basis of this interpretation that THE plus the stimuli produced by a novel (therefore, nonsense) word response would tend to elicit the response IS. For example, if subjects were given the stimulus THE WUH in a word association task it would be expected that the response IS would (among others) tend to occur. The stimulus properties produced by THE and another word response would tend to elicit IS on the basis of stimulus generalization. It is suggested that it is this type of word association which accounts for the fact that THE MAFF VLEMS OOTHLY UM THE GLOX NERFS is more easily learned than MAFF VLEM OOTH UM GLOX NERFS. That is, THE plus a word response has been paired with verbs such as SWIMS, CLIMBS, SUMS, SLUMS, BUMS, RAMS, JAMS, and as a result tends to elicit responses ending in the vocal response MS. If that is the case there would already be associations between THE MAFF VLEMS; on this basis, learning this sequence *should* require fewer trials than verbal response sequences which are completely unconnected. The same type of mechanism would operate in other parts of this sequence. These very complex acquired verbal mechanisms function in memory tasks, taking tests, solving problems, and so on.

Word Endings as a Function of S–R Associations

It is also suggested that grammatical word endings depend upon the formation of the appropriate response associations. However, in this case, vocal responses that form parts of words seem to be involved. Let us take plural endings as an example.

> The rule in English is: a word ending in a voiceless consonant forms its plural with the voiceless sibilant . . . as in *cats, cakes,* and *lips;* a word ending in either a vowel or a voiced consonant forms its plural with the voiced sibilant . . . as in *dogs, crows,* and *ribs;* a word ending in the singular with either /s/ or /z/ forms its plural with /z/ plus an interpolated neutral vowel as in *classes* and *poses.* We all follow these rules and know at once that a new word like *bazooka* will have, as its plural, bazooka/-z/, even though most speakers of English will never know the rule in explicit form. (Brown and Fraser, 1961, pp. 5–7)

The word "rule" as used here can only be thought of as a descriptive term; a person does not ordinarily say things *because* he is following a rule. Actually, in this case the S–R account is rather simple. It is suggested that the stimuli which come to control the voiceless sibilant /-s/

vocal response are, for example, the plural stimulus object and the naming response which ends in the voiceless consonant. After the child has had many, many trials where he is reinforced for the voiceless sibilant /-s/ following the voiceless consonant, this stimulus would elicit the appropriate response. After the appropriate associations have been formed between the ending of a word and the "plural" response, the appropriate ending would be expected to occur even when a novel word was introduced. Berko (1958) showed this to be the case by constructing a figure of an imaginary animal, for example, and showing it to a child with the instructions, THIS IS A WUG. NOW THERE ARE TWO _____? The child's task was to supply the word response, including its plural ending, and would usually do this correctly by responding WUG/-Z/. The child's ability to do this would be accounted for on the basis of word associations.

ORIGINAL, BUT LEARNED, BEHAVIOR

A frequent criticism that is made of learning conceptions of human behavior is that they cannot account for novel behavior, that is, behavior that emerges without prior training. Any conception of human behavior that cannot deal with original behaviors, it must be stated, is inadequate. For many of the most significant behaviors are ones that other individuals have not yet emitted, and thus the person emitting the original behavior could not have received specific training for the behavior. This admission may be made with confidence, however, for it is quite possible to treat original behaviors within the context of the present approach. The present very short section will briefly describe one way that original behaviors may arise and will give several examples of varying complexity. (An experiment on one subject—called a micro-experiment—to be presented in a later chapter, will verify this analysis in the context of concept formation. In the experiment the concept stimuli are letters presented in different combinations in a reading acquisition task.)

To begin, Miller (1965) has presented a challenge to a learning analysis of language, suggesting that this type of analysis cannot account for original sentence generation. He states, for example, "Since the variety of admissable word combinations is so great, no child could learn them all." (p. 18) Miller thus suggests, in essence, that the child could not acquire language according to known learning principles. This criticism of learning approaches has also been leveled by other psycholinguists, again as though criticizing one learning formulation is like criticizing all learning theories (Bever, et al., 1965).

This, however, is a critique of fragmented, simplistic, learning theories. There is nothing in principle that suggests the present approach is not capable of accounting for novel sentence generation, as well as other novel behavior—*based upon the past learning of the individual*. Actually with the concepts of response hierarchies, word associations, and complex environmental stimulus control, the way in which past learning produces novel sentence generation can easily be seen. The following simple example will suggest how a child could have learned specific S–R connections, and on this basis emit entirely novel combinations of words in generating a sentence.

Let us say that the child has been reinforced for saying MAN in the presence of different "man stimulus objects" and such a stimulus has come as a ^DS to control the vocal response MAN. Let us also say that the child has also had the same experience with respect to the vocal response RUNNING. That is in the presence of a running dog, a running boy, a running girl, and so on, the child has been reinforced for saying RUNNING. This response, however, has never been reinforced in the presence of a man running. Let us also say, however, that the child sees a man who is running. Under these circumstances the child would be likely to say MAN RUNNING or RUNNING MAN. The total response would be entirely novel, since the child would never before have emitted the sequence.

It may be suggested that a complex stimulus composed of components can elicit *original* behavior when the component stimuli each control a separately learned response. The originality consists of the emission of the behavior in a new configuration. A somewhat more complex example will illustrate the principle more fully and demonstrate the role of word associations in such original behaviors. Let us say that a child has had experience with the statement GIVE HIM HENRY'S PAPER. This experience, among other things, would be expected to form the word association $R_{\overline{GIVE}}S\text{----------}R_{\overline{HIM}}S$. This would occur whether the child was told the sentence by someone else or read it himself. Let us also say that the child has experience with IT WAS IN HIM THAT I PUT MY TRUST, forming the word association $R_{\overline{HIM}}S\text{--------}R_{\overline{THAT}}S$. From the sentence THAT BLUE BALL IS MINE the word association $R_{\overline{THAT}}S\text{--------}R_{\overline{BLUE}}S$ would be formed. And, finally, let us say that the sentence I WOULD LIKE TO HAVE A BLUE CAR results in the formation of the word association $R_{\overline{BLUE}}S\text{--------}R_{\overline{CAR}}S$. These associations to be very strong might require, of course, more than one learning trial.

Let us say that the child has also been trained to say each of the above words in the presence of the appropriate stimulus circumstances.

With these givens, also resulting from specifiable training conditions, it would be expected that in the presence of an appropriate stimulus situation—for example, two other small children, one of whom has just taken a toy blue car from the other—the child in the present example would look at the aggressing child and emit the original sentence $R\overline{\overline{GIVE}}S$ ------$R\overline{\overline{HIM}}S$------$R\overline{\overline{THAT}}S$------$R\overline{\overline{BLUE}}S$-------$R\overline{\overline{CAR}}S$. Never having said this before, the sentence would be entirely novel, but it would have been based upon the word associations, and vocal responses under environmental stimulus control, which the child had previously learned.

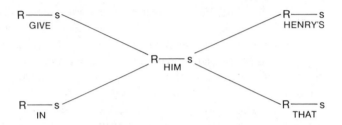

FIGURE 10.3.   The word association hierarchies formed by the language experience given in the example. From Staats' chapter in B. Kleinmuntz, Ed., *Problem Solving*, New York: Wiley, 1966 by permission of the publisher.

The function of the above child's word associations could have been evidenced in other original ways than in the above situation. Having the word association structure, for example, the child would be able to remember such a sentence more easily than if he had not had the subsidiary training. That is, he would have a greater memory span for associated verbal sequences. The same sequence of previously learned responses would also enable the child to answer a grammar test item correctly. That is, asked to underline the correct statement, the child would select GIVE HIM THAT BLUE CAR rather than GIVE HE THAT BLUE CAR. He could also select correctly among new items such as GIVE HIM A BALL versus GIVE HE A BALL. Thus, important aspects of language achievement would be thought to depend upon the richness of the individual's word association repertoire.

It should be indicated here that we actually have hierarchies of responses at each step of our learned sequences of verbal responses—formed by our past conditioning experiences. Just by virtue of the training the child in the preceding example had, the word response hierarchies depicted in Figure 10.3 would have been formed. Both convergent hierarchies, where various stimuli come to elicit one response, as well as divergent hierarchies, where one stimulus comes to elicit various responses, as shown in the figure, must be considered to be formed and to function in complex cognitive behaviors.

Thus, it must be concluded that upon the basis of the child's experience with language through reading, being spoken to, being prompted to repeat things, through being reinforced when he says certain things and not others, and so on, the child acquires word associations, that yield sequences of hierarchies of responses. Under suitable environmental conditions, or verbal conditions (as in tests), the child will emit the one appropriate sequence from the various possible combinations— simply on the basis of his past training. As the author has indicated in the previous section, this analysis may serve to indicate how the child learns grammatical word orders, as well as to indicate how original sequences of language behavior occur.

Novel Problem Solving Behavior

The author has also suggested (Staats, 1965; Staats and Staats, 1963) that the principles involved in the preceding analysis have implications for understanding even complex cases of original problem solving. Several examples were presented and the following material is taken from these accounts.[3] It deals with an "original proof" in geometry and attempts to show the types of experiences upon which such novel behavior might be based.

First, the following verbal response may be considered to be a complex naming sequence under the control of appropriate stimulus objects and events: QUANTITIES EQUAL TO THE SAME QUANTITY ARE EQUAL TO EACH OTHER. This response sequence might have been acquired, for example, in a situation where each of two bags of sugar were successively balanced with the same weight and then with one another, and the individual described the situation as IF THE TWO BAGS BALANCE WITH (EQUAL) THE SAME WEIGHT, THE BAGS EQUAL EACH OTHER. Further training would bring the verbal sequence under the control of many analogous stimulus situations involving numbers, angles, lengths, and so on.

Another verbal response, IF EQUAL SUMS ARE SUBTRACTED FROM EQUAL SUMS THE REMAINDERS ARE EQUAL, could also come under the control of appropriate stimulus situations through pro-

---

[3] See *Complex Human Behavior,* pp. 238–242 and Staats, A. W. An integrated-functional learning approach to complex human behavior. *Technical Report Number 28* under Office of Naval Research Contract Nonr-2794 (02) with Arizona State University, 1965.

cedures comparable to those described above. Finally, a third verbal response can also be considered a complex naming response to certain objects, in this case to certain lines and angles: THE SUM OF THE ANGLES ABOUT A POINT ON ONE SIDE OF A STRAIGHT LINE IS EQUAL TO 180°.[4] This verbal response, just as the other two described, might have been acquired through experience in many diverse situations.

On the basis of these complex verbal responses, each of which is itself under the control of complex stimulus situations, the development of an even more complex language structure might be considered, that is, Thales' demonstration that vertical angles of two intersecting straight lines are equal (Shute, *et al.*, 1960). This example is clearly one of "originality" in verbal behavior but may be considered in terms of a number of previously acquired complex verbal response sequences that are controlled by specific situations and are emitted together in a novel manner when the individual is confronted with a complex situation that simultaneously tends to elicit all of them.

Figure 10.4 illustrates the problem showing the intersecting lines and the angles produced.

> To demonstrate that when two straight lines intersect the vertical angles in pairs are equal, Thales was given two straight lines, AB and CD intersecting at 0, forming the vertical angles, $\angle 1$ and $\angle 2$, and the vertical angles, $\angle 3$ and $\angle 4$. Since AB was given a straight line, and since the sum of the angles about a point on one side of a straight line is equal to 180°, Thales knew that $\angle 1 + \angle 3 = 180°$. Similarly, since CD was given a straight line, he knew $\angle 3 + \angle 2 = 180°$. Applying the axiom, quantities equal to the same quantity are equal to each other, Thales obtained the equality: $\angle 1 + \angle 3 = \angle 3 + \angle 2$. Thales next applied the subtraction axiom by subtracting $\angle 3$ from both sides of the equation to get the equality: $\angle 1 = \angle 2$. In like manner, Thales proved that $\angle 3 = \angle 4$. Thus Thales proved that vertical angles in pairs are equal. (p. 25)

The following will attempt a brief account of the "derivation" of the final statement in terms of the behavioral principles that have been discussed. Figure 10.5 which depicts the possible S–R processes involved

---

[4] In these examples, the complex verbal response sequences are probably composed of simpler individual labeling responses. The response SUM is a word under the control of multiple stimuli which can be responded to singly or as a group, usually by making an arithmetic response. The response ANGLES is also under the control of multiple "angle stimuli." The same is true for POINT, STRAIGHT LINE, EQUAL, and 180°. In addition, other S–R processes would be thought to be involved such as those discussed previously in the discussion of grammatical and mathematical response sequences. For the purpose of simplifying the example, these may, however, be described as complex sequences of verbal responses.

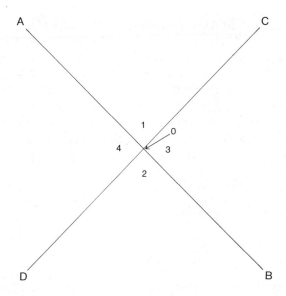

FIGURE 10.4. Illustration used in demonstrating that when two straight lines intersect, the vertical angles in pairs are equal. From *Complex Human Behavior* by Arthur W. Staats with contributions by Carolyn K. Staats. Copyright © 1963 by Holt, Rinehart and Winston, Inc. Reprinted by permission of Holt, Rinehart and Winston, Inc.

in this example, is simplified for purposes of illustration and some steps have been omitted to conserve space.

The first ^DS in the chain of reasoning might be part of the geometric form: Line AB is a straight line intersected at point O producing the angles $\angle 1$ and $\angle 3$, and producing another line OC. As $^DS_1$, this complex stimulus might control the verbal response sequence R_1, THE SUM OF THE ANGLES ABOUT A POINT ON ONE SIDE OF A STRAIGHT LINE IS EQUAL TO 180°. This response sequence could then be considered $^DS_2$, in the chain eliciting the writing response R_2: ANGLE ONE PLUS ANGLE THREE EQUALS 180°. Line CD with the line OB emanating from point O is also a stimulus ($^DS_4$), which elicits R_4, the same verbal response elicited by $^DS_1$, and thus the analogous writing responses with respect to angles $\angle 2$ and $\angle 3$, that their sum equals 180°.

The stimuli produced by the next two written responses ($^DS_3$ and $^DS_6$) combine because of the past history of training to elicit the verbal response sequence (R_6) QUANTITIES EQUAL TO THE SAME QUANTITY ARE EQUAL TO EACH OTHER; ANGLES ONE PLUS THREE EQUAL TWO PLUS THREE. This verbal response sequence produces $^DS_7$, which then elicits the next verbal response (R_7) EQUALS SUB-

TRACTED FROM EQUALS LEAVE EQUAL REMAINDERS; SUB-
TRACTING ANGLE THREE FROM BOTH SIDES LEAVES ANGLES
ONE AND TWO AS EQUALS. This response might then be the ^DS that
would elicit the final statement WHEN TWO STRAIGHT LINES
INTERSECT, THE VERTICAL ANGLES IN PAIRS ARE EQUAL.
It thus seems conceivable that such types of original reasoning could
be based upon S-R processes acquired individually through the individual's past experience and that without such previously acquired
response sequences, the novel response could not occur.

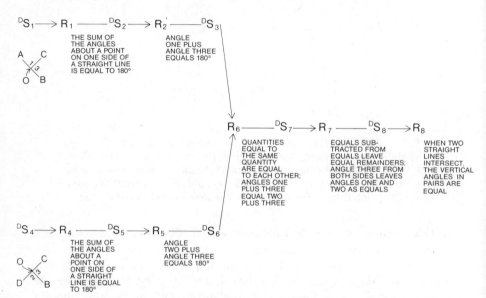

FIGURE 10.5.   An S–R sequence illustrating the elicitation of
previously acquired responses to specific situations that, when elicited
together in a situation that simultaneously tends to elicit all of them,
results in a novel or "original" behavior. From *Complex Human Behavior* by Arthur W. Staats with contributions by Carolyn K. Staats.
Copyright © 1963 by Holt, Rinehart and Winston, Inc. Reprinted
by permission of Holt, Rinehart and Winston, Inc.

Thus, in this example, the response sequences described could be called
"original" reasoning because the extended sequence of responses that
emerges has never occurred before. Each of the components as described,
however, had been conditioned to a more simple stimulus, but in the
presence of a more complicated stimulus the first response sequence
produces stimuli which, in conjunction with the complex stimulus, elicits

the next response and so on, until the final novel response occurs.[5] The final sequence might then become a complex verbal sequence to the geometric stimulus. It should be noted that this is an oversimplified schematization of originality. Rather than the straight line process shown, where each stimulus leads irrevocably to the next and correct response, the process actually involves response alternatives at each step of the process. Many responses are ordinarily emitted before attaining final solution of complex problems. Mathematicians, musicians, or anyone producing original responses, habitually spend much time emitting responses from the various alternatives until the correct combination is attained that constitutes problem solution. Many failures are included in this process.

The scope of the present section will not allow the presentation of the various S–R mechanisms that are important to understanding complex human behavior. Those presented herein may be considered only as examples that characterize the present approach. In addition to the preceding excerpt two further examples will be given here, however, because they are so appropriate to the consideration of higher cognitive behavior, or abstract thinking. Many important types of human behavior involve sets of related verbal responses *under the control of other sets of related verbal responses.* That is, the stimuli produced by a set involving a large number of verbal responses can come to be the stimulus "objects" that control a more "abstract" set of verbal responses that are far fewer in number. Sequences of the "abstract" set of verbal responses can then act as very general "rules" which can then mediate appropriate sequences in the much larger, lower-level, class of verbal responses. This S–R mechanism may sound very arcane; illustrations, however, may be used to suggest the possibilities more clearly.

A previous section of the present paper suggested that a child can be trained according to instrumental discrimination principles to make a verbal response to both a man and to the stimulus events produced by a running mammal. Such a child will respond to the relationship of the two events by saying MAN RUNNING. Well, verbal stimuli are also stimulus objects. The individual trained to verbally respond to verbal stimulus objects will also be able to respond to such verbal stimulus objects when they occur in new combinations. Thus, it would be expected that a child who had been trained to respond to any number

---

[5] For simplicity, the stimulus of the geometric figure is not shown in Figure 10.5 at each step of the chain. It should be remembered, however, that the geometric figure could remain a ^DS at each stage and might be quite important in eliciting the appropriate R in any particular case.

with a literal number response, let us say a, b, or c would be in position to emit certain novel literal number responses when presented with various addition problems (verbal stimulus objects). That is, the child after training on a number of problems of the sort $2 + 4 = 6$, $1 + 3 = 4$, $7 + 8 = 15$, and so on, might respond with the new sequence $a + b = c$. Literal numbers, as one example, may be considered to consist of a related set of verbal responses learned in response to another set of verbal responses. The *concept* of the literal number, it may be suggested, involves both of the types of concept mechanisms previously described in Figure 6.2 and Figure 6.3. That is, the learning of a literal number would depend upon the various number stimuli coming to elicit a literal number response, and the literal number response, in turn coming to have tendencies to elicit each of the number responses. This mechanism is depicted in Figure 10.6. In learning literal number responses the child

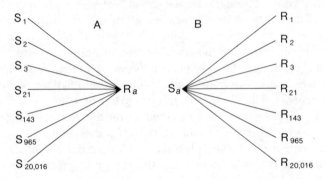

FIGURE 10.6.   Part A of the figure represents a hierarchy of specific number stimuli, each of which tends to elicit the literal number response a. In addition, a as a stimulus comes to elicit a class of arithmetic number responses. This is depicted in part B. From *Complex Human Behavior* by Arthur W. Staats with contributions by Carolyn K. Staats. Copyright © 1963 by Holt, Rinehart and Winston, Inc. Reprinted by permission of Holt, Rinehart and Winston, Inc.

is actually learning a language about (or under the control of) another language.

The products obtainable from creating a whole set of literal number response statements is very evident of course. In teaching a child, for example, the more simple literal number sequences can be presented and they will mediate the much larger number of actual number statements. Furthermore, the individual who has acquired the literal number response statements to the point of fluency could be expected to emit such statements (general rules) that have never before been seen with actual numbers. Thus, we have discoveries in mathematics, the more abstract verbal response repertoire, that were not observed in the empirical world but which have implications for the empirical world. For example, negative numbers were derived from the more "abstract" number sequences. A grammar, or the descriptive statements of linguists may also be considered to be "abstract" verbal responses, in the sense discussed, that have come to be made to other verbal responses. The author has more fully described examples of sets of verbal responses learned under the control of other verbal stimuli (see Staats and Staats, 1963). Because such abstract verbal behaviors are not under the control of environmental events, but rather other verbal responses (stimuli), original abstract verbal behavior more readily gives the impression that mental events are involved that are over and above what the individual could have learned (Staats, 1966).

The manner in which a set of verbal responses under the control of another set of verbal responses can function in producing original scientific behavior can also be illustrated. The author suggests the following with respect to certain aspects of creative scientific behavior.

The important point here, which might also be significant for understanding "originality" in the extension of scientific theories, is that verbal responses which may be developed through experience with environmental stimuli may produce new verbal responses also on the basis of past learning which may have no known environmental counterparts but which may lead individuals to look for environmental events not previously seen. An illustration of the possibility of discussing some of the functions of scientific theories in terms of behavior principles may be useful here.

In a science area a possible example might be the periodic table of elements in chemistry. As verbal responses to environmental events a table of the weights of different elements was formed, let us say. The table itself, however, may be considered to have stimulus characteristics that can be described by previously learned verbal responses. The new set of verbal responses, let us say, described the systematic nature of the table, with weights increasing in a certain fashion from element to element, even though there were gaps in the table. These verbal response sequences might then have elicited the final sequence that perhaps there were elements, yet unobserved, which would fill in the gaps. This verbal response sequence might then have controlled the behavior of making further observations, leading to the discovery of new elements, filling in the table, and so on.

This is another example of a type of complex S–R mechanism. The account suggests that the original table is formed by the elicitation of verbal responses under the control of environmental stimuli as they occur in the act of scientific observation. These verbal responses themselves then elicit further, more "abstract," verbal responses that are descriptive of the first verbal responses (the table), and these abstract verbal responses then elicit the motor behaviors of looking for further elements. Although the mechanisms are complex, and produce original verbal behaviors and new discoveries by leading to additional observations, it appears possible to consider even such unique types of human behavior in terms of the learned repertoires of which they are composed. Other examples of scientific and social reasoning have been analyzed in learning terms by the author (see Staats and Staats, 1963).

Thus, it may be suggested that it is possible to consider even complex cases of originality in terms of the past learning of the individual. In doing so, however, one must be prepared to utilize the various principles of conditioning and to look for the complex ways that stimuli and responses can be organized into complex S–R mechanisms, on the basis of the principles. The author (1965) has also suggested methods by which to investigate actual cases of cognitive originality and innovation within the context of S–R analyses.

LANGUAGE COMPLEXITY AND LEARNING THEORIES OF LANGUAGE

One of the central points to be made in the present approach is that language is complex. Language does not consist of a simple repertoire, involving only one type of stimulus, one type of response, or one type of learning principle. Even within the realm of one specific aspect of language that is the case. The present author in giving a summary example of the complexity of language listed 9 types of language mechanisms. (Staats and Staats, 1963, p. 183) This was not intended to be comprehensive, and in the present book the various aspects of language discussed will total much more.

It must be suggested that whenever we analyze an aspect of language behavior we must be prepared to make a complex analysis. The *various* learning principles and the *various* complex S–R mechanisms may be involved. This is frequently not understood; critics of learning approaches are prepared to see all learning theories as simple-minded, fragmented, and separatistic. For example, Green (1966) and Forehand (1966), in discussing the author's analysis of Thale's proof that the opposite angles produced by intersecting lines are equal, incorrectly thought the analysis suggested that the reasoning involved a simple sequence of responses. Thus, it is worthwhile to state that it is not possible in every naturalistic example cited to make a complete analysis of all the S–R events that must actually occur. While simplification is necessary for expository purposes, the *various* S–R mechanisms that have been described must be considered to more completely account for any particular type of complex human behavior.

The reasons that people are inclined to expect learning approaches to present inadequate theoretical structures for dealing with complex human behavior may be suggested. That is, one of the most prominent weaknesses of previous learning theories of language involves their incompleteness and oversimplification in various respects (see Staats, in press *a*, for a more complete discussion). The number of learning principles used has been too few, for example. Skinner (1957) restricted himself to instrumental conditioning principles and then did not make analyses utilizing complex S–R mechanisms which involve those principles. Osgood (1953) has relied only upon one principle, instrumental conditioning, and only a few S–R mechanisms and has been concerned almost entirely with only one aspect of language—the measurement of one type of meaning. Mowrer (1954) has been primarily concerned with higher-order classical conditioning and the transfer of meaning from word to word within a sentence, and with self-reinforcement in early speech learning. To say this, it should be noted, in no way detracts from the very large contributions made by these theorists to an understanding of language.

To continue, however, in previous learning theories of language the use of experimental methods in developing the theory has been either nonexistent or practically so. Even then, the research has usually been descriptive, rather than experimental in the sense of manipulating conditions and producing a result. Thus, for example, factor analytic studies of meaning only describe language. They do not discover the principles by which language behavior is produced and by which it functions.

Investigators concerned with serial and paired-associate learning have been prolific in research. However, they have not dealt with actual samples of language, nor have the findings been related to actual language learning and function.

It is also true, in general, that the various investigators have not related the findings and concepts in one area of study to those in another area. In many cases the various learning orientations have been critical of each other's philosophy of science, research methodology, concepts, and findings. This deficit by itself has given learning theories their fragmented, oversimplified appearance. Certainly, it has been easy to see that one learning principle and few S–R mechanisms are not sufficient to deal with complex human activities.

It is thus suggested that an elaboration of the various learning principles along with their interactions, in concert with the various derivable S–R mechanisms, constitute a theoretical structure that is capable of reflecting all the complexity seen in human behavior in everyday life. Although there are infinite variations in complex human behavior, the S–R mechanisms are capable of arrangement into infinitely varied arrangements.

One more point may be made in this discussion. Previous learning theories of language have usually been incomplete in one other glaring way. While the basic approach itself, that of learning, tends to constrain our consideration of language to its acquisition or learning, this is shortsighted. Learning principles are as heavily involved in the ways in which language *functions* in human adjustment as they are in the acquisition phase. Communication, grammatical utterances, new verbal learning in educational and other situations, problem solving and reasoning, intelligence, and so on, depend upon the language repertoires the individual has already acquired. Thus, language must also be considered in detail in its role in individual adjustment—that is, as an independent variable—as well as considered as a type of behavior to be dealt with as a dependent variable. Subsequent parts of the book will emphasize and exemplify this suggestion. Before moving on, however, one additional pluralistic analysis of an important aspect of language will be made in the next section.

A PLURALISTIC CONCEPTION OF
WORD MEANING

A good example of the separatistic tendencies of learning theory can be seen in one of the issues that has concerned word meaning. The present author (Staats, 1959, 1961; Staats, *et al.*, 1957, 1960, 1963) as well as other learning theorists (Mowrer, 1954; Osgood, 1953) have described word meaning as an implicit response. Osgood has suggested that the meaning response comes under the control of the word stimulus through instrumental conditioning; the other two theorists have suggested the principle involved is that of classical conditioning.

An opposing view has been that the meaning of a word resides in the word associations that the word elicits. For example, Noble (1952) suggested that the "meaningfulness" of a word is given by the number of word associates the word will elicit. He called this measure m.

Bousfield, *et al.* (1958) elaborated this view to suggest that the *meaning* of a word is given by the type of word associates it elicits.

Osgood, *et al.* (1957) raised the issue between the two views. In their account, the number of word associates of a word was accepted as a measure of the association value of a stimulus word, but the interpretation that the associations could be thought of as word meaning was strongly rejected. The issue was further heated up by the findings and suggestions of Jenkins and Russell (1956). They showed that ratings of word meaning which are used to index the implicit conditioned response concept of meaning were highly correlated with *m*, the measure of the associates of words. They suggested that the two different concepts of word meaning actually referred to the same process.

The present author (Staats, 1959; Staats and Staats, 1959*b*) felt that the issue could be resolved by a closer analysis of the learning principles and S–R mechanisms involved. The analysis suggested that there were two processes involved, notwithstanding the finding of Jenkins and Russell. The high correlation between the two types of meaning occurred because there is language experience that simultaneously strengthens each. Let us take the sentence *The music is lovely.* When stated by someone enjoying a concert, it would be expected that the following two types of learning (at least) would be produced. The emotional response previously classically conditioned to the word *lovely* would be conditioned to the word *music*, in the manner that has been described. In addition, however, on the basis of instrumental conditioning it would also be expected that the word (response) "music" would come to control the word response "lovely." Thus, it would be expected that as a consequence of this experience the person would be more likely to rate the meaning of the word toward the pleasant end of a *pleasant–unpleasant* rating scale. Furthermore, if asked to list the words that *music* brought to mind in a word association task the person would tend more strongly to say "lovely."

If the words with which a word is paired tend to have the same classically conditioned meaning responses, then the word would through pairings with these words acquire that type of meaning. The more of such words, the more intense would be the meaning the word acquired. In addition, of course, the more of such words, the higher would be the *m* measure—that is, the number of word associates elicited by the word. This would account for the correlation between the word association measure and intensity of rated meaning. Thus, the hypothesis was that a word obtains its rated meaning in part from the words with which it is paired and that these words also become the associates of the word. The conclusion that the emotional meaning of a word is generally of the same type as the meaning of the associates of the word was tested with positive results (Staats and Staats, 1959; see also Pollio, 1964; Di Vesta and Bernheim, 1967).

The analysis included other suggestions, however. One was that the rating of the meaning of a word depends upon classically conditioned responses which are separate from or independent of the number of associates the word has. This hypothesis was tested in another study (Staats, 1959). In this study it was shown that word associations to a word could be increased without altering the meaning of the word. That is, when a stimulus word is paired with two words that have no meaning and another stimulus word is paired with four words that have no meaning, the stimulus word in either case acquires no emotional meaning. Thus, the number of word associates can be manipulated while emotional meaning remains constant.

In another case in the same study it was possible to increase the rated meaning of a word without increasing the number of its word associates. That is, a word paired with two words that have positive emotional meaning came also to elicit positive emotional meaning. A word paired with two words that elicit no emotional meaning will remain neutral and will not elicit an emotional response. In each case, however, the m value will be the same—each word will have gained two word associates.

On the other hand, it was also shown that a word paired with four words that elicit a positive, emotional response came to elicit the emotional response more strongly than did a word that was paired with only two words that elicit the emotional response. This finding showed that rated meaning and m could be made to increase in a parallel fashion. That is, when the associates of a word had the same meaning, the greater the number of associates the stronger was the rated meaning.

This topic has been discussed for several reasons. First, it indicates an important point. The same language stimulus of a sentence (a communication stimulus) can produce more than one kind of learning. The same sentence may produce emotional conditioning, for example, while it also establishes or strengthens word associations.

In showing this, however, the analysis helps characterize the present approach. An integration of learning principles allows a fuller conception of language (and other aspects of human behavior). Furthermore, detailed analysis of complex behavior into the S–R mechanisms of which it is composed allows a more profound theory. In this case an integrated learning analysis solved what appeared to be a controversy in learning theories and empirical findings. It also resulted in a better understanding of the learning functions that a sentence may have.

It should be stressed that the present conception of word meaning is pluralistic. This pluralistic approach appears to be necessary to provide an adequate account of language. That is, the common sense notion of word meaning, which implies a unitary process, actually covers a *number* of different S–R mechanisms, as well as the principles of both classical and instrumental conditioning. The preceding discussions and experiments have demonstrated this by example and the mechanisms described may all be considered to be types of word meaning. Some of the types of word meaning may be briefly mentioned to indicate the conception more clearly.

Many words are meaningful because they come to control motor responses through the principle of instrumental discrimination learning. That is, the words are discriminative stimuli for motor responses. Many verbs would have this type of "motor" word meaning.

Many words, also on the basis of instrumental discrimination learning come to control other word responses—and may be considered to have meaning on the basis of their word associations. As has been described, important aspects of grammatical utterances and grammatical speech production depend upon word associations. Some words appear to have a primary function, or meaning, because of their word associations and thus the way they influence the order in which language units are emitted. For example, as has been briefly mentioned, articles such as the word *the* come to be elicited by a large number of words and also come to elicit a large number of words. These associations help dictate the order in which the various words will be emitted. Thus, in the group of words *The daughter of Abraham went to the well,* the association structures of *The* and *of,* for example, dictate that the order of emission will not be *The of Abraham daughter* or *The of daughter Abraham* or some other order. Certain words can follow *The,* not others. That is, there are certain associations in this case which are dominant and which direct the order of speech. Words such as articles are meaningful words because of the associations they have that affect the grammatical order of speech.

Other words have meaning because they are conditioned stimuli (^cS) and they elicit emotional responses. Many nouns (for example, *mother*) fall into this category. Many verbs, adjectives, and adverbs also have this type of meaning, for example, *loved, lovely,* and *loving.*

These words may be considered to be meaningful because they elicit an emotional response—which they can transfer to other stimuli with which they are associated. They are also meaningful because they will function as reinforcing stimuli. That is, it may be said that a word has meaning for a person if the word when applied in a response contingent manner will affect the strength of that response. As already stated, also, the reinforcement value of a stimulus (word) affects its discriminative stimulus value.

Some words have meaning because they elicit sensory meaning responses. The principle involved again is classical conditioning. The words are usually nouns, verbs, and adjectives.

The reader will notice that the same S–R mechanisms are being discussed under the topic of this pluralistic conception of word meaning as were discussed under the heading of communication. It is useful to indicate that this is what occurs when the traditional classificatory system is used. Traditional classification breaks up human behavior in a very arbitrary way. Because of this many behaviors are considered in more than one category. Thus, we would find samples of behavior that some investigators would treat under the topic of concept formation, other investigators under the name of communication, or problem solving, meaning, perception, reasoning, creativity, attitude formation, and so on. This confusion may be eliminated when we attend to the behaviors themselves and to the S–R mechanisms of which they are composed and disregard the category names. *It should be understood that the various S–R mechanisms that have been described are meant to apply to various areas of human behavior regardless of the traditional classificatory system.* Thus, as one example, the topic of emotional word meaning is crucially relevant to the study of attitude formation and function, and both are of concern to the general area of human motivation. It is unfortunate that traditional categories break up into separate areas human behaviors that are actually similar and involve the same principles of learning. One of the primary purposes of the present theoretical orientation is to unify the various areas of study of human behavior with a common theoretical structure.

LANGUAGE AS A THEORY FOR THE INDIVIDUAL AND THE GROUP

For many years the author has been interested in the similarity in function that both a language and a scientific theory have for their "users." This section will present a paper written on this topic in 1956. It was not submitted for publication, but it has formed the basis for some of the author's later analyses of the characteristics of science as well as the role of language in cognition, in areas such as perception, problem solving, reasoning, thinking, and so on. Moreover, the analysis enables a learning consideration of cultural evolution, and cultural relativity and determinism in general as well as the specific area of linguistic events. (References to the other parts of the book and to recent sources have been added to the original article.)

The Conception of Language as Theory

S. S. Stevens has discussed the fact that it is neither an accident nor indeed a miracle that our number system and certain environmental events are isomorphic. That is, when two pebbles are added to two other pebbles there are four pebbles, and the same result occurs when this is done in symbolic form. He points out that arithmetic was constructed so that it would be isomorphic with certain actual events. "The fact is, [man] built a formal model to stand for an aspect of his empirical world, just as an architect draws a plan for a house." (1951, p. 4) Actually, it will be suggested that behaviors such as number sequences were not planned but rather "evolved," according to the principles of learning. To continue, however, Stevens described mathematics as a formal system of signs with rules for relating them—whose significance lies in the fact that parts of the system are isomorphic with certain events in the empirical world. That is, the signs and their relations parallel real events and their relationships. It was also noted that much of mathematics is not isomorphic with any aspect of reality. However, when there is an isomorphism, manipulations of the formal system will agree with the empirical system. When the former occurs first in time it may be called prediction or "anticipation" of the future. When there is faulty isomorphism, faulty predictions will result.

Empirical laws in science may be considered in the same terms. The principle of reinforcement, stated simply as follows, may be used as an example. *When a response is followed by a reinforcing stimulus the response will occur more frequently in the future.* The principle was developed to be isomorphic with the events involved both in terms of labeling the events and in following their rules of relationship. Like any formal theoretical system the individual terms *response, reinforcer,* and *future response,* may be used to label various types of events—the bar-press of a rat with food as the reinforcer, the temper tantrum of a child with attention as the reinforcer, and so on. To the extent that the verbal sequence, the scientific principle, is isomorphic with the relevant events of the empirical world, the verbal sequence will allow the scientist, the practitioner, or the layman to anticipate the consequent event when he has observed the antecedent event. The verbal sequence may also mediate behavior which is appropriate to the events involved.

Languages may also be considered to be formal theoretical systems developed in part because of their isomorphism with empirical events, and significant because of this isomorphism. The development of the isomorphism may be considered in terms of the principles of learning operating over the individual's history and cumulatively over the history of man. To the extent of the ismorphism, language may also generate predictions through manipulations of its symbols (the overt or covert speech of the language user), as would be expected of a formal (theoretical) system. Making predictions about important (reinforcing or punishing) events of the world can lead to gaining positive consequences and avoiding negative ones, for example.

It is thus suggested, as has already been described, that one's sequences of verbal behaviors control or mediate one's behaviors. Complex sequences of language behavior may mediate complex adjustments of various kinds. On this basis the similar functions of theory for the scientist and of language for the language user can be illustrated. The use of the principle of reinforcement was actually one example that could occur in some people's common language today. Additional examples will be given, however, to better illustrate the conception in the linguistic realm.

Linguistic Relativity and Determinism

A person who is given change in a store will count it and, depending upon the counting sequence of responses, will put the change in his pocket, or tell the clerk that there has been an error. The importance of the counting sequence of responses is that it parallels the empirical events of the coins. Furthermore, the culmination of the sequence produces a cue which controls further behavior. This further behavior is appropriate to the extent that the language behavior sequence parallels the empirical events. The relevance of such sequences of verbal behavior for what is called thinking and reasoning should be clear. See the writer's discussions (Staats and Staats, pp. 245–258).

When language is considered in these terms, it is not difficult to find S–R principles also in agreement with Whorfian principles of linguistic relativity and determinism, that is, that language modes differ and shape the thought of the user. When two individuals have quite different response sequences of language which control sequences of behavior, their behavior will be quite different. Using the situation of the individual receiving change in a store, let us say that each of two individuals expects change of thirty-nine cents. Both are given a quarter, a dime, and 4 pennies. One says "Twenty-five plus ten plus four is thirty-four," and the other says "Twenty-five plus ten plus four is thirty-nine." The latter person will put his change away; the former will ask the clerk for more money. One individual's behavior agrees with the world of real events, the other does not. The example is simple, but variations in this aspect of language may have large consequences.

It may be added that the actual responses do not have to be the same. Identical behaviors could be mediated by different specific verbal responses in different languages. That is, different individuals could have the same training history with different verbal responses and the different verbal responses could nevertheless be isomorphic with reality and thus mediate the same behavior. For example, the person who says, "Veinte y cinco y diez y cuatro igual treinta y nueve," will put away his change as will the person who says "Twenty-five plus ten plus four equals thirty-nine." Whether different verbal sequences are actually functionally different will depend upon the experiential history of the individuals involved. On the other hand, the same verbal sequence of responses may mediate entirely different behaviors. For example, one child, alone in the home, standing before a delicious chocolate cake will say, "Mother told me not to touch the cake," and then proceed to take some of the frosting. Another child subjected to different training with respect to the same language responses will have withdrawing responses mediated by his chain of verbal responses. Thus, different language responses may mediate the same concluding behavior. Or, the same language responses may mediate different behaviors.

The Whorfian idea is that different languages lead to differences in thought. Languages contain concepts which others do not and this produces a different "view" of the world. Put into more objective terminology, it might be said that languages will produce different behaviors in their users if one language theory contains terms which, because of the experiential history of the users, will mediate certain behaviors and the other languages do not contain those terms. The fact that the Eskimo has 11 types of verbal response with respect to snow should in certain situations result in mediation of behaviors, qualitatively or quantitatively, which are different than the English speaking person who only has one generic term. Various studies (Birge, 1941; Brown and Lenneberg, 1954) demonstrate that the labeling responses to stimuli that the individual has learned will directly affect his response to (perception of) these stimuli. When a term for a worldly event is absent from the language user's repertoire, it may take several terms to do the same job. Ordinarily, this means that a longer period will be required to emit the response; or the language may contain no such term and behavior dependent upon the emission of the response may not occur.

The following statement of Whorf's which can be readily stated in learning terms, could be used here with good descriptive purpose. "We are thus introduced to a new principle of relativity, which holds that all observers are not led by the same physical evidence to the same picture of the universe, unless their linguistic backgrounds are similar, or can in some way be calibrated." (Whorf, 1956, p. 214). An example might be cited which translates this observation into the present conception in a more naturalistic setting. The Jivaro Indians of South America are said to have no concept of death from infection or disease. The Jivaro man, on learning of the death of a relative is likely to say, "This is the result of evil spirits set into the body of the relative by a Shaman at the instigation of so and so." He has no term for virus infection or disease. His behavior, as mediated by this language sequence, will be different than the Christian who says, "It was the will of God who moves in mysterious ways." And both behaviors will be different than that which is mediated by the language sequence of a third man who says, "It was the result of a flu infection complicated by pneumonia because he got out of bed too soon." This example is analogous to Whorf's statement that the same physical occurrence may give rise to a different picture of the world. Rather, we might say that different learned language sequences mediate different behaviors toward the same physical occurrence.

However, to say that language sequences (including the above) determine thought is redundant. These language sequences *are* types of thought and could be called chains of thought responses. It is suggested that a large portion of what we call thought is composed of such chains (as well as of other S–R mechanisms described in the present book). The author (Staats and Staats, 1963, pp. 199–219) has described various experimental studies and examples which may be used to illustrate the dependence of thinking or reasoning on such chains of responses when set into action by the individual's language responses to a problem situation.

After noting that different languages produce different thought patterns in their users, Whorf also expressed the feeling that though languages differ, this does not indicate that one is better than another. He used examples which state that reality may be broken up differently by different languages, but that the languages adapt equally well. This linguistic relativity suggests that variation from our own thought modes does not mean inferiority. While the author would agree that one should not make prejudicial evaluations of other peoples' culture, the analyses presented so far in this book contain an implication that languages of individuals and of groups *vary in terms of their functional value*. Real differences in languages should mediate behaviors of varying appropriateness for the situation, depending upon how isomorphic the language sequence is with the worldly events involved.

Certainly, a language without terms for disease will not be isomorphic with empirical events involving this process, and will be more likely to mediate behaviors inappropriate to the process. It would be equally sure that languages containing terms which have no counterparts in empirical events (such as evil spirits, nonexistent psychological processes, mystical forces, deities, and so on) would contain language sequences which do not parallel empirical sequences of events. Differences in these and other aspects could occur between languages which seemingly are not greatly different. Individuals *within* a language community will also idiosyncratically have acquired different language sequences because of their experience and these differences will be involved in different thought sequences which mediate different behaviors. It may be suggested that many cases of psychopathology involve idiosyncratic language which mediates inappropriate behavior. The author has given examples of such behavioral problems (see Staats and Staats, 1963, pp. 386–394).

Differences will also occur within one language as it develops over a period of time. Terms which occur frequently in a language at one time and which control certain behaviors will occur less frequently at a later time and in their place will be other sequences which control other behaviors. Thus, languages may *improve* in the extent of their isomorphism with reality, and as a result mediate more appropriate behavior. For example, at one time in our language community when a person behaved in an unusual fashion people said, "He behaves that way because he is possessed by the devil." The response term "devil" is an aspect of the formal system having no isomorphism with empirical events, and consequently, could control behavior which was not appropriate to the actual events. This particular usage, presumably because it led to nonfunctional behavior was replaced in later developments of our language by, "He behaves that way because he is mentally ill." This latter statement has perhaps greater isomorphism with empirical events even though the term mental illness has no distinct empirical correlate. However, because of our training it mediates behavior which is more appropriate to the treatment of psychopathology than its former linguistic counterpart. When the language system has developed to the point where the same unusual behavior evokes the language sequence, "He behaves that way because his parents rewarded only more and more extreme cases of crying as he grew older, and now he has tantrums," then the language sequence may be isomorphic with the actual events, and the principles by which the events are related, and so mediate behavior which can be more appropriate to these events.

This progression is, of course, analogous to the growth of any scientific theory. However, the three examples could have taken place in the common everyday language usage. It is suggested that we may look forward to a time when many "unrealistic" terms or concepts which abide in our language will disappear and be replaced by terms which refer to actual empirical events—and consequently bring our common language into closer isomorphism with reality. To continue the example, yesterday most types of human behavior were described in terms which developed from religious terminology and which paralleled no empirical events. Today the common language system contains terms which derive, let us say from psychoanalytic terminology, with some improvement in terms of mediating adequate behavior. Tomorrow, the common language will reflect empirical variables discovered by systematic study which will allow the language sequences to parallel more exactly the empirical events of behavior. Thus, it is suggested that languages *evolve* as formal theoretical systems isomorphic with larger and larger aspects of reality. The average person today speaks a language which better mediates his social (and general) behavior than did the language of his counterpart in the Middle Ages or in the days of the Roman Empire.

The mechanisms by which languages evolve cannot be treated at length herein (although the various learning principles would seem to be involved). One mechanism which makes for the similarity between scientific theory and language will be described, however. That is, theory develops as terms and principles in the theory are accepted or rejected on the basis of their isomorphism with observable events; as terms and principles make for prediction and control of the empirical events involved. The scientist who generates sequences of theory responses which better yield prediction and control emerges as the foremost scientist in comparison to one whose theory sequences do not. It is suggested that this is also one way a language develops; that is, on the basis of the experience of the various individuals and groups using a language. The individual or group whose language sequences mediate appropriate behavior gains ascendance over the individual or group whose verbal sequences mediate inappropriate behavior. And, over a long period of time, those with the better language sequences will influence more people—their behavior will succeed and impress others in a manner analogous to survival of the fittest, based upon the principle of reinforcement. When the language sequences involving the concept are not predictive and so do not mediate useful behavior, the sequences are not reinforced in the individual nor is the place of the individual who uses the terms improved in his society. This process which would be very complex, of course, may be described as the social evolution of language and the writer has suggested that the principles apply generally to cultural evolution. (See Staats, 1964a, and Staats and Staats, 1963, for more complete statements.)

A comparative study of languages for their efficacy as theories should reveal that different languages, as well as individual differences in language, mediate behavior which is more or less appropriate in the sense discussed. It is suggested that languages which are actually different in their terms and in the rules for relating these terms will differ in their functional value. This does not mean that a language which is superior in one instance will be so in all instances. The fact that the Eskimo has 11 language responses for snow may account for appropriate behavior on his part better than, or quicker than, that of an English speaking person. On the other hand, the speaker of English may have many terms in his language which mediate many behaviors in a better manner than those of the speaker of Eskimo. Over all, nevertheless, one language may be far advanced over another.

In summary, it is suggested that a language is adequate to the extent that it contains terms which stand for the important events of the empirical world (including biological, physical, and social events) with rules (syntax) for relating the terms which also are like the natural principles relating the empirical events. Presumably, a language is also adequate to the extent that it does not contain terms, other than purely formal (syntactic) ones which have no counterparts in the empirical world.

It should be added that the present discussion of language as a "theory" that mediates the individual's perception, reasoning of various kinds, problem solving, and so on, has dealt only with the manner in which empirical events are labeled and with the rules by which the terms of the language are related. The various other S–R mechanisms in language outlined in the present book would also play similar roles in the efficacy of the individual's or the group's language. That is, as another example, if a word has reinforcing value for an individual or group when it is not "realistic" to do so, the word will lead to inappropriate behaviors. A word may elicit an inappropriate image also, inappropriate word associations, inappropriate motor responses and so on—each of these spoiling the "theoretical" (functional) value of the language for the "user."

Finally, the topic of language universals (commonalities that occur in different languages) may be mentioned. Language universals have become a central consideration for many contemporary linguists and psycholinguists. While the topic cannot be dealt with fully herein, it is suggested that the learning analysis of language, and the present conception of language and theory, provides an interpretation of language universals. That is, languages *should* have commonalities in their terms and in their rules for relating the terms, because the different languages have evolved to be isomorphic with the *same* world of events. These events follow the same physical, chemical, biological, and psychological (learning) laws everywhere.

For many reasons there should also be language idiosyncracies, as well as universals. One language may have terms that refer to dimensions of the empirical world that another does not, for example, because of differences in the physical or social environment. The linguistic categories of speech and their rules of relations may also differ in some ways. This would be expected. The same was true in times past in the number area of language. That is, although number systems did arise with different characteristics and symbols (examples may be seen in Arabic and Roman numerals and in the various calendars), there was also commonality because the events with which they dealt were isomorphic. By the same token all languages should have commonalities that refer to the dimensions of the world common to all. It is suggested that even these general aspects of language and culture can be treated productively within the present learning theory.

Functional learning theory and cognitive behavior modification

11

*The functional learning
philosophy
and representative
behavior sampling*

The study of learning, the effects that environmental events have on the organism's behavior, originally stemmed from an interest in human behavior. It was early recognized that man's behavior was influenced by the experiences that he had. Thus, we find that prior to the development of experimental psychology there was a good deal of philosophical interest in the role that experience played in complex human behavior. The British empiricists, for example, on the basis of naturalistic observations, concluded that cognitive behaviors were formed through the individual's experience. Their theories included statements concerning the laws of associations, or learning.

However, the early philosophers did not have an adequate laboratory experimental methodology. It is difficult solely on the basis of naturalistic observation to isolate the basic, analytical, principles by which events are related, at least in a field of science involving events as complex as those in psychology. It is difficult to assess the effect of variable A on an event X unless it is possible to control or take account of other variables that also affect event X. Although there are types of environmental events that lawfully affect human behavior, these combine in naturalistic circumstances in infinitely varied and complex ways. Without the possibility of simplifying the situation through laboratory techniques, it would be impossible to see the lawfulness involved, much less to isolate the basic, analytic principles that are operating.

Thus, as we described in the first chapter, the laboratory scientist simplifies the events with which he deals. The basic researcher in learning takes a simple sample of (1) the environment, a stimulus, of (2) the behavior, a response, and of (3) the various types of organisms. In this way he can manipulate the stimulus and see the principle by which the response is affected.

Thus, it was entirely appropriate for the experimental psychology of learning to concentrate in the beginning upon the discovery of basic principles in the artificial simplicity of the laboratory. However, for many investigators in the field of learning, the discovery of basic, analytical, learning principles, as well as the formulation of theoretical systems to incorporate the findings, became an end in itself. No longer were these investigators interested in the events of human behavior that originally gave rise to an interest in the effects of environmental stimuli. And this again was as it should be. For the basic study of learning is an important area of science in and of itself, and much additional research is needed in this area of study.

However, there is another aspect of the science of learning that is equally important—as the science matures—that is, the extension of the basic, analytic, principles back to the consideration of the more complex events of man's behavior. When the principles of a science are relevant to the events of the real world, one of the criteria by which the generality and importance of the principles of the science are demonstrated is in the extent to which they aid in understanding and solving the problems of the real world. The principles of learning are obviously relevant to the behavior of man—it was in this area that an interest in learning was first derived. Thus, the development of a learning theory in its most general sense cannot be restricted to the laboratory study of basic principles, and to the behavior of simple organisms or simple behaviors. Part of the progress of the science of learning must come from extensions of basic principles back to significant complex human behaviors.

There has not been an adequate philosophy, however, within the field of academic experimental psychology by which to include the study of the significant behaviors of man and the problems of such behavior. In the history of psychology applied and basic work has been divorced. The principles that were studied by the basic scientist were not used in the applied fields of psychology. While the basic worker was discovering his basic, analytic, principles of learning, the applied worker was discovering techniques and principles with which to work with real problems of behavior. The latter did this, however, through the systematic study of naturalistic rather than laboratory events.

Thus, basic and applied work were actually quite separate. The work of the applied psychologist did not have the exact methods of the experi-mentalist—nor were experimentally derived principles used in applied work. The experimentalist, it may be added, also developed negative attitudes toward applied work—for it was not conducted with the same scientific finesse that the experimental psychologist held in high value.

On the other hand, the applied worker saw the development of the experimental psychology of learning as less than of world shaking impor-tance. While it might be a justifiable area of scientific study, it was obvious that it treated events that in the measure of worldly concerns were actually quite trivial. Furthermore the basic worker seemed anxious to indicate that his work had little of practical significance, and was unlikely to develop any soon. Members of applied fields who looked to the experimental psychology of learning in hopes of using the principles in their realm of interest were greeted with the morass of experimental results and conflicting theories. It is not possible to survey the basic literature and to thereby obtain a theoretical framework that is relevant to important human behaviors. Furthermore, it was necessary to develop an experimental methodology by which research on significant complex human behavior could be conducted—before the social relevance of the basic science could be seen.

Without the necessary theoretical and experimental basis for the use of basic psychology in the study of functional human behaviors, the schism between basic and applied psychology has continued to exist to a large extent. Thus, for example, clinical psychology has been largely separated from experimental psychology and educational psychology is not even in the department of psychology of most universities—even though, in both cases, the types of behavior studied in these areas are directly of interest to the experimental study of human learning. The negative attitudes of the experimentalist for applied work, and of the applied psychologist for experimental findings and methods, have not generally abated. Where at first the separation was based upon the lack of development of theory and methods within the basic field for working with complex human behavior, the negative attitudes once formed have become an obstacle in themselves.

Once it is demonstrated that basic learning principles and experimental methods can be used to understand complex human behavior and the problems of human behavior, however, these negative attitudes should become anachronistic. That is, when it is possible to extend basic findings to important problems of the real world, then this type of applied activity becomes an extension and verification of the basic science and both applied and basic psychology become joined with a common interest.

The path of progress in integrating these aspects of psychology, it may be suggested, lies in the direction of extending the basic principles to more complex behaviors significant to the adjustment of the individual, and to his value to society. In this way the science will attain its full social role. Furthermore, as will be discussed later, the effort will yield a classic theory—a learning theory of human behavior. Involved in this progressive development must be progress in obtaining more and more *representative* samples of human behavior—within the confines of the basic learning principles and the experimental methods. Working out learning analyses of significant human behaviors in the necessary detail and the development of experimental methods and treatment procedures with which to deal with those behaviors will be central in developing such a scientific theory of human behavior.

It may be said that academic experimental psychology has been concerned with complex human behavior, which in a sense is true. There have been many studies of verbal learning, concept formation, and problem solving—within the framework of learning analyses. The author (1966) has suggested, however, that the behaviors dealt with under these rubrics are really far removed from what these terms describe in everyday life. The definitions of the terms actually have not arisen from analyses of the behaviors that are called problem solving, concept formation, or language learning. Actually, the experimental studies have been based upon the classificatory system already described and on prior philosophical conceptions of cognitive structures.

This suggestion may be better explained by example. Learning studies of problem solving, to illustrate, have used the same traditional categorizations as those used by earlier Gestalt psychologists, and the same *strategy* in selecting experimental situations for the study of problem solving. Thus, the learning studies of problem solving have tended to use experimental situations (problems) that are based upon a conception of problem solving as a unitary cognitive faculty that people have more or less of. At least this has been implied by the fact that any type of problem task has been accepted as a representative sample of problem solving. Thus, one could speak of problem solving whether the study involved the Maier two-string problem, the Luchins water-jar problem, anagram solution, card sorting, or complex discriminations. However, problem solving, as well as concept formation, perception, communication, reasoning, and the like—may not be considered to be a unitary process, or a unitary type of behavior. Different problem situations call out behaviors learned via different principles, and involving different types of behavior combined into different S–R mechanisms.

One is forced to ask what actual problem solving behaviors of real life are sampled by the two-string problem, by anagram solution, card sorting, and selecting the next stimulus in a series. What, for example, is the relationship of the inductive reasoning task of Long and Holland (Skinner, 1961), where the task is to indicate the next stimulus in a regularly alternating series, to the inductive reasoning that occurs in various scientific problems. In what way are these problem tasks samples of complex human problem solving, and how do the principles and findings generalize to the universe of actual problem solving behaviors in which we are ultimately interested? It is necessary that this be explicated if we are to accept these studies as relevant to problem solving. The best experimental and statistical control goes for naught if the behavior we sample in our experiment is not a sample of the universe of behaviors in which we are interested. Thus, attention to this type of sampling becomes crucial when one is interested in an aspect of complex human behavior.

The question of representative behavior sampling is generally pertinent to much of the academic study of human learning. Take the field of verbal learning, to illustrate the point more fully, although the points to be discussed apply equally well to problem solving, concept formation, and reasoning research, and other areas of the study of cognitive behavior. Verbal learning research originally stemmed from an interest in an aspect of complex human behavior. The hundreds of experiments in paired-associate and serial verbal learning have shown in general terms the relevance of the principles and procedures for this type of human learning. A necessary avenue of advance, however, is to begin to deal with better and better (more and more representative) samples of the behavior we ultimately wish to generalize back to. However, there seems to be little conscious effort to do this. The field of verbal learning has had little contact with the events of complex human behavior for many years, and many hundreds of experiments. As the situation now exists in the field of verbal learning, the research has largely ceased obtaining life-like samples of complex human behavior, the experiments stem solely from other experiments. It may be suggested that experimental fields can also stray away from the events in which they were originally interested in the same way that theoretical endeavors miss the mainstream of scientific development.

One of the criteria by which to assess the worth of the scientific principles and methods of verbal learning will ultimately be in the extent to which they give a better understanding of and control of actual verbal learning. Grammatical speech production, much of mathematical learning, reasoning, reading, writing, communication, are examples of complex behaviors that appear to involve the establishment and function of word response sequences (word associations). What, one may ask, can the science of verbal learning tell us about how the child learns such S–R mechanisms and how they function in his adjustment. These are legitimate demands upon the field. Presumably, the principles obtained by the research must ultimately refer back to the events of original interest. But, this cannot be done without experiments to relate the basic methods and principles to those events.

On the other hand, there has been little progress made in gaining a learning analysis of complex human behaviors, that is a theory of cognitive behavior, from the field of teaching machines and programmed instruction. Although this field was more or less self-consciously devoted to applying operant conditioning principles and methods to problems of teaching, it has not attained the promise of this goal. While the teaching machine movement has been salubrious simply by virtue of showing interest in applying psychological principles to practical problems, the movement has largely been concerned with the exploitation of a relatively few techniques applied to the practical development of curriculum materials.

Furthermore, the foundation of the programmed instruction movement has been parochial, being restricted to the philosophy of science and the principles and methods of Skinner's operant conditioning. In line with his philosophy, even within the confines of its principles, it has not aimed at analysis and understanding, but only at producing a program that works. For example, one of the primary principles of the programmed instruction approach is that the terminal behavioral skill must first be specified. This would imply a behavioral analysis upon which to base the construction of a program, if the S–R mechanisms involved were explicated. However, specification of the skill is ordinarily simply taken from teaching materials that already exist, without a learning analysis. In this respect, there is no more behavioral analysis in programming than there is in the construction of achievement tests—where the same principle of specifying the terminal behavior has existed for some time.

Thus, we find programs to teach complex repertoires when there has been no analysis of the behavior involved in terms of basic principles and thus no confirmation or disconfirmation of principles. As another example, there are programs for teaching algebra. The major point involved will be the use of small steps in introducing material, so the subject has mastered prerequisite skills before new material occurs. In addition, devices may be used to control the learning progress. What principles are involved in algebra learning, however, will not emerge from the programming—or from the research involved in evaluating the program. As with academic experimental psychology's study of cognitive behavior, the conception of the behavior involved is simply taken from what already exists. Thus, in education there are programs for teaching traditional arithmetic and programs for teaching the new math, but no psychological rationale for choosing one over the other as the basic training for the young child.

Because of these characteristics new and penetrating analyses of complex human behavior, which would constitute a psychology of cognition, are not emerging from the programmed instruction work. Although the programs produced may have some practical value, and be well justified on this basis, they are developed in purely applied studies. The studies do not give a general understanding or specific analysis of the behavior involved in terms of some set of principles, do not show how the behavior is acquired, what other skills are first necessary, or how the behavior is the foundation for later types of learning, and so on.

It is suggested that an integrated set of learning principles and methods must be applied in experimental and theoretical analyses in which there is detailed and explicit analysis of the behaviors involved. This type of analysis will extend the learning conception of human behavior and produce understanding of specific types of human behavior that can be used to construct various training programs dealing with that type of behavior, as well as lead to analyses of other types of behavior with varying degrees of relationship.

In summary, it is suggested that those aspects of learning that deal with human behavior meet their final evaluation in the extent to which they are able to compete with other approaches to the study of and dealing with actual complex human behavior. This means the extent to which such behavior can be predicted and desirable behaviors produced (scientific prediction and control). The principles and methods of the science must eventually show superior ability to deal with practical events. To extend the science of learning toward this ultimate assessment, it is suggested that we must begin to work with samples of behavior that are more representative of the behaviors in which we are actually interested—the behaviors we see in everyday life. Exemplification of this strategy for the development of basic and applied learning theory will be made in subsequent discussions.

The author selected several samples of complex cognitive repertoires to work with further in developing the integrated-functional learning theory. These types of behavior were chosen for experimental and theoretical analyses for several reasons. First, they are of great complexity, requiring much training and time in development. They are clearly cognitive in nature and clearly functional—with much adjustmental value. Understanding these behaviors and the ability to solve problems in the development of these behaviors would contribute much toward an understanding of complex human behavior. Methods by which this could be accomplished would seemingly have general implications for the study of other aspects of human behavior.

In addition, however, successful application of experimental principles and procedures to the analysis of these behaviors would contribute toward the necessary rapprochement between the applied and basic aspects of psychology. Thus, on the one hand, the attempt is to show the experimental psychologist that he can study basic principles in the context of actual, functional, human behaviors—usually of interest to the applied psychologist. This can be done in a manner that is consistent with the methods and philosophy of the basic science. Moreover, by dealing with samples of actual behaviors, the experimental psychologist can better treat the areas of study in his field that are concerned with human behavior.

On the other hand the attempt is also to show the educational, clinical, and child psychologist that he can better obtain an understanding of the behaviors in which he is interested through the use of the learning theory and the methods of experimental psychology.

Following this rationale, the cognitive behaviors selected for theoretical and experimental analysis were number concept learning, writing acquisition, and reading acquisition and function. In the traditional classificatory system these areas are usually relegated to applied psychology. The next section will present brief analyses of these three areas of cognitive development. Following this, preliminary and more basic laboratory research on such cognitive learning will be described. Additional research will then be described that deals with the actual cognitive repertoires of number concept learning, writing acquisition, and reading acquisition.

NUMBER CONCEPT LEARNING AND ARITHMETIC

On the basis of his integrated learning theory and personal experience, plus the experience of research with his 1-½-year-old daughter in the very first stages of number concept acquisition, the author projected a learning analysis of number concept learning and arithmetic operations (see Staats and Staats, 1963, pp. 221–236). On the basis of further investigation of this type of learning with his daughter and additional subjects additional parts of the analysis have been experimentally verified. This experimental work has also suggested some modifications in the original analysis, however. The following will present the original analysis as revised on the basis of further experimentation, some of which will be systematically described in a later chapter.

The First Number Discriminations

The acquisition of the very first number concepts appears to take place in a process that is analogous to the instrumental discrimination learning in which the child learns to name objects. The process, however, is somewhat more complex and is like that originally called concept formation by Hull (1920). As was described in the section on concepts in Chapter 9, Hull suggested that if a particular response was made to different complex stimuli all of which had a common component stimulus, the common stimulus would come to control the response. Skinner has since called the same process abstraction (1957).

This type of learning is involved in the child's first number concept learning. He is reinforced for saying TWO in the presence of various complex stimuli, all of which contain a common stimulus element—the element of "twoness." In the presence of complex stimuli which differ in various respects, but have a common stimulus of "threeness," the child is reinforced for saying THREE. A similar experience occurs with the stimulus component of "oneness," for the verbal response ONE.

Although the stimuli, "oneness," "twoness," and "threeness" are quite different, this concept formation type of discrimination learning is difficult. This is the case because the particular response is being reinforced in the presence of complex stimuli, each component of which will come to control the verbal response. Thus, when the child is reinforced for saying THREE in the presence of three oranges, the stimuli of the oranges—regardless of the number—will also come to control the response. Trials must be conducted to extinguish the number response to the oranges themselves while maintaining the response in good strength to the common stimulus component, the *number* of objects present. In general, the size, shape, color, and so on of objects must as stimuli come *not* to control number responses.

The process of producing this complex stimulus control, however, is quite simple. It requires only that the child be presented with numbers of different stimulus objects, be prompted to make the appropriate number response, and then be reinforced. A sufficient number of trials must be conducted so that the particular stimulus characteristics of the objects no longer control the particular number response, only the stimuli of numerosity.

In addition, it should be added, the child has to be trained to make number responses to stimulus objects in the presence of the appropriate verbal discriminative stimuli. Simply training the child on the number responses themselves will not be enough to insure that he make number responses in appropriate circumstances. That is, if training had been conducted only on number responses and the child was then asked "What color are these?" while he was shown two red balls, the child might well respond TWO. Thus, the child's number responses must be brought under the control of the numerosity of stimulus objects *plus* additional stimuli such as the question "How many are there?"

Counting S–R Mechanisms

By virtue of the preceding type of training the child can acquire a simple number response repertoire. When presented with two objects and asked how many there are he will respond TWO. He may in this manner also acquire number responses to one, three, and perhaps four or five objects. However, simple discrimination training of this type is insufficient to produce a number response repertoire much larger than this. As a stimulus, 9 objects are really very much like 10 objects and differentially responding to them would constitute a difficult discrimination. To further advance the number concept response repertoire additional training must be conducted and additional skills learned besides the straightforward discrimination training.

For one thing, the child must acquire a sequence of number (verbal) responses each of which is elicited (or controlled) by the preceding response and each of which controls the following response. The formation of such a sequence is analogous to paired associate and serial learning. If two or more (verbal) responses occur in sequence and this is followed by reinforcement, the first response will tend to elicit the second, the second the third, and so on. Of course, until many trials have been conducted this control will not be perfect. That is, one response may elicit an incorrect response, or no response at all.

In addition to the number response sequence, which at this point would be analogous to having learned the alphabet, the child must come to be able to coordinate the emission in sequence of these number responses with another sequence of responses—the sequential responses of looking at (and pointing at, touching, or moving) objects in a group. Again, the number response sequence and the sensory-motor response sequence must be coordinated and occur in a parallel manner. That is, in counting the child must look initially at one object in the group and say ONE. The stimuli produced by these responses must then control the next pair of responses, that of looking at the next object in the group and also of saying TWO.

The trainer must arrange so that this parallelism of the two sequences of response occurs and then reinforce the child. After a sufficient number of trials have occurred of this type, the child will be able to count in this manner any series of objects. This is a general description of the type of learning involved. The following section will present a more detailed analysis of the S–R mechanisms that must be acquired in the development of number and counting concept repertoires.

After the child, through straightforward discrimination training, has acquired a basic number concept repertoire in which he can respond appropriately to the question of how many when presented with one or two objects, he is ready to be trained to an expanded number concept repertoire, including that of counting. This training may be conducted by presenting the child with three objects arranged in a series. The parent should then prompt the child to point to the leftmost object, let us say, and at the same time to say ONE. Then, the parent should prompt the child to move his finger (and consequently his eyes) to the next object and say TWO, to the next object and say THREE.

After this has been done several times, the appropriate sequences of responses will begin to form and the parent's prompting stimuli can be gradually dropped. It will require many trials, however, before the child performs the complex coordinations of the response sequences involved without error. In the beginning stages the child will make the verbal counting responses at a different rate than he makes his pointing and looking responses. If the verbal responses are too fast, he will count too many, if too slow he will not count enough.

On the basis of this training the child may be expected to begin to acquire the combination of attentional responses, manual responses, and vocal number-response sequences of which counting is composed. That is, the general stimulus of a group of objects would be expected through such training to come to control the necessary eye movements, or observing responses. If the stimuli are in a line the child will look first, let us say, at the leftmost member of the group, because of the training. This stimulus will then control the first number response ONE. The stimuli produced by this response, plus the stimulus of the leftmost object, would then come to control the response of looking at the second leftmost object. This object, plus the stimulus produced by the response ONE, would then elicit the response TWO, and so on. As the child counted further the particular number response to be elicited would be controlled both by the stimuli of the object and especially by the stimuli produced by the preceding number response. This chaining process is depicted in Figure 11.1.

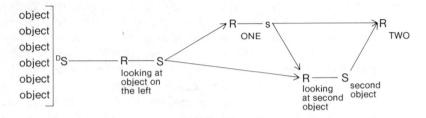

FIGURE 11.1.   Illustration of the sequence of responses involved in counting. A group of stimulus objects is depicted as well as the already formed number responses of the child that control further counting responses. First, the group of stimuli elicit the orienting attentional response, let us say, of looking at the leftmost object. This stimulus then elicits the number response ONE, as well as the response of moving the eyes to the next object. The next stimulus, plus the preceding response ONE, elicit the number response TWO, and so on.

According to the author's analysis, however, the child must receive training in counting groups of objects in many different arrangements before his counting behavior will come under the control of the different arrangements. Instead of just making a series of eye movements (perhaps with pointing responses) in coordination with the number responses, a new set of motor responses must be included in the complex S–R mechanism. That is, the child has to acquire a sequence of moving one object at a time out of the group. Each time he moves one object out, he must at the same time emit the next response in the number response sequence. When these two sequences of responses have been learned in a coordinated fashion, the child can count any group of objects regardless of arrangement—to the extent of the number response sequence he has acquired at any rate. It would be expected that extensive training would be required to establish each sequence. In addition, further training is necessary to make the response of one sequence elicit the next response in the other sequence (so that the sequences occur in a parallel manner), as well as elicit the next response in its own sequence. The complex S–R mechanism that must be established is shown in Figure 11.2. At any rate, it is suggested that the child may be straightforwardly trained to the number concept repertoire involved in counting objects no matter what their arrangement; the learning analysis constitutes an empirical hypothesis.

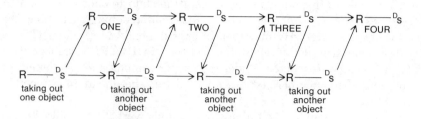

FIGURE 11.2. The S–R mechanism involved in counting any group of objects. The group of objects as a stimulus is left out of the diagram, and the account begins with the first response of taking one object out of the group. This response is the stimulus for saying ONE, and this verbal stimulus along with preceding motor response is the stimulus that controls the next response of taking another object out of the group. This movement, plus the preceding number response, provides the controlling stimuli for saying TWO, and so on until the child has taken all the objects out of the group. When the learning is still not complete, the responses may not precisely control each other in the necessary order and errors may occur.

It may be added that in addition to the types of training already described, other types of experience are also necessary before the child will emit number responses correctly in the appropriate stimulus situation (task). Prior to training, a child who is asked HOW MANY PIECES OF CANDY DO YOU WANT, ONE OR TWO? might not respond appropriately even if he had been trained to count. Ordinarily, it would be expected that the child would have to be trained to make correct number responses in many different types of situations, for example, when the grocer says YOU MUST HAVE FIVE PENNIES FOR THAT CANDY BAR. All these training situations, in addition to the actual counting training, and many more, are the variables that would be thought to underlie the child's acquisition of an appropriate number concept repertoire—"the idea of number."

Verbal Extensions of Counting Mechanisms

Once the child has acquired the preceding repertoire of number responses up to, let us say, ten or twelve, under the control of stimulus objects rather than of their different arrangements, the counting mechanisms can be extended further solely on a verbal basis—simply by adding to the number response sequence the child already has acquired. Although many training trials involve counting objects, the parent or teacher could at this point simply prompt the child to emit these number responses without counting objects and reinforce him each time the repertoire is emitted. He may then prompt the child to say THIRTEEN at the completion of the repertoire, and then FOURTEEN, and perhaps one or two more responses. Under the proper training and reinforcement conditions these number responses would thus be added to the child's repertoire.

Now, even though this training was purely verbal, it would be expected that when the child was counting a group of objects and came to twelve, he could continue on. His counting behavior would be under the control of the objects still left in the group, as well as the words emitted in the verbal chain: TWELVE, THIRTEEN, FOURTEEN, and so on. Thus, the child's number response S–R mechanisms might grow through purely verbal training. It seems apparent that most of our counting repertoires have been partly established through verbal training alone, yet we could actually count an indefinite number of objects should it be required; although most of us have never counted a group of, say, 1713 objects, we could do so on the basis of our verbal training and the general counting S–R mechanisms we have acquired.

Because of the redundancy in our number system it is also relatively easy to extend the number-response sequences through verbal training once a basic repertoire has been established. After acquiring a repertoire up to twenty, counting to thirty is easy to establish because there already are associations between the responses ONE, TWO, THREE . . . NINE. When the child says TWENTY-ONE, and then TWENTY-, the preceding ONE response tends to elicit TWO on the basis of the already learned chain. Thus, establishing TWENTY-TWO takes relatively few trials. This is, of course, also true for other number responses which follow— the 30s, 40s, 130s, and so on. Thus, the S–R mechanisms underlying redundancy (and therefore ease of extension) in the number system seem to be the chains or verbal response sequences which have been previously established.

Reading and Writing Numbers

In the same manner that the child learns to make reading and writing responses to verbal stimuli, he also learns to read or write numbers. These are essential skills that are prerequisite to further training in arithmetic and mathematical repertoires. Data concerning this aspect of the analysis of number concept learning will be presented in a later chapter and no further elaboration will be made here.

One point may be made, however, that is relevant as a general discussion. In any type of complex learning it may many times be necessary that the child be taught additional skills that are related to the specific skill which is of interest, if the specific skill is to be functional in any way. The reading and writing of numbers may be used as an example here. That is, the child could be taught to read numbers without being taught the other number mechanisms that have been described as well as those to be described. In such a case, reading the numbers would be quite an isolated skill and would not contribute to the child's adjustment in other ways. In common sense terms this skill would be meaningless, and thus subject to the criticisms of rote learning frequently made by educators and other individuals who are antagonistic to specific S–R learning interpretations of human behavior. Simple minded learning analyses of human behavior are not adequate to answer such criticisms. To do so a more comprehensive analysis of the behavioral repertoires that are involved must be supplied, including the related repertoires that make a specific skill functional. More will be said later on this topic.

Addition S–R Mechanisms

The child may also acquire a rudimentary "addition" repertoire through what is essentially a process of counting. For example, he might be presented with two marbles and then another two and asked: HOW MANY MARBLES ARE TWO MARBLES PLUS TWO MARBLES? The child may then be prompted to count ONE-TWO-THREE-FOUR marbles, or the parent or teacher may simply prompt the child to say FOUR. From this type of training the number response sequence TWO PLUS TWO IS FOUR will be formed.

Although the first "adding" number response sequences (the concept of addition) may be established in a process involving counting, additional sequences are probably ordinarily established on a purely verbal level. Usually the most important developments customarily await the formal training the child receives in school where he acquires sequences such as SEVEN PLUS TWO IS NINE, EIGHT PLUS NINE IS SEVENTEEN, and the like. In addition, he will ordinarily be trained to read addition stimuli. That is, the stimuli

$$\begin{array}{r} 6 \\ +7 \\ \hline 13 \end{array}$$

will come to control the verbal response sequence SIX PLUS SEVEN EQUALS THIRTEEN. It should be pointed out that this seemingly simple S–R sequence actually includes quite complicated S–R mechanisms. In order for this complex stimulus to control the appropriate responses, the child's observing or attentional responses must be under appropriate stimulus control. He must look at the stimuli in a particular order (as a prelude to further addition training): the 6 first, the plus sign next, the 7 next, then the 13. Each stimulus must, of course, elicit the correct number response. These skills are basic to further addition training. This is depicted in Figure 11.3.

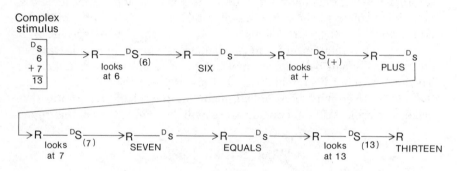

FIGURE 11.3.   A complex chain of observing and vocal responses is involved in reading a simple addition problem. The child must observe the stimuli in the proper order and respond appropriately to them.

After such basic adding sequences have been established, plus the appropriate chains of observing and reading responses, the child may be presented with more complicated number stimuli (problems), such as

$$\begin{array}{r} 18 \\ +19 \\ \hline \end{array}$$

The prompting in this case, as in the preceding one, may require a fairly complex set of instructions involving the elicitation of both vocal and writing responses from the child.

Let us consider an example of a plausible chain in which a child might be trained in order to solve addition problems. Naturally, in this example, and all others considered in this chapter, the sequences established are not the only ones that will result in the "right" answer. Nor is it suggested that the chains discussed are the most efficient. At each stage, the reader should remember that such questions must be answered through experimentation.

To continue, in the presence of the addition problem above, the instructor might say, TO ADD THESE TWO NUMBERS, FIRST ADD THE EIGHT AND THE NINE. HOW MUCH IS EIGHT AND NINE? When the child responds, SEVENTEEN, the instructor may continue, WRITE THE SEVEN UNDER THE EIGHT AND NINE, AND PUT A LITTLE ONE JUST TO THE LEFT SIDE OF THE SEVEN SO THAT YOU REMEMBER IT REALLY STANDS FOR SEVENTEEN. NOW YOU MUST ALSO PUT A LITTLE ONE JUST ABOVE THE ONE IN THE EIGHTEEN. THEN YOU JUST ADD THE ONE AND ONE AND ONE WHICH IS THREE AND WRITE IT UNDERNEATH.

These verbal stimuli provided by the instructor should elicit the correct behaviors of the child (provided the necessary basic responses—"attending"—have been acquired). In so doing a chain of responses to a more complicated addition problem begins to be formed. The response chain is depicted in Figure 11.4.

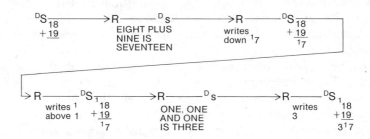

FIGURE 11.4.   An addition response sequence.

After the child has been prompted to respond in this manner to a number of these problems, the child's sequence of behavior might be expected to come under the control of certain *general* stimulus features of the complex stimulus, as well as of the specific stimulus features of the numbers involved. Both types of S–R mechanisms are necessary. As in the previous example, the general stimulus features of the problem consist of the *position* of the stimuli. Ignoring the specific numbers involved, the stimuli have position characteristics as follows:

$$
\begin{array}{r}
XX \\
+XX \\
\hline
XX
\end{array}
$$

These position stimuli must come to control an appropriate sequence of observing responses. In a complex chain the child should come to look first at the upper rightmost stimulus, then the lower rightmost stimulus. The specific number stimuli would control the specific number verbal responses, which culminate with the statement of the sum. Then the writing response would occur following which the position stimuli would again control looking at the upper leftmost stimulus, and so on.

When correct observing responses to the general stimuli of position as well as the correct number responses to the specific number stimuli have been acquired, it would be expected that the child then would respond correctly and without prompting to any addition problem of the type just discussed. The necessary chains of addition responses should be acquired on far fewer trials than the infinite number of different possible problems made up of the various number combinations. Although never having added 78 and 83, as an example, the child who has the appropriate general responses, as well as the individual basic addition verbal sequences should arrive at a correct final response. The motor and verbal responses acquired here are like a system in that the responses acquired are appropriate to a very large number of different stimuli. (Thus, the analysis describes another mechanism for producing original behavior.)

Thus, we see how the sequence of number responses might come under the control of the appropriate stimuli. The responses to a new problem are considered correct or incorrect to the extent that they are the same responses that others have learned to make to the same stimuli. In other terms, the problem is solved correctly if the final response made a stimulus matching that of an authority source.

Of course, in any practical problem, the final authority is whether the addition number responses produce the same final result as would counting the objects directly; for example, the adding chain is reinforced by yielding a final response that is the same as that given by responding to the objects themselves. It seems reasonable to conjecture that it is because of the reinforcement of saving time and effort through emitting the verbal adding chain, in contrast to simply counting the objects, that the adding chain has become more and more frequently emitted in situations in which either response chain would be finally successful, both in the cases of individual's histories as well as in the history of our society.

This would thus be an exemplification of the linguistic evolution conception previously described.

Multiplication S–R Mechanisms

To a large extent the acquisition of multiplication sequences would seem to involve the same types of S–R mechanisms as those discussed under addition. Multiplication deals with a special class of addition problems where the same number is repeated, and added, more than once. To such problems as

$$
\begin{array}{r}
4 \\
4 \\
4 \\
\hline
\end{array}
$$

the child already has acquired number response sequences, such as FOUR PLUS FOUR IS EIGHT, AND EIGHT PLUS FOUR IS TWELVE.

In place of this sequence, he may be trained on a new sequence, consisting first of counting the number of fours, and then emitting the number response sequence THREE TIMES FOUR EQUALS TWELVE. The child may thus acquire another number response chain to these types of number stimuli (problems). It is interesting that in teaching, these new multiplication response sequences are not usually first brought under the control of stimulus objects in the same way that counting and adding responses are. The objects counted in this instance are number stimuli—the child counts numbers. Later, the multiplication response sequences must be brought under the control of the appropriate stimulus objects, perhaps through the use of word problems. That is, in counting there is a stimulus object (or objects) which can control the verbal response. Also, for addition there is a stimulus event of combining two or more objects that can control an adding number response. There is no additional event to control multiplication responses, the event being the same combination that controls the adding responses.

Thus, the child may acquire his multiplication response sequences by responding to the number stimuli of the multiplication tables. In this case, the appropriate chains are acquired by making the responses in sequence (by repeating the teacher or reading the numbers). Problems might be given also in which the final response is absent and the child is correct if his response matches that of an authority source. Formation of the multiplication table sequences seems to be necessary for further

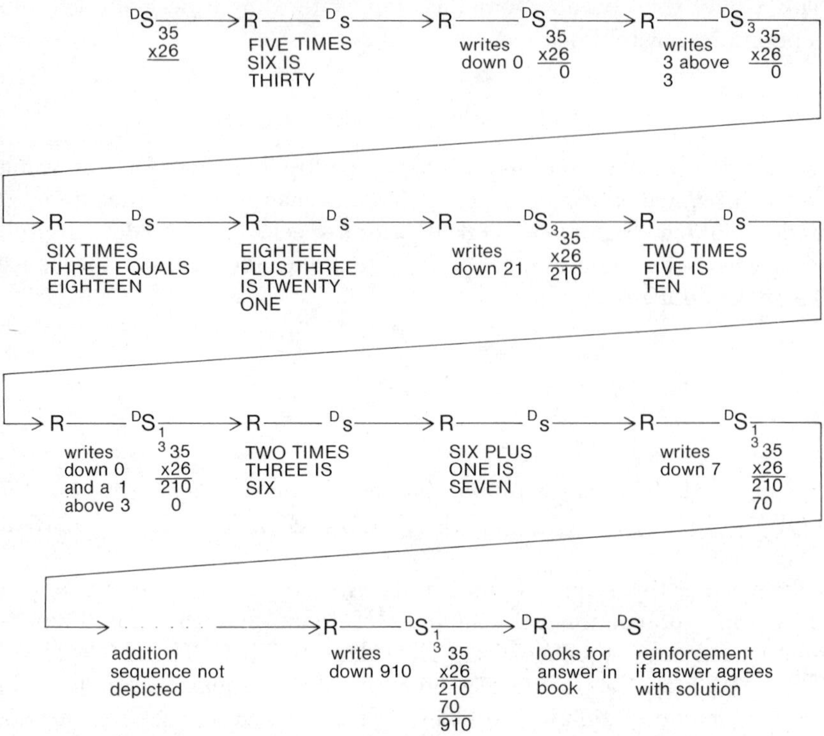

$^{D}S\dfrac{35}{\times 26}$ $\longrightarrow$ R $\longrightarrow$ ^{D}s $\longrightarrow$ R $\longrightarrow$ $^{D}S\dfrac{35}{\times 26}{0}$ $\longrightarrow$ R $\longrightarrow$ $^{D}S\overset{3}{\dfrac{35}{\times 26}}{0}$

FIVE TIMES SIX IS THIRTY   writes down 0   writes 3 above 3

$\longrightarrow$ R $\longrightarrow$ ^{D}s $\longrightarrow$ R $\longrightarrow$ ^{D}s $\longrightarrow$ R $\longrightarrow$ $^{D}S\overset{3}{\dfrac{35}{\times 26}{210}}$ $\longrightarrow$ R $\longrightarrow$ ^{D}s $\longrightarrow$

SIX TIMES THREE EQUALS EIGHTEEN   EIGHTEEN PLUS THREE IS TWENTY ONE   writes down 21   TWO TIMES FIVE IS TEN

$\longrightarrow$ R $\longrightarrow$ $^{D}S_{1}$ $\longrightarrow$ R $\longrightarrow$ ^{D}s $\longrightarrow$ R $\longrightarrow$ ^{D}s $\longrightarrow$ R $\longrightarrow$ $^{D}S_{1}$

writes down 0 and a 1 above 3 $\overset{3}{\dfrac{35}{\times 26}{210}}{0}$ TWO TIMES THREE IS SIX   SIX PLUS ONE IS SEVEN   writes down 7 $\overset{3}{\dfrac{35}{\times 26}{210}}{70}$

$\longrightarrow \cdots \longrightarrow$ R $\longrightarrow$ $^{D}S_{1}$ $\longrightarrow$ ^{D}R $\longrightarrow$ ^{D}S

addition sequence not depicted   writes down 910 $\overset{3}{\dfrac{\dfrac{35}{\times 26}}{\dfrac{210}{\dfrac{70}{910}}}}$ looks for answer in book   reinforcement if answer agrees with solution

FIGURE 11.5. The figure illustrates the complexity of a chain of responses that might be involved in training a child to complete the multiplication problem 35×26. The child might first be prompted to respond to the two right-hand stimuli with a multiplication sequence already acquired: FIVE TIMES SIX IS THIRTY. The instructor might then prompt the child to write a zero under the 5 and 6 and to write a small 3 above the 3 in 35. This writing response should thus come under the control of the stimulus produced by the preceding response, FIVE TIMES SIX IS THIRTY. The child might then be prompted to respond to the bottom right-hand number stimulus 6 and the upper number stimulus second from the right, 3, with the previously acquired multiplication response, SIX TIMES THREE EQUALS EIGHTEEN. This response produces a stimulus (visual, if it is written, or auditory) which with the 3 previously written ("carried"), and perhaps further prompts from the instructor, produces the addition response EIGHTEEN PLUS THREE IS TWENTY-ONE. In the presence of this stimulus, the child may be prompted to write 21 just to the left of the zero. The process might then continue with the pupil reading the number stimulus 2, second from the right in the bottom row, and the right-hand upper stimulus

multiplication learning just as a basic single-digit addition repertoire was necessary for more complicated addition problems in the procedure already discussed.

Although no new principles are introduced, an example of multiplication learning is presented in Figure 11.5 to illustrate the complex chain of responses involved in even a relatively simple multiplication problem. The specific responses are not important, of course, but the figure does show what sort of complex chain might be involved. It would be expected that all the attention, adding, writing, and verbal response sequences we previously described would be included in such a multiplication chain, formed into more complex constellations such as depicted.

In problems requiring many steps in a certain order, as in Figure 11.5, the responses would probably be elicited first by both the number stimuli of the problem and the instructor's prompting. However, after many trials, the complex sequence of responses under the control of the general (position) stimuli and the specific number stimuli would be expected to become firmly established.

In problems as complex as this, it is easy to see that the multiplication response sequences would be more quickly reinforced and be less aversive in terms of effort expended than either addition response sequences or the direct counting response sequence in the presence of the actual objects. That is to say, multiplying 35×26 would be more reinforcing (that is, less effortful or aversive) than adding 35 twenty-six times or directly counting 910 objects. The multiplication response sequence would thus become a stronger behavior than either adding or counting both for the individual and as an example of "societal learning," that is where a behavior grows more dominant in the group over time.

5, and emitting the multiplication response TWO TIMES FIVE IS TEN. In the presence of this stimulus the child might then be prompted to write the zero indented one space to the left of the rightmost number stimulus in the preceding product and to write a small 1 above the 3. He may then be prompted to respond to the 2 again and the number stimulus 3 (second from the right on the top row) with the number response sequence TWO TIMES THREE IS SIX. To the stimulus produced by this response and the 1 written above the 3 the child may be further prompted to respond with the addition response SIX PLUS ONE IS SEVEN, and to respond to this by writing 7 just to the left of the previously written zero. Addition responses then emitted would lead to the terminal response 910. The reinforcement for this complex sequence of events would normally be the matching visual stimulus of seeing 910 in the answer book (or hearing the instructor give 910 as the answer).

WRITING ACQUISITION

The analysis of writing acquisition in learning terms follows very straightforwardly from the previous general discussions of instrumental discrimination learning where a verbal stimulus comes to control a motor response. The example used to demonstrate this principle involved the cat coming to respond to the auditory presentation of its name. In the case of writing acquisition, however, the stimuli are either auditory verbal stimuli, (the sound of the spoken word,) whether given by someone else or oneself, or visual verbal stimuli. The latter are printed or written letters or words. The motor response, of course, is the writing of the verbal stimulus involved.

Ordinarily, by the time the child receives training to write, he will also be receiving training to read. Thus, he will not only be learning to make the proper motor writing response, he will be learning to make the proper motor vocal response to the verbal stimulus—that is, to read it. However, each of these types of behavior—writing and reading—may be discussed separately.

Although this is not usually considered in terms of writing learning, a good deal of the training in the ordinary middle-class family will have taken place prior to the formal training. That is, the child will ordinarily at least have had practice in grasping a pencil or crayon and making marks on a piece of paper. These are motor skills on which the child must have considerable experience to perform proficiently.

At this point, however, the child will not yet have acquired the two basic skills in the acquisition of writing; that is, the skills involved in producing the standard letter forms, as well as learning the stimulus control of these "letter-making" motor skills. Ordinarily, again, these two types of training take place simultaneously, since the child looks at the letter as he writes it. However, a child could be trained to write a letter while blind-folded, as one can learn a maze blindfolded. In this case he would develop the motor skill, but it would not be under the stimulus control of the visual letter, or under control of the sound of the letter, for that matter. Thus, the child would be unable to trace or write the letter on command.

At any rate, at the beginning of writing training the child will not have the chain of motor responses involved in writing each letter of the alphabet. When the child has made the particular letter response a number of times, however, the movements involved in making the letter will come into a smooth chain in which each part movement will then come to elicit the next part movement. Then it will seem as if the total response of making the letter is one response, rather than separate links in a chain.

This type of skill may be produced in the child by having him trace the letter. Actually, tracing also involves sensory-motor learning, or in our terms, bringing a motor response under the control of the visual stimulus. That is, even in tracing the lines must come to control the appropriate movement of the pencil. When the child is individually observed in original training of this type it will be seen that the control of the motor responses by the visual stimuli is quite weak. The child will not keep the pencil on the line, and his response will be hesitating, involve retracings and so on.

After a number of trials, however, the line as a stimulus will come to control the tracing response. Then, repetitions of the tracing response will chain the individual movements together into a fairly smooth total response. After this has to some extent been established, when the child is instructed to copy the letter, not trace it, the letter stimulus will have acquired some control over the fairly smooth motor response. However, ordinarily, the control will be weak, and the specific letter response movements only partially chained into a smooth total response. Thus, the first copying response is likely to be a poor imitation of the letter.

With repetitions of this type of training, intermixed with tracing responses to further establish the total writing response, the control of the writing response by the visually presented letter will occur. At this point there will still be considerable variation in the writing response from trial to trial, some of the products being better than others. Many, many, responses are necessary before the writing skill standard for adult performance is attained.

If the child has been told the name of the letter each time he writes it, that is if the auditory stimulus is also present when he makes the writing response, the name of the letter will also, to a certain extent, come to control the writing response. Further training, as with the copying, will be necessary, however, to bring the writing response under good control of the auditorily presented letter stimulus. Further training will also be necessary to bring the child's writing response under the control of the sound of the letter which he has said himself.

This description applies only to the very first learning of writing. Even when the child has received training in writing each of the letters, writing a word will be done very poorly, even when the word is copied. The letters will be written askance, there will be varying space between them, some of the letters will be larger than others, and so on. The various positional stimuli of the letters must come to control the proper responses. Additional discriminations of this type will also be required when writing sentences. Although the principle involved in establishing the proper stimulus control as well as in increasing the motor writing skills is the same throughout, the complexity and the subtlety of the stimuli and responses, as well as the large number of S–R mechanisms involved make this a very complex type of training. As a consequence the training must be conducted over a long period of time and involve many, many training trials. The duration of the training necessary has special implications that will be outlined further on, and research conducted in the study of this cognitive repertoire will be reported.

READING ACQUISITION

A very extensive analysis of this crucially important type of cognitive repertoire will be given in a later section. Thus, at this point only a very brief statement will be made concerning some of the gross aspects of reading acquisition.

By the time the child is provided with reading training he has acquired many cognitive skills that are utilized in the training. At this point, however, these various aspects of learning may be disregarded and the training may be considered to involve only instrumental discrimination training. Using a discriminative stimulus to control the child's vocal behavior, the parent or teacher will get the child to say a word, for example, while the child looks at the word. It would be expected on the basis of the previous analyses that in this process the written or printed word would in this process become a discriminative stimulus that will control that vocal word response.

This does not begin to make a complete analysis of the acquisition of reading, or of how this cognitive repertoire when once acquired functions in further cognitive development. Even the acquisition phase represents a fantastically complicated training process, involving many complex S–R mechanisms. However, this brief indication of how the important principle of discrimination learning functions in the context of reading acquisition will serve as the basis for beginning research upon this type of cognitive development. Since the principle of instrumental discriminative learning is involved in the three types of cognitive development to be described, the research to be reported at first may be considered to be basic to number concept learning and writing acquisition (and other types of cognitive development) as well as to reading acquisition.

12

Laboratory study of reading learning in children

Following the preceding rationale, the author began the study of cognitive learning in children that is relevant to important, adjustive, cognitive repertoires. The samples of cognitive behavior that were to be of primary interest were those of writing acquisition (as a sensory-motor task), reading acquisition, and number concept learning. In the basic phases of the research, however, the learning task itself was not of primary importance. The principles of learning are the same in the three types of cognitive learning, thus the basic findings and procedures involving those principles should apply to each. That is, the first step was to develop procedures for studying the conditioning principles while children were engaged in an arduous, repetitive, and long-term training task—such as is involved in writing acquisition, reading acquisition, or number concept learning. Corroboration of the principles and the development of experimental methods in the context of one of these types of learning would apply equally well to each—as well as to various types of cognitive learning which are of a long-term, complex, variety.

EXPERIMENTAL INVESTIGATION OF READING DISCRIMINATIONS

Reading learning was chosen as the task with which to first extend the experimental-naturalistic study of cognitive learning which the author had already conducted. It should be pointed out that there have not been analyses of actual cognitive behaviors in detailed stimulus-response terms, or experimental methods that have provided for the objective study of the acquisition of such complex behavioral repertoires. Thus, methodological developments may be considered to be a prominent part of progress which is necessary. These matters will be discussed more fully later, but it may serve to indicate that this is an important part of the extension of a learning theory of language learning and cognitive development.

The aim of the beginning aspect of the learning analysis of reading was to construct a laboratory procedure within which reinforcement principles could be studied objectively with young children over long periods of time, where the verbal stimuli were presented in a controlled manner. The reading stimulus materials devised for the first experimental work were selected to fulfill certain criteria, and these will be summarized before presenting the study. While the task was chosen to be a reading task, to produce good laboratory control the materials were selected to be as simple and as homogeneous as possible. Since words and sentences are of different lengths and difficulty, single vowels and consonant-vowel pairs were selected. In devising this set of stimulus materials the author was also applying a preliminary analysis of the learning to be achieved, that is, the type of stimulus discriminations which must be made and the responses which have to be controlled. This analysis, as will be discussed, by no means solves the problems, but it does begin to confront them.

Many investigators concerned with reading have pointed out that in the English language the same letter stimuli often must come to control different speech sounds when the letters are in different contexts. The letter *a* is responded variously to, as in *father, fate, fat,* and so on. One stimulus must thus come to elicit several responses depending upon the context in which it occurs. This represents a complex type of learning. Although there are some general consistencies or rules according to which the stimuli of context can come to control the correct one of the several responses, there are many exceptions, and even when dealing with only the consistencies of context the child confronts a very complex learning task.

There have been various suggestions for overcoming such problems in the training of reading, for example, (1) the English spelling may be altered and new symbols introduced, but this may make the transfer to normal English spelling quite difficult; or (2) in order to retain the actual English spelling, the system may deal with only a limited number of words, not including the many exceptions; however, this limits the generality of the learning.

The stimuli used in the present study were such that they might later be used in the study of some of these problems. The research method retains the letters used in English. However, a different identifying mark appears in conjunction with the letter for each different sound the letter must come to elicit, for example, *a* controls the "a" response in *father*, and *ā* controls the "a" in *fate*. As a result, each letter with its symbol (when necessary) controls only one response, a method consistent with a preliminary analysis of the learning involved. Once the child acquires such a letter repertoire he should be able to read any word composed of these letters. As the learning progresses, and the context stimuli have come to assume control over the correct phonic response, the supplementary identifying stimuli could be gradually removed from the reading materials. These matters are not actually pertinent to the research that is now to be discussed, but it does indicate the rationale the author used in selecting the reading stimuli—and later discussions will concern a more detailed learning analysis of reading materials.

To continue, however, to obtain good experimental control in this basic experiment an apparatus was constructed in which the phonetic letter stimuli could be displayed in a controlled manner. The apparatus is schematized in Figure 12.1 and a picture of a child operating the apparatus is shown in Figure 12.2. The stimulus presentation apparatus consists of the panel with four plastic covered windows. One of the windows is centered above the other three. Pressure on any of the plastic covers activates microswitches which lead to various experimental contingencies.

The verbal stimuli are presented to the child in a discrimination procedure. The top stimulus is "matched" by one of the three stimuli in the bottom row of windows. The task of the child is to select the stimulus that matches the one in the top window. In the procedure the stimuli are presented, and the experimenter, who is not visible to the child, "names" the top stimulus. The child must repeat the name and then press the plastic cover over the top window. Then he must select the matching stimulus from among the bottom windows, press the plastic cover, and read the phonetic stimulus again. When this reading response occurs, the child is automatically and immediately reinforced. If the child correctly reads the stimulus before the experimenter does so, that is, "anticipates" the correct name, reinforcement immediately follows—it is then not necessary to go through the matching task.

A problem with the study of child learning which is complex and requires long periods of time has also been with construction of a reinforcer system that will maintain voluntary participation (see Long, *et al.*, 1958). One of the things we see on the basis of naturalistic observation, however, is that tokens, like money, become excellent reinforcers for peo-

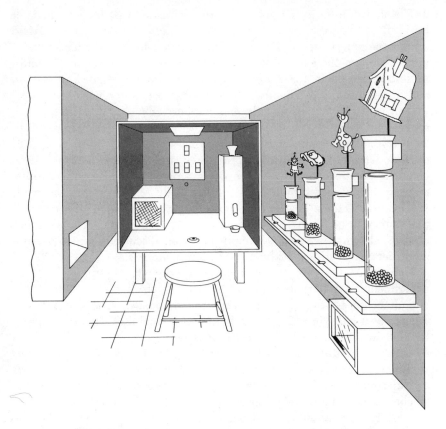

FIGURE 12.1.　The laboratory apparatus for the experimental study of reading behavior. The child is seated before the center panel within easy reach of the various manipulanda which are involved in the reading response sequence. Letter stimuli appear in the small plexiglass windows in front of the child whenever he activates the pushbutton on the table before him. If a correct reading response sequence then occurs, the marble dispenser located at the child's near-right drops a marble into a tray positioned at its base. To the child's left is an open bin in the Universal Feeder cabinet into which are delivered trinkets, edibles, or pennies, whenever the child deposits a marble in the funnel located atop the marble dispenser. A marble may also be "spent" for toys displayed at the child's far right. Whenever the plexiglass tube beneath a toy is filled with marbles the child receives that toy. An intercom speaker at the child's left allows his vocal behavior to be monitored from outside the experimental chamber. The light at the top of the center panel was not used in this study. From *Human Learning* by Arthur W. Staats. Copyright © 1964 by Holt, Rinehart and Winston, Inc. Reprinted by permission of Holt, Rinehart and Winston, Inc.

ple—even without states of deprivation of primary reinforcers. Taking this tip from everyday life, the author developed a reinforcer system based upon the same principle. This consisted of tokens backed up by various items which the children had previously selected—the ratio of tokens to back-up reinforcers dictated by the capacity of the tube in which the tokens are deposited (see Figure 12.1).

Thus, each time a correct response was emitted a token (a marble) was ejected from the tube into the dish in the right corner of the table in front of the child, as shown in Figure 12.1. The tokens were backed up by reinforcers of different value, the difference in value determining the number of tokens that had to be accumulated before the tokens could be exchanged for the reinforcer. In the procedure, the child selected a number of toys from a large class of each value, before he commenced the training program. A toy from each class was then hung in the experimental room (see Figure 12.1), each above a plastic tube. The size of the plastic tube indicates the number of tokens required to obtain the reinforcer. The child could thus "work" for any of the back-up reinforcers; he could obtain an edible or a trinket by depositing the token in the funnel-shaped opening in the right upper corner; he could consecutively deposit 10 tokens in the smallest plastic tube and obtain the reinforcer above it, and the same with the other plastic tubes; or he could work for several different back-up reinforcers at the same time.

The child could thus use his tokens to obtain four different classes of toy reinforcers or the trinket-edible mixture. As soon as he obtained a toy, another that he had previously selected from the same class was placed on display so that he always had a choice among four "for which to work."

After the child had been trained to use the apparatus and to make the phonetic character discriminations, which took ordinarily two of the 20-minute training sessions, the reading procedure proper was begun. The child could press a doorbell-type of button in front of him. That would bring on the next phonetic character which would appear in the top window. The experimenter (who was invisible to the child) would say the name of the character, and the child would repeat the name. This would turn on lights of the bottom windows and activate the switches connected to the plastic covers of the windows. In one of the bottom windows would be the same character as in the top window, the other two windows containing foil characters that differed either in the diacritical mark or in the consonant or vowel letters. The child would have to select the matching stimulus in the bottom window and press its plastic cover and say the character's name again. If the selection was incorrect a buzzer would ring and the lights in the window would go out, and the child would have to begin by pressing the doorbell-type button again.

If the child's response was correct in all aspects, a marble-reinforcer would be delivered. The mechanism would then be turned off until the child had deposited the marble in one of the possible alternatives and had put away any back-up reinforcer that he might have received. Each correct response was recorded automatically with standard cumulative recording equipment. That is, the record consisted of a pen that moved from left to right at a constant speed. Thus, time constituted the baseline of the diagrams representing the child's rate of reading performance. Each time the child made a response, the pen would take a graduated step upwards. The more rapidly the child responded the more steeply would the line slope upward. The steepness of the slope of the line of the records to be presented indicates how rapidly the child is reading.

The first step in the experimental analysis of actual cases of cognitive learning was to test the combined apparatus and procedure. While each phase of developing the laboratory facility involved pilot work, it was important to determine whether the entire system would maintain the child's behavior for a long enough period of time to study significant variables in the learning process, to see if the stimulus materials and apparatus produced control of attentional responses, to establish the feasibility of cumulative recording, and to note the sensitivity of the records, and so on.

For this purpose three 4-year-old children (two boys, one girl) were volunteered by their parents for the study. One of the children was dismissed from the study after 12 training sessions because her behavior tended to be injurious to the equipment. Each of the other subjects voluntarily participated in the forty 20-minute training sessions which were held five times a week for 8 weeks. During this time one subject made 1382 reading responses and the other made 1482 responses. The study indicated by the length and quality of the children's participation that the reinforcer system was effective. That is, although it is usually difficult to get preschool children to attend to a task and work arduously for long periods of time, when this behavior was reinforced as in the present study the behavior was well maintained. It should be remembered that voluntary participation in the training was in competition with free play since that is what the children would otherwise have been doing.

In addition, the apparatus for the presentation of the verbal stimuli, and the apparatus for recording the responses, appeared to function effectively. The child's moment to moment responding could in this way be recorded. Thus, the results for these children indicated that the various procedural developments were functional in producing a laboratory situation within which to study the complex human learning of reading discriminations. Long-term studies appeared to be possible, judging from the behavior of the two subjects in this particular experiment (Staats, et al., 1964b).

FIGURE 12.2. A photograph of the apparatus for the laboratory study of reading acquisition.

Although this study demonstrated the effectiveness of the use of the reinforcement system in maintaining arduous learning behavior of the children, it did not do so in an experimental fashion. That is, the reinforcement was not manipulated during the study to see the effect that its presence and absence would have on the behavior of the children. This would be necessary to more firmly show the importance of this variable in the original learning of small children.

Thus, the next step in the systematic analysis of reading was to use the laboratory facility to begin to assess variables important to the acquisition of reading. As part of this, also, there was the need to test the extent to which the facility was well enough controlled to be sensitive to the manipulation of important independent variables.

An important variable needing more systematic study concerns the schedule of reinforcement. Information from more basic studies indicates that certain schedules of reinforcement will produce better working behaviors than others. On a practical level of dealing with children's learning, can we improve the rate of response by reinforcement scheduling variables when complex learning is involved? Related to this is also a second goal of improving the reinforcer system. That is, it would be advisable to minimize the delivery of reinforcers to prevent satiation. Anything which postpones satiation can be considered to increase the effect of the reinforcer system, and intermittent reinforcement would do this by reducing reinforcer expenditure.

The next study, using additional children, was oriented towards these questions. Two different schedules of reinforcement were applied to each subject, and rates of response under each schedule were compared. The procedure was that of discrimination learning: the child was reinforced in one manner under one room-light condition, and in another manner under another room-light condition, in a manner which has been referred to as a multiple schedule. The principle of instrumental discrimination states that a response that is reinforced in the presence of a particular stimulus, and not in its absence, will come to be controlled by that stimulus. Thus, for example, it would be expected that if the child was reinforced for reading in the presence of one room-light condition, and not in the presence of another room-light condition, the first stimulus condition would come to control the reading behavior, whereas the second room-light condition would come to control "not-reading" behavior. In general, the discriminative stimulus of the room-light should come to control behavior that is appropriate to the reinforcement schedule that is in effect in the presence of that room-light stimulus.

The experiment that is to be reported was conducted with the help of Judson R. Finley, Karl A. Minke, and Montrose Wolf.[1]

Reinforcement Variables in the Control of Unit Reading Responses

Method

SUBJECTS Four 4-year-old children (three boys, one girl) who would be entering kindergarten at the Arizona State University Campus Laboratory School the following fall semester (1962) were volunteered for participation by their parents. The female S failed to exhibit the requisite

---

[1] For the complete study, see Arthur W. Staats, Judson R. Finley, Karl A. Minke, and Montrose Wolf. Reinforcement variables in the control of unit reading responses. *J. exp. anal. Behav.*, 1964, 7, 139–149.

behavior after the pretraining period and was replaced by a male S from the same population. The experimenter transported the children to and from the Language Learning Laboratory.

MATERIALS AND APPARATUS Each tube depicted in Figure 12.1 could hold a different number of marbles: 10, 35, 80, or 150. Above each tube a toy, which S had previously selected, was displayed. When the tube was filled, S received the toy above the tube. Toys were selected before the experimental session from four bins in another room. Each bin contained toys of approximately $0.10, $0.35, $0.80, or $1.50 value.

The automatic contingencies and recording were handled by standard operant conditioning apparatus. A Gerbrands cumulative recorder recorded S's responses, the delivery of a toy, and the operation of the Universal Feeder. Recorder's paper speed was 15 cm per hour and each response double-stepped the recording pen.

Occasionally, the automatic equipment would malfunction during a daily session, causing a brief interruption. At such times S was taken from the experimental chamber to a playroom containing a hobby-horse.

Procedure

The reading task was designed to insure that S said the name of a reading character while looking at it, the basic definition of a correct response. Since the reading characters were presented more than once, however, it was frequently possible in the reading task for S to look at the letter and say its name without waiting for the auditory prompt. This fits the basic response definition. Without requiring the matching and pressing responses, this response was also treated as correct, that is, the stimulus card was withdrawn, and if the schedule called for it, a marble reinforcer was delivered.

When an incorrect response occurred—either vocally or in matching the reading characters—a buzzer was rung and E presented the auditory stimulus which named the character. The S was then required to go through the complete chain of repeating and matching responses.

Thus, three different contingencies were possible. Naming the stimulus in the top window spontaneously resulted in immediate reinforcement. When he did not do this he was prompted to name the stimulus and complete the chain. Thirdly, an error required the S to return to the repeating phase of the chain and then to finish the chain correctly. In this way, only correct vocal responses while looking at the reading character were reinforced.

Before starting the reading task proper, each S received pretraining designed to establish the appropriate responses. A repeating task (consisting of single vowels and words) was presented initially, in which S was required to make a matching vocal response to the vowel or word spoken by E.

Then, 30 matching-to-sample cards, made up of line drawings of simple objects, were used to establish the chain of repeating, matching, and pressing responses described above. After this chain was established, S was instructed to "anticipate," if possible, the name of the picture in the upper window before E provided the verbal stimulus. Correct anticipations were immediately reinforced in the manner described above.

When S had learned to give picture responses without prompting, the reading task proper began and the matching-to-sample cards for the reading characters were presented. Two Ss displayed some breakdown in the response chain when the reading materials were introduced: occasional prompting of the appropriate chain behaviors was maintained for them for the first few sessions.

[Three types of schedules were employed, in different combinations. One schedule was continuous reinforcement for each response (CRF). Another was variable ratio (VR 6), which means the child was reinforced on a varying proportion of the reading responses he made with an average of one reinforcer for six responses. The third schedule was variable interval (VI 2). On this schedule the child was not reinforced for a varying interval of time after he had made his last response. But the first response after that interval was reinforced.]

During the pretraining phases, each correct response of the S was reinforced with presentation of a marble. From the time the actual reading task was introduced, however, each S was run under a different two-component multiple schedule involving nonreinforced responses. The four different multiple schedules were: CRF-EXT, CRF-VR, CRF-VI 2 minutes, and VR-VI 2 minutes. It was initially decided to begin the variable ratio at a VR 6, but as the experiment progressed it became obvious that the ratio was too high. Therefore, it was dropped to VR 2 and raised gradually to VR 6 only after the response rate became somewhat stable under VR 2.

The change of component under the multiple schedule was effected on a reinforcer-contingent basis for CRF and VR components, and on a time-contingent basis for VI and EXT components. The CRF component was in effect for 15 reinforcers, and the VR component for five. The VI schedule was in effect for 10 minutes and the extinction component for 5 minutes regardless of which component was in effect and regardless of the length of time that the component had been in effect. Each S was slated to run for 30 sessions.

Each component of a multiple schedule was correlated with an illumination condition in the experimental room. Under one condition both the light over the apparatus panel and the overhead room lights were on; under the other condition the overhead room light was off. All CRF conditions, as well as the VR component in the mult VR-VI condition, were correlated with the panel-light-only condition. The second component of the multiple schedule was correlated with the panel-plus-room-light condition. During pretraining, an intermediate light condition prevailed which consisted of the panel light and a wall light, but not the room light.

The S was allowed to consume the edibles obtained during the session or he could take them home. When one of the plastic tubes had been filled, the small bulb at the tube's base lighted momentarily, the bell rang and the light flashed in the marble dispenser. The cumulative recorder stopped, the toy was given to the child, and the marble tube was emptied. A new toy was then mounted above the tube, and the recorder started. The delivery of a back-up reinforcer was performed with minimal interaction between S and E. Before each day's experiment, S was taken to the toy room to select enough toys to replace those earned the previous day.

Results

CRF-EXT SUBJECT The daily session record is presented for this S (Figure 12.3), because the rate differences for the components are great enough to see clearly in single sessions. (This is not true for the multiple schedules used with the other Ss, and their daily session records are not presented.) For this S, the actual reading program was introduced at point A in Session 3. Records prior to this point represent performance on the various pretraining tasks. Point B notes the inadvertent reinforcement of a response in the first extinction component. Sessions 4–30 commenced with CRF conditions which then alternated with the EXT condition. At point C the first six responses under EXT were accidentally reinforced. The S was removed from the chamber during repairs, the recorder reset, and appropriate EXT conditions were presented to S. Point D indicates that in Session 18 each EXT component was only of 3 minutes, 20 seconds duration.

Figure 12.3 also shows the operation of the back-up reinforcer system for each session. The event marker on the line below each curve notes the occurrence of a back-up reinforcer: 1 indicates that a 10-cent toy was presented in exchange for 10 marbles, 0 marks the presentation of a 35-cent toy for 35 marbles, and unlettered event marks indicate that S deposited a marble for some items from the Universal Feeder. The record thus shows that S worked primarily for trinkets and edibles and

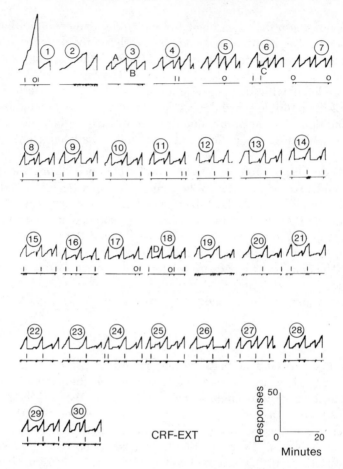

FIGURE 12.3.   The 30 daily session records for the mult CRF-EXT subject show the reading response rates for the various experimental conditions. Lettered points along the curves refer to procedural changes, some of which are described below and others in the results section. Responses prior to point A for this S occurred during the pretraining phases of the study. At this point the reading program was introduced under CRF. Beginning with Session 4 each 20-minute reading session commenced with a CRF component which then alternated with EXT conditions. The event marker on the line below each record indicates the delivery of a back-up reinforcer: I notes the exchange of 10 marbles for a $.10 toy, zero notes the presentation of a $.35 toy in exchange for 35 marbles, and unlettered event marks indicate the exchange of one marble for an item from the Universal Feeder. From A. W. Staats, J. R. Finley, K. A. Minke, and M. Wolfe. Reinforcement variables in the control of unit reading responses. *J. exp. Anal. Behav.*, 1964, **7**, 139–149.

for low value back-up toys which could be obtained with the marbles received during a single *CRF* component. In fact, *S* was often observed to place the first 10 marbles received under the *CRF* condition into the 10-cent tube and to use the remaining marbles for Universal Feeder items.

The record shows ·(Figure 12.3) that the response rate under the two components became somewhat differentiated in Session 6, with responding during *EXT* generally decreasing across sessions through Session 26. From Sessions 27–30 the *EXT* rate accelerated. An overall comparison of the effect of the differing contingencies is obtained when the records for the reading sessions are pieced together by components to give one continuous curve for each reinforcement schedule. This composite record, shown in Figure 12.4, indicates that the *EXT* rate slightly exceeded the *CRF* rate until A, at which point the curves crossed and separated at an ever-increasing pace. A good discrimination was achieved and the child's behavior came under the control of the light stimuli. Unlike the results from more basic studies, however, the child continued to respond to some extent under the "no reinforcement" light condition.

The *S* was presented with a total of 1608 reading trials in the experiment. Anticipation data for Session 23 is not available; data recorded for 1565 reading responses shows that 92.20 percent were anticipated, and 29.65 percent were anticipated correctly.

CRF-VR SUBJECT. In early sessions this *S* worked primarily for items from the Universal Feeder. Then he began to work toward a 150-marble toy and his response rate increased. Although the curves are not shown, it is interesting to note that a marked reduction in responding was evident in this *S*'s daily record after the delivery of this toy. This type of rate decline was also evident later when the *S* received an 80-marble toy. Overall, this *S* employed the Universal Feeder extensively until the last 10 sessions during which he shifted primarily to 10-cent toys.

The composite curves in Figure 12.5 show that in the early reading program sessions the two rates were almost identical, the *VR* rate beginning slightly below the *CRF* rate and crossing only at point A. From this point on a higher rate more appropriate to a *VR* schedule was obtained. *CRF* component responding remained relatively stable while *VR* component responding continued to increase across sessions.

By Session 19, *S*'s rate had risen to such an extent that *E* found it difficult to administer manually the reading program promptly in response to *S*'s initiation of each trial. This was especially evident during the *VR* component. It is possible that a greater difference between the *VR* and *CRF* rates would have been shown if the procedure had been

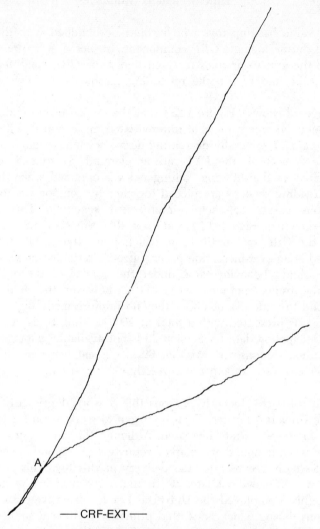

A

— CRF-EXT —

FIGURE 12.4. Composite record for the mult CRF-EXT subject. To compare an S's response rates for the two experimental conditions, the records for reinforcement schedules were separated and re-combined to yield an individual curve for each condition according to daily session sequence. All records commence with the introduction of the reading program. The composite records for the four Ss are directly comparable; however, the size of each record is determined by Ss response rate. The figure shows that for the mult CRF-EXT subject the EXT rate was initially higher, but at point A it declined and crossed the CRF curve. The CRF response rate was relatively rapid and stable throughout. From A. W. Staats, J. R. Finley, K. A. Minke, and M. Wolfe. Reinforcement variables in the control of unit reading response. *J. exp. Anal. Behav.* 1964, **7**, 139–149.

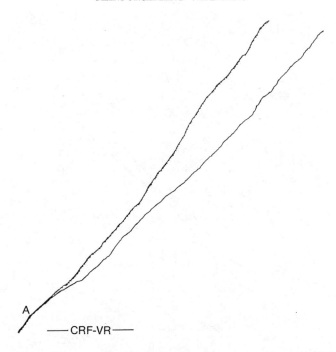

— CRF-VR —

FIGURE 12.5. Composite record for the mult CRF-VR subject.
The VR curve (shown with slash marks on the record) was initially
lower than the CRF curve. However, from point A the VR rate is
the more rapid. From A. W. Staats, J. R. Finley, K. A. Minke, and
M. Wolfe. Reinforcement variables in the control of unit reading
responses. *J. exp. Anal. Behav.* 1964, **7**, 139–149.

automated to a greater extent. In Session 29 the highest number of
responses emitted by any S in this procedure was obtained during a *VR*
component—92 reading trials in the 20-minute session.

The S was presented a total of 1519 reading trials during the experiment. Correct anticipation figures for Session 26 were not recorded;
however, an analysis shows that of 1476 reading trials, 46.14 percent
were anticipated, 43.36 percent correctly.

CRF-VI SUBJECT. Figure 12.6 presents the composite curves, indicating the rate differences that developed between the two schedules.
Responding during *VI* components remained essentially at a stable rate
throughout—which was initially higher than under *CRF*. The rate under
CRF accelerated after the first quarter of the curve, at which point the
CRF rate was higher than the *VI*. The rates were retained in this
relationship and at a point A the cumulative records crossed with the

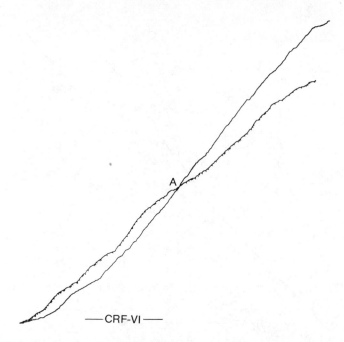

FIGURE 12.6. Composite record for the mult CRF-VI subject. The VI curve (with slash marks) is depicted above the CRF curve until point A on the record, at which point it becomes the lower. From A. W. Staats, J. R. Finley, K. A. Minke, and M. Wolfe. Reinforcement variables in the control of unit reading responses. *J. exp. Anal. Behav.*, 1964, **7**, 139–149.

CRF, retaining the lead thereafter. Data for Sessions 17–19 do not appear on this record. A special procedure was used during that period to extinguish a "random pecking" type of behavior which had developed.

During the initial session S deposited all his marbles for Universal Feeder items. In subsequent sessions S used only the tube system. This S worked from Session 2 until the latter part of Session 7 without a single back-up reinforcer, and then until Session 10 before receiving another. Response rate decreased after each toy was earned. The value of the back-up toys earned decreased systematically as the sessions progressed; that is, S first deposited his marbles for the highest value toy, then for lesser value toys, and finally only for 10-cent toys.

A total of 1234 reading trials were presented during the experiment, 22.93 percent of which were anticipated correctly. Data for anticipatory behavior for Sessions 17–30 is not comparable to that of Sessions 3–16 due to the special contingency initiated in Session 17. However, in

Sessions 3–16, 581 reading trials occurred, 75.39 percent of which were anticipated, and 24.96 percent were anticipated correctly.

VR-VI SUBJECT. The composite curves in Figure 12.7 show that response rates for the components were essentially parallel, the VI curve beginning lower than VR until point A, then crossing and remaining above the VR curve until point B, where the VI rate declines slightly. Thus, differential responding was not controlled by the multiple schedule for this S.

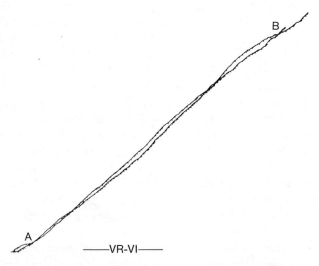

FIGURE 12.7. Composite record for the VR-VI subject. The VI curve begins lower than the VR curve until point A, then crosses and remains above the VR curve until point B, at which point the VI rate declines. From A. W. Staats, J. R. Finley, K. A. Minke, and M. Wolfe. Reinforcement variables in the control of unit reading responses. *J. exp. Anal. Behav.*, 1964, **7**, 139–149.

The S received relatively few reinforcers for reading program sessions during the experiment—an average of 11.40 per session (excluding Sessions 6 and 7). Numbers varied from only 1 in Session 4 to 16 in several later sessions. The S worked initially for an 80-cent toy, the receipt of which in Session 9 produced a decline in response rate. He then obtained a number of 35-cent toys. In Session 23, S shifted to Universal Feeder items and the overall rate gradually dropped, accelerating again in the final two sessions during which S employed the 10-cent tube.

Anticipatory behavior was extremely weak for this S, only seven such responses occurring even in pretraining. Half of the anticipations to reading material were emitted in Sessions 3–9. Most of the remainder occurred only after prompting by E, even though S sometimes declared his intention to say them ahead of E. Only 1066 reading trials were presented during the experiment, the absence of anticipatory responding requiring the 10-second delay period on most trials. Of the total responses, 3.56 percent were anticipated, 2.81 percent correctly.

Discussion

Several general implications are indicated by the results. First, the principles and techniques of operant conditioning apparently can be extended to the study of significant complex human behaviors—specifically, to the acquisition of reading. The multiple schedule design proved valuable for the study of individual schedule effects and the results were generally as expected on the basis of previous work with animals (for example, Ferster and Skinner, 1957). However, the differences in rate produced by the different schedules were not as great as those obtainable in more basic animal studies. This might be expected on the basis of the type of behavior under study. Rather than a quick and easy bar-press, knob-pull, or pecking response, the present procedure required close discriminations which had to control a chain of motor responses and a class of vocal responses. In addition, this "response" did not take place instantaneously but required more time than is usual. These factors would be expected to dampen the effect of different reinforcement schedules, for example, in a ratio schedule higher rate "bursts" of responses could not attain startlingly more immediate reinforcement because the responses themselves required so much time.

Nevertheless, in each case where a CRF schedule was used as the comparison schedule, the appropriate results occurred. When the opposed schedule was EXT, the discrimination was rapidly acquired and the greatest difference between component schedules of all Ss was evidenced. Under the CRF-VI schedule the VI component did not produce as high a rate of response as did the CRF. For the CRF-VR subject, on the other hand, the VR schedule produced a rate of response higher than that produced by the CRF.

Only the VR-VI schedule did not produce the expected results—and that appeared to be an artifact of the experimental procedure; that is, when an S did not anticipate there was a 10-second delay period for the trial. Thus, an S who consistently failed to anticipate could attain only the rate limited by this delay procedure, which was the case with VR-VI subject. Both components of this schedule appeared to maintain the S's behavior at a maximum rate, within the limitation imposed by the lack of anticipation responses. This conclusion is supported by a comparison to an S from the previous study who also did not anticipate. The S in the present study averaged 42.4 responses per training session, whereas the S in the previous study, under CRF conditions throughout, averaged 38.7 responses per session. Thus, it is quite possible that under a procedure where the rate is not limited by the 10-second delay, the expected differences between VR and VI schedules could be obtained, for example, it would be possible for a VR schedule to result in the customary more rapid rate of response.

It is also of interest to note that this experiment included conditions which represent one of the few attempts to apply a VR schedule to human behavior. Sidman (1962) states that "Orlando and Bijou (1962) are the only investigators who have reported on this schedule and their work was with developmentally retarded children" (p. 184) [and simple responses]. Salzinger, et al. (1962), have more recently reported an experiment in which speech rate in normal children was subjected to such a schedule.

Although there are improvements to be made in the procedure, and the qualifications already noted, the results of this study indicate that the general procedure and apparatus provide enough experimental control so that the dependent variable (acquisition of reading responses) is sensitive to the manipulation of important independent variables. This suggests that these developments may be extended to the study of a number of types of significant behavior acquisitions, such as, speech learning, arithmetic learning, and so forth and to various special populations, such as deaf children, mutes, mental retardates, and so forth. Much instrumental research with humans has tended to involve only simple responses such as knob-pulling and button-pressing, and simple controlling stimuli. The present facility would seem to be useful in the study of the acquisition of complex responses of more immediate significance to human adjustment. This could also involve work which had remedial objectives, such as, remedial reading problems, the training of autistic children, general training problems in children resulting from deficient "motivation."

As this discussion implies, in addition to studying the principles of general psychology in the context of this particular type of behavior, other goals of the project are the study of reading itself and the study of child learning in general. Thus, the project is interested in developing an experimental situation which maximizes behavior acquisition, a primary aspect of which is the development of the most efficacious reinforcement system. As noted by other investigators (see Long, et al., 1958) it has been difficult to develop a reinforcer system which both maintains children's behavior well and is durable, that is, does not weaken over time. The present reinforcement procedure appears to have solved this problem, but a great deal of study remains in order to maximize the procedure. What is desired is a reinforcement system which will (1) produce maximal rates, and (2) minimize the expenditure of reinforcers. The last stipulation involves both economy as well as the consideration that the fewer reinforcers given, the longer it will take the S to satiate on the available reinforcers.

The experimental results which have so far emerged from the laboratory study of reading acquisition have implications for these problems. That is, a number of Ss have been run under various schedules, both single and multiple. The results are interesting for their effects upon the average overall rates of behavior produced per session, and for the cost in reinforcers in producing these rates. These effects can be seen by comparing the rates, reinforcers, and so on, of the multiple schedule Ss to each other, as well as to the results of Ss run in the previous experiment which utilized strictly CRF conditions. These various results are shown in Table 12.1.

As can be seen, the highest average rate per session was produced under CRF-EXT; the next highest, in order, were CRF-VR, CRF-VI, VR-VI, and then the CRF subjects. On the other hand, the VR-VI schedule involved the least expenditure of reinforcers. The CRF-VI and CRF-VR schedules involved about an equal frequency of reinforcement and yet the rates produced were higher for the latter, as would be expected. While the CRF-EXT schedule produced the highest average number of responses per session, the percentage of reinforcement for the responses was also high. Nevertheless, it is interesting to note that the highest CRF rate of any S (including the straight CRF subjects) was produced when this schedule was paired with extinction. This finding would be expected from Reynolds' (1961a, 1961b) study of the relationship of reinforcement frequency and behavioral contrast.

These data and the comparisons must be considered to be tentative since, as a consequence of the experimental procedure, rate was not independent of the number of anticipations S made. An anticipation, correct or incorrect, obviated the 10-second delay period. Thus, Ss who made many anticipations were afforded the opportunity of moving more rapidly. It is also true that any individual differences in rates were not controlled in these comparisons, since only one S was run under each multiple schedule. Nevertheless, in broad outline, the results seem to contain some information. For example, the three CRF subjects appeared to produce highly similar rates. In addition, the results indicate that the multiple schedules which involve intermittent reinforcement generally produced higher rates for less expenditure of reinforcers than

TABLE 12.1

COMPARISON OF PERFORMANCE OF SUBJECTS RUN UNDER DIFFERENT SCHEDULES OF REINFORCEMENT*

| Subject | SESSIONS | | Total Responses | Average Responses/ Session | Average Tokens/ Session | Average Responses/ Token | % Responses Reinforced | % Total Anticipations | % Correct Anticipations |
	Whole Days on Reading	Total for Computations							
CRF #1	4-11	8	294	36.7	36.7	1.00	100	76.4	40.5
CRF #2	3-40	38	1473	38.7	38.7	1.00	100	2.3	2.1
CRF #3	3-40	38	1305	34.5	34.5	1.00	100	47.4	45.3
CRF-EXT	4-30 less session 23	26	1530	58.8	44.5	1.32	75.6	94.0	30.1
CRF-VR	5-30	26	1394	53.6	34.5	1.56	64.3	50.0**	46.9**
CRF-VI	4-30 less sessions 17-19	24	1075	44.8	29.3	1.53	65.4	75.7***	25.0***
VR-VI	4-30 less sessions 6-7	25	1060	42.4	11.4	3.72	26.9	3.6	2.8

* Results of seven Ss run in the laboratory facility. Subjects CRF #1, #2, and #3 were employed in a procedure comparable to the present study, but were administered only continuous reinforcement conditions (see Staats, Minke, Finley, Wolf, and Brooks, 1964b). Computations are based on full-length reading sessions; sessions omitted include pretraining phases, major deviations from normal procedure, or sessions for which complete data were unavailable.
** Session 26 omitted.
*** Sessions 17-30 omitted.

did *CRF*—a very important finding in this situation for both practical and scientific purposes.

As Herrnstein and Brady (1958) point out, the effects of schedules upon behavior can be studied in a short time through the use of multiple schedules. However, there appears to be an interaction between the components of a multiple schedule (see also Reynolds, 1961*a*, 1961*b*). This is a limiting factor in generalizing the effects of a component in a multiple schedule to its effects in isolation. As a consequence, there has been interest in studying the effects of interaction on the individual component. However, the effects of interaction upon the overall rates produced under multiple schedules (as well as other types of combinations) have not yet been systematically studied. (See Herrick, *et al.*, 1959, for an indication that overall rates of response under an ^{D}S-$^\Delta$S multiple schedule may be greater than under *CRF*.) The tentative suggestion which has emerged from the laboratory study of reading acquisition to date is that multiple schedules can also have significance in terms of maximizing rates of response produced in the individual components and thus result in higher overall rates. At the same time, multiple schedules may also offer the possibility to reduce the expenditure of reinforcers. This is important in the study of human learning, where the reinforcer system may be a problem.

Extensions to Educable and Trainable
Retarded Children

Following the development and test of the apparatus, principles, and procedures in the preceding study, another study was conducted using retarded children as the subjects. This was done with two major purposes in mind. First, the study was conducted to begin the exploration of the learning of retarded children on a long-term learning task that was of the type that is important to normal cognitive development. The fact is that we do not know what retarded children are capable of learning because such research has not been conducted. We do not know what, if any, are the special learning deficits of retarded children. Until we have conducted such research we cannot readily say whether the deficits in cognitive skills that we observe in retarded children are due to unfortunate environmental (training) circumstances, or due to some personal defect.

It is also the case that we need further development in laboratory research methods with which to work with children over long periods of time, engaged in complex cognitive tasks that are representative of those the child faces in everyday life. And we need to make detailed, systematic, objective, observations and records of the process. This section will summarize some of the findings of a study with retarded children which provide information relevant to these points. The research was conducted under the direction of the author by William G. Heard, as part of his doctoral dissertation.

Methods

The same laboratory apparatus was used as that described in the preceding study. It will be recalled that the child in the reading discrimination task did several things. He was free to simply sit in the room. There was nothing that compelled him to engage in the learning task, and when reinforcement was not forthcoming the child's rate of engaging in and completing reading discriminations was low. The reading discrimination task began, however, when the child pressed the button which resulted in the presentation of the reading stimulus. The child then had to repeat the name of the reading stimulus and perform the sensory and motor tasks involved in making the reading discrimination. Or, if he had already learned the name, he had to say it and press the cover of the window. This sequence took a certain amount of time— and this was the time actually involved in making the reading discrimination. This period was of course susceptible to a good deal of variation depending upon how difficult the reading discriminations were for the child.

Once the reading discrimination had taken place, however, a marble was delivered. The child could use the marble to obtain (or work for) any one of the types of reinforcers that has been described. There was also a certain amount of time which was involved in securing the marble and depositing it, receiving the reinforcer, consuming it, or putting it away. In the present study this sequence and the time involved was made more explicit in the following way. To the right of the child, under the plastic tubes, a box was arranged that operated automatically. When a marble was delivered, the lid of the box opened and it remained open until the child deposited his marble, received his reinforcer, and put it away in the box (or ate it if it was an edible). Then the child could close the box lid and this act constituted the end of the period during which the child was occupied with the reinforcers. This period was also susceptible to a good deal of variation depending upon how long the child spent with the reinforcer before putting it away and closing the box lid.

After closing the lid of the box the child was free to sit and do nothing, to perform some irrelevant behavior, or to press the button which would bring on another reading stimulus and make possible responses that would lead to another reinforcer. Thus, there was a specific period of time during which any responses that were competing with the reading responses could occur. This period was also susceptible to variation depending upon how strong the reading behavior was in comparison to other "fooling around" behaviors.

Since there was a specific event that began (and ended) each of these periods it was possible to measure the amount of time spent by each subject in each activity—over the training sessions in which the child participated. The record then indicates how much time the child spent (1) in the reading trials, (2) in time with the reinforcers, (3) in emitting nonreading responses that competed with the reading. These results were an important part of the data of the study.

Subjects

Six noninstitutionalized mentally retarded children who were in special classes were volunteered by their parents as subjects. The children had no reading skills or special emotional problems, according to their teachers. One educable retardate was a Negro girl of 9 years and 7 months of age. She came from obviously culturally-deprived circumstances. Her IQ was 67 (all IQs except one were Stanford-Binets) and her MA was 6 years and 5 months. The other educable retardate was a Negro boy of 9 years and 5 months, IQ 65, MA 6-1.

The other 4 children were white, two displaying no physical abnormalities, and two displaying the physical characteristics of mongoloidism. Of the first two, one was a girl who had an IQ of 50, and MA of 5-4, and was 10 years and 8 months of age. The other was a boy who had an IQ of 45, an MA of 3-11 (Wechsler Intelligence Scale for Children), and was 8 years and 8 months of age. Of the mongoloid children, one was a white girl with an IQ of 52, an MA of 3-9, and was 7 years and 3 months old. The other mongoloid child was a white boy, age 9, with an IQ of 36 and an MA of 3-2.

Results and Conclusions

Not all of the results can be presented here. A summary can be made, however, and the data for some of the subjects can be shown in more detail.

As described in the preceding study the reading discriminations required in the task were quite difficult, more difficult than those required with the usual alphabet. That is, the child not only had to discriminate letters from each other, but in addition, had to discriminate a letter with one diacritical mark from the same letter with another diacritical mark, and also from a different letter with the same diacritical mark. Thus, both diacritical mark and letter had to be discriminated.

Now it has been suggested that one of the differences between normal and retarded children may lie in their ability to make sensory discriminations (see House and Zeaman, 1960). In the context of cognitive learning an important question arises concerning whether retarded children are capable of the complex visual discriminations involved in learning to read, to count, to write, and so on. The present results bear importantly upon these questions.

The results for the first two educable retardates showed that they performed very well in the complex task. They came to make the reading discriminations with ease. They attended well and worked hard. In both cases, their cumulative records as well as the records of the amount of time spent in the three different phases of the task showed this clearly. That is, relatively little time was spent in making the reading discriminations, little unnecessary time was spent with the reinforcers, and practically no time was spent in competing behaviors—the children went right to the next reading trial after putting the reinforcer away.

The child with the IQ of 67 emitted 2,466 correct responses, 2,224 of which were reading responses. Of these, 22 per cent were unprompted reading responses. The other child with the IQ of 65 emitted 2,143 correct responses, of which 1,831 were reading responses. Of these, about 16 percent were unprompted reading responses. Both children's performance was more rapid than that of the normal, but younger, children in the previous studies. On the other hand, it took longer to train the retarded children in the complex sequence of responses involved in the discrimination task. It required 4 and 5 sessions, respectively, for the two retarded subjects to learn the sequence of attentional, verbal, motor, and discrimination responses involved in the task. The younger children customarily required only 2 sessions.

One of the difficult points in the training to use the apparatus came at the introduction of the letter-diacritical mark discriminations, although there were also other difficult points. With normal children, and with the educable retardates, it was possible to introduce these tasks with the liberal use of verbal instructions. Changes were introduced in the pre-training procedures and materials to make the training less difficult for the trainable retardates. A more detailed description of procedures used to train these children to make the complex reading discriminations will be presented, along with the results of one of the children. The subject was the child with the IQ of 50. The description of the material will refer to the points on the child's cumulative record where the procedures were introduced (see Figure 12.8). In this way it is possible to see how the child was responding during the various tasks and the effect that the introduction of a new procedure has upon the child's responding.

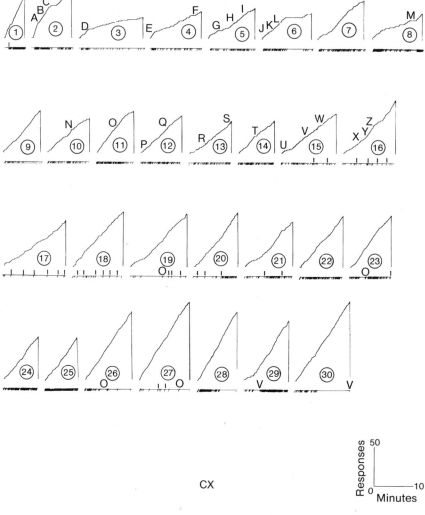

FIGURE 12.8.   Cumulative record of the daily reading sessions of CX.

Thus, whether or not the step in the training program is too difficult, for example, may be seen from the way that it affects the child's rate of responding.

In the new procedure the button press was first introduced as part of the vocal imitation task, at point A. Thus, the child had to press the doorbell to get the experimenter to say the next word. In addition, when the experimenter said the word the empty standard stimulus window was illuminated, and when the child repeated the word that illumination was brightened and then the child was reinforced. At point B a picture was introduced into the standard stimulus window and the child had to name it. At point C the child then had to press the cover of the window. At point D the matching picture stimulus was introduced into one of the bottom windows. Only this bottom window was illuminated, the other two were dark and blank. As the record shows, the child's rate of response decreases as each new task is added, especially the task of responding a second time to the matching picture. At the beginning of the next session the procedure was returned to the previous phase and at E the matching picture was again introduced and the child began naming the picture. At F the child named the picture and then pressed the window cover. At point G illumination was introduced in another one of the bottom windows but it was left blank. Even this constituted a discrimination of some difficulty for the child as the response rate shows. At point H the second foil window was illuminated. The first foil picture was introduced at I, but was withdrawn from the procedure when the child experienced difficulty and was not re-introduced until point J. At this time the child experienced no great difficulty and at K the second foil picture was introduced. The transition at this point was also smooth and occasioned no decrease in response rate. It should be noted here that the child now had the full chain of attentional, motor, verbal, and discrimination responses required.

However, at point L the general procedure to introduce the phonetic reading material was commenced and a few trials later the first phonetic reading symbol was presented. This was the procedure that had been developed for the normal children and used with the educable retardates. As can be seen from the record, the introduction of the phonetic symbol discriminations resulted in the disruption of the chain of responses the child had acquired and the response rate fell off sharply. The introduction of the phonetic reading characters so abruptly was too large a step, and it was necessary to return to the picture matching task. This was continued through Session 9. As can be seen, the child's response rate began increasing, with the exception of a period at M where the child began jumping ahead in the chain of responses. Training on this chain was continued until it was again well acquired.

This evidence given by the cumulative records thus indicated a source of difficulty with the training materials at the point of introduction of the phonetic symbols. On this basis, new materials were designed with which to more gradually introduce the characters. The new materials first presented the diacritical marks in the familiar picture matching task. Once

FIGURE 12.9. Samples of the cards designed to gradually train the trainable retardates to discriminate the phonetic symbols (letter-diacritical mark combinations).

discriminations on the basis of the diacritical marks had been established in this context, the diacritical marks were presented with vowel and vowel-consonant letter stimuli. The introduction of the various materials took place in 12 steps. The new material in each step was gradually worked in among discriminations the child had already acquired, until at the end of the step the child would be working entirely in the new material for the step.

The first step, introduced at point N, included 27 picture discrimination cards with 9 of these displaying matching diacritical marks over the standard picture and its matching picture (the diacritical marks were unnecessary to the discrimination). At point O the next step consisted of 9 simple picture discrimination cards, 9 cards with diacritical marks and pictures, and a new set of 9 cards which had a foil that differed from the matching card only in not containing the diacritical mark (see Figure 12.9a). Thus, a discrimination on the basis of presence or absence of diacritical mark was required. At point P the next step included cards from the previous two steps, plus 9 cards in which there were two foil pictures in the bottom windows which differed from the matching stimulus only by the absence of the diacritical mark. This type of discrimination card is shown in Figure 12.9b.

The following steps continued the practice of including 9 cards from each of the two preceding steps as well as 9 new cards. Thus, at point Q the new cards had two picture foils each of which contained the same diacritical mark (Figure 12.9c). This mark was different from that on the matching stimulus, and thus the discrimination had to be made upon the basis of the difference in diacritical marks. The new cards introduced at point R included discriminations in which each foil had a different diacritical mark which was different in turn from that in the matching stimulus (Figure 12.9d).

At point S letter-diacritical mark stimuli were introduced as one foil. The child was told that the phonetic symbol had a name, like a picture had, and the sound was given and echoed by the child. At point T the phonetic letter symbol was used as the standard and matching stimuli, with pictures as foils (Figure 12.9e). At point U the phonetic letter stimulus had to be discriminated from another phonetic stimulus that differed only in having a different diacritical mark, as shown in Figure 12.10a. At point V there were two identical phonetic stimuli as foils that differed from the matching stimulus only on the basis of their diacritical mark, as shown in Figure 12.10b. At point W one of the phonetic letter foils had a different diacritical mark than the matching stimulus, and the other foil was composed of a consonant-vowel combination, rather than the single letters that had been previously used, as is shown in

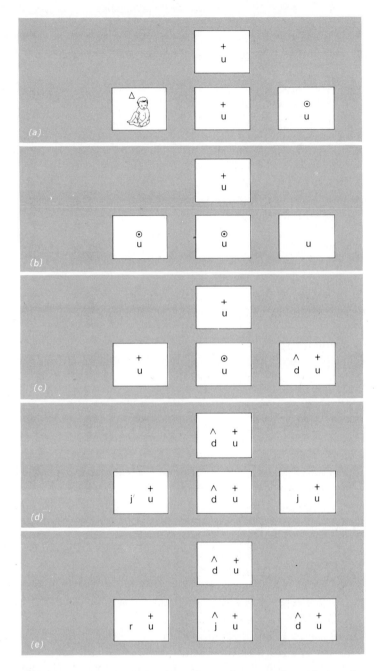

FIGURE 12.10. Additional cards in the procedure designed to gradually train the trainable retardates to discriminate the phonetic symbols (lettered-diacritical mark combinations).

Figure 12.10c. At the point commencing Session 16 the standard and matching stimuli were composed of consonant-vowel combinations, each having its separate diacritical mark, and the foils were consonant-vowel phonetic stimuli like each other and different from the matching stimulus (Figure 12.10d). At point X each of the foils was a consonant-vowel combination different from the matching stimulus combination, and different from each other (Figure 12.10e). As can be seen, difficult discriminations were involved.

Finally, at point Y the child was presented with cards designed to train anticipation responses—without waiting for the experimenter to name the phonetic stimulus. For this purpose 11 cards were selected from those that had already been presented to the child. At point Z the phonetic reading program proper was commenced.

As can be seen from the cumulative record for this S, none of the points of introduction of these new materials resulted in disruption of the chain of behaviors that had previously been established, illustrating that proper procedures for introducing the discriminations removed the point of difficulty and this was reflected in the cumulative record. In fact only in two cases, at points T and U, is there much of a decrease in rate of response. During this period of the introduction of the various stimulus materials responding was maintained at a moderate rate of response with fair consistency. Nevertheless, further practice makes the reading discriminations less difficult for the child.

After entering the reading program proper in Session 16, the child's rate of responding shows a gradual increase through the next 14 sessions. The rate of response in the last 7 sessions is consistently high, almost attaining the high rates produced by the two educable retardates.

The additional information obtainable by the several measures of performance shown in the histograms is clear for this child, as is shown in Figure 12.11. As can be seen this child spent relatively little time between trials almost from the beginning of the training. It is interesting, however, that as the training progressed less and less time was spent between trials—as the task becomes less difficult the reading behavior becomes stronger and competitive behaviors less dominant. At the end this trainable retardate wasted as little time between trials as the two hardworking educable retardates—although taking longer to develop such good work habits.

These findings are paralleled by the results for *Reading Trial Time*. This child took somewhat longer than the educable retardates in performing the response task at first, but improved so that at the end of training he was making the discriminations involved in the reading program about as rapidly as they did. It is interesting to note that this child's results

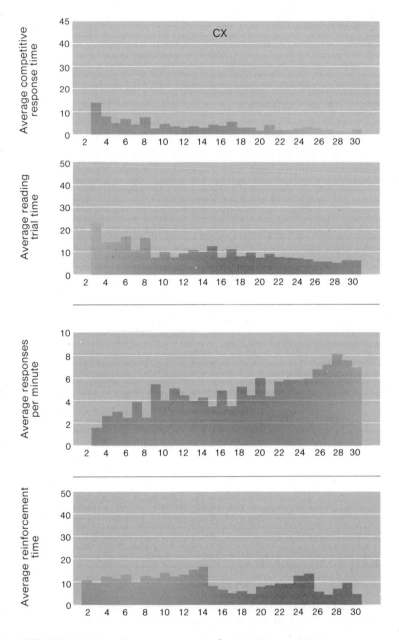

FIGURE 12.11.   Response rate and intra-session time measures given by sessions, for CX. Time measure given in seconds.

show an increase in *Reading Trial Time* in Session 6 where the phonetic symbols were first introduced. Except for the upward fluctuation that occurred in Session 8, as a result of jumping ahead in the response sequence, the *Reading Trial Time* decreased slightly until the introduction of the diacritical marks in Session 11. From this point there was slightly more time spent in *Reading Trial Time,* presumably due to the more difficult discriminations required. However, after a few sessions the *Reading Trial Time* returned to its former level and then gradually decreased as the child became more proficient in making such discrimination. Again, the work habits of this child appeared to be very good, the variance appeared to be due to the difficulty of the discriminations, with little pausing or playing around within the reading trials.

The average number of responses made by this subject per minute also increased over the training sessions as was also shown by cumulative record. In the later sessions the rate of response was comparable to the rates produced by the educable retardates. The child appeared to spend more time "consuming" the reinforcers than either of the educable retardates, but less than the other trainable retardates. Nevertheless, there was a decrease in *Reinforcement Time* over the training, an occurrence that is related to the use of the reinforcer system. During the first 15 sessions when *Reinforcement Time* was high, this S used the Universal Feeder exclusively. Across the remainder of the study this child alternated between the Universal Feeder and the toy tubes. In Sessions 21–25 the Universal Feeder was used almost exclusively, and again there was a higher *Reinforcement Time.* This child used the reinforcer system through the \$.80 toys, obtaining the second toy of this value before the end of training.

This child made 1,698 responses, of which 1,020 were correct reading responses. Twenty per cent of the reading responses were made without prompting.

One other child's records will be presented so that the possible differences in behavior can be seen. This child was the mongoloid retardate with the IQ of 52. Figure 12.12 presents her daily cumulative records. The records show the effects of introducing new components of the response sequence. New additions resulted in lessening the response rate in this child, and this appeared to be progressive up to the ninth session (except in Session 5 where there was a temporary return to an easier level), when the child had finally acquired the whole complex sequence and no further components were introduced. In addition to the low rate, long pauses appeared in the record.

As the record also shows, by the point where the diacritical mark material began to be introduced in Session 11, the child's response rate

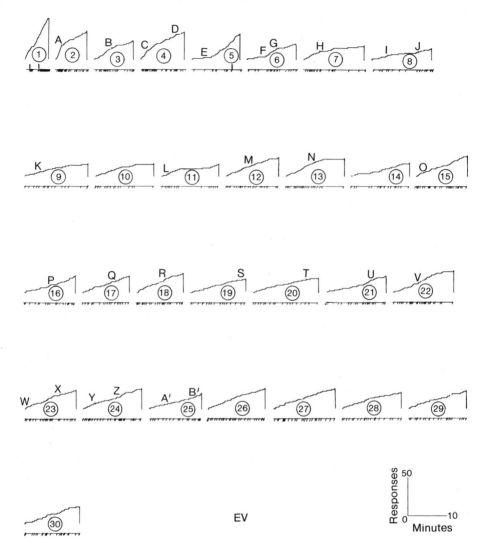

FIGURE 12.12. Cumulative record of the daily sessions of EV.

was very low and her behavior was interrupted by long pauses during which no reading responses occurred. However, the pausing dropped out by the end of Session 14, and over all there appeared to be a gradual increase of rate throughout the remaining sessions with the exception of a slow down in Sessions 19, 20, and 21. This indicated, again, that the new materials for the introduction of the phonetic symbols did not involve especially difficult steps, but that the task was generally difficult for this child. On the other hand, the slow-down in Sessions 19, 20, and 21 coincided with the introduction of the phonetic symbols themselves and this indicated that the introduction of this material constituted a more difficult learning task for this child.

This suggestion is shown more clearly in the histogram data of Figure 12.13 which breaks down the time the S spent in the different activities. Figure 12.13 indicates that the response rate of this subject as shown by average responses per minute tended to increase after Session 9, after the child had learned the whole response sequence. However, the rate was very low throughout. This child and the trainable retardate with the IQ of 45 had the highest *Competitive Response Time* of the various children. This indicates, of course, poor work habits with much time spent between trials in irrelevant behaviors.

On the whole, however, relatively more time is spent within trials. The results of this measure support the indications given by the daily session record. That is, *Reading Trial Time* increased with the addition of the various responses in the sequence required by the discrimination task. From the point where all of these responses had been acquired in sequence, Session 9, *Reading Trial Time* tended to show a decrease. This measure also shows the difficulty the child had with the discrimination of the phonetic symbols, giving greater specificity than the cumulative record. That is, the introduction of the discriminations between phonetic symbols on the basis of different diacritical marks constituted a difficult discrimination for this S. As a result there was an increase in *Reading Trial Time* in Session 19, where the standard stimulus was a letter with a diacritical mark and one of the two foils was the same letter with another diacritical mark (the other foil being a picture). In Session 20 both foils consisted of the letter with the same diacritical mark which was different than that of the standard stimulus. Again these discriminations were shown to be difficult for the child by the high *Reading Trial Time*. In Session 21 the two foils were different phonetic symbols and had the same effect. It is interesting to note here that the difficulty in the discrimination task had an effect upon the child's *Competitive Response Time* also. That is, when the discriminations became difficult, *Reading Trial Time* increased, but in addition, the S took longer in making the response necessary to bring on the next card.

Inspection of the results of the present child suggests that this child has not had a history of being presented with complex, effortful tasks, and of being reinforced for working at such tasks. Her record indicates, however, that the reinforcer system was effective and suggests that her response rate would have continued to improve in the experimental situation. This suggestion is gained from the fact that the child's rate goes down gradually as she is required to add new components to the complex response sequence of the task. However, after acquiring the sequence, the response rate showed a gradual increase (with the exception of 3 sessions) throughout the rest of the sessions, even though new types of discriminations were demanded.

In general, the picture for this child is one of very low response rate, with much time spent with the reinforcers, and with irrelevant behaviors both within and between trials. The work and attentional behaviors of this child were very poor. It would have been interesting to have continued this child for a greater number of sessions after entering the phonetic reading program proper. Since no new types of response had to be learned, and no behavioral disruptions thus caused, the rate of response might have increased. More reinforcement would thus have been forthcoming, with less effort expenditure—a situation likely to boost response rate—and the child's behavior could well have come under better control of the reinforcement system. A consequent lessening in irrelevant behaviors would then be expected. However, these possibilities will have to await future studies.

This child earned only three $.10 toys (given for only 5 marbles for this child) during the study, the remainder of the marbles being deposited for Universal Feeder items. As shown in Figure 12.13, the average reinforcement time for each session tended to decrease slightly over the training, another indication of the progressive strengthening of the reading behavior.

This S responded 676 times during the study with 113 reading responses, 15 percent of which were correct anticipations.

The trainable retardate with the IQ of 45 performed in a manner that was very similar to the performance of the preceding child. His rate of response became very low as the various aspects of the task were introduced—26 training sessions were required before the child could fully perform the complex sequence in the task and make the difficult reading discriminations. Over the 30 training sessions he completed only 651 responses, of which 99 were reading discrimination responses involving the letters and diacritical marks. Of these 22 percent were correct reading responses which required no prompting.

The last child to be described presented an entirely different circumstance. This child had such a meager repertoire of cognitive skills that the procedures used to train the other children in the task would not suffice. The child could not perform the picture naming task, for example. The mother of the child and his former school teacher were contacted and questioned with respect to the child's verbal repertoire. It was found

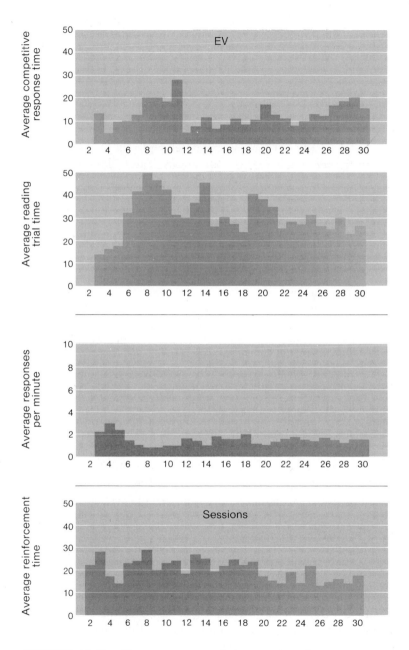

FIGURE 12.13. Response rate and intra-session time measures given by sessions, for EV. Time measures given in seconds.

that the child would never spontaneously name objects. His verbal repertoire consisted of two or three vocal responses, indicating he wanted something, which only his mother could understand, and approximately 15 object words which the child would repeat when prompted by his mother. There was no evidence that he could name pictures.

Ten of these 15 word responses were selected for use in the construction of special materials for work with this child. Pictures were made up of the objects, and the child received training in naming the pictures. The pictures (a cat, cup, television set, car, block, apple, dog, pie, loaf of bread, and a telephone) were alternately displayed in the standard procedure in the top window of the apparatus. The child would at first not respond to a picture spontaneously, emitting only one of his stereotyped vocal responses. However, when the experimenter gave the name of the picture, the child would repeat the word. Later the experimenter gradually began dropping these prompts, saying only "Guess its name," while pointing to the picture. In subsequent trials both the verbal and pointing prompts of the experimenter were gradually removed from the procedure until the child would spontaneously name the picture as it appeared in the window.

This picture naming repertoire was then employed in training the child to the complex response chain involved in performing the picture matching task. Twelve training sessions were involved in training the child to name pictures and later to go through the sequence of naming the picture, pressing the plastic cover of the window, selecting the picture in the window below that matched the top picture, saying the name again, pressing the plastic cover of the window, and also in the use of the reinforcer system. During this time the child's response rate grew steadily less each time a new step was introduced in the task. However, at this time no new steps were introduced into the task for 5 additional sessions —and the child's response rate steadily increased back to a high rate of response. He had mastered the matching task with pictures.

At this point the procedure to introduce the phonetic symbols was used, with no success. In Session 27 it was decided to first establish discriminations to the diacritical marks, made in a larger size. By Session 30 he had been trained to correctly name and discriminate the several diacritical marks used. Following this, the diacritical marks were combined with larger sized letters—the resulting characters were about a half inch in size. The introduction of these letter-diacritical mark symbols was done gradually and by the end of training (37 sessions) the child was making the same type of reading discriminations as the other children, albeit with larger stimuli. This child had an IQ of 36.

During the training the child emitted 1,465 responses, of which 32 were reading discrimination responses. The child's work behaviors were very good, with little time spent between reading trials, although a good deal of time was spent with the reinforcers. His rate of response was directly related to the difficulty of the task. When his time per trial went up his rate of response went down. Over the period of the study, and after he had acquired the matching task behaviors, he showed an increasing response rate except when difficult discriminations were introduced.

One of the important findings of the present study with the various retarded children was the indication that the ability of such children to discriminate letter stimuli will not constitute an obstacle in learning to read—with either a standard or a phonetic alphabet. The question arises in the context of these results why retardates have shown less than normal abilities in discrimination. It may be suggested that such findings are an artifact, arising because the retardate does not respond to the general features of the task as normal subjects do. (This suggestion could also be applied to other special populations of subjects, for example, psychotic subjects.) Thus, although all the children in the present study could make the complex discriminations, they came to the task with varying degrees of skill in several aspects; for example, in the extent to which the children had a repertoire of verbal stimuli (instructions) that would control various sensory and motor behaviors, in the extent to which environmental stimuli (like pictures) controlled appropriate verbal responses, the extent of their imitative vocal repertoires, the quality of the child's attentional repertoire (that is, looking where directed, and so on), the quality of the child's working behaviors when involved in a complex and arduous task versus the strength of "fooling around" behaviors, and so on. These and other behavioral skills may be considered to form a basic behavioral repertoire (or intelligence) that will determine how well the child will respond in a complex learning task.

Thus, the last child described had severe defects in his basic language repertoire. Before his discrimination skills could be observed it was necessary to put him through long-term training in making verbal responses to pictures, and so on. To lesser extents this was also true of the other children; they did not respond to verbal stimuli very well and it took longer to get them to respond appropriately to the task.

Rather than thinking that there are personal qualities of intelligence, or ability, talent, and the like, it is suggested that individuals have varying degrees of development of behavioral repertoires that will determine how successful they are in a particular task. (The concept of the basic behavioral repertoire will be outlined later.) The implication, of course, is that we look to the individual's learning circumstances if we wish to know what limits his performance and if we wish to maximize children's performance.

Several conclusions are pertinent to this. First, it is important to conduct studies on how retardates learn the types of repertoires they actually need in life—for example, reading, writing acquisition, number concepts, and so on—within the laboratory where it is possible to insure that learning conditions are appropriate (for example, reinforcement conditions) and the process may be studied in detail. In this way we will be able to discover what retardates are actually capable of learning; the present findings suggest it is much greater than has been thought. Such findings will also indicate what deficits in behavior can be attributed to poor environmental conditions of training. Furthermore, such study should eventually culminate in findings which will allow us to devise methods of training retardates with which to bring the retardate to his maximal level of behavioral development. Many special populations of children could only profit from such research. In addition to these cognitive skills other important behaviors should be studied within the present framework, for example, general language development and the basic behavioral repertoires yet to be described, as well as various sensory-motor, social, and emotional behaviors.

It is interesting that the two children with the least developed behavioral repertoires, the mongoloid children with the Mental Ages of 3–9 and 3–2, used the reinforcer system in a less developed manner than did the others. In both cases the mongoloid children used the tokens almost entirely for the immediate back-up reinforcers obtainable on a 1 to 1 ratio from the Universal Feeder. Perhaps this indicates these retardates have not had past experience with a token reinforcer system, such as most children have had with money. Another possibility, supported by certain subsidiary results, is that the reinforcer system also depends upon the language development of the child. The verbal directions by which the reinforcer system is introduced must control the appropriate behaviors, or the child is forced to learn directly that putting the tokens in a tube ultimately results in the receipt of a more attractive back-up reinforcer. Further study of differences in reinforcement systems and the determinants of such differences should be made.

In addition to these findings the study with the retardates yielded some suggestions concerning methodological points. Traditionally, in human learning research the learning conditions are applied, usually to a group of subjects, and the subjects are later tested to see what they have learned. The subject's moment-to-moment learning is not recorded. It may be suggested that in dealing with long-term complex human learning it is necessary to make more detailed observations of the learning process, that is, the specific effects of stimulus materials on the behavior of the subject. Only in this way is it possible to make a specific stimulus-response analysis of the learning and to corroborate and extend such an analysis. More will be said later of possibilities for doing this while dealing with actual samples of cognitive learning. However, the present study also yielded some interesting findings.

The present study showed that the cumulative record may be used to assess the effect on learning of additional types of independent variables; that is, the effect on rate of response of different types of stimulus materials. These findings indicate that the cumulative record was sensitive to the difficulty of the reading materials. When new discriminations were introduced, for example, the records showed pauses, or slowdowns in rate. As the child had practice in the sequence of responses involved, or in the type of discriminations required, the rate increased. In essence, through the use of the continuous records it was possible to see what parts of the program were more difficult, what parts resulted in pausing and poor performance, and so on. Thus, this type of information should be invaluable for working out instructional materials, in reading as well as in other subjects. Points of difficulty, the relative interest of materials, and other variables within a training program should be detectable from such continuous records.

It should also be possible to better compare different types of instructional materials in greater detail through the use of this type of measure. The relative merits of different *parts* of two programs could be compared, not only the overall merits. For example, two independent programs of reading materials (using different letters) could be worked out based upon different theories and alternately presented to one child. Measures could be taken, through the use of a cumulative record, of the rate of response to the two different materials as well as the rate of response to different aspects of each of the programs. It would be expected that such a dependent variable could give more detailed information concerning the effect of various stimulus materials on learning. And the relative economy of this research methodology—versus methods involving whole classrooms, schools, or school districts in comparing reading programs—is an important characteristic that has many implications.

The cumulative records show the reinforcement variable and rate of response, but give little detail concerning what the subject is doing that accounts for his rate. The timing measures were introduced into the experimental procedure to obtain more detailed information on an objective, automated, basis. The results showed that these types of observations do give information on important aspects of the child's behavior *during* the learning—and with greater detail in some respects than the cumulative records. Some of the children were characterized, for example, by low *Competitive Response Time*, low *Reinforcement Time*, with a greater proportion being spent in *Reading Trial Time* (although this could also be high or low depending upon the difficulty of the discriminations for the child). *Average Responses Per Minute* were high for these children. They were the hard-working ones, who demonstrated good attention, with little irrelevant behaviors of any kind—including the time spent with the reinforcers. On the other hand, some of the records were characterized by relatively long *Competitive Response Time*, and *Reinforcement Time*. These children were displaying poor work and attentional behaviors, with many irrelevant behaviors, and much time wasted with the reinforcers.

The progress of the children's performance could also be assessed more specifically. As examples, one child's work and attentional behaviors clearly showed improvement over the course of the training sessions, and another showed progressive decrement in performance until the complex sequence of responses had been acquired—thereafter this child's performance showed a gradual increment. It may be suggested that the time measures may be used to objectively describe important differences in the behavior of children engaged in a complex learning task, and perhaps differences in the behavior of types of children.

Furthermore, these objective measures indicated a good deal about the nature of the materials that were being presented to the child. When the materials were difficult, either in learning new responses in the sequence or in the complexity of the discriminations, *Reading Trial Time* was seen to increase. There was also a correlated increase in *Competitive Response Time* indicating that as the learning task became more effortful, thus more aversive, the behavior of bringing on the task became weaker —and irrelevant behaviors were elevated to a relatively more dominant position.

These methods of recording thus have important implications for the further study of training materials for various types of complex cognitive learning. *Reading Trial Time* in the present procedure gave information on this aspect of the training materials. When the step was difficult *Reading Trial Time* increased. As the child became proficient with a type of material *Reading Trial Time* decreased. Thus, various parts of a training procedure could be assessed for difficulty—as in the present study. For example, different reading materials, like the phonetic symbols used herein, versus ordinary letters, would seem to differ in difficulty. This could be more precisely shown by the measures suggested. Or, reading programs that differed in the number of repetitions of their stimuli should show differing levels of difficulty on the various time measures (as well as on the cumulative record of the rate of response). Although the present data were gathered for a session, if different conditions were manipulated *within* a session, records could be taken which were specific to each condition. Or a record could be taken for *Reading Trial Time* that was practically continuous. That is, by use of a print-out counter, the time for each reading trial (or other task) could be recorded.

The *Competitive Response Time* represents, of course, most clearly an index of the extent of hard-working behaviors, or conversely of "fooling around" behaviors. The strength of such behaviors, as has been suggested in the previous studies (Staats, *et al.*, 1964; Staats, *et al.*, 1962), is a function of the conditions of reinforcement. In addition, however, other independent variables, as previously indicated, seem also to be important. That is, the better the training material, which means that it will not be too difficult to be aversive, nor too easy so that it is boring (and thus aversive), the shorter should the *Competitive Response Time* be—other conditions being equal.

The greater detail and specificity of these observations, by indicating the improvement shown by some of the subjects during the training, has further implications. First, it supports previous results indicating that the strength of working behaviors varies according to the principles of learning. Furthermore, the present results, by showing that working behaviors are partly a function of the experimental conditions, suggest that conditions could be established in the experimental situation to bring about an improvement in the working behaviors of the children. Thus, it would be possible to introduce contingencies in the present procedure that would penalize desultory behavior and strongly reward good attentional and working behaviors. For example, a contingency could be introduced in which a delay in the reading trial period of too great a duration would result in the ringing of the error button and necessitate beginning the trial all over again. This type of contingency could also be introduced into the between trials period by having a retractable starting button (or some means of manipulating the availability of the button). Then if the child did not press the starting button soon enough after the preceding trial the button could retract for a certain period of time—delaying the opportunity for gaining another reinforcer. (These possibilities are actually adaptations of what in basic conditioning terms is called a limited hold contingency.) The time limits would, of course, have to be applied in accordance with the child's performance and only gradually demand better work behaviors. Since these procedures would cut down on the amount of reinforcement received by the child, a countering procedure could be introduced which would further strengthen good working behaviors. That is, correct responses, within the specific time periods, could be reinforced more heavily than correct responses made after a delay.

However, these are methods to be worked out in further research. The general suggestion here is that this basic type of behavior, the quality of work habits, can also be subjected to controlled laboratory experimentation using the methods described herein.

Extensions to the Acquisition of a Small Reading Repertoire in Preschool Children

The author and associates (Staats, *et al.*, 1962) conducted an additional study to formally test the principles and procedures in the context of learning a small reading repertoire. In the experiment the children were first presented with training trials on single words. When they had learned to respond correctly to the single words the words were combined into sentences. Later the sentences were combined into short stories. Reinforcement consisted of a mixture of trinkets and edibles and of pennies. When twenty-four pennies had been acquired they were exchanged for a small toy.

The training sessions were 40 minutes in length divided after the first 20 minutes by a 5-minute break. Three four-year-old children were introduced to the training but were at first given no reinforcement. Two of these children asked to go home before 15 minutes had elapsed, the other child completed one training session, but asked to go home after 15 minutes of work in the next day's session.

At the time the children requested cessation of the activity the reinforcement procedures were introduced. In all cases the children's attentional and working behaviors, which had been poor, began to increase in strength. The children then attended well, worked hard, and learned easily for the remaining sessions (about seven). In this time the children acquired respectively sixteen, seventeen, and seventeen word reading vocabularies—where the words could be read singly, in sentences, or in short stories.

Another group of three children was run under the opposite reinforcement condition. They received reinforcement for each correct reading response for the first two training sessions. Then the reinforcement was cut off until the child requested cessation of the activity—at which time the reinforcement was reinstituted. The results showed, again, that the children attended well, worked hard, and learned easily when under appropriate conditions of motivation. When the motivational conditions were not good (with no reinforcement) their attentional and working behaviors extinguished in only two or three sessions and their learning ceased. Then, reinstitution of reinforcement again strengthened the reading behavior.

The results have several implications, as did the qualitative observations of the children's working behaviors. The importance of motivational variables was again shown in this cognitive learning task involving actual reading acquisition. It was shown, contrary to many traditional assumptions, that young children are capable of good, sustained, attention and work behaviors when the motivational system is appropriate. Moreover, such young children are capable of complex learning, again contrary to many assumptions.

In addition, the study had methodological significance. It was possible to study learning variables reliably in *each* child using a design in which each child was subjected to two experimental conditions. Thus each child received both the reinforcement and the no-reinforcement conditions and the systematic effect of the variations was evident in each case. As the study with the multiple schedules also showed, it is possible to study complex learning using a few children, or only one child—when "heavyweight" learning principles are manipulated. This possibility is of central significance to research on complex learning which must extend over a long period. The method is also important for clinical study of behavior problems (see Harris, Johnston, Kelley, and Wolf, 1964).

It may be suggested also that in any training situation the child's behavior may be conceptualized as consisting of two classes. One class of behaviors may be called working behaviors, the other class may be called competitive behaviors. If reinforcement is contingent upon the former, that class of behavior will to that extent become dominant. If this class of behavior is not reinforced, however, it will weaken relative to the other class of behavior. Since working behaviors involve an aversive energy expenditure, absence of reinforcement for either class favors the emergence of the competitive behaviors (one of which is doing nothing) as the more dominant class.

The research to be reported in the next chapter makes a more profound experimental exploration of these and the other types of cognitive development.

13

The experimental-longitudinal study of cognitive learning

At the same time that the author was involved in conducting the more formal experiments on cognitive learning just presented, he was also conducting experimental-naturalistic studies in which the theoretical analysis was being developed and informally tested. This study was instructive for the author and for those who were acquainted with it. Thus, the author utilized the findings of this research in many of his theoretical analyses (such as Staats, 1957, 1961, 1963, 1964a, 1966; Staats and Staats, 1963)—for example, in analyses of early language learning, early sensory-motor learning, abnormal language, social learning and so on. However, the research findings were not systematic enough, with the detailed recording that would be necessary for presentation in the scientific journal literature.

It became clear to the author, however, that psychology needed research methods by which to make these experimental-naturalistic types of study more systematic and objective, acceptable to a laboratory science, while retaining the possibility of studying and manipulating complex behaviors important to human adjustment. The development of such research methods would enable the study of better samples of functional human behaviors in a manner that would be capable of general dissemination; that would lead to direct test of the theoretical learning approach and to general knowledge. The development of such methods would enable the field to begin the objective study of important behaviors within the confines of experimental psychology.

Thus, when the author began research on the reading acquisition, writing acquisition, and number concept learning with his daughter, he began at the same time attempts to develop objective methods for conducting such long term experimental research. The studies to be reported herein constitute the phase of the project in which the theory of learning and the analyses of cognitive learning that have previously been presented, as well as some of the experimental and experimental-naturalistic procedures developed, were adapted for use in actually training children in the several aspects of original language learning. These studies were conducted over sufficient lengths of time to sample realistically the problems involved in long term complex training and treatment programs as well as to study the various aspects of the training and the stimulus materials. It is felt that these types of study are essential to the formulation of a learning theory of cognitive development (and cognitive behavior modification) —that is, that actual samples of cognitive behavior must be investigated. Furthermore, the study attempts to indicate that this type of research can be conducted in an objective, experimental, manner where the stimuli presented and the responses made are recorded and the experimental findings are capable of replication.

Actually, the present line of inquiry had a number of different goals and purposes. As described, one was methodological; to develop methods for the study of complex, functional, behaviors. Another purpose was theoretical; to verify and extend the learning theory. In addition, as has been suggested, part of the verification and generality of a set of scientific principles and methods is gained in the demonstration that the principles and methods pertain to worldly problems, and that the principles and methods are advantageous in the solution of such problems.

In the present case the author was interested in demonstrating that the learning theory and experimental methods could actually be used in the training of a child to complex, functional, cognitive behavior repertoires. In addition, as later studies will also demonstrate, the author wished to show that the procedures that were developed could actually be used to solve some of the problems that occur in cognitive development.

A skeptic might ask what can be proved by the use of the learning theory in training a child to read, as one example. Children have been trained to read for some time—without the use of learning theory and experimental methods. The answer to this is similar to that which has occurred in other sciences. Many times practical skills will have developed prior to scientific knowledge—for example, men were accomplished sailors prior to the development of appropriate scientific laws, such as those of mechanics. When the scientific analysis did develop, however, it provided improved practical skills, including better designed sailing vessels and better sailing skills.

Furthermore, when we only have the practical skill, it is frequently in the category of an art. That is, since there is no precise analysis of what is occurring, the central points cannot be clearly distinguished and thus imparted on a verbal level to a novice who wishes to learn the skill. As a consequence the novice must go through a long practical training experience in which he is immersed in the field and gradually acquires himself the artistic (and many times nonverbal) skills. When the scientific analysis is made, on the other hand, it cuts to the heart of the matter, separating the scientific wheat from the folklore chaff. Furthermore, the scientific statements are couched in clear verbal terms which enables them to be transmitted to others, enables the statements to be tested, and allows for the derivation of additional implications. Since an experimental method is ordinarily associated with a set of scientific principles, such an approach also provides for the systematic acquisition of even more knowledge and discovery.

In the present case, whereas the cognitive behaviors of reading, number concepts, writing and other cognitive skills have been taught for many, many, years, the knowledge of the process has been in the category of an art, rather than in science. Even the people specially interested in the study of reading as one example, have not been able to say what the process of reading really is, or the principles by which it is acquired. The field of programmed instruction has also failed to provide this knowledge, and its methodology will not lead to the acquisition of this knowledge. The same may be said for mathematics, as well as other intellectual areas. It was interesting to the author in attending a conference devoted to the topic of reading, that among the psychologists, educational psychologists, educators, linguists, and so on, at the meeting, no one was prepared to make an analysis of reading—that is, to answer the question of what reading is. And the question was asked several times.

Thus, there have been only superficial statements concerning what reading is, for example, and these statements are in conflict. There is no clear statement of what is involved in such cognitive learning. As a consequence, it is not possible to derive explicit training procedures from theoretical analysis—and the present training procedures are far from perfect and yield a good percentage of failures. That is, there are many individuals who do not learn to read, or do so only to a minimum level of skill. Furthermore, because there is no straightforward analysis of the cognitive repertoire, there are not straightforward means of training individuals to impart cognitive skills to others. For example, teachers take many courses which are hoped will give them a background in the area, and this is coupled with extensive practical experience—as is the case in most artistic areas. Lastly, since the knowledge of reading has been derived from practical experience, there has been no research method developed from which to conduct continuing study that will bring us closer and closer to the precise knowledge we need, as well as closer and closer to the development of materials with which to solve some of the problems of the field.

The present approach, in contrast, attempts a specific analysis of the repertoire and its learning, using stimulus materials that derive straightforwardly from the theoretical analysis. And, as would also be expected from the nature of the approach, it points the way toward continued investigations which will lead to even more precise knowledge. An important aspect of the study is to develop the analyses and the materials so they can be generally applied by various individuals in a straightforward way. The production of such standard procedures is seen to help verify the approach, and, of course, to also have wide practical value.

These, then, are some of the secondary aspects of the research to be discussed. That is, in addition to the study of the S–R analysis of reading acquisition, number concept learning, and writing acquisition, the studies are concerned with dealing with problems of cognitive learning using the theoretical framework and experimental methods, with the aim of better solving some of those problems.

THE INNOVATIONAL STAGE: EXPERIMENTAL STUDY OF NUMBER CONCEPT, WRITING, AND READING LEARNING

In the first experiment to be described, conducted with the author's little girl, one of the goals in mind was to work with training procedures that could be used in the home by other parents, as well as by professionals in the educational and mental health fields. As the author has suggested (Staats and Staats, 1963), and as will be discussed later, parents are very important trainers of the child's basic skills—yet there is little information to give them concerning the training problems they face. One goal of the present line of research is to develop standard methods by which parents can train their children to repertoires that will be basic to their later cognitive learning. Such standard methods would also be important in the treatment of children from culturally deprived homes, or from homes with other deficits, as well as in treatment of children whose behavior problems prevent them from learning in ordinary training situations, for example, emotionally disturbed or autistic children.

Thus, while the author's main purpose in the research with his daughter—and its replication with other children—was the elaboration of the theory, the procedures were also designed to serve the above described purpose. It should be indicated that the author was only interested in procedures by which a *basic* repertoire in the several areas could be established; a repertoire that would serve as a basis for the later cognitive learning tasks the child would meet. There was no intent, as a consequence, to give the child entirely complete cognitive repertoires that would accelerate the child too markedly and make her school work unchallenging and boring. It was expected, however, that the training would provide the child with a considerable advantage on entering school.

This rationale was also consistent with the goal of producing training procedures that could be used by parents in general. That is, few parents have the time or desire to spend large blocks of time with a child—with the aim of producing an extraordinarily accelerated child. But many parents would be happy to spend a few minutes a day with a child to train the child to a repertoire of skills that would insure marked success for the child in his later cognitive learning in school—that is to give the child (1) a basic reading repertoire that would take him past the most difficult part of this type of learning and would enable him to learn a full reading repertoire in school with relative ease, (2) a basic number concept learning repertoire that would do the same in this area, and (3) a basic writing repertoire that would provide an entree into this type of learning as well as provide a basis for the other types of cognitive learning.

Methods, Results, and Conclusions

Subject

The subject was the author's daughter Jennifer. The study commenced when she was 2 years of age. Although the author is still conducting the cognitive training, when Jennifer is 6 years of age, the systematic data collection occurred in the period up to the age of 4 years and 10 months. It was at that time that the present manuscript was first drafted. Thus, the study describes 2 years and 10 months of research.

Actually, as has been mentioned, the author had previously made a number of analyses of early child learning and these were applied to Jennifer beginning when she was only a few months old. Due at least in part to this training Jennifer was somewhat accelerated in her cognitive behavioral development. Thus, for example, she spoke her first words earlier than is customary (beginning at 9 months of age). The author also conducted basic sensory-motor training involving such things as eye–hand coordinations, walking, and swimming. And Jennifer walked alone at the age of 9 months, swam alone at the age of 3 years, and so on. These training programs were of the experimental-naturalistic variety, however, and objective records were not kept of the results. They do have relevance here, however, in describing the subject.

Apparatus

In the beginning of the study a piece of apparatus was used with which to present the visual stimuli as well as to deliver the reinforcers which were used. Essentially, the apparatus provided a partition between the experimenter and the child. In the "partition" there was a window into which 5 by 8 cards could be placed and thus shown to the child. To the child's lower right, also in the partition, there was a chute which led into a small receptacle. The beginning of the chute was on the author's side of the apparatus and a reinforcer when dropped into the chute on this side would emerge and fall into the receptacle in front of the child. This apparatus was the prototype of the one shown in Figure 13.5 later in the present chapter. However, the present apparatus did not have the tubes.

The apparatus enabled the author to establish the isolation for his activities and materials that was desirable. That is, various cards and reinforcers were used by the author. If these were directly displayed they could have controlled the child's attention, as well as the behavior of reaching for them and playing with them. After the essential behaviors of the child had been acquired, however, as we shall see, it was no longer necessary to use the apparatus.

Reinforcer System

The reinforcer system was changed as the study progressed, and the use of the various reinforcers constitutes one of the significant findings of the study. However, the reinforcer system will be discussed in this section although some aspects are also pertinent to the results section. In general, in the present study, methods, results, and conclusions are intermixed to some extent. Thus, later in the results section, the various procedures which were used will be described along with the behaviors of the child produced by the procedures. The methods and procedures were variegated and it is not possible to cleanly separate procedures from results.

At the beginning of the study a mixture of small trinkets, toys, and edibles (for example, raisins, peanuts, potato chips, M & M candies, and the like) was used as the reinforcer system. When Jennifer made a correct response, one of the reinforcers was delivered into the chute on a continuous reinforcement schedule. At first, only one trial was conducted during a training session. Soon a few training trials were conducted each session. After a couple of months when Jennifer had acquired the necessary behaviors under the control of the experimental situation, slightly larger toys were used as reinforcers. These consisted mostly of the miniature toys described in the laboratory procedure for the study of reading discriminations. And at this time the procedure involved ratio reinforcement rather than continuous reinforcement. That is, when one of these toys was used as the reinforcer it was not given until several training trials had taken place. Since the number of training trials varied, sometimes being only 3 and sometimes being as much as 7 or 8, a variable ratio schedule was actually involved. Rarely, however, did the number of training trials exceed five in any one training session. And, in the training sessions where trinkets or small edibles were given as reinforcers continuous reinforcement was used for the several trials involved. Thus, the ratio schedule was gradually introduced into the procedure.

After several months of the training had elapsed under the control of this reinforcer system, a token system was introduced. This was done using a small ($1\frac{1}{2}$ by 7 in.) piece of wood that had five holes drilled in it. When Jennifer made a correct response a penny was delivered into the chute and she was instructed to put it in one of the holes. She was told that when all the holes were filled she would get a toy. The first time this procedure was employed Jennifer was guided in the placement of the pennies. And when the holes were filled, supporting instructions were given such as "Now you have all the holes filled and you get your toy. Very good." Under these circumstances it would be expected that the stimuli of "filling the board," as well as the words *very good,* would become conditioned reinforcers.

Later on additional boards were used in the training. In addition to the 5-hole board, which was used most frequently, a 10-hole board was used sometimes, and a 24-hole board occasionally—when a more valued back-up toy or other reinforcer was to be given at the end of the session. During this progression into the token reinforcer system, which at first was mixed in with the previous procedures, the same back-up reinforcers were used—with the addition of somewhat larger toys from time to time. Thus, whenever a new toy was going to be given Jennifer anyway, it was given in the "reading game" rather than simply as a present. This procedure was followed even when the toy, or what have you, was a present that had been sent to the child by relatives. When such a present was given to Jennifer after a training session, she was told who had sent it to her as she would have been under ordinary circumstances, and the present appeared to have the same effects as if given under ordinary circumstances.

Even some Christmas and birthday presents played a part in the procedure (although it would have been quite feasible to have conducted the study successfully without this source of reinforcers). This was done in the following way. Jennifer would have free access to the presents during the actual event in the customary manner. However, when she was satiated on a particular present—as is likely to occur quickly with some when there are many presents—the author would put the present away. A day or two later it would be given again after a reading session. Thus, a present that was hardly looked at when there were many around could have considerable reinforcement value when presented a few days later when there were no other competing reinforcers.

Gradually, another procedure was introduced into the reinforcer system. It became customary to play the reading game after dinner—this time being both available to the author and an appropriate time to let Jennifer have some form of sweet. As the research progressed various forms of dessert—ice cream, cookies, cake, pie, jello, candy, and the like— were introduced as the back-up reinforcer for a training session. Since these were ordinarily larger and more attractive (reinforcing) than the small edibles, they were very appropriate for use as back-up reinforcers for the token-system.

As will be described more fully in another section, Jennifer also received training in counting the pennies as they were delivered as part of a training program in which the author trained her to count. Shortly after Jennifer was 3 years old, an additional procedure was introduced to train her to count further, as will be described later. Of significance here, however, is that the penny-boards were dispensed with in the procedure. Using a toy cash register, previously given as a "present-reinforcer," the reading procedures were modified to "play" as if Jennifer was buying something with her pennies. Thus, for example, several miniature products and small toys would be shown Jennifer and she would indicate one that she wanted to work for. A price would be set on the reinforcer and she would begin to accumulate pennies in the reading training. When she had a pile she was prompted to count them and see if she had enough—and this was done several times until she did have enough.

When the goals of counting training had been reached in this procedure, and the procedure had lost some of its reinforcing value, it was abandoned. However, the reading training did not again make use of the token-boards. By this time (when she was a little over 3 years of age) she would make a number of reading responses without any explicit token reinforcer. Her behavior was adequately maintained by the one back-up reinforcer she received after the training session. It should be noted that requirements of a reinforcer system may be expected to change in a long-term training program. At the very beginning more immediate reinforcers may be necessary with very young children or children with special problems. Later the immediacy of the reinforcers becomes less important. Additional changes in the reinforcer system in long-term training will be discussed later.

By the time Jennifer was 4 years old, through a gradual and natural progression, the reinforcement procedure had simply come to consist of having dessert after completing the reading game. Each evening, sometime after dinner was over Jennifer would customarily ask to play the reading game. After the completion of the training session dessert would be served. When there were alternatives available for dessert, Jennifer would select her choice. At times when it was not possible to play the reading game because of the presence of visitors and so on, dessert would be served as usual anyway. This had no effect upon the procedures involving the reading game. It was simply accepted that unless there were obstacles, the reading game would be played after dinner and this was followed by dessert of some kind.

One additional point should be made. Abundant use was also made of social reinforcers—attention, approval, and so on. Thus, the author would personally give these reinforcers. In addition, he would have Jennifer display her skills to the family from time to time, with consequent attention and approval. These reinforcers were effective and served a useful purpose in bringing achievement behaviors under the control of social approval. However, these were not the "bread and butter" reinforcers that were used—and experimental and naturalistic evidence indicates that such reinforcers are not effective with young children engaged in long-term, arduous, learning tasks that involve many, many training trials— not to mention with children with special problems of learning and behavior.

It may also be indicated in making this point that except for the period in which the cash register was used, as mentioned above, there was really nothing of a game-like quality to the training. That is, the training was not set up to have reinforcing qualities itself, such as playing store, or playing school, or what have you. The 5 or so minutes devoted to the reading activity consisted solely of concentrated study. This by no means is described as a means of denigrating the use of other reinforcers. However, for research and theoretical purposes it is clearer to use well recognized reinforcing stimuli. Furthermore, in many situations these are the most effective reinforcers, or the only ones possible. So it is important to indicate that they alone can be effective in producing complex cognitive development.

Training Sessions, Work Habits, and Motivation

Although this might superficially appear to. be a relatively insignificant aspect of the procedure, the length of the training sessions involved several points that are intimately involved with the rationale and the purposes of this study. First, the author has suggested in brief already (see Staats, 1964a) that one aspect of the difficulty of learning to read is the intensity with which the training is conducted. To illustrate this it may be indicated that in learning to speak the training is dispersed throughout the day in very short training sessions which occur naturally. The speaking responses are also individually reinforced with relatively strong reinforcers. This natural procedure constitutes a very effective training method. On the other hand, reading training customarily commences relatively abruptly and the training sessions are longer—concentrated in short periods.

When this is done, however, it can be expected that very strong positive reinforcers will be needed—unless the child is restrained, or aversive stimuli are used to force him to continue working. The latter two conditions are operative for many children in the usual school situation.

This rationale and the author's research findings may be summarized in the general statement that *it is necessary to match the power of the reinforcers to the amount (number or effortfulness) of the responses demanded.* When the reinforcers are very strong more behavior can be required. As had been shown in child studies (Staats, *et al.*, 1963) when the amount of reinforcement given falls below a certain amount, the behavior "breaks down," that is, the rate of emission of the behavior falters, becomes erratic, and may largely disappear. It may generally be concluded that the motivational system and the length and effortfulness of the task interact. When the latter increases, the strength of the motivational system must be increased.

There are a number of variables that affect the amount of reinforcement requisite to maintain the working behavior of an organism. Some of these will be discussed later. It is relevant to indicate here, however, that an organism can be gradually trained to put out a relatively large number of responses before getting his reinforcer. That is, although at the beginning of training the organism's behavior might not be maintained, as an example, when an average of 100 responses are necessary prior to receipt of the reinforcer, if reinforcement is first given for only a few responses and the requirement gradually raised, the organisms can be trained to the desired "work habits." Thus, another variable in the effort expenditure that can be demanded involves the organism's previous work training.

At this point, another generalization, borne out by the results of the present study, may be stated. The less the previous work training, the stronger the motivational system must be, and the shorter and easier must the task be. When the child is quite young, when he has not been trained in long working sequences, less behavior may be demanded in the task than will be possible later on, when his work habits have been increased through training. This relationship would be expected to hold when the strength of the reinforcer system is held constant.

This limitation could be counteracted in a training program by presenting reinforcers more profusely. In short term studies, or in studies lasting only several months, or in cases of special learning problems, such as the other studies to be included further on, a reinforcer system may be used that is stronger and will maintain attentive behavior in longer training sessions. In the present study, however, the author's purpose was to conduct only short training sessions, appropriate for the busy parent, as well as to use reinforcers that were appropriate for the home situation and very long-term training programs. Thus, one of the aspects of the study was to commence with short sessions, an easy learning task, and to gradually train an increased ability to work, up to the limit of the length of the training session desired, which was not long.

Thus, the training began with only one training trial which was immediately reinforced. A little later a few trials were conducted in a training session. Later more reading responses were required. Even when the sessions were rather standard at about 5 minutes in length the difficulty of the training was varied by the number of picture cards introduced into the training. Picture trials required little effort other than attention. At first the picture cards were used more profusely, then their use was decreased. Finally, after 8 or 9 months they were rarely if ever used.

A 5 minute reading session is not very long and does not provide an opportunity for extensive training. Assuming that four training sessions on the average were conducted per week, a year of training would only involve about 17 hours of training. However, it is this limitation that (1) makes the procedure feasible for application by busy parents, and (2) it insures that although the child will learn a great deal he will not be accelerated in a fashion that could produce problems of adjustment in later learning situations.

The author would like to insert one qualification here. There were occasions in which Jennifer made errors that were "aggravating" to the author and where the author mistakenly repeated the material and exceeded the limitations on the training sessions that had been set. It must also be confessed that aversiveness was also used several times— for which there is no justification in terms of the theory underlying the procedures used, and which served no productive purpose in the training. In fact the converse resulted in each case. A by-product was also a certain timidity about making errors. There were also occasions, before the author learned better, where Jennifer did so well on materials that the *amount* of material presented was advanced too rapidly. This did not usually result in markedly longer training periods but rather in the attempt to cover too much material within the training period, with too few picture trials.

The result in both cases was the same. Jennifer's reading behavior weakened. She did not request playing the reading game with such alacrity and enthusiasm as before. And, her attention and working behaviors in the session were seen to weaken, while competing and obstructing behaviors of other types increased in strength. In each of these cases, and because of the author's familiarity with the principles involved, the procedure was changed and until Jennifer's behavior again became strong the training sessions were made very short, involving only a few training trials, with the same amount of reinforcement being given in many cases.

Several conclusions may be drawn from these findings. In training situations in which the participation and attention of the child is maintained by positive reinforcers, the requirements for the behavioral output of the child on which reinforcement is based, that is, the difficulty and the length of the task, must be sensitively attuned to (1) the child's work repertoire—that is, his past history of learning with respect to sustaining good work and attentional behaviors as well as to (2) the strength of the reinforcers that are being used. When the reinforcers are lightweight, as in the present case, the training periods must be short and the amount and effortfulness of the behavior demanded must be low. In addition, when working with a very young child the behavioral demands must be minimal and only very gradually increased. The trainer must also be very sensitive to signs that the participation and attentional behavior of the child are weakening. When this occurs this means that reinforcement must be increased, or when, as in the present case, this is not desirable, reinforcement should be given for smaller units of behavior. When a weakening in desirable behavior has been detected the behavioral demands should be markedly reduced until the participation and attentional behaviors increase to good strength. Aversive stimulation should rarely be used. These can be considered to be general statements concerning child training in sensory-motor learning tasks, such as an athletic skill, as well as in the intellective learning tasks of special concern here.

In the present procedure, up to the child's age of 4 years and 10 months, the training sessions with few exceptions did not exceed 5 minutes in length. Increases in accomplishment involved only increases in the behavioral ouput during that period of time. And this rate of response in the training sessions varied cyclically with the newness of the material being presented. Whenever new material was presented fewer responses were made in a training session. When the responses had been well acquired, however, many more responses were made in a training session.

The number of training sessions conducted with Jennifer were not precisely tabulated, nor was the time per session. As stated, the training commenced when Jennifer was two years old and at the time of the first writing of the present article she was 4 years and 10 months of age. In the early stages of training there were fewer sessions conducted per week. At the end, 4 to 5 sessions were conducted per week under ordinary circumstances, although many times no sessions were conducted, for example, during trips, when entertaining, one complete summer, and so on, and many weeks contained fewer than 4 training sessions. Although this is only approximate, it may be estimated that in about three years of training, with an average of 4 training sessions per week, and an average of 5 minutes a training session, about 50 hours were spent in the program of training. Although this is an estimate, since the time spent was so short in continuous time, it is probably not in error more than 10 or so hours in either direction. This point is stressed since it is the very reasonable contribution of time that makes the present procedures appropriate for use in the home by interested parents, as well as in other ways that will be elaborated.

Pretraining of Basic Skills

Considered in terms of the child's repertoire, the task required certain basic skills. That is, the child had to be brought to the point where she would respond appropriately to the apparatus, stimulus materials, and procedures. The training was going to involve the presentation of visual stimuli to which the child had to attend, and this behavior was to be maintained by the delivery of reinforcers which the child had to reach for and obtain. It was necessary that the child stand or be seated on the proper side of the apparatus, not go around to the author's side or to other parts of the room. The child had to wait for the stimulus, not play around with other items or the apparatus. The child had to "direct" his eyes toward the visual stimuli on the cards, rather than attending to other stimuli in the situation. And the verbal stimuli (instructions) presented by the experimenter had to control the behavior of listening and sometimes repeating (imitating) the verbal stimuli, or doing other things such as placing the pennies in the token board.

In common sense terms, the child had to follow directions, cooperate in the task, attend to the stimuli, and wait for his rewards, obtaining them when they were presented, and so on. Such behaviors are many times taken for granted, as something children spontaneously develop, but they are end products of training. Without appropriate training they will not be present, as many parents (and teachers) have quickly realized when trying to train a young child. Actually, these various behaviors may be considered to be instrumental responses that must be brought under the control of the appropriate stimuli through the use of reinforcement, as will be described more fully later.

Without this basic repertoire, the training could not have commenced on the level which it did. However, the author had worked on many of the basic behaviors with learning procedures prior to the present phase of the study and, also as a consequence of usual family interaction, many of the requisite behaviors were already in Jennifer's repertoire. Nevertheless, the necessary repertoire was by no means fully established and the first part of the training procedures further engendered the necessary skills.

For example, the first formal procedure in the reading training, as will be described, involved naming pictures. The ability to do this, however, depended upon previous training given to the child. Although it is not unusual for the following training to occur in the home, or for the training to occur in informal action of the parent and child if the necessary materials are available, the author explicitly trained Jennifer to respond verbally to pictures of various objects that she had previously learned to name. This was done simply by selecting a realistic and simple picture of an *object* for which she had a naming response. She was then shown the picture and told its name, and asked to repeat the name while looking at the picture.

Since we as adults have such well learned responses to pictures, it is difficult for us many times to realize that the responses have to be learned. A picture does not have the same stimulus properties as the object. An object as a stimulus may control the appropriate verbal response of a young child when the picture of the object still will not—or when the picture control is still very weak. Establishing the picture control must involve learning trials, at least at first, over and above those involved in naming the object. Ideally, such training would involve pictures that were almost identical as stimuli to objects the child could already name. Gradually, then, pictures of the objects could be used that were more and more different than the object. If such a graduated series were shown to the child, it could be largely self-instructive and not require an adult to name the picture for the child. It is interesting to note that such pictures are not available at the present time. In fact it is difficult to get picture books for young children that contain pictures of common objects—the objects to which the child first acquires verbal responses. And, unfortunately there is a popular custom of cartoonizing children's picture books so that many of the pictures bear little resemblance to the objects they represent. While cartoons are very pleasurable for the child later on, at the age where the child needs to learn to respond to pictures, cartoons constitute a stiff obstacle to learning—the desirable picture is one that is very like the object it depicts.

The author found, thus, that a more munificent source of realistic and simple pictures—those not involving many other distracting stimuli—was available in magazines, especially women's magazines where there are pictures of many foods and household items, many times in color. It should be pointed out that at first—if this training is commenced when the child is still quite young, for example, from 15 months of age to 2 years of age—the child will not respond spontaneously to pictures. Even though he will respond to the stimulus object, he will not respond to pictures of the object, although as stated this type of training could be introduced using materials specially constructed for the purpose.

To continue, however, the parent may introduce a picture to the child from time to time and say its name and get the child to say the name while looking at the picture. Thus, although the procedure is simple, a number of such training trials are necessary before a child will come to respond correctly to new pictures. However, if the training is spaced there is sufficient reinforcement in seeing the pictures and of being on the parent's lap and receiving his attention and affection to maintain the training. When the picture is a reinforcing object, which is usually the case, looking at the picture and saying its name can be considered to be reinforcing. It may also be pointed out at this point that after the child has learned to look at pictures and name them, his speaking vocabulary can be enlarged through this training. This is one of the by products of the training to be discussed here and applied in the later studies.

In the present case, by the time the reading training program was started Jennifer had a picture naming repertoire, which was an important basis for training her in the reading procedures. Thus, the first phase of the training involved the use of 35 pictures that had been clipped from magazines. Each one was pasted upon a 5 by 8 card and could thus be displayed in the window of the apparatus. The pictures were chosen to be clear representations of the object involved, and to be uncluttered with other distracting or confusing stimuli. This was done so the picture would tend to strongly control a single verbal response. Some objects occurred in several pictures. For example, there were several different pictures of cars, children, and so on. The classes of objects represented were: cars, buses, food objects, eating utensils, furniture, animals, people or parts of people (for example, a hand), a train, other household objects, boats, clothing, airplanes. Jennifer was familiar with these objects and she was able to name the pictures spontaneously with only a few exceptions. She quickly learned to respond to these few as part of the training.

The pictures were also chosen to vary in size. For example, one (a bus) was $3\frac{1}{2}$ in. by $2\frac{1}{4}$ in. The smallest stimulus object in a picture was a car $\frac{5}{16}$ in. by $\frac{5}{16}$ in. Variations in picture size were arranged to include small objects so that the child's "looking responses" would come under the control of small visual stimuli on the 5 by 8 cards. The letters which were to be used later, although of primary type, were of course quite small, and the selection of the pictures was made to prepare her to read the small letters.

In this pretraining procedure the apparatus and the pictures were used to establish the behaviors necessary for the later reading training and to introduce the system of reinforcers. The apparatus was placed upon a low table and Jennifer was instructed to stand in front of it and to look at the window in the apparatus. It took several moments before she complied since she was "interested" in what the author was doing. However, using instructions liberally it was possible to get her to look at the window and then a picture was presented. The picture controlled the appropriate verbal response and a plastic trinket and a small edible were delivered. The author then explained that this was the "reading game," that the author would present pictures to Jennifer in the window and when she said what they were she would get something she liked.

This procedure was repeated the next day and several times later. Sometimes in the pretraining period, and also later on, Jennifer would go behind the apparatus, or play in some way before settling down properly in front of the apparatus. The author insured that this behavior was not reinforced, that is, he did not present reinforcers or pictures or a view of them, and did not stimulate conversation or give attention. After a moment or so, and a request or two to see what she was going to get, and the like, she would get in position when told that when she did so she could play.

Jennifer's behavior gradually came under better and better control of the experimental procedures. In a short time several pictures were presented during one training session, with one of the small reinforcers being presented for each correct response.

In the beginning training sessions were not conducted as frequently as occurred later on. Not more than 3 training sessions were conducted in a week. Thus, although not many training sessions were involved, the time over which the training extended was long. This procedure was continued until Jennifer had gone through the picture cards several times and responded appropriately to every picture.

Reading Training

At this point the introduction of alphabet training commenced. After a picture had been presented in the apparatus at the beginning of a session Jennifer was told, "I am going to show you a letter next. It is the letter A. When you see this letter you read it by saying A." The letter was then shown and the verbal prompt "Can you say A?" was given.

The next picture was presented. After this trial the author said "I'm going to show you A again." It was shown and Jennifer was asked "Can you say A?" Then the next picture was shown. After this trial Jennifer was asked "Remember the A?" After a pause she was prompted "Can you say A?" Her correct response concluded the session.

This procedure was repeated the next session, with the same results. On the following session the procedure was repeated. On the third presentation of A, however, the instruction was "I am going to show you the A again. Tell me its name as soon as you see it." The letter was shown in the apparatus and Jennifer said A. That concluded the session.

In the next session the prompt was "When you see the A, say its name." The A was then shown and Jennifer gave its name. A picture trial was presented and then the A was presented again and the author said A. Another picture trial was presented and then the A was presented and Jennifer said A. This occurred again on the next letter trial.

At the first of the next session the author again said "A" on the first trial and on the next two trials Jennifer responded correctly spontaneously. From here, in subsequent training sessions, presentations of the A card were intermixed with picture presentations until it was clear that the letter A strongly controlled the A response.

At the beginning of the next session Jennifer was told that she had learned the first letter—which she was shown and which she named— and that now she was going to be shown the next letter which was B. She was asked to say the name of the new letter and was shown the letter. Then she was told that the letter A comes first—it was shown and she was prompted to say A—and the letter B comes next. It was shown and she was prompted to say *B*. Then Jennifer was shown a card with an *A* on the left side and *B* on the right and she was prompted by pointing to look at *A* and to say its name. Then *B* was indicated and Jennifer was prompted to say *B*. This was repeated 2 more times. Picture trials were intermixed before concluding the session.

This procedure was repeated several additional times. The author then said that the letters would be shown one at a time, first *A* then *B*. Jennifer was asked to repeat *A* . . . *B*. Then an *A* card was shown and the experimenter said *A*. The experimenter then said "Remember the *B*?" and presented that letter. Jennifer responded correctly. This was repeated several times.

Then Jennifer was told that she would be presented with *A* first then *B* and to "remember that *A* is first." *A* was presented and she said *A* and *B* was immediately presented. These trials were intermixed with the presentation of the card that had both *A* and *B* on it as already described.

When the training had progressed to the point where errors no longer occurred, the presentation of the two cards was gradually mixed up. That is, at first *A* occurred first followed by *B*. Then trials were presented in which two *A* trials occurred followed by two *B* trials. Then the letter cards were randomly presented intermixed with picture cards. In addition, however, the card with the *A* and *B* on it was also presented from time to time.

Whenever Jennifer made an error she was prompted to give the correct answer and then trials were presented with prompts so that further errors would not occur. In addition, Jennifer was asked such questions as "What two letters do you read now?" At first the answer was given by the experimenter, until she would say *A* . . . *B*, or *A* and *B*.

When this learning was well acquired the next letter was introduced. Jennifer was told "You have learned *A* . . . *B*. Now I'm going to show you the next letter. Can you say *C*?" When she had repeated the letter, she was asked to say *A* . . . *B* . . . *C*. Then Jennifer was shown a *C* card and was prompted to say *C*. This was repeated several times interspersed with picture cards. Then an *A-B-C* card was presented and the previously described procedure of pointing to the three letters and prompting the correct response was again followed. In addition, the three letters were presented singly, in order at first, and gradually in different orders—interspersed with picture cards. This was continued until Jennifer could read each letter singly as well as in the proper order. The letter *D* was then introduced in the same manner as was *C* and learned to the same criterion.

At this point Jennifer was introduced to the alphabet (at least the letters that she was to learn at first) which had been arranged upon a poster board. The letters were 1¼ inches in height, arranged in rows. There were 5 letters to a row, with spaces for letters that were left out. The letters on the board were *A, B, C, D, E, F, H, L, M, N, O, P, R, S, T,* and *U*. The experimenter pointed to *A* and asked the child to read it. Then *B, C,* and *D* followed.

Then the experimenter pointed to the *E* and said what its name was and asked Jennifer to say it also. Then a card with the *E* on it was presented in the apparatus and named with Jennifer repeating the name. A picture was presented, then another trial with *E*. This was continued until Jennifer said the name spontaneously when *E* was presented. Then an *A-B-C-D-E* card was presented and Jennifer was prompted to read the *E* until she could read it in a series without prompting.

These procedures were continued until Jennifer could read the 5 letters when presented singly on cards in any order, when presented in a series on a card, or when presented in a series on the poster board alphabet, or when pointed to individually on the poster board.

The other letters in the 16 word upper case alphabet were introduced in the same manner. However, after the first 6 letters, one additional feature was added to the procedure. After first naming the letter on the poster board and then learning to respond to the single letter on a card, Jennifer was presented with the letter in a series which included only the two preceding letters, rather than in a series including all the previously learned letters. This allowed the establishment of word associations between the new letter and those just preceding it more rapidly than would have been the case if on each trial it was necessary to repeat the entire alphabet already learned. Then when the associations between the last three letters had been well established trials would be presented in which Jennifer would go through all the letters she had learned. Then the other types of learning trials would be presented to remove dependence on the letter associations and to bring, instead, the entire control of the letter response under the letter itself.

When the 16 letters had been well learned so Jennifer could read them in series as well as when individually presented, words were introduced into the reading training. This was done simply by presenting the word on a card and prompting Jennifer to say the word as she looked at it. After several trials, picture cards were presented alternately with the word. Then another word was introduced under the same procedure.

When both words had been learned, the words were presented following one another, with the experimenter prompting Jennifer to insure that errors did not occur. Upon seeing that the responses were well learned, the word cards were presented with no prompting. After Jennifer showed that both words were well learned, a third word was introduced and so on. Five words were learned first: JENNI, MOMMY, DADDY, HAS, A, and CAR.

At this point the words were combined into sentences which were individually typed on a card. This type of card was presented in the apparatus and the experimenter would point at each one in succession and Jennifer would read the word, or be prompted to do so when her reading was not spontaneous. These words then formed the three sentences JENNI, MOMMY, or DADDY, HAS A CAR.

When Jennifer was able to read these sentences easily and correctly another word was introduced, the word DRIVES. This word was introduced like the others. When it had been learned, all of the words that had previously been learned were presented in alternating orders until they were all well learned. At any time that it appeared that one word was not well learned, extra training would be given on the word until it could again be mixed with the other words and presented. Following this Jennifer was presented with the three sentences JENNIE, MOMMY, or DADDY DRIVES A CAR. Word reviews continued to be conducted as were alphabet reviews—to insure the continued strength of these repertoires.

Then the word THE was introduced in the same type of procedure and the three sentences JENNI, MOMMY, and DADDY DRIVES THE CAR were presented. Following the customary reviews of previously learned material, the word TO was introduced. The three sentences JENNI DRIVES THE CAR TO MOMMY, MOMMY DRIVES THE CAR TO JENNI, and JENNI DRIVES THE CAR TO DADDY were then presented. The customary reviews followed. Then the word STORE was introduced which lent itself to the sentences. JENNI, MOMMY, or DADDY DRIVES TO THE STORE. When these sentences had been successfully read, the following three were presented. JENNI, MOMMY, or DADDY DRIVES THE CAR TO THE STORE.

All of the material, including the different sentences, were then reviewed. Following this the first "story" was presented to Jennifer. The story was presented on a card as follows:

> JENNI DRIVES THE CAR.
> JENNI DRIVES TO MOMMY.
> JENNI DRIVES TO THE STORE.

Then the word SEES was introduced and learned. The sentences JENNI, MOMMY, and DADDY SEES THE STORE were presented.

At this point—December 14, 1962, 10 months after beginning training—it was concluded that the major principles and methods were applicable to the task of training a child to read and that the preliminary S–R analysis of this type of cognitive learning was sound. Using the reinforcer system and the printed stimuli and the vocal prompts it was possible to train the child to a rudimentary reading repertoire, beginning with the first alphabet learning. The procedures were adequate for shaping and maintaining the child's attention and cooperation in long term training procedures. Single letter responses could be taught as well as word, sentence, and paragraph reading.

In continuing the research, it was deemed desirable to use lower case letters, as well as upper case, in the usual pattern. Thus, the training returned to the alphabet learning phase. Before summarizing these procedures, however, a moment may be spent on some of the other findings that had occurred up to this point.

First, at this time the token reinforcer system was still being utilized. A penny was given for each response ordinarily, whether it was a letter-response or a word-response. When Jennifer read a whole sentence, or a sequence of letters, she would be given more than one penny. Thus, a four word sentence would merit the delivery of 4 pennies. During one session, as a consequence, Jennifer could make from 15 to 35 responses, and various combinations of the 5, 10, and 24-hole token boards were being used.

It should be pointed out, however, that it was in this phase of the training that the first ratio strain occurred. That is, the training seemed to be going so well that the experimenter had the impression that higher demands upon responding could be made than was actually the case. Pictures were no longer presented, and the sessions consisted of solid reading. As a consequence of these overly demanding training sessions, however, poor attention, lackadaisical participation, and poor performance began to occur. The training was too concentrated, the amount of reinforcement was insufficient for the amount of work demanded, and the basic behaviors maintained by the reinforcement began to deteriorate. It was thus necessary to decrease the effortfulness of the task—that is decrease the reading responses involved in each session. This adjustment brought the basic behaviors back to full strength and helped in creating the general rule that the number of reading training trials must remain well within the power of the reinforcer system and the child's work repertoire.

One further point may be made here. In terms of the actual reading units acquired as a function of training time, the training progressed more slowly at the beginning and then became increasingly more rapid. Thus, when the basic attentional responses, following directions, and so on, are being acquired there is relatively little reading learned. After these basic behaviors have been acquired, however, and a few reading responses have also been learned, the speed of acquisition increases. This progression was also seen in the other children yet to be described, where, as in the present case the most difficult reading responses to learn appeared to be the first 3, 4, or 5 letters presented. After learning these, however, the others were acquired much more easily. There appear to be basic behaviors that have to be acquired which later yield general improvement in the remaining task.

Thus, in the present case 10 months were utilized in training the basic repertoire, a 16 letter alphabet, and 10 words which could be read individually, in sentences, or in short paragraphs. These reading responses were well learned and Jennifer could read the sentences and stories with fluency and understanding. Nevertheless, as the subsequent description will show, the speed of learning accelerated later. Thus, as one example, although it took 8–9 months to teach the first 16 letters of the upper case alphabet, Jennifer later acquired a 20 letter lower-case alphabet, plus an additional 4 upper-case letter responses, in less than a month (actually, within a 20 day period). In this study these figures are not precise since in the beginning few training trials were conducted in a month, and more later on. In the replication studies to be presented, however, more exact data demonstrate the effect quite clearly. Within the context of simple discrimination learning this acceleration of learning has been descriptively termed "learning how to learn." In the present learning theory, however, it may be suggested that what is being acquired involves the basic behavioral repertoire that has been briefly described, and will be elaborated upon later on.

The method which was used to produce the lower-case alphabet was like that already described, which may be summarized as follows. After a few lower-case letters had been learned, at the beginning of a session these would be presented in sequence. Then the next letter to be learned would be added to the sequence using a large alphabet on the poster-board. Then the new letter on a card would be presented several times gradually interspersing picture trials with presentations of the letter. Then the new letter would be interspersed with the last previous letter learned—insuring by prompting at first that an error did not occur. Then the new letter would be interspersed with the last two previous letters learned, again using prompts to prevent errors. Then the three letters, including the new one, would be presented in sequence until the sequence was well learned. Then the entire sequence that had been learned up to this point would be presented until it was shown that each response, and the sequence, had been well acquired. Whenever an error occurred on an "old" letter Jennifer was prompted. After the sequence was completed, however, that letter was pulled and presented several times alone until it had been well learned again. Then sequence trials were run again.

As would be expected from the difficulty of the discrimination involved, Jennifer would say *b* for *d* and the reverse. This discrimination problem was solved by adding a small pencil mark to the *b*, changing it to *B̵* which made it faintly resemble the upper-case *B*, and served to aid the discrimination. Later, when Jennifer had strongly acquired the *b* and *d* discrimination, this extra stimulus mark was deleted. Jennifer also had difficulty learning the *l*, calling it *i*, and the same procedure was used to make the discrimination easier. That is a small mark was made on the *l*, changing it to *l̵*, which made it resemble the upper-case *L* as well as making it different from the *i*. This was also done to the *h* changing it to *h̵*. In each case, this procedure solved the problem.

Thus, after 11 months of training Jennifer had acquired the 20-word alphabet, *A, B, C, D, E, F, G, H, I, J, K, L, M, N, O, P, R, S, T, U*, in both upper and lower case letters. At this point the training returned to the word, sentence, and paragraph reading materials already de-scribed—this time printed in lower case letters and utilizing upper case letters only in their appropriate place.

Training at this time proceeded very rapidly, since the words and sentences at first were the same as those she had learned before, except they were now in lower case letters. This might be expected because there was generalization from the upper case letters, because Jennifer had already learned the word associations involved (in common sense terms would have remembered some of the sentences), and had already acquired some of the basic behaviors such as the necessary eye movements. Because of the ease of learning here, the experimenter again went too rapidly at times, and the result was a deterioration in the strength of participation and so on.

Nevertheless, by March of 1963, after about 12 months of training, Jennifer could read the alphabets described as well as the following words presented singly, in sentences, or in "stories:" *at, a, to, the, and, milk, bread, store, car, school, boys, girls, Jenni, Mommy, Daddy, sees, eats* and *drives*. An example of one of the stories is presented below.

> Jenni drives the car to the store.
> Jenni sees milk at the store.
> Jenni sees bread at the store.
> Jenni sees bread and milk.

In addition, a "story book" was constructed for Jennifer with the title "Jenni at school," with an appropriate picture (clipped from a magazine) on each page. The book was quite reinforcing and Jenni later read it many times. The story was as follows:

> Jenni drives to school. (p. 1)
> Jenni sees a girl at school. (p. 2)
> Jenni sees a boy.
> The boy eats bread. (p. 3)
> Mommy sees Jenni at school. (p. 4)

At this time procedures were introduced to teach some phonetic responses, that is, unit responses (phonemes) under the control of unit stimuli (graphemes). The first stimulus unit selected was *s* which was to control the sibilant "s" response (or as we shall see, the *two* sibilant "s" responses).

The task was introduced in the following manner. A card was presented with the word *car* typed on the left side, and the word *cars* typed on the right side. Jennifer was asked what the first word was, with the other one covered. After she read it the experimenter pointed to *cars* and said that when it had the *s* on the end it was *cars*. She was prompted to read this word.

Following this a number of cards were individually presented each of which had two words on it, one with an *s* and one without. The cards were: *boy-boys, girl-girls, stores-store, sees-see, drive-drives,* and *school-schools*. Sometimes the non-*s* word was on the left side, sometimes on the right.

Jennifer was then presented with these materials and when she made an error she was corrected. She quickly began to make the discrimination, that is, the *s* stimulus began to control the appropriate sibilant response. By the middle of the thirteenth month of training this discrimination was well on its way to being learned. At that time it would also occur when the words were presented in sentences. It was interesting to note that Jennifer spontaneously began at one point to emit the grammatical rule involved. Thus, when the card *eat-eats* was presented she said "When there is no *s* you say *eat*, when it has an *s* you say *eats*." (The same behavior occurred with another child, to be described later, who was 5 years old and had an IQ of 90.)

A "micro-experiment" was conducted to see if the *s* phonetic unit would transfer to a new word. This was done by presenting the following paragraph on a card.

> Jenni sees a cat at school.
> Jenni sees a cat at the store.
> Jenni plays with the cats.

Before reading this story the word *cat* was presented to Jennifer until she could read it easily. The results of the micro-experiment indicated that the expected transfer (generalization) did occur. On *first* presentation, the word *cats* was read properly after a moment's hesitation. After this a *cat-cats* card was presented to Jennifer and she also read each word correctly. This is an example of novel, but learned, behavior.

At this point it may serve to make a few general points. First, the card presentation apparatus and the token-reinforcer system were no longer in use. The cards were shown to Jennifer by hand. The reinforcers were more and more coming to depend solely upon the dessert which Jennifer consumed after the "reading game." In addition, Jennifer was beginning to acquire other general habits. Although this was far from complete, she was spontaneously coming under the control of the position of the word stimuli in a sentence and reading without prompting from left to right. Although the experimenter many times pointed to the word to be read when a sentence or paragraph was involved, Jennifer was learning to do this to some extent herself, although this control was far from complete. Thus, sentences that were continued on the line below were not followed without prompting, and so on. In addition, as has been described, one phonetic response had been established, in part, in addition to the letter and word reading responses. It was also noticed that Jennifer's general observing behavior was developing as a consequence of the reading training. She began to notice words that were presented on television, for one thing. For example, she would indicate product names she had seen on television, like CRISCO, when she was in the store. This was by no means a well developed skill, however, and it was not until much later that she began asking what such and such a word spelled. Although this type of responding was not in this case used as a way of training new words, it is interesting to see that the reading training did transfer in this manner—a manner that would be expected to pay dividends later on in school.

One point may be briefly indicated here. It should be noted that an *s* at the end of a word actually has to control two vocalic responses, not just one. That is, when the *s* follows certain letters (unvoiced consonants), such as *t* or *p*, the *s* has to control an unvoiced sibilant response such as the sound the *s* controls in *cats* or *tops*. However, when the *s* follows certain other letters (voiced consonants or vowels), like *d*, *g*, or *m*, it has to control a voiced sibilant response such as occurs in *schools, cars,* or *sees.*

It may be said briefly at this point that it was not necessary to provide any specific training so the *s* stimulus controlled the proper sibilant response. That is, although a child is trained on words such as *drive-*

drives, car-cars, store-stores, all of which involve voiced consonants, and thus voiced sibilants, no further training in reading is required for words which end in an unvoiced consonant and an *s*. Although alphabets have been proposed where there is a separate symbol to represent the unvoiced sibilant as well as the voiced sibilant (see Downing, 1964), this is an unnecessary complication. A later analysis will indicate more fully why only one symbol is necessary even though it must control two responses.

Following the training on the final *s*, materials were presented to extend the *s* control of the sibilant sound when the *s* occurred at the beginning of a word. Cards were prepared each of which included a pair of the following, *eat-seat, and-sand,* and *at-sat*. The single words without the *s*, also each on a card, were first introduced and presented until they had been learned. Sentences were then composed that included these words and further training was given on them.

After the words with the *s* had been well learned, the cards with the word pairs were presented. Jennifer was prompted to read the cards correctly until her performance was without error. Then single cards were presented which had the various words on them, *eat, seat,* and *and, sand,* as well as *at, sat*. In addition, sentences were presented of the following type, which in the present case constituted a story.

> Mommy and Jennifer drive to a school.
> Jennifer sees boys and girls at school.
> The boys and girls play in the sand.
> Jennifer sat in the seat in the sand.
> I eat in the seat at the school.
> I sat in the seat to eat.

The *s* letter was also presented alone on a card and Jennifer received training in responding to the letter with the unvoiced sibilant response. She was also trained to say that the letter was an *s* and it was pronounced "s-s-s-s."

In addition to this training additional words had been singly introduced and then combined with the other words into sentences and stories. Jennifer's reading repertoire at the end of 16 months of reading training consisted of the following words read singly or in sentences and stories. In addition, she had learned the upper and lower case 20 letter alphabets already described. The words were: *Jenni, Mommy, Daddy, boys, boy, girl, girls, car, cars, store, stores, bread, milk, school, schools, zoo, animals, animal, the, and, a, with, at, to, drives, drive, play, plays, see, sees, eat, eats, seat, sat, sand, Jennifer, Staats, in, I, stop, has, cat, cats,* and *can*.

In addition, she could read the *s* letter alone by making the unvoiced sibilant sound.

The next procedure extended this training by introducing materials to develop additional phonic responses as well as to further indicate that words are composed of parts and units; that is, bring part responses under control of part word stimuli, and have them pronounced in series. The same type of discrimination methods were used. A card was typed with the words *and, sand,* and *hand* spaced in a row. Another card contained *at, sat, hat,* and another contained *it, sit,* and *hit.* The new words *hat, hand,* and *it, sit,* and *hit* were first introduced as single words on cards and then were presented in sentences until they were well learned. Then Jennifer was given training on the discrimination cards. She read the three words on a card, for example, *at, sat,* and *hat,* and then the single words were presented to her. On different trials the order of the singly presented words would be varied.

During this time the experimenter would also describe the fact that without any other letter in front of it the word *and* was read as *"and."* It was added, however, that when an *s* was added to the word *and* you pronounced the *s* and that made it "sand." The same procedure was done with the other words and the other letters.

Following this the words *sit, sat,* and *sand,* as one example, were presented in series and Jennifer was told that words beginning with an *s* began with an *s* sound. *Hit, hat,* and *hand* were also presented in the same way and the same instructions were given concerning *h.* Then the single letters *s* and *h* were presented and Jennifer was trained to respond to each with the appropriate phoneme. She was also told that this was the way to pronounce the letter. During this time sentences and stories containing these words were also presented to Jennifer.

Following this type of training a group of words that Jennifer had learned (or was first taught for this procedure) which all began with the same letter were presented in series. Then she was shown the single letter on a card and asked its name and how it was pronounced. For example, the words *hand, house, has,* and *hit* were presented and read. Following this the *h* was presented and Jennifer had to say its name and the way it was pronounced in the words. This was also done for all the *s* words she had learned as well as all the *c* words.

The words *bed, ball, blocks,* and *baby* were then introduced, each upon a card in the usual manner. When they had been learned, these words were also introduced into sentences. After they were well learned, these words, along with the previously learned *boy* and *bread,* were presented in the phonetics type training described above. Thus, through the use of these *b* words Jennifer was given training in the *b* phonetic sound.

Following this a procedure was introduced by which to bring the appropriate response under the control of the letters -*ing*. This was done by taking each verb that Jennifer had learned and typing it on a card. On one side of the card the verb was typed without the ending and on the other side with the ending. There were two cards for each verb so that the position of the verb with and without the ending could be varied. Thus, one card as an example had *eat* on the left side and *eating* on the right side. For another card this was reversed.

The cards were shown to Jennifer and she was prompted to read the verb she knew first and then to read the one with the ending. She was told how the *ing* was pronounced, and that when a word had that on the end she was to say the *ing*. After a few trials, her response began to come under the control of the -*ing* stimulus.

Another procedure was introduced to study the possibility that the individual phonetic responses (the grapheme-phoneme correspondences) could be combined into words. Jennifer could pronounce *s, h, c,* and *b,* for example. She was trained to also pronounce *a* and *t*. Then a card was prepared on which the letters *s, a, t* were typed on the left side and the word *sat* on the right side. Then, first the *s* was exposed and she was asked to pronounce it. Then this was done for the *a* and *t*. Jennifer was also instructed on how to run the vocal responses into the word *sat*. This procedure was followed using *cat, hat,* and *bat*.

Transfer of this type of learning was tested by training Jennifer to pronounce *p* and *f* and then testing her ability to read *p a t* and *f a t*. Transfer did occur but it was not perfect and it was concluded that although a good deal of learning did occur, it was a difficult task. When the training was extended to include *sit, hit, pit, fit, is,* and *has,* there was negative transfer. Training was conducted, however, until the performance was good on the specific materials but not to a point where the general sounding out repertoire had been acquired. Later training trials were conducted in this type of phonetic training with Jennifer and by the time she entered first grade she did have a partial repertoire of this type that was functional for her.

These are but the highlights of some of the reading training procedures that were conducted. As can be seen, in addition to the goal of producing a rudimentary reading repertoire, a primary purpose of the work involved the test of the possibility that the S–R procedures and analyses could be used to produce the cognitive learning and to test the possibility that reading stimulus materials could be studied in an experimental manner.

During the period when these materials were presented to Jennifer, she was also learning the other letters of the alphabet, and additional single words, as well as reading these words in sentences and stories. Most of the stories consisted of five to seven lines typed on a single card. Some of the stories were longer, two to four cards in length. One of them that she learned to read quite well is presented below.

Mommy and baby and Jennifer sit in the house.
Mommy drives Jennifer to school.
The baby is in the car too.
They stop for Peggy.
Mommy, Peggy, Jennifer, and baby drive to school.
They see stores, cars, houses, and animals.
At school Peggy and Jennifer play in the sand.
They sit in the seats with boys and girls.
They can see a boy and a girl play with a ball.
They play with blocks and animals.
Peggy and Jennifer eat at school.
Peggy has milk and bread.
Jennifer eats milk and bread too.
Peggy has a ball.
Jennifer and Peggy play with the ball.
They play in the sand at school.
Peggy's Mommy is at the school.
Peggy's Mommy drives the girls to Jennifer's house.
Jennifer sees her Mommy and Daddy.
Jennifer sees her baby too.
The baby eats milk.
Jennifer eats too.
The baby is in bed.
The baby is playing with a ball.
Jennifer sits in the bed with the baby.

In summary, then, after 2 years and 3 months of training Jennifer had a reading vocabulary of 121 words (including the variations of a word as different), 52 letters (upper-and lower-case) and 6 phonetic responses. During the period of training approximately 409 cards were used (excluding pictures) each one containing different reading materials. There were about 1,998 single word or letter stimuli on these cards, and of course responses to each one of these were made a number of times.

This was not the end of the training program, however. Following a summer during which a family move and other distractions had resulted in a cessation of the training, the program was reactivated in the fall of 1964. The training from this point until the time of the first writing of the present manuscript (a period of 4 months) was devoted to two purposes. First, the research concentrated on training Jennifer to write the upper- and lower-case alphabets. This was a continuation of a brief training program conducted earlier in which the author trained Jennifer to print her name. The writing training will be described in the next section.

Although the nightly training sessions with Jennifer still continue, and will be conducted more or less indefinitely, the semi-systematic recording of the materials and behaviors was dispensed with after the writing training. On the basis of the work with Jennifer the author had developed methods for work with children in general, as well as ideas for an improved research methodology. The main focus of the research thus moved to replication of the methods and procedures with other children and other experimenters, as will be described further on.

Writing Training

In addition to reading acquisition, the present research was concerned with the acquisition of a writing repertoire as well as with number concept learning—areas that will now be described. Again, the research was in part derived from the analyses of these two types of cognitive development that have already been summarized. In part, however, the present research contributed to those analyses.

In general the same type of principles are involved in a writing repertoire as is involved in the acquisition of reading. The acquisition of writing may be considered to be a special case of discrimination learning in which, when a response is reinforced in the presence of a particular stimulus, that stimulus will come to control that response.

In addition, a learning analysis of writing acquisition must specify what the responses are and, especially, what the stimuli are in the training process. The responses are straightforward and objective, the motor responses that produce written verbal stimuli. The controlling stimuli are of several types. We want a child to be able to copy any letter; in this case the letter is the visual stimulus. In addition, we want him to be able to write any letter on command, which is another way of saying that auditorily given verbal stimuli must also come to control the correct writing responses. Furthermore, we want his own verbal stimuli to control the correct writing responses. That is, in the act of composition, the things the individual says (to himself or out loud) must also be capable of controlling the correct writing responses. This last skill does not represent a very big training step, since if the writing responses are under the control of auditory verbal stimuli delivered by someone else, it is not a large generalization for the individual's own verbal responses to control the same behavior. Nevertheless, it must be considered as an aspect of the training.

At any rate, the previous analysis of writing formed the basis of the procedures that are now to be discussed. The procedures moved in correspondence with the analysis. The first goal was to bring the writing responses under the control of the written letter stimuli. This was actually broken down into two steps. The first was to have the child copy the stimuli by writing on top of the stimuli, that is, to trace. This training was used to establish the movement skills that are involved in writing, somewhat under the control of the visual stimulus. (Another way of doing this, which can even precede the tracing procedure is to guide the child's hand oneself or through mechanical implements such as a "letter maze.") Following the development of some motor skill in holding the pencil and making movements on the paper, the next step was to transfer the responses to the control of the visual verbal stimuli, without actually tracing the stimuli. This is the more traditional form of copying.

After the child can adequately (more or less) copy the verbal stimuli, the next step is to bring the responses under the control of verbal stimuli presented auditorily. It should be possible to present the auditory verbal stimuli (by naming the letters) as the child is writing the letter, and thus establish the auditory stimulus control. The last step is to get the child to give himself the auditory verbal prompts while writing and thus establish his own vocal control of his writing behavior.

By the time Jennifer was 3, the author had given Jennifer some training in writing, or printing, letters of the alphabet. This was not done, however, as part of a continuing training program but merely to tentatively test the feasibility of this type of training at an early age, as well as to tentatively assess some simple techniques for beginning the training of writing.

The technique used was to lightly write a letter and have Jennifer trace the letter more heavily using a darker pencil or a crayon. The letters were first written in a very large size. Later, this training progressed in two ways. The model to be traced was removed somewhat by making the lines lighter yet and then making the lines intermittent. In addition, the size of the letters was reduced.

Although the records of these early training sessions with Jennifer were lost and cannot be shown here, data of this type will be presented in the replication studies that follow. Complete records have been kept for these children so that each response the child made is available for study.

Although only a few early training sessions were conducted with Jennifer this was done over a considerable time period, during which time her motor skills were improving as a result of other activities. As a consequence of the training, and the general improvement in motor skill from drawing and copying, improvement was shown in tracing the letters over this period. It should be noted, however, that even the tracing was quite irregular and poorly done. On a few letters, in the beginning those of Jennifer's first and last names, there was especially good improvement, since the training concentrated upon this material.

When Jennifer was 4 writing was again taken up with the goal of continuing the 5 minute training sessions until Jennifer could print on her own all of the letters of the upper-and lower-case alphabets. The first technique, at this time, was to print a letter and have the child copy it below. Verbal directions were also given when a letter presented difficulty to her, or when she indicated difficulty in beginning a letter. In Figure 13.1 the letter stimuli presented to Jennifer are shown in the top of each double row, Jennifer's copying responses are shown in the bottom half.

Following this type of procedure Jennifer was trained to write letters on command. She would be asked to make an *A*, then *B* and so on. When she could do this she was no longer given the verbal direction. At this point, however, she could not independently write the alphabet. When she did not know what letter came next she was asked to read through her whole alphabet until she came to that letter. Ordinarily, at that point, the letter response would be elicited by the preceding letter responses and she would say the letter and then write it. If she still could not say the letter she was told its name and then wrote it. Later, she was asked only to read the preceding *three* letters when she did not know what came next and thus could not write the letter.

Through this training Jennifer learned the sequence of alphabet responses very strongly so that she could say what the next letter was after reading (or hearing) the preceding several letters. Moreover, she learned each letter writing response under the control of the appropriate auditory verbal stimulus—whether given by the author or by herself. Figure 13.2 is an example taken on January 13, 1965 in which Jennifer has written the upper-case alphabet completely independently. At this time she could write the alphabet rapidly, going back a few letters whenever a verbal stimulus was required prior to doing the next letter. In most

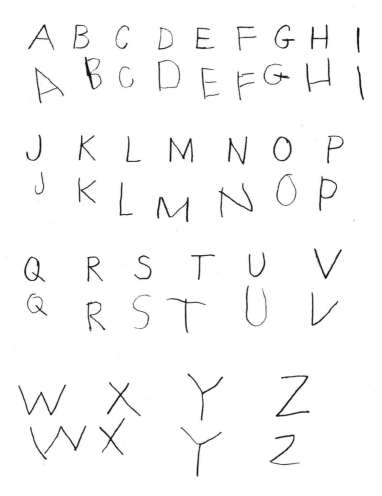

FIGURE 13.1.   An alphabet copying training trial (September 21, 1964), reduced 75 percent.

cases, however, the preceding writing response already controlled the next writing response.

Lower-case writing response training had also been begun by this time. This training moved much more rapidly since some of the general behaviors involved had already been acquired through the preceding training. Following the acquisition of this writing repertoire, Jennifer was given training on writing words, and later on numbers as well. Figure 13.3 presents a sample of some of the word-writing training. As the figure shows this training involved the writing of *at, cat, sat, fat, hat, bat,* and

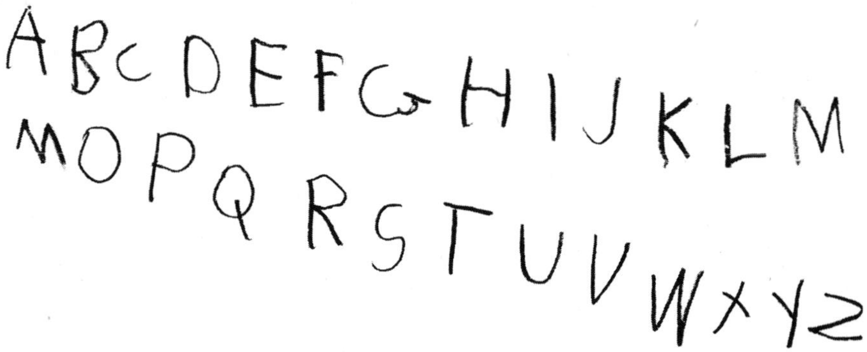

ABCDEFGHIJKLM
MOPQRSTUVWXYZ

FIGURE 13.2. A completely independently done alphabet (January 13, 1965), reduced 75 percent.

at   Pat

cat

sat

fat

hat

bat

FIGURE 13.3. Prompted and unprompted word writing trials (January 18, 1965), reduced 75 percent.

pat. She had already learned to read these words and could sound out the initial letters phonetically. Thus, at this time she could write most of the words upon verbal pronunciation of the word. On others some additional prompting was necessary. For example, she asked how to write *pat* and the author said in return, "What does *pat* begin with, *pat, puh_____ puh.*" At this point Jennifer repeated the *puh* sound, then said the letter *p* and wrote the word. This also occurred with the word *bat.*

Number Concept Learning

The S–R analysis of number concept learning has already been summarized. Again the analysis led to the exploratory research to be described, but in addition the first parts of the analysis were affected by the research. The research that will now be described had the same goals as did the study of reading acquisition and writing acquisition.

In the present case the beginning of the training began before Jennifer was 2 years of age—prior to the commencement of the reading acquisition training. As a consequence, the first part of the training was not as formally conducted as with the other two types of cognitive development. The training was not held regularly at that time. The results, however, did indicate the possibilities of more systematic efforts.

The first step in training a number concept repertoire, as already described in the theoretical analysis, was to bring the verbal response TWO under the control of two objects and the verbal response ONE under the control of one of those objects. This was done by holding up one object, let us say an apple, and saying ONE APPLE. When Jennifer repeated this she was reinforced either with an edible or object, or with some reinforcing experience, usually attention and approval but sometimes with a romp or some other reinforcing social interaction. When two apples were presented she would be prompted to say TWO.

This procedure was repeated using many different objects. In addition, later, when only one object was used the experimenter would say ONE MARBLE, or what have you. Following this, the name of the objects was gradually removed so that the words ONE and TWO were used alone. That is, the experimenter would say HOW MANY APPLES DO I HAVE, ONE OR TWO? After some trials where Jennifer was prompted to give one or the other response, the stimuli themselves began to control the correct response.

After a number of such trials one object began to control the ONE response and two objects the TWO response. Then training was commenced to bring the THREE response under the control of three objects. Many trials were conducted, also, in which the author would ask Jennifer if she wanted 1 or 2 desirable (that is, reinforcing) objects, and at other times whether she wanted 2 or 3 such objects. As an example, she would be asked if she wanted 2 or 3 raisins, and she would be given the number indicated by her answer. At first she was shown the objects of her choice; later the learning trial was conducted solely on a verbal level. As has been suggested, this type of experience also underlies the acquisition of the "concept of number."

Much later, after this learning had been completed and Jennifer had the appropriate responses well under the control of the appropriate stimuli, procedures were introduced to begin counting training and at the same time to introduce additional number responses into her repertoire. This training was conducted during the reading sessions, as mentioned, using the penny reinforcers as the objects that were counted. First, Jennifer was asked to respond to the one, two, or three pennies as described above. Then, after several reading responses had been made 3 pennies would be delivered one after the other. She was prompted to say ONE when one penny had been delivered, TWO when another had been delivered, and THREE on the delivery of the third. Then the session was devoted from this point on to counting training. The pennies were arranged in a row and Jennifer was prompted to touch the penny on the left and say ONE, then the next penny and say TWO, and finally the last penny and say THREE. Following several repetitions and variations of this procedure, Jennifer was given her reinforcer for that session.

This procedure was thus instituted for the first three pennies delivered in subsequent reading training sessions until the attentional, motor, and verbal response sequences were well established under appropriate stimulus control—that is, would be emitted in parallel sequences. In addition, during this same period, the experimenter would conduct trials at various times in which the verbal sequence itself—ONE, TWO, THREE—was prompted and reinforced (mostly by social approval) until the verbal sequence was well acquired. When this sequence had been acquired this type of training was extended by prompting Jennifer to make the next response, FOUR.

When this latter response had been acquired in sequence it was then possible to prompt Jennifer to count to four pennies in the reading session. This process of verbal and then counting training was continued until Jennifer could count to thirteen, both on a purely verbal level as well as by the parallel verbal and pointing sequence. This repertoire had been acquired by Jennifer by the age of 2 years and 10 months and involved relatively few actual training sessions.

Shortly after Jennifer was 3 years old, as was described in the section on the reinforcer system, a procedure was used involving a toy cash register. Jennifer would select the reinforcer she wished to work for that evening and a price was put upon the object. Then a penny was given for each of her reading responses. After she had accrued a pile of pennies she was asked to count them to see if she had enough to "buy" the reinforcer. This was done after she had gotten a few more pennies than she could count. When she got to the end of her repertoire, which at first was THIRTEEN, she was prompted to count FOURTEEN, FIF-TEEN, and perhaps SIXTEEN. Ordinarily, Jennifer would count her pennies (with some prompting) several times before she had obtained the number required for the reinforcer.

In this procedure the pennies were not arranged in a row. The pennies were put in a pile. Thus, Jennifer had to be trained to pull one penny at a time out of the pile and to give the next number at the same time. It took some time for this parallel response emission to be learned. That is, Jennifer would sometimes count—emit the verbal responses—more rapidly (or slowly) than she would take pennies out of the pile. At this time she would have to be prompted to "Say the number only when you take a penny out." When this type of error occurred Jennifer would have to recount the whole pile. An essential feature of this type of training is that the parallel sequence of responses not be conducted too rapidly—otherwise confusion results. Thus, a frequent instruction was given to go more slowly.

Through this type of training Jennifer's counting repertoire was increased to thirty by the time she was $3\frac{1}{2}$ years of age. Following this her verbal number response sequence was increased through purely verbal training much beyond this. Since the general counting behaviors had been established, however, as her verbal number response sequence was extended so was her actual counting repertoire.

Following this, Jennifer was given training in reading numbers. The procedure was like that used with the alphabet training already described, except that it went more rapidly at this time. The training program extended only up to the number 10. However, Jennifer informally asked about the additional numbers on television channels 11, 12, and 13 —and thus learned these numbers.

Jennifer was also given training in a small *addition* repertoire. The author presented trials in which Jennifer was first asked "How much is one and one," presenting first one object and then another. Then Jennifer was prompted to count the objects out loud. When she had done so he would say "One and one are two." This was done with various combinations of a few objects. Besides the actual verbal response sequences which she acquired in this manner, for example, TWO AND TWO ARE (MAKE) FOUR, Jennifer also learned to prove or test her verbal response sequence by counting. In common sense terms it could be said that her addition verbal responses were meaningful, in contrast to what is sometimes pejoratively called "rote learning." As an example, 2 months before her fifth birthday she asked the author how much 6 and 6 were. He replied "twelve." She proceeded to count 6 of her fingers and then continued to count an additional 6. She finally concluded, YOU'RE RIGHT DADDY.

Although by no means a complete repertoire, through this specific stimulus-response training Jennifer had acquired a functional "concept of number." She could count, make a few additions, and it was quite evident in many ways that she understood very well (responded appropriately to) the stimuli of numerosity—for example, she "understood" that numbers referred to magnitude, and her behavior was mediated accordingly.

Conclusions

Various goals of the research have already been outlined. Although it is not suggested that the goals were fully met with the one child, progress was made towards each goal—progress which became the basis for the studies yet to be summarized which together with the present and preceding studies do constitute substantial support for the approach. The conclusions to be outlined at this point are specifically relevant to the preceding research. The more general points and the general concepts which the research supports will be discussed later.

At the end of the approximately 3 years of the research Jennifer had acquired elementary skills in the 3 areas of cognitive development. For example, although her reading repertoire was not complete, the main aspects of the reading skills were present in rudimentary form. It may be suggested that she had learned many aspects of cognitive development that would be of great adjustmental value to her. It is instructive to spend just a moment considering in general terms the cognitive and emotional (attitudinal) learning that had taken place. First of all, she had acquired many of the basic attentional and working behaviors that are so generally important to learning. The nature of these behaviors will be described more fully later on. To summarize, however, at the age of 4 years and 10 months she had learned to follow directions, to attend and work in a concentrated manner, to make close discriminations of various kinds. In addition, she had an increased picture naming repertoire; a rudimentary writing repertoire; a rudimentary number concept repertoire; she could copy abstract symbols; she could read all the letters and numbers; and she could read words and sentences, and paragraphs made up of those words; and she had a small phonetic reading repertoire as well as some of the skills involved in sounding out words.

In sum, although the work was conducted primarily for research purposes, she had acquired by virtue of the training a better repertoire than most children have by the time they enter the first grade in the areas of cognitive development that had been treated. This has since been further verified; Jennifer at the time of the final writing of this manuscript has entered and completed the first grade. Although she entered school a year early, her skills and general adjustment to the formal learning situation proved to be very good. She showed advanced performance in reading, spelling, writing, and arithmetic at the start, and her deportment and general behavior were very good. At the end of the year she was working above grade level in reading, arithmetic, phonics, and spelling.

Moreover, she liked school. This point is made here also to indicate that there was no difficulty in moving from the training situation as it has been outlined to the formal school situation. Frequently, the question arises concerning the child's future adjustment in learning situations when he has previously been given material reinforcers for learning and then these are no longer given. The results showed that there were no adjustmental problems or difficulties at all. It was quite apparent that the training had produced a child with advanced cognitive development and with attitudes toward learning and achievement that were propitious for continued progress in the educational situation.[1]

Most parents would be willing to spend 5 minutes a day to insure that these positive circumstances would be provided for their children. And many institutions would like to provide such experience for their charges —provided the training could be economically administered. One of the suggestions of the present research was that the methods, because of their straightforward nature and their simplicity, could be widely applied by relatively untrained individuals. The studies that follow will provide

[1] At the time of reading this manuscript in galley proof Jennifer has completed another year of school which has produced some additional follow-up data. Her second grade school records showed the results of one achievement test, the C.R.T. (presumably the California Reading Test), and her performance was at the 99th percentile. It is worth noting that Jennifer who is now 7 years old has been in the final "stage" of reading proficiency for some time. That is, as will be described later, reading itself can come to provide the "intrinsic" reinforcement for the behavior, which then occurs spontaneously. When this had fully occurred the reading game sessions were dispensed with. The author now simply ensures that the child has a supply of library books available—Dr. Doolittle books being one current favorite.

further information about this possibility. It should also be indicated that there was no question of "pushing" the child in the present, preceding, or the following studies. Participation was always voluntary.

Another finding with applied implications may be mentioned here. The training program did not involve expensive instrumentation such as computers or teaching machines and so on, elaborately worked out stimulus materials that involved the skills of curriculum experts, and the like. The materials were simple, inexpensive, and effective. This is not to say that the stimulus materials were as effective as could be devised. With appropriate investment of the necessary time and money, however, it may be suggested that the learning theory and the training methods could be used to produce a very effective cognitive training program for young children.

A theoretical issue that frequently arises in the context of specific child training is whether real cognitive development has occurred, or only "rote learning." The totality of the present theory and findings is really an answer to the question. However, it may be productive to address the question in the context of the present research findings.

First, it should be said that what is called rote learning in child and educational psychology usually refers to incomplete learning of a cognitive repertoire that involves various complex subskills. For example, the vocal sequence of number responses (verbal counting) is a type of complex learning. This skill may be imparted to the child in a straightforward manner as has been discussed. It is an essential type of cognitive development. By itself, however, without being incorporated into the other cognitive skills involved in what has been called the concept of number, the verbal counting alone is nonfunctional.

Parents and teachers (or psychologists) may in certain cases not be aware of the other skills of the concept of number, and their function, and thus may give the child training only in verbal counting. When this occurs the learning may be termed "rote learning" in a pejorative sense. The child will not have the "concept of number," that is will not be able to respond to the various circumstances and problems requiring the other more comprehensive number skills. Furthermore, in some cases this type of part learning may even be an obstacle to further cognitive learning if it has occurred out of order in the training process—and in this way may actually be a handicap.

This is not to say that it is not important to understand how the child learns to say numbers in the appropriate sequence, following along with the same example. This skill is a necessary part of the child's cognitive development. However, it is not the whole repertoire involved in the "concept of number." As long as the theoretician or experimentalist understands this, nothing negative is involved in the study of such fragments of a larger repertoire.

It may be suggested that in all likelihood not all of the training involved in acquiring a full concept of number repertoire was provided in the present study. However, a number of such cognitive skills were produced through the training—enough so that it would be inappropriate to call the results "rote learning" in the pejorative sense. The theoretical analyses and the training procedures were sophisticated enough that the several subskills produced were related and thus formed a larger functional repertoire that was useful in the child's adjustment and generalized to other problem or novel situations. Several examples of this indication of general cognitive development may be given.

For example, after Jennifer had learned to count objects, respond to the "more" or "less" properties of numbers, and could read the numbers from 1 to 10, she learned to read the numbers 11 through 13 on her own. That is, she asked what these numbers were when she noticed them on the television set. Thus, after a child has acquired a functional repertoire, the physical and social environment itself may provide circumstances for learning new skills.

A more specific example of the functionallity of Jennifer's concept of number occurred when she was 5 years old. During a visit her grandmother quickly taught her how to play the card game called *War*. Jennifer was able to learn this almost immediately since the only learning required over and above what she had already learned was that the *jack, queen, king,* and *ace* were "more than" 10, in that order of magnitude. She had already been trained to count and respond to numbers in terms of relative quantity, and she could read the numbers from 1 to 10. The little that remained to be learned could be acquired with a reasonable few training trials under the control of the social reinforcement of the game and the approval of her relatives. To play the game, however, required that these cognitive skills, forming part of the concept of number, were functional and would transfer.

(Thus having a functional concept of number she was prepared to acquire additional cognitive skills in this domain. This is also an example of how previously learned behaviors form the basis for later learning in a hierarchical structure—which is what the concept of readiness refers to, or should refer to. The concept of a hierarchical cognitive "structure" will be elaborated further on.)

More extensive exemplification of the generality of Jennifer's number concept learning occurred when she entered school. Many of the tasks in school involved counting and matching numbers of objects and so on. She utilized her previously acquired cognitive skills very directly in these tasks.

The study that has been described, even with the single subject, also has many implications for research methodology. While these will not be spelled out here, a few points will be made. For one thing, the study suggests that it is possible to conduct experimental-longitudinal research —long term studies of a manipulative character—with objectivity. Furthermore, this can be done in the context of the development of a theoretical framework. Using materials based specifically upon the strict S–R analysis, it was possible to record the stimuli that were presented as well as the responses that were made, thus testing the effects of the presentations. This was not done with great detail and a high degree of systematization in the present study, but it was evident that there were no obstacles to refining recording methods to be more systematic so that each stimulus that was presented could be recorded as well as each response made. Thus, the present study indicated the potential for experimental-longitudinal research dealing with complex cognitive development. This suggestion will be elaborated in further research findings and discussion.

Furthermore, the possibility that specific experimental hypotheses could be explored within the context of this type of experimental-longitudinal research was tested. For example, Jennifer was trained to respond to the *s* letter at the end of words by presenting the word with and without the *s* on it and prompting Jennifer to in each case read the word properly. The question that arises in this context is whether or not the *s* stimulus can in this manner, as a common part of the various stimulus words, come to control the part (phonetic) response of the voiced sibilant (in this case).

The test of this possibility was made by having Jennifer learn a new word, *cat*, and then presenting the word *cats*, with which Jennifer had had no previous experience. Would the letter stimulus *s* in this new situation control the sibilant response. This type of transfer did occur. (Incidently, this is evidence in support of the previous analysis of a type of original or novel behavior. That is, two separate stimuli each of which has separately come to control a response can when presented together control an original total response.) This micro-experiment indicated that experimental hypotheses can be tested within the conduct of long-term research. More systematic use of the micro-experimental technique as part of some of the later experimental-longitudinal research will be described further on.

REPLICATION: FURTHER TEST OF THE
COGNITIVE THEORY AND TRAINING
PROCEDURES WITH ADDITIONAL
SUBJECTS

Although the preceding study indicated that a child may be presented with specified stimuli and this will produce various cognitive repertoires —it is true that only one subject was involved, and one experimenter. Questions may arise concerning the generality of the findings. Perhaps the child was unusual, or perhaps the training was of an artistic type; perhaps the procedures could not be concisely communicated, or readily applied by other people.

One of the purposes of the present line of research was to produce specific analyses of the behavior involved and the way the behavior could be produced. This demands communicability of the theory and methods. It also demands that other individuals can apply the theory and the methods. It thus becomes important that, in addition to the learning of the children, the factors necessary to make people into good trainers of children be studied. That is, one of the objects of the research is to produce training materials that are standard and can be generally applied by nonspecialists. In this phase of the research the experimenter applying the procedures must become a subject as much as the children who are being trained. (It may be suggested that this type of study will have to be conducted in various fields of psychology concerned with behavioral analysis of human problems, for example, behavior modification practices in clinical psychology, various child training practices, and so on.)

Thus, the author although observing many of the training sessions through a one-way mirror did not work individually with the children. The procedures to be applied were presented mostly in written form to the experimenter. Although the experimenter employed in the present study had run subjects in experimental work and had a background in the psychology of learning, he was not experienced with children and had no experience or training in teaching.

The research methodology in the present studies was improved in that each stimulus presented to the child was recorded, as was every response that the child made, each reinforcer, and so on. Data sheets for this purpose were not well worked out yet as they were for the research to be presented in the next chapter. However, although it was cumbersome in some respects, and consumed a portion of the experimental time, it was possible to very objectively record what had taken place in the cognitive training sessions.

In general, with a different experimenter-trainer and with different children, the results supported the findings obtained with Jennifer. It will not be possible to give in any detail the various results of the children who served as subjects, one of whom served in the study for $7\frac{1}{2}$ months. Since all of the stimuli presented to the children, as well as their responses, were recorded the data was voluminous. However, something may be said of their performance and a few aspects of the training will be described to indicate how hypotheses may be tested in this type of experimental-longitudinal research. In addition, one micro-experiment will be summarized.

There were several differences in the procedure from that employed with Jennifer. First, the training sessions were longer, lasting about 15 minutes. This was necessary for practicality since the children were transported to and from the laboratory. Since the sessions were longer, the more powerful reinforcer system already described was employed. That is, the children were given marbles for their responses. A marble could then be used to obtain a small edible or trinket, or it could be deposited in a tube in working for the toy hung above the tube.

The first subject was run the longest, to test the various procedures. He had an IQ of 90 (which must be considered an inflated score since it was taken after 5 months of the training) and his age was 5 years and 1 month. He came from a Mexican-American home and was considered to be a behavior problem by his parents—difficult to train and control and a slow learner.

In toto this child participated in 170 training sessions, ordinarily one each week day, for a total of 43 hours and 7 minutes of experimental-training. During this period he emitted 5,593 responses, some of which actually consist of multiple responses since reading a sequence of letters or words was considered to be one response. During this period he was given 3,235 marbles which if valued at a penny each (an overestimate) would be equal to $32.35.

It required this child, whose intelligence measure was at best low normal, only 8 hours and 49 minutes to learn to read the upper-and lower-case alphabets through the letter T (excluding G and Q). It is interesting to note the rate of progress of the child in learning to read the letters. That is, it was qualitatively noted in the research with Jennifer that it became less difficult to learn new letters as the training progressed, after the first 4 letters at any rate. As a consequence of the detailed records kept of the child's performance in the present study, it was possible to check this hypothesis.

Table 13.1 presents the child's results in learning to read the upper-and lower-case alphabets in a manner that indicates his rate of learning.

TABLE 13.1

SUMMARY OF THE ALPHABET LEARNING
PERFORMANCE OF ALBERT

Letters Learned	Time in Minutes	Mean Time in Minutes Per Letter	Number of Responses	Mean Number of Responses Per Letter	Number of Sessions	Mean Number of Sessions Per Letter
a, b, c, & d	204	51.00	499	124.75	14	3.50
e, f, h, & i	86	21.50	187	46.75	6	1.50
j, k, l, & m	55	13.75	114	28.50	4	1.00
n, o, p, & r	40	10.00	166	41.50	3	.75
s & t	32	16.00	58	29.00	2	1.00
A–T	112	6.22	255	14.17	8	.44
Totals	529		1,179		37	

For the lower-case letters the time required to learn the first 4 letters may be compared to the time required for the next 4 and so on, for the first 16 letters. Then the time required to learn the last 2 lower-case letters is shown and then the time to learn all 18 of the upper-case letters. In addition to the time involved the number of responses (training trials) required is shown as well as the number of sessions required. In each case the mean number required to learn each letter is also given.

The results strongly support the hypothesis. For example, it took a mean time of 51 minutes per letter to learn the first 4 letters, 21.50 the second 4, 13.75 the third 4, 10.00 the fourth 4, and 16.00 minutes on the average to learn the last 2 lower-case letters. (There was a review conducted here, prior to moving on to the upper-case letters that inflates the indices of the time of learning these two letters.) On the upper-case letters, in continuing the acceleration in learning rate, it required only a mean of 6.22 minutes to learn each letter. It required about 4 times as much time to learn the first 18 letters as it required to learn the second 18 (417 minutes versus 112 minutes).

The same results are shown using the indices of number of responses or number of training sessions. As we shall see, the same finding was made with the other two subjects in the present study, and in the next study to be reported the finding is duplicated in the cognitive repertoire of writing. This appears to be a "learning how to learn" phenomena demonstrated with children involved in complex cognitive learning—a very important finding. To say this, however, is only descriptive; later discussions of the cognitive skills of attention and discrimination and so on (see the discussion of the basic behavioral repertoire) will provide a theoretical explanation of how and why this learning how to learn occurs.

In addition to the alphabet reading training this child was also trained in word, sentence, and story reading of the type already described. It required 5 hours and 49 minutes to learn to read 21 words, presented alone, in sentences, or in paragraphs. Further training of this type was conducted so that by the end of the study the child had a reading repertoire of 53 words.

In addition, writing training was conducted in which the child learned to write his name. This training consumed 2 hours and 51 minutes.

One of the main focuses of the work with this child, however, involved an exploration of the learning of *reading units,* in linguistic terms grapheme-phoneme units. Grapheme refers to the written letter units, phoneme to the vocal response units. The child was given discrimination training in which the letter *s* at the end of a word came to control the sibilant vocal responses. This training required 3 hours and 34 minutes. The course of progress in this learning was measured by presenting the child with sentences in which the words appeared with and without the final *s*. In the last 92 of such sentences the child made only 3 errors in reading the *s*.

The child was then given discrimination training to bring the *s* and *h* grapheme-phoneme units under control when the letter occurred at the beginning of a word. This required 7 hours and 51 minutes for training the child and testing the learning.

These are examples of some of the types of possibilities for the study of this type of learning in experimental-longitudinal study. One further example will be given to indicate how this type of research may be conducted more formally. This example is actually an experiment in and of itself, although it can only be summarized at this point.

A MICRO-EXPERIMENT IN CONSONANT CONCEPT FORMATION   Sessions 139 to 170 were spent exploring the possibility that the formation of phonetic responses (consonant concepts in the present case) could be studied more formally. In this manner it would also be possible to relate the study of reading acquisition to the area of concept formation in traditional experimental psychology and thus indicate how classical problems in experimental psychology can (and should) be studied within the context of functional human behaviors.

Concept formation has been experimentally studied in psychology for some time and there are many, many published investigations in this area. However, the experimental tasks as well as the theories of concept formation which have been employed have rarely been related to representative samples of human behavior—that is, to concept formation as it occurs in everyday human adjustment. This section will describe a study in which some of the S–R mechanisms involved in concept formation and the generation of original behaviors were studied within the context of reading acquisition. This is an example of how principles, methods, and concepts, which are important to experimental psychology must be elaborated in the context of complex, adjustive, human behaviors.

Hull (1920) suggested that concept formation involves the process whereby a common part of a number of otherwise different stimuli comes to control a common response. That is, the common elements in a number of stimuli come to control the concept response; the common elements are "abstracted" out of the total stimulus in each case in the sense that they come to control the response. The elements of the various stimuli that do not occur commonly do not retain control of the concept response. An example may be given in the learning of number responses. Two objects as a stimulus, as has been described, will come to control the vocal response TWO when the response is reinforced in the presence of the two stimuli. The response will at first, however, also come under the control of the other stimulus attributes of the objects which are irrelevant to the stimulus quality of "twoness." Nevertheless, if a number of different complex stimuli are presented to the child, the only common elements of which consist of "twoness," then these common elements alone will come to control the number vocal response—which fits the definition of a concept.

Thus, the acquisition of such a number concept may be seen as a form of instrumental discrimination learning involving the stimuli of numerosity coming to control a vocal number response. While the present author would contend that this type of learning by no means encompasses what in everyday life would be considered to be examples of concept formation, it is suggested that the development of such S–R mechanisms are important for understanding various aspects of complex human behavior. Thus, it is important to demonstrate the mechanism experimentally in the context of significant, functional, behaviors.

The aspect of behavior to be dealt with in the present case concerns the acquisition of a phonetic reading repertoire. In learning to read it is necessary that the graphemes (single letters) and other parts of words (syllables) come to control phonemic (part) word responses. In order to sound out a new word in reading new material, the child must be able to respond to the letter and syllable units with a correct sequence of vocal unit responses, the sequence then completing the word response.

This type of repertoire could be trained in different ways. For example, Bloomfield (1961) has suggested that unit reading repertoires come about in a way that can be seen as a more complex example of the type of concept formation outlined above. Using the present procedures as an example, it would be expected that if the child was presented with the letter stimuli *d, g, l, k, n,* and *w* in combination with the vowels *a, e, i, o,* and *u*—the various combinations being presented—and was trained to read such syllables, the single stimuli involved in each combination would come to control the appropriate response unit involved in each total response. As an example, the *d* would be presented as the one common part of the stimulus compound when combined with the vowels, as in *da, de, di, do,* and *du.* The response of saying "duh" would only be re- inforced in the presence of the letter *d.* It would be expected that this stimulus, which was a common stimulus in each case, would be "abstracted" out of the stimulus compound and come to control the "duh" response. The control of the vocal response by the common stimulus would be a reading "concept." The same should happen to the other consonants and the vowels as well.

The present experiment actually only concerned the acquisition of the consonant vocal sounds (consonant concepts) under the control of the consonant letters. The learning of the consonant responses (phonemes) under the control of the consonant symbols (graphemes) was tested by teaching the child to respond to two new vowels, *y* and *a.* The new vowels were then combined with the consonants and presented to the child. These constituted novel syllables, that is, novel stimulus combinations. If the consonant *concepts* had been learned, these *new* syllables should be read correctly, without further training.

In the training procedure, to test the consonant concept formation, a stimulus (one of the 2-letter stimuli) was presented, the experimenter said its name, the child repeated the name while looking at the stimulus and then a marble was delivered. He was also reinforced when he read the stimulus without prompting. At the time the phonetic training (concept formation) began in the present study, the child had already been trained to read the vowels: *a* as "aye," *e* as "ee," *i* as "eye," *o* as "oh," *u* as "oo" (this one required some additional training since the child previously had learned to pronounce *u* as "you").

In the concept formation phonetic training the characters *da, ga, la, ka, na,* and *wa* were presented in random order. The child was prompted to make the appropriate vocal response while looking at the character and was reinforced when he had done so. These characters were presented until the child had read each of the six without error for four consecutive times. The same process was then repeated with the other vowels in combination with the same consonants. When this was finished for all of the vowels, the total procedure was then repeated twice more to the same criterion level. The child's performance on this task is shown in Table 13.2.

TABLE 13.2

LEARNING THE CONSONANT CONCEPTS

Consonants with the Vowels	FIRST PRESENTATION TO CRITERION		SECOND PRESENTATION TO CRITERION		THIRD PRESENTATION TO CRITERION	
	Number of Trials	Number of Consonant Errors	Number of Trials	Number of Consonant Errors	Number of Trials	Number of Consonant Errors
a	54	7	114	9	36	0
i	108	16	66	4	36	0
e	90	12	36	1	42	1
u	138	15	36	0	30	0
o	42	4	42	0	36	0
Totals	432	54	294	14	180	1

The table shows for each of the three presentations of the five vowels the number of trials necessary to reach the criterion as well as the number of errors made on the consonant involved. Thus, it took 54 trials to learn the consonant-*a* syllables (*da, ga, la, ka, na,* and *wa*) on their first presentation, with seven consonant errors occurring. The number of consonant errors increased with the next consonant-vowel series, the *consonant-i* series. This would be expected from what is known about retroactive inhibition. That is, presentation of the *consonant-a* series has a negative transfer effect upon the subsequent learning. By the time the *consonant-e* series is presented, however, the errors began to fall. Nevertheless, more trials were necessary to reach criterion for the *consonant-u* series, and more errors were made on the consonants in this series. It is possible this increase in errors was influenced by the vowel *u*. That is, the child had just been trained to make a new response to this vowel (the "oo" sound rather than the name of the letter) whereas he already had well learned responses to the other vowel stimuli, and this probably contributed to the complexity of the learning involved here.

In any event by the time the *consonant-o* series was reached the errors had decreased markedly. Again, however, this may have reflected the ease of learning the vowel involved. In the second presentation of the *consonant-a* series the effects of negative transfer may be clearly seen. More errors were made on the consonants in the second presentation than in the first presentation. At this point it is clear the concept learning was incomplete. However, with additional learning trials, the number of errors continued to decrease with the presentation of the other consonant-vowel series. By the time the third presentation of the various consonant-vowel sets occurred, the child was making almost no errors on the consonants. At this point it would seem that the consonant letter stimuli had come to control the correct vocal responses, that is, that the consonant "concepts" had been formed.

This was tested for generality by training the child to read two new vowels, *ã* as "ah," and *y* as "ee." If the concept formation had actually taken place, that is, if the common consonant stimulus which was part of various "syllable stimuli" had come to control the consonant response, then the consonants when in combination with new vowels would result in the reading of new syllable vocal responses. (*This would, of course, be an example of an original behavior since the child would be making a novel total response to a new combination of stimuli.* This is an important consideration for the author's conception or originality as it has already been discussed.)

This possibility was tested in the following manner. The child was trained to read a new vowel *ã*. This was done by presenting the letter singly and prompting the child to say the correct sound, this being followed by reinforcement. The sound of the *ã* was "ah." The card was presented in this manner until the child read it correctly three times. Then in the test of the concept learning, the new vowel was paired with each of the consonants to yield *dã, gã, lã, kã, nã,* and *wã*. These characters were randomly presented five times each for a total of thirty trials. This procedure was completed for the new vowel *y* also. In both cases the results showed almost perfect transfer of the concept consonants. There was only one error in the 30 presentations of the syllables with the *ã* and only one error with the *y* syllables.

In summary then, the micro-experiment (with one subject) presented objective evidence that grapheme-phoneme reading units could be acquired according to a learning conception of concept formation. Thus, a common part of a number of word responses, which was reinforced in the presence of a common part of a number of otherwise different compound word stimuli, would come under the control of the common stimulus element. The consonant-concepts that emerged from this type of learning could then function in reading new combinations of letters.

It is important to indicate that besides its implications for the consideration of concept formation, the micro-experiment also bears upon a traditional controversy concerning the way that reading should be taught. Thus, some educators have favored a "whole word" teaching method. It is assumed the child will learn reading units as well as the ability to read whole words—simply through the presentation of whole words. Bloomfield and Barnhart's (1961) method is a systematic whole word teaching method. The present results show experimentally that a child will learn grapheme-phoneme reading units when he is presented with whole word types of learning trials. The experiment thus has many implications for the further study of reading training procedures.

In addition, the previously presented analysis of a type of original behavior was given experimental demonstration. That is, responses separately trained to separate stimuli will occur together in a novel response combination when the separate stimuli occur together. This S–R mechanism has been employed by the author (see also Staats, 1966; Staats and Staats, 1963) to describe aspects of novel sentence generation, as well as social, scientific, and mathematical reasoning. The present results thus show that behavior may be strictly learned (determined), yet under the appropriate stimulus conditions *novel* forms of behavior can occur.

In addition to these results additional training was conducted with this child to systematically test the possibility that reading units could be directly trained, not arise through a concept formation task, and that the child could be trained to combine these units in sounding out words. (This possibility had also already been explored with Jennifer.) This method is analogous to what is called the phonic method of teaching reading. It was found in the objective experimental procedure that reading learning could also occur in this manner.

Thus, *both* whole word and phonic methods of training can be used to produce S–R reading units, as well as whole word reading repertoires. The present study and the experimental-longitudinal method of experimentation was important in indicating that this complex learning could be investigated in detail in the laboratory. Through use of the methods it should be possible to resolve some of the educational issues that have appeared to be insoluable. Furthermore, the study indicates that hypotheses of importance to experimental psychology can be studied in the context of functional human behaviors. A rapprochement is thus possible in which basic theory is advanced at the same time that functional human behavior is studied and applied questions resolved. It may be suggested that it is the function of an experimental educational psychology to conduct analyses of educational materials in terms of learning principles and S–R mechanisms and to study these analyses in laboratory experimentation and later in developing and improving cognitive training procedures and materials. This suggestion will become clearer in later discussions. It may also be noted that the present micro-experiment was an example of obtaining a representative sample of functional human behavior. There have been many published studies of concept formation using artificial experimental tasks whose significance for understanding actual concept learning is open to question. Simply naming a task concept formation, as one example, does not insure that the study is relevant to (a sample of) any of the behaviors we call concept formation in real life. The sterility of such studies may be removed by dealing with actual samples of concept learning—as in the present example. Through self-conscious extension of its principles and methods to functional human behavior, general-experimental psychology will not only improve its basic science value but will also provide a foundation for its applied-science fields in a manner that can remove the present basic-applied schism in psychology. More will be said of this later.

In the 32 training sessions devoted to this micro-experiment the child learned 6 consonant phonetic reading responses and several new vowel phonetic reading responses. Furthermore, he received further training in reading syllables in series, thus, in the sounding out of new words. This training consumed 8 hours and 24 minutes and involved 1,420 reading responses. During this period Albert earned about $13.45. His attentional and working behaviors were well maintained in this long and arduous learning task—as they had been for the preceding training.

It may be added that the parents were very pleased with the effects of the experimental-training on the child. They felt that he was learning in a manner that they had not expected. As a matter of fact the writing training was undertaken toward the end of the study because the child had entered kindergarten and could not learn to write his name. The mother had been requested to train the child in this repertoire but was having no success. In the experimental procedures the training was accomplished easily. It is also interesting to note that the mother used the threat of not allowing the child to participate further in the training program as a means of controlling his behavior at home—further testimony of the attractiveness (reinforcing value) of the training for the child.

ADDITIONAL RESULTS   Two additional children's results will be summarized. These studies were not continued for as long a period once it was established that the learning was proceeding in the same manner as with the two subjects already dealt with so extensively. The first of these children to be described was 5 years and 5 months of age. He had an IQ on the Stanford-Binet of 105—however, the test was given following the training which in all likelihood inflated the score.

The results of this child's alphabet learning are shown in Table 13.3.

TABLE 13.3

SUMMARY OF THE ALPHABET LEARNING
PERFORMANCE OF HAROLD

Letters Learned	Time in Minutes	Mean Time in Minutes Per Letter	Number of Learning Trials	Mean Number of Learning Trials Per Letter	Number of Sessions	Mean Number of Sessions
a, b, c, & d	172	43.00	470	117.50	12	3.00
e, f, h, & i	93	23.25	257	66.25	7	1.75
j, k, l & m	81	20.25	166	41.50	6	1.50
n, o, p, & r	64	16.00	143	35.75	5	1.25
s & t	66	33.00	183	91.50	5	1.25
A–T	64	3.55	162	9.00	6	.33
Totals	540		1,381		41	

Again, it took more time, more learning trials, and more training sessions to learn the first letters than it did those that followed. This appears to be progressive at least through the 36 letters dealt with in the present procedures.

In summary, during the 46 training sessions, involving a total of 10 hours and 56 minutes, this child acquired a reading repertoire of the 18 upper- and 18 lower-case letters, as well as 12 words which he could read singly, in sentences, or in stories. This child made 1,491 reading responses during this period. For this he received 1,954 marbles which may be estimated to value $19.54.

The child's mother stated that he enjoyed the training very much, which was typical for the various children, and she thought that it helped him when he got into kindergarten. One other observation is relevant here. The child had a brother who was only slightly older than he was. This child had had trouble in learning how to read in school and was behind in developing this repertoire. There seemed to be some feeling of regret in the family that the child used in the present study was surpassing his older brother in learning to read. How this situation may have affected the child's learning cannot be surmised. It is interesting to note, however, that the child used in the present study performed in a superior fashion when he got into kindergarten. This was ascertained at the time that the intelligence test was given to the child when he was 6 years old. Again, how much of his advanced performance was due to the experimental training cannot be estimated, but in view of the fact that the experimental training provided him with a better repertoire than most children in his age group, and in view of the fact that his brother had not done well in school, it might be suggested that the experimental training was a considerable asset.

The last child to be described here was selected for the study because he was 3 years and 1 month of age. Five to 6 weeks after the beginning of the study the child was given a Stanford-Binet and he received an IQ score of 130.

It required 17 hours and 21 minutes for this child to learn to read 14 letters of the lower case alphabet. This involved 71 training sessions, during which 2,353 responses were made and that number of marble reinforcers given. The summary of his rate of progress in this learning task is shown in Table 13.4. The acceleration in rate of learning is again shown very clearly by this child, which is of special interest because he is so young. Thus, the mean time spent per letter is 14.50 minutes at the end, versus 135.75 minutes spent on the average in learning each of the first 4 letters.

It is interesting to note that this child who is about 2 years younger than the other subjects described learns at a considerably lower rate. However, by the time this child had completed learning the 8 letters, after about 12 hours of training, he was learning the letters more rapidly than the other two older subjects were when they began the training.

TABLE 13.4

SUMMARY OF THE ALPHABET LEARNING
PERFORMANCE OF MARK

Letters Learned	Time in Minutes	Mean Time in Minutes Per Letter	Number of Responses	Mean Number of Responses Per Letter	Number of Sessions	Mean Number of Sessions
a, b, c, & d	543	135.75	1,557	389.25	36	9.00
e, f, g, & h	332	83.00	383	95.75	16	4.00
i, j, k, & l	198	49.50	312	78.00	15	3.75
m & n	58	14.50	101	25.25	4	2.00
Totals	1031		2,353		71	

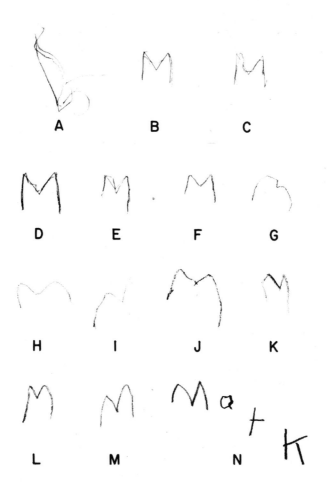

FIGURE 13.4.   A summary of Mark's writing performance.

This point is relevant to the traditional claim that it is better to wait until the child is physiologically "ready" to learn things and that introducing the training early is actually wasteful, if not harmful. The present results suggest, in contrast, that very young child can learn complex cognitive repertoires much earlier than previously thought. Moreover, this training appeared to accelerate the rate of cognitive development of the child.

In addition to the alphabet training the child was given training in writing his name. Although he was above average on his intelligence test, he had scored below average on the skills involved in writing. Figure 13.4 shows some of the results of this training. In point A of the figure the child was asked to write his name. In point *B* the child's first unguided tracing of the letter *M* is shown. Additional tracing responses are shown in figures up to point *F*. At *G* the child makes his first unguided writing trial, where there are no lines to trace. Improvement through additional tracing and writing trials is shown up to *L* and *M* where the letter is being reliably written in a legible manner. This required 205 training trials. In an additional 351 training trials the child has learned to write the three additional letters, *a, r,* and *k,* and to also write all 4 letters in making his name. Thus, the first letter required 205 training trials. The next 3 letters, however, required on the average only 117 training trials each. Thus, the cognitive learning acceleration occurs in this area also—a fact that will be shown more clearly in the next section.

Twenty-two sessions were devoted to this training. A total of 566 training trials were conducted involving 6 hours and 28 minutes. The child received 1,520 reinforcers, worth $15.20. Again, the parents were very pleased with the training provided for the child and were very anxious to have the child continue.

Conclusions

The results for 3 children who had been presented with the cognitive training were described. The children ranged in intelligence measures (given in each case after they had undergone a good deal of training) from borderline normal to superior, with one of the children being average. In all three cases the straightforward training procedures, derived from the learning theory and experimental methods, appeared to produce cognitive development in reading or in writing, or both.

These children under the appropriate training conditions quickly acquired good attentional behaviors and worked diligently. As a consequence they were presented with many learning trials and acquired important, functional, cognitive behaviors. Moreover, the children engaged in this arduous learning activity voluntarily, and enjoyed the activity.

There are many theoretical and practical implications of the present findings—some of which will be spelled out further on. One of these implications may be foreshadowed here, however, in pointing out one aspect of the findings. It is frequently said that it is wasteful, and perhaps harmful, to begin training a child too early—the correct time being the traditional one when the training commences. These assumptions are based upon the concept of maturation and short-term developmental studies comparing no-training to training simple behaviors (behaviors like climbing stairs or remembering a sequence of numbers, and the like).

The present results in general do not support the conclusion that training is unimportant in cognitive development. The children already dealt with, as well as the 12 children to be described in the next study, were capable of learning cognitive material which ordinarily would not be systematically presented to them until they were older. This was done with no harm to the children, but rather with evident enjoyment and with positive learning.

In this respect it was interesting to compare the performance of the 3-year-old subject to that of the 5-year-olds in the present study. It is true that the very young child had a slower learning rate than the other two. Thus, he required about 9 training sessions to learn to read each of the first 4 letters, whereas the other two required only 3.5 and 3, respectively. This indicated that the learning was more difficult for the younger child. However, this cannot be taken as a reason for delaying the training, since the 3-year-old learned complex cognitive skills easily and with enjoyment. Furthermore, the cognitive skills were important in and of themselves as well as basic to the acquisition of other very important intellectual repertoires.

Moreover, after only 17 hours of training this child was learning letters at a rate that more closely approximated the learning rates of the other children. While for letters 12 and 13 of the lower-case alphabet the youngest child required 2 training sessions, the other children required 1 and 1.25 training sessions respectively. It is certainly quite clear that the youngest child after this brief training was functioning better in learning rate than the others had at the *beginning* of their training. In view of the basic nature of the cognitive skills involved in this performance it must be concluded that the training was to the advantage of the 3-year-old child.

The "learning how to learn" phenomenon demonstrated here in the context of these important aspects of cognitive development in young children is also quite significant. The earlier we can accelerate the child's cognitive learning the better. It may be noted here that the term "learning how to learn" has been developed in short-term studies with animals and children, rather than in studies of functional cognitive behaviors. Moreover, the term has been a descriptive one, rather than an explanatory one. It is important, however, to indicate what are the determinants of the acceleration in learning that takes place when children are provided with cognitive training of the present type. That is, we need to know more about the mechanisms which we can provide the child with so that his cognitive learning will accelerate in the various areas of behavioral development important to later adjustment. These topics will be discussed further in the section on the basic behavioral repertoire.

COGNITIVE DEVELOPMENT (BEHAVIOR MOD-IFICATION) IN CULTURALLY-DEPRIVED PRE-SCHOOLERS: METHODS AND FACILITIES FOR RESEARCH ON LEARNING AND TREATMENT OF LEARNING PROBLEMS

Another study has been completed in the development of the experimental-longitudinal method of research which has had the following purposes: to check the reliability of the observations that had already been obtained, to test further the potentiality of the experimental-longitudinal method for producing replicable findings, and to further develop the apparatus, experimental facilities, and procedures for general application.

With respect to some of the methodological progress to be described, it may be said that basic research on learning has been able to advance because there has been an experimental population with which to conduct its laboratory studies. Because the subjects of the experimentation were primarily animals it was not necessary to conduct the research with the animals' benefit in mind. Humans have also been used as subjects in basic experiments in studies where the principles involved were simple and the experiments were thus quite short in duration.

However, it should be noted that there have not been laboratories, apparatus, and procedures available by which to study the various types of complex human behavior in which we are most deeply interested. The development to be described here has wide generality both with respect to the institutions within which such a laboratory facility could be constructed, as well as with respect to the numbers of types of behaviors and the numbers of types of populations that the laboratory makes accessible for controlled, experimental study.

To study the way that cognitive learning takes place it must be possible to work with individual children over long periods of time during which the various stimuli that are presented to the child are objectively recorded as is the nature of the behavior change (responses) that occur as a result of the stimulus conditions. Since the children are to be treated for long periods of time, however, the treatment must have adjustmental value. Long term, human studies cannot be conducted without regard for the welfare of the individual subjects.

However, there are practical considerations involved in conducting such long-term research. In the studies that have already been described the children were transported to and from the laboratory at considerable cost. In one case—the study with the mental retardates—the children were brought to the laboratory in a group and cared for there while individual children were taken out to participate in the experiment.

A more economical procedure is to take the laboratory to the children, or to construct a laboratory where the children come and stay for a considerable period of time. Previous research with children has utilized techniques where children were taken out of schools for experimentation. This is possible with short-term studies. A house trailer can be fitted as a laboratory and placed where children are available. However, the children under such circumstances have not participated in the research for long periods.

The ideal type of laboratory facility would accept the responsibility for the children. However, this could only be done where the goals of the research were consonant with the adjustmental needs of the children. It was because of the previous development of apparatus, procedures, and methods by which to conduct experimental work, while still contributing to the child's adjustment, that the author could design the present cognitive learning laboratory for children. The purposes of the laboratory were for research; but within that purpose the procedures are also designed to be of value to the child.

The laboratory facility was set up in a public school; however, the same type of laboratory could be constructed in departments of psychology, educational psychology, or child development, or for that matter, in many public institutions such as orphanages, homes for children, reformatories, psychiatric institutions, and so on.

In the present case the children were 4-year-old culturally-deprived children. The central aspect of the laboratory was that the children were in a nursery-school program in a group situation. In this situation they received training in the same type of activities that are beneficial to children in nursery school. The children painted, danced, played games, listened to music, and so on. In addition, however, each child during the $3\frac{1}{2}$ hours of the daily program also participated in three experimental-treatment sessions. That is, at regularly scheduled times the child would leave the nursery school room and go to one of three experimental rooms where he would participate in the type of training sessions already described. He would participate in experimental number concept learning training, writing learning training, as well as alphabet reading training. The child's cognitive development in these three areas was produced and studied in the manner previously described. No activities were conducted in the group situation that would overlap with the cognitive learning studied in the individual experimental rooms.

The results of the study for number concept development and writing development will only be summarized at this time. Full presentation will require a monograph publication. However, a brief description at this point is relevant to the goals of the present part of the book.

The 12 children who served as subjects were selected from culturally disadvantaged homes to participate in the study. They ranged in age from 3 years and 10 months to 4 years and 9 months at the beginning of the study, with a mean age of 4 years and 4 months. Seven of the children were from negro parents, one from white and negro parents, one from white and Polynesian, and 3 from white parents. Several of the children had emotional or behavior problems of various degrees of severity. One girl had severe tantrums where she would bite, kick, scream, lie on the floor, and so on. One child would at times feign a comatose state for long periods of time whenever he was dissatisfied with something, for example, when he had been reprimanded. One child was a mild conduct problem. Several children were observed to be very backward in speech development and in the comprehension of instructions—they seemed retarded in their cognitive skills and their intelligence test results indicated they were borderline normals.

The laboratory facility consisted of a large classroom in the Franklin school in Madison, Wisconsin. Two rooms close by were used for the experimental training. One of the rooms was large enough to contain two apparatus set-ups; thus 3 children could be run simultaneously.

Each child would leave the classroom 3 times a day for training sessions, at regularly scheduled times spaced over the $3\frac{1}{2}$ hours they participated. The periods were scheduled for 13 minutes. During the 13-minute period, however, there was on the average only from 5–7 minutes actually involved in the training. The child had to leave the classroom activity and to walk to and from the class; and the experimenter-trainers (or therapy or instructional technicians) had many tasks to perform to prepare for the child.

The apparatus, which can be constructed so that it has its own legs or so that it can be placed upon an appropriately sized table, is depicted in Figure 13.5. In front of the child there is a chute, which is just below the window in which the stimuli are displayed. When the child makes a correct response a marble is delivered by the experimenter. The experimenter simply takes a marble out of the container fixed to the back of the partition separating the experimenter and the child, and drops the marble down the chute. The marble falls into the container below the chute.

The child then takes the marble and deposits it in one of the 5 places. He can put it in the hole to the right and above the chute, in which case the marble drops into the container on the other side of the partition that holds the marbles for the experimenter. When the child de-

FIGURE 13.5.   The child learning apparatus used for the study of complex behavior.

posited a marble through that hole, the experimenter would drop an item from the trinket-edible mixture down the chute. Or the marbles could be deposited in the tubes in the manner already described. The various alternatives were gradually introduced.

The present apparatus was constructed to have a window in front of the child in which 5 by 8 inch cards could be placed. Some of the stimuli were presented to the child in this manner. Writing and counting training also involved the use of objects which the child manipulated in the space in front of him.

The experimenters employed in the individual training sessions were not trained in teaching, nor had any of them experience in training children of their own. They were not provided with a psychology of cognitive learning as it appears in this book, but were simply given the training materials and an opportunity to study them. One experimenter-trainer (or instructional technician or therapy technician) dealt with each of the 12 children in one of the three areas of cognitive training.

Data sheets were composed for the number concept learning and the alphabet reading learning task. Thus, each stimulus presented to the child could be noted quickly, as well as the child's response, the reinforcer that was given, and so on. Each child's written responses to the reading materials were kept and represent a graphic record of the child's progress in this cognitive learning.

Number Concept Training

The materials derived from the analysis of number concept learning, previously used with Jennifer, were employed in this phase of the study. The children thus first learned to discriminate one object from two objects and to say ONE or TWO in the appropriate circumstances. This was done using pictures instead of objects.

Following this the child was trained to count objects arranged in a series. Objects were used, such as pennies, rocks, and so on, as well as dots printed on a 5 by 8 card.

When the child had learned to count to 10 by these methods he was trained to count objects presented in an unorganized pile. Thus, each object in the pile had to be pulled out, one at a time, while the child emitted the appropriate counting response in each case.

When the child had learned to count 10 such objects correctly, as well as any lesser number, the child was trained to read and then write the numbers in order. Following this the child was trained to read the numbers presented in any order. Each of these types of training involved specific stimulus materials and instructions for presentation.

The S–R analysis and the training procedures were supported by the results with these 12 culturally-deprived children. Moreover, the findings obtained with the one child, Jennifer, were replicated—thus indicating the reliability of the research method. In each case the progress of cognitive development in number concept learning occurred as predicted in accordance with the theory and previous experimental results. In 11 of the 12 cases the cognitive learning progressed rapidly. In one case with a boy who measured 88 on the IQ test, the training progressed slowly as compared to the others and the author conducted the training to study the requirements of a training program appropriate for a child with less well developed cognitive skills; for this child was markedly behind the others in various spheres of behavioral development. In any event the procedures used all followed the straightforward learning analysis and this child was able to acquire the number concept repertoire up to counting 5 objects, regardless of the arrangement of the objects; a not inconsiderable advance. This training consumed approximately 12 hours.

Table 13.5 presents a summary of the results for the other 11 children taken in the first 4½ months of the study. Under the heading *Learning Tasks* in the table there are three steps listed. This is a somewhat arbitrary breakdown in certain respects but it can be used to characterize the progress of the 11 children's results depicted in the table. The numbers in the cells of the table indicate the number of training sessions conducted to attain that level of proficiency, as well as the number of individual stimulus presentations (training trials) involved. The number of sessions is given first, followed by the number of training trials. In both cases the numbers are cumulative so that the number indicates the total number of sessions, or trials, required before the child gained that level of proficiency. The point at which the child had acquired a particular level of proficiency was taken as the last training trial prior to the introduction of another new learning material.

Thus, for child number 1, who had an IQ of 88, 11 training sessions and 284 training trials were required before the discrimination of numerosity for 1 or 2 objects was firmly established. Thirty-three additional sessions and 455 training sessions were required before this child learned to count a series of 10 objects correctly. This type of performance is shown for each child, for each of the levels of proficiency in the number concept repertoire.

The results summarized in the table are of interest in several ways. First, it is important to note that each of these children, whose IQ measures extend across a range of 42 points, appear to be capable of this type of cognitive learning. Furthermore, it was possible to produce this learning in a standard manner. One of the unusual results, however, is the fact of the great similarities in the progress of the children. Thus, the total number of training trials necessary to produce the repertoire dealt with did not vary a great deal among the various children. For example, if the results of the children are considered only up to the point where they learned to count a randomly arranged set of 10 objects, the differences were quite small. That is, the 3 children in the table with the lowest IQ's (mean of 89) took a mean of 628.7 training trials to learn number concepts to this level. The 3 children with the highest IQ's (mean of 118.3) required 570 trials to reach the same level of proficiency.

A strong source of variation which does appear, however, is in the

TABLE 13.5
SUMMARY OF THE CHILDREN'S PROGRESS IN NUMBER CONCEPT LEARNING
CHILDREN RANKED BY IQ

Learning Tasks	2 IQ 88	3 IQ 89	4 IQ 90	5 IQ 93	6 IQ 99	7 IQ 100	8 IQ 104	9 IQ 105	10 IQ 108	11 IQ 117	12 IQ 130
Discriminates 1 and 2 objects	11 / 284	7 / 196	7 / 201	9 / 245	10 / 285	9 / 272	7 / 215	11 / 296	11 / 309	7 / 241	8 / 246
Counts 1–10 objects in series	44 / 639	49 / 738	27 / 425	64 / 821	19 / 449	29 / 488	28 / 446	35 / 571	24 / 471	28 / 512	25 / 458
Counts 1–10 objects randomly arranged	48 / 676	50 / 756	29 / 454	67 / 839	34 / 641	34 / 546	31 / 487	38 / 602	38 / 613	31 / 548	31 / 549

rapidity of responding in the training sessions. Thus, the 3 children with the lowest IQ's in the table required a mean of 42.3 training sessions to attain this level of proficiency, whereas the 3 children with the highest IQ's required only a mean of 33.3 training sessions to reach the same level of proficiency. Although these results can only be considered to be suggestive, they do agree with the findings in the previous study with the educable and trainable mental retardates in which the greatest difference that appeared in performance was the *rate* of response. Further results in writing learning will also show that the children, regardless of their measured intelligence, were generally capable of acquiring the cognitive repertoire in a standard manner.

One final point may be made in discussing the learning of the cognitive repertoire up to the point of counting an unarranged group of 10 objects. Under the S–R presentation methods of the study the 11 children acquired this level of cognitive development in a mean time of 5 hours and 28 minutes. Thus, under the appropriate stimulus conditions and motivational conditions, the 4-year-old culturally-deprived children acquired this type of cognitive development rapidly. As will be discussed later, this is an important finding in view of statements that have been made regarding when these cognitive skills can be expected to develop customarily (Piaget, 1953).

In addition to learning the aspects of the number concept repertoire that have been described, most of the children were also trained to write and read the numbers from 1–10. Child #5 in Table 13.1 learned to write and read the numbers only from 1–5, and child #9 from 1–9. More detailed data on this type of learning is presented in the next section.

Writing Learning

Each child's complete set of writing responses constitutes the data in this part of the study. The problem is how to provide a general picture since it is not possible to present all of the data. The general progress of a child's learning in this cognitive skill can be seen by sampling his responses during the training. It is also possible to compare the progress of various children by looking at their writing responses and by tabulating the number of writing responses (learning trials) involved in attaining that level of skill.

In the present summary the results for one child will be presented, and then the final level of skill for each child will be given. In addition, information may be obtained by indicating the length of time involved and the number of learning trials required for the various children to read and write the alphabet.

Figure 13.6 presents a summary of the writing progress of a child who

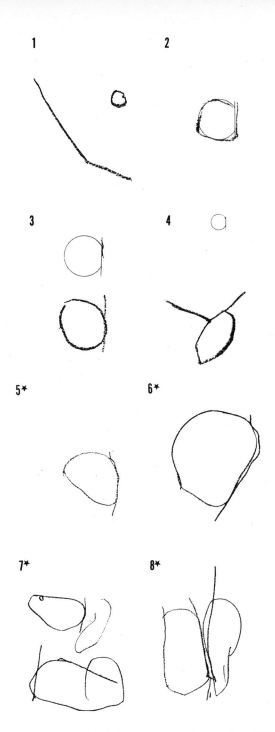

FIGURE 13.6.   Records of the writing training of a child with an IQ of 89.

9

10

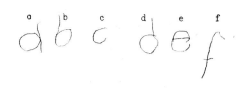

11

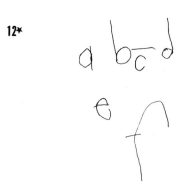

12*

FIGURE 13.6 (Continued)

13

14

15

16

FIGURE 13.6 (Continued)

had an IQ of 89 and a Metropolitan Readiness test score in the lowest hundredth (1st percentile)—on tests given prior to the commencement of training. He scored zero on the copying portion of the Metropolitan test indicating that the first skills in the acquisition of writing were not in his repertoire. This child was also seen as one of the most retarded in the group. His speech was very poor, hardly understandable. In terms of home background, the child had 5 young siblings, and lived in a poor, unkempt home environment that would be considered disadvantaged. His father was a laborer and the child had previously been selected as a culturally disadvantaged child for participation in a summer Project Headstart program.

This child's records were selected for presentation from among the 12 children because his performance was average for the group, because it demonstrates what can be done with a child who was at least verging on retardation, and because his records show a fairly typical picture of the progression that occurs in this type of cognitive learning. An indication of his relative progress can be gained by noting that 5 of the other children had attained the same level of skill in writing as had this child at the time of this writing, or were just slightly behind this child, 2 were very much behind this child and 4 children had progressed more rapidly than this child.

The first response in Figure 13.6 occurred when the child was asked to write his name. (Each child was tested to see if he could write his name, or any letters—none could.) The next response was his first tracing of a large letter *a*. He had had 185 learning trials in tracing lines and circles preceding this response. The third response shown (#206) is his first copying of a large *a*. Response #216 shows the child's first attempt to copy a middle-sized *a*, and response #370 is the first attempt to copy a primary sized *a*. Response #375 is the child's first attempt to write *a* with no stimulus present. (This response is starred to indicate that it was reduced in size by one half in comparison to the size of the unstarred responses.) From this point on the child's responses are sampled by taking the first copying response of primary sized letters and the first free writing response made at various times when a new letter had been added. Thus, the seventh sample (#407) is the first copying of *a* with the *b* added and the eighth sample (#419) is the first free writing of these letters. The response numbers of the remaining samples are 527 (sample 9), 533 (10), 595 (11), 599 (12), 631 (13), 640 (14), 788 (15), 792 (16). The child's 929th writing trial is shown in #3 of Figure 13.7.

As Figure 13.6 shows the child has difficulty in the training program at the point where he must first copy the small letter stimuli and it is not until he has had 527 training trials (sample 9) that he is copying these

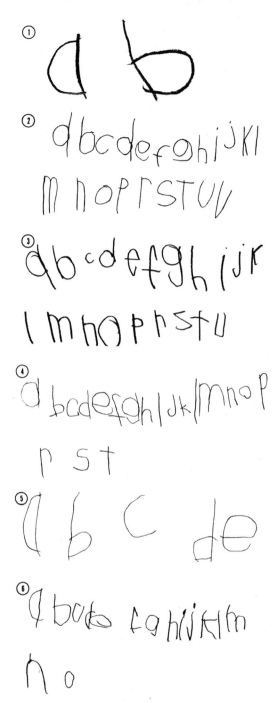

FIGURE 13.7.   Samples of the writing (and reading) skills for the 12 children. The order of IQ scores from first to last is 88, 88, 89, 90, 93, 99, 100, 104, 105, 108, 117, and 130.

FIGURE 13.7 (Continued)

letters very well. These results indicate the training procedures could have been presented much more smoothly. The child does not freely write the letters in their correct order until later.

Great improvement is shown by the twelfth sample. By the end the child is freely writing the letters with no help. At this point if the child has any difficulty at any point in the alphabet he reads the preceding 3 letters he has written and thus provides his own instructions for continuing on. He is at this time able to read the letters that he has written or to read the letters in primary sized type. The training which produced his final performance consumed 120 training sessions involving 17 hours and 18 minutes. This was the most time spent with any child in this training. The mean time for all the children in this type of cognitive training was 15 hours and 42 minutes.

A sample of the reading and writing repertoires of each of the 12 children is presented in Figure 13.7. The first sample shown is of a boy IQ 88, and the training time involved was 15 hours and 31 minutes. The same information will be abbreviated for each of the others as follows: Child #2, IQ 88, 15 hours and 22 minutes, #3, IQ 89, 17 hours and 18 minutes, #4, IQ 90, 15 hrs. 9 mins., #5, IQ 93, 16 hrs. 25 mins., #6, IQ 99, 14 hrs. 37 min., #7, IQ 100, 14 hrs. 36 mins., #8, IQ 104, 15 hrs. 15 mins., #9, IQ 105, 15 hrs. 28 mins., #10, IQ 108, 16 hrs. 3 mins., #11, IQ 117, 15 hrs. 59 mins., #12, IQ 130, 16 hrs. 43 mins.

Subject #1 was the child that required the special procedures in the number concept training. Again in the writing task he required special treatment to first train him in some of the skills which were basic to the actual learning to write the letters. For example, this child's tracing and copying skills were very poor (as were his attention and discrimination skills). Thus, extensive training was given to this child in these repertoires before introducing the letters. The same was true of one other child (#5, who also demonstrated deficits in the number concept learning.) In each case, however, the child acquired the basic skills and was progressing into the alphabet training. With child #5 the training at the end of the study appeared to be rapidly accelerating into a normal rate of progress. This was also true of child #1, but to a lesser extent. He was, however, able to copy lines well, copy the letters a, b, c, and d on command and to independently write the a, b, and c and read the letters.

The emotional and behavior problem children were #9, who had the severe tantrums, #5 who was intransigent in training at first, took reinforcers he was not supposed to have, and displayed the sham comatose state, and #7 who was unruly, hyperactive, and aggressive. In each case, as in the number concept learning, these children did not perform well in the training situation at the beginning. However, after a few weeks they began to respond normally in the training situation. After that time their behavior, except for flurries, which came less and less frequently, was very much like that of the other children in the training procedure. The results in this training and in the classroom indicated that emotionally disturbed children may be treated for their behavioral problems, and can also receive training which will prevent the development of cognitive deficits, through the use of the present types of facilities and procedures.

With respect to the results of the writing training there are several more points to be made. First, the performance of the children, excluding the two cases requiring special training procedures, was very similar— even though there were wide differences in measured intelligence among them. That is, it took a mean of 655.7 training trials for #2, #3, and #4 children with the lowest IQ's (with a mean IQ of 89) to learn to write and read the letters from *a* to *n*. The 3 children with the highest IQ's (mean IQ of 118.3) required a mean of 652.0 trials to acquire the same cognitive repertoires. Over the entire training the mean number of training trials required to learn each letter was 37.0 for the low IQ children and 37.1 for the high IQ children. Thus, even though the mean IQ difference for these two groups of children was 29.3, the cognitive learning was very similar. The results thus support the previous findings with the educable and trainable mental retardates. (The mean number of trials required for learning each letter of the remaining subjects—the middle group, with a mean IQ of 102—was 50.1. However, this group of subjects included 2 children who had behavior problems that slowed the learning process, especially at the beginning.) The mean number of trials to learn each letter for the 12 children, with the IQ of each child written in parentheses, are listed as follows: 430.5 (88), 35.7 (88), 46.4 (89), 28.9 (90), 196.0 (93), 61.1 (99), 48.7 (100), 34.5 (104), 56.0 (105), 37.9 (100), 33.2 (117), 40.3 (130). (The correlation between these learning scores and the IQ scores will be discussed further on.)

It has been suggested several times already that there is an acceleration of rate in cognitive learning; that is, the first part of a cognitive learning task is more effortful and requires more time and more learning trials than does later learning. This hypothesis was supported by the present writing training results. The number of trials required to learn the first half of the children's writing and reading repertoires was tabulated and compared to the number required to learn the other half of the letters. The mean number of trials required was 409.4 trials for the first half and only 221.7 trials for the remaining letters. An even sharper "learning how to learn effect" can be seen by comparing the trials to learn the first 4 letters versus the trials to learn the last 4 letters. For the first 4 letters it required a mean of 287.8 training trials; for the last 4 letters it required only a mean of 76.4 training trials.

These results again suggest that it is to the benefit of the child's cognitive development to begin his training early. Not only does the child through such training acquire important cognitive skills, but he also becomes better at acquiring additional cognitive skills. In the negative case children who are deprived of cognitive training at an early age can be expected to suffer in both of these ways.

Test Results

Just prior to the beginning of the research the children were given Stanford-Binet (Terman and Merrill, 1937) Intelligence Tests and Metropolitan Readiness Tests (1948). About 3 months later the tests were repeated, and they were repeated again about 3 months after that. They were given for the last time 1 month later. The mean scores for the group of children are shown in Table 13.6. The score for the Stanford-Binet tests is an IQ. The score for the Metropolitan is a percentile; that is, the child's position in a group of children is given in terms of percentages of children that score less. A score at the fifth percentile indicates 5 percent of the norm group have a lower score. The children in the norm group were about 2 years older than the present children, being in the first month of starting the first grade.

As the results show there appears to be a considerable gain both in the intelligence measures as well as in the cognitive skills involved in readiness for school. It may be pointed out that these results are tentative —there may be practice effects in the intelligence tests, at least for the last time it was given. Nevertheless, the indication is that the training in

TABLE 13.6

INTELLIGENCE AND READINESS TEST SCORES
DURING THE STUDY

	September	December	Beginning April	End April
	IQ	IQ	IQ	IQ
Stanford-Binet (1937)	100.9	106.3	104.2	112.5
Metropolitan	%tile	%tile	%tile	%tile
Readiness Tests	2.3	4.5	14.3	23.8

the areas of cognitive development had effects that were reflected on the children's general intelligence measure. This finding is enhanced because the general expectation is that culturally-deprived children fall progressively behind on intellective measures as they grow older. It should be noted that the third time the intelligence test was given the examiners were inadvertently mixed and the examiner that systematically tended to give lower scores tested 7 of the children rather than the 5 this examiner tested the other three times. This may well have resulted in the lowness of the mean score relative to those of the other testings.

It is also of interest to examine the children's progress in cognitive readiness as measured by the Metropolitan. The Metropolitan tests the areas of *Word Meaning, Sentences,* and *Information,* as well as the areas of *Matching, Numbers,* and *Copying.* The results show that the children's overall scores increased considerably in these important areas of cognitive development. Moreover, examination of the children's improvement in the 6 areas showed that the major increases came in the areas of *Matching, Numbers,* and *Copying.* This is especially interesting since it was in these areas that the children received the cognitive training in the study. That is, the area of *Matching* tests the child's ability to discriminate stimuli, the *Numbers* area tests the child's number concept development, and the *Copying* area tests the child in the types of skills he received training on in the writing procedures.

In any event, the rate of the children's improvement on this test was marked and if continued would have made this group of children superior by the time they would enter the first grade—which would be about 1 year and 4 months after the final testing. In view of the fact that children such as these may be expected to lose ground in intellective development as measured by tests, the results on both of these intellective tests were very encouraging. Additional research should be conducted to more precisely examine the tested cognitive changes that occur as a result of the type of training that has been described.

Intelligence test measures are considered by many people to be indices of some basic, personal, attribute of intellectual quality such as a rate of learning (that is, ability to learn). According to the view, two children with different basic learning rates who are subjected to the same training circumstances will have different rates of cognitive development. With respect to this it was interesting to correlate the rapidity of learning to write with the children's intelligence measures. This was done by computing the mean time consumed per letter in learning to write and then relating these scores to the childrens IQ's. The Pearson correlation was .377, which means that 14 percent of the variation of the children's cognitive learning in this case could be accounted for by differences in

IQ scores. It should be noted that this statistic included the results for 2 children who actually worked for the greater part of the time on different materials aimed to prepare them to learn to write—and these children's scores contributed heavily to the size of the correlation.

This was also done for 11 of the 12 children in the number concept learning task by taking the number of responses required to learn all the skills up to the writing of the numbers 1 through 5. The Pearson correlation was .398, which means that 16 percent of the variation in this cognitive learning could be attributed to IQ score. In both of these cases it should also be pointed out that the children with the higher IQ's were better learners, especially at the beginning of the study, because of skills that had nothing to do with learning rate, for example, such things as rate of response, the quality of their attention, and so on.

Additional Conclusions

The major finding is that both the integrated-functional learning theory of these cognitive behaviors, and the associated experimental-longitudinal research method, received additional support. Cognitive development in these young children was produced through the presentation of specific stimulus circumstances, employing a motivational system that produced good attention and work behaviors.

The present experimental investigation of number concept learning and writing acquisition was conducted in greater detail, with greater systematization, and with a larger number of subjects, than the author's previous studies. The results of the number concept training appear to clearly suggest that this important cognitive repertoire is acquired according to the stimulus-response analysis. The various children, including the most difficult learning problem of them all, were trained to count objects regardless of the arrangement of the objects. The progress of this training occurred as predicted from the S–R analysis.

Moreover, all of the children, except the most difficult learning problem, learned to count unarranged objects up to 10. The other child learned to count five unarranged objects. Eight of the children also learned to write and read the numbers from 1 to 10, another child could do this from 1 to 9, and another from 1 to 5. There is no reason to doubt that the children could be presented with training materials of the present type that would give them full mathematical cognitive repertoires. This, of course, would require additional years of training, and further research is necessary to test this hypothesis.

Thus, the present results have wide implications for a consideration of cognitive development in general and of mathematics concepts in particular. It may be suggested that this type of cognitive development can be dealt with in very straightforward learning terms. This conclusion in turn suggests that learning analyses and experimental procedures of the present type should be elaborated and extended to provide a full and detailed treatment of this type of learning. It may be confidently expected that such a development would provide a complete scientific theory of this type of cognitive development which would give us understanding as well as have much practical value in terms of developing teaching materials—beginning as in the present case from the very onset of the acquisition of the repertoire.

The same types of results appeared to be true in the area of writing acquisition. The various children appeared to learn this cognitive repertoire in a straightforward stimulus-response manner, progressing similarly, at about the same rate, except for two children who required additional training in copying. Again, as with the other two types of learning it was possible to employ simple stimulus materials in a standard manner—administered by individuals not trained in working with children or in teaching.

It should be noted that the stimulus materials were really quite primitive and only sparse instructions were given to the trainer-experimenters. Much improvement could be made in both of these areas of research development.

In addition to providing support for the learning theory of cognitive development, the study also indicated the value of experimental-longitudinal research and the ability of the methods to produce replicable findings. Furthermore, the procedures also appeared to be of therapeutic value for the children. As suggested in the introduction to the present chapter, the fact that the theory and methods could be used effectively in the child's own interests has implications for the further development of a science of complex human behavior. That is, long term research with children cannot be conducted unless the children also benefit from the research. This requirement appeared to be met by the procedures, apparatus, and general laboratory facility that has been described herein.

One of the most important developments of the present line of research is methodological, that is, in the general strategy of research, the development of the apparatus, the general procedures (especially the reinforcement system), and in the general laboratory facility including the group classroom as well as the individual work rooms. This topic will not be discussed fully here. However, it may be suggested that this development represents a breakthrough in the experimental study of human intellective behavior. Using these methods and the learning theory it should be possible to investigate with the precision approaching that of the laboratory some of the most complex types of cognitive development. The present studies may be considered to have only touched upon the various possibilities of the development as a general research method.

Let us consider the apparatus and reinforcing system and its general applicability in a little more detail. One of the paths of progress in an area of research involves the development of apparatus and procedures by which new types of objective data may be collected. Much early work on instrumental conditioning utilized various adaptations of the maze, and the apparatus devised by Skinner for work with animals also represented a significant step forward. The latter apparatus offered a situation in which the dependent variable of the animal's behavior was easily obtained, and objective data produced. Furthermore, the dependent variable was sensitive to the manipulation of independent variables of various kinds.

The apparatus also was adaptable for the study of different types of behavior and different principles of learning. That is, it could be adapted for bar-pressing behavior in rats, key-pecking in pigeons, knob-pulling in primates, and so on. And, in addition to the principle of reinforcement, the principles involving discrimination learning, stimulus generalization, schedules, superstitious behavior, and so on, could also be objectively isolated and studied.

There is an implicit motivational aspect of animal research apparatus which is not easily reproduced with children, however, especially the very young or children with various behavioral difficulties. The participation and hard-working behaviors of the lab animal may be guaranteed by deprivation operations, or by the use of aversive stimulation and negative reinforcement. Those procedures are undesirable with children. Thus, an apparatus and reinforcement procedure of similar generality, in which complex learning can be studied objectively over the long durations necessary is not derivable from the animal procedures. The straightforward presentation of edibles (especially candy) to children has been useful for some research and treatment purposes, but it is restricted. There is a limit to how much can be given to a child under ordinary conditions. Furthermore, candy is ineffective with many children in long-term, arduous learning tasks.

One of the primary lines of progress of the present research has been the development of an experimental situation within which children could be run in long-term research, involved in complex learning tasks, without deprivation or the use of aversive stimulation. The apparatus has to be economical and easy to construct, generally applicable and effective, simple to use, and be capable of adaptation to the study of various types of learning with children of various age groups. The earlier laboratory procedures of the author lacked some of the necessary characteristics stated above, especially those of simplicity, ease and economy of construction, and generality of application.

The author's present apparatus, however, does fulfill these needs. This apparatus, developed in long-term research with the author's daughter, is susceptible, moreover, to considerable adaptation to fit various types of research needs. Various degrees of mechanical and electronic sophistication can be used in adaptations of the basic apparatus and procedures. Counters can be mounted above the tubes to make the marble count precise and automatic. Furthermore, the stimuli can be presented to the child automatically. (Where it is desirable to retain the free operant characteristics of the apparatus, activation of a button by the child can be included as the event that dictates presentation of a stimulus.) Programming equipment can be used with this basic design. Memory drums could be used also. Furthermore, the response of the child can be automatically recorded in cases where the response involves the activation of a piece of equipment. Automation of the stimulus presentation and the recording of the response (and the delivery of the toys) would make it possible to remove the experimenter from the situation. This is technically quite possible and was approached in several of the preceding studies.

The simplest apparatus is depicted in Figure 13.5, however. As the preceding study demonstrated, the entire research operation can be handled by one experimenter. This only requires that the stimulus materials and presentation procedures be specified beforehand, as well as the recording procedures. The experimenter can devise data sheets for recording responses easily, and well controlled experiments can then be conducted in which each stimulus presentation is recorded as well as each response. It is this simplicity that gives the basic apparatus its flexibility and generality of use.

It may serve in this context to briefly summarize some of the types of research that can be conducted with this apparatus as well as some types of populations of children that can be investigated. In the first use of a modification of the present type of apparatus, the acquisition of reading responses to letters was studied as a type of discrimination learning. It is suggested that the presently described apparatus would lend itself to the investigations of any kind of complex stimulus discrimination which requires many learning trials and long-term participation.

In addition, as in the present study, the apparatus may be used to study complex cognitive learning, like reading acquisition, writing acquisition, and number concept learning, and other types as well. For example, as part of the letter reading discrimination study with retarded children, one mongoloid child who previously had no spontaneous language, although he would repeat a few words, was trained to name ten objects. The apparatus could easily be applied to the systematic study of speech development in preverbal children, or the study of further vocabulary acquisition in children who already speak. The apparatus could also be used in the study of the treatment of speech pathologies.

The author has adapted the reinforcement procedure for work with adolescent children who are remedial reading cases, as will be described in the next chapter. For younger children with school learning problems, the apparatus could be used with no alterations.

In addition, the apparatus would lend itself well to the study of more traditional areas of child learning. For example, paired associate and serial verbal learning could be studied in young children hitherto unavailable for such learning studies. Moreover, this use of the apparatus with children before they have acquired the extensive word associations of the adult, as well as various strategies of word learning, should enable verbal learning to be studied in a much more controlled manner, unconfounded by individual differences in word associations or strategies.

The same advantages would be available for investigating "concept formation" in children, as well as various types of complex stimulus discriminations. As summarized in the micro-experiment already described, it was possible to study the formation of "consonant" concepts where the consonant letter concept was presented in different consonant-vowel pairs and had to be abstracted in a manner analogous to Hull's (1920) original analysis of concept formation. Various analyses of reading acquisition could be studied and compared in the present type of research.

In addition, the basic conditions of reinforcement may be studied through the use of this apparatus. The previously presented study of reinforcement schedules explored this possibility using a more elaborate apparatus. However, questions regarding the schedules best for long term learning of complex skills by young children are largely unanswered. Furthermore, interesting questions arise in the individual differences shown by the subjects in their use of reinforcers. Rough data seems to suggest that younger children, and more retarded children, use the marbles for more immediate back-up reinforcers. This suggests that the extent to which longer term goals come to be effective is learned and this possibility can be studied using this apparatus.

Furthermore, the apparatus and procedures lend themselves to the study of various kinds of populations of children as has been implicit in some of the above examples. That is, the author has employed the apparatus and procedures with children ranging from 2 years of age through 14 years of age. The learning of educable retarded children and trainable retarded children has also been investigated. It may be pointed out that the apparatus enables the study of *complex learning* with these children—such as language development, number concept learning, and so on. It is the long term study of such complex skills that must be conducted to ascertain the potentialities and limitations in learning of various types of children. The apparatus has also been employed with culturally-deprived children, and with disturbed children who represent special learning problems. It may be suggested that the apparatus could generally be used in treatment and research with a wide variety of cases of psychological disorders in children which are of interest to clinical psychology and psychiatry.

It may be concluded that the apparatus and reinforcement procedure, with adaptations in terms of type and kind of stimulus presentation and recording and type and kind of behaviors and recording, appear to enable the collection of objective data over long periods of time, dealing with repertoires of varying degress of complexity. It has the same advantages for work with children and the study of complex learning, as the Skinner box has for animals and the study of simple learning. The general laboratory situation involving the general classroom and adjoining experimental rooms, has the same value for research and treatment work with children. These implications, however, will be discussed further on.

Another point will be raised at this time which will receive further attention later on. One of the important findings of the studies already presented, as well as those to follow, has been that children, regardless of measured IQ, appear to be capable of complex cognitive learning— and in a manner and at a rate which is relatively similar. This strongly suggests to the author that personal differences in learning ability are probably much smaller than has heretofore been considered. A not unlikely tentative hypothesis is that *any* normally constructed human is capable of the most complex cognitive learning, when the learning conditions insure the necessary participation, attentional, and work behaviors, and so on. It would seem quite probable that any group of children, such as those who have participated in the research so far, provided with properly motivated learning conditions and appropriately constructed stimulus materials could acquire the most complex of verbal and mathematical cognitive repertoires.

This is not to say that children cannot and do not ordinarily learn wide differences in basic skills—as was evident in the children treated so far—and that these differences do not produce very wide variations in the children's ability to learn in the traditional classroom situations. Thus, in the present study, the two "brightest" children (with IQ's of 117 and 130) did show differences from most of the other children in behaviors that would be important to classroom learning. One aspect of advancement involved their immediate adjustment to the learning situation. They had well acquired attentional and learning behaviors to begin with —they followed instructions well, attended well, and so on. Many of the other children were much slower in the beginning, until the requisite behaviors necessary for learning had been acquired.

Moreover, these two children, and later on some of the others with them, were very concerned with their progress. They would compare how much they had gotten in the training sessions, and they would "boast" about what they had learned and what they could do. It was evident that these two had received training that in common sense terms made them "want to learn" (competitively so in fact). Other observations seemed to indicate that the children were reinforced for their accomplishments at home also.

As a consequence of these basic behaviors, these children were also more capable in various types of things as was clearly shown in the classroom. They followed instructions better, and learned more quickly to paint better and to dance better, and so on. On the basis of this type of general performance, these children were easily spotted as the "brightest" of the group.

It may be suggested that in the usual classroom situation these two children, because of these cognitive and attitudinal skills, would ordinarily have learned much more than their companions. The present results, however, suggest that when individually good learning conditions were presented the other children were also capable of learning in a manner more closely on a par with the two most capable children.

The implication is, of course, that the major differences between these various children involved the conditions of learning which their life circumstances had presented to them. The author has previously suggested that we can train our children to be intelligent and that we must conduct long term research to assess the limits within which this is possible (Staats and Staats, 1963). The present findings provide support for this assertion, and also suggest methods by which to further investigate these possibilities. This conception will be elaborated further on.

One further point will be made concerning the present methods and findings. The nursery school situation in the present laboratory has not been described, and it was not the subject of systematic study. However, learning principles were applied in this group situation, and with good affect. For example, the behaviors of the children were reinforced when desirable and extinguished or mildly punished when undesirable. The mild punishment was one that the author first used in training Jennifer a number of years ago, and which has since been employed systematically in research (Wolf and Risely, 1964). It has a long history of use by some parents and could be called "banishment from reinforcing activities" or time out from such activities. In the present circumstances it was employed with especially good effect with the child who had severe temper tantrums. Whenever she had one she was sent to a corner of the room. At first it was necessary to physically restrain her so that she remained there. There she would cry, kick, scream, and so on. The other children quickly adjusted to this and paid no attention to her. In addition to this use of punishment, a systematic effort was made to single this child out for attention and approval when she was behaving well. This treatment plus the experimental training resulted in a marked improvement in the behavior of this child; her temper tantrums became very infrequent and of less intensity. It is significant to note that this child has since, in her first few months of public school, returned to being a severe behavior problem. She is now being evaluated for psychological treatment. This demonstrated clearly that the special classroom procedures in conjunction with the special individual training procedures could function to reduce the child's behavior problems. Of equal importance, the procedures could be employed to prevent the child from developing cognitive behavior deficits.

It may be suggested again that the present facility and procedures could be used to good effect for research and treatment with emotionally disturbed children. In this manner therapeutic treatment of their emotional, social, and cognitive problems could be dealt with in a manner that would also produce scientific data. It is the author's contention, based upon the present types of objective findings as well as the general rationale, that children with behavior problems should be treated in the context of the learning environments which constitute a child's most important areas of adjustment. "Emotional disturbances," "behavior problems," or whatever the term, are important in large part because they interfere with the child's adjustment to learning situations and thus prevent learning. Thus, cognitive, or social or emotional, deficits are commonly the concommitants of "emotional disturbance." Moreover, it makes no sense to attempt to treat a child in an artificial therapy situation. The child should be treated where his inappropriate behaviors occur and where his behavioral deficits would ordinarily be acquired. As the present studies have indicated, it is possible to conduct this type of treatment (and research) with children, either in the home or the school, or both. The following chapter will provide material which supplements this analysis.

14

Learning theory and behavior modification

The philosophy of the present approach is that a science of complex human behavior must rest upon basic, analytic, principles—which must be found in the laboratory, not in the naturalistic observation of society or naturalistic observations obtained in the clinic. The present book, except for the just preceding chapters, has dealt more with the learning theory of human behavior than with clinical and social applications of the theory and its research methods. This is simply a strategem, however, since once the theory and research methods are established it becomes equally important in the extension and elaboration of the theory to extend these developments to clinical and social problems. Although this is not the place for a full presentation, it is relevant within the present context to mention a few points involved in a learning theory which intends to deal with problems of human behavior.

First, it may be suggested that what we call personality refers to the individual's learned repertoires of behavior—most of them of fantastic complexity, when subjected to a detailed S–R analysis. It is quite conceivable that people could genetically inherit certain emotional response differences as well as differences in rate of learning, the total number of S–R mechanisms that can be learned, physical characteristics such as health and strength, sensory acuity, speed of response, and so on, and perhaps other basic response capacities. However, *what* the individual comes to be, on the basis of these response variations, must be accounted for in terms of learning principles.

For example, it may be that one child responds more strongly to an aversive (painful) stimulus than does another child (although it should be added that all physically normal children will respond similarly to the same unconditioned stimuli). What neutral stimuli will become aversive for either of the children, however, will depend entirely upon the nature of the child's conditioning history. The emotions (or values, attitudes, needs, interests) he feels towards various people, ideas, customs, activities, statements, issues, and so on—in short, the nature of what the author terms the individual's reinforcing (motivational) system—will be determined by the individual's conditioning history, according to the principles of classical conditioning. The variability that is possible between people on the basis of their conditioning histories is fantastically large in both the intensity of the emotional conditioning as well as in the variety of stimuli involved.

And, as complex as the effects of the individual's classical conditioning history are, there are equally or more complex effects of his instrumental conditioning history. The individual's motor, sensory-motor, social, and intellectual repertoires can all be considered to be a function of the individual's conditioning. Again, although there could be basic differences in the rapidity with which an individual can acquire instrumental S–R associations, or in the total number he can acquire, whatever is in the individual's repertoire depends upon his conditioning history. What the individual says, what he does, how he works, how creative, how intelligent, and so, whether he is a criminal or a saint, whether a college professor or a skilled worker, and so on, all involve a fantastically complicated instrumental (and classical) conditioning history.

The individual, or the individual's personality—which in the present terms may be called his total behavioral repertoire, including all of his infinitely complex and unique S–R mechanisms—is formed by the nature of his experiences, according to the principles of learning. Furthermore, at any time the individual "functions" according to these same principles. That is, his repertoire is of such and such a sort because of his conditioning history, but in addition present stimulus circumstances elicit those parts of the repertoire in accordance with those principles. This, of course, will also create new experiences which will affect the nature of the individual's total repertoire in future stimulus circumstances. Thus, at any time, the individual's experience dictates what his behavior is at that time and also produces learning that will effect the way he will behave at a later time.

But these are very general statements concerning the theory of human behavior. In order to deal effectively with various aspects of human behavior, and in order to understand human behavior, it is necessary to have specific and detailed analyses of the various repertoires—social, emotional, cognitive, sensory-motor, and so on. The task of a learning theory of personality is to provide such analyses. The task of a learning theory of clinical psychology includes working out through research well specified analyses and procedures for understanding and dealing with the problems of such behavioral repertoires. This must be done so the product is scientific—communicable and replicable in a standard manner by the trained person—not artistic in the sense already mentioned.

The progress we have had so far in the fields of behavior therapy and behavior modification represents only the barest beginning. This research and treatment has been largely limited to simple behaviors and short-term studies which have had their major significance as demonstrations that learning principles do apply to human behaviors of an abnormal variety.

The lack of conceptual development of behavior therapy and behavior modification is related to the separatism that has already been described —with the field of behavior therapy deriving largely from a Hullian theoretical framework, and using classical conditioning principles, and the field of behavior modification presently depending on applying operant conditioning principles and the operant conditioning philosophy, including its antipathy for theoretical analyses. The necessary integration of the various learning principles has not been evidenced by the investigators involved in clinical psychology. (See Staats, 1967b, for a more extensive analysis of behavior therapy and behavior modification in terms of the integrated learning theory.)

Moreover, the theoretical elaboration of the learning principles in the context of behavior problems has not previously been carried very far. The most developed theoretical effort outside of the author's account (see Staats, 1967b; Staats and Staats, 1963) was provided in the work of Dollard and Miller (1950) and this approach stressed psychoanalytical analysis more than it did an intensive application of the principles of learning.

The present author (Staats and Staats, 1963) applied his integrated learning theory to the problems of human behavior and their treatment in an outline attempting to resolve the divergent views and indicate some of the possibilities for a more detailed learning analysis. In completing a learning analysis it must be expected that although the learning theory provides the basic principles of a personality and clinical theory, the application of the principles will also involve the elaboration of new conceptions, ones that derive from clinical and social observations (see Staats, 1967b).

Thus, for example, the author has suggested that behavior problems can arise, because (1) there is a deficit of behavior necessary for adjustment in our society, (2) because behaviors considereu undesirable by the society are present in the individual's repertoire, or (3) because the individual's motivational (reinforcement) system is inappropriate in some respect.

Actually, it should be indicated that there may be interaction between these classes of behavioral defects. Thus, the individual who has deficits in behavior may not as a consequence gain positive reinforcement—the receipt of which in contiguity with other stimuli would produce additional development of his motivational (reinforcement) system. For example, the male with deficits in social behaviors may not be able to interact with normal women so that he experiences sexual reinforcement necessary to further develop his learned "sexual" reinforcement system. Homosexuality, thus, may at a primary level involve a deficit in social behaviors. As another example, certain deficits in behavior (for example, the lack of intellectual or social skills) are punished socially and the punishment may help produce an inappropriate "social" reinforcement system.

On the other hand, a defective motivational system can lead to behavioral deficits. A child for whom learning something new, doing well in comparison to others, an adult's approval, and so on, are not positive reinforcers—a defect in achievement motivation—will not adjust well to one of his most crucial cognitive learning situations, the classroom. That is, his work and attentional behaviors will not be maintained. As a consequence, he will later evidence deficits in his cognitive repertoires.

As another example, the individual with unpleasant inappropriate behavior may as a consequence be shunned and not obtain the social experiences necessary to learn an adequate social repertoire. Moreover, the deficit in social experience may leave deficits in his motivational system. *Ordinarily, with severely abnormal individuals these various processes occur and interact producing various deficits and inappropriacies in the behavioral repertoire.*

The author as a student at UCLA had worked with children with emotional and learning problems in the late Grace Fernald's clinic. In the course of this experience he became convinced that the major problems of learning for these children were motivational (reinforcement problems) and involved the poor maintenance of their working and attentional behaviors. That is, in the present terms, it was felt that the children's primary difficulty was a motivational deficit and that introduction of a functional reinforcing system would treat the cognitive deficit. In the late 1950's the author began to extend the learning principles to the systematic consideration of cognitive deficits and by 1959 completed a pilot study with six retarded readers. One of the articles to follow describes a study that elaborates and extends the analyses and procedures, beginning a series of studies of "motivated learning" behavioral treatment methods. The cognitive deficit dealt with is reading, but the procedures have a wide applicability to the treatment of other behavioral deficits as well. It has also been suggested herein that a learning clinical psychology must produce procedures for the treatment of complex behaviors that can be standardly applied and are replicable. This paper attempts to give an example of such standard procedures to employ in research and treatment. The explicitness of the principles and the procedures employed should make them capable of easy communicability and use. Because of this it should be possible to make standard applications by subprofessional individuals trained solely in the specific therapeutic procedure. Thus, William H. Butterfield, an officer of the Maricopa County Juvenile Probation Department (Phoenix, Arizona), although not a therapist or teacher, applied the author's treatment procedures in the study. The article appeared in the 1965 volume of *Child Development*. In the follow-up study (Staats, Minke, Goodwin, and Landeen, 1967) volunteer housewives and high school seniors were used as the therapy-technicians. This study is briefly summarized at the end of the chapter.

The above concept that is important to an understanding of abnormal behavior is that the behavior can be a result of deficits, or inappropriate aspects, in the individual's learned reinforcement system. (The manner in which differences in individuals' learned reinforcement system will cause differences in their behaviors will be discussed further on.) In addition, however, abnormal behaviors may arise because of the way that "normal" reinforcers are applied—that is, the "rules" for the application of reinforcement that are in effect. For example, the attention of other people is a "normal" reinforcer for all of us. However, if attention is given for inappropriate behaviors then those behaviors will increase in frequency. This can be seen very readily with children where many undesirable behaviors are learned because the behaviors get attention. Many children learn, for example, to whine and cry and make objectionable noises because the busy parent does not look at them when they request something in an appropriate, well modulated tone of voice.

As another example, many years ago the author, as a Veterans Administration trainee in a neuropsychiatric hospital, observed that many times it was the bizarre behaviors of the patient that attracted attention. When the patient made some symptomatic behavior, the psychologist or psychiatrist would become interested and attend to and respond to the patient in an attempt to explore the "psycho-dynamics" of the symptom. It appeared that it was the social reinforcement of this attention that was in many cases maintaining abnormal behavior—and perhaps was also responsible for the origin of the symptom. (In a more complete analysis, this type of symptom learning would also have to be discussed in terms of deficits in behavior usually employed by the "normal" person to get attention.)

The author wrote the original version of the following article when a case that involved this process occurred in the literature. This was published in the *Journal of Abnormal and Social Psychology* of 1957, at a time when clinical applications of instrumental conditioning principles had not yet commenced, and it anticipates the form that the early behavior modification studies later took. Actually, the author, with the help of John Michael, had in 1956 already conducted a behavior modification procedure to improve self-confident speech in a fellow graduate student. This was done by the addition of systematic positive social reinforcement contingent on the confident speech and the deletion of argumentative aversiveness that had more customarily been given. (Like the author's other experimental naturalistic findings, however, the study was never published, but it served as the basis for subsequent research.) Later, Ayllon and Michael (1959), in a very influential paper, showed very clearly in an experimental fashion the several major points suggested in the article to be presented in the next section: (1) abnormal or undesirable behavior may be decreased through extinction, (2) desirable behavior may be strengthened through social reinforcement, and (3) there may be nontherapeutic interactions between patient and hospital personnel in which abnormal behaviors are reinforced and thus learned. It is also worth noting that this early paper demonstrates the possibilities of integrating diverse theoretical concepts in the analysis of complex human behavior.

The two papers to be presented are only examples, it should be indicated. The first of them is an example of the analyses we must have to begin to work with abnormal behaviors. The second, along with the preceding experiments, attempts to suggest that we need detailed theoretical and experimental analyses of complex behaviors which are of adjustmental value and that we need then to work on procedures for producing these behaviors—both with normal and abnormal populations.

LEARNING THEORY AND "OPPOSITE SPEECH"

Laffal, Lenkoski, and Ameen (1956), have recently reported the case of a schizophrenic patient demonstrating what they call an "opposite speech" syndrome. The authors state that the syndrome is basically a reversal in certain language usages, especially in the use of "yes" and "no." Feeling that the speech reversal is an expression of repressed hostility, they suggest that opposite speech copes with the hostile impulses by disrupting communication and rejecting other people or by allowing the "verbalization of ideas which the patient consciously rejects." (1956, p. 412)

Laffal, et al. conclude that learning theory has little to offer in this instance or others of pathological speech."The so-called pragmatic and interpersonal functions of language behavior have been largely neglected by learning theorists in favor of the meaning or semantic aspects." (1956, p. 412)

However, a number of recent experimental and theoretical studies (such as Cohen, et al., 1956; Dollard and Miller, 1950; Greenspoon, 1950; Staats, 1955; Verplanck, 1955) have been very much concerned with similar problems of language behavior. Several points can thus be made from a learning theory approach which have relevance for "opposite speech." Instead of asking, as do Laffal, et al., "what uses (needs) the opposite speech may serve," (1956, p. 412) learning theory is concerned with the conditions which increase the probability that the response will occur again in similar stimulus situations, that strengthen the response.

It has been shown experimentally that social reinforcement which follows verbal responses has the effect of increasing their frequency. These studies have used various social reinforcements. The question is thus raised regarding the reinforcements involved in opposite speech. It is suggested that attention, operating as a reinforcer, could account in part for the origin and maintenance of opposite speech. The interview quoted by Laffal (1956, p. 411) is a good demonstration of how the patient's opposite speech could elicit attention from others. The therapists strongly attended to the patient when his speech reversals occurred. They asked questions about the reversals, about why he said one thing when he meant another, and so on. The particular attention paid to his disordered speech can be expected to have strengthened that type of speech. His "realistic" speech was by contrast given little reinforcement and would be expected to extinguish as a consequence. Other reinforcers would also be effective in strengthening reversed language. For example, the patient's reversals were said to "not extend to thought or action. Thus, if asked if he wishes a cigaret, the patient may say, 'No' instead of 'Yes, I do,' but he accepts and smokes the cigaret" (1956, p. 412). Giving the cigaret to the "No" response is a reinforcement and would be expected to strengthen that response, that is, raise the probability that the patient would again say "No" in the same situation. Reinforcements such as these, without concomitant admonition, would be unlikely to occur in the normal person's social environment.

Certain implications are derivable from this interpretation. If the opposite speech is maintained by positive reinforcement, then lack of such reinforcement should lead to extinction of such behavior. For example, withholding the cigaret should weaken the strength of opposite speech, and giving the cigaret to correct speech should strengthen that type of response.

Another example of learning theory formulations applicable to opposite speech is offered by Dollard and Miller (1950). They discuss repression in terms of reinforcement theory. Certain thoughts arouse anxiety. Cessation of thinking those thoughts reduces anxiety. Thus, stopping thinking about that topic becomes a well-learned response. The same analysis can be applied to speech. Dollard and Miller (1950) give an example of a group of people who change the topic of a conversation because it arouses anxiety, and state, "people tend to learn to avoid unpleasant topics of conversation." (1950, p. 199)

It could be said that the schizophrenic patient's verbal behavior, when it is not confused by reversal, elicits an anxiety response in him, perhaps because of its typical content. Confused ways of speaking, and perhaps even of thinking, would therefore be anxiety reducing. This rationale could be extended to obsessive thinking in addition to other types of confused schizophrenic speech and thought. In addition, for the schizophrenic, communication with others which is understandable probably introduces touchy subjects which arouse anxiety. Reversed verbal behavior and other confused speech may reduce anxiety when it produces breakdown of the communication and cessation of the anxiety producing subject matter or of the bothersome conversation itself.

Why the schizophrenic's speech might elicit anxiety in him need not herein be elaborated, since the speech symptom is the relevant topic. It could be stated, however, that the unhappy life situation of an adult schizophrenic probably elicits thought and speech which are not positive secondary reinforcers, but instead arouse anxiety. It is also probable that the lack of success of the schizophrenic's life behavior evokes verbal behavior from others which is anxiety producing for the schizophrenic. Verbal and nonverbal behavior of the schizophrenic which would avoid this anxiety would thus be well learned.

In concluding, it should be stated that this note is not intended as a complete analysis of the opposite speech of the schizophrenic patient. Perhaps it points out that hypotheses which apply to pathological language can be derived from a learning theory approach. At any rate, it is suggested that learning theory has reached a state where it has some-thing to offer clinical theory *and practice.* The complex activities to which contemporary learning theory addresses itself, and not without success, indicate that the approach can no longer be ignored.

TREATMENT OF NONREADING IN A CULTURALLY DEPRIVED JUVENILE DELINQUENT: AN APPLICATION OF REINFORCEMENT PRINCIPLES

Staats (1964d; Staats and Staats, 1963) has previously discussed be-havior problems and their treatment in terms of learning principles. In doing so it was indicated that problem behaviors can arise in part (1) because behavior that is necessary for adjustment in our society is absent from the individual's repertoire, (2) because behaviors considered un-desirable by the society are present in the individual's repertoire, or (3) because the individual's motivational (reinforcement) system was inap-propriate in some respect.

Although a complete account is not relevant here, several points perti-nent to the above conceptions will be made in introducing the present study. The notion that many behavior problems consist of deficits in behavior is important in the study of child development. Behaviorally speaking, a child is considered to be a problem when he does not acquire behaviors as other children do. It is conceivable that a deficit in behavior could arise because the child simply cannot acquire the behavior in-volved, even though the conditions of learning have been entirely adequate.

It would be expected, however, that behavioral deficits would also arise in cases where the conditions of learning have been defective. Learning conditions can be defective in different ways. For example, the child may never have received training in the behavior he must later exhibit. Or the training may be poor, even though the "trainers," parents or teachers, and so on, have the best intentions.

In addition, however, a child may be exposed to learning conditions that are appropriate for most children but, due to the particular child's past history of learning, are not appropriate for him. It is especially in these cases that people are most likely to conclude erroneously that since other children learn in the same circumstances, the child's deficit must be because of some personal defect. For example, in cases where the training is long-term, adequate reinforcement must be available to maintain the attentional and work behaviors necessary for learning. As Staats has indicated (1964d; Staats and Staats, 1963; Staats, *et al.*, 1962), the reinforcers present in the traditional schoolroom are inadequate for many children. Their attentional behaviors are not maintained, and they do not learn. Thus, a deficit in an individual's behavioral repertoire may arise although he has been presented with the "same" training circumstances from which other children profit. Learning does not take place because the child's previous experience has not provided, in this example, the necessary reinforcer (motivational) system to maintain good "learning" behaviors. It would seem that in such a circumstance the assumption that the child has a personal defect would be unwarranted and ineffective.

However, after a few years of school attendance where the conditions of learning are not appropriate for the child, he will not have acquired the behavioral repertoires acquired by more fortunate members of the class—whose previous experiences have established an adequate motivational system. Then, lack of skilled behavior is likely to be treated aversively. That is, in the present case, the child with a reading deficit (or other evidence of under-achievement) is likely to be gibed at and teased when he is still young and ignored, avoided, and looked down upon when he is older. Although the individuals doing this may not intend to be aversive, such actions constitute the presentation of aversive stimuli. Furthermore, this presentation of aversive stimuli by other "successful" children, and perhaps by a teacher, would be expected to result in further learning, but learning of an undesirable nature. These successful children, teachers, academic materials, and the total school situation can in this way become learned negative reinforcers, which may be translated (see Staats, 1964d) to say the child acquires negative attitudes toward school.

At this, point, the child is likely to begin to "escape" the school situation in various ways (daydreaming, poor attendance, and so on) and to behave aversively in turn to the school and its inhabitants (vandalism, fighting, baiting teachers and students, and the like). Thus, a deficit in behavior, resulting from an inappropriate motivational system, can lead to the further development of inappropriate reinforcers and inappropriate behaviors.

The foregoing is by no means intended as a complete analysis of delinquency, dropouts, and the like. However, it does indicate some of the problems of learning that may occur in school. In addition, it does suggest that an analysis in terms of laboratory-established learning principles, when applied to problems such as in classroom learning of the above type, can yield new research and applied hypotheses. It was with this general strategy that the study of reading acquisition employing learning principles and reinforcement procedures was commenced (Staats, 1964a; Staats, et al., 1962; Staats, et al., 1964a; Staats, et al., 1964b). The present study is a replication and an extension of these various findings to the development of a program for training nonreaders to read. The program, which adapts standard reading materials, is based upon the principle of the reinforcer system employed in the previous studies with the younger children, thus testing the principles of reinforcement in the context of remedial reading training, as well as the feasibility of using the type of reinforcement system with a new type of S. As such, the study has implications for the study of nonreading children of preadolescent, and young adult ages. In the present case, S was also a culturally deprived delinquent child—and the study thus involves additional information and implications for the special problems associated with education in this population of children.

Methods

Subject

The S was a 14-year-and-3-month-old boy of Mexican-American ancestry. He was the fifth child in a family of 11 children and the mother and father. The parental techniques for controlling their children's behavior consisted of physical and verbal abuse. Both parents described their own childhood conditions as primitive. The father was taken out of school after completing the fifth grade to help with his father's work. Each of S's four older brothers had been referred to the juvenile court for misbehavior. The parents appeared to be at loss as to how to provide effective control for family members.

The S had a history of various miscreant behaviors, having been referred to the juvenile department nine times for such things as running away, burglary, incorrigibility, and truancy. During the course of the study S was again referred on a complaint (with three other boys) of malicious mischief [vandalism] for shooting light bulbs and windows in a school building with a BB gun. He associated with a group of boys who had been in marked difficulty with the law. The S smoked, and on occasion he drank excessively.

The study commenced when S was residing with his family. However, after the complaint on malicious mischief S was sent to a juvenile detention home. During his stay there he was allowed to attend school in the daytime. The study was finally concluded when S was committed to an industrial school for juvenile delinquent boys. This occurred because S baited the attendants at the detention home and caused disturbances which, although not serious, were very unpleasant and disruptive.

On the Wechsler Bellevue Form 1, given when S was 13-10, he received Verbal and Performance IQ's of 77 and 106, respectively, for a Full Scale IQ of 90. The examiner concluded that S was probably within the normal range for this test. On the basis of this test and HTP Projective Drawings, S was characterized as having a poor attention span and poorly integrated thought processes and as lacking intellectual ambitiousness. He was also described as seeking satisfaction in fantasy and as having good conventional judgment.

The S had continually received failing grades in all subjects in school. He was described as having "been incorrigible since he came here in the second grade. He has no respect for teachers, steals and lies habitually and uses extremely foul language." The S had been promoted throughout his school career simply to move him on or to "get rid of him." He was disliked by the teachers and administrators in grade school because of his troublesome behavior and was described by the principal as mentally retarded even though one of the tests taken there indicated a score within the normal range. Another test taken there gave him an IQ of 75. During the study S was attending a local high school and taking classes for low-level students.

Reinforcer System

In previous studies (Staats, 1966; Staats, et al., 1964a; 1964b), a reinforcer system was demonstrated that was capable of maintaining attention and work behaviors for long-term experimental studies. This system worked well with preschool children of ages 2 to 6 and with educable and trainable retardates of ages 8 to 11. The principle of the system was based upon token reinforcers. The tokens were presented contingent upon correct responses and could be exchanged for items the child could keep. In the previous studies toys of various values could be obtained when a sufficient number of tokens had been accrued in visible containers.

This system was adapted for use with the adolescent S of the present study. In the adaptation there were three types of tokens, distinguished by color. The tokens were of different value in terms of the items for which the tokens could be exchanged. A blue token was valued at $\frac{1}{10}$ of one cent. A white token was valued at $\frac{1}{3}$ of a cent. A red token was worth $\frac{1}{2}$ of a cent.

The child's acquisition of tokens was plotted so that visual evidence of the reinforcers was available. The tokens could be used to purchase a variety of items. These items, chosen by the subject, could range in value from pennies to whatever the subject wished to work for. Records were kept of the tokens earned by S and of the manner in which the tokens were used.

Reading Materials

The reading material used was taken from the Science Research Associates (SRA) reading-kit materials. The SRA kits consist of stories developed for and grouped into grade levels. Each story includes a series of questions which can be used to assess the reader's comprehension of the story. The reading training program was adapted from the SRA materials as follows:

VOCABULARY WORDS   A running list was made of the new words that appeared in the series of stories. The list finally included each different word that appeared in the stories that were presented. From this list, the new vocabulary for each story was selected, and each word was typed on a separate 3 × 5 card.

ORAL READING MATERIALS   Each paragraph in the SRA stories was typed on a 5 × 8 card. Each story could thus be presented to S paragraph by paragraph.

SILENT-READING AND COMPREHENSIVE-QUESTION MATERIALS   Each SRA story, with its comprehensive questions, was typed on an $8\frac{1}{2}$ × 13 sheet of white paper.

Procedure

VOCABULARY PRESENTATION   The procedure for each story in the series commenced with the presentation of the new words introduced in that story. The words were presented individually on the cards, and S was asked to pronounce them. A correct response to a word-stimulus card was reinforced with a midvalue token. After a correct response to a word, the card was dropped from the group of cards yet to be presented. The S was instructed to indicate words that he did not know the meaning of, and this information was provided in such cases.

When an incorrect response to a word stimulus occurred, or when S gave no response, E gave the correct response. The S then repeated the word while looking at the stimulus word. However, the word card involved was returned to the group of cards still to be presented. A card was not dropped from the group until it was read correctly without prompting. After an error on a word stimulus, only a low-value token was given on the next trial when the word was read correctly without prompting. The vocabulary-presentation phase of the training was continued until each word was read correctly without prompting.

ORAL READING Upon completion of the vocabulary materials, each paragraph was individually presented to S in the order in which the paragraph occurred in the story. When correct reading responses were made to each word in the paragraph, a high-value token was given upon completion of the paragraph. When a paragraph contained errors, S was corrected, and he repeated the word correctly while looking at the word. The paragraph was put aside, and when the other paragraphs had been completed, the paragraph containing errors was again presented. The paragraph was repeated until it was done correctly in its entirety—at which time a midvalue token was presented. When all paragraphs in a story had been completed correctly, the next phase of the training was begun.

SILENT READING AND COMPREHENSIVE QUESTIONS Following the oral reading S was given the sheet containing the story and questions. He was instructed to read the story silently and to answer the questions beneath the story. He was also instructed that it was important to read to understand the story so that he could answer the questions.

Reinforcement was given on a variable interval schedule for attentive behavior during the silent reading phase. That is, as long as S appropriately scanned the material he was given a low-value reinforcer an average of every 15 seconds. The exact time for reinforcement was determined by a table of random numbers varying from 1 to 30 seconds. Whenever he did anything other than peruse the material, no reinforcement was given. The next interval was then timed from the moment S returned to the silent reading, with the stipulation that no reinforcement be given sooner than 5 seconds after S returned to the reading. If the interval was less than 5 seconds, a token was not given until the next interval had also occurred. Timing was done by a continuously running stopwatch. The S was also given an extra midvalue token at the end of the silently read story on those occasions where he read without moving his lips.

Upon completion of the story, S wrote his answers to the questions typed below the story and gave his answers to E. For each correct answer, S received a high-value token. For an answer with a spelling error, S was reinforced with a midvalue token when he had corrected the answer. For incorrect answers S had to reread the appropriate paragraph, correct his answer and he then received a midvalue token.

VOCABULARY REVIEW   Some of the vocabulary words presented to S in the first phase of training were words he already could read. Many others, however, were words that the procedure was set up to teach. The oral-reading-phase performance indicated the level of S's retention of the words he had learned—and also provided further training trials on the words not already learned. A further assessment of S's retention of the words that he did not know in the vocabulary training was made after each 20 stories of the SRA materials had been read. This test of individually presented words, for each story, was started about 3 days after completion of the 20 stories and constituted fairly long-term retention.

This test was also used as a review for S, and further training on the words was given. This was first done by reinforcing S with a low-value token for every word he read correctly. However, S's attention was not well maintained by this reinforcement, and the procedure was changed to provide a midvalue token for correctly read words. When S could not read a word, or missed one, he was prompted and had to correctly repeat the name of the word while looking at the word. This word card was then put aside and presented later, at which time S was reinforced with a low-value token if he read it correctly. If not, the procedure was repeated until a correct unprompted trial occurred.

ACHIEVEMENT TESTS   Prior to the commencement of the training, S was tested to assess his reading performance, and during the period of experimental training he was given two additional reading-achievement tests. The first one given was the Developmental Reading Test. (At this time the S's vision and hearing were also tested and found to be normal.) After 45 training sessions another reading test was given S, this time the California Reading Test, Form BB, for grades 1, 2, 3 and L-4. Twenty-five sessions later, just before the termination of the study, S was given the California Reading Test, Form BB, for grades 4, 5, and 6. The S's performance on the three reading tests constituted one of the measures of his progress. The tests were given at the Arizona State University Reading Center.

TRAINING SESSIONS   The training sessions would ordinarily last for 1 hour or less, although a few sessions were as short as 30 minutes or as long as 2 hours. Not all of this time was spent in reading, however. A good deal of time was spent in arranging the materials, recording S's performance, keeping count of the reinforcers, plotting the reinforcers accrued, and so on. The time spent actually reading was tabulated. During the $4\frac{1}{2}$ month experimental period, 70 training sessions were conducted, with an average of about 35 minutes spent per session for a total of 40 hours of reading training.

Results and Conclusions

During the period of training S made many reading responses. Figure 14.1 shows the number of single-word reading responses S made as a

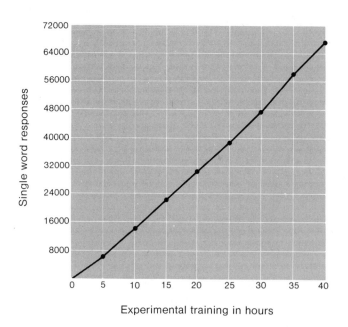

Experimental training in hours

FIGURE 14.1.   Number of single-word reading responses as a function of the time in experimental training. From A. W. Staats and W. H. Butterfield. Treatment of nonreading in a culturally deprived juvenile delinquent: An application of reinforcement principles. *Child Development*, 1965, 4, 925–942. Reprinted by permission of the Society for Research in Child Development.

function of the hours of time spent in training. An estimate of the number of single-word reading responses was obtained from tabulating each presentation of a word card, the number of words in the stories, and the reading-comprehension questions at the end of each story, as well as the words presented to S in the later single-word retention test. Actually, the number of words in the stories was an estimate obtained from the mean number of words in two out of each five stories. Thus, rather than giving the true absolute number of reading responses made, the figure gives an estimate. However, the most important aspect of the figure is to indicate the rate of this single-word reading-response measure as a function of time in experimental training. As can be seen, as the training progressed S covered the reading material at a slightly more rapid rate, as is shown by the slight positive acceleration in the curve. The importance of this result is to indicate that the child's behavior of attending to the task and making the appropriate reading responses did not diminish throughout the period of training. Thus, the reinforcement system employed was capable of maintaining the behavior for a long period of time. During this time the attentional and cooperative behaviors instigated resulted in many, many learning trials—a *sine qua non* for the acquisition of achievement in any skill.

Before reading each story S was presented with individual cards for all the words included in that story which had not been presented in a previous story. When these words were presented, S would read a certain proportion correctly on first presentation, the other words being missed on the first presentation. The ones missed were considered to be new words for S, words that he had not previously learned. These words were separately tabulated. The cumulative number of these new words as a function of every 5 SRA stories read is shown by the top curve of Figure 21.2. (The data for the first 10 stories are not presented since they were not available for all three curves.) As this curve indicates, 761 new words were presented to S during the training.

Thus, S missed 761 words when they were first presented to him. However, he was given training trials on these words, and then he read them again in the oral reading of the paragraph. The number of these words that he missed in this oral-reading phase is plotted in the bottom curve of Figure 14.2. This curve then indicates the number of errors made on the second reading test of the words that had been previously learned. Thus, only 176 words out of the 761 (about 23 percent) were missed in the oral-reading phase—showing retention for 585 words. The results indicate that the criterion of one correct unprompted reading trial in the original vocabulary-learning phase produced considerable learning when the words were read in context.

The middle curve in Figure 14.2 involves a measure of long-term retention of the words that had been learned. This measure was obtained by testing S on the words, presented singly, that had been learned in the preceding 20 stories. This test was given 10 to 15 days after the training occurred. The training thus included the previous single-word presentations of the words, as well as those same words read orally and silently.

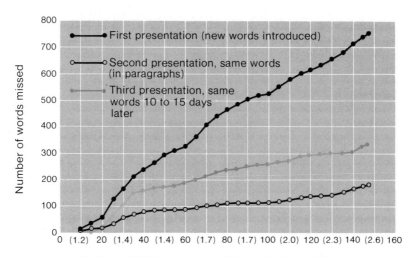

FIGURE 14.2.   Number of words missed on first, second, and third presentation for the 150 SRA stories. From A. W. Staats and W. H. Butterfield. Treatment of nonreading in a culturally deprived juvenile delinquent: An application of reinforcement principles. *Child Development*, 1965, **4**, 925–942. Reprinted by permission of the Society for Research in Child Development.

In addition, however, S had also learned a considerable number of other words by the time of this test. As the middle curve shows, when tested 10–15 days later, S read 430 of the 761 words correctly, or, conversely, 331 words (about 43 percent) were missed. Thus, the procedures produced retention when the words were later presented out of context after a considerable intervening period.

The results appearing in Figure 14.2 indicate that the child covered a considerable amount of reading material, that he learned to read a number of new words when presented individually or in context, and that he retained a good proportion of what he had learned. The results also indicate that the child improved during the training in his retention. That is, his rate of getting new words in the first-presentation phase continues at a high rate throughout the study. (This supports the results shown in Figure 14.1 indicating that the child's behavior did not weaken during the training.) However, his "rate" of missing the new words on the second and third presentations decreased, that is, he retained more of the words he had learned. Thus, tabulation indicated that for the first 35 stories only about 33 percent of the words learned were retained 10–15 days later, whereas S's subsequent retention increased to about 55 percent. It should be noted that this improvement occurred even though the difficulty of the words (as shown in Figure 14.3 by the numbers in parentheses) became progressively greater during the training, moving from the 1.2 grade level of difficulty to the 2.6 grade level.

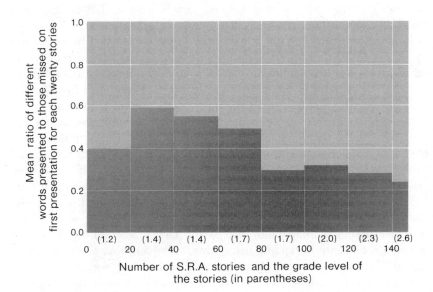

FIGURE 14.3.   Ratio of words presented to those missed on first presentation for the 150 SRA stories. From A. W. Staats and W. H. Butterfield. Treatment of nonreading in a culturally deprived juvenile delinquent: An application of reinforcement principles. *Child Development*, 1965, **4**, 925–942. Reprinted by permission of the Society for Research in Child Development.

These results receive support from the data presented in Figure 14.3. As already indicated, on the first presentation of the vocabulary of a story, some words were missed out of the total presented—and S was then presented with training on these words. Figure 14.3 shows the number of the words presented and missed in ratio to the total number presented, as this ratio is related to the number and difficulty of the stories presented. A smaller ratio indicates that S missed fewer of the total vocabulary words when they were presented for the first time. As can be seen in Figure 14.3 as the child read more stories in his training (even though they become more difficult), he missed fewer and fewer words that were presented to him. It should be stressed that he was thus improving in the extent to which he correctly responded to new words on first presentation. This improvement appeared to be correlated with other observations that indicated that S was also beginning to learn to sound out words as a function of the training. For example, he remarked when in the judge's office that he thought a sign said "information," because he could read the "in" and the "for" and the "mation." In addition, S reported a number of times that the training was helping him in school, that reading was getting easier for him in school, that he liked the reading training better as he went along, and so on. It would be expected (as will be supported by other data) that as the reading training improved his reading in school, the things he learned in school would also improve his performance in the reading training. It is this effect that may also be reflected in his increasing ability to read the new words presented to him.

In addition to this direct evidence of the child's progress in reading training, and the foregoing indirect evidence that the reading training was having general effects upon the child's behavior, the study was formulated to obtain other sources of information concerning the child's progress. One means of doing this was to give the child reading-achievement tests before beginning the reading training as well as during the training. The results of these tests are shown in Figure 14.4. The first point on the curve is a measurement obtained by use of the Developmental Reading Test giving a total score of reading achievement showing that S was performing at the grade 2 level. After 45 reading-training sessions, S's performance on the California Reading Test showed a gain to the 3.8 grade level. By the end of the training, after 25 more training sessions, S had advanced to the 4.3 grade level on the California Reading Test.

Another indication of the general effect of the reading training came from the child's performance in school, both in school achievement and deportment. The period of reading training coincided with a school term. The boy received passing grades in all subjects: A C in physical education, a D in general shop, a D in English, and a D in mathematics. It should be emphasized that these grades represent the first courses that this child had ever passed, and thus his finest academic performance.

Furthermore, S began to behave better while in school. The boy had always been a behavior problem in school, and this continued into the period during which S received reading training. As Figure 14.5 shows, during the first month of the training S committed 10 misbehaviors that resulted in the receipt of demerits. The behaviors were as follows: disturbance in class (2 times), disobedience in class (5 times), loitering (2 times), and tardiness. In the second month he was given demerits for scuffing on the school grounds and also for creating a disturbance. In the third month he was given demerits for cutting a math class and for

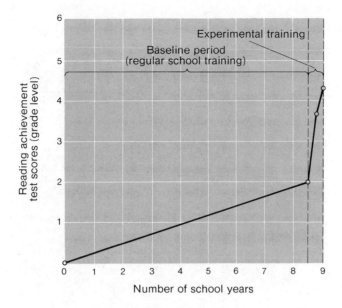

FIGURE 14.4.   Reading-achievement test scores as a function of
8½ years of school training and 4½ months of experimental training.
From A. W. Staats and W. H. Butterfield. Treatment of nonreading
in a culturally deprived juvenile delinquent: An application of reinforcement principles. *Child Development*, 1965, **4**, 925–942. Reprinted by permission of the Society for Research in Child Development.

profanity in class. As the figure shows, however, no misbehaviors occurred
in the fourth month or in the half month after this until the conclusion
of the school term.

The S requested that the tokens be exchanged for items that he wanted
in Sessions 12, 17, 25, 31, 35, 43, 49, 55, and in the last session he was
given the value of the remaining tokens in cash. Items included were a
pair of "beatle" shoes, hair pomade, a phonograph record, an ice cream
sundae, a ticket to a school function, money for his brother who was
going to reform school, and so on. Further information regarding the reinforcement system is given in Figure 14.6. The vertical axis of the graph
represents the ratio of the number of tokens obtained by S relative to
the number of single-word reading responses which he emitted. Lesser
ratios thus indicate more reading responses per reinforcer. This ratio was
plotted as a function of the progress S made in the training program, as
given by the number of SRA stories he had completed. As the training
progressed S gradually made an increasingly greater number of reading

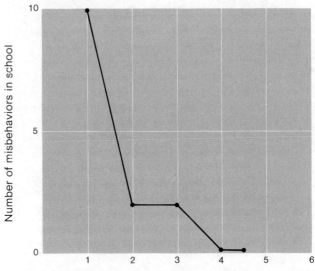

FIGURE 14.5. Number of official misbehaviors in school as a function of time in the experimental training. From A. W. Staats and W. H. Butterfield. Treatment of nonreading in a culturally deprived juvenile delinquent: An application of reinforcement principles. *Child Development*, 1965, 4, 925–942. Reprinted by permission of the Society for Research in Child Development.

responses per reinforcer. This effect was not accomplished by changing the rules by which the reinforcers were administered. The effect, which was planned in the training program, resulted from the fact that the SRA stories became longer as the grade level was raised. Since, for example, paragraph reading was reinforced by the paragraph, the longer the paragraph, the greater the number of reading responses that had to be emitted before reinforcement was obtained. At the end of training, thus, S was getting about half as much reinforcement per response as at the beginning of training. It should also be indicated that the stories were more difficult as the training progressed, so the effort involved in reading was increasing—although reinforcement for the reading was decreasing.

During the 4½ months of training, which involved 40 hours of reading training and the emission of an estimated 64,307 single-word reading responses, S received $20.31.

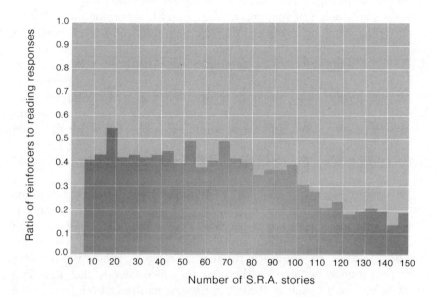

FIGURE 14.6.   Ratio of the number of tokens received divided by
the number of reading responses made, as a function of the number
of SRA stories that had been read. From A. W. Staats and W. H.
Butterfield. Treatment of nonreading in a culturally deprived juvenile delinquent: An application of reinforcement principles. *Child
Development*, 1965, 4, 925–942. Reprinted by permission of the Society for Research in Child Development.

Discussion

In this section the various aspects of the reading-training procedures
will first be discussed. Then the implications of the results and analysis
will be outlined both for further studies of remedial reading training as
well as for a learning conception of certain aspects of cultural deprivation
and delinquency.

The method of reading training used in the present study was derived
from previous study (Staats, 1964a; 1966; Staats, *et al.*, 1962) with preschool children in which words were first presented singly, then in sentences, and finally in short stories. The present study indicated that SRA
materials can be adapted for a similar type of presentation in conjunction
with the type of reinforcer system previously developed (Staats, *et al.*,
1964a; 1964b). From the SRA materials it was possible to present single-

word training trials and oral-reading training and to develop a silent-reading training procedure, all involving reinforcement.

When the training of reading, at least in part, is considered as instrumental discrimination learning, the learning task consists of having S emit the correct speech response while looking at the verbal stimulus—this process being followed by reinforcement. This basic procedure was elaborated in the present study to include two levels of reinforcement. An unprompted reading response on the first trial was reinforced more heavily than one that had been previously missed. This procedure appeared to produce learning that was retained very well when the child later read the words orally in a paragraph, with considerable retention also occurring when the child was tested on the individual words 10–15 days later.

It may seem incongruous at first to attempt to reinforce silent reading, since this behavior is not observable. However, it should be remembered that the subject actually has two types of behavior in the silent-reading act. He looks at the verbal stimuli—that is, attends—and he makes "reading" verbal responses to the verbal stimuli. While the reading responses cannot be monitored when they are covert, the attending behavior can be. Of course, there is a danger involved in reinforcing the behavior of just looking at something. Perhaps the child will do nothing else. If he is heavily reinforced for sitting and looking at a page, and the actual reading responses are effortful, he may not emit the reading responses. The present procedure was set up to eliminate this possibility by using a double contingency. The child was reinforced for simple attention, but the reinforcement was low in value. The opportunity for a greater amount of reinforcement came during the answering of the questions. Thus, although simple attention was reinforced lightly, attention and reading responses were reinforced much more heavily. In this way it was possible to use reinforcement in a procedure designed to maintain reading for "understanding" in addition to simple "word-naming." (These results could be generalized to other types of learning.) Furthermore, this procedure provided an opportunity to train the subject to read silently. Although he had a tendency to make vocal or lip responses while reading, it was possible to strengthen reading without these other responses through differentially reinforcing the correct silent reading.

Thus, it may be concluded that the reading program increased the child's reading vocabulary as shown by the various measures of retention used in the study, the tests of reading achievement, as well as the child's improved school performance and his verbal description of improved attitude toward and performance in reading in school. There were also suggestions that the child was acquiring a "unit-reading repertoire," that is, the general ability to sound out words through making the correct response to single letters and syllables. Thus, for example, the child made errors on fewer and fewer of the new words presented as the training progressed, even though the words were of greater difficulty. In addition, he retained a greater proportion of the words he learned as he went on. Further research of the present type must be conducted to test the possibilities for using a more phonic system of remedial reading training with the present type of subject.

A final point should be made concerning the training procedures used in the present study. The procedures are very specific and relatively simple. Thus, it was not necessary to have a person highly trained in education to administer the training. In the present case the trainer-experimenter was a probation officer. It might also be suggested that anyone with a high-school education and the ability to read could have administered the training. This has implications for the practical application of the present methods, since one of the questions that arises in this context concerns the economy of the procedures. Although the procedures as described involved a one-trainer-to-one-student ratio, as many remedial teaching procedures do, in the present case the simplicity of the procedures suggests the possibility that savings may be effected because the trainer need not be so highly trained. Thus, the procedures could be widely applied or adapted by various professionals, for example, social workers, prison officials, remedial teachers, tutors, and so on. In an even more economical application, helpers of professionals could be used to actually administer the procedures; for example, selected delinquents (or prisoners) could administer the procedures to other delinquents. Thus, the procedures could be utilized in various situations, such as settlement houses, homes for juvenile delinquents, prison training programs, parts of adult education, and so on. All that is needed is a suitable system of reinforcers to back up the tokens. These conclusions are supported by the studies with the preschool children.

In the same context, it may be worthwhile pointing out that the results indicated that the child advanced as many years in reading achievement, as measured by the tests, during the experimental training as he had in his previous school history. A comparison of the relative costs—in the present case, about 40 hours of time of a person not necessarily trained in teaching and $20.31 for the reinforcers versus $8\frac{1}{2}$ years of trained teachers' time, albeit in a group situation—suggests that the procedure introduced in the present study may not be uneconomical, even without improvements in the method. And, as will be further described, the child's failure in school may in many cases be considered as a contributor to the child's delinquency—which also carries a high cost to society. The present results, in suggesting that the training procedures may also effect general improvements in behavior, including misbehaviors in school, thus have further implications concerning the economy of the procedures.

The present study, among other things, tests the feasibility of using the type of reinforcing system, previously applied successfully to younger children, to the study of learning in older children—in this case a 14-year-old juvenile delinquent. The reinforcer system worked very well with the present S, maintaining his attention and working behaviors in good strength for a long period of time. And there was every reason to expect that the study could have been continued for a much longer period, probably as long as it would have taken to train the child to read normally.

It should be noted that although the amount of reinforcement given decreases during the training, as shown in Figure 14.6, the reading behavior is maintained in good strength throughout the study, as shown in Figures 14.1 and 14.2, thus less and less reinforcement is needed to maintain the behavior even though the material increases in difficulty. As already described, this occurred because a progressively greater number of reading responses was necessary per reinforcer. This is analogous to gradually raising the ratio of responses to the reinforcers as considered in terms of ratio schedules of reinforcement. Staats has suggested that this type of gradual increase must occur to produce good work behaviors in humans (Staats and Staats, 1963).

This result in the present study is in part an answer to the question whether the use of extrinsic reinforcers in training will produce a child who is dependent upon these reinforcers. It is not possible to discuss this topic fully now. However, it may be said that the extrinsic reinforcement can be gradually decreased until, as was happening with the present child, reading becomes reinforcing itself, or other sources of reinforcement maintain the behavior.

A word should be said concerning the relevance of reinforcement variables in the treatment of nonlearning in culturally deprived children. Typically, as in the present case, such children do not, as a result of their home experiences, acquire "reinforcer systems" appropriate for maintaining learning in the traditional classroom. Rosen (1956) has shown that, in the present terminology, lower-class children do not have experiences that make school achievement and learning itself positively reinforcing. This deficit, among others that affect the reinforcer system, can be expected to lead to poor school learning and other behavioral deficits. In such cases, there are increased opportunities for other poor social attitudes and undesirable behaviors to develop, as suggested in the introduction and exemplified in the present case.

The present study suggests that these conditions can be reversed through the application of learning principles and reinforcement variables to the task of repairing the child's behavioral-achievement deficit. There were indications that this treatment resulted in improvement in the reinforcement value of (attitudes toward) school for this child and consequently in the decrease in incidence of misbehaviors in school. The results thus suggest that under appropriate conditions the deficit in behavior stemming from the child's inadequate reinforcing system may be, at least in part, repaired by a properly administered, effective reinforcement system, resulting in a decrease in undesirable behaviors.

A comment should be made about the possibility of a Hawthorne effect, that is, that the social reinforcement by the E and possible extra-experimental reinforcement contributed to the results in the present study. It would be expected that such reinforcers could contribute to the overall effect—and in the present case the expenditure for the material reinforcers was small. In general, it can be expected that individuals will vary in the extent to which social reinforcers will be effective. For example, in preschool children social reinforcement is ineffective for long-term training (Staats, 1964a; Staats, et al., 1962), and the same would be expected for many individuals with behavior problems. Ordinarily, it might be expected that the weaker other sources of reinforcement are for the individual, the stronger must be the reinforcer system of the treatment procedure.

In conclusion, the present study helps support and replicate the previous findings and extends the general procedures and principles to the study of an adolescent child who is culturally deprived, and is also a juvenile delinquent. The various sources of data used suggest that the present procedures and principles are applicable to this population also. Based upon these suggestions, further studies will be conducted on culturally deprived children, delinquent and nondelinquent, as well as studies of other types of nonachieving or underachieving readers.

It should also be indicated that the present study indicates the possibility for developing procedures for the objective application and test of laboratory-derived learning principles within the context of an actual problem of behavior. As previously indicated (Staats, 1964b), verification of learning principles in the context of a problem of human behavior constitutes one way to further the generality of the principles themselves. It may thus be suggested that such studies have two types of implication: they have implications for people interested in dealing with the problems of human behavior, as well as for those interested in the extension and verification of the basic science. [It is suggested that it will be through such studies, because they (1) employ basic principles in (2) the context of important human behaviors, that the basic-applied schism in psychology will be dissolved. This will be discussed further.]

REPLICATION OF THE COGNITIVE BEHAVIOR MODIFICATION PROCEDURES WITH SUBPROFESSIONAL THERAPY- OR INSTRUCTIONAL-TECHNICIANS

As has been mentioned, experimental-clinical and experimental-educational psychology must strive through research to produce procedures that can be applied in a standard manner to the treatment of problems of behavior. When this has been achieved it should be possible in many instances to employ subprofessional people who have been trained in the treatment procedure. To demonstrate these points, as well as to replicate the findings with the first subject, the cognitive behavior modification procedure already described was used on 18 additional subjects.

The use of instructional-technicians (in educational settings) or therapy-technicians (in clinical settings), as already suggested, has practical implications. It is not possible to provide highly trained personnel for extensive work with individual patients or students, yet many children for various reasons do not progress satisfactorily in the group educational situation. One strategy has sought a solution to this problem through the use of apparatus—this is the basis of the teaching machine interest, including variations of this approach that use such elaborate apparatus as computers. The fact is, however, that no computer has as many features as the human trainer in many circumstances. Take the simple feature of being able to monitor the speech or writing responses of a student. Any literate, responsible person can do this with precision. But an exceedingly complex and expensive computer would be necessary to perform the task—and then its range and flexibility and accuracy would not be as high as the human "machine." To introduce a computer that would judge whether a child had read a sentence correctly would require an exorbitant expenditure.

It may be suggested that one possible way of solving some of our glaring clinical and educational problems is through the use of people to administer the training materials. When the materials are simple and straightforward the people need only be literate and responsible. This means that individual instruction can be provided for problem learners while remaining within an economic monetary expenditure.

The author designed the experiment to be described to further test the possibility that children with special learning problems could be treated by high school students and adult volunteers, when the training materials were specific and could be applied in a standard manner. The high school students were paid $1.25 an hour for serving as instructional-technicians, the adult volunteers received expense money of $2.00 per day.

The subjects selected for training were junior high school students who were retarded in this area of cognitive development. The 18 subjects included cases who were mentally retarded (7 were from classes for the retarded) as well as several who were behavior problems or emotionally disturbed. The mean IQ of the children was 75.3 with a range from 50 to 94. The results of the study have been described more fully (Staats, Minke, Goodwin, and Landeen, in press), and only a brief summary will be made here.

The procedure and the reinforcer system appeared to be generally functional. The attention, attendance, cooperation, and diligent work behaviors of the various children were maintained in good strength throughout the length of the study. In fact these behaviors appeared to be gaining strength. Thus, the methods have proved successful with an incorrigible juvenile delinquent and with the present group of 18 children which included mentally retarded children and emotionally disturbed children. In addition, the procedures have also been tested with the same success in clinical work with several psychiatrically referred children, one of whom was diagnosed as a schizoid, as well as with ongoing research with a larger group of Negro, culturally-deprived, problem learners, using unemployed literate adults from the same population as the therapy-technicians (as a means of upgrading these individuals as well). Thus, the present method is one of the few in the field of behavior modification that has been tested with a substantial number of subjects treated for the same behavior problem, with the same reinforcement system.

Moreover, in the present study not only was the behavior of these children very appropriate in the 38.2 hour training situation, but the behavioral measures indicated that the children covered a great deal of material and learned a number of new words. They covered a mean of 94,425 reading responses. A mean of 593.5 words were presented that the children did not at first know. After training, in the long term retention measure, the children retained a mean of 70.9 percent of these words. This represents a straightforward indication that the children (including 7 children in classes for the retarded) were learning the material on which they were being trained. In addition, the curves that indicated the rate at which the children were reading was accelerating even though the difficulty of the material was increasing.

These findings were supplemented by the differences between the experimental group and 18 control subjects on their respective ability to read a sample of 100 SRA words when individually presented to each child. The experimental group increased in this index of reading ability to an extent that was significantly greater than the increase of the control group.

The reinforcement system used in the Staats and Butterfield study as well as the present study was designed so that the amount of reinforcement given per unit of behavior decreased over the period of the training. Thus, during the training each child was gradually getting less reinforcement for his reading. Nevertheless, his behavior was maintained in better strength as the training progressed.

There are several points concerning the supervision of the training that should be mentioned. The procedure was set up so that the therapy-technicians were observed from time to time (especially in the beginning) in a systematic manner. This was done in general to supervise the correct application of the procedure. In addition, the monitoring provided observations concerning the information needs of the therapy-technicians as well as a means of assessing the manner in which the procedures and materials functioned with various subjects. In one case (which was unique) the author observed practices of a therapy-technician in the first couple of weeks of training that were leading to deterioration in the training interaction. This led to replacement of the therapy-technician and to additional instructions to the other therapy-technicians. That is, they were instructed that they were not to urge the child to do better, or to expect better or faster performance in any case. The reinforcer system and materials were to take care of the child's good work behaviors, attention, and learning. When a child attended and worked well he was performing maximally regardless of his errors or rate of reading. The therapy-technicians were instructed that they could give positive social approval, but no aversive stimulation was to be given of either a direct kind or by implication through saying such things as "You can do better than that," "Try harder," "You knew that before," and so on.

The child who had been subjected to this type of urging, which was administered with very good intent and was so natural that it was not noticed by the other supervisors, was becoming more disturbed and hostile in action and difficult to control as the training progressed. (As it happened he was a child with acting out problems.) He stated he was going to withdraw from the program. When the difficulty was discovered two of the experimenters alternated as the therapy-technicians until another volunteer adult was obtained and trained. When the aversive training circumstances were removed by this adjustment, the child's behavior and learning improved quickly and he continued in the training in a normal manner throughout the experiment. It is suggested that an effective way to apply the present procedures is to have a child-clinical psychologist set up and supervise the program, having direct training and supervisory contact with the therapy-technicians. Larger programs could also be conducted in which the child-clinical psychologist had adjunct professional personnel (such as social workers, probation officers, prison personnel, special education teachers, and so on) who supervised the therapy-technicians. In any event, it would seem necessary to have the specialist in child learning and behavior problems in a position to handle the special problems of the children, or the therapy-technicians, which could be expected to arise on occasion.

An aspect not insignificant to the present treatment is its economy. Although a professional trained at the doctoral level, or even a lesser trained professional, cannot provide long-term individual treatment to children, it would be economical to have a professional train and supervise therapy-technicians; in specific treatment responsibilities. Related to this is the cost of the treatment itself. In the first study the $4\frac{1}{2}$ months of training cost $20.31 in reinforcers. This was closely paralleled in the present study. That is, the mean cost for the children over a similar period of time was $22.29. In many cases this would be a very minimal price to pay to insure that ordinarily untrainable children would not only be amenable to various types of training, but would also work diligently and learn well.

Achievement tests were also given to the children in the present study. They could not be used, however, primarily because they were given in a group situation and the children randomly guessed at the answers. The test procedures were thus altered and utilized to assess the hypothesis that improved test-taking behaviors could be produced by reinforcing the child for correct answers (with 2 cents) and punishing him (by taking away 1 cent) for each incorrect answer. The children who had previously randomly scored items began to peruse the items more carefully under the extrinsic reinforcement procedure. The results showed that when the good test-taking behavior was reinforced and poor test-taking behavior punished the desired behavior increased in strength to a statistically significant extent. When reinforced, the children scored better on intelligence and achievement tests even while answering fewer test items. This has theoretical implications; for differences in "motivation" are not usually controlled when testing different groups of subjects, even though there are many categories of disturbed individuals whose poor motivational circumstances would no doubt adversely affect their test results. For example, there are many, many studies that compare patient populations, such as schizophrenics, with normals on some learning, cognitive, word association, or other task or test. The differences obtained in such studies are, it is suggested, many times affected by differences in reinforcement variables and thus in the lesser extent to which the attention, cooperation, and diligent work behavior of the schizophrenics are maintained. It may be suggested that *any* group comparisons on tests or tasks made for theoretical purposes should take into account likely differences in behavior as a function of motivational differences. The present results suggest, of course, that this source of variation could be controlled by insuring that the subjects of the experiment are reinforced for good test-taking behavior.

These results also have similar significance for diagnostic testing. There are many cases in which test results are part of diagnosis and treatment and where the test-taking behaviors of the subject prevent accurate appraisal because of motivational deficits. It is suggested that more valid test results could be obtained through the use of reinforcement to strengthen "good test behavior." If poor test performance is a function of motivational variables, it is important to know the source of the difficulty.

It is suggested that the present general procedures are ready to be extended widely in research-treatment studies in clinical work with children with various problems. The methods have been tested sufficiently with various types of children to indicate that children who are otherwise untrainable will respond appropriately to the present type of training situation. When the procedures can be administered in a standard manner, subprofessional therapy-technicians can be employed. It may be suggested that clinical psychology must begin through research to develop procedures that can be administered by adjunct personnel in standard treatment programs. The clinical psychologist would then set up the treatment program and supervise the therapy and be an expert in dealing with any special problems that arise. Research to develop training procedures by which to treat deficits in various complex adjustive repertoires in patients who under traditional procedures are untrainable may be seen as an important task of learning oriented clinical psychology.

Clinical psychology in following the "illness model" that has pervaded the field of "mental health" has tended to concentrate on the intrapsychic life of the child, his gross social-emotional adjustment, and grossly aberrant behaviors, sometimes neglecting consideration of his cognitive learning. If cognitive training is regarded "as it is in many mental health programs, as something that can wait until the child gets better," (Hobbs, 1967, p. 1111) the child can develop severe cognitive deficits that will preclude later adjustment regardless of any diminution of other difficulties. The complex cognitive skills the child must learn require long periods of training and innumerable training trials. It is suggested that clearing up some other form of behavioral disturbance will not provide the child with those skills—as one might erroneously assume from a "mental block" interpretation of cognitive deficit.

"Underachievement in school is the single most common characteristic of emotionally disturbed children." (Hobbs, 1967, p. 1110). It may be added that perhaps the most important significance of what is called emotional disturbance in children is in the manner in which the behavioral difficulty prevents normal social learning, cognitive learning, sensory-motor learning, emotional learning, and so on. In general, it is thus suggested that clinical psychology in developing a *learning model* of human problems and their treatment must become interested in these problems for the part they play in producing repertoirial deficits. In addition, emphasis must be given to the development of methods of treatment of these deficits, methods which diverge from traditional psychotherapy procedures and involve an additional role for the clinical psychologist.

part
5

*An
integrated-functional
learning conception
of cognitive
development*

15

Hierarchical child development, the basic behavioral repertoire, and conceptions of human motivation and imitation

Thus far, the account has begun with a consideration of the manner in which the principles of classical conditioning apply to important aspects of complex human behavior, especially in the area of language and attitude learning. The basic principles of instrumental conditioning have also been elaborated as they apply to language learning. In addition, the theory has also indicated how these two major principles must be integrated in a common theoretical terminology and how more complex S–R mechanisms are derived from the basic principles.

Then it was suggested that this structure of basic principles and derived S–R mechanisms forms a theoretical basis for consideration of various types of cognitive behaviors, and that part of the elaboration and verification of the theory lies in demonstrating the theory's utility in accounting for and dealing with actual behavior. Thus, preliminary analyses of three areas of cognitive behavior were made in terms of the theory. Research was also conducted to verify the theoretical analyses and to show that understanding of and functional solution to problems of cognitive learning could be produced.

A muted but reoccurring theme in this formulation has been a notion of cognitive development as learned in a hierarchical fashion. That is, basic behaviors must be learned before additional cognitive repertoires can be acquired, and so on. This theme will be developed in the next section of the present chapter and subsequent discussions will elaborate the conception. In doing this, what will be called the basic behavioral repertoire will be described in a more complete manner. After this, the way a particular cognitive repertoire (reading) is built upon the basic behavioral repertoire will be described in a following chapter. The account will give a description of the way that this latter repertoire is fundamental to the acquisition of even higher-level cognitive repertoires *—that is, a major feature of the present approach is that a human behavior is both a dependent variable, a result of preceding conditions (independent variables), as well as an independent variable, a determinant of the acquisition of additional behaviors.* This aspect of the theory actually removes a major point of difference between so-called cognitive approaches to human behavior and the learning approach.

This more detailed consideration of the cognitive repertoire of reading will be made for several reasons. First, it demonstrates more fully the value of the integrated-functional learning theory in extending our understanding of human behavior. Moreover, by making a more detailed analysis of this one very important cognitive repertoire the conception of the hierarchical nature of cognitive learning can be illustrated. Not all of the various cognitive repertoires will be dealt with in this detail in the present book, although this type of analysis would be possible. Reading was selected for special treatment because its acquisition depends upon previous cognitive learning, and once acquired it serves as the basis for much further cognitive development as well as the learning of other aspects of behavior such as social and emotional behavior, sensory-motor skills, and so on. It should also be indicated that this elaboration of the theory in one particular area of cognitive behavior is intended as an example of what can be done with the theory—an example suggestive for conducting analyses of other aspects of human behavior, cognitive and otherwise. Finally, this cognitive repertoire was particularly selected to indicate the need for experimental and theoretical analyses of actual human repertoires which are customarily ignored because they are labeled *applied*. Actually, basic principles can and should be tested in the context of functional behaviors. This type of study has greater generality than do many artificial laboratory tasks, which speciously *seem* to be more general because they are labeled concept formation, problem solving, and so on. More will be said of this later.

THE HIERARCHICAL LEARNING CONCEPTION 385

THE HIERARCHICAL LEARNING CONCEPTION
OF COGNITIVE DEVELOPMENT

It has already been suggested herein that all complex human behaviors are learned. None of them comes about through biological maturation. Nevertheless, it is commonly believed that special cognitive skills or "talent"—or indeed artistic, sensory-motor, motivational, or other skills, aptitudes, personality traits, intelligence, characteristic behaviors of various kinds, and so on—are due to some special personal, usually biological, factor. However, it may be suggested that *whatever* the complex repertoire, it is learned. For example, the individual who has a complex higher mathematical repertoire has learned a fantastically complex set of S—R mechanisms in a training program that includes innumerable conditioning trials stretching over a period of many years. While it is customarily thought that only individuals with special genetically based qualities ("intelligence," "ability," or what have you) can acquire such complex repertoires, in view of the lack of evidence we have to entertain the possibility that any normally constructed person could acquire such a repertoire if exposed to the appropriate learning circumstances.

Actually, naturalistic evidence suggests that a very, very, complex training program is necessary for the development of complex cognitive repertoires. The whole history of man indicates that such repertoires did not simply spring from maturational processes. When there was no body of mathematical training to give children, they did not acquire this repertoire. And the repertoire itself was only painstakingly developed, with certain cognitive repertoirial developments being necessary before the next original step could be taken. Moreover, the development of man's tremendous cognitive repertoires has taken place over a period when his genetic structure has remained unchanged.

The naturalistic evidence that a complex set of training circumstances is the *sine qua non* in the development of complex cognitive (and other repertoires) is all around us. Peoples and groups who do not receive appropriate training circumstances do not evidence members with the highly-developed cognitive repertoires—nor does the people as a whole produce the products of such cognitive repertoires. Perhaps, however, the clearest naturalistic evidence is available in our own schools. Perusal of the teaching materials which are presented to children to train them to cognitive skills shows that they are straightforward S–R presentations, although this is not usually recognized. The repertoires involved, of course, are very complex and even at the beginning levels an analysis into S–R terms becomes exceedingly complex. Furthermore, observation indicates that complex and subtle reinforcing events are involved—which themselves depend upon complex prior conditioning histories.

In addition, of course, there are many experimental studies that show that the well established basic learning principles apply to simple responses in humans. And, to be sure, the preceding extensions of learning analyses and experimental methods to the consideration of the various types of language and cognitive learning take the development of the theory further. That is, the preceding studies may be considered to be preliminary experimental exploration of the general theory. Thus, even at this point it may be said that the present learning theory of cognitive development is more closely tied to a set of basic laboratory derived principles which have been extensively explored and rigorously tested than any other competing biological or maturational theory. The S–R theory is the most explicitly set forth, in greater detail, and is more comprehensively applied to the realm of phenomena. And, it is more closely tied to the experimental methods of the laboratory from which its basic principles were derived. Finally, in the tradition of its laboratory foundation, independent variables (determinants) have been isolated, and cognitive behaviors have been experimentally *produced* in accord with theoretical expectations, by S–R presentations and learning procedures.

Thus, as has been suggested, it is time that we review our biological and maturational conceptions of complex human behavior, including cognitive development. The evidence for such conceptions is actually very slim, and that evidence is mostly "circumstantial." There is little, if any, in the way of isolation of anatomical structures or differences, physiological functioning, or genetic mechanisms, that can be independently and directly observed and whose presence or absence produces some type of complex human behavior. There is no ability existent to dig into the organism and do something neurologically or chemically, or what have you, and thereby *produce* a human behavior such as counting, or the discrimination of two letters, let alone some more complex or original behavior.

Because a learning analysis of various complex human behaviors has been lacking should not increase the credibility of a biological explanation of the development of human behavior. Only the direct evidence of biological determinants should do that. We cannot infer biological or maturational causes when all we have observed is the behavior itself. This is true in the clinical case where we are concerned about knowing and treating the cause of the problem, and it is true in establishing a general conception of human behavior.

Actually, biological explanations of behavior which involve specification of determinants which can be manipulated to produce behavior are much less developed than the learning theory. As the present volume has illustrated, there are numerous experiments where human behavior of complex forms has been produced, according to the specified principles of the learning theory. These are demonstrations of explanatory, causative, theory and should yield great confidence that additional work will lead to further ability to account for, produce, and improve the development of human behavior. An analysis of a human behavior in terms of learning principles—where the controlling stimuli, the responses, and the training principles and circumstances are given—constitutes an empirical hypothesis which includes the independent and dependent variables and their laws of relationship. Test of the hypothesis will support or disconfirm it, and when the results support the hypothesis we have procedures for *producing* such behaviors. It is this quality which shows the productivity and advancement of the learning approach and gives it the status of true explanatory theory.

It is important to assert this issue in a definitive way—because the biological conception of human behavior has considerable social as well as scientific significance. When we accept that a human behavior is biologically determined, then we attribute problems of that human behavior to the personal defects of the individuals involved. If language or cognitive development comes from biological determinants, then the child who does not develop normal language, or what have you, is biologically inferior. It is but a short step to consider groups of individuals, or races, inferior when we observe that they do not display the behaviors we desire. Certainly, the type of indirect evidence that has been used to support the biological conception of a type of cognitive human behavior (see Lenneberg, 1966, and McNeil, in press, for an example in the area of language) could, by the same reasoning, be mistakenly applied to other types of social behavior.

Furthermore, acceptance of a biological conception of complex human behavior aims to turn our attention away from environmental or learning causes (an effect which again has professional and social significance). Although the biological view in the realm of complex human behavior has not approached the state where it can account for the vast individual differences that exist, or solve problems of complex human behavior, the conception as developed in various areas of psychology and other social sciences has a primary thrust in directing us not to attempt to find learning principles that can potentially produce the necessary type of knowledge. The fact is that learning principles are much more advanced as an explanatory theory than is biological theory—it still remains to be seen, for example, if *any* complex human behavior develops through the growth of biological structures. It may help to review briefly several biological conceptions in the area of cognitive development and to indicate a competitive learning theory. The concept of intelligence (which takes many forms) has been a foremost obstacle to our thinking in this area and the discussion may begin with its consideration. (It should be noted that the present view is not a denial of the importance of biological variables. Behavior is *learned* on the basis of the biological structure of the organism and it is important to study the mechanisms involved.)

First, it is quite evident that the concept of intelligence, as generally used has no explanatory value. That is, the major observations that define the concept are ones of human behavior—we see that people as individuals and groups differ in the skill with which they respond to various of life's tasks and problems. These differences are vast, and vastly important. It would thus be very important to know something about the determinants of these differences. The differences could conceivably be due to biological variations. Although this remains a possibility, little direct evidence has been uncovered to relate observable biological variations to the intelligence behavioral differences. The evidence of the biological determination of intelligence in the field of child development is not acceptable for methodological reasons (Fowler, 1962) and it is only of the "circumstantial" variety. The tremendous intellectual differences we see in human behavior have no neurological correlates when the small percentage of grossly impaired individuals are excluded.

Tests of intelligence are very useful and important but contribute no theoretical understanding or explanation of the intellectual differences we see in people. This fact remains, regardless of the sophistication of the statistical and measurement techniques that are used. That is, intelligence tests consist of standardized observations of intellectual skills—they are observations of the behavioral events we wish to explain. They cannot be used to explain themselves; no amount of factor analysis of test items will give us information about, and ability to manipulate, the determinants of intellective differences. The field of the measurement of intelligence and other intellective differences in general has remained essentially unchanged for some time. It has not produced a theory or a set of experimental treatment procedures by which to produce desirable changes in human behavior. And the field will not yield such knowledge or such methods; for the field of psychological measurement is not in contact with the independent variables (the causes) that determine human behavior. While it must be stressed that psychological measurement has much to contribute to the study of human behavior, its role is in the measurement of *human behavior itself*, not in accounting for the origins of that behavior, or indeed in accounting for the function of that behavior in human adjustment.

We must look elsewhere for an explanation of the intellective differences we see in people—and, incidentally, we must look elsewhere for a psychological theory upon which to base our construction of intellective tests, since it cannot come from the field itself. If the concept of intelligence productively refers to anything besides a test result *it may be considered to refer to a wide sample of the basic behavioral skills the child (or adult) has acquired which are important to the acquisition of further skilled behaviors.* Looked upon in this manner certain enigmas concerning intelligence and intelligence tests can be clarified.

To elaborate, behavioral psychology has at one time attempted to remove some of the ambiguities in the use of the term intelligence by stating that intelligence was what intelligence tests measured. This is in agreement with what was said above—that is, that intelligence refers to behavioral differences but does not explain them. However, this statement is incomplete, for intelligence test results also index an independent variable for, or a general determinant of, human behavior. That is, for example, people can be selected who score high on an intelligence test, along with a low scoring group. As an independent variable in an experiment, the intelligence test differences will produce effects. That is, the first group will learn many things more rapidly, will read more rapidly, will make higher grades in school, and so on.

Intelligence seems to have the status of a determinant of human behavior. This is not a paradox, however, nor is it inconsistent with the present analysis. Intelligence may be considered as a dependent variable (an effect) and an independent variable (a cause) within the same analysis. When the concept of the basic behavioral repertoire is related to the concept of intelligence, the seeming paradox is resolved. The child through learning experiences acquires a basic behavioral repertoire (intelligence). This basic behavioral repertoire, and its measurement, is a dependent variable. If we wish to account for it we must look to the conditions and principles of learning.

However, we are interested in this basic behavioral repertoire in the first place because we can observe that children who have the constituents of such a repertoire do well in their life tasks and problems. They do better in school and so on. In the study with the preschool children, for example, it was easily seen that the children who had the higher intelligence scores had better basic behavioral repertoires. They paid attention, followed directions well, were eager to acquire skills and to exhibit them (found both reinforcing), and so on. Their learning under the conditions where there was an adequate reinforcement system for all the children was not remarkable, as the results showed. However, under traditional classroom circumstances their basic behavioral repertoires would insure that they would learn more rapidly and that their attentional and working behaviors would be maintained.

The author (Staats and Staats, 1963) has made an analysis of the types of items on intelligence tests for young children which helps support the present contentions. The items all involved behaviors that are very straightforwardly learned; for example, naming pictures and objects, repeating words and sentences, counting, complex spontaneous utterances in terms of number of words, and so on. Moreover, doing well on an intelligence test heavily involves the child's attentional responses, the verbal control of the child's behavior (following instructions), and so on. Again, these are all themselves learned behaviors, but at the same time they are basic to any further learning that the child will acquire.

It may also be suggested that the same rationale may be extended to other areas of intellectual development and intellective tests. That is, there is a concept of readiness in the fields of child and educational psychology to which the present analysis may be applied equally well. The concept of readiness has also been heavily influenced by a maturational approach to human development. The child, according to this view, walks when he is physiologically developed, talks when maturationally developed, and so on. While in this approach it would be admitted that the experience of the child plays a part, the role given to learning is relatively unimportant and is left unspecified as though learning opportunities are relatively similar for all children. The following passage illustrates this type of conception.

> Most accomplishments of a child require a certain level of skeletal-muscular-neurological development (or a certain level of organization of the electrometabolic field). When this level of development has been reached, we say that a child biologically is "ready" to perform a certain task. Although he may not perform it even when he is ready, he cannot perform it before that time. . . . It remains a controversial matter whether attempts to induce a child to perform a task before physiological readiness have any effect in speeding up the rate of growth toward readiness. (Bigge, and Hunt, 1962)

It is worth noting that such maturational approaches have no independent means of observing biological readiness. Readiness, or intelligence, or what have you, is inferred from the behavior of the child. Thus, the thing which is to be explained, the behavior, is used to verify the explanatory concept—true circular reasoning. While in theory learning has been discounted in psychological conceptions of intelligence and readiness, and so on, in practice there has been recognition of its effect. Thus, today nursery schools and kindergarten may use materials that attempt to provide the child with readiness skills through training. These efforts, however, have been of a practical nature and have not affected current conceptions of cognitive development. Using an integrated learning theory such as has been explicated herein, it may be suggested that the basic behavioral repertoire (readiness) which is necessary for further learning is *acquired* according to learning principles. The child comes to school with good "readiness" for certain tasks only if his home environment has provided the complex training that is necessary.

When we consider intelligence and readiness to actually consist of a basic behavioral repertoire, it is easy to see that we must have specific analyses of the repertoires involved. We need to know how such cognitive repertoires are acquired from the beginning (and we must further design procedures by which to *produce* such repertoires). In the task of assessment of the basic behavioral repertoire (intelligence or readiness) it may be treated as a dependent variable. Tests devised to assess the basic behavioral repertoire would be very important—they would tell us where children were in the development of their repertoires, which aspects of the repertoire they still needed training on, and so on.

In addition, however, we need more analyses of and research on the way the various aspects of the basic behavioral repertoire are *necessary* for the cognitive learning tasks with which the child will have to contend. What cognitive skills does the child have to have before he can begin to learn a number concept repertoire, for example. And what type of number concept repertoire should he have before he is introduced to number operations.

Tests that were based upon such analyses would indeed be extremely useful tools in composing effective programs of training for children. They would serve as measurements of behavioral skills—as measurements of dependent variables—indicating how much and how well a child has progressed. Furthermore, the tests constructed upon the basis of such S–R analyses would also better serve as measurements of behavioral skills as independent variables. That is, the test information would indicate what children could profit from certain levels of cognitive training, or, as another example, what training materials the child was prepared to work on.

Test results today are performing these functions. But the measurement concepts and the tests themselves are not embedded in a theoretical and experimental framework along with the training materials. Thus, to a large extent, measurement and learning research move along independent paths. It may be suggested that we must drop our conceptions of *intelligence, abilities, talents,* and so on, as well as motivational concepts such as *interests, values, needs,* and the like, and instead elaborate S–R analyses that indicate how the relevant behavioral repertoires are *learned.* It may be suggested herein, albeit in only outline form, that an integrated-functional learning theory of cognitive (and motivational) development could serve to integrate the fields of developmental, clinical, and educational psychology with the field of psychological measurement —all within one theoretical and experimental framework.

In this brief consideration there has implicitly been a conception of a progressive type of cognitive development. This suggestion has also been made in some of the preceding discussions. Several characteristics of this conception of cognitive development, as well as some of the particular principles involved may be outlined here. Then more specific analyses of some cognitive repertoires will be made to elaborate the conceptions.

The concept of a hierarchical type of progression is an important aspect of the consideration of cognitive development. Stage, or hierarchical, conceptions have abounded in the field of developmental psychology. But such conceptions have always relied solely, or heavily, on hypothesized physiological maturation, or nonlearning concepts of cognitive (mental) development. Furthermore, these conceptions have remained on a very general level. They have not become specific in terms of detailing the cognitive repertoires present at any level, nor have they indicated in any detail the determinants of the cognitive levels. The research has mainly been oriented toward supporting the general conceptions. Nevertheless, the naturalistic evidence upon which these general hierarchical conceptions of behavioral development were based seems pretty clear. Children must in many cases acquire one skill before progressing to the next, whether the skill is cognitive, sensory-motor, or social.

When the repertoires are considered in terms of specific S–R mechanisms the suggestion of the naturalistic evidence that cognitive development is hierarchical is enhanced, and can also be seen in detail. Examples may be taken from the analyses already made herein, even the more simple ones. Thus, the higher-order classical conditioning of the meaning of many words rests upon the prior conditioning of the meaning of other words. Thus, the child may be told "Swimming out too far is dangerous." This will condition a negative (aversive) meaning response to the action of swimming out too far, provided that the child through previous conditioning has acquired an appropriate meaning response to the word *dangerous* for example. In general, communication, which is a common sense word for many different verbal interactions involving different language S–R mechanisms, is a type of social interaction that rests entirely upon the previous development of fantastically complex language repertoires.

There are many other examples in the preceding experimental work. For example, one mongoloid mental retardate had to acquire a picture-vocabulary of 10 words before he could learn to discriminate letters. In the number concept learning, the culturally-deprived children were first trained to discriminate "twoness" in objects from "oneness" and "three-ness." This training was followed by training to count increasing numbers of objects. Later, the children learned to read and count the numbers themselves. Thus, the prior training provided the children with S–R mechanisms that made the reading and counting of printed numbers more than a "rote-learning" task. And, as has been described, the functionality of the "number concept" basic behavioral repertoire was shown with Jennifer where she was able to employ the skills in further learning.

Another example may be drawn from the experience with Jennifer. When she was in kindergarten the teacher would allow the children who were able to do so to write and read stories. That is, if they asked the teacher how to write a word she would do so. They could then copy the word and use it in the story. In order to participate in this activity, however, the children had to have the relevant aspects of the basic behavioral repertoire—all the rudimentary writing, copying, and reading skills. Other children in class did not participate before they had the requisite skills (they were not "ready"). Those children thus lost the opportunity for the same type of training. In general, in the school setting children who have acquired more advanced behavioral repertoires are given more advanced training by grouping them into sections and so on.

Problem solving, also, involves the functioning of previously acquired S–R repertoires of diverse kinds. Although the field of problem solving in psychology has tended to imply that there is a unitary process that underlies problem solving ability in various situations, it may be suggested, rather, that there is an infinite number of different problems which require different types of repertoires for solution. For example, it must be concluded that the problem-solving ability of the physicist depends upon such previously learned basic repertoires, as counting, adding, reading words and numbers, his mathematical verbal response sequences, and the like, rather than upon some personal quality of excellence, some personal cognitive ability, aptitude, or what have you.

The acquisition of a repertoire of literal numbers, as another example, appears to rest upon the previous acquisition of a repertoire that has been called number concept learning, with all the complex S–R mechanisms this involves. And the acquisition of the number concepts themselves takes place only on the basis of the previous learning of attentional and discrimination behaviors, work behaviors, and so on—not to mention the learning of a motivational system.

These are only specific examples to indicate that all of the learning that has been considered so far is not isolated. The experiments are samples of types of complex human repertoires, all of which are important to the individual's cognitive, social, and motivational (emotional) development. In many cases one type of learning is necessary before another repertoire can be developed in the everyday life learning circumstance. The extent to which the basic conditioning principles interact in complex learning, and the manner in which previously acquired S–R repertoires allow for additional learning, will be indicated in more detail in the rest of the present part of the book in dealing with a more detailed analysis of the basic behavioral repertoire and the acquisition and function of reading. At this point, however, a few general characteristics of the hierarchical conception of behavioral development will be described.

First, as the present author has seen in long-term experimental-naturalistic research and has been shown in short-term studies (Rheingold, et al., 1959), the learning of the infant begins very early. There is thus much opportunity for acceleration, or retardation, to occur as a consequence of early childhood training, or its absence or distortion.

This becomes very clear when one considers the hierarchical (or cumulative) nature of behavioral development. A child who more quickly has developed a good attentional repertoire, has learned to follow directions, and so on, can be given training in other skills sooner than a child who has not learned these basic repertoires. Then, having acquired the additional skills he can again be trained to the next type of skill. The general statement here is that acceleration in the acquisition of one repertoire accelerates the acquisition of the next. Because of this cumulative effect, vast differences in the level of behavioral skill of different children can be produced. The same is true also of the quality of the training given the child. The better, as well as the more quickly, a repertoire is acquired, the more quickly will the next repertoire be acquired. It may be suggested that this is what explains the "learning how to learn" phenomenon that was shown in the present case in the cognitive learning of young children. Specific aspects of the basic behavioral repertoire that would accelerate the rate of learning in many situations will be described. At this point it should be indicated, however, that the present analysis sug-gests that there are many basic behavioral repertoires that once acquired accelerate the rate and increase the quality of learning in further tasks the child faces. Although not all areas will be dealt with here, it is likely that such learning how to learn acceleration occurs in areas of sensory-motor skill, artistic skill, social skills, and so on as well as the vast number of cognitive skills.

To continue, however, this cumulative effect of cognitive training has led to misconceptions concerning behavioral development. That is, when one deals with a group he is dealing with children who have reached different levels and qualities of cognitive learning. At this point, even though comparable training is given to all the members of the group there will be large differences in learning produced, because their differ-ent levels of previous cognitive learning will determine how they will do in the new learning. Since at this point the children are all given equal treatment, it is easy to conclude erroneously that there must be personal differences in the "ability" of the children to learn—some internal, probably innate, quality. It is thus important to suggest that very large differences in behavioral skill would be expected upon the basis of the learning conception of cognitive development, and it would be expected that there would be different learning *rates* for children, purely upon the basis of their past training.

It is also because of the cumulative nature of cognitive learning that many of the short-term studies conducted in the nature-nurture contro-versy have been inadequate. The vast differences in skill that can be produced by learning can be shown only when the study is of sufficient length to allow such large differences to be produced. To give one twin special training for a short period—or training in a task which is not the basis for another type of cognitive learning—will not produce large differ-ence through learning. The short-term training in a skill that leads no-where is inconsequential relative to the training received in the children's life experiences. (This is true for sensory-motor and motivational skills or repertoires as well as cognitive skills.) That is, for example, a few weeks of special training in climbing stairs may not produce significant effects. However, if a child was presented with systematic training in learning to walk at an early age, and then in running, swimming, riding a bicycle, throwing and catching a ball, jumping—in short, training in many basic sensory-motor coordinations—and then was introduced to special training in a sport or a physical art form, and this was done in a progressive manner, differences could be produced that would clearly throw the twin without special training into the category of duffer, and the trained twin into the category of skilled athlete or performer. Life presents possibilities for such long-term, cumulative, skill acquisitions. Furthermore, once a child has acquired a skill that is a little out of the ordinary—there are many factors that will tend to insure that he gains even more skill. For one thing he will receive much extra reinforcement for the behavior involved, from various sources. Since this is informal, and people do not generally record the events or know their effects, the individuals involved will ordinarily deny that there were any special training circumstances in the person's life experience.

To understand the tremendous effects of learning on all types of complex behavioral development we must consider the circumstance where the acquisition of one repertoire in rate and quality affects the acquisition of the next repertoire, and the next affects the following one, and so on, in a snowballing effect *for good or bad.* The very able person is the lucky one who has had an advantage in his training which has cumulated— he is called intelligent, talented, able, and so on. The retardate (excluding, in this example, individuals with detectable physical abnormalities) is the person who has suffered the cumulative deficits of poor training. The retarded individual is one who for one reason or another has not acquired the basic behavioral repertoires, cannot emit them in new learning situations, and thus cannot respond in a manner that will enlarge his repertorial skills.

It must also be remembered, that most cognitive training past the age of 5 will move in a manner that is pitched not at the child's individual level of cognitive learning—but at some average point. Thus, once he falls behind, the retardate's life circumstances will almost guarantee that the cumulative effect will produce a "snowballing" low level of development. Moreover, a home environment is likely to have a constant rate and quality of cognitive training. That is, the child who has an accelerated or retarded cognitive development because of his early home training is likely to continue to get the same type of boost in later stages of cognitive development, again in a manner that enhances the cumulative effects of the child's training experience. There are exceptions, of course; for one reason or another parents may be good trainers at one level and poor ones at another. Certainly, in these and other respects there is room for infinite variation in parents.

One point may be made here. It is not suggested that these levels of cognitive learning are discrete and separable. It would seem quite likely that the S–R repertoires in many instances are not cleanly separated. Nevertheless, in other cases, the skills that must be acquired before another type of learning may be undertaken seem to be fairly clear. The next section will describe some of the aspects of the basic behavioral repertoire that appear to be necessary for later cognitive learning. These repertoires are relevant to considerations of such concepts as intelligence, readiness, and the learning how to learn acceleration in new skill acquisition.

THE BASIC BEHAVIORAL REPERTOIRE

The whole preceding book has been concerned with language—which is an important part of the basic behavioral repertoire. The following discussions will not duplicate previous discussions but will show how language learning and function is relevant to the concept of the basic behavioral repertoire.

The Basic Language Repertoire

The development of language in children has been described in the previous chapters. The present discussion will only summarize some of the types of language repertoires that are important to the child's successful adjustment in various types of learning situations. That is, many learning situations will depend heavily upon language repertoires, which if not previously acquired will make the learning situation impossible; these are thus aspects of the basic behavioral repertoire.

Speech Development

As previously described a long process of reinforcement for vocal responses that produce appropriate speech sounds is necessary in the first development of understandable speech. Ordinarily, it is a year or so before the child's vocal responses produce such sounds. This process may be considered to be like the acquisition of any skilled motor response. In this case, as in many, a large number of different muscular responses are involved, including those of the respiratory system, the larynx, the mouth, tongue, and lips. Thus, considerable sensory-motor coordination is necessary.

The repertoire the child has to acquire in this area of learning includes the unit speech responses that make up the language sounds—these unit speech responses are called phonemes in the study of linguistics. It is from these response units that the word responses of the language are "constructed."

In addition, these phoneme responses must also be formed into response chains—when they have not been initially learned this way. Thus, to summarize, the child must acquire unit speech responses—the phoneme responses. In addition, these phoneme responses must be linked into word and, later, sentence sequences. Thus, the child may have learned to emit the response *a* as in *ask*. In addition, in making the word responses AT, ASK, and APPLE, for example, it is necessary that this phoneme response —or the muscular and auditory stimuli the response produces—comes to control the vocal responses that produce the "t," "s," and "p" sounds.

Thus, the learning necessary for the child to make the response AM would not be complete when the child had learned only to emit the "a" response in saying AT and the "m" response in saying MAN. Even if the child had learned to say the phoneme response "a" and "m" alone this would not guarantee that he would be able to emit the two phoneme responses together in the correct sequence in saying AM. Emission of the *sequence* of responses would require additional learning. Once the two phoneme responses have been well learned in sequence, however, the sequence should occur with ease and appear to function as a single response itself in further learning. As an illustration, all of us can emit the phonemic units in the word "ultramicroscopicsilicovolcanicconeosis," however, it takes training (practice) to be able to pronounce the whole word.

It would be expected that the child would require extensive training (ordinarily of an informal sort) in the process of acquiring the phonemic response repertoire as well as the repertoire in which the various phonemic responses are joined into sequences in the large number of combinations that occur in our language. Moreover, these repertoires would be essential in learning new words, that is, new combinations of phonemes.

The Imitative Speech Repertoire

The speech repertoire itself is an important aspect of language development, and this aspect could be studied independently. However, in the process of developing a functional language it is important that the speech responses occur at the appropriate times—that is, under the appropriate stimulus controls. One of the most important types of stimulus control involves auditory stimuli which come to control vocal responses that yield a sound which matches the original auditory stimulus. That is, the child has to learn to emit phoneme responses like that of some source—to make responses that produce imitative sounds.

The manner in which this type of speech repertoire is acquired has already been outlined and further discussions of the general topic of learning through imitation are to be made. It will only be stated here that the child has to acquire a repertoire so that he can repeat any phoneme response that occurs in his language, as well as whole words and phrases of various types. When the parent or teacher manipulates two objects, saying "One and one are two, now you do it," the child must be able to imitate the verbal responses as well as perform the other responses involved. As we will see, a great deal of formal education, including reading acquisition, is squarely based upon the child's imitative speech repertoire.

The Labeling Speech Repertoire

As has been described many speech responses occur under the control of various stimulus objects and events in our world. When a stimulus object (a car, a man, a boat, and so on) controls the speech response, the speech response may be a noun or an adjective, for example. When the stimulus event is the response of some organism or object, the speech response that is controlled is more likely to be a verb or an adverb.

A large and important aspect of our functional speech involves responses under the control of these types of stimuli. Without an adequate repertoire of this type the child is crippled with respect to additional learning of all kinds including educational training. In addition, problem solving and reasoning heavily involve the labeling repertoire. The author (see Staats and Staats, 1963, p. 205–207) has suggested that many problem solving processes commence with a verbal response which labels the problem solving objects. As another example, the difficulty of some of the retardates dealt with in Chapter 15 was an example of the learning problems produced by an inadequate "labeling" repertoire.

Since the training necessary to produce a labeling repertoire is extensive, there is much opportunity for variation and there are many children whose repertoire is inadequate for normal progress in a formal training program. A child who has to learn this repertoire, which other children already have, while he is also learning other tasks appropriate for his age level, will be under a considerable handicap.

It should be noted that after proper training in this repertoire the child himself will ask the parent to tell him the name of many things and will repeat the name while looking at the object. That is, after being reinforced for "naming" many objects and events, it will become reinforcing for the child to make such a naming response. If *asking* for the name of objects is also reinforced along with the rest of the process, this "asking" behavior may become strong enough to result in many training trials for the child with various adults and other children in addition to the parents. The child also may repeat new names to himself when they have been said by other people without an overt training trial being observable. These will also be important general aspects of the child's basic behavioral repertoire that will aid in his learning in many situations.

(In addition, new labeling speech responses can be learned under the control of the appropriate stimulus object without ever having seen the stimulus object itself, but only a "verbal representation." This possibility, however, will not be described until the acquisition of word meaning has been summarized.)

Verbal Stimuli Controlling Motor Behavior

Another aspect of language development concerns language as it functions as a stimulus itself, rather than as a response. That is, not only does the child have to learn to produce language responses, it is very important that he come under extensive control of verbal stimuli. Much of our behavior occurs appropriately under the control of the language stimuli produced by others and also by ourselves.

The same principle is involved, that of instrumental discrimination learning. It may only be added here that again this is a very important repertoire for formal education. The child in common sense terms must follow instructions to learn many things. When the child is told to look in a certain direction he must do so. When he is told how to hold a pencil, the appropriateness of his response will depend upon the extent to which the verbal stimuli control the necessary motor responses. When the child is told to add two objects to two other objects the verbal stimuli have to control the appropriate motor responses for training to proceed smoothly.

It may be suggested that this type of training produces general habits. That is, if a child has been reinforced for "following instructions"—that is, reinforced for certain behaviors following a verbal stimulus—verbal stimuli given by new people will also control his behavior. Thus, if the child has been appropriately trained by his parents, the verbal stimuli given by a teacher will have a similar effect.

At any rate, this repertoire, as with those already described, is what the instructor in any learning task depends upon to conduct his training procedures. However, there are many parents who have only partially trained their children in this basic repertoire. In fact, in extreme cases the child may have been reinforced by the parents' increased attention, for example, for *not* responding to the parents' verbal stimuli (instructions). When there has been such a deficit in training, or a distortion of the basic behavioral repertoire through inadvertent and inappropriate training, the child's ability to adjust to learning situations will be disastrously impaired. The child will be seen as intransigent, dull, undisciplined, unresponsive, unmanageable, and untrainable, and, in cases of severe deficit or distortion, as psychotic or autistic. It may be noted here that deficits or distortions of any of the basic behavioral repertoire described herein will result in behaviors in the child which, depending upon severity, will be viewed as maladjustments or psychopathology.

One further point may be made. It should also be possible to produce a person who follows instructions too well. There are many requests given by other people that would control behaviors that are not advantageous to the individual, or which are inappropriate in some other way. If our behavior was perfectly controlled by all verbal stimuli to which we were exposed, for example, we would be in a sorry state simply with respect to TV commercials. Thus, a child has to be trained to a repertoire in which verbal stimuli control motor behaviors. This is part of his basic behavioral repertoire. Later, however, he also must receive training which provides additional controls over behavior. For example, the verbal stimuli must exert stimulus control only when other social stimuli are also present.

These two types of training may be considered to be conflicting to a certain extent. The child is originally trained to do whatever the adult says. Later, he will be trained to first respond to other stimuli before making the final motor response. He will be told, for example, even at an early age, not to take candy from strangers and not to get into their cars or go away with them. This will modify the controlling quality of the verbal stimuli produced by an unknown person. Thus, additional training is necessary so the child comes to respond to instructions but also to additional social stimuli. Without such training the child would be too compliant.

Before concluding this section it should be emphasized that the number (richness) of the child's basic (language) behavioral repertoire is a crucial item. For the child to respond appropriately to a large variety of situations, he must have a repertoire that includes responses relevant to the various situations. This applies to the next basic behavioral repertoire to be described, and to most of the others as well.

The "Word Stimulus-Meaning Response" Repertoire

It was just stated that words come to control appropriate motor responses in the child—and this repertoire is very important in the child's adjustment. Some words have "meaning" because they control motor responses. The principle involved in this type of learning is that of instrumental conditioning. In addition, as has been described, words come to elicit responses in the individual according to the principles of classical conditioning in the manner that has been described.

This is a most important aspect of language in several ways that are important to his further learning. First, since both stimuli, the word (^cS)

and the object (^{uc}S), elicit the same response they become functionally equivalent as has been described. That is, whatever happens to one stimulus will generalize to the other. If the child is reinforced for saying SPINACH, for example, he will also eat more spinach (Lovaas, 1961). If the child is reinforced for saying FAST he will respond more rapidly (Lovaas, 1961). The process by which this functional equivalence, or generalization, takes place between word and object has been described earlier in the present book under the heading of mediated or semantic generalization.

More specifically, since the word and the object both elicit the same response, when a new response is conditioned to this common response, both stimuli will elicit the new response. Let us say, for example, that the child has had conditioning trials in which the word *blue* is paired with blue objects. Both the word and the objects as a consequence would elicit the sensory response originally elicited by the blue objects themselves. Following this, let us say that the child is told "Things that are blue are also called azure, can you say azure?" When the child says the word and is reinforced it would be expected that the image (conditioned sensory response) elicited by the word *blue* would come to control the labeling response *azure*. (In addition, it would also be expected that the pairing of the words *azure* and *blue* would condition the sensory response or meaning of *blue* to the new word.) Since any blue object also elicits that type of sensory response on an unconditional basis, any blue object would now also tend to elicit the labeling response AZURE. *Thus, the child could learn a new labeling response for an object without having any training trials with the object itself.* But to learn in this manner he would have to have the necessary basic behavioral repertoire which included the meaning responses to the relevant words.

The foregoing example was a simple one. The process is actually more important in terms of acquiring new vocabulary than the example shows. Let us say, for example, that a child has never seen a zebra, has no labeling response for the animal, has no meaning response to the word *zebra*. If this child reads a story with the word *zebra* in it, he will not profit from the story as he would if he had the necessary repertoire. If he is told to select a zebra from among several other pictures of animals he also does not know, such as on an intelligence test item, let us say, he will not respond correctly. If he is told draw a zebra and so on, he will have no appropriate response.

Let us say, however, that this child has had conditioning experiences in which the words *four, legs, striped, horse, tiger, donkey, white,* and *black* have come to elicit conditioned sensory responses (images). Upon the basis of this basic language repertoire the child is then prepared to learn the labeling response ZEBRA and the other responses implied in the above paragraph. That is, let us also say that someone says to the child "A zebra is a black and white animal that has four legs and is striped like a tiger; the zebra has a head like a horse and the size and shape of a donkey; can you say zebra?" This language experience would have the following effect. The various words would elicit conditioned sensory responses that would roughly form the total conditioned sensory response of an animal like a zebra. The vocal response ZEBRA would then be elicited and *conditioned to this total sensory response.* Later, when the child was shown a picture of a zebra it would elicit the total sensory response to which the vocal response ZEBRA had been conditioned and the child would say the appropriate name. This could happen although the child had never before seen a zebra. If the child read a story with the word *zebra* in it, the word would now elicit the appropriate conditioned sensory responses (meaning), and the child would comprehend the passage. He could also discriminate a zebra from other pictures of animals. All of these skills could give him a higher score on an intelligence test, language test, and so on. It should also be indicated that many of these skills would be types of "original" behaviors. That is, the child would be responding appropriately to situations with which he had had no previous direct experience. Thus, these mechanisms give additional examples of "originality" that are nevertheless based upon past learning. These various hypotheses could be tested experimentally.

A sort of naturalistic support for this analysis may be obtained by reading the following words to someone else who closes his eyes: *warm, four-legged, active, furry, friendly, loyal, playful, panting, wagging tail.* Although some of these words may have acquired their conditioned meaning responses other than through being paired with stimulus objects themselves, most people will find that conditioned sensory responses are elicited and they will see a dog before the last word is read.

It may thus be suggested that the child has to acquire a basic set of word meanings in order to profit from much of his language experience. For example, if the teacher says that a "zebra has stripes. . .," and so on, and these words elicit no meaning responses in the child, then he will not be able to learn the new labeling response of ZEBRA under the proper stimulus control, nor the meaning of the word *zebra* upon the basis of this experience. Thus, having a large repertoire of words that elicit meaning responses is basic to much additional language learning. It would also be expected that a child who begins by being retarded in the development of this basic language repertoire will fall even further behind as he goes on. That is, he will learn fewer new words from spoken and written context, in an ever increasing process of retardation.

Aspects of this process will be explicated further in later passages that deal with reading comprehension, and communication through reading.

VERBAL REINFORCERS   Before leaving the discussion of word meaning and its function in further learning, a word should be said here about verbal reinforcement although the topic of motivation will be discussed generally later. A great deal of the reinforcement for humans involves words that are either positive reinforcers or negative reinforcers. As has been discussed the child normally acquires a large repertoire of such words because the words are paired with other reinforcers in a classical conditioning process.

Much of our behavior is learned under the action of words that are either positive or negative reinforcers, according to the principles of instrumental conditioning. The parent decreases the strength of certain undesirable behaviors by saying "That is dangerous." This may be done, of course, only if the child has previously learned the meaning of *dangerous*, that is, if the word has been paired with negative reinforcing stimulus objects or words and is thus a conditioned negative reinforcer itself. For the child who has not learned the meaning of the word *dangerous*, however, the statement "That is dangerous" will have no effect upon his behavior.

It is thus important that the child learn a large repertoire of words of this type—that is many words must come through the child's conditioning experience to elicit meaning responses that have either positive or negative reinforcement value. This is a necessary aspect of human motivation and will take part in much learning in the child who has such a repertoire. Without such a repertoire the child will be seen as "dull," "disinterested," "lacking in motivation," and so on, in many situations in which he could learn. Later on, of course, he will as a consequence suffer achievement deficits.

(Moreover, as will be discussed further on, reinforcing stimuli also have controlling [discriminative] value. Thus, a child with a deficit in his repertoire of reinforcing words will also show deficits in following directions. For this he will also be considered stupid.)

Furthermore, as with the other repertoires, severe *distortions* in this repertoire, rather than deficits, will also lead to distortions in the behavior exhibited by the child—that is, psychopathological conditions can result from *unusual* learning as well as from deficits in learning. The person for whom the word *dangerous* has strong positive reinforcing value will respond differently to the statements involving the word than will a person for whom the word has strong negative reinforcing value.

If we are to behave appropriately in this very verbal world, we must have a basic repertoire of reinforcing words, both positive and negative, which is in large part like that of others in our community.

Word Associations

The importance of word associations in the complex adjustments of human behavior have not been fully realized—although the experimental study of word associations has proceeded for many years. It may be suggested in the present context that there is a very, very extensive network of associations between word responses. These associations constitute a basic behavioral repertoire important to the child's further progress in informal and formal educational circumstances. Various types of S–R mechanisms occur in the associations between words: sequences of word associates, hierarchies where one word elicits multiple word associates, sequences of hierarchies of word associates, and so on. Several aspects of this repertoire will be summarized in this section.

The term memory, or memory span, is frequently used in a manner that implies that the individual in some way has a certain internal faculty or capacity that determines how much he can repeat of material that has been presented to him. Used in this way the term suggests that learning variables have relatively little to do with the process of acquiring and repeating material—with the act of memorizing—but that personal (biological) factors predominate.

It may be suggested, however, that although it is quite conceivable that there are individual biological limits between people in this area of behavior, learning variables do indeed play an important part. And, word associations, or the tendency for one verbal response (or the stimulus it produces) to elicit another, appear to be important in this process.

Perhaps an illustration can be used here to indicate the importance of word associations in acts of memory. If we were to ask someone to repeat the numbers 5, 5, 5, 2, 2, 7, 2, 0, 1, many individuals would have a difficult time with this 9-digit memory task. It would then be said that their memory span was not as long as that of some other individuals. It may be suggested, however, that the task would be easier for some individuals than for others. For the author, for example, the task would be extremely simple, since the digits compose his own social security number which he learned as a sequence of word associations long ago. Since the verbal response sequence is already quite strong, the author would have no difficulty in "memorizing" it.

In the same manner, most of us could repeat the sentence "Now is the time for all good men to come to the aid of the party" with little difficulty. Our memory for this sentence would be quite good, much better than it would be for many 16 word sentences. The reason, again, is quite clear. For most of us, each word response in the sequence as a stimulus has come to elicit the next response in the chain. Thus, it is not necessary for these word associations to be formed in the "memory" task itself. For the individual who does not have such already formed word associations, the memory task actually involves the learning of the word associations—a much more difficult task.

It is not difficult to translate this analysis into other learning problems. Let us say, for example, that two children in school have both been taught to read numbers. Following this, let us say, they are given a series of number statements to read and learn, such as $1 + 1$ is 2, $1 + 2$ is 3, $2 + 2$ is 4, $2 + 3$ is 5, and so on. Let us say that one child has previously received training by his parents in making the speech response sequences ONE PLUS ONE IS TWO, ONE PLUS TWO IS THREE, TWO PLUS TWO IS FOUR, TWO PLUS THREE IS FIVE, and so on. Now, even though the training may not yet be complete, this child will be able to learn to read and remember the sequences much more easily than the other child who has not received any training in the necessary word association sequences.

It is by no means suggested that the establishment of word associations is the sole basis for arithmetical and mathematical learning. The example does indicate, however, that word associations are involved and that children faced with the same task may be able to learn and retain it more or less easily depending upon the basic repertoire of word associations that they have already acquired.

As another example, the ease with which a child reads, which will be discussed more fully later, will depend in part upon how many of the word associations he covers are already in his language repertoire. Thus, in reading "A stitch in time. . ." it is not necessary for most of us to look at each word in the complete sentence. After the first few words have been responded to, the rest of the word responses occur automatically. A person without the appropriate word associations would have to read the whole sentence, however, which would require more time and effort. The same thing pertains to listening to lectures. If the listener has a rich repertoire of word associations, other things equal, which are like those of the lecturer, he will follow the lecture more easily—and retain more of what is presented.

Thus, the richness of the individual's word association repertoire will help determine his ease of learning verbal material in general, the extent to which he retains verbal material that has been presented to him, and so on. It is also true that the *type* of word associations he has, in addition to the number (or richness) in his repertoire, will be an important factor.

If his associations are like those of the source of the verbal material he will find the material relatively easy. If his word associations are atypical, the converse will be true. Or if the verbal material is atypical, or unsuited for the child, the learning task will be more difficult.

The author, in the present book and elsewhere (Staats, 1955, 1963, 1966; Staats and Staats, 1963), has indicated the importance of word associations to the individual's problem solving and reasoning (including social reasoning), sentence generation and grammar, originality, scientific behavior, and so on. The author has also indicated (Staats and Staats, 1963) that measurement of word associations is heavily involved in intelligence testing. For example, the child scores a point on the age 2 level items if he demonstrates two-unit sequences of word responses (two-word word associations) on the Stanford-Binet (Terman and Merrill, 1937, p. 77 and 198), for example, if he says BYE MOMMY, ALL GONE, or SEE MAN. Many vocabulary items also test the child's word association repertoire. For example, in response to the task of stating what *envelope* means, the child scores a point if he says AN ENVELOPE IS FOR A LETTER. This correct response could have been acquired as a word association sequence simply from having heard a parent, sibling, or friend say "An envelope is for a letter." Word associations are also important on many of the reasoning items found on intelligence tests. It may also be added that a child who comes from a home where he has acquired good grammatical word associations will perform better on tests and in learning tasks with which he is confronted.

The Number Repertoire

In the preceding section several examples have been given of the importance of "number" word associations. Number word associations alone, however, do not account for the full basic "number repertoire." As has been described, the acquisition of the concept of number involves the formation of complex S–R mechanisms. The child first must acquire vocal responses under the control of the stimuli of numerosity in a difficult kind of concept formation training. In addition, the child has to acquire sequences of eye movement responses, motor responses, and vocal responses, under the control of the visual stimuli of the objects being counted—and these sequences must be under the control of each other so that the sequences occur in a parallel manner. The formation of this type of repertoire is important to the later learning of the child. For the purposes of the present discussion, however, the analysis that has been made so far will suffice. It should be stated, however, that this is a basic behavioral repertoire that deserves detailed individual treatment in and of itself.

Attention: Stimulus Control of
"Sense-Placing Behavior"

The aspect of the basic behavioral repertoire to be described now is at certain points related to, or involves, language development. As a matter of fact, it should be indicated that the various aspects of the basic behavioral repertoire are not as independent as their separate discussion would suggest. Although it is convenient to discuss the acquisition of the various repertoires separately, it should be understood that the several types of learning overlap and at points are interrelated.

One category of behavior that enters into almost all informal and formal education of the child involves what is called *attention* in common sense terms. In a manner similar to the general use of the term *memory*, which has been previously mentioned, the term attention is frequently used as though there were some inner entity or process which determines whether or not the individual will attend appropriately. This concept has also acquired a developmental flavor in much common usage. That is, many people feel that this internal entity or process matures or develops with age. Thus, it might be stated that children of 4 years of age are not yet mature in the development of their attention, and thus they have a short attention span.

The discussion that follows will attempt to show how learning principles underlie the development of attention. This type of analysis is basic to an understanding of much cognitive learning. Moreover, until the analysis of the development of attentional behavior is made, many problems of cognitive learning cannot be dealt with. Thus, the learning analysis of attention, as with the other learning analyses made herein, is intended to yield applications as well as understanding.

To begin, the sense organs of the human body are placed in anatomical structures whose "movement," in many cases, results in variation in what stimuli will affect the organism. These movements have an important influence on what is commonly called attention. Thus, as an example, the organs sensitive to light stimuli are concentrated in the eyes. The position of these structures is varied by the various movements of the eyes, eyelids, neck, back, as well as the general movements of the body. Any independent variable that controls these various "sense-placing responses" affects the stimulus input to the eye. Thus, two individuals may be in the same general environmental situation, however, different past histories of conditioning with respect to attentional behaviors, or indeed different present variations in variables such as motivation, may result in the two individuals receiving markedly different stimulus conditions because of variations in their "sense-placing," or attentional, behavior.

Moreover, these differences, will markedly effect the way that individuals will learn, in both formal and informal training circumstances. It may be suggested that one of the variations in the learning ability that we see in children will depend upon the previous history of learning with respect to these sense-placing responses. This section will begin a discussion of this important type of behavior.

Attention, discussed on this level, may be considered to involve a kind of "competition" between stimuli. Let us say that the individual is in a situation which involves a multitude of stimuli. Let us say that in the past he has been trained to respond to one of these stimuli much more strongly than he has been trained to respond to the others. In such a circumstance this one stimulus will control his response, and thus be described in everyday terms as having "gained his attention." In very general terms then, attention in the naturalistic situation will be influenced by the relative strengths of the stimuli in the situation for eliciting a sense-placing response.

An individual who has, for example, been reinforced in the past for looking at a particular color, in contrast to others colors, will "attend" to this color more than to the others. Ordinarily, this training would probably take place in the process of training the child to name colors, so that the stronger attentional response to the color would include a stronger verbal response to the color.

Furthermore, besides there being "competition among stimuli" of one particular sensory modality for the control of the individual's response, there may be competition *between* the senses in this respect. That is, in a situation in which the individual is presented with both auditory and visual sources of stimulation, if he has been reinforced more for responding to the visual stimuli than to the auditory stimuli, he will respond (attend) to the visual stimuli. Of course, ordinarily it would be expected that there would be considerable overlap in any case, since some stimuli in the "weaker" sense would be stronger than some of the stimuli in the "stronger" sense.

(As will be described more fully further on, stimuli in one sense also have to come to control attentional responses important for a different sense. That is, there are auditory stimuli that come to control auditory attentional responses. In addition, however, auditory stimuli must also come to control attentional responses for better placing the visual sensory organs. Thus, as an illustration, the *sound* of an approaching car for the hiker along the road will control turning of the head so that the eyes are brought into position where they can sense the approaching car.)

The important thing to suggest here is that what we call attention, a very basic form of behavior, is subject to influence by the individual's conditioning history. This suggestion may be elaborated in the context of discussing an important type of attentional learning that must take place in early child training. That is, it is important, if further learning is to be effected in many different training circumstances, that certain stimuli have come to more strongly control attentional responses than do other stimuli. The untrained child will not differentially respond in this way—and this may mean that no new learning occurs.

For example, one of the things that must occur for the child if he is to learn well in school situations is that certain auditory stimuli must have come to strongly control his behavior. At a very basic level the sound of the human voice must become a stimulus that strongly controls "stopping and listening." Vocally produced stimuli must gain strong control over the behavior of the child in "competition" with other auditory stimuli as well as stimuli of other kinds.

A child for whom this is not the case will be considered abnormal—if the deficit is severe enough. For example, a child that continues to respond to other stimuli in a situation when an adult speaks to the child will be considered dull, or autistic, or uncontrollable. Many autistic children suffer from this deficit in learning. A child in a preschool or kindergarten group that does not respond with attention to the teacher's words as do the other children will be considered backward or abnormal Furthermore, he will not be subject to the same training circumstances as the other children and will not learn well. As anyone who has worked with children can attest, there are large differences among children in the extent to which their attentional behaviors are controlled by the auditory stimuli of an adult's voice, a frequent underlying reason for the label of mentally retarded.

At this point it will serve to describe examples of the manner in which attentional responses come under the control of appropriate stimuli in the process of instrumental discrimination learning. A description of a case involving visual defect may be first used as an example here. There are retinal diseases that result in tunnel vision (the absence of peripheral vision). The individual so afflicted may have good central (foveal) vision, but see nothing a short distance in any direction away from the center of his visual field. When this is the case, the "sense-placing responses" of the eye become very, very important, and this example can be used to illustrate several points. That is, with normal vision the individual receives stimulation from objects in the periphery of his visual field; after the child's early training objects approaching the individual may be sensed without directly looking at them. This cuts down on the amount of movement necessary to bring the eye into "contact" with the relevant objects in the individual's physical and social environment.

An individual who becomes afflicted with tunnel vision, however, must develop a new and more vigorous set of "sense-placing responses" for his eyes. He should acquire strong scanning responses under special types of stimulus controls. When walking down the street in conversation with a companion, for example, this individual should not look continuously at the other person, to the extent that is customary. He must under such circumstances make movements that will result in visually sensing obstacles of various kinds that might occur in his path, he must sense stimuli that maintain geographic location, and so on.

This individual in any new situation should make responses that bring his visual senses into contact with the various aspects of the situation that are relevant to his movements in the situation, as well as the aspects of the situation that are moving with respect to him. This will demand a great deal of responding not required of the normal seeing person for the same degree of safety and skill in orientation. The controlling stimuli of the faces of other individuals, their lip movements, and their sounds, to some extent, must in certain situations come to *not* exert such strong stimulus control over the attentional behaviors of individuals afflicted with tunnel vision. This would mean relearning attentional behaviors under the control of new stimuli—that is conditioning trials (or instructions) would have to be presented to change the individual's extensive past training, which has produced attentional responses that are no longer maximally adjustive.

In the infant and young child, of course, the normal adjustive attentional behaviors must be learned for the first time. A word may be said about some of these general habits, and the circumstances under which they are acquired. First, long before the child can emit language himself, the auditory stimuli produced by others will under usual circumstances come to elicit responses. For example, the parent will usually talk when administering to the child, that is, providing the child with positive reinforcers and removing negative reinforcers. This means the various "positive" responses elicited by the reinforcers will be conditioned to the parent's voice. The parent's normal voice, as has been mentioned earlier, will thus become a positive conditioned reinforcing stimulus.

Consequently, as the child is awake lying in his crib and the parent is in another part of the house talking or singing, head movements that result in a clearer auditory signal of the parent's voice should be reinforced. If the child moves in one direction he hears the reinforcing sound more strongly, if he moves in the opposite direction he hears the sound less strongly. Such conditioning experiences would be expected to result in general habits. Weak auditory signals could come to control the attentional behaviors of "cocking" the head in the way with which we are familiar, for example. It may be suggested that this type of attentional training, informal as it is, and depending upon the parent's voice becoming a reinforcing stimulus, may be thought to commence its development at very early ages.

Furthermore, early in life also, visual stimuli also come to control visual attentional responses; responses that bring the eyes into appropriate position, and function. This would be expected on the basis of learning as the following example will illustrate. In addition to the parent's sound becoming a positive reinforcer, the sight of the parent also becomes a positive reinforcer. As a consequence, movements within the eye as well as movements of the eye that result in a better visual stimulus of the parent would be reinforced. It would be expected that some of the learning of the movements of the child's lenses, his eyes, and head, and so on, would occur through the action of this type of reinforcement.

That is, for example, when the parent is out of focus, certain particular changes in the muscles controlling the curvature of the lens of the eyes will be strengthened by providing a better visual stimulus of the parent. These responses will thus be reinforced. Movements of the lens muscles in the wrong direction, however, will result in a less clear visual image and consequently would not be strengthened. Under this training it would be expected that a blurred image would come to control movements of the lens muscles that clarified the image. As with other types of sensory-motor learning, after a sufficient number of conditioning trials, it would be expected that these visual attentional responses would occur rapidly and surely. In general, it should become reinforcing to have sharp rather than blurred visual sensations, since these types of sensations allow successful (better reinforced) sensory-motor behaviors.

Similar circumstances would also involve movements of the muscles attached to the eyeball itself, as well as movements of the muscles of the neck and other parts of the body. It is thus suggested that the child learns his basic attentional behaviors of visual perception, which in themselves constitute a very complex type of repertoire. It may be added that although the parent has been used as the stimulus in the example, as was also the case in discussing auditory attentional learning, it would be expected that many other stimuli would be involved with this type of learning.

To continue, it would also seem that there are attentional responses learned under the control of stimuli of the other senses as well. Thus, when the individual turns his head in the presence of a faint odor, he may receive either a stronger or weaker contact with the molecules stimulating the sensory response. A more dramatic response that has an even greater effect upon olfaction is the response of sniffing. Sniffing may be considered to be an attentional response that is learned under the control of faint olfactory stimuli.

Faint, or incomplete, tactile stimuli also appear to come to control tactile attentional responses. That is, the individual will acquire a repertoire of "feeling" things by which to improve contact with objects. When he has received a "partial" tactile stimulus, for example, he will respond by moving the hands in such a way as to receive additional stimulation. These responses have been acquired in situations in which it is positively reinforcing to make such hand movements as well as in situations in which such tactile attentional responses have escaped or avoided aversive stimuli.

These various repertoires may be considered to be very basic types of attentional responses under the control of stimuli in the same modality as the attentional responses being controlled. It would seem likely that everyone would acquire a repertoire of these types of attentional responses, except perhaps in exceptional cases. On the other hand, it is not unlikely that it is possible to acquire these attentional repertoires in varying levels of skill. Thus, it would appear that some athletic skills, as one example, involve special development of such attentional skills, and these skills are an essential feature of the athletic ability. Take the baseball player, for example. The visual stimulus of a rapidly moving object, in this case the baseball, must come to control appropriate eye movements that follow the ball as well as movements of the muscles of the lenses of the eyes that maintain the ball in good focus. The same would be true of the tennis player, as another example. It is certainly true that the tennis player's eye must track the moving object and part of the player's skill resides in his visual attentional responses. Keeping one's eye on the ball is an essential constituent of any sport involving a ball.

The development of the appropriate eye movements for such athletic skills can be readily observed in young children. In the beginning a child will not track a ball that is thrown to him, even when told to "Watch the ball." Only after many, many training trials will this attentional skill begin to emerge. By the time the player has become expert, however, these attentional responses are well acquired and it is said that a tennis player will keep his eye on the ball until it strikes his racquet. Obviously, there will be great disparities in these attentional skills of adults, depending upon their histories of conditioning. (It may be inserted here that the manner in which the attentional repertoire is acquired is being described as it occurs under normal circumstances. It should be remembered, however, in this as in other repertoires analyzed herein, that there is opportunity, even at a very basic level, for development to be retarded or distorted. The training circumstances, for example, may be absent or awry; the parents may not have or employ properly the necessary reinforcement system, and so on.)

Cross-Modal Control of Attentional Behavior

In addition to the case where the stimuli of a particular sense come to control attentional responses relevant to that sense organ, there are various mixtures where the stimuli of one sense come to control movements that orient a different sense organ. Thus, for example, the child is reinforced for attentional responses that bring his mouth into contact with objects that he has *seen*. In this case, the visual stimulus object has to control muscular responses that orient the tactile and gustatory senses of the mouth, lips, and tongue. Ordinarily, we also acquire a vast repertoire of movements that are attentional responses for our tactile senses, under the control of visual stimuli. Thus, for example, we acquire eye-hand motor coordinations of various kinds in which the movement results in better tactile stimulations. (See the author's discussion of the acquisition of sensory-motor coordinations in Staats and Staats, 1963). Additional examples of cross modal control of attentional responses will be given in the following discussions.

VERBAL STIMULUS CONTROL OF ATTENTION BEHAVIOR   An even more important repertoire of attentional responses, at least for the later learning of the child, involves control by auditory verbal stimuli. Although attentional responses of the various sensory modalities are involved, perhaps it is the control of visual attentional responses that is most important. That is, the child must receive extensive training (usually informally conducted in the home) for making varied visual attentional responses under the control of verbal stimuli (instructions).

Thus, he must be trained to respond correctly to such stimuli as "Look to your right," "Look up," "Look at the small one," "Look at the third one from the right," "Look at the red one," "Look at the triangle," "Notice that the letter m has two humps while the letter n has only one." In addition, of course such verbal stimuli must also come to control other types of attentional responses. The following are examples of the control of auditory attentional responses, gustatory attentional responses and tactile attentional responses. "Listen for the high note," "Taste the bitter after-taste," "Feel the rough spot here."

It is also true that the verbal control of attentional behaviors becomes very subtle. Thus, verbal stimuli from some people will ordinarily gain control over the attention of the child to a greater extent than will the verbal stimuli from other people. For example, the same words from another child will not control the child's attentional responses as when the verbal stimuli are produced by a parent. Later in life, of course, complex and subtle social stimuli will differentially control the adult's attentional behaviors. The words of one's employer, wife, mother, children, the grocery-store man, an expert, and so on, will have differential amounts of control over the individual's behavior including his attentional behaviors. Some of these differences must be learned early if the child is to succeed in a school, as one example. Thus, it is important that adult's instructions gain strong control over the child's attentional responses; stronger than the control of other children and various environmental stimuli. When this is not the case, as will be described more fully, the child may be seen as difficult to control.

These, of course, are variations of the verbal-motor repertoires previously described. The difference is that the behaviors involved in the present case are sense-placing responses so basic to the later learning of the child that the repertoire deserves separate discussion. This is especially true since deficits in this basic repertoire seem frequently to be at the root of learning problems of children (as in mental retardation and autism) and thus behavior problems of the adult.

The suggestion here is that this repertoire of attentional behaviors, like the others, is learned. The child has to receive experiences which train him to the repertoire. Since this is not done formally, we tend to think of this type of behavior as given through maturation. Closer observation and analysis indicates, however, that the child's attentional repertoire develops through training, not through physiological maturation. He must learn to attend under the control of the appropriate stimuli. It is interesting, for example, to take a young child and give him attentional instructions such as calling the child's name or saying "Close your eyes," "Move your eyes to the right," "Look up," "Look down," "Turn around," and so on. Depending upon the previous training of the child he will respond appropriately or not. In addition, it is quite easy and informative to take a child that has not learned an attentional response under the control of the verbal stimulus and teach him this aspect of the necessary repertoire.

An especially amusing thing is to give a child an instruction of this type when some learning has occurred but it is incomplete. The partial response usually produces a very cute result. For example, if you ask the young child to "Close one eye," or to "Move your eyes to one side," before the skill is perfectly acquired the child will emit some very ludicrous behaviors. The learning of these repertoires does not always progress in the same manner. In the first example, with the instruction "Close one eye," the verbal stimuli will ordinarily have gained control over the child's behavior before the skill of closing one eye has been acquired. Thus, the child will attempt the response with various facial contortions. In the second example, "Move your eyes to the side," the response is in the child's hierarchy when he is quite young but does not come under the control of the verbal stimulus until much later. That is, even when the child cannot move his eyes on command, he will be able to look to the side when the eye movement is controlled by the stimulus of a moving object.

At any rate, a good repertoire of verbally controlled attentional behaviors is absolutely essential for later formal and informal learning situations. However, even though it is easily seen that there are vast differences in this repertoire among preschool children, little attention has been directed toward investigation of the conditions that produce the necessary repertoires of attentional behaviors. One of the main reasons for this seeming disinterest in the manner in which such attentional skills are learned seems to be in the common conception that individual differences among children are a function of differences in physiological maturation. Following the present analysis, however, it may be suggested that learning variables account for very large differences in this essential repertoire.

It may be productive to sketch out the principles involved in the establishment of the auditory control of attentive behaviors for the visual apparatus, as well as some of the first types of training involved in elaborating this repertoire. To continue with the previous example, because the sight of the parent is frequently paired with positive reinforcers the sight of the parent becomes a conditioned reinforcer—especially when there has been a period of absence (deprivation) of the parent. Let us say that the child has been isolated from the parent for a time and the parent has then entered the child's room, and has made some type of vocal response. If in the presence of the parent's auditory stimulus the child turns his head and eyes a certain way, he will see the parent, and these movements will thus be followed by the reinforcement involved in seeing the parent. This experience would be expected to produce instrumental discrimination learning. The stimulus is the vocal sound. The responses are the "sense-placing responses" of turning the head and eyes. The reinforcement is the sight of the parent. As a consequence of a wide variety of this type of experience, auditory (verbal) sounds will come to control attentional responses for the visual apparatus. This is thus an example of the way that certain sound stimuli come to control responses that move the visual apparatus so the source of the sound is seen.

Of course, a great deal of conditioning experience is necessary before the wide varieties of sounds, emanating from a wide variety of locations, will come to control the appropriate attentional responses. To continue with examples involving parent-child relations, this type of conditioning will ordinarily include the production of a complex repertoire by which verbal stimuli come to control specific attentional responses. When the parent has said the child's name, or said "Look here," or "Look at me," or some such things, there will be many instances when the attentional responses of turning eyes and head will be reinforced by something more than just the sight of the parent. That is, many times when the parent is offering some object (reinforcer) to the child the parent will say the child's name or utter one of the other sounds that must come to control the visual attentional responses. When this training first begins the control of the child's attentional behavior will be weak and it may be a moment or more before the child makes the appropriate attentional responses. The parent (trainer) may also be forced to produce some other stimulus that already has strong control over the attentional responses—such as saying loudly "Hey," or clapping his hands. With additional training trials, however, the verbal control of the child's attention will become stronger until eventually simply saying the child's name will immediately elicit the responses that result in the child looking toward the source of the auditory stimulus. In the above example, the parent who is a poor trainer may not bother but simply walk over and dangle the reinforcer in front of the child—thus losing an opportunity for enhancing development of this crucial repertoire.

Further training is necessary to bring the child's attentional responses under the control of specific verbal stimuli such as "Look here," "Look under the bed," "It is on the table," "You will find it in the hall," "See the difference between the one on the right and the one on the left," and so on. A long history of conditioning involving many training trials would be expected to be necessary to produce the correct repertoire of visual attentional responses under the control of vocal stimuli. As already suggested, in the early stages of establishing this repertoire, the parent may also use other visual stimuli that already control attentional responses. That is, through the same type of conditioning already described, pointing will come as a stimulus to control attentional behaviors

—the child having in the past been reinforced by seeing reinforcing objects when following a pointing finger with his eyes. The pointing finger, once it has come to control attentional responses, can be used as a stimulus that gets the child to make an attentional response at the same time that the parent is providing a verbal stimulus like "Look here." After this has happened a number of times, sometimes followed by reinforcement, the vocal stimulus "Look blank" itself will thus acquire control over the visual attentional responses.

It would be expected that it would be necessary to insure that adequate reinforcement was made contingent upon the attentional responses— otherwise this type of behavior under the control of the verbal stimuli would extinguish. If the child is many times told to "Look here" and what is seen is not reinforcing, or if some form of extrinsic reinforcement is not given, the child's attentional responses will weaken. Many parents are surprised to find that this is the case when trying to teach their children to read or to count or something of that sort. Although they may at first get the child's attention through verbal control, this will weaken very quickly if the behavior is not reinforced.

A good type of training in this area of behavioral development, which utilizes a good source of reinforcement, consists of simply pointing out things to the child that have become reinforcing to him. Thus, after the child has played with a dog, or watched a horse, or even seen moving pictures of the animals, it will be reinforcing to see one. Thus, the parent may have a good training trial in which he says to the young child "Look at the horse," and then insures that the child direct his head and eyes in the right direction. After a program of this kind of training, when the parent says "Look at such and such," the child being reinforced when he does so, these verbal stimuli will have control over the appropriate looking attentional responses.

As has been suggested this repertoire of attentional behaviors under appropriate stimulus control is basic to early cognitive learning. For example, this repertoire is what the teacher's procedures rely upon. Where children have this repertoire well developed, the teacher need only present the verbal stimuli (instructions) to control the correct attentional behaviors. Where the repertoire has not yet been developed by the pupil it must be trained or the child will not learn.

Both of these results frequently occur. That is, when the teacher has classes in which the pupils customarily do not have well developed attentional repertoires, a primary aspect of training must involve training attentional behaviors. It is not infrequent, for example, to observe that many of the activities of the kindergarten teacher constitute attentional training. The teacher will say, for example, "Everyone look here," strike a chord on the piano (which controls attention), and wait for the appropriate attentional response before introducing a new and reinforcing activity.

When a child has a deficit in the verbal control of his attentional behaviors, many types of training are impossible, and it is not likely that the child will gain as much from learning experiences as do other children with better attentional repertoires. In many cases it is necessary that a child look at (attend to) a specified stimulus and also make a response. This is certainly true in the acquisition of reading, writing, and number concept learning—as well as many other social behaviors. If the child does not attend to the stimulus, if the adult's words do not control the looking responses, the child does not see the stimulus and learning does not occur; that is, the child is "retarded" or "disturbed."

Since the acquisition of basic attentional responses requires extensive training it must be expected that many children will not have an adequate repertoire. That is, many parents do not, for one reason or another, provide the conditioning experiences that will yield the necessary repertoire. This deficit would be expected to occur more generally in families subjected to suppressed circumstances in socioeconomic-cultural factors; in families whose members have special problems such as parental instability, maladjustment, or retardation; in families where the child through illness or injury presents special problems of training; and so on. At any rate, before children can be expected to profit from many learning situations, including our traditional formal educational training circumstances, it would be expected that training in this repertoire would be necessary.

In support of this rationale, it may be noted that the first training that was necessary with Jennifer in the preceding study, when she was two years old, involved gaining control of her attentional responses. It was necessary that she receive training to look at the card as it was presented in the apparatus, versus looking at other things or doing other things. Moreover, the printed stimulus on the card had to more specifically control her visual attentional responses. Furthermore, it was necessary to train Jennifer to respond to the vocal stimulus provided. Other sounds and distracting stimuli had to exert less control. As the results of that study indicated, the acquisition of the requisite attentional responses took place over a period of time with continued progress even after the basic control had been established.

It also appeared in the work with the other children, particularly the retarded children, that there are large differences in the quality of these attentional repertoires. That is, with the normally developed children verbal stimuli (instructions) controlled the appropriate visual attentional responses. The child could be told "Look at this picture first, then look at the pictures below," and so on, and the appropriate attentional behaviors would be elicited. With some of the more retarded children, it was necessary to physically guide the child to make the necessary looking responses, or to use other controls of the attentional behavior such as pointing. When this was necessary the learning task was immensely more difficult.

It was also shown in the two studies which put the children under two different conditions of reinforcement that the quality of attentional behaviors can vary widely depending upon the conditions of reinforcement for the behaviors. When the young children were reinforced for attending, the behaviors were maintained in good strength. Under conditions where there were weak reinforcers these basic behaviors deteriorated and the learning ceased. Many of these children had already acquired the basic attentional behaviors. However, adequate reinforcement is still necessary in any particular situation to maintain attention. Thus, it did not take very long for the preschool children's attentional behaviors to extinguish in the training situation, when only social reinforcers were presented contingent upon the behaviors.

It should be indicated, however, that the attentional repertoire does not customarily remain dependent upon immediate reinforcement, after it has been strongly learned. Although the attentional behaviors of preschool children cannot be maintained for long when they are voluntarily participating in an arduous and unreinforcing task, by the time children begin school many of them will have such a strongly acquired attentional repertoire that immediate reinforcement is not as necessary. That is, when the child has had a long history of being reinforced for attentional responses under verbal control, the verbal stimuli will maintain control for some time even when no reinforcement is forthcoming.

In summary then, it is true that once appropriate stimuli have come to control behavior, these stimuli can be presented and learning will occur, even without reinforcement. Much formal education, for example, depends upon the prior establishment of these sources of control for attentional and working behaviors; that is, school training procedures rest upon the child having a repertoire which the parents have hopefully developed in the child. If this type of control has not been previously established no learning will take place in the usual educational situation. Furthermore, if in any learning situation the attentional behaviors do not result in reinforcement, the control will be weakened and learning will be negatively affected.

Discrimination Skills

Attention has been discussed as the fairly general movements involved in placing the sense organs so they may be more effectively stimulated. In addition to these important aspects of attention, there are even finer skills apparently involved in much discrimination learning that is important to the child's further learning.

That is, what is commonly called discrimination appears to involve attentional responses that are more subtle than simply looking in the general direction of an object—as some of the previous discussion has implied. Thus, the task may involve acquiring a different response to a complex stimulus that is only slightly different from another complex stimulus, or of making a different response to two complex objects just slightly different than two other objects. In such cases it may be observed even on a naturalistic level that the individual will scan the two objects, and move his eyes back and forth from one object to another. That is, it may be suggested that the child if properly trained acquires general skills such that when he is faced with a problem of discrimination he makes scanning eye movements, and comparing eye movements looking from one to the other of the objects involved, and so on. Furthermore, many stimuli are of such a nature that they must be scrutinized in fine detail before the important stimulus is seen that controls the relevant behavior. It may be suggested that the detailed scrutiny of stimuli, the comparing of stimuli, and so on are attentional behaviors that must be learned.

Although there are probably general discrimination habits acquired simply through being trained to make many discriminations involving slight differences in complex stimuli, in any particular situation new responses may have to be learned. For example, although a child may have learned to discriminate complex stimuli such as letters and words, there are additional responses that must be acquired in learning to read. That is, the child has to learn to look at the letters in a word successively, for example.

Some of these discrimination habits that are relevant for reading acquisition will be discussed later in that context. It may suffice to say at this point that there seem to be additional attentional responses that sharpen the stimulus, or the differences between stimuli, that involve sequences of attentional responses, and so on. It may be suggested that a repertoire of such fine attentional responses is also of great importance in the child's further learning. It should be noted that such attentional "comparing" responses may involve other senses than vision. The individual may sniff a cantaloupe for example, while shopping, and then quickly sniff another—in this way bringing the two stimuli together for comparison (differential response). Obviously these discrimination skills can be developed to a high degree through training—as for example, with the professional wine taster.

Sensory-Motor Skills

The principle of learning involved in the acquisition of sensory-motor skills appears to be the same as that involved in acquiring the repertoire of attentional responses—namely, the principle of instrumental discrimination learning. In the present case, however, the responses of interest are not attentional responses, but rather instrumental responses of other types.

Again, prevailing conceptions about child development are that early acquisition of sensory-motor skills result largely from maturation. From the author's observation and research, however, a different conception can be formulated. The author has suggested that such basic coordinations as walking, and balance itself, involve complex stimulus controls acquired through the individual's reinforcement history. The stimuli that come to control balance, for example, arise in the eyes, the sensory nerves in the muscles and tendons, and the sensory nerves in the semicircular canals of the ears. Appropriate "righting" responses to the "off-balance" visual stimuli should also be learned according to the principles of reinforcement. Thus, in the presence of the visual cues of the room deviating too far from the vertical, if certain responses occur, the aversive stimulation of a fall is avoided. If the "righting" responses do not take place, the child falls. The visual cues, as discriminative stimuli (and reinforcing stimuli as well), should in this way come to control the appropriate responses which maintain us in an upright position.

The same would be true of the stimuli controlling balance that arise in the semicircular canals of the inner ear. These canals, which extend in three planes, contain fluid. Any movement of the head results in movement of the fluid with respect to the walls of the canal. Extending from the walls into the fluid are hairlike organs that are activated by movement of the fluid. The activation of these organs produces some of the stimulation of balance. Since being off-balance (a certain pattern of stimulation from these organs) would frequently be paired with the aversive stimulation of knocks and bumps, it would be expected that the off-balance stimuli would become negative reinforcers. Any "righting" response would be reinforced by eliminating these stimuli (as well as avoiding the primary aversiveness of a fall). In common sense terms, it could be said that it should become "unpleasant" for the child to be off-balance, and this source of negative reinforcement would be a factor in learning to make correct upright movements when walking and standing, sitting, and so on.

Observations of other sensory-motor developments of the child suggest that responses which one may feel are naturally present in the human actually have to be acquired in childhood. For example, a child must *learn* to lower his head upon walking under an object, such as a table, when he grows too tall to walk under it upright. Many trials that result in aversive stimulation may be required to complete this visual discrimination involving the sight of the object toward which the child is walking. If the child does not duck his head, aversive stimuli follow. Then, if the child lowers his head sufficiently, aversive stimulation ceases. It would therefore be expected that through a number of negatively reinforced head-lowering responses, the child would finally acquire the discrimination, and the approach of visual objects on the level of one's eyes would control the ducking response. This coordination seems so automatic for an adult that it is somewhat surprising to observe a child going through a long course of training before it is acquired.

The same variables also appear to play a role in simple "eye-hand" coordinations. Stimuli in various positions with respect to the body must come to be ^DS for various hand movements. Prior to training, the child does not respond appropriately to such visual stimuli. He cannot without training reach unerringly for objects he sees. However, in the presence of an object in a certain position a particular movement will be reinforced by the consequence of obtaining the object, whereas other movements will postpone reinforcement. After a number of trials in which differential reinforcement is contingent upon these responses, the child should finally come to quickly reach in any required direction and obtain the reinforcing object. Stimulus control would then be considered complete.

Again, this class of behavior should develop in roughly similar patterns for all children because the physical principles of the world (as well as the psychological principles of behavior) are the same for all. On the other hand, these interpretations also suggest how some individual differences in locomotor development would arise as a function of training variables. For example, parents may provide different opportunities for the discriminations and chains of behavior to occur and be reinforced—thus influencing the speed of behavioral development. Some parents, when the infant makes a slight movement toward an object, or looks at an object and emits a vocal response, obtain the object for the child; others allow the infant to fend for himself when the task is not too great, to make struggling movements toward an object within his reach. The latter procedure would allow locomotor movements to be followed by reinforcement in the presence of the appropriate stimuli. It would be expected that a systematic training program in which reinforcing objects were gradually placed further and further from the child and were gradually placed in different positions as well, would result in more rapid locomotor and sensory-motor development.

At any rate, it would appear that large individual differences in this type of behavior could be produced by varying training conditions, and a long term training program which reinforced increasingly complex sensory-motor coordinations could lead to a superior individual in this type of behavior. Furthermore, it is suggested that some of these elementary sensory motor skills are basic to other learning in the same manner that has been discussed for language and attentional repertoires.

For example, the child who has acquired skilled throwing responses will learn to serve in tennis more easily than a less skilled child; for the tennis serving stroke involves a throwing movement. In general it may be suggested that a child who has acquired the basic skills involved in running, dodging, and sliding, and so on, receiving, throwing, and kicking moving objects, and so on, is in a better position to learn new games involving these basic skills.

There are other basic sensory-motor coordinations that appear to be more closely related to early verbal learning. Grasping a pencil or crayon properly and making marks in various directions involves sensory-motor skills that are basic to the ease with which the child will learn to write. In addition, the eye-hand coordinations involved in drawing lines according to visual specification are important, and constitute a basic behavioral repertoire. This would include tracing lines and copying lines and figures. A child who has these sensory-motor skills is of course prepared to learn to write more easily than would otherwise be the case.

While it may at first appear that a discussion of sensory-motor skills is only peripherally related to a conception of cognitive development, it should be pointed out that in some areas of human behavior there is really a fine shading between sensory-motor and cognitive skills. For example, artistic skills may be considered to involve highly developed sensory-motor repertoires—as do many other high-level professional endeavors. This is seen clearly with the dancer and the singer. The musician, however, also has to acquire complex motor skills under the control of complex and subtle sensory stimuli—repertoires that could be subjected to detailed analyses and experimental study. In addition, of course, the musician has to acquire a "verbal" repertoire also, a repertoire that may be considered to be similar to the types of cognitive learning already discussed. Dancers, also, although their art heavily involves sensory-motor repertoires, depend heavily upon verbal stimuli for learning new routines—a fact that has been made explicit with the modern invention of a language system for representing, *and controlling* (in choreographic instruction), various dance movements.

It is suggested that the interrelated nature of sensory-motor and cognitive skills may perhaps be best illustrated by stressing the fact that the child must acquire a vast repertoire of sensory-motor skills *under the control of verbal stimuli*. On the basis of these verbal-motor mechanisms or units the child may learn new sequences of sensory-motor skills in a manner that short-circuits the original development of the skills. Also, through the production of *original* verbal sequences which control motor behaviors, the person (such as a choreographer) can originate novel sensory-motor skills. These are as much cognitive acts as they are sensory-motor acts and constitute an important part of the basic behavioral repertoire.

At any rate, this brief mention of the arts may be a good point at which to indicate that terms like cognitive and sensory-motor are only loose terms to be used as descriptions for loose categorizations of types of human behaviors. The use of the labels should not imply that there are any basic differences in the principles involved in learning cognitive repertoires as contrasted with sensory-motor repertoires, social repertoires, and so on.

Imitation as a Sensory-Motor Repertoire

What has been labeled as imitation is an important aspect of the basic behavioral repertoire. It is on the basis of the imitation repertoire that much learning takes place, cognitive learning, sensory-motor learning, emotional (or motivational) learning, social learning, and so on. The importance of the imitation repertoire cannot be underestimated.

There should be several facets of any theoretical analysis that attempts to deal with imitation, however. Traditionally, imitation has been considered to be a basic propensity of "human nature" which is not analyzable into lower-level principles. As such the concept of imitation was used to explain behavior—which in one manner of speaking is quite acceptable. That is, as a constituent of the basic behavioral repertoire, imitation skills will indeed determine how the child will learn in many different situations. Thus, the varying quality of children's imitational repertoires could be selected as an independent variable in a study to see what the effect of the independent variable would be on cognitive learning, sensory-motor learning, social learning, and so on.

However, the imitation repertoire is itself explainable on the basis of the higher-level basic laws of conditioning. That appears to be something which some of the current treatments of imitation have neglected (Bandura, 1962; Bandura and Walters, 1963). That is, as was originally suggested by Miller and Dollard (1941) in beginning an S–R analysis of imitation, this behavior may be considered to be learned itself. It may be suggested that imitation, or modeling, is not basic; imitative behavior considered as an aspect of the basic behavioral repertoire is derivable from the principles of the learning theory, including the S–R mechanisms described.

A point that should be stressed here is that imitation has several aspects. Thus, imitation can be considered as it is part of the basic behavioral repertoire that is important to much of the child's further learning. In addition, imitation must be considered in terms of the manner in which the imitation repertoire is itself acquired. That is, the acquisition of imitation skills involves instrumental discrimination, but in addition an important part of imitation learning involves motivational considerations—that is the consideration of the reinforcement value of imitation *as well as the ways that reinforcement value of the imitated person effects the act of imitation*. Because the imitation repertoire is so closely related to a consideration of motivational (reinforcement) topics, the present section will only mention the importance of the imitation repertoire as a sensory-motor skill. The discussion of the manner in which an imitation repertoire is acquired as well as the more complete theory of imitation will be left for the next section.

Several points may be made here, however, concerning the manner in which the child learns through imitation. An important aspect of the imitation repertoire is that the child will have learned in certain situations to look at the actions of other people *and the stimuli that are controlling those actions*. With proper training, a child when in a situation where his own behavior is not controlled by the stimuli—that is, problematical situations where the child has no learned responses that solve the problem—he will look at the ways that others behave. These attentional responses are very important to his learning, for if there is someone else who has learned a response the child will see (or hear, and so on) this response.

Thus, basic to an imitational repertoire are the attentional behaviors that allow the child to sense the actions of another person, and the relevant stimuli that control the person's response. Two children could be in the same problem situation, see someone else solve the problem, and yet profit differently because one closely observed the action and the controlling stimuli for the action and the other did not.

We learn to observe other people's behaviors when we have had the appropriate conditioning history. A child may be instructed, for example, to "Watch how I do it." This can be done in great detail, with the trainer drawing attention of the child to the relevant stimuli of the problem solving objects, as well as to the stimuli of his own behavior. A child who has had a rich experience of this kind—where he observes and imitates and is then reinforced when he behaves in kind—will acquire a rich attentional repertoire for observing other people's behavior, as well as a rich imitational repertoire.

(It should be indicated that in many cases the first step in imitating a behavior that is different from one that we have in our own repertoire may be to first discriminate the difference. That is, before we can imitate a spoken dialect that is slightly different from our own, we must be able to discriminate the dialect—be able to respond to it differentially. This again, can involve close attentional behaviors. Following the discrimination one can practice imitating the different speech.)

The child in class, for example, who watches the teacher closely, as well as the stimulus objects she manipulates, and so on, as she performs actions which later on she will want the class to also perform, will learn rapidly. The child who does not have this repertoire will not even observe what has occurred, let alone be able to imitate the action. In addition to the observation of other people's behaviors, of course, the child must have learned the actual imitational repertoire that is involved, even though this learning may not yet be complete. That is, he must to some extent be able to repeat what the teacher has written, said, or done, for the learning to be complete.

It may be added here, however, that we can *overlearn* the imitation repertoire, or we may not learn other skills that should later replace the imitational repertoire in many situations. That is, in addition to learning to imitate, the child must also be reinforced for working things out by himself, and he must be trained so that he imitates selectively. For example, he should imitate some people (some people should control the repertoire) and not others. Moreover, some situations should control his imitational repertoire—and not others. Thus, during an examination his imitational (copying) repertoire should not be elicited.

Without giving additional examples at this time, it should be realized that the sensory-motor repertoire of imitation, including attentional responses, constitutes a very important aspect of the basic behavioral repertoire. The most difficult learners in the group of children in the previous experiments were those who among other things did not appear to observe and imitate the trainer's actions well—although the training programs did not attempt to maximally utilize this type of learning.

Principles of the Reinforcement System: a Conception
of Human Motivation

Motivation has been a prime concern of many approaches to an under-standing of human behavior. Clinical psychology and social psychology theories of human behavior heavily involve motivation, and the same is true of the other behavioral and social sciences, both in theory and practice. Experimental psychology has also been focally concerned with the study of motivation in the laboratory. However, the concepts that have arisen in the naturalistic observations of the social and behavioral sciences have not formerly been integrated with the conceptions from experimental psychology—thus motivational conceptions concerned with significant aspects of human behavior have largely been separate from the basic principles of motivation as they have been studied in the animal laboratory.

The author has attempted to set forth a general conception of human motivation (see Staats, 1964a, in the introduction to Chapter VI and VII; Staats, in press b; Staats and Staats, 1963, Chapters VII and VIII). The au-thor's strategy has been to employ the observations made of motivational conditions in the context of significant human behavior, as taken from the behavioral and social sciences, but to derive the theory from the basic prin-ciples of the experimental laboratory. Neither the view of the experimental psychologist or the social scientist has been complete itself, and a combi-nation of the approaches yields a more complete picture while retaining the potential predictability and control of the basic laboratory. Actually, the integration has suggestions for both areas—for further experimentation in the basic laboratory, as well as for further work in the social and be-havioral sciences. In the present context the motivational system may be considered an essential aspect of the basic behavioral repertoire.

Several themes are involved in this conception of human motivation, which should be elaborated in the context of the present concerns. First, it may be stated that there are stimuli which have reinforcement (motiva-tional) value simply by virtue of the organism's biological structure. Air is a reinforcing stimulus to the oxygen deprived individual, and food, sexual stimulation, and other stimuli are also reinforcers because of the manner in which the organism is constructed.

As with other types of behavior, as we go lower in the phylogenetic scale we see more uniformity in the stimuli that are reinforcing for the particular species. We see that wild animals of a particular species con-sume very similar reinforcing stimuli, even the higher mammals. Although this could no doubt be subject to a good deal of training, even in lower animals, in man the variegated experiences of different individuals and different groups allows for the development of wide differences in this sphere.

Although man, as is the case with other organisms, has a biological structure that determines that some stimuli will be reinforcers—food, sex stimulation, water, warmth, air, and so on—his reinforcement system appears to be largely learned. Many of man's most potent reinforcing stimuli are ones which would have no special reinforcement value unless man had received training that made them reinforcing. This applies not only to neutral stimuli that have become reinforcers, but also to the special types of primary reinforcers that have special reinforcement value. That is, for example, nutritive substances (food) have reinforcement value for the human organism who is deprived of such substances. This is the case because of the biological structure of the organism. However, through a vast conditioning history, for the ordinary human many other stimuli will acquire the same reinforcement value through learning. The sight and smell of various foods, which are unrelated to their nutritional function, will come to have powerful reinforcement value on the basis of learning—so powerful that even under great deprivation these naturally neutral stimuli may have even greater reinforcement value than the biologically fulfilling food substance itself. This is also true of the other primary reinforcing stimuli. As one other example, sexual stimulation is a primary reinforcer. However, the stimuli of the various senses that will come to have sexual reinforcing power for different individuals are subject to wide variations on the basis of conditioning history. These variations can be seen as the basis of many of the problem sexual behaviors that we see in man.

We see these learned differences in motivational stimuli in the variations that occur in individuals within and between particular cultural groups or subcultures. Some stimuli are very reinforcing for some people, but not so reinforcing for others. The terms used in the description of these differences are varied. People are said to differ in values, needs, desires, emotions, interests, attitudes, ambitions, goals, and so on. All of these terms and others refer to the fact that people find different stimuli reinforcing. There are no biological or physiological differences in men that can be used to account for these differences.

The same thing is true when people in different cultures are compared. There are vast differences in the motivational systems of groups of people. A child raised in one society or group will acquire a motivational (reinforcement) system that is quite different from a child raised in another. Anthropology and sociology are replete with the descriptions of such differences. Often stimuli that have positive reinforcement value in one culture will have negative reinforcement value in another. This occurs with the so-called biological needs (primary reinforcers) as with learned reinforcers. Thus, in Egypt (at least among royalty) one's siblings of the opposite sex could as a stimulus object become a strong sex reinforcer. In our culture one's experience is ordinarily of a type that will make one's sister or brother a negative sex reinforcer. As another example, one man's food is another man's poison—foods that are positive reinforcers to the people in one culture will be highly aversive to the people in another.

One may ask why the nature of the individual's or group's reinforcement system is so important. The answer is that the nature of the individual's, or group's, reinforcement system will determine the behavior that is acquired by the individual, or the group. A more detailed analysis of how the reinforcement system determines behavior will be made further on. At this point it will suffice to indicate that two individuals in exactly the same situation, where a particular stimulus is presented contingent upon a particular behavior, will acquire that behavior in a very different manner if the stimulus for one is a positive reinforcer and for the other a neutral stimulus. Even more dramatic differences in what the individuals learn will be shown if for one the stimulus is a positive reinforcer and for the other a negative reinforcer.

The relationship of the motivational (reinforcer) system to the types of behavior *produced* is so lawful that in the social and behavioral sciences, which depend upon naturalistic observation, the two types of events are often treated as the same. That is, some motivational terms such as needs, desires, goals, interests, and the like, are inferred at times from observations of behavior and at other times from observations of the reinforcing stimuli themselves. Sometimes, of course, the motivational term is defined by both types of events.

At any rate, if we are interested in solving some of the problems of human behavior we must be concerned with the problems of the individual's as well as the group's reinforcer systems. Many of the problems of the development of undesirable behaviors, or the lack of development of desirable ones, stem from the nature of the reinforcer system. This is many times not recognized in its full importance, and even when it is recognized the lack of an adequate conception of human motivation leads to erroneous interpretations and actions.

Thus, poor motivation is frequently considered to be a personal or moral defect. There is a strong common conception that if the child or adult does not find learning itself reinforcing, does not find achievement, excelling, cleanliness, working hard, or whatever, reinforcing that the person is personally weak, and also responsible for his personal weakness. It may be suggested, however, that poor motivational systems have not been shown to be due to personal defect. Moreover, the learning analysis would suggest just the reverse. Poor motivational systems are formed in individuals who have had poor histories of conditioning experience. If we want people with motivational systems that are more desirable in our society, then we have to furnish them with the experience that will yield such a motivational system. There are many people who because of poverty, isolation, the effects of prejudice, ill health, and so on, do not provide experiences for their children that produce desirable motivational systems. The author, for example, has indicated how racial prejudice that has prevented Negroes from gaining employment in high paying and high status jobs, even when they were able by virtue of education and skill to handle such jobs, will have the effect of producing a deficient motivational system in the individual and the group. That is, learning and achievement only will be conditioned reinforcers if such attainments are paired with other reinforcers—that is, only if they lead to good jobs, status, housing, and so on (Staats and Staats, 1963, pp. 296–298). These are societal problems—but an amelioration of the problems awaits an understanding of the relevant conditions and principles of motivation.

The Several Functions of Motivational Stimuli

One last point will be made in this general discussion. That is, a complete account of human motivation must explicate how the motivational system affects behavior in different types of ways. The treatment of motivation that arises from experimental psychology has treated only one of these ways. That is, experimental psychology has dealt with reinforcement—the manner in which certain stimuli can effect the future strength of a response when they are presented contingent upon that response.

In the social and behavioral sciences and professions, however, the concept of motivation has included another effect upon behavior. In various ways it is said that motivational stimuli bring on, or direct, behavior as well as reward the behavior after it has occurred. It is because motivational stimuli, like goals, serve to "bring on" behavior that human behavior is frequently described as purposive.

The dilemma that has existed is how to account for this aspect of motivation with only the one concept of reinforcement, as has been the attempt within experimental psychology. Actually, however, the various aspects of motivation that are important to the social and behavioral sciences can be treated within the framework of basic learning principles —but the analysis requires more than one principle.

Thus, the analysis must indicate that motivational stimuli have both a reinforcing as well as a directing (or controlling) function. This occurs because motivational stimuli are discriminative stimuli (^DSs) as well as conditioned reinforcing stimuli ($^{C\cdot R}Ss$). As will be described, by virtue of a stimulus acquiring reinforcement value through the process of classical conditioning, the stimulus also acquires discriminative stimulus value which affects the individual's instrumental behaviors. Any stimulus that acquires reinforcement value will also through this acquire controlling value for certain behaviors. As the reinforcement value is increased or decreased, so will be the discriminative stimulus value for these behaviors. The analysis that yields these secondary principles is a little complicated. But the analysis is important and at this point a summary of these principles of human motivation is in order.

Classical Conditioning and the Reinforcement System

Although the stimuli that have motivational power are referred to under a variety of terms—attitudes, needs, drives, motivations, desires, interests, values, emotions, and so on—these stimuli may all be considered to acquire this power according to the principles of classical conditioning. This is no doubt one of the primary areas in which classical conditioning principles have their significance. Many times in these various areas of study we direct our attention *away* from the principles by which stimuli come to be emotional, attitudinal, interesting, needed, and so on (and also, as we shall see, away from the effects these stimuli have on our behavior), and focus instead upon the internal feelings these motivational stimuli engender. Although the internal responses elicited by such stimuli are important (and constitute one of the functions of motivational stimuli), as well as the individual's reports of those feelings, we must also focus upon the principles by which the stimuli come to have this effect and the relevance of the stimuli for our adjustment.

It has already been suggested that stimuli come to be reinforcing stimuli (goal stimuli, attitudinal stimuli, valued stimuli, emotional stimuli, and so on) through the process of classical conditioning. A stimulus acquires reinforcement value, becomes a conditioned reinforcing stimulus ($^{C\cdot R}S$), as it is paired with other stimuli that are unconditioned or conditioned reinforcing stimuli. A stimulus that is already a reinforcing stimulus (conditioned or unconditioned) can acquire more reinforcing value from being paired with other reinforcing stimuli. The reinforcement value of the stimulus would be expected to increase as a function of both the number of conditioning trials and the number of different reinforcing stimuli with which the stimulus is paired.

It should be pointed out that one of the primary processes by which stimuli acquire reinforcement value involves language. Language stimuli that are already conditioned reinforcing stimuli (that is words that elicit what we call evaluative meaning, or attitudes, or emotions) will impart this property to stimuli with which they are paired—as was shown in the experiments in the first part of the present book. Thus, objects, events, and other words may become conditioned reinforcing stimuli through being paired with words that are already reinforcing stimuli. Of course, as has been described, some words must first gain their reinforcement value through being paired with objects and events that are reinforcing.

"Rules" of Application of Reinforcers and the Motivational System

Thus, the principles of classical conditioning underly the acquisition of the individual's motivation (reinforcer) system. But, as has been indicated, a theory of human motivation must not only analyze how motivational stimuli are formed and changed, but also how motivational stimuli *function* in determining the type and strength of the individual's behavior. The principles by which reinforcing stimuli effect behavior have already been stated—they are the principles of instrumental conditioning which have been well specified in the laboratory.

However, there are some additional considerations for a more comprehensive account of human behavior. Thus, in the animal laboratory we take for granted the "rules" of the "society" in which the organism is investigated. That is, the experimenter provides the "rule" by which he will apply the reinforcing stimulus. For example, the "rule" may be that when the animal presses the bar in the apparatus he will get a reinforcer—or he will get the reinforcer for so many bar-press responses. The "rule" concerning *what behavior will be reinforced* is thus not the variable being studied; it is the principle of learning involved, the principle of instrumental conditioning, that has been of concern. The behavior selected is one that can be objectively observed, is simple, is natural to the organism being studied and thus likely to occur, and so on. These rules are only of peripheral interest to the investigator studying the basic principles of learning.

In the realm of human behavior, however, the rules for the application of reinforcers become very important variables. The rules will vary depending upon the culture, the subculture, and the family unit—to abstract several entities as examples. It should be emphasized that *regardless of the stimuli that are reinforcers for the group, there may be differences between groups in the rules by which the reinforcers are applied.*

Thus, there are several considerations in discussing human motivation whose implications do not arise from the study of reinforcement in the laboratory. Two considerations are the nature of the stimuli which as reinforcers are effective for the individual or the group, and the other concerns the "rules" by which the group will apply the reinforcers.

For example, in our society some of the stimuli that have a good deal of reinforcing value are social and personal attention, acclaim, and respect; money, fine clothes, expensive cars, and horses; and various tokens such as awards and honors. In our society, also, there are "rules" (not formal or explicit) for the application of these stimuli. That is, they are delivered contingent upon some kinds of behavior but not upon others. Thus, large amounts of these stimuli are delivered contingent upon exceptionally skilled baseball, football, acting, dancing, or comic behaviors, among others. Relatively small amounts are delivered contingent upon the behaviors of skilled manual work, teaching, unskilled manual work, nursing, and many others.

These characteristics of our reinforcing system and its rules of application, to continue with the example, have an effect upon the manner in which behavior in our society is shaped. Consider, thus, a boy who has two classes of skilled behaviors, one a set of intellectual skills consisting of knowledge and well-developed study and scholarly work habits, and the other consisting of some form of fine athletic prowess. Let us say that either behavior could be developed to "championship" caliber. Now, in a situation in which the larger amount of reinforcement is made contingent upon the one behavior, this behavior will be strengthened, and as must be the case, at the expense of the other to the extent that the behaviors are incompatible. In our society, of course, many of the strongest reinforcers are more apt to be more liberally applied to athletic rather than scholarly behavior.

When groups are considered, it would also be expected that the reinforcer system and its rules of application will determine the types of behaviors that are dominant. A society that has a differing set of reinforcers and rules will evidence different behavior over the group of people exposed to that set of conditions. A society, for example, whose reinforcers are made contingent upon scholarly research behaviors to a larger extent than another society will create stronger behaviors of that type, in a greater number of people, than will the other society. In general, many of the different cultural, national, and class behaviors that have been observed in sociology, anthropology, and other behavioral sciences, can be considered to involve this aspect of human motivation—the reinforcer system and its rules of application.

The reinforcer system, including the many social attitudes, must also be considered of great importance in understanding abnormal behavior. An individual who has a markedly different reinforcer system than those in his group is likely to develop abnormal behavior. Thus, the male for whom other males are strong sexual reinforcers is more likely to develop homosexual behaviors, for such behaviors will be strengthened by contact with those reinforcers. *The problem of behavioral treatment may thus involve changing the nature of the individual's reinforcer system.*

These, of course, are simplified examples and take no account of other variables that will also contribute to the eventual outcome. However, in principle, it can be suggested that (1) the nature of the individual's or group's reinforcer system and (2) the rules of response-contingent application of the system are crucial determinants of individual and group behavior. Thus, a description of those events, and an understanding of the principles by which reinforcers affect behavior would be expected to yield a great deal of knowledge of individual and group behavior. While the above examples, as well as those to follow, involve positive reinforcing stimuli, it should be remembered that the implications hold also for aversive stimuli in the individual's reinforcing system. These stimuli, of course, strengthen behavior that is followed by removal of the negative reinforcing stimulus.

Rewards and Goals: An Integrated Motivational Hypothesis

At this point, however, only the manner in which motivational stimuli can affect behavior when applied in a response contingent way has been described. Earlier it was stated that a theory of human motivation must account also for the goal-directed nature of behavior. Many motivational stimuli have their effect *before* they are applied, that is, they *elicit* striving behaviors in the individual—either striving to get the (positive) motivational stimulus, or striving to get away from or to get rid of the (negative) motivational stimulus. This is obviously not a result of the reinforcement value of the stimulus, *a reinforcing stimulus has its effect when it is applied following a behavior.* Reinforcing stimuli are not defined in terms of the behaviors they elicit or control—but in terms of the behaviors their application *subsequently* strengthens. For an adequate theory of human motivation, however, the controlling function of motivational (reinforcing) stimuli must also be accounted for.

To begin this account, when a stimulus object is a reinforcer for a child, it is very likely to become a discriminative stimulus (^DS) that will control various responses whose result is obtaining the object. Let us say that the stimulus object is a reinforcer for the child but does not yet control any instrumental behavior. (For example, the bottle will be a reinforcer for the child before it controls a "reaching response.") In this case, if the child makes responses that take him away from the object, he is not reinforced by obtaining the object. However, some responses, for example, crawling or creeping toward the object, will result in receiving the object, thus reinforcing that behavior in the presence of the visual stimulus of that stimulus object. This of course fits the principle for establishing a discriminative stimulus that controls a response. That is, when a response is reinforced in the presence of a stimulus, the stimulus will come to bring on or control the response.

As a result of such experience, a stimulus that was at first only a conditioned reinforcing stimulus ($^{c \cdot R}S$), let us say, would also have become a ^{D}S. The stimulus would have acquired an additional function; it would control a motor approach response.

The general point is that all reinforcing stimulus objects have the power to reinforce responses that result in obtaining those objects, and thereby are likely to become discriminative stimuli that control motor approach responses. Thus, in the child's experience a wide variety of stimulus objects that are reinforcers will come to control responses that result in obtaining those objects. These responses will also be quite varied—crawling toward, walking toward, running toward, climbing over and around obstacles, reaching and grabbing for, fighting and struggling for, asking, and crying for reinforcing stimuli. Later on, even more complex behaviors will come under the control of the reinforcing stimuli— working for, wheedling for, arguing for, flattering for, being ingratiating for, being respectful for, as well as competing for in various ways, acceptable and otherwise.

Thus, a wide variety of reinforcing stimuli will come to control a wide variety of these behaviors, which can be called "striving" behaviors. It should be noted also that although a stimulus will tend to control a wide number of "striving" responses, the specific response that occurs will also be a function of other controlling stimuli that are present in the situation. Although a reinforcing stimulus may control walking for and asking for behavior, the latter will be more likely to occur when there is another person present.

It would also be expected that the amount of reinforcement value of the stimulus as a variable would come to control variable strengths of these "striving" behaviors. For example, when the stimulus has much reinforcement value it will reinforce strongly the behavior that obtains it, and thus come to control strong behavior. When the reinforcer is weak it will only weakly control striving behavior.

To continue, however, after the child has had a number of conditioning experiences in which a stimulus that has reinforcing value—that is, a stimulus that elicits a reinforcing (emotional) response—comes to control instrumental "striving" behaviors, it would be expected that *all* stimuli that elicited such an emotional response would control such striving behaviors. Any *new* reinforcing stimulus would also control the striving behaviors because the reinforcing stimul· s would elicit the same type of emotional response that other reinforcing stimuli elicit.

The critical S–R mechanism here is mediated generalization as it has previously been described. In making the analysis, let us recall that reinforcing stimuli have a reinforcing property because they elicit a certain type of response—positive reinforcers elicit one type of emotional response and negative reinforcers elicit another type of emotional response. Unconditioned reinforcing stimuli ($^{UC \cdot R}S$) elicit such a response without training, conditioned reinforcing stimuli ($^{C \cdot R}S$) come to elicit a reinforcing (emotional) response through classical conditioning. It should also be indicated again that responses, including reinforcing (emotional) responses have stimulus characteristics, and thus "positive reinforcing responses" would be expected to have different stimulus characteristics than "negative reinforcing responses."

With this as the basic theory, the way generalization of stimulus control (^{D}S value) established with one reinforcing stimulus will occur to a new reinforcing stimulus can now be outlined. That is, although several reinforcing objects may have very different stimulus characteristics otherwise—that is different size, shape, color, texture, smell, and so on—they may still have a similar characteristic in that they all elicit a "positive reinforcing (emotional) response" with its special type of stimulus properties. This may be schematized as follows:

$$^{C \cdot R^+}S \longrightarrow r^+ \text{————} s.$$

That is, a positive conditioned reinforcing stimulus elicits a positive emotional response that has characteristic stimulus properties. The same would be true of negative reinforcing stimuli, except the emotional response and its stimuli would be different.

Now, whenever such a reinforcing stimulus is involved in the process whereby it becomes capable, as a ^{D}S, of controlling striving responses (making the stimulus a $^{C \cdot R \cdot D}S$), its reinforcing or emotional response (the r^+———— s) will also to the same extent come to control the striving responses. The emotional response and its attendant stimuli will also become a ^{D}S that will control striving responses. Thus, the process whereby the reinforcing stimulus becomes a ^{D}S will make the *emotional response elicited by the reinforcing stimulus* also capable of controlling the striving responses. When this has occurred, the striving responses will be brought on by any stimulus that elicits that emotional response. For example, a boy may see a new girl who elicits in him positive emotional responses. Although his "striving" behaviors have never before been reinforced in the presence of this new stimulus object, he will "strive" for her immediately. The positive emotional response (or more correctly the stimulus properties of that response) will act as the ^DS and control the striving behaviors that the boy has learned to other reinforcing objects—in this case "sex" reinforcing objects.

Even more complex cases of mediation may be considered to occur on the basis of language. That is, the girl may simply be described to the boy with words that elicit positive emotional responses, and the positive emotional responses will control "striving" behaviors. That is, the words *beautiful, shapely, affectionate, friendly, fun,* and so on, will elicit positive emotional responses in him which will control such striving responses as calling the girl for a date.

Thus, after the child has had a history of being reinforced for striving for (or away from) reinforcing stimulus objects by the receipt (or avoidance) of the objects, his striving behaviors will come under the control of the emotional responses elicited by such reinforcing stimuli. Although this analysis has been derived directly from the present basic theory, there is experimental evidence that substantiates the analysis. For example, Lott and Lott (1960) found that when child A has been reinforced in the presence of child B, child A will later select (strive for) child B as a companion. In the study, it should be remembered, the behavior of selecting child B, or otherwise "striving" toward child B, was not learned. The experimental conditions simply increased the reinforcement or positive emotional value of child B, and as would be expected from the preceding analysis this emotional conditioning increased the control the child exerted as a controlling (^DS) stimulus. This analysis indicates, incidentally, that the concepts of group attitudes and group cohesiveness can be accounted for within the integrated-functional learning theory, especially by the concept of the relationship of discriminative stimulus and reinforcing value.

The results thus support the suggestion that increasing reinforcement value increases discriminative stimulus value. This opens the study of social power to the experimental methods and principles of learning. Change in the reinforcing value of an individual would be expected to change his power as a stimulus in controlling other people's behavior in various ways. An increase in the reinforcing (emotional) value of an individual will increase verbal and motor approach or companionable responses, respectful responses, affectionate behavior, sexual behavior, following behavior, smiling, pleasant conversation, sympathetic responses, and other "striving" behaviors—depending upon which behavior is also elicited by the other stimuli in the situation. (That is, it should be realized that the emotional response elicited by a stimulus is not the only event that controls what behavior is actually elicited. The author, see Staats and Staats, 1963, has discussed the additional control of striving behavior under the heading *Socially Controlling Stimuli,* p. 384 ff.)

All of the examples employed in the above account have involved the way in which positive reinforcing (attitudinal or emotional) responses control a wide variety of striving behaviors. It should be recalled, however, that the principle would be expected to hold also with negative reinforcers. Negative reinforcers rather than controlling a class of approach striving responses will come to control the opposite, responses that carry one away from the emotion eliciting stimulus object, or that drive the stimulus object away. These responses, both verbal and motor, will include cruel behavior, derisive or insulting comments, obstructionistic behavior, antagonistic responses, oppositional voting, and the like. In addition, servile, cringing, afraid behavior, and so on, may also be acquired under the control of the negative reinforcing response. An increase in the negative reinforcing value of an individual for others would be expected to insure that he would control these types of overt responses more strongly.

The experiment of Lott and Lott shows that the reinforcement value and hence controlling value of a stimulus for striving responses is changed by pairing the stimulus object with reinforcing stimuli. The experiment involved the straightforward process of the classical conditioning of conditioned reinforcement value. It can be added, however, that there are also other means by which the reinforcement value of a social stimulus could be changed through conditioning procedures. For example, the same process could be accomplished via moving or still pictures. A person, or a group (let us say a racial or ethnic group) that was shown in a film to "possess" many reinforcers in a film would come to have greater reinforcement value and controlling value for the viewers of the film. This suggests that reinforcement and discriminative stimulus value can be changed through pictorial mass communication media.

The same process should be possible purely through the function of language. It has already been shown in previous experiments that a stimulus that is paired with words that elicit evaluative (emotional, reinforcing, or attitudinal) meaning responses will come also to elicit these evaluative meaning responses. A person paired with positive meaning words should, for example, become a stronger positive reinforcer and thus more strongly control striving behaviors. Again, it would not even be necessary that the individual himself be paired with the word reinforcers. The same end could be achieved by pairing his *name* with the word reinforcers, a suggestion that receives support in an experiment of DiVesta and Stover (1962). Or the individual's picture could be paired with reinforcing words and produce the conditioning effects. For these reasons the change of reinforcer and ^DS value and the ways these influence group cohesiveness and other social interactions could be made via mass communication media—film, radio, television, newspapers, magazines, and books—as well as through face-to-face communication.

The learning analysis also appears to have other implications. For example, concerning group prejudice, if a group's distinctive physical features, name, dress, language, or other behavior, elicits little positive reinforcing value, the members of the group will have little social controlling power. That is, members of the group will not be listened to, imitated, followed, chosen as a companion, and so on, or even hired, promoted, and so forth to the extent that members of groups will who have more reinforcement value. If the group, or its name, elicits negative reinforcing responses its members will be more likely to be insulted, avoided, opposed, arrested, rejected, fired, and so on, and in extreme cases, killed, lynched, and fought against. Verbal passages, films, or direct experience that presents members of the group, or its name, in contiguity with negative reinforcers would be expected to enhance the undesirable behaviors controlled by (made to) members of the group.

Matters of concern in the field of propaganda and advertising can also be incorporated into this learning analysis. One of the common techniques of the political editorial, for example, is to present the name of a political figure in contiguity with positive reinforcing words when the writer favors the politician or with negative reinforcing words when the writer is opposed. Each one of the pairings of name and reinforcing word may be considered to be a conditioning trial that changes the reinforcing value of the political figure's name and person. When that name or its owner appears on later occasions, the individual who has been so conditioned, taking the negative case as an example, will speak against the political figure and his principles, vote against him, fight against him, and so on.

Deprivation and Motivation

One additional general aspect of motivation should be indicated here. This concerns the effect of deprivation on the motivational system. It has been recognized from naturalistic observation, and verified in the laboratory, that when an organism is deprived of a reinforcing stimulus (such as food) the reinforcement value of the stimulus is increased. The implications of this principle for understanding human behavior can be elaborated upon on the basis of the preceding analysis. That is, since deprivation increases the reinforcement value of the stimulus the organism is deprived of, a hypothesis that could be derived from the theory would be that the "striving" behaviors controlled by the stimulus would as a consequence also become stronger. The food-deprived organism would struggle harder through obstacles toward a food stimulus. The sex deprived individual would strive harder under the stimulus control of a sexual object. The individual deprived of social status and social approval would struggle more toward social stimuli that had this type of reinforcement value for him.

It should be added, upon the basis of the principle that deprivation increases the reinforcement value of a stimulus, that *differential* deprivation for different reinforcers in the individual's reinforcement system should have important effects upon the *relative* values of the reinforcers in the system. Thus, deprivation of sex reinforcers would be expected to increase the reinforcing value of this class of stimuli, at the expense of other reinforcers in the individual's system. For the adolescent, for example, under sex deprivation, other reinforcers may be relatively weak and the behavior reinforced and controlled by those reinforcers—study, reading, family activities—may weaken. The child from the lower socio-economic class home who has the same reinforcer system as a child from a wealthier home may nevertheless be more strongly reinforced and controlled by the reinforcers of material wealth because he is deprived of those things.

These are general aspects of a theory of human motivation that should be considered in the context of discussing the importance of motivation in the cognitive learning of the child. By no means has the discussion exhausted the examination of human motivation in terms of learning principles, nor is this possible in the present book. The sections that are to follow, however, will treat several additional, more specific, topics concerning children's motivational learning that are of special relevance to cognitive learning and which may be considered as important aspects of the basic behavioral repertoire.

Imitation (or Modeling) and Self-Reinforcement

It is frequently said in the context of cognitive learning that "learning is (or should be) its own reward." This general expectation, for example, appears to be generally accepted in the field of education. The author's own work with cognitive learning that has employed extrinsic rewards has at times been questioned on the basis of the expectation; when extrinsic rewards are used to produce cognitive learning, some individuals will label the process bribery although it is a misuse of the term.

The conception that learning must be self-reinforcing can be criticized for impracticality, as well as on the grounds that there is no biological structure in man that makes learning reinforcing in and of itself. However, there are certain points in this area that should be explicated. For one thing, much learning does take place where the attentional and working behaviors are apparently maintained by the products of the activity—the learning itself, or related products. The nature of the processes involved should therefore be understood. It is this understanding which will suggest what the variables are that determine why some children do learn through this type of self-reinforcement and why other children do not.

Imitation, which involves a type of self-reinforcement, has been a topic of considerable interest to psychology for some time. In more recent times Miller and Dollard (1941) have suggested that imitational behavior occurs when the stimulus of one organism's behavior comes (in the present terminology) as a discriminative stimulus to control a similar (matching) response on the part of another organism. More recently, imitation (or social learning or modeling) has been discussed in a somewhat inconsistent way; as though it were a basic principle (Bandura, 1962), and at other times in terms of the straightforward application of the principles of reinforcement—without including the explanatory principles of discriminative stimulus control (Bandura, *et al.*, 1963) or other S–R mechanisms such as verbal behavior.

At any rate, comprehensive analyses of the learning principles and S–R mechanisms involved in imitation have not been made. It may be suggested, however, that application of an integrated learning theory can provide a more complete account. Again, a pluralistic approach is necessary to understand what is called imitation. The author (Staats, 1964; Staats and Staats, 1963) has suggested several principles and S–R mechanisms which can be used towards this end. The more complete account must consider imitation (1) as a sensory–motor skill in which certain social stimuli directly (or mediated by language or symbolic behaviors) come to control imitational behavior, (2) as involving the reinforcement value of matching or imitational stimuli, and (3) as involving the manner in which the reinforcement value of social stimuli controls imitational behavior. In general it may be said that imitation may be considered to consist of learned S–R mechanisms, rather than involving new, basic, principles.

IMITATION BEHAVIOR ACQUISITION   It will be remembered that a response reinforced only in the presence of a particular stimulus will come under the control of that stimulus. That is, the organism will "discriminate" the particular stimulus from other similar stimuli and will respond only in the presence of that one. For example, Ferster (1960) has shown that pigeons can be conditioned to peck a key which matches another key in color. Because the response is reinforced in the presence of the matching stimuli, the stimuli come (1) to control the response and (2) to have reinforcing value.

To continue, if a rat was reinforced when two white circular forms of equal size were presented and not when one of the forms deviated from the other in size, the animal would soon discriminate two matching circles from two nonmatching circles. In fact, if presented with a device constructed so that the variable circle would be adjusted by the rat himself, he could be trained to adjust the variable circle until it equaled the other one by presenting reinforcement only when the rat had adjusted the circles to match one another. Thus, the rat should be able to learn to match a stimulus produced by his own responses to a stimulus produced by someone else.

It appears that children normally learn to match their speech responses to the speech responses of others in an analogous manner. When the parent states, "Say water," a response that produces a sound like that made by the parent is reinforced immediately. If a different sound is emitted, however, the request is repeated and reinforcement delayed. In other words, in the presence of matched sounds, one of which he has produced (imitated) himself, the child receives reinforcement—but no reinforcement is presented in the absence of a matched pair of sounds. It has already been suggested that the child thus comes to discriminate matched (imitated) from unmatched sounds.

IMITATION BEHAVIOR UNITS   This process as described would mean that each new word the child became able to match would involve an elaborate conditioning process. This process of gradually learning the matching imitational response becomes short-circuited, however, as the child acquires a basic imitational repertoire. An analogy for this type of training may be seen in the suggested example of the rat producing matching white circles of equal size. It would be expected that not only could matched circles become reinforcing for the animal, but the specific responses involved in producing the matched stimuli could be learned, that is, come under the control of the stimuli themselves. For example, under the action of the reinforcement, the rat could come to make one type of response if the variable circle was *smaller* than the standard, and another type of response if the variable circle was *larger* than the standard. That is, in time, the disparity of the stimuli would immediately elicit the response appropriate to the direction of the disparity. No matter the size of the variable stimulus, the two stimuli would immediately control an appropriate imitational response—that is, a response which produced matching stimuli.

In a similar manner, the child learns many matching responses in units, in various areas of behavior, so that later the more tortuous original learning is no longer necessary every time the child "imitates" someone else's behavior. Thus, in an example analogous to the rat's stimulus matching (imitative) repertoire, a 6-year-old child can immediately imitate a high note, a low note, and so on, albeit imperfectly. In general, language is an area in which imitational learning becomes important at an early age. Although the infant begins by emitting sounds of a widely varied sort, by the age of six months or so he commences more and more to emit sounds composed of syllables appearing in the language of his parents.

Let us take imitative speech as an example and treat it in greater detail. As has already been described, the vocal sounds made by the parents become conditioned reinforcing stimuli because they are frequently paired with the positive reinforcers involved in caring for the child. When the parents' vocal stimuli have become reinforcing, the stage is set for the development of a verbal imitation repertoire in the child. That is, whenever the child makes a reinforcing sound (one like the parents' sounds) the vocal response that has produced it will be reinforced. In this way the child's speech is very gradually conditioned to be more and more like that of his parents until finally the child begins to say some recognizable words.

This process as described would mean that each new word the child became able to match would involve an elaborate conditioning process. This process could be short-circuited, however, if the child had already acquired the necessary response *units* under the control of the appropriate speech sound. It seems that imitative verbal behaviors are capable of division into units smaller than a whole word. That is, having learned to discriminate the various vowel and consonant sounds and to make responses that produce those sounds, the child is then prepared to learn new word responses simply on the basis of matching the sound produced by an adult. Thus, the child, when told "Say daughter," will be able to do so more quickly if he has already been trained to match his responses to the sounds /d/og and w/ater/ produced by adults.

After the various response units have been formed, and imitation, or matching, has itself become reinforcing (both aspects of the basic behavior repertoire), it will be easier for a child to be helped in developing precise speech by the coaching given to him by adults and other children who have more precise speech. When the child has emitted some speech response and has been instructed in a more precise pronunciation, it will be reinforcing for him to repeat the word. The closer the match, the more the response will be reinforced.

The same analysis can be applied to the manner in which other imitative behaviors are learned. That is, the parent, because he is paired so many times with positive reinforcers and the removal of negative reinforcers, becomes in general a positive conditioned reinforcer. His physical characteristics become positive reinforcers. Thus we see the child who dresses like one of the parents and so on.

In addition, of course, the behaviors of the parent (as stimuli for the child) become positive reinforcers. We see the child behaving in ways that are like the parent, imitating actions of the parent in various ways, and so on. This imitative repertoire is further developed because the child will customarily be additionally reinforced for matching his behavior as a stimulus to the stimulus of someone else's behavior. It is quite usual for a parent who sees his child emit a behavior that is a match for a behavior in the parent's own repertoire to find this reinforcing to himself and consequently heavily reinforce the child in return.

The use of the imitation repertoire in training a child can be profuse. The parents say "Can you do such and such like Charlie?" (an older or more skilled child) and will reinforce the child when he has made a reasonable match of the behavior. This is a powerful tool for training when used intentionally as well as when it occurs informally in some learning circumstance. That is, a child who has a strong imitative motivational repertoire will have strong reinforcement for learning in many situations. Let us say, for example, that such a child goes to school and there are children there who read although he does not. The stimulus produced by the other child will control attempts to match the behavior on the part of the nonreading child. Then, when the opportunity to learn to read is presented, the reading behavior of the other child will control studying the reading materials.

Additional Imitation Mechanisms

It should be indicated, of course, as the author has previously described (Staats and Staats, 1963) that speech behavior and other aspects of language may be involved in imitational behavior. That is, the observing child may make verbal responses to the social events he experiences, and the verbal response sequence that is thus established may later mediate imitational behavior. The observing youngster may say to himself WHEN HE STARTS THE CAR HE TURNS THE IGNITION KEY FIRST, and so on, in describing his father's complete act. Later, the youngster may again make these verbal responses, and the verbal stimuli produced could control his own imitation behaviors of starting the car.

The types of conditioned sensory responses described in Chapter 3 may also play a part in controlling imitational behavior. An example will be used that illustrates that imitation—behavior that is controlled by the stimuli of some other person's behavior—can be of a negative or avoidant kind as well as a positive kind. That is, *the child may be affected by someone else's behavior in such a way that he is less likely to perform the same action.* The principles are the same so that negative as well as positive imitation should be included in the same analysis.

At any rate, in the example a child has just observed another child take a bicycle away from a third child and push him down. Let us also say that an adult then punishes the offending child. Such a sequence of events will produce a sequence of conditioned sensory responses in the observing child. Thus, later when the sequence of conditioned sensory responses is elicited the child could describe what had happened—that is, the sensory responses (images) would control the appropriate verbal responses. Or, in certain other circumstances the conditioned sensory responses could be elicited and mediate avoidance of performing actions like that of the previously punished child. This would then be a case of negative imitation.

The major point to be made by these last examples, however, is that like any other complex human behavior imitation may involve complex language and symbolic S–R mechanisms. Although this may not be illustrated in each category of human behavior that is dealt with, because of the limitations of space, it must be considered to be implicit in any particular case. A more complete analysis in such cases only demands a specific extension of the more complete integrated learning theory.

Imitational (Matching) Stimuli in Self-Reinforcement

Although the focus in the just preceding sections has been on the instrumental behaviors of imitation and the manner in which they are acquired and come under stimulus control, running through the discussion has been the concept that the imitational or matching stimuli produced by the behavior is reinforcing. The fact that the stimuli of matching one's behavior to the behavior of someone else is reinforcing constitutes a very important aspect of the human motivational system and should be given individual attention.

It has been said repeatedly herein that other people as stimulus objects become positive conditioned reinforcers. This occurs because people are paired with many other positive reinforcers. The principle involved is classical conditioning, as is involved in the establishment of any conditioned reinforcer.

Furthermore, through the same experiences and the same principle, the behaviors of other people become conditioned reinforcers. The behaviors of another person constitute stimuli—visual, auditory, tactile, and so on—and pairing them with reinforcers will make these stimuli conditioned reinforcers. This holds also for the accoutrements associated with people, for example, their clothes, jewelry, cars, and so on.

Although this is quite simple to describe, the various social stimuli of this type constitute a compendium of reinforcing stimuli for most people that is an extremely important aspect of their reinforcing system. Many behaviors, and many fine skills, as has been briefly summarized, are acquired on the basis of reinforcement by imitational stimuli. Children learn behaviors from other children and from adults—and this learning through imitation continues throughout life. Conversely, the child who has suffered some deficit or inappropriacy in his imitational reinforcing system will to that extent display deficits in behavior or inappropriate behaviors that will be considered abnormal.

Furthermore, imitational reinforcing stimuli constitute a form of "self-reinforcement." That is, there appears to be no extrinsic reinforcement involved. The child imitates another child or adult, the behavior being acquired or maintained solely by the fact that his behavior is like that of the other person. The individual may dress like, speak like, obtain possessions like, go to the same places, engage in activities and recreations like some other individual or group—his behavior reinforced by the fact that he is producing stimuli that match those of the other individual or group.

Thus, the source of motivation appears to be within the person himself. However, the analysis of the motivational stimuli reveals the learning principles involved in their creation. This is thus another case where human behavior appears to be self-initiated, because there is no clear external reward that is provided the behavior. Furthermore, people vary in the extent and types of social stimuli that are reinforcing for them and that they will imitate. This again gives the appearance that individuals "select" the things they do. In general, in fact, it may be suggested that human behavior in this case appears to be spontaneous, or self-initiated, because different individuals have learned different reinforcement systems and thus strive for different things.

THE REINFORCER-DISCRIMINATIVE STIMULUS RELATIONSHIP IN THE CONTROL OF IMITATION   It has been suggested already that one of the primary aspects of motivational stimuli is that they *control* behavior, in addition to their function as reinforcers. Perhaps it is the effect upon the control of behavior that makes the reinforcement value of stimuli so important. This has not been fully realized in the field of learning, where the functions of reinforcing stimuli and discriminative (controlling) stimuli are usually separated. For this reason the analysis of imitation (modeling or social learning) and the interpretation of some experiments on imitation have been inadequate. It will be productive to indicate some of the pertinent points involved here.

The theory underlying the present discussion has previously been presented. That is, it was suggested that emotional (or reinforcing) responses (or rather their stimuli) come to be discriminative stimuli which control a large number of striving behaviors. An important type of striving behaviors consists of what we term imitational or modeling behaviors, as well as the closely related class of behaviors that might be called "following." Thus, it may be hypothesized that when we increase the reinforcement value of (emotional response to) a social stimulus we increase its controlling value as a discriminative stimulus for a large number of responses, including those of imitation or following.

In addition to the discussions already made showing why this is the case, a few examples that are specific to imitation may be described. The account may be simply stated, when we imitate someone who has high reinforcement value (that is, elicits positive emotional responses) our imitational behavior is reinforced in the presence of that reinforcement value. As a consequence high reinforcement value (positive emotional responses) comes to control imitational behavior.

For example, it would not be hard to see how, in primitive societies, the individual who was keen of scent and vision and swift of limb, who had acquired the skills necessary in hunting, might become a "leader." If this individual continually returned from the hunt with game, whereas others failed, it might be expected that "imitation" of his behavior would soon be acquired. By traveling with this person and using the same hunting techniques, the others in the group would also gain the crucial reinforcers and the pattern of following this man would be correspondingly reinforced. The behavior of the leader would thus become a discriminative stimulus for further following. Moreover, since he would be associated with positive reinforcing stimuli he would come to elicit positive emotional responses. The third result would be that the stimuli of those positive emotional responses would also come to control imitative behavior. This last product would be the mechanism by which the imitation behavior would generalize to other behaviors of the leader. Moreover, *other* people who elicited positive emotional responses in the individuals so conditioned would also to that extent control their imitational behavior.

We can see that in everyday life the same process operates. That is, when an adult or an older child makes a response of a certain type which is more skilled than that of the younger child, the younger child receives more reinforcement when he matches the behavior of the more skilled person. This is one of the essential types of reinforcement for imitational behavior, and it is not restricted to imitation in children, but is also important for understanding social behavior in general.

The same type of development of leader-follower interaction would occur in more "abstract" realms of behaviors—such as reasoning and thinking—where imitational behavior would be more strongly reinforced with high-valued people. That is, there are "status" or high valued people whose verbal behaviors when imitated result in more reinforcement than when the statements of low-valued people are imitated. As a result, for example, we see that the child soon comes to repeat the statements of more valued people to a greater extent. This continues throughout life; that is we are more likely to mold our statements after some high-valued person.

In general, through this and other types of experience, the *reinforcing value* of social stimuli will come to control behavior of the child—including imitative behavior. The stronger the positive reinforcing value of a stimulus, moreover, the stronger will it have discriminative stimulus value and control behavior.

This analysis indicates that the reinforcement value of other people is an important variable which determines the extent to which the child will imitate people, and thus in many situations the extent and content of what he will learn. In the schoolroom, as another illustration, if the teacher has much reinforcement value for a child her behavior will control imitational behavior in the child. The same is true, however, for other children in the class. If for a particular child other able, hardworking, children are positive reinforcers, then their behavior will be more highly imitated by the child. Anything that lessens the reinforcement value of these able children will lessen the controlling effect they have in producing like behaviors in the child. On the other hand, if a group of rebellious, negligent, students have a good deal of reinforcement value for the child he will imitate their behavior.

Once the mechanism is formed, however—that is, the mechanism whereby the reinforcement value of other people controls imitational behavior—the individual's imitational behavior may be manipulated by manipulating the reinforcement value of the social stimulus. It is then not necessary that the imitator have any direct experience with the social stimulus. The analysis thus indicates why celebrities, leaders, and so on are imitated. It is not necessary that a person be reinforced for imitating or following a leader. The only thing necessary is that the reinforcement value of the leader be made positive. This may be done on the basis of words, through communication procedures, through pictures and so on, as has been described.

For example, let us say that negative meaning (negative reinforcing) words are paired with able, hard-working, students, or words representing them. As a consequence these students will lose some of their positive reinforcing value—perhaps become negative reinforcing stimuli. This will affect the extent to which the child who is so conditioned will emulate those students. A parent who says to his child "Those college kids are sissies and loafers who only know how to study" will be lessening for his child the reinforcement value of "college type" youngsters and their behavior. And this will lessen the extent to which his own child will match his behavior to theirs in school. By the same token the parent who gives relatively high verbal praise to baseball players, fighters, and so on, will be ensuring that these types of individuals are reinforcing for his child and consequently that his child will emulate the behaviors of these types of individuals.

Thus, different children, exposed to different conditioning experiences, will acquire different reinforcement systems—that is different types of people, among other things, will become reinforcing to them. The self-reinforcement the children get from imitating these people will thus differ, as will the extent to which these people will *control* imitative behavior. Thus, the way that people come to be reinforcing for the child is very important—in fact, it deserves separate treatment in the study of human behavior.

It should be indicated that contemporary learning conceptions of imitation or modeling suffer because the theory has not made a detailed analysis of the principles involved. One important inadequacy has been in not recognizing the relationship between the reinforcing value of a stimulus and its discriminative stimulus value for controlling imitative behavior. Thus, for example Bandura, *et al.*, (1963) while conducting a very significant experiment on imitation, interpreted their results in terms of the simple principle of reinforcement. The experiment in general varied the extent to which two adults were paired with reinforcers and noted the effect of this pairing upon the extent to which the adults' behaviors were imitated. The children imitated the adult who "possessed" the reinforcers more than they imitated the adult without reinforcers. Bandura, *et al.*, suggest a secondary reinforcement theory of imitation (or identification). This interpretation indicates that the adult associated with the reinforcers becomes more reinforcing. Thus, the children's behavior of imitating this adult's behavior should be more reinforcing. The analysis is taken from Mowrer's learning approach. The analysis is incorrect, however, for a reinforcing stimulus only has its effect *after it is applied.* Just because a child's imitational behavior *would* be reinforcing if it occurred cannot make the behavior occur. It would be teleological to think that it would. The principle of reinforcement is that a reinforcing stimulus presented *following* a response will strengthen *future* occurrences of that response. Reinforcement does not have an effect on responses that have not yet occurred. This is a weakness in the general learning theory involved (Mowrer, 1960a) and in this specific interpretation of the experimental results.

The present set of principles, however, indicates how varying the reinforcement value of a stimulus will also affect the *controlling* or eliciting effect of the stimulus. Thus, in the experiment of Bandura, *et al.,* the reinforcement value of the one adult was increased by pairing him with other reinforcers. The reason this adult will then better control imitation in the children, however, is because *the increase in the adult's reinforcement value increases his potency as a discriminative stimulus which will bring on the imitation.* To understand the results it is necessary to understand the relationship between reinforcement value and discriminative stimulus (controlling) value that emerges as a function of our conditioning histories. Again, an integrated-learning theory showing the relationships of classical and instrumental principles is necessary.

A question may arise in the context of the present general analysis of imitation which demands a corollary statement. The question is, if positive emotional (reinforcing) responses control imitative responses, why does the young boy not imitate his mother in the same manner that he does his father? The answer is that he does, until he has been trained not to. Additional experience is necessary to produce discrimination learning. That is, a young boy of 3 years of age, for example, will make imitational responses under the control of his mother's actions, dress, and so on. The customary aversive stimulation that is brought to bear on such imitational behavior, however, as well as the relative lack of positive reinforcement, weakens the imitation. Thus, the mother, and other female social stimuli as well, come to be discriminative stimuli that control not-imitating, at least for certain behaviors. This control overrides the control of the positive emotional responses elicited by some female social stimuli. Thus, this is another case in which a detailed S–R analysis must be made if one is to see the lawful functioning of the various learning principles and S–R mechanisms.

Achievement, Standards, and Rivalry as Self-Reinforcers

In the preceding section one type of self-reinforcement was discussed, the matching stimuli produced by imitative behaviors. It is because the matching stimuli, one of which is produced by the child's own behavior, "carry" the reinforcement value that the term self-reinforcement is used. In addition to imitation, however, there are other types of self-reinforcement for the child who has had the necessary past conditioning history— self-reinforcement that is produced by the same process of making a response whose stimulus properties match another stimulus. In each of the cases to be described, as with the preceding one, the training that produces a motivational system that makes matching stimuli reinforcing can be considered to result in a basic behavioral repertoire which is fundamental to much of human learning.

Perhaps the motivation (reinforcement) that has been discussed the most frequently in the context of human learning is that of achievement. However, the fact that achievement is more reinforcing for some individuals than others is customarily discussed in terms of personal qualities, or needs, that the individual has. The author has analyzed this aspect of the reinforcement system in learning terms in the following manner.

> . . . Murray's (1938) definition of achievement may be paraphrased in the following manner: "To accomplish something difficult. To master, manipulate, or organize physical objects, human beings, or ideas. To do this as rapidly and as independently as possible. To overcome obstacles and attain a high standard. To excel one-self. To rival and surpass others. To increase self-regard by the successful exercise of talent" (p. 164). This definition includes descriptions of behavior, but certain reinforcing stimuli are also implicitly described in the definition.
>
> Consider the stimuli associated with attaining a high standard. Certainly in a naive organism, overcoming obstacles and doing something difficult is not itself originally reinforcing. Effortful behavior produces stimulation that is aversive (Azrin, 1961; Hull, 1943). Without some change in these aversive features, it is to be expected that an organism would escape from hard work, that is, the cessation of work would act as negative reinforcement (Azrin, 1961). The same might be true of working as rapidly as possible. Since rapid responding is not itself reinforcing, unless such behavior has been shaped in the individual's learning history, the behavior would not be expected to occur (Staats and Staats, 1963, pp. 293–294).

The same is true of accomplishment, attaining high standards, and achievement. Objectively these various terms refer to behavior that produces stimuli or stimulus objects that the language community responds to as achievements, accomplishments, and what have you. Ordinarily, these achievement products are positively reinforcing to the group.

These achievement stimuli, however, have no unlearned reinforcing properties. Their reinforcement value for the individual, if any, is customarily entirely learned. Thus, for example, the act of a child in reading letters may be very reinforcing to the parents, to employers, to the teacher who obtains her livelihood (reinforcers) from teaching children to read, and so on, but it would not be expected to have reinforcement value in and of itself for the child. Acquisition of new skills of many types by the child is ordinarily reinforcing to the middle-class parent. Thus, the middle-class parent will consequently reward the child heavily for behavior that produces achievement stimuli of various kinds. Many, many times, when the child has learned to walk, to go to the toilet, to dress himself, to learn new words, to tell stories, to count, and so on, he will have been given many social reinforcers and perhaps material reinforcers of various kinds. Under such a circumstance it would be expected from the learning analysis that for such children the products (stimuli) of acquired skills would themselves become very reinforcing. In common sense terms, for children with such fortunate backgrounds, learning (or its products) would itself become reinforcing. And there are many observations that have been made in social psychology, sociology, anthropology, and education (see, for example, Goldman, 1937; Rosen, 1956; Carter, 1964; Maccoby and Gibbs, 1954) that support this analysis and the suggestion that practices that produce such reinforcers for children vary from family to family and from social class to social class.

What it means to say that learning has become "its own reward" should be examined further for a moment in terms of S–R principles. It has been suggested that one mechanism that appears to be involved is that of matching stimuli. That is, to a large extent, the "proof" of having learned something is when the product of the behavior (the stimulus produced by the behavior) matches the standard stimulus provided by an authority source. In these terms, much of the reinforcing value of learning may be seen as analogous to imitational reinforcement.

In addition, however, "improvement" in performance may also be expected to become reinforcing in the child who has had the appropriate experience. Thus, a child may be reinforced for improvement, even before his behavior *matches* a standard very well. Thus, improvement, which is actually the behavioral production of a stimulus that is closer to the standard stimulus than could be formerly produced, can come to have reinforcement value.

Not all reinforcement for learning (behavioral acquisition) appears to be based upon matching a standard, however, and the present discussion may be considered to be a brief exploration of "achievement motivation." To include an example that does not involve reinforcement in the presence of matching stimuli, let us say that a child's parent has told the child that the world is round and has given the child a rather complete explanation of the earth as a planet. Let us also say that later on, when the child is in a group of young children, the question arises concerning where the "end of the earth" really is. At this time the informed child may give his account and if it is more comprehensive, more reasonable, and more impressive in the terms in which it is stated, the account may "win" out óver the accounts of the others and the child may receive social reinforcement. Having such verbal skills which we call "knowledge" would in this case be expected to become reinforcing, because the emission of the verbal behavior is reinforced. Such sources of reinforcement may also serve to maintain the learning behaviors involved in acquiring the verbal skills, in fact, it is suggested that this is a common source of reinforcement for successful students.

One further point may be made in this context. It is frequently said that children differ greatly in the "standards of performance" which they hold. This is commonly thought to result from a "personal" selection by the child, as the following quotation indicates. "Children differ dramatically in the standards of performance which they set for themselves. Some children decide that performance just a bit above average for their class is adequate to meet their standards; others demand of themselves the top position in the class. The child's commitment to work and persevere will be a function of the standard that satisfies him." (J. Kagan, 1965, p. 558–559) The observation that children find different standards to be reinforcing certainly appears to be the case. However, the present analysis would suggest that the individual differences that we see in children's standards, and the consequent work and study habits created by this source of reinforcement, are produced through their individual experiences according to the principles of conditioning. The child does not set standards for himself spontaneously; although he may carry them "within," they are learned and it is important for a human learning theory to indicate the mechanisms involved. Thus, as one example, we may observe a boy alone practicing a certain "move" in football, until he is "satisfied," that is, until he has attained some internal standard. The standard stimulus within, as one example, may be a conditioned sensory response (image) which the boy has acquired from observing a more skilled player. The novice actor may practice a walk or gesture in the mirror until he attains the standard of an internal image. The painter or musician acquires similar sensory standards through a long history of conditioning and continues working on a piece until the standards are matched and reinforcement produced. In other cases the internal standards are of a verbal nature. The individual continues responding until his own behavior elicits in him verbal responses that match some standard the individual holds. Thus, in a simple example, the child might continue to practice reciting a poem, after missing one word, because he says to himself "Last time I recited and missed a word I got a 'B' instead of an 'A.'" When at last he recites perfectly he says to himself "Now I will get an 'A'" and is reinforced. The subject of verbal reinforcers, which is relevant to the present discussion of internal standards, will be treated in the next section. It should be indicated here, however, that *internal standards that have reinforcing value will to that extent also have discriminative stimulus value and will control behaviors that strive to attain the standard.*

Another important source of reinforcement for child learning is to be found in "rivalling and surpassing others," in fact, the *act* of competing may itself be reinforcing. These stimulus consequences by themselves, however, prior to learning, would not be expected to be reinforcing. Such events become reinforcing because they have in the past been paired with other positive reinforcers. Children have to be trained to find "winning" reinforcing, to find competition reinforcing, and so on. The author remembers vividly his undergraduate experiences as a counselor in day camp attempting to teach 4- and 5-year-old children group games. The competitive events involved that are reinforcers for adults were quite neutral to these children. Winning a race, for example, can be a very neutral stimulus for a young child, and the verbal stimuli "Run as fast as you can and try to win," may have no controlling value whatsoever. It is very frustrating to attempt to teach something to such children when your selection of reinforcers has no reinforcing value. The same children after appropriate conditioning experiences can become very competitive, with well developed competitional reinforcement systems, well under control of instructions "to try and win."

Again, there is much evidence from the other social and behavioral sciences that familial, social, and cultural groups provide different training conditions for their children of the sort that produce different types and strengths of this type of reinforcer. This, of course, means that some children will have more fully developed reinforcement systems (or repertoires) in this respect.

It is traditionally assumed that these three types of reinforcement are present for all pupils, or should be, apparently on the basis of genetic factors; witness again the old saw, "Learning is (or should be) its own reward." However, in view of the preceding analysis, these reinforcers cannot be counted upon for every child, or in certain cricumstances for even a large percentage of children. Many children do not have a past history which has made learning itself reinforcing, which has established many achievement stimuli as reinforcing, or made the stimuli of competition and winning reinforcing. When this is the case, it is ineffective simply to invoke the plea that learning *should* be reinforcing.

One further point should be made herein. Achievement motivation has been discussed solely in terms of the principle of reinforcement. It has been stated that some children because of their conditioning histories come to find achievement stimuli reinforcing. Thus, when they do something that produces such an achievement stimulus the behavior is strengthened or maintained in good strength. However, the principle by which achievement stimuli direct behavior—that is, can bring on (control) working behaviors before reinforcement has occurred—has not been described.

The principle is the same as has been outlined in preceding discussions. That is, the reinforcement value and discriminative stimulus value are related. As the reinforcement value is increased the discriminative stimulus value is increased. It is suggested that this is true also in the context of the present discussion. When achievement stimuli become reinforcers they also come to *control* the behavior of the child involved. That is, when achievement stimuli reinforce the child's behavior, it may also be observed that they will bring on his working behaviors. When achievement stimuli are reinforcers the child when seeing someone else's achievement will work harder himself. Seeing someone else ahead of him in some competition, the child will try even harder. When a high standard is presented to him it will control diligent working behaviors. This refers to the directing aspect of the stimuli, which must be considered in terms of the principle of instrumental discrimination learning.

The same principle applies to the other reinforcers yet to be discussed. That is, another, major, aspect of the human motivational system involves the language repertoire. This aspect of the system actually involves both self-reinforcement as well as externally given reinforcement—so the topic could be discussed under both headings. That is, many words may be considered to be stimuli (produced by vocal responses) that have reinforcing value. Words which the individual says himself can have this reinforcing value. Or, the same word given by someone else can have the reinforcing value. Although the next section can by no means describe the importance of this source of human motivation, several points can be made. It should also be stated here that each of the aspects of motivation already discussed can be formed on the basis of language experience.

Verbal Stimuli as Reinforcers

The fact that words come to be reinforcers through the process of classical conditioning has already been described. Words that are paired with reinforcing stimuli (either $^{UC \cdot R}S$ or $^{C \cdot R}S$, including verbal reinforcers) come to be reinforcing themselves, as they come to elicit the same responses the reinforcing stimuli elicit.

Furthermore, when a word has come to be a reinforcing stimulus itself (a $^{C \cdot R}S$) it can make other words, other objects, events, and other actions reinforcers too. That is, these other occurrences have stimulus properties. And, if a reinforcing stimulus (a word or material reinforcer) is paired with these objects, events, or actions then these new stimuli will come to be reinforcing stimuli for the individual who has been so conditioned. Once words have come to be reinforcing stimuli for the individual he is prepared to learn many new aspects of his reinforcing system. For example, let us say that the child has had the word *good* paired many times with positive reinforcers of various types and the word has come to be a strong positive reinforcer. After this has occurred, when the parent says to the child "Learning is good, working and studying are good, school is good, the teacher is good," and so on, these social objects, events, and actions will also become positive reinforcers. (Actually, the words *learning, working, studying, school,* and *teacher* would become positive reinforcers. But the effect would transfer to the actual stimuli through the principle of mediated generalization.)

In the same manner, other words become negative reinforcers and these words can make other stimuli negative reinforcers through being paired with them. Let us say that the word *bad* has come to be a negative reinforcer and that the word *bad* has been paired with the word *fail* a number of times so the latter word is also a negative reinforcer. After this conditioning has taken place when the teacher says to the student, "If you do not study you will fail," the words *If you do not study* will become a negative reinforcer, and so will the actions of not studying. The responses elicited by negative reinforcing stimuli ("anxiety" or negative emotional responses) will be elicited by "not studying" behavior. Escape from this negative reinforcement may then be obtained by studying and in this manner studying behavior may be maintained.

Many of the reinforcers that maintain learning behavior, following the educational example, are verbal reinforcers delivered by the teacher, the parent, or the student himself, as well as by many other avenues of communication. That is, when the child is told that he must have a college degree to get a "good" job and career, that only "good" positions furnish enough money and leisure to have a "good" life, that if he does not study well and make "good" grades he will not get into school, and so on, verbal reinforcers are being established that will serve to maintain much appropriate behavior.

These types of statements, as has been suggested, can come from many sources and occur in many different forms. Of course, this varies according to the life circumstances of the individual. For example, it is more likely that statements relating the positive verbal reinforcers about the "good life" with various aspects of education will be made to the middle-class white American citizen. These statements are simple descriptions of what has occurred to middle-class white people. On the other hand, even if the negro individual obtains a college degree, especially in a southern university, there is less likelihood of obtaining the "good things of life." As a consequence, the statements relating positive reinforcers with education are not as likely to occur since they would not describe actual conditions and thus it is not as likely that a negro youth will as strongly be conditioned to educational stimuli as positive reinforcers.

The general point that is involved here is that there are large numbers of words in our language that have either positive or negative affective meaning that are intimately involved in our experience in producing other positive or negative reinforcing stimuli, verbal and otherwise. The principles involved are those of classical conditioning. The significance of this process for the formation of the individual's motivational system cannot be underestimated. The examples above concerned the formation of the child's "values" for education. It may be suggested in general that the individual's values are largely formed on the basis of verbal conditioning of this type and that what we mean by values concerns the reinforcement value of various verbal and nonverbal stimuli.

It should also be indicated here, albeit only briefly, that the various aspects of the individual's motivational system are established by verbal conditioning as well as direct experience. For example, although not directly relevant to the present considerations of cognitive development, the individual's "repertoire" of sex reinforcers is heavily influenced by language conditioning. Long before a child has had any direct sex experience with another person, he will ordinarily experience a great deal of language conditioning that will affect his sex reinforcing system. As a consequence of the verbal conditioning other individuals with certain characteristics will gain stronger sex reinforcement value for him than individuals with other characteristics.

One further point should be considered in the context of the verbal reinforcement system and its effects. As with the other reinforcing stimuli that have been discussed, it may be suggested that words that have affective meaning (reinforcement value) also have as a consequence discriminative stimulus value and control a large class of striving behaviors. This has been mentioned in some of the previous examples, but the general implications should be indicated. Positive emotional words may be expected to control "approach" striving behaviors, and negative affective words may be expected to control "avoidance" striving behaviors. As one example, when the child is told, "Don't cross the street because it is dangerous," the word *dangerous* as a stimulus that elicits a negative emotional response (sometimes called anxiety) will control avoidance behavior.

In general, it may be suggested that any stimulus event that comes to elicit a word response in the individual that has emotional meaning, will be responded to by the individual in a manner that is influenced by that emotional meaning. In common sense terms, when any stimulus event (social, physical, or what have you) is "labeled" with a word that has reinforcing value, the way people respond to the stimulus event will be influenced by the reinforcing value of its label.

It should also be indicated that reinforcing words would be expected to control instrumental behaviors whether the words have been said by someone else, or whether they have been said by the individual himself. This has a good deal of significance for understanding certain aspects of human reasoning, including social reasoning. For example, sequences of verbal behavior are many times elicited that are relevant to future events. The student is asked to accompany a friend to a show and this and other stimulus circumstances elicit a long sequence of verbal responses. He says, let us say, "It is a very funny picture; however, I have not studied for my exam tomorrow and if I do not I will fail the course." The word stimuli *very funny* are positive conditioned reinforcers, for the individual with the appropriate conditioning history, and would tend to control the "approach" striving behaviors of attending the movie. The word stimuli *fail the course,* on the other hand, will control conditioned negative emotional responses in the individual with the appropriate conditioning history, and these emotional responses will in turn control behaviors that avoid the proposed activity. What the individual does in this problem situation, as one of many examples, will be influenced by his sequence of verbal behaviors *and* the reinforcement (and thus discriminative) value of the words.

This and other discussions in the present book cannot be considered to have completed the detailed analysis that should be given to the development and functions of verbal reinforcing stimuli. However, the main principles have been outlined as well as the main S–R mechanisms involved. To summarize, it has been suggested that word reinforcers have three distinct and important functions. (1) In an earlier chapter it was stated that words with emotional meaning can function as reinforcers and will strengthen or maintain (in the case of positive words) any instrumental behavior upon which they are contingent. Since much human behavior is shaped and maintained by verbal reinforcers, a very basic repertoire for the individual consists of a repertoire of such words and the affective responses they elicit.

(2) In addition, it has been shown how words that elicit affective meaning responses may serve according to the principles of classical conditioning to impart reinforcement value to other stimuli, both verbal and nonverbal stimuli of all kinds including various social stimuli. Thus, verbal reinforcers have great importance in the manner in which other aspects of the individual's reinforcement system develop.

(3) Furthermore, word stimuli that have reinforcement value because they elicit emotional responses have an important function in directly controlling approach and avoidance behaviors. Vast amounts of such behaviors are controlled by verbal stimuli presented by other people, *or in the individual's own reasoning*. Various areas of human motivation variously labeled *attitudes, interests, needs, norms, values, emotions,* and so on involve these language aspects of the human motivation system.

Social Approval

The fact that the responses of other people to our behavior affect our behavior has been stated many times in many different ways. That is, the individual has been said to strive for other people's support and social approval, to desire praise, affection, attention and the like. Various theories of personality have posited as a crucial concept that man has a "need" for these social stimuli.

In more objective terms we can begin to observe what the behavior of one individual constitutes as a stimulus for another individual. Thus, one individual as a behaving object presents visual, auditory, tactile, and thermal, stimulation, among others, for other individuals with whom he is in contact. These stimuli can have the same properties that other environmental stimuli have. If the stimuli presented by one individual to another are conditioned or unconditioned stimuli, the other may be classically conditioned to new responses. If the stimuli of one's behavior and physical being are unconditioned or conditioned reinforcers the other person will be affected according to instrumental conditioning principles. It is with the latter that the present section will be concerned.

Because of our past history in which these stimuli have been paired with positive reinforcers, smiles, soft spoken words, and caresses—as examples of visual, auditory, and tactile stimuli from another—ordinarily become strong positive reinforcers. Certain types of these stimuli are called social approval. Considered in terms of reinforcing stimuli, however, the function of such stimuli can immediately be suggested. Rather than saying that people have a "need" for social approval, it may be said that "social approval stimuli" that occur following a particular response will increase the strength of that response. That is, that type of response will be instrumentally conditioned and will occur more frequently in the future in that same situation.

Let us consider the manner in which simple attention from another person usually becomes a conditioned reinforcer for children. Actually, on first presentation when the child is a new-born infant, the sight or sound of other humans has no reinforcing value, but these stimuli later develop into very strong reinforcers. It may be commonly observed, for example, that many young children develop very strong "attention-getting" behavior and may be observed on occasion to demand of their parents, LOOK AT ME. Because this type of behavior has been so widely observed, it was suggested by early investigators that everyone has an "inborn need" for attention. When it is understood, however, that the stimuli of someone looking at us or listening to us become reinforcing through the operation of the principle of conditioned reinforcement, the inference of an "inborn need" becomes an unnecessary concept. It may be said that being looked at and listened to is reinforcing because in our past histories these stimuli have been presented along with primary reinforcers. It is when the mother is "paying attention" to the child that he is fed, uncomfortable pins are removed, warmth is provided, and so on. Each situation pairs the "attention" with primary reinforcement. Thus, the "attention" of other people should become a very strong secondary or conditioned reinforcer. It may then be observed that behavior which is followed by the attention of others (which "gets attention") is strengthened. It is interesting to note in this connection that the phrase "to attend to" may mean to take care of someone as well as to "pay attention" to him.

Imagine, however, a child for whom attention was always accompanied by the presentation of aversive stimuli, in other words, where punishment was delivered each time other people attended to him. Later in life this child's behavior would not be strengthened by attention. He would not be likely to have a strong response of saying, LOOK AT ME. Rather, this child's behavior would be reinforced by the removal of attention because attention for him would be a conditioned negative reinforcer. Attention would also function as an aversive stimulus in weakening some action of the child when attention was given. Of course, this history of experience is not likely to occur, at least not in quite such a one-sided manner. Unless the infant is provided with a certain number of primary positive reinforcers by parents he will not survive, since he cannot obtain these for himself. The more usual case is that the presence of others is paired with both positive and negative reinforcers, although more often with the former. Because of the duality of this experience, attention of others becomes both positively and negatively reinforcing. That is, in the individual's past history, being looked at when the "looker" is smiling, nodding, and so on, has been accompanied by positive reinforcers such as good things to eat and drink, complimentary words, and other conditioned reinforcers. On the other hand, when the "looker" is frowning, shouting, snarling, and so on, aversive stimuli have usually been present.

Thus, though simply being looked at usually becomes a positive conditioned reinforcer, "social approval" usually becomes an even stronger positive reinforcer, and "social disapproval" becomes a strong negative reinforcer.

Much learning in children is accomplished through the use of social reinforcers such as attention and approval, or conversely through disapproval. This is one of the types of reinforcement that is available in cognitive learning. For example, the approval and attention of the parent or teacher can be a strong source of reinforcement for maintaining the attention and working behaviors of children. In addition, if attention and approval as positive reinforcers are made contingent upon the achievement of some skill, the surpassing of some standard, or the winning of some competition, these stimuli will also acquire reinforcement value in the process—in addition to the behavior that produced the achievement being itself strengthened.

However, as is implicit in the preceding description of the formation of social reinforcers such as approval, the extent to which social reinforcers will be reinforcing will depend upon the past conditioning history of the child. For a child who has been rewarded many times as he gets attention or approval, these social stimuli will become strong positive reinforcers. However, many children will not have had such a conditioning history.

Many children will not have received as many conditioning trials when rewards have been dispensed in contiguity with attention. There are many parents who use relatively little positive reinforcement in training their children. For example, the study with the juvenile delinquent presented in a preceding chapter was such a case. His case study revealed that the methods of training used by the mother and father of the boy were primarily those of physical and verbal abuse. For such a child, social approval and attention of authority figures may have little positive reinforcing value.

It appears that there are large differences in the social classes in terms of such differences in training. Maccoby and Gibbs conducted a study of child rearing practices in which it was found that (1) lower-class mothers used more physical and verbal punishment in toilet training their children; (2) lower-class mothers also used more punishment in sex training; (3) lower-class mothers used physical and verbal punishment, deprivation of privileges, and so on, as a means of training socially acceptable behavior in general; (4) middle-class parents appeared to use reasoning and praise and possibly some forms of withdrawal of love more often.

Thus, children can be expected to vary widely in the extent to which the attention and social approval of adults will constitute positive reinforcers. For some children, for example, the teacher's attention and approval will be strong reinforcing stimuli. However, if the child comes from a home which has not paired learning with reinforcing stimuli, where through a deficit in language conditioning, especially, educators and their approval have not become secondary reinforcers, he will suffer a decrement in "motivation" for appropriate school behaviors and be said to have little "value" for education. That is, one of the important sources of maintaining the child's working and attentional behaviors will be absent.

The attention and approval of the child's schoolmates may also be reinforcers for the child. That is, if the attention and approval of other children has in the past been paired with reinforcement, then this type of attention and approval will be reinforcing. This type of conditioning is likely to have taken place in the usual middle-class child's training.

Furthermore, the attention and approval of middle-class children is likely to be gained by "achievement behaviors"—working hard, playing skillfully, studying, and so on. For example, the child who studies and works well and thus exhibits high-level student behavior (information) is likely to receive social reinforcement from his schoolmates as well as from his teacher. One thing should be stressed here. As has been pointed out, not only is the nature of the reinforcement system important in determining the individual's behavior, but in addition the "rules" by which the reinforcement is presented is an important determinant. In most school situations the rule is generally that skilled student behavior (knowledge) will be reinforced. This is customarily based upon a relational criterion. Behavior that is *better* than the other student's behavior is reinforced most heavily and most frequently. It is the especially skilled student that receives the social approval of the teacher and that of the other students.

For the poor student, who probably is a poor student because there have been inadequate sources of reinforcement, there is little social reinforcement. His student behavior is relatively poor and he will rarely be told things such as "You are an exceptionally good student," "Your work is very good," "That was a wonderful performance," and so on. Thus, there is a snowballing effect, since the child for whom there are weak reinforcers learns slowly. Because he accomplishes little, he receives less reinforcement contingent upon his classroom performance, and his behavior which is important to school success weakens even more.

One further point should be made in the context of describing this source of reinforcement for complex child learning. "Subcultures" can form within a society or community or neighborhood, or other group, which develop motivational systems that are different from that of the larger group. Although an adolescent child may come from a home, for example, which has a certain motivational system, he may become a member of a peer group that has a markedly different motivational system. As a consequence of the conditioning he undergoes in the group his motivational system may change. And, as a consequence of the way the group reinforces him, he may acquire behaviors quite at variance with those considered desirable by his family—or in fact by the larger society.

Thus, as a specific example, it is quite frequent that a group of children in a classroom will have a different system of reinforcement than has been described for the usual middle-class child. For these children the social approval of the teacher will not be a positive reinforcer. Indeed, the social disapproval of the teacher, which may be much milder than the aversive stimuli used in the child's experience, may not even be aversive. It may, as we shall see, even become a positive reinforcer.

These children, whose performance is likely to gain them little social reinforcement anyway, may be thrown together as "outcasts" from the larger group. In their interactions with each other they may become positive reinforcers for each other and also develop a reinforcer system that is different from and antagonistic to the reinforcer system that applies in the classroom. That is, the approval of the teacher can become a negative reinforcer. A child in this group who does something that merits teacher approval may be derided by other members of the sub-group. Under such circumstances teacher approval will become a negative reinforcer and behavior that escapes and avoids the teacher approval will be learned, for example, baiting the teacher, misbehaving in class, and so on. An analysis of any group situation that involves sub-groups must include an analysis of the reinforcement systems functioning in the subgroups. It may be suggested that investigation of the characteristics of group reinforcer systems, within the present theory, would be a fertile field of research.

Additional Sources of Reinforcement

There are many other types of reinforcers present in the individual's reinforcement system which effectively determine his behaviors in the ways that have been described. For the child there are special privileges of various kinds, games, play, toys, companionship, movies, television, stories, travel and other recreative activities, snacks, and so on. For the most part, these various reinforcing circumstances are delivered "free." That is, they are not delivered contingent upon any specific behaviors, at least to a large extent.

This is also the case in the formal situation for conducting cognitive development, the school. There are many additional reinforcers in school, some of which have been innumerated above, but many of them are not delivered in a response-contingent manner and thus are not used effectively. Take the school recess, for example. It has been shown that relief from work is a strong reinforcer (Azrin, 1961). However, recess is delivered on a completely temporal schedule—with no regard to the behavior of the children. The child could be pulling the hair of the girl seated in front of him as the recess bell chimes. A more likely occurrence, often seen in college classes where there is no bell ending the class, is that restless behavior will be learned under the control of temporal cues —the moving of books, the shuffling of papers, moving one's feet, and so on. This behavior is learned because it controls the professor's behavior and he ends the class, thus providing positive reinforcement or the cessation of negative reinforcers.

Motivational Deficits

In general it may be suggested that the preceding experimental findings and theoretical analyses suggest one conclusion very strongly. It may be suggested that there are no differences among people in their motivation for which they are personally responsible, or which (in the absence of clear cut physical abnormality) should be considered as a sign of biological inferiority. A widely held conception is that the poor and seemingly unambitious are that way because they are naturally shiftless, lazy, unmotivated, and so on. Racial groups may also be characterized in this manner, also with an implication of biological inferiority.

However, these are inferred conceptions, based only upon the behaviors which are displayed. Biological interpretations of motivational differences are made without having direct evidence of biological events which could cause such differences. No anatomical structures have been found to which differences in motivational systems can be attributed. And behavioral evidence indicates quite the contrary. That is, in every group and every race of people there are stimuli which have reinforcement value only through the conditioning experience of the individual. For all peoples there are stimuli that are positive reinforcers and stimuli that are negative reinforcers, and many of these are social stimuli.

Biological interpretations of motivational differences in people are simply unacquainted with the differences that can occur on the basis of learning. Thus, from the biological approach, 4-year-olds' lack of motivated learning behavior is usually interpreted in terms of biological maturation. It is said that the child has not yet "matured" and thus has a short interest (or attention) span. This interpretation, in principle, is similar to the one which sees the backward child who has not learned anything, who comes from poor and shiftless parents, and so on, as biologically inferior.

However, the experimental results with the preschool children cited herein shows that long-term, arduous, complex, learning tasks can be pursued by very young children when adequate reinforcement is provided. When such reinforcers are introduced, the behavior of such children becomes interested, motivated, hard working—and good cognitive learning results. The sudden increase in such behavior was independent of biological change or maturation.

In essence, then, it may be suggested that differences in "motivated" behavior are a function of the past conditioning history of the individual and the reward conditions of the situation in which the individual finds himself. If we want "motivated" learning behavior (good attention, consistent and rapid work, and so on) we must be prepared to guarantee that motivational conditions are arranged to produce these behaviors. *If we want motivated behavior in traditional learning situations—like the classroom—we must guarantee that the child has the appropriate training so that the reinforcers present in that situation are potent. If this training is not provided, then we must be prepared to alter the situation so that it includes reinforcers that are appropriate for the reinforcer system that the child has learned.* It must be concluded that the organism (the child) is never responsible for his behavior—he behaves in accord with lawful principles. It is the nature of his experiences and the nature of the situation that determine what his behavior will be.

THE PARENT AS THE TRAINER OF THE BASIC BEHAVIORAL REPERTOIRE

In summary, a learning analysis of the acquisition of behavior in general, and especially the basic behavioral repertoire, leads to a focus upon the parent as a *trainer*. Whether the parent intends to or not, he manipulates many conditions of learning that will determine to a large extent the behaviors the child will acquire. As long as the child's behavioral development consists of innumerable training experiences, many of which occur in the home, then the parent has many of the controlling variables in his hands and cannot relinquish them regardless of his philosophy of child development.

The author has previously described various aspects of child development (Chapter 9, Staats and Staats, 1963), albeit without as much detail concerning the basic behavioral repertoire. As part of this analysis the author indicated the important role played by the parent in the early development of his child, an excerpt from which will be quoted.

> This suggests that the parent could be an active participant in arranging circumstances to most efficaciously produce an abundant, rich, adjustive, behavioral repertoire using a minimum of aversive stimulation and a maximum of positive reinforcement. Good working behaviors, good studying behaviors, the ability to work without immediate reinforcement; reasonable, cooperative, not overselfish behavior; a good language system about the world, his own behavior, and that of others; a good system of reinforcers, including words of positive and negative reinforcement value; social stimuli that appropriately control striving and nonstriving behavior; social behaviors that reinforce other people as well as oneself; these seem to be some of the behaviors that the parents help determine by the conditions they present to the child. Thus, to a large extent the learning conditions that occur in the home would seem to determine whether the child will grow into a "well-adjusted," "happy," "productive," individual.
>
> Faced with a training task of such imposing responsibilities, it would seem that the parent would need an understanding of the principles of behavior by which children learn. In addition, it would seem that the parent would require an analysis in terms of those principles of the various specific training problems he faces. The parent needs to know how not to shape undesirable behaviors, or, when they have developed, how to decrease them benignly; and he needs to know how to shape the many adjustive behaviors the child will require. (Staats and Staats, 1963, pp. 412–413)

It may be suggested that this is the weakest link in the child's cognitive development and thus in our educational system, and is the one that is subject to the greatest amount of variation. We leave the training of the various aspects of the basic behavioral repertoire in the hands of individuals who have no special training with respect to what the child needs in his basic behavioral repertoire, or of the principles by which the repertoire is acquired, or indeed of methods to produce the learning.

If the parent has himself had a fortunate history of training, including experience that has made him a good trainer, and barring other obstacles, he will duplicate this type of training for his children. Parents who have not been fortunate in these respects will not. But whether the parent is good or poor is relatively uninfluenced by any systematic study conducted in the field of psychology or education or medicine. There is at present no institution or set of materials to which the parent can turn to find methods and principles which he can use to help him train his children to a better basic behavioral repertoire. He must fumble along on his own, many times in an inadequate manner even when he meets no special problems of child training.

Although the training he provides is the basis for the child's whole social, emotional, and cognitive educational progress, there is no systematic program to improve these aspects of mental health and education. With few exceptions, improvements in educational practices are aimed at the educational institutions and children of school age. Thus, one of the purposes of the preceding and following analyses is to produce information yielding training procedures appropriate for utilization by parents. It is one of the author's contentions that one of the foremost goals of an adequate learning theory of human behavior should be the production of a set of methods, principles, and apparatus (materials) by which professionals *and* parents, may understand and deal with problems of child learning. The present theory lends itself to that goal.

Adjustment and the Basic Behavioral Repertoire

These analyses may be considered as examples of the basic behavioral repertoires that are important to the child's further learning; emotional, social, and cognitive learning. This is by no means intended as a complete analysis of the various components of the basic behavioral repertoire that are important to the child's adjustment, and to his normal development. However, the discussions may be considered as an illustration of the general conception as well as the general approach, and also serve as the basis for the discussion of more advanced cognitive repertoires in an elaboration of the hierarchical conception of cognitive development.

In this account, the stress has been on the *normal* development of these essential repertoires. It should be noted, however, that the analysis also provides a basis for an abnormal psychology. Even though the analysis is not complete, it may be suggested that deficits in the development of any of the basic behavioral repertoire will yield severe maladjustments. Usually, such maladjustments will result in further unfortunate experiences that will produce additional behavioral deficits and inappropriate behaviors—in the manner exemplified with the culturally-deprived delinquent child in the previous study.

In addition, *distortion* of any of the components of the basic behavioral repertoires through atypical conditioning histories will also lead to the same consequences as behavioral deficits. Thus, the child who has a behavioral deficit in that his behavior has not come under the control of verbal stimuli will be grievously maladjusted. A good portion of useful social interaction will be lost to him, and he will be unable to learn in situations in which other more fortunate children progress rapidly. The same would be true if, rather than a deficit in the basic behavioral repertoire, the child responded to verbal stimuli but in highly atypical ways.

As another example, a child whose word associations are awry, that is, a child who has not acquired logical language (and hence thinking) will be very handicapped in many situations, depending upon the severity of the distortion in his repertoire. It may thus be suggested, although this is not the place for a full development of the theme, that we must begin the analysis of the behavioral repertoires of man; to assess the adjustmental value of the repertoires, to see what happens when the repertoires are benign and when they are not, and thus to gain a specific knowledge of normal and abnormal behavior. Although the learning principles, and the S–R mechanisms, have been elucidated, as well as sample analyses of the various repertoires—a great task lies ahead in this endeavor. A central point in this task, however, is to stop considering deficits and distortions in cognitive (and social and emotional) behaviors as symptoms of abnormality, but rather as the "abnormality" itself. It may be suggested that the principles provided herein would serve productively as the foundation for an abnormal psychology that would analyze various behavior disorders, mental retardation, autism, various forms of psychosis, and so on. (See also the author's account in Chapter 11, Staats and Staats, 1963.)

This present book can by no means complete such a task, but can only indicate examples and suggest a method. By way of doing this, one further repertoire—more advanced than the basic behavioral repertoire—will be analyzed in some detail. This analysis (of the development and function of reading) is intended again as an example, to indicate how the basic behavioral repertoire is involved in more advanced learning, and to illustrate further the hierarchical learning conception of human development by showing how the more advanced repertoire is itself basic to the learning of even more advanced repertoires. The analysis also demonstrates the utility of the integrated learning theory in providing useful accounts of functional human behaviors. It may be added that we must have such detailed S–R analyses of various human repertoires before we will have a comprehensive psychology of human behavior with attendant procedures for dealing with human problems.

16

The cognitive repertoire of reading: an analysis of its acquisition, function, and motivational aspects

The act of reading involves more than one type of behavioral repertoire. This fact is illustrated nicely by the following anecdote. The story is that during the Second World War there was an intelligence team operating in Europe which included among its members a Pole who had in childhood learned to speak but not to read Russian. The team also included an American who had attended a language school for a short while and learned to read the Russian alphabet, but no more. The other members of the team had no experience with the Russian language.

As it happened, the team intercepted a message written in Russian. The American was shown the message and he stood there and sounded out the Russian letters. The Pole heard the words and wrote out a translation for the other members of the team. The question is, which one was reading?

The answer, of course, is that neither one alone was reading; but both together were. In the present terms, the American had acquired part of a reading repertoire, the Pole another part. Together, their repertoires yielded what could be called reading.

The analysis of reading will first deal with the type of reading that the American had acquired; that is, with the instrumental discrimination learning involved in bringing vocal responses under the control of visually presented verbal stimuli. Later sections will deal with those aspects of reading that involve comprehension, communication, learning through reading, motivational aspects of reading acquisition and function, and so on. It may be noted here that reading is an exceedingly complex human behavior, as are most repertoires in which one is interested, and thus involves the various learning principles and S–R mechanisms.

DISCRIMINATION LEARNING AND
THE READING REPERTOIRE:
READING ACQUISITION

The manner in which particular vocal sounds, that is, word responses, come under the control of environmental stimuli has already been described. In addition, it has also been said, and demonstrated experimentally, that the same principle is involved in bringing vocal responses under the control of printed and written verbal stimuli. Normally, people think of reading as involving abilities, capacities, or talents other than those involved in the learning of seemingly different aspects of language such as the naming of objects. However, it would appear that there is no difference in the principles of learning involved; both the naming of objects and the "naming" of verbal stimuli involve the principle of instrumental discrimination learning.

Furthermore, the nature of the stimuli are not different in these two types of language learning. Both are visual stimuli—in naming objects environmental stimuli are involved, in naming letters or words the stimuli are external and visual. The environmental stimuli that the child learns to name are complex, as are the letter stimuli. Ordinary language behavior requires that verbal responses be under the control of very subtle, evanescent, aspects of one's stimulus environment. The same thing is true of reading, that is, the stimuli are no more complex or subtle.

This appears to be the case on rationale analysis. In addition, the foregoing experiments have corroborated the analysis very strongly. Even the very retarded children studied in the previous chapter were capable of discriminating the letters—in fact, as indicated, the stimuli used in that experiment were even more complex than those normally used.

Probably the foremost reason that reading is generally thought to be different from comparable forms of the language repertoire involves the difficulty in acquiring a reading repertoire. Virtually every intact individual seemingly acquires adequate speech behaviors, yet there are many individuals who, although they display adequate speech, appear unable to learn to read, or do so only with great difficulty.

It is commonly suggested that such uneven development is a result of some biological defect, such as neurological impairment. In fact, we have medical terms, alexia and dyslexia, by which nonreading and poor reading is considered to be due to neurological impairment. However, unless there is some independent observation of this neurological defect, not just the fact that the child cannot read, this type of concept is simply *ad hoc*.

Perceptual tests that measure attentional and discrimination repertoires do not constitute this type of independent evidence. Although particular "perceptual" behaviors may be necessary before the child will learn to read readily, the "perceptual" behaviors are learned also.

The author suggests that if the child is capable of acquiring differential speech responses under the control of the ordinary visual stimuli in a normal manner—if he has acquired normal speech—then it should be possible for visual verbal stimuli also to come to control the verbal responses in the act of reading. On the other hand, on the basis of the present analysis, it would seem that, exclusive of personal defect, there are several very real reasons why some people do not under usual circumstances learn to read even though their speech development is otherwise normal. Actually, for everyone, learning to read is accomplished only with great difficulty in comparison to the acquisition of speech under the control of other stimuli. To indicate the reasons, several important characteristics of the acquisition of speech responses and the process whereby speech responses come under the control of external and internal stimuli should be emphasized.

First, as has been implicit in the previous discussions, the process of speech acquisition is very gradual. Beginning with the strengthening of the general speech class in early infancy, more and more precise speech responses are gradually refined through learning until the exact word responses of the language community occur. These responses are only gradually brought under the control of the appropriate stimulus objects in a long program of training. Learning sessions occur intermittently and are dispersed throughout the day. In addition, new objects are introduced over a period of years in building up verbal discriminations.

Secondly, there are strong sources of reinforcement involved. When the child first says WAHTAR, the strong reinforcer of a cup of water is presented. When the child says BAYBEE, the strong reinforcer of a baby doll is presented. In addition, strong reinforcers are abundantly available in the attention and approval of people in the environment. When the child says LOOK and another child responds by looking, this is a reinforcer for the verbal response.

Thirdly, these strong reinforcers are individually applied, and they are applied immediately following the speech behaviors involved. It is most important at an early age that the reinforcing stimulus be presented quickly after a response has occurred. If no reinforcer is presented, or if the lag is too great, the response will not be strengthened.

Comparing these characteristics with those involved in the acquisition of reading behavior, it becomes obvious that the learning of reading would be more difficult for everyone. Unlike speech behavior itself, and speech behavior under the control of other types of stimuli, reading is not gradually acquired in the preschool years. It is customary to introduce training in the acquisition of speech responses to visually presented verbal stimuli only when the child enters school. Although there is some attempt to make this more gradual through the use of nursery schools, kindergartens, and reading readiness programs, in comparison to the learning of speech responses, the onset of reading training is sudden and intensive.

This major difference between speech and reading learning has important consequences. For example, intensive periods involving the acquisition, or the performance, of responses may be considered to have aversive characteristics. It has been shown that discriminative stimuli acquire aversive characteristics after an extended period of "working" in the presence of the stimuli, even when the responses involved are reinforced. That is, another response which will remove the discriminative stimulus will be maintained in some strength. Furthermore, the more intensive the "work" is (that is, the greater the ratio of responses to reinforcement), the more aversive the discriminative stimulus becomes (Azrin, 1961).

Naturalistic observations also suggest that the intensive rather than gradual training of reading has aversive aspects. Many children describe school and school activities as "work," and in aversive terms. Although the language learning which takes place prior to school training is just as complex, and in these terms just as difficult to acquire, it is not described as being trying or difficult to the same extent as is formal training. The child does not say that he is having, or has had, a difficult time in learning to speak—or learning his extensive repertoire of discriminated verbal responses.

In addition, to the extent that the school situation is aversive, it will be reinforcing to "escape" the situation. Any behavior which removes the child from the aversive situation will be strengthened. Thus, behaviors such as talking to other pupils, cutting up, doodling and playing quiet games, teasing other pupils, daydreaming, and so on, will be strengthened by providing an escape from the aversive training situation.

Of course, it is possible to make the behavior of leaving the situation in these ways more aversive through punishment and, in this manner, maintain good participation in learning. Education in former times utilized these methods. However, unless some reinforcement system is employed to maintain attention and participation behaviors, no matter how long the child is in the learning situation, no learning will ensue.

The major point here, however, is that reading acquisition involves the same principles of learning as the other types of discriminative stimulus control in language. Thus, a child who can learn to speak under appropriate environmental control should be able to learn to read. Nevertheless, there are aspects of reading learning that are not nearly as propitious as those usually involved in ordinary language learning.

Thus, although reading learning is no more difficult than learning an appropriate speech repertoire, it should be emphasized that a reading learning repertoire is a fantastically complex repertoire. Thus, the acquisition of such a repertoire constitutes an extremely difficult learning task—even when the task is commenced when the child already has a good basic behavioral repertoire. To fully appreciate what is involved in reading acquisition, it is necessary to analyze in learning terms what a reading repertoire consists of. This is the subject of the following analyses.

Discrimination of Letters
(Alphabet Training)

It has been mentioned that the stimuli involved in reading are complex and subtle. Another reason reading acquisition is so difficult, as we shall see in greater detail, is that there are so *many* stimuli that must come to control vocal responses of various sorts. In addition, however, the stimuli themselves present problems.

One of the major problems lies in the area of discrimination learning. It has been stated that if a response is reinforced in the presence of a particular stimulus and not in the absence of the stimulus, the stimulus will come to control the response. This is the simple case of instrumental discrimination learning.

A corollary statement is necessary, however, that is called the principle of stimulus generalization. The fact is that when a response has been brought under the control of a stimulus in the manner described above, any stimulus that is physically similar will also bring on the response— to the extent this stimulus is physically similar to the one used in the conditioning process. For example, a child trained to call his father DADDY may also call the father's brother DADDY. By the same principle the child who has been reinforced for saying THE in the presence of the word *the* will later err in reading *this, then, their, there, they, thus,* and so on as THE.

Whenever stimulus generalization causes errors, when the child makes a response to a stimulus that is appropriate for some other stimulus, further discrimination training is necessary. That is, let us say that stimulus *A* is the stimulus to which the organism has been conditioned, and stimulus *B* is the stimulus that is similar to *A* and which inappropriately controls the response also. We could get the organism to respond to *A* and not *B* by conducting trials where both stimuli are alternately presented but the organism is reinforced only for responding to *A*. In this case *A* will continue to control the response, whereas the response to *B* will extinguish. When this training is complete there will be a sharp discrimination and the organism will respond to one but not the other.

Nevertheless, if we have a learning task in which many of the stimuli are similar to each other but must come to control different responses, then we know the learning will be quite difficult. When a response is conditioned to one stimulus (*A*) the other similar stimuli will tend to elicit the response. In addition, if we condition a different response to another similar stimulus (*B*) then this response will tend to be elicited by the other stimulus (*A*) also. Error responses will occur in both directions.

This type of difficulty in discrimination occurs to a large extent in the learning of reading, as has been noted on a simple observational level. For example, the letters *b* and *d* are quite similar, as are the letters *p* and *q*. The letters *r, n, h, m,* and *b* are also similar. The letters *C, O,* and *Q* are similar as are *M* and *N, P* and *R, K* and *H, M* and *W,* and *V* and *W,* and so on. It would be expected on the basis of the learning analysis that the more similar two letters were the more difficult it would be to establish one response specifically under the control of each letter.

By way of indicating the difficulty of establishing the discriminations involved in learning the alphabet, it should be added that there is more than one way of printing several of the letters. Take the letter *g,* for example. It is printed in upper case as *G,* in lower case as *g* or in many children's books as *g*, and is written as *g*. That means that four different stimuli must come to control the "g" vocal response; thus the child must learn four S–R associations for the one letter. In learning to read whole words, for example, the different ways of printing and writing letters may combine to produce many different forms of the word. Thus, as Downing (1964) has pointed out the word *dog* may be printed as *DOG, Dog, dog, Dog,* and *dog.* It may also be written.

For reasons which will be more clear after succeeding discussions, in the process of acquiring a reading repertoire the child must come to be able to look at the various letter stimuli, presented in their various forms, and respond differently to each stimulus; that is, the child must learn to discriminate the letters. This is the function of the alphabet training the child is given at the beginning of virtually all reading training programs. The responses which are learned to the letter stimuli are ones that will later be a part of the reading repertoire, but, as will be shown, are only a small part.

At any rate, it may be suggested that alphabet learning, the discrimination of the letters, is a very important part of the total learning process. This is not to say, however, that our present alphabet training is the best way of producing the letter discriminations. As the next section will elaborate, in addition to the alphabet responses, the letter stimuli must also come to control other vocal responses.

The Unit Reading (Grapheme-Phoneme) Repertoire

The fact of the matter is that the child cannot be presented in his training with every word that he will later be expected to read. If it were necessary to present the many thousands of words in our language to the child in a random order in training aiming to produce a single word reading repertoire, the task would be insuperable. Although the child can easily learn a limited single word reading repertoire, it becomes evident very quickly that it is not possible to increase the repertoire beyond a primitive level in this manner. Not only would this be an ineffective method of training, but the training time involved would be exorbitant. The child must receive training which forms a basic reading behavioral repertoire which will enable him to "train" himself when encountering new words with which he is unfamiliar. As such the training of reading offers a fine example of the display of a type of "originality," that is, the learning of a repertoire of stimulus-response units which in the presence of new stimuli result in novel (combinations of) responses. It is quite evident that such cases of originality can, and must, occur in great multitude in the learning of reading.

The type of reading unit repertoire that is necessary may be easily illustrated. Let us say that the letters *at* have come to control the vocal response AT in the process of learning to read the words *mat, bat, cat, sat,* and *rat.* Let us also say that the letter *f* has come to control the vocal "F-F-F" response in the process of learning the words *fate, father, fast, far, farm, first,* and so on. With these two grapheme-phoneme reading units, when the novel stimulus *fat* is presented to the child he should respond with the vocal response elicited by the *f* and the vocal response elicited by the *at* to form the original reading response FAT. (As will be described in the next section, the child will also require training in the "sounding out" repertoire in order to accomplish the task.)

In order for the child to have a serviceable unit reading repertoire, by which he can sound out new words, he must acquire a very large number of S–R (grapheme-phoneme) reading units, all according to the principle of instrumental discrimination learning. To realize the size of the repertoire and the difficulty of the learning involved, at least as far as the English language is concerned, a few examples may be given. The major complication concerns the fact that a single letter stimulus must come to control more than one vocal response. Furthermore, the same vocal response must come to be controlled by different letter stimuli. The learning thus involves complex hierarchies of responses, both convergent and divergent. For example, Soffieti, (1955) has indicated that the vocal response "oo" must come to be controlled by nine different printed letter or letter combinations; *u* as in *rule, ue,* as in *flue, ui* as in *fruit, eu* as in *maneuver, ou* as in *group, ew* as in *grew, o* as in *move, oe* as in *canoe,* and *oo* as in *moon.* This type of learning could be schematized in a figure in which the nine different letter stimuli control the same response (a convergent hierarchy). As large as it is, this list does not actually indicate fully the number of different letter stimuli that must come to control the "oo" vocal response. Thus, Downing (1964) has indicated that 18 different letter stimuli actually must come to control this response, not just the nine suggested above.

Furthermore, single letter stimuli, and combinations of letters, must come to control different vocal responses. Each of the vowels, singly and in combination, must come to control various vocal responses. And the same is true of consonant letters and letter combinations. Thus, for example, the letter *a* must control the vocal response A as in *at* when the letter is preceded by *f* and followed by *t.* When the letter *a* is preceded by *f* and followed by *te* the letter must control the response long A response. When the letter is preceded by *f* again and followed by *t* plus *her* as in *father* the *a* must control the sound made in pronouncing this word. This learning could be schematized in terms of a divergent response hierarchy concept—a single letter stimulus controlling the several different vocal responses.

Many of these divergent and convergent response hierarchies must be learned in reading English. And, on the basis of a learning analysis, it must be realized that this represents a very difficult learning task. The sheer number of S–R units that must be acquired is imposing, and the possibilities of error responses because of stimulus generalization are great. Some of the difficulties will be described in the next section.

The Sounding Out Repertoire

The fact that the child has learned to give the appropriate phoneme response to various letters does not in itself provide the ability to sound out words. As the experiments with Jennifer showed very clearly, the child can have several grapheme-phoneme units but not be able to pronounce a new word composed of the graphemes—that is not be able to respond to the graphemes in series in a manner that produces a word that is recognizable to the child. For example, the child may be trained to respond with the "p" sound when a *p* is presented, to the *a* with an appropriate sound, and to the *t* with a "t" sound. On the basis of this training alone, however, the word *pat* will not control the word response PAT. As a matter of fact the sounding out sequence is a very difficult skill to train using these particular types of grapheme-phoneme units since the three phonemes vocalized *discretely* in a series do not produce a sound much like that of the ordinary word response PAT.

However, as the results with Jennifer and the other subject showed, after the child has been trained to make vocal responses to individual letters, he can be trained to respond to letters in combination, from left to right, to produce a total sound that is a word. This process is very similar to what the child has to do in learning to count. He must first look at the leftmost letter, say its "name," look at the next one and say its "name," and so on. These form an important part of the basic skills that go into the reading repertoire and are especially important during the process of reading acquisition.

The example above is, of course, a simple case. The child had been given just those grapheme-phonemes that were involved in the word to be sounded out. And this is a necessary part of the training, since it is by doing this that the child learns the sequences of response (the left-to-right order of looking at the letters, and so on) that are involved in sounding out words.

However, additional skills are also involved before the child can sound out a large number of actual words. It should be remembered that in a particular word the letter must control a particular vocal response—although, as mentioned, the letter may have to control another type of vocal response in a different word. Whenever more than one letter in a word is a letter that controls more than one vocal response under different circumstances—that is, controls a hierarchy of responses—then it should be evident that the alternatives may be quite large. Thus, the word *familiar* has four vowels in it each of which comes to control a hierarchy of reading responses in the child, let us say. The child who then sees this word for the first time, who has the necessary reading unit repertoire, may still not be able to read the word. He may say, for example, FAY-MY (rhymes with eye) -LY (rhymes with eye) -AIR, for example, or any of the other combinations that is not the usual pronunciation of the word.

In order for the child to read this word with "understanding," however, it is necessary that the child continue to sound out the parts of the word until he produces a whole word that is sufficiently like *familiar* to assume the functions of that word. (These functions will be discussed in later portions of this chapter.) This persistence in sounding out involves certain skills itself. The child must look at the printed syllables and emit one of the responses controlled, and do this for each syllable. However, if the word which he produces does not match any that he has in his repertoire, he must go back and repeat the process. On each repetition, however, he must emit a different response in his hierarchy of responses to each vowel. Using the above example, he might say FAH-MY-LY-AIR and still not produce a word response that was functional.

At this point the child would have to repeat the process emitting other possible vowel responses. Let us say that the child finally says FAH-MEE-LEE-ARE and this word response is sufficiently similar to the word response FAMILIAR. The child will then try out the total word response by reading the word over again by syllables saying FA-MI-LI-AR and if the series of syllabic responses produces the word this time, if his word response matches the usual sound of the word *familiar,* the child will be reinforced (or in common sense terms, know that he is correct).

When this performance is broken down this way it can be seen that a rather extensive set of repertoires is involved, just considering the skills involved in learning to sound out words. This type of performance has been called a "strategy" by some individuals, but the learning analysis suggests that it is a learned repertoire involving (1) first looking at the letters and syllables successively, (2) then emitting one of the responses from the hierarchy controlled by each letter or syllable, (3) listening to the word stimulus he has in this manner produced, (4) comparing this stimulus to those with which he has had experience, and (5) failing to achieve a match with a familiar word, repeating the process by emitting different responses to the letters and syllables until a match is produced.

This is a very complex sequence of skills. And before it can be effectively acquired it is necessary that the child have in his repertoire the hierarchies of vocal responses under the control of letters and syllables.

The Whole Word Reading Repertoire

It is quite apparent, however, that the accomplished reader performs in the above manner relatively infrequently. That is, after much reading experience, the words themselves, as well as combinations of words, come to control whole word responses. At this stage in the learning of reading it is rare that the reader encounters a word with which he has not had experience and which does not as a consequence immediately control the appropriate vocal response (and, as we shall see, other types of responses as well).

Actually, the performance of the accomplished reader is much like that which would result if the child had simply been trained to read whole words. For example, in one of the preceding studies with preschoolers the reading training procedures consisted of presenting a word, prompting the child to say the word, and then reinforcing the child. As a function of such conditioning the word as a complex stimulus unit came to control the word response as a unit. In training of this type, however, a single letter, or a pair of letters, could be the stimulus controlling the word response. Or the general configuration of the word could control the response, as is probably the case with the accomplished reader. In the case of the children in the study, however, not having the necessary letter discriminations and the grapheme-phoneme repertoire, they would be unable simply on the basis of a few whole word training trials to distinguish similar words from those they were trained on.

It should be pointed out, in addition, that much of the word reading repertoire of the accomplished reader has been acquired upon the basis of his previously learned grapheme-phoneme repertoire. That is, using the word *familiar* as the example again, let us say that the word is seen for the first time by the child who has a grapheme-phoneme repertoire. He looks at the *fa*, and as a stimulus it controls the appropriate vocal response, as previously described. He responds to each syllable in series and finally produces a word response. After several trials he gets the correct word response. Then the child reads the syllables several times to himself saying FA-MI-LI-AR. And, finally while looking at the word he says several times, FAMILIAR, FAMILIAR, FAMILIAR. These training trials are depicted in Figure 16.1.

The final product of the training as is shown in the figure, however, is that the word stimulus as a unit comes to control the word response as a unit. The next time the child comes across the word he will read it as FAMILIAR, perhaps still with some hesitation and while looking successively at the letters. With a sufficient number of these training trials,

(a)

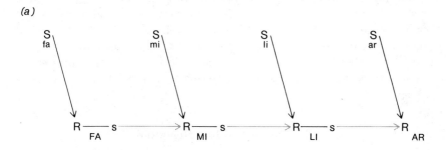

(b)

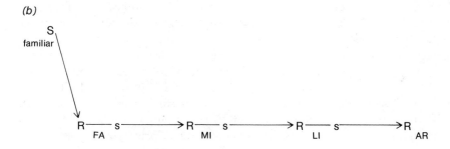

(c)

FIGURE 16.1. The process of learning to read a new word on the basis of reading syllable units. In (a) the child sounds out the successive syllables and this begins to establish the syllable responses as a chain. Through further learning trials, as shown in (b) the chain becomes more firmly established and begins to come under the control of the whole word. As shown in (c) the whole word has come to be the stimulus controlling the whole word response.

however, the whole word will ultimately come to control the whole vocal response. It thus appears that a whole word reading repertoire, and ultimately a phrase reading repertoire, can be acquired on the basis of a grapheme-phoneme type of reading repertoire.

Thus, it is suggested that children can be trained to letter and syllable phonetic responses which can be used in sounding out novel words. The repertoires involved in sounding out words include not only the grapheme-phoneme repertoire, but also the chain of responses just described upon which the sounding out skills depend. The basic point of the present section, however, is to emphasize the point that reading training must be carried to the stage where there is a very good whole word reading repertoire. A child could have a well formed ability to sound out new words and yet be a very poor reader. The whole word stimuli, with few exceptions permissible, must quickly elicit the appropriate reading responses if the reader is to read rapidly, easily, and with "understanding."

The Phrase Reading Repertoire

It has sometimes been assumed by linguists and psycholinguists that an S–R analysis of language can consider words as stimuli, but not larger language units. There is no reason to draw this conclusion, however. As has been suggested, the child may learn vocal responses to single letter stimuli. But later he may sound out single letters which produce a whole word vocal response. When this occurs the word response comes under the control of the configuration of letters which is the word stimulus. Thus, larger responses can be composed of smaller units, and through training come under the control of larger stimuli which are themselves composed of smaller units. There is nothing in principle that limits the complexity of the stimulus that comes to control a response—nor indeed that limits the complexity of the response itself. Empirical findings, for example, suggest that very simple responses can be instrumentally conditioned, as well as responses that are formed from combinations of separate responses.

The same expectations would occur when words were the units rather than letters. That is, it would be expected that word stimuli that occurred together a number of times would come as a unit to control the word responses, as a unit, that the individual words would themselves control. Thus, one look at the phrase would control the unit response (composed of several word responses). One of the reasons the expert reader does not have to look at each word, it may be suggested, occurs because phrases have come to be stimuli that elicit the necessary word responses. The reading is then no longer dependent upon looking at each word stimulus. *Coca cola* and *Pepsi cola* may be used as examples of multiple word stimuli that come to be responded to as a unit by most Americans, as are the combinations *United States, General Motors, stormy weather,* and so on. It might be suggested in fact that there are many such phrase stimuli that control unit responses—and that there is probably a dimension of strength of control. Thus, the unit *Coca cola* probably has more unit control than would *The blue sky*. It may be suggested that the extent to which a group of words had come as a unit to control a unit reading response could be observed by presenting the stimuli tachistoscopically—that is, for very short intervals. Thus, it would be expected that it would take longer to read *hots tend* than it would to read *Coca cola*, although both combinations of stimuli contain the same number of letters.

Although this and other aspects of the analysis should be more specifically tested in the laboratory, the suggestions derive directly from the theory, and they are supported by various types of naturalistic and experimental evidence. This aspect of the learning of reading will not be elaborated, however. There is a later section on the importance of word associations in reading that touches upon related matters. It may only be added that the skill of the reader will be affected by the extent and quality of his phrase reading repertoire, as is also the case for his whole word reading repertoire.

Stages of Reading Learning

Implicit in this analysis has been the suggestion that at different stages of the child's development of reading different aspects of the discrimination repertoires described have varying degrees of importance. Thus, for example, in the accomplished reader the repertoire of whole word and phrase reading discriminations would seem to be the most important aspect of his skill. Only on infrequent occasions is the grapheme-phoneme repertoire of the accomplished reader called into play. And, only on those occasions also is the accomplished reader required to emit the sounding out sequences described.

On the other hand, when the child is still in the acquisition stage of reading, the sounding out repertoire and the grapheme-phoneme repertoire are more crucial. A larger proportion of the words he encounters in reading are new. At this point the child's speaking repertoire is much larger than his whole word reading repertoire. He needs to learn the large whole word and phrase reading repertoire of the accomplished reader. And, it should be stressed, he must do much of this on his own. At this point he is dependent upon his sounding out skills, composed as has been described of various repertoires. Because of these more basic behavioral repertoires he can respond to novel printed material appropriately and can in this manner learn the whole word responses to the whole word stimulus.

This analysis, then, indicates that there is a complex interweaving of learning involved in these aspects of reading discrimination learning. For example, as shown in the previously described micro-experiment on consonant concept formation, consonant reading units may be learned from whole word tasks. It may be suggested in general that the child learns aspects of his grapheme-phoneme repertoire from whole word training, *and from the employment of this repertoire in reading that he does on his own,* for it should be emphasized that the child learns reading units from reading, as is the case also with other aspects of his reading repertoire. Discrimination learning trials occur here as well as in formal tuition.

In addition, however, the child learns some of his whole word reading repertoire on the basis of his grapheme-phoneme repertoire. It is no doubt because of the complex interweaving of learning of these repertoires that the oft repeated controversies concerning whole word versus phonetic methods of teaching reading have continued to occur again and again without much resolution. While the research and theory reported in the present book do not settle these issues of the method of teaching reading, they do clarify the issues by providing the type of learning analysis which is necessary to this task. Furthermore, the theory, when combined with the research methods, provides a means by which the issues may be resolved through experimentation. An additional analysis of some of the current approaches to the teaching of reading in terms of learning principles may lend impetus to the use of the present learning theory and experimental methodology in the study of some of the issues involved in the process of reading acquisition. Thus, the next section will be devoted to a brief summary of some of the learning considerations involved in an analysis of methods of teaching of reading. While additional analyses are still to be presented in completing the learning theory of reading, controversies in teaching methods habitually involve only those aspects of reading that have already been presented, which justifies the next section although actually it is a digression from the main purpose of the present chapter.

Discrimination Learning and Teaching Methods

Controversies concerning methods of teaching reading have arisen and continued because there have been no specific and detailed analyses of what constitutes a reading repertoire, nor what principles of learning are involved. Nor has there been a method of experimentation that could explore the learning of a reading repertoire in systematic detail and with laboratory objectivity. While the present research does not involve a comparison of training methods, it does suggest a general experimental method by which to answer some of the questions and controversies concerning such training methods. It may also be suggested that in addition to appropriate research methods (which will be discussed more fully in a later section) definitive research on different methods of training will depend upon a detailed analysis of the reading repertoire in terms of the principles by which the complex and inter-related responses are learned. It is the purpose of the present section to discuss a few topics important to reading materials by way of demon-strating the relevance of a learning analysis to the problems which reside in the practical teaching situation.

LETTERS AS STIMULI   The way in which the similarity of the letters in the alphabet makes learning different responses under the control of the letters so difficult has already been described. That is, a vocal response conditioned to one letter will also be controlled by another letter to the extent of similarity between the letters. Thus, a vocal response condi-tioned to *n* would to some extent be elicited by *h*, and *r*. One of the greatest errors of stimulus generalization, and thus one of the greatest difficulties in learning, occurs with *b* and *d*. As has generally been ob-served with children, and as was shown in the results described in the last part of the book, the child has great difficulty in learning the *d* when he has just learned the *b*. He will say B when the *d* is shown and he will say D when the *b* is shown, which would be expected on the basis of the principle of stimulus generalization.

The child's learning task would be easier if there was little similarity in the letter stimuli. If we were to construct an alphabet now, on the basis of what we know about learning principles, and on the basis of detailed experimentation, we would certainly design our letters to mini-mize difficulty because of similarity and the stimulus generalization which results. Actually, there are movements afoot to change our orthog-raphy, which will be mentioned. However, whether they fulfill the requirements of being based upon knowledge of learning principles as well as detailed and systematic research are matters that should be questioned.

In addition to the physical similarity in the letter stimuli, a learning analysis also suggests certain other matters of relevance—especially when the language is English. As has been suggested, simply acquiring 26 S–R mechanisms, as in learning to sound letters, plus the skill involved in sounding out words letter by letter, constitutes a very difficult learning task. Thus, just learning *one* response each to the 26 English letters as well as how to read them in series would be enough of a learning task. However, every letter that has to control more than one response increases the difficulty of the learning task. Every case in which there are several letters controlling a single response also adds to this difficulty. When these complexities are involved it means that other stimuli besides the letter itself have to come to control the response that is elicited.

While there have not been systematic analyses in terms of learning principles, and the experimentation has not been of the laboratory variety with the detail and control it offers, some of the difficulties involved in written English have been recognized. In addition, there have been many suggestions pertaining to the solution of some of the difficulties. It may be helpful to consider some of the issues involved in some of the solutions to these problems.

Sir James Pitman designed a new alphabet (initial teaching alphabet, or *i.t.a.*) and a new method of spelling in the attempt to develop "a more simple and more consistent initial teaching medium . . . for the early stages of learning to read" (Downing, 1964, p. 11). This method was based upon the 40 sound analysis of English speech forms made by Isaac Pitman. The *i.t.a.* method simplifies the alphabet and spelling, so that there is a greater proportion of one-letter-one-sound S–R mechanisms—and there are relatively few cases where one stimulus controls multiple responses, or where multiple stimuli control the same response.

In addition, however, the method was devised so that the words are not as markedly different from normally spelled English words as some reform spelling methods that have been suggested. That is, Pitman's system was also devised to ease the child in his transition from reading in *i.t.a.* to reading in traditional orthography.

The best way of describing the system is to depict its alphabet and a sample of a passage printed in the alphabet. Table 16.1 is taken from Downing (1964, p. 15). It shows the *i.t.a.* alphabetic characters, gives an example of the character as used in a word, and gives the word spelled in the traditional alphabet. Figure 16.2 also gives an example of a passage printed in *i.t.a.*

As Table 16.1 shows, the multiple control of vocal responses by vowels is largely eradicated thus attempting to simplify the reading task. That is, there are 15 vowel characters, almost all of which must control a response that is different from the responses controlled by any of the other vowel characters. In a few cases, however, the difficulties of multiple control are unfortunately retained. Thus, for example, *a* controls the "ah" response, as in *far;* the character *au* controls the "au" response, as in *autumn;* and the character *o* controls the "o" response, as in *hot.* There is no difference in the responses of the latter two, and there is (as we shall see) such a small difference between these two and the first that we can consider them all to involve the same response.

In terms of a learning analysis, of course, one stimulus should in most instances control a particular response, and there should be as few S–R elements as are necessary. Thus, we see that in retaining unnecessary complexity the *i.t.a.* methods retain some of the defects of traditional

TABLE 16.1

THE AUGMENTED ROMAN ALPHABET.

Number	Character	Name	Example	Traditional spelling
1	æ	ae	ræt	rate
2	b	bee	big	big
3	c	kee	cat	cat
4	d	dee	dog	dog
5	ɛɛ	ee	mɛɛt	meet
6	f	ef	fill	fill
7	g	gae	gun	gun
8	h	hae	hat	hat
9	ie	ie	tie	tie
10	j	jae	jelly	jelly
11	k	kae	kit	kit
12	l	el	lamp	lamp
13	m	em	man	man
14	n	en	net	net
15	œ	oe	tœ	toe
16	p	pee	pig	pig
17	r	rae	run	run
18	s	ess	sad	sad
19	t	tee	tap	tap
20	ue	ue	due	due
21	v	vee	van	van
22	w	wae	will	will
23	y	i-ae	yell	yell
24	z	zed or zee	fizz	fizz
25	ʒ	zess	houʒes	houses
26	wh	whae	when	when
27	ʧh	chae	ʧhick	chick
28	ʧh	ith	ʧhaut	thought
29	ʃh	thee	ʃhe	the
30	ʃh	ish	ʃhip	ship
31	ʒ	zhee	meʒuer	measure
32	ŋ	ing	siŋ	sing
33	ɑ	ah	fɑr	far
34	au	au	autum	autumn
35	a	at	appl	apple
36	e	et	egg	egg
37	i	it	dip	dip
38	o	ot	hot	hot
39	u	ut	ugly	ugly
40	ω	oot	bωk	book
41	ꞷ	oo	mꞷn	moon
42	ou	ow	bou	bough
43	oi	oi	toi	toy

From *The Initial Teaching Alphabet Reading Experiment* by John Downing. Reprinted by permission of Scott, Foresman and Company.

orthographies. It may be suggested that it is not necessary to have a different symbol to control responses that are only slightly different. This conclusion was made on the basis of the research results discussed previously. It will be remembered that Jennifer was trained to make an unvoiced sibilant response to the letter *s*. This response is the one that is properly controlled by the *s* when it appears in a word following an unvoiced consonant like *t* or *p*. On the other hand, when *s* follows a voiced consonant like *d* or *b* the letter must control a voiced consonant response (*z* sound) as in *lids* or *bibs*.

It might be thought that it would be necessary to introduce two letters to control the two different vocal responses—the unvoiced and voiced sibilant responses. However, a detailed learning analysis, as well as the experimental results, suggest otherwise. That is, although Jennifer was trained to respond to the *s* with an unvoiced sibilant response, when a word was introduced in which the *s* should control a voiced sibilant she would read it correctly without further training. There was no need to train the two responses each one under the control of a different stimulus.

Since ordinarily a learning analysis would suggest that one stimulus-one response learning would be less difficult, a moment may be given to indicating why in this type of case it appears that it is more efficient to have only one stimulus for two responses. The rationale involves consideration of the control over the reading response which occurs on the basis of word associations. In simple form only one letter *s* is needed *because the child's previously established word associations will guarantee the emission of the correct sibilant response.* In fact, the control is so strong that most people do not even realize that the printed *s* character actually controls two different responses.

The learning analysis goes as follows. In the child's language experience he learns very strongly the "word association" sequence of responses T——→S, P——→S, K——→S, and so on, where the *s* response is a voiceless sibilant. Thus, whenever he says a word that ends in one of these consonants, this *response* controls the pronunciation of the voiceless *s* when a sibilant response is called for. It would make no difference if the word response CATS was controlled by the visual stimulus of several cats or by the word *cats*. The type of *s* sound the child makes is guaranteed (controlled) by the type of consonant it follows. That is, the voiceless consonant and voiceless sibilant responses may be considered to be joined into a unit by virtue of numberless practice trials in everyday language experience, and the same is true for the voiced consonant and voiced sibilant response unit. Since we can depend upon this control by the time the child begins to read, we do not have to add the additional difficulty of another letter to the training task of the child.

Thus, although the system of Pitman is based upon a close inspection of written and vocalized English, an analysis based upon learning principles and experimental results gives us opposing suggestions for improving the teaching of reading. That is, following the present example, the *i.t.a.* system has three different characters to control the sibilant (voiced and unvoiced) responses. It would seem that two of these characters are unnecessary and needlessly complicate the child's learning to read.

Furthermore, this case is not the only one that involves this analysis. *I.t.a.* has two characters to control the "oo" sound as in *rule,* two characters to control the sibilant responses in *measure* and *ship,* two characters to control the "th" sounds in *thought* and *the,* and so on. It should be remembered that in each of these cases the unnecessary additional characters in the alphabet make the learning task more difficult in two ways. The sheer increase in number of S–R mechanisms increases the difficulty of the task. In addition, the similarity of the letter stimuli involved in each case guarantees that a very difficult discrimination will be involved—with many errors through stimulus generalization. It is apparent that the principle of stimulus generalization, and the errors caused on the basis of this principle, did not figure into the development of the *i.t.a.*

Lest the reader feel that this account is entirely critical of *i.t.a.*, it should be stated that many of its propositions are in sound agreement with a learning analysis. Its basic purpose of simplifying early reading learning, allowing it to be more regular so that the child learns one response to one stimulus, is well supported by the present experimental and theoretical analysis. Moreover, some educational data has been collected (see Downing, 1964) which supports the advantage of use of *i.t.a.* materials over traditional materials in the teaching of reading. Apparently, children taught with *i.t.a.* materials learn to read more rapidly than children taught with traditional materials. There is evidence that the children taught with *i.t.a.* do better in accuracy and comprehension of reading after they have been transferred to traditional materials, and on speed of reading they do as well as children who have been trained with traditional materials all the time. This evidence suggests that beginning the training with *i.t.a.* materials does not involve a difficult change to the traditional alphabet and spelling. However, these conclusions must at this time still be considered as tentative.

In addition, there is good reason to make the reading acquisition task easy at the beginning even though the system means that there will be some problem of transfer to regular materials later on. This conclusion rests upon several aspects of the analysis. First, it is in the beginning that the child has such a great many general (basic behavioral) responses to learn. In addition, to the immediate learning of the letter-sound S–R mechanisms, the child has to learn the complex attentional repertoire involved in studying reading materials and following the teacher's instructions, and the complex "sounding out" repertoire; the order of the words as positional stimuli must come to control the order of eye movements, the stimulus control of the initial capital letter and the terminal period must be acquired, and so on, as will be discussed more fully later on.

In addition, if the child has learned to read in one set of materials, transfer to a similar set will include the carry over of word associations that have already been established in the original reading. The passage in Figure 16.2 is a good example. For many readers the word *fiet* in the

wee ʃhall fiet

bie ſir winston ɖhurɖhill

ɛɛven ſhœ larj tracts ov uerop, and meny œld and fæmus stæts hav faullen or mæ faull intœ ſhe grip ov ſhe gestapœ and aull ſhe œdius apparætus ov nazi rœl, wee ʃhall not flag or fæl. wee ʃhall gœ on tœ ſhe end, wee ʃhall fiet in frans, wee ʃhall fiet on ſhe sees and œʃhans, wee ʃhall fiet wiſh grœiŋ confidens and grœiŋ streŋſh in ſhe ær, wee ʃhall defend our ieland, whotever ſhe cost mæ bee, wee ʃhall fiet on ſhe beeɖhes, wee ʃhall fiet on ſhe landiŋ grounds, wee ʃhall fiet in ſhe feelds and in ſhe streets, wee ʃhall fiet in ſhe hills; wee ʃhall never surrender, and ɛɛven if, whiɖh ie dœ not for a mœment beleev, ſhis ieland or a larj part ov it wer subjœgæted and starviŋ, ſhen our empier beyond ſhe sees, armd and garded bie ſhe britiʃh fleet, wœd carry on ſhe struggl, until, in god's gœd tiem, ſhe nue wurld, wiſh aul its pouer and miet, steps forſh tœ ſhe rescue and the liberæʃhion ov ſhe œld.

FIGURE 16.2.   From *The Initial Teaching Alphabet Reading Experiment* by John Downing. Reprinted by permission of Scott, Foresman and Company.

title will not immediately elicit the word response FIGHT. The accomplished reader will first pronounce it FEET, based upon his past training in traditional English. However, this response does not produce a usual word association, in common sense terms the phrase WE SHALL FEET is meaningless. Based upon the general habits he has acquired, however, the accomplished reader might look down and see that the quotation is from a statement by Winston Churchill—and the words "Winston Churchill," along with the WE SHALL beginning to the title, would tend to more strongly elicit the word response FIGHT.

Or, the accomplished reader may acquire the correct response to the *ie* letter stimulus by looking at the *bie Winston Churchill*. The name and the position of the words underneath a title, plus the *bie* itself, would tend to elicit the response of saying BY. This would only occur if these S–R mechanisms had already been established in the reader through past training. At this point it is still necessary that the reader look at the *ie* alone and emit the response EYE. Then he has to return to the word *fiet*, look at the first letter and emit the *f* sound then look at the *iet* and emit the *ight* sound.

This is a complex analysis even for this simple piece of transfer. What the example demonstrates, however, is that the training on the traditional orthography transfers to the passage written in *i.t.a.* on the basis of very complex repertoires of responses that the accomplished reader has acquired in his extensive reading learning. The transfer of training takes place easily because of these previously acquired repertoires. It may be added that the transfer in the opposite direction, from *i.t.a.* to traditional orthography, may be thought to take place on the basis of the same repertoires. The point is, however, that since these repertoires are so important in reading, and so difficult to acquire, that it makes good sense to train the child to the complex repertoires using the simplest materials available. After the child has acquired the complex repertoires, the materials can be changed back to their traditional complexity.

While *i.t.a. appears* to better accomplish the training of the repertoires necessary to good reading through the use of simplified materials, and while transfer to regular materials apparently occurs while maintaining an advantage over traditional teaching materials, this is not to say that the transfer is made without any drawbacks. Nor is this to say that *i.t.a.* materials are the best training materials that can be devised. The fact of the matter is, no research has been conducted which will yield either of these types of information. The research done so far suggests that *i.t.a.* is better than traditional methods. Where its strengths and weaknesses are, including the difficulty of transfer to traditional methods, cannot be gotten from the research, or indeed from traditional types of educational research in general. And, nothing is known about the value of alternative types of reading training materials. *It would be premature to change to this system, which has not been investigated in detail or in depth either experimentally or theoretically.* Even on the basis of the present analysis it is quite evident that *i.t.a.* itself will not be anywhere close to the final set of initial training methods we will develop. More will be said of the need for more exacting experimentation. First, however, it will be productive to mention shortly several other attempts to solve the training problems involved in reading acquisition.

Another system for guaranteeing a one letter-one response type of learning materials underlay the use of the diacritical marks in the laboratory studies presented in the preceding part of the book. That is, in each case where a letter has to come to control more than one response, the letter could be joined with diacritical marks so that each letter and diacritical mark combination would control a different response. On this basis, regularity in reading could be gained. That is, this system would make it relatively simple to acquire the sounding out repertoire, each letter always eliciting the same response in forming the word.

As the child received more training in reading whole words the combination of stimuli in a word would acquire controlling properties over the response, in addition to the letter and diacritical mark. When these "contextual" stimuli had acquired sufficient control the diacritical mark could be eliminated, leaving only the standard letters as the alphabet.

As an example, although the *a* might be introduced with a diacritical mark to control the A response in the word *dad*, after the child had said the whole word many times while looking at the word, the *a* in combination with the other letters would control the proper A response. At this point the diacritical mark could be removed.

Thus, there would be relatively little difficulty with transfer from a diacritical mark alphabet to a regular alphabet. However, there would be problems of the original complexity of the alphabet learning, unless additional modifications were introduced. That is, when each letter-diacritical mark character is supposed to control a different response, a very large original alphabet results. Moreover, there would be great similarity between the characters that were formed from the same letter, or letter combination, and this complicates the learning task. And different letter-diacritical mark characters would still have to control the same response.

Thus, to achieve a maximally effective system, additional simplification would be necessary. This could be done by introducing only a functional set of characters at the beginning and then slowly adding characters. As an example, the *á* might at first be the only character to control the *ah* response. Let us also say that the slash mark would be used for silent letters—letters not to be pronounced. Following this example, words like *father, autumn, awful, hot,* and *bought* would be spelled variously as *fáther, áμtumn, áμ̈ful, hǎt,* and *báμ̈g̈ht.* Gradually, the regular letters could be introduced so that *autumn* became *autumn* after a sufficient number of training trials, and then finally *autumn,* again after a sufficient number of training trials. In addition, the letter *o,* or the letter *o* with a diacritical mark, would later have to be introduced and equated with the *ǎ.* Thus, the child would have to have training trials in which he said the same word to both *hot* and *hǎt.* The efficacy of this type of training would of course have to be demonstrated experimentally.

In addition to these methods of training reading, Bloomfield and Barnhart (1961) have suggested that complications in acquiring reading may be lessened through removing the irregularities in spelling in the early materials presented to the child. This "linguistic" method is actually a way of establishing letter and syllable units that control vocal response units beginning with simple words and progressing to the more complex Thus, the child is presented with words like *ban, can, fan, man, tan, san, lan,* and so on. Later he is trained to read *bat, cat, fat, mat, tat,* and so on, and then these two types of words are combined in the following manner: *A fat cat ran.* This type of training can be expected to yield reading units where consonant letters will control the consonant phonemes and the syllables *at* and *an* will come to control the appropriate syllabic responses. This method can be seen to be a modification of the whole word teaching methods: that is, the letters are not presented separately, but in letter combinations. Through the type of "concept formation" presentation of the words the child learns unit responses to the letter units of which the words are composed. This process was demonstrated experimentally in an earlier chapter.

In addition, there are more traditional methods of training children to read based upon whole word, or "look-say" presentation procedures. And there are traditional methods of training the child to read which involve a concerted attempt to directly train reading units. These are usually called phonic methods. The types of repertoire that the various methods must produce in the child, analyzed in terms of learning principles, have already been described. In addition, experimental results were cited to indicate that the child could learn the various repertoires with either whole word, phonic, or "linguistic" training methods.

This is by no means meant as a comprehensive discussion of different methods of training reading. However, on the basis of this brief summary, as well as the preceding analyses, it is possible to derive some conclusions concerning the development of a more profound analysis of reading materials as well as practical procedures for applying the materials. First, in all the time that methods of teaching reading have been studied, we have not gained a detailed analysis of what reading is, what acts constitute reading, or what are the principles by which the acts are acquired. The naturalistic observations gained from teaching the child to read do not yield either type of information. The traditional research conducted on reading merely compares methods. There has not been detailed and systematic study of the learning which takes place within a particular method of training. Furthermore, we have not had an experimental method which could tell us, except in a very gross way, which method is better or why it is better. Nor have we formerly had a method for studying in detail the nature of the complex learning task.

More will be said of the present methodology and research possibilities in the final section of the book. At this point is is only suggested that the traditional research in reading does not provide the basis for crystallizing either an orthography, for example *i.t.a.*, or methods of teaching reading—even in use as a beginning instrument. Taking *i.t.a.* as the example, while it probably improves the traditional orthography, the preceding analysis indicated that it was not by any means a finished product arrived at after detailed and systematic research.

Thus, *i.t.a.* cannot be considered a maximal improvement. Moreover, widespread introduction of this type of training method materials would tend to fix progress. A major reason preventing reform of the English orthography is the tremendous expense of reprinting new materials and so on, and of the relearning involved for the mass of people trained on traditional orthographies.

Since there is such tremendous expense involved, it would be folly to make changes that would themselves require large scale changes at a later time. Any changes that are introduced should be done so on the basis of systematic, detailed research which involves observations made upon each aspect of the learning task—not simply on the basis of grossly comparing one set of materials to another. With the methods of experimentation outlined herein, it should be possible to work out an orthography that maximizes the learning conditions involved—which as the preceding analysis has demonstrated is not the case with the *i.t.a.* On the basis of such research it should be possible to tell how many characters should go into an initial teaching alphabet; when new characters may be added since it is not mandatory that all characters be introduced at the beginning; when modified characters (for example, *i.t.a.* type characters, or diacritical mark characters) should be gradually eliminated and replaced by standard letters; and so on.

This type of research is now distinctly possible, based upon detailed learning analyses of the complex act of reading and the experimental methods of learning. More will be said of this later. At this point the discussion will return to the analysis of remaining aspects of the reading repertoire.

Eye Movements in Reading

Eye movements have been discussed in the context of attention as motor responses which can be brought under the control of discriminative stimuli according to the principles of reinforcement. The same type of analysis may be extended to consideration of the types of eye movements that must be learned in acquiring a reading repertoire.

Speech as an auditory stimulus does not have spatial characteristics of order. The ordering of vocal responses occurs on a temporal dimension. In presenting stimuli that are to control sequences of vocal responses, however, there must be stimuli that control the order of emission of the responses. Since order is a prime consideration in vocal speech, it must be present in visual verbal stimuli in some manner so the stimuli control the correct order of responses.

As we all know, the primary visual stimuli that control the order of emission of reading responses are spatial. The letter stimuli in a word must be responded to in our language from left to right if the subject is to finally emit the correct word response sequence. This means that the child in sounding out a new word must look first at the leftmost letter or syllable, then the next leftmost, and so on. This type of attentional responding will require prompting at the beginning, until the spatial stimuli themselves, the relation of the letters to each other in a left–right dimension, acquire stimulus control.

The same is true for reading words. The words as stimuli must be looked at beginning with the leftmost and moving word by word to the right. The child will not necessarily do this at first and training trials are required until the position of the words, regardless of the words involved, will control the sequence of looking and vocalizing.

In addition, of course, there are spatial stimuli in the top to bottom visual dimension that must also come to control the child's looking and vocalizing sequences. That is, the child must be trained not only to commence with the leftmost word, but also with the leftmost word at the top of the page. Thus, the positional stimuli of the printed page must come to control attentional responses that begin at the top, go from left to right, then to the next leftmost word that is second from the top, and so on. This constitutes a learning task in itself that has a certain amount of complexity and the child who is learning to read will continue to make errors for some time until the stimulus control has been acquired.

In addition to the spatial stimuli that must control the attentional-vocalizing sequences, there are several other visual stimuli that acquire some control over these sequences and hence the order of emitting reading responses. Thus, in English the beginning word in the sentence is capitalized and sentence termination is indicated by a period. As a consequence, it would be expected that if a subject were shown a group of words one of which was capitalized on the initial letter, that word would tend to be looked at first and responded to vocally, and the word followed by a period would be looked at and responded to later—even in the case where the spatial order has been distorted. Take the following sentence as an example.

party.
    the
       of
          aid
             the
                to
                   come
                      to
                         time
                           the
                             is
                             Now

Someone asked to read this group of words as a sentence will first look at the topmost, leftmost, word. This response will occur because of our training to respond to those spatial stimuli. The individual will probably also read several more words in the left-to-right and top-to-bottom direction. Not attaining problem solution, however, the stimulus of the period following *party* would be expected to control a response to this word as the lastmost word stimulus to respond to and the subject is likely then to look all the way down the line of words to the word *Now*. Since the first letter of this word is capitalized the subject now has two stimulus controls for responding to the words in a right-to-left and bottom-to-top manner. If he does so the word responses he emits will match a sequence he has already learned and this will constitute problem solution.

This little exercise indicates that the capitalization of initial letters and the period at the end of a sentence come to also exert stimulus control over the order of the reading responses. In addition, and for the same reasons it may be suggested that words that many times occur at the beginning of sentences will acquire some control over the order of attentional responses involved in reading. Articles such as *the*, for example, and the personal pronouns, although they occur in various positions in sentences have a greater frequency in initial positions in sentences than do certain other word stimuli. As such they should come to control attentional responses more strongly than the other types of words.

EYE-MOVEMENTS WHILE READING   It has been reliably observed a number of times that expert readers do not look at each word they read, much less each letter they read. The expert reader's attentional response will fall on only a proportion of the words he reads—that is, his eyes will stop on only a few words in a sentence. Apparently, the expert reader responds to phrases as stimulus units rather than just to words. (This analysis is more complicated as will be shown in the next section discussing word associations and the next chapter discussing reading comprehension.)

The poor reader on the other hand tends much more to look at each word he reads. He also goes back to words he has already read more frequently. Thus, there is a definite difference between poor and accomplished readers on the types of eye-movement responses they make in reading. It is on this difference that one method for improving reading skills is based. That is, one method of improving reading is to provide training to subjects in moving their eyes not from word to word but in jumps that take in multiple words. The method thus attempts to teach the type of eye-movement responses that expert readers make.

It is certainly conceivable that a person could have acquired the various repertoires involved in being an expert reader and thus only require in addition that he make expert eye movements. This is unlikely, however, since the training that would provide the various repertoires of an expert reader would be likely to train eye movements of at least minimal expertness. Furthermore, it is likely that the individual who is a poor reader *is* a poor reader not only because of his poor eye movements, which in themselves are simpler responses than the other repertoires involved in reading. That is, it is likely that for the poor reader other aspects of the complex repertoire are poorly developed, for example, the verbal stimuli have not strongly come to control appropriate word and phrase responses (as well as the other responses to be discussed).

If this is the case the individual could be trained to move his eyes properly, but this would have little effect on his reading ability. The reading repertoires already described are much more complex and thus difficult in acquisition than the eye-movements themselves. The eye-movements, and the rapidity of reading, are a function of the strength to which the words and phrase stimuli strongly control word responses and sequences of word responses, as well as the meaning responses to be described. It is for this reason that even expert readers read with poor eye-movements when the verbal passages are new and difficult.

It is likely, following this analysis, that training supposedly to produce better eye-movements probably has its greatest effect in providing the subjects with general reading training—as well as improving the attentional responses themselves. Actually, the effects are probably largely motivational and ephemeral.

Word Associations in Reading Acquisition

Word association sequences that the individual has acquired in his general language experience play as important a role in an analysis of reading comprehension as they do in understanding reading acquisition. In fact, the function is so similar it is difficult to consider the topics entirely separately. However, the description of the importance of this S–R mechanism for reading acquisition can at least be enjoined at this time, saving discussions of reading comprehension for later.

In describing the learning of reading it has been suggested that "stimulus word-vocal response" mechanisms must be established so that presentation of the word stimulus controls the appropriate vocal response. In the act of reading, at least in the beginning stages, the reader looks from word to word, each stimulus controlling (hopefully) the appropriate word response. The formation of word associations in this process should have a considerable effect upon the skill of reading.

Let us say, for example, that the child is reading the phrase *The table and chair.* Each word stimulus has some tendency to control the appropriate word reading response, let us say. However, as a function of the child's language experience, in our culture at any rate, it is likely that the word association sequence TABLE AND CHAIR will have been established in some strength. As a consequence, there will actually be two sources of response strength for the reading responses AND CHAIR. That is, after the child has read the words *The* and *table* when he looks at the word *and* it will tend to control the saying of AND. In addition, the previous response the child has emitted, that is TABLE, will also tend to elicit the response AND as a word associate. It is thus more likely that the child will read the word *and* correctly than it would be if he has no word association strength between the word responses TABLE AND.

The same analysis is true for reading the next word in the phrase, the word *chair.* Having just said TABLE AND the word associate CHAIR tends to be elicited, thus contributing to any tendency the printed word has as a stimulus for eliciting the response CHAIR.

The author (Staats and Staats, 1963, p. 463) first suggested this as an hypothesis. However, Samuels (1965) has since provided experimental verification of the hypothesis showing that children can read the second of two words, previously unknown, when that word is an associate of the first word which they are able to read. It may be suggested again that the role word associations play in the reading acquisition should be studied closely. It may be suggested again, as Samuel's study exemplifies, that a theoretical analysis of a complex skill like reading into its S–R components can lead to experimental hypotheses. Furthermore, the hypotheses could be used as a basis upon which to construct improved reading materials.

Word association sequences also play an important part in the learning process in another way. It has already been stated that the accomplished reader learns to read in phrases, that is, combinations of words become stimulus units that control groups of word responses as units. It was suggested that this is the type of repertoire that underlies the ability to acquire eye movements that focus only on a proportion of the word stimuli covered. It may be suggested that one way a group of word stimuli become joined into a unit is initially influenced by the strength of associations between the word responses they control. Thus, the individual's word associations in reading may be considered to be one of the determinants of his speed of reading and retention of what he has read.

For example, how many words have to be focused upon in the following phrase: *I pledge allegiance to the flag of the United States of America* . . . ? Very few. The word associations are so strong that one look is enough to elicit the several responses that control the entire sequence.

It may be suggested in general that when we read material where the word stimuli control word responses that have strong tendencies to elicit one another in the order read, these word associational tendencies are a strong source of control for what is read. The reader is then not as strongly dependent upon the word stimuli themselves. This will be reflected by his eye-movements—which will take in more words per stop—as well as by the rapidity with which the individual reads. An individual may read very rapidly and well when the verbal material is of this type, but not nearly as well when the verbal material does not control word responses that are associated.

Thus, the individual's repertoire of word association sequences, established in his general language experience, play an important role in learning to read and in the extent to which the individual reads rapidly and comprehends well. In addition, the word associational repertoire contributes to the learning of reading in another way. Any condition that enhances reading rapidity and ease of reading means the child will read more given the same opportunity—and this produces more additional learning. Moreover, as will be apparent later, the greater the ease and rapidity of reading the more reinforcement is available for reading—thus, promoting more frequent reading behavior and its products of additional skills.

For these reasons, it can be seen that this aspect of what is usually called general language facility—the child's word associational repertoire —contributes greatly to reading acquisition and, as we shall see, to reading function.

One point of qualification should be inserted here. Word associations can be so strong in reading material, as in the case of the pledge of allegiance example just given, that the reader does not have to look at the words. While this may aid reading performance, this type of material is not appropriate for the beginning reader. If the child can make the verbal responses without looking at the letters and words, then he will not be learning vocal responses under the control of the printed stimuli. Thus, an actual reading program should be designed to utilize word associations productively, but not so they interfere with the learning. The present discussion aims only to indicate the function of word associations in learning to read and in the performance of reading.

MEANING RESPONSES CONTROLLED BY PRINTED VERBAL STIMULI: READING COMPREHENSION ACQUISITION

As the anecdote used to introduce the present chapter suggested, the control of vocal responses by printed and written verbal stimuli is not the only repertoire involved in reading acquisition. The preceding section has given a detailed analysis of how letters, words, phrases, and other stimuli come to control vocal responses in the acquisition of a skilled reading repertoire. However, a child could easily be trained to make vocal responses under the control of visual verbal stimuli in an entirely nonfunctional manner—as the American intelligence agent in the anecdote had been trained to read Russian letters and words.

For the America intelligence agent, the words he read were in common sense terms "meaningless," or nonfunctional. Reading acquisition obviously involves more than the control of vocal responses by printed and written words. The present section will discuss certain aspects of this learning that in various ways result in "meaningful" reading. This section, and several to follow will thus deal with the topic of "reading comprehension" and the learning that is involved in reading and comprehending what is read.

Word Meaning and Reading

In the first part of the present book the classical conditioning of word meaning was described. It was suggested that words come to elicit responses in the process of classical conditioning. A word paired with a stimulus that elicits a response will also come to elicit at least part of that response.

In this discussion the term *word* referred to words as auditory stimuli spoken by someone else or by oneself. The present discussion will be concerned with consideration of the learning of word meaning when the stimuli are the visually presented verbal stimuli involved in reading.

As has been suggested, when a new word is presented to the child it will at first control no particular response. If, however, the child has a grapheme-phoneme reading repertoire, the word stimulus, or its parts, will control a series of part word responses. At this stage of the process, then, the word controls a series of syllable responses.

However, the properly trained child will continue to sound out the syllables until he finally says a word that he has already experienced. At this point he will repeat the word response while looking at the word stimulus. In this process he is providing himself with training that will bring the word response under the control of the word stimulus.

Let us say, however, that the word response (as an auditory stimulus) has come in the child's past conditioning history to elicit a meaning response. *This being the case, the meaning response elicited by the word response would be conditioned to the written word stimulus.* That is, the word stimulus elicits the spoken word response, the word response (as an auditory stimulus) elicits the meaning response, and the meaning response is classically conditioned to the printed word stimulus (higher-order classical conditioning).

This three stage process of learning word meaning on the visual (reading) presentation of the word may be recapitulated in the following example. In stage one the written word stimulus *chocolate,* let us say, as a discriminative stimulus controls the sounding out sequence of responses. In stage two the word comes to control the whole word response, CHOCOLATE. In stage three, through repeated reading of the word, the meaning response, elicited by saying the word, is conditioned to the written word stimulus.

When this conditioning has taken place, it is suggested that the printed word stimulus itself will directly elicit the meaning response. It is no longer necessary that the word stimulus first elicit the vocal word response; the vocal word response then eliciting the meaning response. Since one link in the chain has dropped out, it would be expected that the process could now occur in less time. That is, when the meaning response has been directly conditioned to the written word stimulus the process of reading should occur much more rapidly.

The importance of this may be recognized more fully when it is realized that not just one word is involved but rather a vast repertoire of words. That is, the individual who has been conditioned to directly respond with meaning responses to a vast number of visually presented words will read much more rapidly, with "comprehension," than the individual who has a lesser repertoire of this sort. The latter individual will have to *say* the word before the passage becomes meaningful. On this basis, it would be expected that part of the ease and rapidity of reading would depend upon the extent to which the individual has acquired a repertoire of printed words that directly elicit meaning responses. (Of course, many words would still involve vocalization.)

The process of conditioning meaning responses to printed words probably also involves combinations of words. Thus, the words *raining cats and dogs* could come to be a unitary stimulus which would directly control a meaning response in the reader who has a meaning for the phrase on an auditory basis and who has reading experience that has conditioned the meaning to the printed phrase.

Thus far, in describing the process of conditioning meaning responses directly to printed word stimuli, the types of meaning responses have been left unspecified. It may serve at this time to briefly mention several of the types of meaning that printed verbal stimuli should come to directly elicit.

Evaluative Meaning

As described in the first part of the book, one of the important types of word meaning involves the responses made to positive reinforcing stimuli or negative reinforcing stimuli. There is a large class of words whose members are paired with diverse stimuli that have positive reinforcing characteristics, for example. It would be expected on the basis of classical conditioning that the reinforcing emotional response in each case, or part of the response, would be conditioned to the word. Responses other than emotional responses are customarily also conditioned to different words. However, all words that have been paired with reinforcing stimuli may be considered to elicit a reinforcing emotional response which in part forms the meaning of the word.

It would be expected that in the process of reading acquisition described above many printed words would also come to directly elicit reinforcing meaning responses. For example, it would seem that words like *fun, gift, smile, joy, money, home, happy, friend, food, candy, music, sweet,* and so on, when presented as visual stimuli would directly elicit a positive reinforcing meaning response in the accomplished reader. As a later discussion will outline, the reinforcing meaning of words would seem to play a part in the act of reading as well as in reading acquisition.

An analogous repertoire must also be established for words with negative evaluative (reinforcing) meaning. Thus, printed words like *ugly, pain, bitter, die, sad, hate, sick, ashamed, worry, suffer, dirty,* and the like, come to directly elicit the negative meaning response in the accomplished reader. When this has happened simply looking at the word should elicit the negative meaning response.

Denotative Meaning

As was discussed in the first part of the book, however, there are additional types of word meaning, that is, other types of response that are conditioned to words to form their meaning for the individual. One other type that appears to be conditioned according to classical conditioning principles has been called *denotative* meaning. This refers to the hypothesis that sensory stimuli elicit sensory responses in the individual, and that these sensory responses can be classically conditioned to words with which they are contiguous.

It may be suggested that printed words may also come to elicit these conditioned sensory responses. Thus, single words such as *bell, train, screech, lemon, thunder, hot,* and so on would seem to come to elicit the responses in reading training that the spoken words themselves have come to elicit. That is, the printed words would come to elicit part of the sensory response process that the objects as sensory stimuli elicit.

Written passages that string together words with denotative meaning may be expected to elicit sensory responses that may as a result come to constitute a larger, elaborate, sensory response. Take as an example, the words *hot, path, grass, stream, trees;* or instead the words *cold, path, snow, stream, trees.* It would be expected that each word in each group would elicit a type of conditioned sensory meaning response. The words read in each group in a series would be expected to elicit a group of sensory responses that constitutes a larger sensory response, or scene; the meaning response elicited by each word would be a function of the meaning responses elicited by the other words also. That is the word *trees* in the first group of words would be expected to elicit a different conditioned sensory response than the word *trees* in the second group, at least for individuals who have lived in climates where trees change in summer and winter.

It is thus suggested that words that elicit conditioned sensory responses can be arranged in written material (and spoken also) to produce composite sensory responses of a more complex nature. These word stimuli, through the conditioned meaning responses they elicit, are the building blocks for verbal descriptions. Through language, and in this case through reading, the individual because of these conditioned sensory responses can have sensory experiences in a vicarious way—without ever contacting directly the primary stimulus conditions. We know that this occurs, of course, from our common sense experience. The present analysis suggests, however, how this type of occurrence takes place according to lawful, predictable principles—the principles of classical conditioning.

It is also worthwhile indicating that the composite sensory response a group of words elicits may have reinforcing properties that each of the words by itself does not have. Thus, *path, grass, stream,* and *trees* may have as individual words relatively little reinforcement for a person. However, when put into a passage that elicits a composite sensory image of a country scene, the words may have much greater reinforcement properties. The reinforcement properties are elicited by the composite sensory image—not the words themselves.

It would seem that one of the dimensions of literary success involves the creation of such "composite sensory images" which themselves have reinforcement properties for the reader. It should also be pointed out here that although words may have negative reinforcing properties as individual words, in combination with other words this negative reinforcing value may not be elicited. A simple case is found in the word *bad.* When presented alone it elicits a negative evaluative meaning response. This is because it has been paired with negative reinforcing stimuli. The word when combined with *not,* however, as in *not bad,* does not elicit a negative reinforcing response. This would be expected according to classical conditioning principles since the words *not bad* are usually paired with more positive reinforcing stimuli than is the word *bad* alone.

In a similar fashion composite sensory images that have positive reinforcing properties may be created by putting together words with sensory meaning that is not positive, as mentioned above, or with words that actually elicit negative evaluative meaning. Thus, the words *fear, suffer, lost, hurt, starving,* and *cold,* while each has negative reinforcing meaning, could easily be put in a passage involving a lost hunting party, for example, which would have the positive reinforcing value of a story.

This short section does not intend to provide an analysis of literary composition and the like. However, it does suggest that questions pertinent to these types of topics are not inappropriately treated in the language of learning principles. In any event, it is suggested that an important aspect of reading involves the fact that words as printed stimuli come to elicit the meaning responses that the words elicit when presented auditorily.

Motor Response Meaning

The types of word meaning that have been discussed that appear to be conditioned to the printed word have involved classical conditioning. It is this type of response that has most frequently been called word meaning in psychology. The other types of responses that words as stimuli come to control through instrumental discrimination learning, however, can just as readily be treated under the term word meaning. That is, it has been suggested that the common term "word meaning" really refers to the functions that words have as stimuli, as $^{c \cdot r}S$, ^cS, and ^DS. Words come to elicit some responses according to classical conditioning principles—and this makes the words meaningful. Words also come to control other responses through operant conditioning principles and this may also make the words meaningful. This type of word meaning will now be discussed in the context of reading acquisition.

It was stated that words as discriminative stimuli come to control various motor responses. In fact, one of the important aspects of the child's basic behavioral repertoire involves the acquisition of a large number of responses under the control of word stimuli. The child who has had an adequate training will respond appropriately to verbal stimuli given by someone else.

It has also been stated that discriminative control of motor responses could be "transferred" on the basis of contiguity. That is, if one discriminative stimulus controls a motor response, the motor response will come under the control of other stimuli with which the discriminative stimulus is paired. This analysis may be applied to certain aspects of reading acquisition. Following the example used in Chapter 8, let us say that the auditorily presented word stimulus *close* has come to control the "closing" motor response. Let us also say that the child has learned to read the word *close* so that when it is presented he will say CLOSE. As was the case for the other types of word meaning, it would be expected that each time the child said the word CLOSE while looking at at the word, the discriminative control of the motor response would be transferred to the visual stimulus *close*. After a sufficient number of these reading training trials it would be expected that the printed word would also come to have the same kind of discriminative stimulus control over the motor response. Thus, as another example, the husband on returning home and reading his wife's note saying *Turn off the stove* will perform the relevant motor responses under the control of the written verbal stimuli.

In the child's spoken and reading repertoire there must be a large number of words that as auditory and visual stimuli come to have control over specific motor responses. The following passage is an example taken from a book instructing the reader in the motor skills of golf. For the reader to profit it is necessary that the verbal stimuli control the appropriate motor responses.

EACH TIME YOU WAGGLE THE CLUB BACK, THE RIGHT ELBOW SHOULD HIT THE FRONT PART OF YOUR RIGHT HIP, JUST ABOUT WHERE YOUR WATCH POCKET IS. WHEN THIS TAKES PLACE, THE LEFT ELBOW, AS IT MUST, COMES OUT SLIGHTLY, THE LOWER PART OF THE ARM FROM THE ELBOW DOWN ROTATES A LITTLE, AND THE LEFT HAND MOVES THREE INCHES OR SO PAST THE BALL TOWARD THE TARGET. AS THE HANDS MOVE BACK TO THE BALL ON THE FORWARD WAGGLE, THE LEFT HAND ALSO MOVES AN INCH OR TWO PAST THE BALL TOWARD THE TARGET (Hogan, 1957, pp. 66–67).

As we shall see, one of the important functions of a reading repertoire involves this type of control of motor responses by the printed word.

Word-Associational Meaning

As has been described previously words occur in contiguity with other words in our natural language experience. Because of this experience complex constellations of word associations are formed. A word response will come to elicit many other word responses, each of which itself elicits many other word responses. These word association structures help determine the nature of our speech production, thinking, reasoning, and so on.

One of the important types of learning that would seem to occur in the learning of a reading repertoire is that printed word stimuli would in the process acquire such word-associational meaning in the same manner that they acquire evaluative (or emotional) word meaning. That is, a printed word stimulus on first presentation would elicit no word associates. In the first step of the learning, the printed word stimulus must come to elicit the correct reading response. When this occurs, however, the vocal reading response would be expected to elicit its word associates. Thus, while the child looks at the printed word, various word associates would be implicitly elicited and conditioned to the printed word stimulus. It may be suggested that this is one of the processes that occurs in learning to read and in reading so that printed word stimuli come to directly elicit various word associates that the individual has acquired in his natural language experience. This must be part of the learning that produces skilled reading performance; that is, the skilled reader must acquire a large repertoire which involves printed and written words directly eliciting well learned word associates and which form part of what is called reading comprehension.

NUMBER RESPONSE MEANING A child could easily be trained to say ONE, TWO, THREE, and so on upon the presentation of the appropriate number. In addition, the child could be trained to read $1 + 2 = 3$, $2 + 5 = 7$, and so on, without in either example the reading being "meaningful." That is, meaningful reading of numbers, as with words, does not consist solely in bringing the appropriate vocal response under the control of the appropriate printed arithmetic stimulus.

Numbers as auditorily presented stimuli must first come to elicit meaning responses in a manner similar to the conditioning that takes place with words—if the number stimuli are to be meaningful. That is, the word *two* as an auditory stimulus will be different if the child has had a conditioning history in which the word *two* has been paired many times with *pairs* of various objects. With this type of conditioning history it would be expected, for example, that the sensory responses elicited by *pairs* would be conditioned to the word *two*.

Moreover, the stimulus *ten* will have been paired with the responses of counting to ten, both as a conditioned stimulus and as a discriminative stimulus. It would be expected that the stimulus word ten would as a consequence come to elicit certain sensory responses, as well as to control the motor responses involved in counting.

It may be suggested that these are the responses that come to be elicited by number stimuli and which constitute, at least in part, the meaning of those stimuli. It may also be suggested that in learning to read numbers these meaning responses are conditioned to the visually presented number stimuli and when this happens the child no longer has to say the numbers to himself, or to actually perform the responses involved in counting, and so on. Thus, at one stage of learning to read numbers it might be necessary for the child to stop and count and add before being able to profit from the printed statement $9 + 10 = 19$. Later on, however, each stimulus in the series will elicit the appropriate meaning responses and may be read very quickly.

This may only be considered to be a tentative outline of this type of meaning. No doubt the topic of the learning of a number repertoire demands a detailed analysis in terms of conditioning principles. The present discussion only suggests some of the S–R mechanisms that are likely to be involved and is intended to indicate, along with the preceding discussions of this repertoire, that an analysis in learning terms is not inappropriate.

CONCLUSIONS   In conclusion it may be said that words (produced by oneself or by someone else) are learned stimuli. Except by virtue of the individual's prior conditioning history these are neutral stimuli. This is true whether the mode of presentation of the word is auditory or visual. Originally, word stimuli are meaningless, they do not elicit the varieties of responses described. Whatever behavior they come to elicit or control depends upon conditioning experiences (other than the responses they elicit as members of the general class of visual or auditory stimuli).

Thus, bringing a vocal response under the control of a printed word stimulus imparts no additional functions to the printed word stimulus than just that—unless the vocal response (or the stimulus it produces) has already acquired other functions (meanings). If the vocal response already has other functions, that is, elicits other responses, then bringing the vocal response under the control of the printed word will impart these "functions" to the printed word according to the learning principles involved. At this point, the individual will read the printed word with comprehension. That is, the printed word will elicit the various "functions" that the auditory word elicits. Thus, printed verbal stimuli may become conditioned stimuli and elicit various types of responses such as conditioned sensory responses (images). In addition, the printed word may become a conditioned reinforcing stimulus and elicit either positive reinforcing responses or negative reinforcing responses. Furthermore, the printed word may become a discriminative stimulus and come to control various types of motor responses. Finally, the printed word may elicit word association responses, and responses involved in number concept learning. These various types of word meaning are involved in reading comprehension. When many, many, printed words have come to elicit or control such responses directly—without dependence upon the individual making a vocal response, or by making only a minimal vocal response —it is suggested that the individual can read more rapidly and more easily. His ability to read rapidly, with "comprehension," thus depends upon establishing a large repertoire of such word stimuli.

THE BASIC BEHAVIORAL REPERTOIRE
AND READING ACQUISITION

A moment may now be given to reconsidering the role of the basic behavioral repertoire in reading acquisition, to better emphasize the hierarchical nature of cognitive development. This will only be done in a "footnote" fashion, since the relevant discussions have already been made —but the reader could profitably review those discussions in the light of the description of reading acquisition that has just been presented.

By way of summary, the importance of the attentional repertoire the child brings to school may be seen more fully. The instructions of the teacher, as discriminative stimuli, must control the child's looking and listening responses. Otherwise the stimuli that the teacher provides will not affect the pupil. This control of attentional behaviors must be strongly established and maintained in the child's home life—for the reinforcement for this behavior in school is apt to be rather sparse. Thus, formal education depends heavily on the prior establishment in the child of a repertoire of social discriminative stimuli that will control his attentional behaviors, and other motor behaviors as well, and this is one of the responsibilities of training that the parent must largely assume.

The child must also have a well developed repertoire of vocal responses, and these vocal responses must be under good discriminative control. That is, when the teacher instructs the child to repeat a word or sound, the verbal stimuli must control the appropriate vocal response if the child is to learn. A child with articulatory problems, or a child whose vocal behavior is not under the control of verbal instructions will be retarded in his learning in school. Again, the responsibility for this type of training falls largely upon the parent.

Furthermore, the child must have a large repertoire of meaningful words. Getting the child to make the appropriate vocal response under the control of the appropriate printed word stimulus means little if the vocal response (as a stimulus) does not itself elicit or control other responses. The vocal response must elicit or control other responses for the vocal response itself to be functional (meaningful). In the process of reading, these other responses will be conditioned directly to the printed word, and then reading will become a more rapidly occurring process, capable of directly affecting the child's behavior.

The importance of the child's repertoire of word associations has also been indicated. Word associations play a role in "getting out" vocal responses that are as yet only weakly controlled by the printed word. When the child reads a word because of the preceding words he has read—this is something called knowing a word because of its context—it constitutes a learning trial in the same way it would if the teacher had had to tell the child the new word. In this way the child may learn many new words, based upon his own previous word associational learning. The other aspects of reading comprehension already described also depend upon previously learned repertoires which are of great complexity.

Even this short summary which neglects many aspects of the basic behavioral repertoire, shows why the child's experiential history is so important to the way he will progress in his later learning. If he has been fortunate in having adequate conditions of learning he will have an adequate repertoire and will be capable of profiting from the stimuli with which he is provided. If not, the stimuli will not produce the additional learning that is necessary for success.

Nothing has been said in this summary about the child's motivational repertoire. Since this is a topic that will be treated independently in another section, it will suffice to indicate here that motivational conditions for maintaining attentional and working behaviors are of utmost importance. And, most of the stimuli that are important reinforcers for the child in his learning are conditioned or learned reinforcers. Again, the nature of the child's motivational (reinforcement) system, as it pertains to his learning, will largely be a result of his home experiences, and the motivational system is an important part of the basic behavioral repertoire.

Reading Acquisition Through Reading

Before leaving the topic, we must make explicit a point that has been implicit in many of the previous descriptions of reading acquisition. It has been stated, taking one example, how the child who has learned a grapheme-phoneme reading repertoire will sound out new words. The auditory word stimulus produced in this manner will elicit a meaning response of some type which will be conditioned to the printed word.

The important thing to point out, however, is that this conditioning process takes place without external tuition. The child is *training himself to a reading repertoire,* upon the basis of his own previously learned repertoires. That is, the greater the number of these independently conducted sounding out trials, both in terms of the frequency with which one word is sounded, as well as in the number of different words read in this way, the larger and the more well learned will be the child's repertoire of word stimuli that directly elicit meaning responses. If he has many of these self-training trials, many words will quickly and surely elicit the correct meaning response upon visual presentation. If there are few of these self-training trials, the child's reading repertoire will remain a slowly occurring and laboriously conducted activity.

That the child learns reading from reading is certainly apparent if not well understood or exploited. It is important also to know in detailed learning terms what is involved in this type of self-learning both in terms of the repertoires that are necessary before it can take place, as well as the repertoires that are produced by self-learning. Furthermore, based upon such an analysis, it would seem important to design procedures for insuring that this type of learning will occur. Present school methods, while urging the child to read, do not provide for any standard self-training—much of it being left up to the child and his parents. Thus, there are children that read hundreds of books on their own, and other children that have read only a handful by the time they are ready to enter college.

Almost all of the learning of the accomplished reader in the various repertoires described, occurs after he has acquired a basic sounding out reading repertoire, that is, on the basis of the self-training involved in actually reading. Thus, the importance of the activity cannot be overemphasized and the topic will be mentioned again in describing the functions of reading as well as in describing some of the motivational aspects of reading acquisition and function.

COMMUNICATION THROUGH READING: READING FUNCTION (COMPREHENSION)

An important part of a learning analysis of language concerns the *function* of the behaviors analyzed. The preceding sections have described research and theoretical analyses of reading acquisition. To complete the account it is necessary to describe the manner in which the complex repertoires that constitute reading may function in producing new learning, new repertoirial skills. Only in this manner can the importance of this repertoire in the cognitive development of the individual be fully appreciated, and the hierarchial learning conception of cognitive development demonstrated.

The previous discussions of word meaning concerned the functioning of some S–R mechanisms commonly spoken of as "reading comprehension." This is also true of the types of learning now to be dealt with; reading as an act produces additional types of learning and this is also central to what is meant by reading comprehension.

Meaning Response Sequences

A traditional index of reading comprehension is that the reader "comprehends" when he can indicate the "sense" of the passage although he can not reproduce the actual words in the passage. This phenomena gives the impression that some ineffable "mental" process is involved. However, some of the S–R mechanisms that have been described can be used to account for the phenomenon. Moreover, the process involves an important type of learning that is produced through reading—the formation of sequences of meaning responses.

In Chapter 5, in describing how conditioned sensory responses may control sequences of verbal responses, it was indicated that direct experience can produce sequences of conditioned sensory responses where each response elicits the next. Thus, the person on a sight-seeing trip would acquire a sequence of conditioned sensory responses. This sequence could later control a sequence of verbal (labeling) responses which would be similar to the verbal responses that could be controlled by the actual events. It may be suggested that we can also acquire sequences of conditioned sensory responses from reading passages of words when some of the words in the passage each elicit a conditioned sensory response.

It may be suggested also that such a sequence of conditioned sensory responses may be learned from looking at the words in a passage even though word associations (word response sequences) are not strongly formed from this experience. (Young and Bousfield, 1959, have shown that meaning responses may be conditioned when word associations have not been formed.) Thus, the individual in reading a passage once may not have strong word associations formed as a result, and thus not be able to reproduce the passage. However, if a sequence of meaning responses has been formed, the individual can describe the "sense" of the passage. That is, the individual asked to describe what he has just read could then experience the sequence of conditioned sensory responses which would then control an appropriate sequence of verbal responses. As was described in the analysis of the verbal habit-families, in our language learning each conditioned meaning response comes to control not just one but rather a hierarchy of word responses. Thus, when an individual has learned a sequence of conditioned meaning responses the sequence of word responses emitted under the control of the meaning responses is subject to many variations. The individual may "describe" his conditioned meaning response sequence with various combinations of words—which may differ largely from the passage from which the sequence of conditioned meaning responses was acquired.

It should be stressed that the act of reading is important for its function in producing new sequences of classically conditioned meaning responses. These sequences may involve conditioned emotional responses (connotative or affective meaning), conditioned sensory responses (denotative meaning or images), or mixtures of the two. It should also be realized that reading a passage may produce other types of learning as well. Although the various types of S–R mechanisms formed through reading will be discussed separately, a reading passage may actually produce the various types in various combinations.

Word Response Sequences: Verbal Knowledge

The manner in which printed and written word stimuli come to elicit whole word responses has been described. When the child has acquired a repertoire of such S–R mechanisms one type of new learning can take place through the presentation of printed words. That is, each printed word stimulus in a passage, as it is looked at, will control a word response. As the child looks successively at the verbal stimuli he will thus emit a sequence of word responses. As a consequence, each word response (or the stimulus it produces) will come to tend to control the next word response—thus forming a word association sequence.

This is actually the process that takes place in paired-associate and serial verbal learning. Two or more verbal stimuli are presented in contiguity, each of which as a discriminative stimulus controls a vocal response. The vocal responses occurring in contiguity become associated in the sense that the first will tend to elicit the next as a response. Paired-associate and serial verbal learning is thus a paradigm for the acquisition of new verbal response sequences on the basis (in the usual case) of a previously acquired reading repertoire. Unfortunately, this research methodology has not been extended to the study of this type of communication—although it would lend itself to the task admirably.

To continue, however, much of what is called knowledge consists of the acquisition of word response sequences through reading. The child is presented with the word stimulus series *Columbus discovered America in 1492*, for example, and each word stimulus controls a vocal response, let us say. This experience would constitute a training trial in which each word response that was so elicited would come to tend to elicit the next one.

In the child's school training he will also probably learn that the verbal response sequence can be acquired more strongly if after reading the sentence he repeats to himself COLUMBUS-AMERICA-1492 and so on. In this manner he will insure a strong word association sequence—again, just like the training that occurs in verbal learning experiments.

Much academic learning consists of acquiring just such verbal response sequences. Sometimes, as we shall see, it is necessary that these verbal response sequences also control other behaviors, and this is the main value of acquiring the verbal response sequences. Many times, however, it is the verbal response sequence itself that is of concern. Thus, most written passages in history courses are read by the student to produce sequences of verbal responses (knowledge) which will be emitted under the appropriate circumstances. Learning in such fields is complete when the verbal response sequence has been acquired.

Ignoring the issue of whether the verbal response sequences themselves are sufficient, it is also useful to point out that much learning in arithmetic and mathematics takes place through the same process. Let us say, for example, that the child has learned to make the appropriate vocal response to the numbers from 1 to 10 and also to the signs $+$ and $=$. Let us say that he has also been trained to make the appropriate reading response sequence in several statements like $1 + 2 = 3$, his eye movements controlled by the position of the number stimuli. On the basis of this repertoire he will be able to acquire a basic set of adding sequences just through reading. Thus, when new numbers are presented in this manner, he will read them, that is, make a sequence of vocal responses which will be formed into a sequence. Through this type of self training, based upon his reading repertoire, he will acquire sequences of verbal responses which will later be the basis for his arithmetic addition repertoire. In this way, the child will acquire a repertoire of verbal number response sequences like THREE PLUS FOUR EQUALS SEVEN, TWO PLUS SIX EQUALS EIGHT, and so on.

Once the child has acquired this number reading repertoire, plus the appropriate vocal response under the control of the multiplication sign, he will also be able to acquire his multiplication tables through "self-conducted" reading training. The same processes are also involved in learning the sequences of verbal responses involved in much of mathematics. This discussion does not, of course, imply that the learning of arithmetic and mathematical verbal response sequences constitutes all the learning that is involved in these areas of study. In the preceding section on number meaning, for example, it was pointed out that the number responses had to control additional responses for the number reading to be meaningful. A full exposition of this topic is not of concern here. However, it may also be said that mathematical response sequences are many times important for the other behaviors they mediate in problem solving situations.

The word associations established through the reading repertoire also figure prominently in the analysis of what is generally termed communication, and propaganda. The author in the preceding passages and elsewhere (Staats, 1963, 1966; Staats and Staats, 1963) has given a more complete account of the importance of word association sequences in these areas as well as in problem solving and reasoning, and scientific behavior. In general it may be said that word associations constitute one of our important "thinking" mechanisms in our life adjustment in both intellectual and social problems and interactions. Furthermore, we acquire many of our word associations on the basis of our reading experience when we are literate. The printed verbal stimuli to which we respond constitute an important influence that determines our thinking, according to the principles of learning described.

Motor Response Sequences: New Skills through Reading

When we tell a child *stand up, close the door, come here,* and so on, if he has a conditioning history in which these stimuli have come to control the appropriate motor behaviors, he will behave in such a way that we say he "understands" or "comprehends." In the process of reading acquisition, as has been described, the same discriminative control is "transferred" to the written verbal stimuli. As the child looks at a written passage including words that control different motor behaviors the word stimuli will tend to elicit the respective motor responses in the sequence in which the words are looked at. (The word "tend" is used here because other supporting stimuli will ordinarily be necessary before the motor responses are actually performed.)

At any rate, with the appropriately trained child, when the individual words are read each one elicits a motor response, overtly or covertly. When the motor responses occur in a sequence this provides a learning trial in which each response (through the stimuli it produces) will eventually tend to elicit the next response. If this process is repeated the individual may acquire a smooth chain of motor responses simply on the basis of the printed verbal stimuli, provided of course that he has acquired the essential reading repertoire. When the sequence of motor responses has been repeated a sufficient number of times, it is no longer necessary for the individual to attend to the written verbal stimuli— the skill now becomes independent of that type of stimulus control.

This type of learning through reading occurs very widely. For example, manuals for various occupations consist of sequences of verbal stimuli whose main function is to control motor responses. The complex motor skill of driving could easily be imparted upon the basis of writing (provided the individual has also been trained to respond to the names of the stimulus objects involved, such as *ignition key, gear shift lever,* and so on). Mechanics acquire new sequences of motor responses through training manuals when new cars are introduced, and so on.

The passage on "waggling" which was quoted in the section on Word Meaning and Reading is a good example also. This passage includes a number of words many of which function to control a motor response. The aspiring golfer in reading this passage will respond appropriately when each of these words is attended to, and ultimately he will acquire the sequence so that he is independent of the manual. (He will have to do this for the other motor response sequences involved in the sport, of course, to become proficient.) This is not to say that the individual can in this manner become an expert at the game. Much more training is required than this. However, he will be able to gain in this manner the rudiments of the motor response skills required in this manner. And he will be able to improve his game later on by correcting some of his errors in performance through again consulting the written material. It must be said that on the basis of reading he will be much, much, further ahead than if his only experience with the game was an explanation of rules and goals involved—where he had to build up from scratch the entire motor skills involved. The acquisition of these skills, or those in any sport, customarily have required years and years in their development—and much of the progress in each case can be imparted on a verbal level, through the presentation of printed verbal stimuli to the individual with a reading repertoire.

It should also be indicated that this type of learning through reading may be provided by printed material of somewhat different types. That is, a blueprint or figure may function in the same manner as described. For example, when the individual has been trained to "read" blueprints these also will control his motor behaviors. The carpenter or other artisan will look at the blueprint in accord with his training and emit responses in a certain order that will result in a finished motor skill.

Learning Word Meaning from Other Words (Context)

One of the most important types of learning produced by reading is the applying of meaning to words not already meangingful. This process of learning new word meanings through reading may take place in a simple way when one consults the dictionary. For example, Webster's (1965) dictionary lists the word *tenebrous* as "shut off from the light:

gloomy, obscure." (p. 909) The reader who consults the dictionary and looks upon these word stimuli will receive as part of his learning the following type of conditioning. Let us say that he looks first at *tenebrous* and then at *gloomy*, to simplify the explication. *Tenebrous* as a visual word stimulus is a nonsense word, meaningless. *Gloomy*, on the other hand, let us say, elicits part of the sensory response that darkness elicits (as well as other meaning responses that may have been conditioned to it from pairings with other words). The meaning response to *Gloomy* will as a consequence be conditioned to *tenebrous*, at least to some extent. The subject of this example will ordinarily have learned to ensure that this conditioning to the written word will be made strong by repeating the word GLOOMY several times as he looks at *tenebrous*.

Of course the process just described would also condition the word response GLOOMY to the word *tenebrous*, besides conditioning the meaning of the word *gloomy* to tenebrous.. After sufficient conditioning experience with the word *tenebrous*, however, this word as a printed stimulus will directly elicit its meaning responses and the individual will no longer say the word GLOOMY to himself every time he encounters *tenebrous*.

It may be suggested that some of the individual's repertoire of meaningful words may be established in this manner, through reading definitions in a dictionary. However, an even more important type of learning of word meaning involves the conditioning that takes place in one's general reading—the process commonly referred to as learning from context. As an example, take the following passage. *He was a very hufod animal, always running here and running there, never still for a moment. Hufod animals are the healthiest, however. Choose one that is hufod and you will always be glad you did. Hufod ones are more fun besides.* The first sentence has the effect of pairing the new word *hufod* with *always running* and *never still*. The meaning responses elicited by these words would be conditioned to *hufod*. On such an occasion, the reader will ordinarily also have learned to go back and give himself repeated trials so that the meaning responses are strongly conditioned to *hufod*. He may then look in quick succession at the following words; *hufod-always running*, and *hufod-never still*. *Always running* and *never still*, moreover, will elicit the word associate *active*, for example, and the reader may say *hufod-active* several times, thereby providing himself with additional conditioning trials. In this process the meaning of the words *always running, never still*, and *active* would be acting as unconditioned stimuli and the meaning responses they elicit would be conditioned to *hufod*, giving this formerly meaningless word meaning.

Again, the various conditioning trials in this process would condition the sensory responses elicited by *always running, never still,* and *active* to the word *hufod.* In addition, direct word associations would be established between *hufod* and these other words. Thus, the word *hufod* would become meaningful in the process both by coming to elicit conditioned sensory responses (images) as well as through coming to elicit the meaningful words as associates.

The same process would occur with the other sentences in the passage. The second, third, and fourth sentence would provide pairings of *hufod* with *healthiest, glad,* and *fun.* Because of our common language training, however, for most English speaking individuals the words *healthiest, glad,* and *fun* all elicit a common response—a positive evaluative response or in other terms a positive reinforcing response. It would be expected as a result that the three sentences, among other things, would condition this common meaning component of these three words (acting as unconditioned stimuli) to the word *hufod.* As a consequence, the word *hufod* would itself become a positive reinforcing stimulus—that is a word that had positive emotional meaning.

Because of the great significance of the suggestion that words with positive evaluative meaning act as reinforcers, this analysis should be more fully explored. The above example described the manner in which the new written word stimulus could acquire reinforcing value—positive evaluative meaning. However, at the same time, it should be added, the process would be expected to make the vocal (or auditory) word response reinforcing also. That is, the reader was not only looking at *hufod* then saying the other words *healthiest, glad,* and so on, he also was saying HUFOD as well. That is, the reader would ordinarily look at *hufod* and sound out the word in the manner previously described, for part of the learning of a new word is to bring the proper vocal word response under the control of the new word stimulus. This would provide ample opportunity for the vocal word response (as a stimulus) to come also to elicit the positive emotional meaning that would give it reinforcing properties. This is complex learning but it could be diagrammed quite straightforwardly.

It is this somewhat complex mechanism that accounts for the fact that one's reading will effect one's general language behavior and thus one's behavior to the relevant social and physical events of the world. That is, through reading, let us say, a new word has come to be a positive reinforcer. Whenever this word is presented by someone else in the individual's everyday life it will now have its reinforcing effect as was demonstrated experimentally in an earlier chapter.

The importance of this type of learning and its effects upon our behavior can be realized by stating that the higher-order conditioning of meaning that is a type of communication can take place through reading in the same manner as through speech communication.

Thus, it may be generally suggested that attitudes and values towards the physical and social stimuli in everyday life can be established purely through the act of reading. When the individual looks at a printed word and makes a vocal response covertly and then looks at another printed word which elicits a meaning response, the meaning response will be conditioned to the first word. When the meaning response involved is a reinforcing response the new word will also become a reinforcer and will function in that manner in affecting the individual's behavior.

Thus, the writer, propagandist, and so on, may be considered to produce conditioning that has a determining action on the individual reader's general behavior. This process may be considered to be as lawful as any other type of conditioning. When the reader responds to written verbal stimuli he is being conditioned, perhaps in adjustive ways, perhaps in nonadjustive or maladjustive ways. This is not to say that the only source of conditioning that affects the individual's attitudes and values, for example, is the individual's reading. Many other experiences will also condition the individual, perhaps in ways incompatible with the conditioning he receives from reading some pasage. The S–R mechanisms by which the communicatee effectively counters the conditioning of the communication stimulus have already been mentioned in Chapter 8. Thus, to say that one's reading experience lawfully conditions one in the same manner as direct experience, does not suggest that the process is simple. There are many conditioning determinants of the individual's behavior, and the way he has been conditioned in the past may effect behaviors that change the way he will be conditioned by additional experiences—reading or otherwise. It should be understood, however, that the various conditionings are quite complex, perhaps antagonistic, and yet occur according to lawful principles.

It should be emphasized that all of the types of word meaning and all the types of communication that have been previously described may be involved in learning through reading. That is, it has been stated at length how the evaluative meaning response elicited by one word can be conditioned to another word stimulus in the act of reading. In addition, however, the other types of meaning responses can be conditioned to new words through context in the act of reading. For example, a motor response under the control of a written word would be conditioned to a new written word with which it was paired. Thus a young man might read in the dictionary, OSCULATE - KISS. The word *kiss,* let us say has come to control certain motor responses. After reading the two words in contiguity, the young man would make those motor responses when told by a suitable partner "Osculate me, please." As another example, word associational meaning can be learned in the same manner. The new word would be expected to come to elicit the same word association responses as the words with which it is paired in written passages. The power of the reading repertoire is that it opens such vast possibilities to the literate person for additional classical and instrumental conditioning. These processes of classical and instrumental conditioning contribute to what comes in common sense terms to constitute the individual's intellectuality or intelligence, and so on, as well as his social and emotional repertoires— in short, the nature of the individual's personality.

MOTIVATION AND COGNITIVE LEARNING

A frequent question that arises in the context of the training programs previously described which utilize explicit reinforcement concerns the effect that these procedures will have on the later behavior of the child. In the present context, for example, someone might ask whether a child who has learned to read through a reinforcement system such as described in the research will "want" to read when he is not so reinforced. Questions in this area are crucial to an understanding of human learning and to endeavors to improve systems for producing human learning. Thus, this chapter will discuss matters that are relevant to the specific question of reading acquisition as well as to the general question of reinforcement in human learning training systems.

Learning without Reinforcement?

It should be stated at the beginning of this discussion that the present author is not a classic reinforcement theorist such as Hull (1943), Osgood (1953), or Skinner (1953). It has already been suggested herein that language learning can take place in several ways without the use of reinforcement. Classical conditioning takes place upon the principle of contiguity—the simple paired presentation to the individual of two stimuli. This can produce word meaning, for example, including denotative (or sensory) word meaning, which is usually considered within the realm of cognition.

Furthermore, it has been suggested that instrumental conditioning may take place through contiguity—also by simply pairing two stimuli, one of which is a discriminative stimulus and controls a response. In the process the response will be conditioned to the new stimulus. No reinforcement is necessary to produce this conditioning.

It may generally be suggested that much cognitive learning may take place on this basis. Thus, for example, if the parent or teacher's instructions are discriminative stimuli that control the child's attentional responses so that he looks at the stimuli presented and responds as told to, then he will learn—regardless of whether reinforcement is provided for his attentional responses. However, it must be realized that reinforcement was originally involved in making the instructions discriminative stimuli in the first place. That is, as has been described, attention consists of instrumental responses. (This does not deny that there are physiological correlates to attention, and that there may be classically conditioned responses involved in what is called arousal.) Thus, the attentional responses came under the control of verbal instructions through the use of reinforcement, and reinforcement ultimately must be employed if the attentional responses are to be maintained. When attentional responses of the individual in a training program are not maintained learning ceases. Thus, while reinforcement at a theoretical level may not be necessary for learning to occur, on the practical level on which we deal with human learning the conditions of reinforcement are of paramount importance.

It is important to clarify these matters, because they are relevant to theoretical issues in learning, but also because there are conflicting conceptions of human learning which have had a strong impact upon our practices. For example, there have been experimental studies whose conclusions are that organisms acquire or perform behaviors without material reinforcement. As an illustration, it has been shown that monkeys in a darkened cage will repeatedly make a response maintained by the consequence of a door opening allowing a view of the outside (Butler and Alexander, 1955). Furthermore, monkeys will manipulate (and "solve") mechanical puzzle devices over and over again (Harlow, et al., 1956). In addition, rats satiated on food and water—thus removing this source of reinforcement—will nevertheless make exploratory behaviors when placed in a novel environment (Berlyne, 1955). The intent of the experimenters has usually been to isolate and study a type of reinforcing stimulus. However, their results have led people to conclude that organisms have a curiosity "drive," a "need" for novelty or discovery, a "need" for sensory stimulation, or what have you. In fact such studies have led to a current emphasis upon "discovery" types of teaching methods in educational procedures.

These and other types of observations have been used to support the traditional conception that learning is possible, in fact better, when no extrinsic rewards are involved. The conception must be examined closely, however, since there are crucial issues involved. Of most concern here, of course, is the question of the conditions that produce effective learning of complex cognitive behaviors. In addition, the conception is tied in with general conceptions of human behavior that have social significance. That is, for example, if learning or novelty or curiosity do not maintain a particular child's learning behavior adequately, does this imply that he is personally deficient in some manner?

The conception that one has of human behavior will determine what he does about problems of human behavior. In the present case a conception that some children have personal or constitutional weaknesses in their "motivation" for learning has different social implications than would a conception that the children's difficulty in learning is a consequence of the use of reinforcement systems that are inappropriate for the child because of his experiential history. The social implications can be seen readily when it is realized that it is groups such as lower-class children, racial minorities, or the culturally disadvantaged in general, who are deficient in the display of "learning for learning's sake." Again, constitutional interpretations of such deficiencies lead to different solutions to such social problems than do learning interpretations.

It is suggested that conceptions that there are inborn differences in people which provide some with superior sources of motivation are unfounded. The facts upon which such conceptions are based must be examined more closely. Many times it is concluded that there are no sources of extrinsic reinforcement for an individual—that the motivation from learning is self-determined—when in fact there are such reinforcing stimuli, or when there are learned discriminative stimuli that control the behaviors that result in learning. The misconceptions involved here may be clarified by examining some examples when learning seems to occur without reinforcement, but where reinforcement is actually present.

Take the college student who works and attends for long periods of time with no reinforcement contingent upon his behavior. It is not difficult to see here that there may be abundant sources of "extrinsic" reinforcement which maintain good "student behavior." Attending college may be maintained by the presence of friends (conditioned social reinforcers). If that is the sole reinforcer, however, it may be found that classroom attention and solitary studying are not maintained in good strength. Social reinforcement may also maintain the student behavior in that the verbal repertoires acquired in this class attendance and study may be reinforced in bull sessions outside of class. For many students this is a strong source of reinforcement. Furthermore, the student's own verbal behavior may serve as a strong source of reinforcement. That is, the student may "tell himself stories" about the advantages of a college education and the rewards he will achieve by attaining such an education. In addition, if the individual has been reinforced many times in the past for "knowing" things—as in the bull sessions mentioned above—acquiring new knowledge (verbal behaviors) may be in itself reinforcing. These same sources of reinforcement may have developed for the child in his early school years.

Something should also be said with respect to the experimental work which suggests that sensory stimulation or novelty is a reinforcing stimulus. It was stated that rats will explore a new environment even though satiated for food, that monkeys will manipulate a latch device for long periods, and that monkeys will perform a response to open a door in a dark cage when the consequence is the sight of the outside. However, it must be asked whether there are learned reinforcers operating to maintain such behaviors rather than, as is sometimes assumed, that organisms have an inborn novelty or curiosity drive, or a drive for sensory stimulation. In each case the stimulus maintaining the behavior could have been a conditioned reinforcer. With the rat, there are many occasions where exploratory behavior has been reinforced. Thus, for example, it is much more likely that the rat will come across a bit of food on the floor when he has not explored that part than if he has just explored that part. Parts of the environment which have not just been seen should thus become reinforcing. Visual stimulation should become a mild reinforcer also because it is when the individual, monkey or man, is being visually stimulated that he ordinarily obtains positive reinforcers and avoids negative reinforcers. Furthermore, manipulating physical and social devices many times is followed by reinforcing events and this behavior and the stimuli it produces should become positive reinforcers. The possibility that these types of events—novelty, sensory stimulation, and the like—are learned is by no means absent.

But whether or not there are reinforcers of this type that occur on an unlearned level (so that it might be assumed that people would differ, for example, on a constitutional basis in the extent to which novel occurrences were reinforcing to them), there are additional reasons to discount the importance of possible constitutional factors in the type of complex learning the child is faced with in his cognitive development. In fact it is quite likely that dependence upon novelty as a reinforcer in school training would be a handicap for the individual. For most early learning in school has little novelty, and special procedures have to be constructed to reduce the grinding monotony of the learning tasks.

Let us take the task of learning to read. In the early years, the only novelty in the learning task itself comes in the first few trials, where the procedure is being introduced. After that it is a matter of presenting each stimulus—all of which are quite alike in general stimulus value—

and getting the child to make the correct response as he attends to the stimulus. Because of the complexity of the learning task this essential procedure must be conducted many, many, many times in a long drawn out, very arduous, very monotonous learning task. It is quite evident from exploring the nature of the learning task in terms of basic principles that the task consists of a fantastic number of discrimination training trials.

When you look at the other original learning tasks with which the child is presented—certainly all those in his formal education—the same thing holds true. The learning consists of many, many, training trials on homogeneous material. It is only after the basic repertoire involved in the subject matter has been learned that there may be intrinsic (not necessarily unlearned, however) reinforcement available for the performance of the skill. A training program which depended exclusively upon the intrinsic (natural) reinforcement involved in these learning tasks would be a failure with all children.

As was shown in the previously described experiments when we present children with concentrated learning trials, without a source of extrinsic reinforcement, behaviors deteriorate, and the child makes escape responses of various kinds. In short, the novelty in the very complex and difficult learning tasks of the child is entirely inadequate even where it has become a reinforcer for the child. The first few trials of material may be of interest, but does not remain that way through the many training trials necessary. Certainly, any program with young children in which learning is long-term and concentrated and where natural reinforcers are not present requires the introduction of some means of reinforcing the attending and participating behaviors of the child. This conclusion has eluded many people because they do not recognize the reinforcers usually involved. By way of illustrating this point, it may be useful to examine some current practices of training with respect to making explicit the extrinsic reinforcement that is involved.

First, it should be said that training techniques introduce sources of extrinsic reinforcement in various ways, even though the authors of the methods may be unaware of this fact and opposed to the principle involved. Thus, a teacher who might object to the use of material reinforcers in training children will nevertheless intersperse her training trials with stories, games, and the like, which are reinforcers that maintain the child's participation in the group activities. This is the most prominent part of the nursery school and kindergarten programs and is only gradually decreased as the child's attentional and participation behaviors come under the control of other discriminative and reinforcing stimuli.

Social reinforcers, privileges of various kinds, snacks, rest periods, and the like are also used profusely by many teachers. There are systematic means of using social approval also such as grades, gold stars, organizing the class's approval of individual students, and presenting tokens of various kinds. Ordinarily, however, these will not be reinforcers for all children, nor, as we will see later, will all children gain these reinforcers.

A favorite method of introducing reinforcers in the primary school is to insert the training trials as part of a reinforcing activity. Let us say, for example, that the teacher announces that the class will take a trip to a farm in the near future. The teacher will then use verbal means for creating reinforcers connected with the farm. She may describe the farm in terms of the fun that a child can have on the farm—telling stories that are reinforcing in nature. Then as part of this activity she may introduce the printed words having to do with the farm, relating the words to the story. And she may present pictures of the farm life and its objects and events and relate these to words the children must learn to read. The teacher may also utilize her own social approval and the classes approval in conducting training trials about the farm—calling on children to recite. Finally, the teacher may take the children to the farm, conducting training trials during the visit and repeating the previous training when the class has returned from the visit.

It should be noted that this procedure is no different in principle from the introduction of material reinforcers in a training program. If we want to train the child to read the word *farm*, let us say, the most direct training is to present the word as a stimulus and to get the child to say the word. The fact that a complex activity is used to maintain the child's attention is no different in principle than the use of some other reinforcer system for this purpose. One could say that the child has learned additional things in the activity centered procedure, and that *could* certainly be an advantage. It is also true, however, that a great deal of time, effort, and money may be spent upon what is actually a relatively few reading training trials, as one example. In any event, since this procedure for introducing reinforcers is no different in principle from other methods, including the use of material reinforcers, the ultimate evaluation of the procedure resides solely in its efficacy.

Another way of teaching children to read and write, especially, involves the use of somewhat different social interactions as reinforcers. Thus, the procedure will be set up in which the child is not given straightforward reading training trials—he is told he may write a story. Since he cannot read or write the child must get the words for his story from the teacher. The teacher will have the child look at the word, and write it, and then make a story out of the words given in this manner. When the child writes his "story" the teacher may also arrange social reinforcement by having the child read it to the class—this behavior being followed by class and teacher approval. The child may also take his story home where his parents reinforce him when he reads it.

As an undergraduate psychology major the author gained some experience in applying the Fernald method for teaching reading to nonreaders. The main features of this method were similar to the one just described. In addition, the child had to trace the word before writing it, a procedure based upon the rationale that these nonreading children were kinesthetic learners, but which can be better seen as a method for insuring the visual attention of the child.

In the Montessori method of teaching reinforcement procedures are handled differently. The teacher waits until the child demonstrates an interest in something—in the present terms indicates that something is reinforcing. Then the teacher uses this reinforcing stimulus to introduce training trials as the child has contact (plays with) the stimulus. This system depends upon having the child in a structured situation in which the objects available are those that lend themselves to instructional purposes. Within his required attendance the child is "free" to respond to the object that has the most reinforcing value for him.

The methods of O.K. Moore in teaching reading to young children, as exemplified in his movie, appear to be very similar in principle. That is, the children are kept in a nursery school type of atmosphere which has a certain set of activities. In addition, the children have available another set of materials consisting of an electric typewriter with special attachments to guide the child's responses, as well as an instructor. The child types materials and reads them and so on.

Thus, the child is in a situation where there are a finite number of reinforcing events and objects, one of which involves the reading. In such a circumstance it would be expected that the child would contact the most reinforcing objects first and continue this contact until satiated on the reinforcer. Then he would go to the next, and the next, and so on. In terms of the satiation weakening reinforcing value, if there was not too much disparity between the reinforcing values of the various objects and events, it would be expected that the child would "play with" each in a cyclic fashion of some sort. In the O.K. Moore method the reading materials and apparatus constitute the training program. Reportedly, the apparatus and procedures are reinforcing for many children, and this is enhanced by other means such as writing stories and so on. In this case, as with the Montessori methods, the methods are in concert with a learning analysis to the extent that the systems are based upon the use of a variety of reinforcers among which the child selects. The authors of these and other methods ordinarily interpret their methods in common sense, nonlearning terms, however.

There is also a current enthusiasm with the "method of discovery" learning. Theoretically, this method is close to the conception that the child has "needs" for novelty, curiosity, or discovery. Based upon this conception one seeks to develop methods by which children can be presented with materials and find the answer or principle themselves. In practice, using our terms, it appears that these methods rest upon procedures that are like those already described. That is, a game-like atmosphere is set up in which the children are presented with stimuli and they must "discover" the rule or regularity involved or some such thing. In addition to the materials themselves, the usual social reinforcers involved in games are present. That is, the children are socially reinforced for contributing to the development of the answer both by the other children in the game and by the teacher. In addition, when the subject matter is related to mathematics or physics the children will be reinforced by the suggestion that they are learning very recondite and important material.

Thus, it is suggested that there are sources of extrinsic reinforcement used in training the child to the various repertoires he must acquire in formal education, regardless of the method used. Robbed of these sources of extrinsic reinforcement the stimulus materials themselves are straightforward cases of presenting stimuli and demanding responses from the child. As such they constitute in most cases long and difficult learning tasks. This is not to suggest that these reinforcers be removed from the training procedures. Many people, however, delude themselves into thinking that such methods do not involve extrinsic reinforcement. This is possible because the reinforcement is worked into the training trials and is thus not seen as clearly as an "extrinsic" reinforcer system. However, there is nothing different in principle or practice among social reinforcers, game reinforcers, reinforcement through the use of apparatus like electrical typewriters, and the use of reinforcers like tokens backed up by various kinds of material rewards.

The cold fact is that the stimulus materials by themselves in such learning tasks as reading, writing, arithmetic and mathematics are not naturally reinforcing. They demand many, many, training trials which require attention to stimulus materials and the emission of responses. It is true that they may become reinforcing in later stages—as will be discussed—but there is a long arduous learning program in each case before this occurs.

Thus, it is suggested that the type or types of reinforcers which are used in any particular training method should be based upon various practical considerations—since there is no difference in principle. First, of course, one must consider the adequacy of the reinforcer system— which includes both the adequacy of the reinforcers used, as well as the manner in which the reinforcers are dispensed. This involves questions concerning the generality of the reinforcers. Thus, stories and verbal approval may be reinforcers for some children but not for a verbally retarded child. Frequently it has been said that children learn differently and that teaching methods must be individualized—although the principles involved have been left unstated. It may be said in the present context that actually the principles involved in child learning are the same for all children (for example, the principle of reinforcement). However, there are many individual differences in such things as the objects and events that will be reinforcing for children. The design of training methods should systematically study the topic of effective reinforcers and effective reinforcer systems for various types of children. Practical systems in the school should be designed to be variable with respect to reinforcer systems—so that a child who is not progressing under one can be provided with a more appropriate system. More will be said of these matters later on.

In addition to the reinforcers themselves there are questions concerning the ease and economy of application of the reinforcer system. The commonly used types of reinforcers interwoven into our teaching methods as just outlined have certain weaknesses. For one thing since a group situation is involved it is difficult to administer reinforcement contingent upon the behavior of any one child in an appropriately scheduled manner. Only when the child recites individually may his behavior be immediately reinforced by other persons, and, of course, only a small proportion of school time will be occupied with the behavior of any one child.

Furthermore, reinforcement in the group situation almost has to be on a relative basis, making it impossible to adequately reinforce the behavior of the child who needs it most—the unskilled, behaviorally retarded child. Even though a teacher might want to reinforce the child's "demonstration of knowledge," this cannot be done if the child has no response, or an incorrect one. It is possible many times to prevent negative social reinforcement—derision of other students, for example. However, it is not possible in the group situation, with its relative standards, to give hearty social reinforcement in such cases. This absence of adequate reinforcement is likely to have a snow-balling effect. The child who begins with a poor basic behavioral repertoire learns slowly. Because he learns slowly he gets little reinforcement. Because he gets little reinforcement his attention and participation are poorly maintained and he learns even more slowly.

Another item in terms of the efficacy of the reinforcer system concerns the concentration of training trials that may be conducted using the particular system. *Thus, over a constant period of time one has to ask which method of reinforcement contains the greater number of training trials.* How much time is spent with the reinforcers and how much time with the training? In the method in which training is worked into an activity, as in the example concerning the visit to the farm, a great deal of time may be spent on items that are really irrelevant to the training itself. Contrasted with this is the case where the child obtains a token and puts it away in a matter of a second or so.

This section is not intended to cover the questions and problems involved in the development of adequate reinforcer systems for child learning. The main point is that all methods of training children involve "extrinsic" reinforcement and cannot be compared on that basis. However, it is germane to ask about the relative efficacy of the reinforcer systems, and to begin to think and investigate systematically the advantages and disadvantages of various systems with the aim of developing more effective systems. The author has suggested this generally (see Staats, 1964a; Staats and Staats, 1963). It appears that additional researchers have begun to investigate such possibilities.

One further point or question may be raised—that is the ease of transfer from the reinforcer system used in training to the natural reinforcers that will be available when the skilled performance has been acquired. There could be differences in this area also. The next section will answer this question in a specific area of training, that of reading. In so doing it is necessary to describe the natural reinforcers that are involved in the act of reading—a matter that is also part of the general learning analysis of this important repertoire.

Reinforcement in Reading Acquisition and Function

The question quoted at the beginning of the chapter asked whether a child trained to read with material reinforcers would later read without them. At this point, however, it can be seen that this question applies to all methods of reading training. For example, will the child trained to read under the action of social reinforcement read on his own later on, when social reinforcement is absent? Will the child who learns to read on elaborate electric typewriters, whose effect is in part a reinforcing one, later be content reading a mundane book? and so on.

The fact is that our present methods of training, based upon traditional reinforcer systems, fall far short of producing children with adequate reading repertoires. Many children do not learn to read, some only minimally, and probably a great majority never read as we would like —that is, voraciously, independently, and with zest and reported pleasure. Most people, it must be remembered, even those with functional reading repertoires, only read when this is demanded in some way in their everyday lives. That is, they read signs, labels, and messages as these occur in their work and so on. Thus, they read in most cases only when there is some system of extrinsic reinforcement operating. This is said only to indicate that present methods of training do not produce the "self-motivated" reading we desire.

For convenience of exposition, the types of reinforcement that the individual is subjected to in reading acquisition and later on in reading function may be broken down into three types. (1) There is the reinforcement system under which the reading repertoire is acquired, (2) there is a stage in reading development in which the reading behavior is intrinsically reinforcing in several ways, and (3) there is the system of natural reinforcers for this activity that pertains in one's everyday life, which is also a system of extrinsic reinforcement. The first type of reinforcement system has already been described and will only be described now in its general features to characterize the conditions of the original learning of reading.

The Artificial, Extrinsic, Reinforcement System of Original Reading Training

As has been stated, the behavior involved in acquiring a complex repertoire such as reading is not self-reinforcing. The learning task is arduous, long-term, and concentrated in training trials. It is work. For the behavior of attending and studying to be maintained, some type of extrinsic reinforcer system must be introduced. The system is introduced solely for that purpose and in this sense it is not only extrinsic but also is artificial—the system is not based upon the natural reinforcers that occur in the child's extra-school life. (As will be mentioned, however, there are methods that attempt to use such natural reinforcing systems.)

The essence of such reading training systems is that the child is placed in a room on a compulsory basis. This immediately removes reinforcement systems that might compete with those present in the classroom. This should be made explicit, because for many children the reinforcing systems outside of the schoolroom—including such items as free play —are much more potent than those in the classroom. Except for coercive measures the behaviors of escaping and avoiding the class would be dominant, maintained by the more potent natural reinforcing system.

However, provided that compulsory attendance in class is assured, the demands upon the classroom reinforcement system are reduced. The system in the classroom need only provide stronger reinforcers for appropriate pupil behavior than is provided for inappropriate behavior. Even while ruling out the competition of the outside reinforcers, however, the problems are not solved. The child may still emit behaviors that are reinforced by inappropriate reinforcers. The boy may pull a girl's hair, reinforced by her response to the action. The child may daydream and be reinforced more strongly by imagery (conditioned sensory and reinforcing responses) than he is by attending to classroom stimuli and emitting appropriate behaviors. Thus, the classroom reinforcement system is still in competition with other stimuli that have become reinforcing for the individual child.

The main point in this short discussion, however, is that classroom methods of training the child to read (as well as to his other repertoires) involve an extrinsic reinforcement system that has been specially evolved for the educational purpose. The individuals who apply the artificial, extrinsic reinforcement system may not realize this aspect of their training methods. When the training trials are worked into other activities, and when the reinforcers are verbal and social stimuli, it is easy to consider these reinforcers a natural part of the learning process. But that is a matter of historical familiarity rather than anything else. The fact is the methods of requiring school attendance as well as the use of the other types of reinforcers have been specially developed because they are effective in maintaining attentional, work, and studying behavior among at least a certain percentage of school children—and as a consequence these children acquire the complex repertoires desired by their parents and utilized by the society.

Intrinsic (Self) Reinforcement

As has been described the laborious, repetitive, task of learning to read is not in itself reinforcing. However, an abundance of naturalistic evidence indicates that the behavior of reading can become intrinsically reinforcing. That is, the accomplished reader will perform the behavior in the absence of extrinsic reinforcers. Moreover, the child may perform arduous responses of various kinds, this behavior maintained by the activity of reading. That is, the child may walk a long way to a public library, move up and down rows of books, take out various books, attend to various pages of each such book, finally select several books, walk home carrying the books, and finally at home select one of the books and proceed to read it until forced to abandon this activity by some exigency of home life. The long sequence of behaviors is maintained in strength by the word stimuli in the book.

It is incumbent upon a learning analysis of the complex behavior of reading to indicate the manner in which these word stimuli become such potent reinforcers. Furthermore, the topic is an important one for several reasons. Much of the child's later facility with language, his reasoning ability, and so on, comes from the amount of reading that he does. The child who reads a great deal, other things equal, will develop a greater general language facility—as indicated by intellective tests, writing ability, learning ability in various subjects involving language learning, and so on. And, the amount that a child reads—outside of his school work—will be a direct function of how intrinsically reinforcing this activity becomes.

The manner in which the activity of reading becomes reinforcing may be derived easily from the analyses that have already been presented. Words as stimuli come to elicit other responses. Thus, it has been suggested that printed words may elicit conditioned sensory responses (images). It has also been stated that several words, each of which elicits a conditioned sensory response, can when presented together elicit a composite conditioned sensory response or image. Thus, words such as these can be brought together in different combinations and produce different composite (larger) conditioned sensory responses. Stories may be considered in terms of this analysis. Series of words which elicit conditioned sensory responses are presented and what is elicited in the audience is a running sequence of conditioned sensory responses like actual objects and events. When these objects and events as actual stimuli are reinforcing, the story (the word stimuli) that elicits conditioned sensory responses like those the actual objects and events elicit will also be reinforcing. Thus, if the stimuli of a forest path leading to a grassy area by a brook elicits sensory responses that are reinforcing, then the words "forest path leading to a grassy area by a bubbling brook" will elicit a composite conditioned sensory response that is also reinforcing. This is not to say that the reinforcement value will be large, certainly not necessarily as large as the actual stimulus objects.

Naturalistic examples of story telling in this sense at a very primitive level can be gained from demonstrations with very small children. The author's two-year-old son, for example, had a language repertoire that included such words as *car, driving, Daddy, Peter* (his name), *dog, lick,* and so on. *Driving* and *car* and *Peter* together elicit sensory responses that were reinforcing for the following reason. The author has let Peter sit on his lap and hold the wheel several times when driving on an unused street, at which time the author and the boy have said things such as PETER IS DRIVING. Furthermore, the word *dog* elicits a reinforcing conditioned sensory response because it has been paired with actual dogs which Peter found reinforcing indeed.

Based upon this type of language repertoire the author told Peter a story consisting of "Peter and Daddy go driving. Peter drives. Brm-brm-brm-brm. Peter sees a dog. The dog licks Peter." Actually, in beginning storytelling with Peter many of the nonfunctional words were left out so the story consisted mostly of the words that elicited the sensory responses. At any rate, the reinforcing nature of the words could be seen in the child's laughing and general enjoyment, and in his requests for such a story.

Experimental evidence that auditorily presented words can function as reinforcing stimuli was presented in an earlier chapter. In this experiment whenever a motor response was made it was reinforced for one group of subjects with a positive evaluative meaning word (positive reinforcing word). When this occurred the frequency of the response increased in contrast to a similar response that was not so reinforced. Negative evaluative meaning words had a suppressive effect and neutral words had no effect.

It would be expected that visually presented words would have the same effect for individuals who were skilled readers. For these individuals the visually presented word could be a positive or negative reinforcing stimulus. It is suggested that it is the ability of a word to elicit positive or negative reinforcing responses, or images that have reinforcing value, that enables reading behavior to be intrinsically reinforced.

Thus, many stimulus objects and events are reinforcers for the individual. Words that have been paired with these stimulus objects or events, or with parts of the stimulus objects and events, will come to elicit conditioned sensory responses and conditioned reinforcing responses. Thus, when the words are presented the responses are elicited, and this acts as a reinforcement for the individual. Storytelling is at least in part the art of putting together words which will elicit conditioned sensory and reinforcing responses which are strong for many people. This art would involve the manner in which the words were strung together to elicit the most vivid and the most reinforcing responses. One of the reasons that the author is a good storyteller with his son is that he is aware of those experiences of the child that have formed his language repertoire as well as which experiences are the more reinforcing. In concluding this account, it may be suggested by way of illustrating, that pornography is a good example of word stimuli that elicit both conditioned sensory responses (images) as well as conditioned reinforcing responses that have observable physiological components.

The terms "intrinsic" and "extrinsic" reinforcement have been used in the present analysis. It should be noted that these terms do not refer to learning principles in the way that unconditioned and conditioned reinforcement do. The terms are simple labels for the fact that there are some activities that are intrinsically or self-reinforced, whereas there are other activities that have no intrinsic reinforcement value and will only be performed if there is a source of external reinforcement or some other controlling variable.

This is not to say that intrinsic reinforcement is unlearned or unconditioned reinforcement; that the activity is reinforcing in and of itself on a biological level. The term intrinsic reinforcement refers to the case where the behavior itself results in stimuli that are reinforcers (that is, elicit reinforcing responses). Reading is in that category when the reader looks at the series of words and these stimuli elicit reinforcing responses—thus strengthening and maintaining the behavior of looking at the words.

It should also be indicated that any behavior can become reinforcing that has been reinforced many times in the past. That is, each behavior can be considered to produce distinctive stimuli. If the behavior is reinforced the responses elicited by the reinforcement will be conditioned to the behavior. Reading would be no exception here of course. Thus, if the child has many instances where reading behavior is reinforced, either through some extrinsic reinforcement, or more likely after reading has produced much intrinsic reinforcement, the reading behavior itself may become reinforcing. Thus, it may be observed that people will read at times when the material read is not particularly reinforcing. The person with nothing else to do may pick up a newspaper and read advertisements, or read a magazine article which is not reinforcing by virtue of the meaning responses it elicits. This type of reinforcement is usually not strong, however, and will not ordinarily compete favorably for long with the other reinforcers available in life—although in cases of confinement or other restrictions on other natural reinforcers we may see the individual read the same materials over and over again, although they result in only relatively little reinforcement.

At any rate, it should be understood that what has been called intrinsic reinforcement in reading is actually learned reinforcement. A few considerations of the variables underlying the extent of intrinsic reinforcement that will be available for the individual should also be mentioned. First, the nature of the individual's reinforcing system depends largely upon one's conditioning history. For example, reading about swimming is not likely to be as reinforcing for the person who has suffered aversive conditions in this activity as it will be for a person for whom, because of his history, swimming has become very reinforcing. It may be concluded that individuals differ both in the type and number of different stimulus events that are reinforcing to them, as well as in the intensity of the reinforcing value of particular events.

Furthermore, in order for words to have reinforcing value like that of actual objects and events the individual must have conditioning experiences in which words come through conditioning to elicit the appropriate responses. The individual could have a good reading repertoire in terms of eye movements, for example, and could pronounce each of the words he looked at. However, unless the meaning responses elicited by the words were reinforcing, the activity would not be intrinsically reinforcing.

Moreover, *printed* words must come to directly elicit the reinforcing meaning responses that the auditory words elicit if maximal reinforcing effects are to occur in reading. If the process of reading still demands that the individual say the word to himself first the reinforcing effects are weakened because then it is the stimulus of *saying* the word that elicits the meaning response.

It has already been suggested in general that the more arduous a response is the more reinforcement is necessary to maintain the emission of the response. For the individual who has a very skilled reading repertoire in the various senses previously described, little effort is involved in reading. The activity is not arduous. Many words directly elicit the various meaning responses and the process proceeds smoothly. The poor reader on the other hand still must say each word to himself, and in many cases this may involve sounding out words. If his language repertoire is poor he may also have to ask the meaning of words or look them up in a dictionary. The act of reading can thus be a slow and arduous activity, and therefore one which demands relatively strong sources of reinforcement to maintain the activity.

The speed of reading alone is a variable in the amount of reinforcement obtained in the activity—although this may not be a simple linear relationship at least at the upper levels of reading speed. At any rate, slow readers in covering fewer word stimuli per unit of time obtain less reinforcement, since it is the meaning response to the words that provides the immediate reinforcement.

The relationship between ease and speed of reading and the strength of the reinforcers needed to maintain the reading behavior cannot be overemphasized. The reinforcement involved in reading is frequently not large—at least in comparison to the other sources of reinforcement available to the ordinary middle-class child. Thus, the behavior of reading cannot be too arduous, or the reinforcement will not be sufficient to maintain the behavior in competition with other behaviors.

It may be concluded that these are some of the variables involved in the reinforcement the individual will derive from reading, and hence the extent to which he will read when no other source of extrinsic reinforcement is available. If the child has acquired the complex reading response repertoire to a sufficient level of skill and ease, if there are stimulus objects and events that are reinforcers, if he has a repertoire of word responses that elicit the conditioned responses to these objects and events, and if the reinforcers for behavior that compete with reading are not too strong, it would be expected that the child when presented with suitable reading material will read, the behavior being maintained by intrinsic reinforcement. It may be suggested that this is the highest level or stage of reading—where the child's reading behavior is maintained by the intrinsic (self) reinforcement his responses produce. When this stage is attained much reading occurs, behavior which profoundly affects the child's intellectual development in a positive direction.

Natural Extrinsic Reinforcement

In addition to the type of intrinsic reinforcers for reading just described, there are other sources of natural reinforcers of an extrinsic nature. These sources are important to some extent in the acquisition of a reading repertoire as well as for the maintenance of the repertoire once it has been acquired. This source of reinforcement is termed "natural" in contrast to the "artificial" system of reinforcement that is set up in the formal school situation for the purpose of maintaining attentional and studying behaviors that will lead to a reading repertoire. The natural reinforcement system, on the other hand, involves the conditions that are no doubt involved in the original development and maintenance of a reading repertoire—the reasons that reading is an adjustive behavior for mankind.

The functions of a reading repertoire have in part at least already been summarized. A word should be said, however, about how these functions also may have reinforcing value of the sort that maintains the behavior that yields the functions.

REINFORCEMENT RESULTING FROM PRINTED WORDS AS CONTROLLING STIMULI The individual who has a full reading repertoire is prepared to be controlled by printed verbal stimuli in a way that will produce reinforcement for him. In our complex society there are many verbal stimuli which control behaviors that are adjustive in the sense that the behaviors result in obtaining positive reinforcers or avoiding or escaping negative reinforcers.

The person who can read the word *poison* avoids behaviors that could result in very aversive contingencies. The child who does not have the reading repertoire in its full sense may consume objects labeled with the word *poison* and suffer the consequences. Once the person has a rudimentary reading repertoire he may respond appropriately to many verbal stimuli. Our daily lives are full of such occurrences. The housewife responds to the advertisements in the newspaper and is reinforced by getting sale items at a cost below what she would otherwise pay—her behavior strengthened by the positive reinforcers (money) she gets to keep. We read the movie section of the newspaper, our behavior reinforced by the movie we see when we have gone to the theatre. The "do-it-yourself" habitué reads directions on a project, his behavior reinforced by the product he creates.

These are a few examples of a type of source of reinforcement for reading that is so straightforward that little elaboration is required. In general, it may be said that when various written signs, labels, and directions, control appropriate behaviors in the individual the consequences of this control will amply maintain the strength of the reading behaviors involved.

COMMUNICATION AND SOCIAL REINFORCEMENT AS SOURCES OF REINFORCE- MENT The previous chapter described a number of learning functions that a reading repertoire can result in. That is, the individual on the basis of looking at word stimuli can acquire new word associations, new conditioned meaning responses, and so on. It is worthwhile to indicate that the formation of these new S–R mechanisms can result in reinforcement —this reinforcement serving to maintain the reading behaviors by which the S–R mechanisms were formed. Several examples may illustrate this process.

When the student reads the assigned text he acquires new verbal response sequences as a consequence. The reading behavior may also change the meaning response elicited by certain words, condition new meaning responses and word associations to new words which previously were meaningless, and so on. Later, when the student takes an examination he can answer questions on the basis of these new S–R mechanisms. Answering a question on a test is a reinforcer for most students.

In addition, however, as has been mentioned, the same newly learned S–R mechanisms may be socially reinforced in conversations with other students and faculty members. The same type of social reinforcement is available for the academician or scientist. Through reading behavior new verbal S–R mechanisms are acquired, these verbal behaviors then being reinforced later when the academician lectures to a class or discusses a problem with a colleague, or when the scientist writes a paper.

The same process of social reinforcement for verbal behaviors acquired through reading may be seen throughout various parts of society—in addition to academic-scientific pursuits. As has been described, new motor skills can be acquired by the athlete or dancer through reading, these new motor skills then resulting in social reinforcement. Reading newspapers, books, and magazines may also be maintained through the social reinforcement obtained by the "knowledgeable" person in his normal social interactions. Furthermore, most skilled trades, businesses, and professions provide circumstances in which the reading behavior that the individual makes is reinforced because of the new skills he has acquired.

It may be concluded that once the individual has acquired a reading repertoire there are many sources of reinforcement of a social and non-social sort that will serve to maintain the behavior in some strength. It should be indicated, however, that having a functional reading repertoire of the type included in these examples is not necessarily the same as having a full, extensive, rapid, and effortless reading repertoire that allows intrinsic reinforcement to be obtained in great enough measure to maintain a high strength for the reading behavior.

An individual could be a mathematician with a Ph. D., for example, who is a university professor, and still not have a completely adequate reading repertoire in this sense. The mathematician could have his special reading repertoire but a fairly restricted one in other respects and still get by quite adequately. This is true for many other professions also. The housewife or tradesman or skilled worker also needs only a restricted reading repertoire to meet life's exigencies although new sources of re-inforcement could be opened up if the individual involved had an entirely complete reading repertoire of the type already described.

Before leaving the topic of motivation in the acquisition and main-tenance of reading, a point should be made concerning the social inter-action that is involved between the writer and the reader in terms of the reinforcers that maintain each type of behavior. Let us start with the writer's behavior. Although there is intrinsic reinforcement involved for many prolific writers—who would state that they "enjoy" writing, like to read their own material, and so on—there are also ordinarily strong sources of extrinsic reinforcement involved. The writer's behavior is main-tained by social reinforcers and material reinforcers provided him by his readers. Depending upon the field the writer may be reinforced by increases in professional status, money, replies from correspondents, and so on. This is not always univocal, of course, since aversive stimuli may also be delivered.

The reader on the other hand, because the effect of what he reads has some reinforcing consequence for him, will provide the writer with reinforcers. In doing so the reader may be giving away reinforcers such as money. This being the case the reading must be more reinforcing than the reinforcers he loses, otherwise the net result is a diminution of the reader's reinforcers. At any rate, this can be seen as a typical case of social interaction involving positive reinforcers in which the behavior of the one individual has reinforcing aspects that maintain the behavior of the other individual—and this is reciprocated.

A similar type of interaction is involved between the teacher, the pupil, and the pupil's parents. The teacher may provide the child with new skills that the parents find reinforcing. The teacher is actually paid by the parents to do this, and the pupil's acquisition of skills is also reinforcing for the teacher's behavior. The teacher, on the other hand, is one of the important sources of reinforcement for the child's attentional and studying behaviors.

Conclusions

Thus, in terms of the reinforcers that are effective, the acquisition and function of a reading repertoire seems to involve stages of learning. The first stage is largely dependent upon the use of an artificial, extrinsic, reinforcement system. Although for some children learning itself may have become rewarding and this source of reinforcement may help maintain attentional and studying behaviors, for the most part it is necessary that some source of extrinsic reinforcement be employed.

If the system of reinforcers is adequate enough and the training is carried on sufficiently long with adequate materials, the next stage may be reached where reading becomes extrinsically reinforced by the natural contingencies pertaining in life—not through the artificial system employed in school. Under certain circumstances the reading repertoire will be acquired to the point where reading behavior is maintained in high strength by "intrinsic" reinforcement. This circumstance is propitious for the child acquiring a great deal of "knowledge" he would not otherwise gain. This most advanced stage is not reached until the intrinsic reinforcement of reading is large enough and the effort involved in reading is slight enough for the activity to be reinforcing enough in sum to compete favorably with other alternative activities. Many people, including college graduates, never reach this stage of development. Thus in their life times each reads but a handful of books under the control of the intrinsic reinforcement of reading itself.

Thus, the reinforcement system that is used in the first stage is important along several dimensions. It must be adequate to produce the skills that make it easy to read so the other two systems can come to function. In addition, the reinforcer system used must make a transition to the natural reinforcement system of everyday life, as well as to the intrinsic reinforcement system involved in reading itself. It may be said that the traditional reinforcement systems presently used in education do this for many children. However, there are many children for whom the reinforcer systems are not nearly so propitious. A great deal of interest has gone into designing improved stimulus materials for teaching this all important repertoire. Almost no systematic research outside of the present effort has gone into the development and evaluation of new reinforcer systems to use in the training of reading. It is suggested that this is an open field for research and improvement, and that reinforcement or motivational conditions in the context of early education must be systematically studied with the intensity provided for the study of other human problems. The fact is, many problems of human behavior lie in early school failures which are of a motivational nature.

Thus, in answer to the question posed at the beginning of the chapter, it must be said that all methods of training of reading (and other basic skills) involve some system of artificial, extrinsic, reinforcement. This is so because there is little intrinsic reinforcement available for the long and arduous task involved. Our task then is to use an effective extrinsic reinforcement system so the child can be trained to the point where natural reinforcers will take over. It must be expected that with any particular type of human repertoire an analysis of the behavior is required as well as an analysis of the conditions that can produce the behavior— in detailed S–R terms. This is true for various cognitive behaviors as well as social behaviors, sensory-motor behaviors, and so on. In this task we must be concerned with the conditions of reinforcement involved in the original learning as well as with the reinforcement system that will pertain in the later life situation when the repertoire has been acquired. There may be "stages" in the functional motivational system as well as in the skills which are being acquired.

Implications for applications, research, method and theory

17

Applications and research

The author has attempted to indicate in the present work as well as elsewhere (Staats, 1964a, 1966; Staats and Staats, 1963) that learning principles have been verified in the context of many different realms of human behavior. In recent years we have seen also an upsurge in interest in applying the principles of learning to the treatment of human behavior problems. This movement is demonstrated in the fields of programmed instruction and in behavior therapy and behavior modification treatment methods.

While these movements have been productive, especially in getting large numbers of psychologists interested in a learning approach as well as in stimulating increased research efforts, the fields of programmed instruction and behavior therapy and modification have not yet generally included the analyses of complex human behavior and methods for their treatment that are required for a comprehensive theory. Most work has been empirically rather than theoretically oriented. However, this is not the place for a full explication of these matters. It may be suggested, nevertheless, that progress in developing theories of the relevant human behaviors will demand detailed behavioral analyses and attendant research programs which both verify the analyses and produce methods for dealing with the behaviors involved.

It has been the author's intent to demonstrate some of the possibilities for this type of analysis and research in some of the preceding chapters.

It is felt that this work exemplifies a method (which will be characterized in the next chapter) that can be generally applied in various areas of human research and treatment activities. In this chapter, some areas for the extension of the method in research and applied work will be briefly outlined.

IN THE HOME

As has been described, the child must acquire fantastically complex repertoires of behavior if he is to adjust in our society. Much of the training necessary to produce these repertoires takes place in the informality of everyday living, and we customarily do not realize the tuition that is necessary for producing a normal child. Nevertheless, when the basic behavioral repertoires are described, even restricted to cognitive development, it becomes clear that a great deal of the child's basic behavioral repertoires are acquired in the home and the parents are primarily responsible for the training.

The training task involved in producing normal development in the child may be considered to be a prodigious one. This is true in a large number of areas of behavior not the focus of interest herein, as the author has already indicated (Staats and Staats, 1963, Chapter 9). And, this is also true even when the subject of interest is limited to cognitive learning and related repertoires.

It must also be evident on the basis of the preceding analyses that our educational system, and our society, depend upon the training that the parents give to their children. This is only implicitly recognized, however, and the implications and ramifications of this aspect of our educational system have not been delineated. When an analysis of the child's early learning is made, however, it can be seen that early child learning is an area of fundamental weakness in our whole educational system. When the child's emotional and social learning are generally considered, we may see that problems of child training by the parent are fundamental to other social institutions in addition to education. There are several points that should be made in emphasizing the responsibilities and problems the parent faces in the early training of his children.

First, it appears that a most, perhaps *the* most, crucial part of the child's training is the responsibility of "teachers", the parents, who have themselves no systematic training in the skills or knowledge that are necessary to conduct the child's training. Second, we provide no materials, procedures, or understanding with which to approach this prodigious task. In fact, if the parents encounter difficulty in training their children, there is no agency to which the parent can turn for detailed instructions concerning what he should do. Thirdly, we expect the population of parents to treat widely divergent training problems, many of them of a special nature. That is, for the most part, we expect the parents of a deaf child to provide the unusual training necessary to give the child a basic behavioral repertoire, as we do also for the parents of a child handicapped in other ways, the child who has special illnesses, the child who is a special training problem because of the behavioral deficits from whatever cause, and the child who for similar reasons has developed inappropriate behaviors that interfere with his learning.

Our equanimity in designing our educational system with little regard for the foundation upon which it must rest could only be a result of an inadequate conception of human behavior. That conception of human behavior, it may be suggested, is erroneous in considering the parents' role only that of providing a benevolent environment—rather than that of being an active trainer who is largely responsible for the basic behavioral repertoire which is so important to the child's further learning. It may also be suggested that part of this inadequate conception of human behavior is derived from the conception that the development of the basic behavioral repertoire takes place through physiological maturation rather than through complex learning experiences.

The present conception of the basic behavioral repertoire and the way it is developed on the basis of learning experiences suggests an alternative view. When we look at the parents as the trainers of a repertoire that is crucial to the child's later learning, we have to expect large divergences in the parents ability to teach their children and hence in the ability of the children to profit from later training. Furthermore, we would expect that many parents would not be able to do as good a job of training children as could be done based upon systematic knowledge. Nor, could we expect parents to be able to handle special problems of learning which require knowledge and competencies with which they would ordinarily have had no experience.

These conclusions contain the strong suggestion that our total educational system, as well as the cognitive, emotional, and social adjustment of our children, could be strengthened by extending public education downward to deal with younger children—so that children of 4, 3, and perhaps 2 years of age could participate. This would mean that the problems of assessing the repertoires that should be acquired at these ages could be systematically studied, as would the problems of providing experiences to train children to these skills. To some extent the development of nursery school programs in general and preschool programs for children with special problems such as culturally deprived children represents movement in this direction.

This is a development which will no doubt involve cultural lag. However, at this time we should at least begin as an area of research the analysis of the repertoires learned by the preschool child which are essential to his later cognitive development, as well as research to develop schooling procedures for training the children to those repertoires. Some of the present studies may be considered to be a foundation for that type of research.

The other possibility for removing the deficits in many children when they enter school is to work through the parents to more uniformly make them better trainers. It was in part to demonstrate this possibility that the author developed the training procedures for working in his home with his daughter. Further research should be conducted in which both parents and their children are the subjects. The experimenter would provide the parent with methods and procedures for training his child. The experimenter would then begin the experimental study of what parents need in the way of instructions and materials to become proficient trainers of their children. The author plans such research.

Once established, the methods would be valuable to professionals (child psychologists and psychiatrists, pediatricians, social welfare workers, and so on), providing them with a means for working with parents of children with special learning problems. This type of research should be conducted on a wide front, dealing with the *various* repertoires the child must acquire to be normal—repertoires that are involved in social interaction, emotional (reinforcing) learning, sensory-motor activities, self-care, toilet training, and so on, as well as the cognitive learning that has been the present focus.

IN THE CLINIC

The demonstration that long-term research on children is possible while producing positive behavioral results has many implications for areas dealing with clinical problems. Many patients, children and adults, are placed in institutions in which they receive little if any treatment to improve their behavior problems. Many times, at best, they receive a few hours of psychotherapy of some type during a week's time. For those, however, who have suffered profound learning deficits in their preceding lives, or have acquired extensive and ingrained repertoires of inappropriate behavior, long-term and intensive training programs would be a requisite. This type of treatment would be necessary to correct the behavioral problems that had been acquired over an extended period, or in the case of young children, to insure that such deficits and inappropriate behaviors did not arise.

Using the type of methodology that has been described herein, it is suggested that research should be begun in clinical institutions, upon a wide variety of problems. Take institutionalized mental retardates, as an example. In most institutions the children do not receive enough treatment so that it is possible to say that their behavioral repertoires have been developed to anywhere near the fullest extent. Research of the type described herein, which would have a treatment purpose as well as a research purpose, would certainly be in the children's best interest. Moreover, from this type of research it would be possible to establish what these types of children can or cannot learn. At the present time we do not know.

Another category of institutionalized patients is that of autistic children, who have behavioral disturbances that are of the severity of the mental retardate. In addition to the learning deficits displayed, however, autistic children have also acquired extensive inappropriate behaviors of various kinds many times including self-destructive behaviors. Again, the extent to which these children could acquire normal adjustive behaviors, cognitive and otherwise, will not be known until learning procedures are applied to these children which will maximize good attention and cooperation and which will insure the establishment of basic behavioral repertoires before advancing to more complex tasks.

In addition, there are many children who are variously labeled, for example, as emotionally disturbed or conduct disorders, who do not adjust to the usual situations of life and who as a consequence develop severe learning deficits. Although we focus upon the inappropriate behaviors these children display, of at least equal importance is the fact that the inappropriate behaviors result in learning deficits. If we do not present the child with special training circumstances so that the deficits do not occur, the child will later be a behavioral cripple even though the "emotional disturbance" or "conduct disorder" is removed. More usually, the learning deficits that result from the inappropriate behaviors leave the individual unable to adjust to society, and the pressure which results prevents the successful treatment of the inappropriate behaviors. The learning deficits may actually be the locus of the individual's adjustmental problems, as was demonstrated to some extent with the nonreading in the juvenile delinquent.

At any rate, the present results suggest that even children with inappropriate behaviors can still learn normally if they are subjected to special learning procedures which involve an adequate reinforcement system. It may be suggested that through the use of such procedures it may be possible to prevent learning deficits from occurring in such children, to provide these children with adjustive repertoires which will replace the inappropriate behaviors, and thereby to treat the inappropriate behaviors. These suggestions, however, must be fully explored in extensive research.

In one last example, it may also be suggested that language disorders are many times at the heart of behavior pathology. We see this in each of the types of cases just described as well as with paranoid patients and other schizophrenic patients, in speech pathologies in children, and so on. When we consider these cases of language deficits and disorders in terms of learning, however, it follows that long-term research on identification and treatment should be commenced. We do not know the extent to which such behavioral repertoires can be changed in a benign direction, and we need long-term research on individual patients to establish these possibilities, even though it would have to be with a relatively few patients at the beginning. Speech pathology in children, of course, could be very straightforwardly treated and researched with the cognitive learning procedures already described.

At present, at any rate, we have relatively few detailed analyses of the behaviors involved in behavior pathology, even with relatively simple behaviors, and have very few well developed learning procedures for dealing with the pathology. Research and theory in this area is sorely needed.

When the analyses have been made explicit, and when procedures have been developed for treating the behavior, it is likely that it will be possible for subprofessional personnel to administer the treatment procedures, as was done in some of the research reported herein. A central task of clinical psychology should be the development of treatment-research procedures that can be widely, easily and economically applied. Although the examples just described concerned institutionalized populations, the same type of research could be conducted with outpatients as well.

IN THE SCHOOL

Some of the research that has already been reported may be considered to be a demonstration of an experimental educational psychology conducted in the school setting. It should be indicated, however, that this research did not commence in the school, but was preceded by a rather extensive series of experimental-naturalistic, and experimental-longitudinal laboratory studies. It may be suggested that this may be considered to be a usual expectation. Procedures already researched may then be extended to the laboratory school and finally to field tests in various schools.

The present section will thus not be concerned with describing the cognitive learning research that should be first conducted in the laboratory—but only with several examples of research that concern general areas of education.

The Reinforcement System

Our system of reinforcement in the school situation has developed in the practical task of educating children. It has never been subjected to systematic study and to research and development that is based upon basic principles of behavior. While this is not necessarily a condemnation, the fact is that many children do not profit from their educational experience. For some children the experience in its aversiveness and failure engenders behaviors that are undesirable to society. For many others educational experience does not produce maximal development of the various skilled repertoires.

It is suggested that one of the reasons for this concerns the inappropriate nature of the reinforcement system in the school for many children. While it is important to examine ways of making childrens' reinforcement systems appropriate for the school, it is also reasonable to examine the possibilities for producing more effective reinforcement systems in schools, at least for the children for whom the present system is ineffective.

This discussion is not a call for a revolutionary change in our present system. It is suggested that we systematically consider the motivational aspects of learning, that we realize the possible variations and the fact that some variations are more appropriate for some children than others. Most importantly, however, it is suggested that we must open up this area to study. We must commence systematic research on the various possibilities for devising effective educational circumstances in this area —without preconception or prejudice, guided only by objective criteria such as producing effective learning with economical outlay.

The previous research has described a reinforcement system based upon the use of tokens and back-up reinforcers of a material nature. This reinforcement system has demonstrated its efficacy in promoting rapid learning in young children from families of various socio-economic levels and various ages and levels of cognitive development (intelligence). This system has direct implications for dealing with certain types of learning problems. It has been suggested that such a reinforcement system can be important for problems of special education: with remedial reading, with adult education, with the emotionally disturbed, with institutionalized children of various types, and so on. It has also been suggested that adaptations of this system can be used in the home by parents.

However, it may also be said that this by no means suggests that the study of adequate reinforcement systems has yet been scratched. Many other possibilities are present, other than the use of material reinforcers —which in many cases might be undesirable for various reasons. Ingenuity and research must be applied in the study of these possibilities. One possible type of reinforcer system will be sketched out here by way of example.

There are many activities that are reinforcing to children. Physical exercise, games, stories, moving pictures, free play, television, painting, dancing, and so on. The list of these activities is quite large. Many of them are more available outside of school. Many of them are more available in school. For example, the school ordinarily has equipment for athletic activities that exceeds that which most children have available in their homes.

While many of these activities are strongly reinforcing, and present in the school situation, they are not used as reinforcers, except in the grossest way. The child has a gym period, or recess (free play), both of which constitute large reinforcers. But the large reinforcer is delivered all at once, according to a criterion that has no relationship to the learning activities of the child. When the time comes for the recess the child is as likely, if not more likely, to be pulling someone's hair, daydreaming, or some such, as he is to be attending and studying. The manner in which these large reinforcing activities are delivered makes them contingent only upon coming to school. They could, however, be arranged in a reinforcement system that would make much more effective use of their power through the use of tokens.

Education is compulsory because many children would not attend otherwise. With proper use of the reinforcers available, however, it would probably be possible to construct an experimental school situation to be positively reinforcing to the extent that children would go, with few exceptions, on a purely voluntary basis, as was the case in the child research that has been cited. The basic idea of the school would be to have many types of reinforcing activities and to use these as the basis of the reinforcing system. That is, a token system would be established such that so many tokens were necessary for admittance into each of the reinforcing activities. There could be a free play area for example, access to which for a certain period would require so many tokens. Moving pictures could be run which would require so many tokens, and so on.

The tokens, on the other hand, would be acquired by the child contingent upon his performance of learning tasks. For example, the kindergarten child on entering school in the morning might go into a study room where he was presented with a reading learning task such as has been described herein. After making so many reading responses and acquiring a certain number of tokens he would be able to go into the general classroom where reinforcing activities were being conducted. After some time in this situation it would be time to acquire more tokens and the child would again work on some learning task. These periods could even be scheduled, that is a child would go to a work room at a particular time. However, how long he stayed there would be entirely a function of how rapidly he worked, that is, on how many learning responses he made. When the learning situation involves the reinforcement of each response, not many learning trials are necessary and the child would spend far more time in the reinforcing activities than he would in working. The relative time spent in work versus the time spent in the reinforcing activities would of course change as the child advanced in school. That is, relatively more time would be spent in work as the child advanced.

This is a general suggestion, and would of course require a great deal of engineering. Learning materials would have to be provided that could be individualized for the child. We are getting some such materials from the programmed instruction movement, and many of these can be automatically applied. In addition, reorganizations of other kinds would be required, some of which will be mentioned in the next section. However, there would seem to be no obstacles to the development of such an experimental school program. Based upon the preceding research it can be suggested that a reinforcer system utilizing these types of back-up reinforcers would be effective in maintaining strong studying behaviors and would produce good learning in children for whom the traditional reinforcers are not present as well as for children for whom they are effective.

Experimental classrooms would have to be designed with individual work rooms for children as well as larger rooms for the reinforcing activities. Such a complex would provide for classroom research in which groups of children were involved, for classroom plus individual learning studies, as well as provide experimental rooms for various individual learning experiments. The actual experiment with the preschoolers in the public school that has been described did not have such an elaborate setting. It consisted only of a large classroom and separate rooms that provided individual research rooms for the training of three different children. However, the study did demonstrate the potentialities.

It may be concluded that the time has arrived for developing a full experimental educational psychology by the application of an integrated learning analysis of complex cognitive behaviors and the application of experimental procedures. The type of research conducted should be prepared to make large changes in personnel, facilities, educational materials, and reinforcement systems, along the lines suggested by the previous research. This experimental educational psychology should be prepared to use these innovations in the study of various types of behaviors including the full basic behavioral repertoire which we would expect the child to acquire before he goes to school.

School Organization

Thus, the learning analysis and the research on reinforcement procedures seems to suggest that changes can be introduced into school situations for the purpose of research that would require changes in basic school organization. This emerges from a number of the studies that have been presented herein.

That is, in several cases educational training was conducted in which the materials and reinforcement system were so simple and mechanical that it was not necessary for a highly trained person to administer the training. The most general implication of this result is that as scientific learning principles and laboratory procedures are applied to the problems of educational learning, utilizing the technology which is presently available, training children will become less of an art and will involve more the mechanical presentation of materials and procedures that have been precisely worked out in research. To the extent that this becomes the case, as well as the extent to which reinforcer systems of the type already mentioned are introduced, reorganizations of the personnel and physical facilities of the school can be expected. That is, if training procedures are introduced involving administration by less highly trained individuals, this would suggest that such individuals become part of the personnel of the school. The teacher would then be responsible for those aspects of the training that did require the more intense training, and the teacher might also be an individual who was a specialist in learning who could evaluate and deal with the special problems of training, and supervise and train the less highly trained instructional-technicians. Use of subprofessional personnel could enable individual training sessions rather than the traditional group methods, at least for certain ages and for certain problems.

The research and training techniques that have been described herein may also be considered to be a step in the direction of exploring such new types of school organization. That is, in the study in which the culturally deprived 4-year-olds were involved in a training program in which they were in a large classroom and also received individual training in separate rooms, the author performed the role of the learning specialist. Graduate students untrained in working with children administered the training based upon the written procedures and the materials. In addition, the author monitored the training sessions, especially with the children who were not moving along as easily as the others. On the basis of these observations, instructions were given to the trainers and modifications were made in the materials.

With well worked out materials a teacher could perform the responsibilities of the learning specialist, and subprofessional personnel could serve as the actual trainers as well as the nursery school attendant. One teacher could thus handle a good sized group of children and still have time for work with children who had special learning problems. The teacher in supervising the whole operation could also see that the individual training sessions were coordinated with the classroom activities, and arrange for learning trials in the classroom based upon what the children had learned in their individual sessions.

The possibilities must be investigated more extensively and intensively. Certainly, the theoretical background and research and training procedures are now available for conducting this type of study. There are many situations in which such research could also serve the dual purpose of solving educational problems, such as in the education of the mentally retarded, culturally deprived, emotionally disturbed, and so on. It should also be indicated that these procedures also offer solutions to other types of social problems. That is, the use of subprofessionals to administer training materials could provide white-collar type of employment for disadvantaged adults who were literate or who could become literate. The opportunity for such employment could be used to good advantage in many large cities where there are special problems of education as well as special problems of employment for the adults who are beyond school age.

Special Training

It has been suggested that various aspects of education be subjected to research along the lines outlined. Depending upon the extent to which the proposals differ from traditional methods of education, it might be expected that varying lengths of time would be involved in instituting any innovations that were suggested. Some of the preceding research, however, appears to suggest additional applications that should be of use in solving educational problems now, or at least in beginning applied research which also has a problem solving function. Two of these areas may be briefly mentioned.

Remedial Training

The remedial reading treatment procedures that have been described appear to provide a general method for use with school-age children who are special learning problems. It may be suggested that many such children are not actually learning problems in any way, but rather have problems of motivation in the traditional school situation. The numbers of types of learning problems that could be treated simply by the institution of an appropriate reinforcer system cannot be estimated, but it would seem to be worthwhile to indicate a few of the more obvious ones.

For one thing, the possibility of applying the methods throughout the range of school ages would be important. That is, the remedial reading training was conducted primarily with children in junior high school. Further studies should employ the methods with younger and older school-age children and in adult education as well.

In addition, the methods should be applied to various types of subject matter, in addition to reading; that is, arithmetic, mathematics, spelling, and so on. In each of these cases, as in the area of reading as well, a full program of materials should be formulated to lead the children in the research-treatment programs to a fully normal cognitive repertoire.

Finally, however, the studies should be conducted upon a large scale to the end of producing programs that could be generally applied. It may be suggested that the methods could be used with good effect to remove the learning deficits among the culturally deprived groups who at the present time leave their public schooling with such grievous handicaps.

It may also be suggested that early detection of behavioral deficits that are developing in children and early application of a more effective training program based upon extrinsic reinforcement would be expected to have many positive virtues. The earlier the detection the less the problem of the remedial training, the less the problem of the learning of negative attitudes, the less costly the reinforcers required, and so on. Following this rationale, it would be even wiser to select children *before* they develop behavioral deficits that hinder their school learning. This, of course, is the principle behind the attempt to provide culturally deprived children with special training before they enter school—the topic of the next section.

Preschool Training and Research

It has been stated that one of the weaknesses of our educational system is that it depends upon the child's parents to provide training which will produce an adequate basic behavioral repertoire. One way of solving that problem is, as has been described, the provision of explicit procedures to the parent that can be easily and straightforwardly applied. Many, many parents would use such procedures to insure that their children were well prepared in their basic behavioral repertoires necessary for educational success.

There are many parents, however, who because of their own deprived learning circumstances and the resulting behavioral deficits simply do not have the repertoires or interests (reinforcement system) necessary to apply such procedures. There are many other parents for whom life is too difficult to undertake such responsibilities, and there are others who have other behavioral difficulties (alcoholism, "emotional" difficulties, and so on) which would prevent them from providing adequate training for their children even if the methods were available.

In view of these circumstances additional means must be instituted to provide training for children for whom we can expect there to be inadequate training in the home. To some extent this has been recognized by our society and we have seen the development of Project Headstart, which is a summer nursery school program for culturally deprived children. The present analysis would suggest that this is a step in the right direction, but its effectiveness in repairing the behavioral deficits in the children depends upon the efficacy of its procedures. Effective procedures, and the analysis upon which the procedures are based, has formerly been lacking.

It may be suggested that the procedures for training preschoolers that have been described could be introduced as a training program with very little development research. The materials could be used by subprofessionals working with single children. An organization of the type previously described, with one teacher and a number of helpers, in conjunction with the method of individual training and an appropriate motivational system would in all likelihood be very effective and relatively economical.

It may be suggested, however, that we should move in the direction of providing preschool training for all children—to solve the major weakness of our educational system. Above all, research on cognitive learning in children aged 2, 3, and 4, within a school situation, should be commenced. Such work would have social goals as well as scientific goals. Through use of the types of experimental-longitudinal methods, within the context of the laboratory complex that has been described, it should be possible to develop a psychology of cognition, and related teaching materials, to a much more refined level. The findings would then serve as the basis for moving in an experimental fashion throughout the realm of cognitive learning.

IN THE LABORATORY

The preceding experimental and theoretical analyses of various types of complex human behavior suggest that it is now possible to deal with representative samples of actual human behaviors in the laboratory. This is only possible when the research methodology can include studies of long duration which involve objective, replicable, experimental studies.

Because it has not been possible to conduct this type of research in the past, research in the areas of experimental psychology, child psychology, clinical psychology, and educational psychology has been confined to the study of nonrepresentative samples of behavior. Thus, these fields have attempted to deal with artificial experimental tasks that were simple and did not require long experimental periods. The implicit assumption, of course, has been, using problem solving as an example, that a problem solving task is a problem solving task is a problem solving task is a problem solving task; that one task is as good as another. This was possible because the investigator was never confronted with the demand to demonstrate how his task related to the types of problem solving we are interested in in everyday life—nor with the manner in which the principles involved in the research could be extended to actual human problem solving.

It will only be suggested here that it is the task of psychology to complete theoretical analyses and experimental analyses of *actual* human behavior. It is also possible to begin the laboratory study of various complex human behaviors; social, emotional, cognitive, and sensory-motor. Laboratory researchers, it is felt, must now select types of behavior with which they wish to work and to begin intensive, long-term studies and series of studies of those behaviors. It is suggested that laboratory complexes like that used in the study of cognitive learning of preschoolers should be located in relevant academic and professional departments of universities. In this manner the actual repertoires could be studied with laboratory precision, while still providing the child with a profitable learning situation. This type of study could be concerned more with the basic questions than research which is conducted in institutional facilities which have a particular purpose.

That is, the basic learning principles and S–R mechanisms should be used to analyze actual complex human behaviors. Then, on the basis of the analysis, stimulus materials and training procedures should be devised by which to produce the behavior in question. Thus, for example various complex cognitive behaviors could be studied in the type of methodology outlined. Examples of such behaviors are the various aspects of language development, reading, counting, arithmetic sequences, writing, and the like as well as samples of such complex activities as real problem solving, concept formation, communication, grammatical learning, originality, and so on. The analyses of such complex behaviors presented herein could serve in that role; since they are based upon empirical (explanatory) principles they constitute empirical hypotheses. For example, creative problem solving of an actual nature has never been studied in the laboratory, but it would be possible. Thus, in Chapter 10 it was suggested that an original geometric proof of Thales occurred on the basis of the constituent elements already learned. There is no reason children could not be trained to such constituent elements and the possibility of the children producing an original geometric proof studied. The experimental psychology of learning must begin to deal with such analyses and such experimentation—the present methodology and findings suggest that it is now possible to do so. (This is not to suggest that short term studies of simplified aspects of human and animal behavior should no longer be conducted. Many of the studies described in this volume were of such a type. The emphasis in this discussion, however, is on representative samples of complex human behavior and long term research because these aspects of psychology require development and support. Traditional methods and interests are already developed and popular.)

The behaviors to be investigated in this manner are too numerous to be listed here. Moreover, the suggestion that psychology should move in this direction is intimately tied in with questions concerning research methodology and a philosophy of psychology and psychological theory. The next chapter will be briefly concerned with some of these topics in further indicating some of the implications of the present approach.

18

Research and
theoretical methodology

As already stated, in the development of psychology a schism was formed between experimentalists and applied workers, which if anything has been intensified in recent history. One of the important reasons this has occurred is that the two types of psychologists have not ordinarily worked with each other's concerns. For example, the methods of the experimental psychology of learning have been appropriate, primarily, for dealing with lower organisms or very simple human behaviors. Even when topics with interesting names like problem solving, concept formation, verbal learning, and the like, have been treated in experimental psychology, the tasks have been so nonrepresentative of functional human behaviors that little relevance was seen by the professional concerned with human behavior. Attempts to construct theory in the experimental field of learning have been concerned with the events of the animal laboratory, or very simple behaviors, and thus have had little relevance for complex human behavior.

From the other side, however, the work of the applied psychologist was of little interest to the basic experimentalist. The applied worker did not draw his principles from the basic field, so his results did not bear upon the concerns of the basic field. (Actually, much so-called basic research, because it is not founded upon basic principles, is no more basic than such applied studies.) More frequently, the principles or theoretical approaches used in applied work were drawn from naturalistic (clinical) observations, rather than from experimental observational methods. The principles and theories of the applied worker were consequently accorded a lesser value in terms of contributing to the growth of the science.

Some of this separation between basic and applied psychology may be seen as the inevitable result of the development of psychology. The experimental field had to first work out its basic principles in the artificial simplicity of the laboratory, for example. The applied worker, on the other hand, could obtain no help in the solution of his problems from the methods and principles of the basic field—so he developed his own methods and principles. These did not have the qualities of a natural science but they did deal with the problems with which the professional was concerned.

Thus, the separatism that grew between these interests can be seen to have had a rational basis. However, it may be suggested that today much of the separatism is uncalled for, and is actually an obstacle to growth. Crucial to the suggestion that a rapprochement is possible and productive is ample demonstration that the experimental and applied worker may have a common basis, in methodology and in theory and in the events which they study.

The author believes strongly that this is the case, that as the basic field develops to the point that its principles and methods and theory apply to and solve human problems, the separatism between *basic* and *applied* will dissolve. One of the goals of the present approach is to demonstrate these possibilities.

This chapter will be concerned with summarizing some points of research methodology and the philosophy of theory construction involved in the present approach. In addition, however, since the approach is founded upon the use of basic laboratory principles and methods to gain an understanding of complex human behavior and its problems, the discussions are also relevant to the predicted rapprochement. As such the discussions contain a philosophy of psychology that suggests the possibility of greater unity of endeavors within the field.

RESEARCH METHODOLOGY

One of the problems which appears to be an obstacle in dealing with significant, functional, human behavior within the context of scientific method has been that of research methodology. We have not had ways of working with such behaviors using our basic principles. This shortcoming of our presently accepted major methods of research for working with complex human behavior should be recognized, so that we can search for new methods. It must be realized that our methods have neither been complete nor sufficient for the task we face.

The discussion to follow is by no means intended to fully explore this topic. It only opens the problem for consideration, and also leads to the suggestion that the experimental-longitudinal type of research method fills a gap in presently accepted research methods in the study of functional human behavior.

Short-Term Group Research Methods

The reliability and generality of a set of scientific principles depends upon the reliability and generality of its observational foundation. For example, in testing the effect of an experimental manipulation upon the behavior of the subject, we must insure that other extra-experimental conditions do not affect the behavior in ways that would interfere. Where there are many extra-experimental conditions that affect the behavior of the individual subject, the experimental condition may in a relative sense be very weak. In such cases, the effect for any one individual could easily be that of an extra-experimental condition rather than that of an experimental manipulation.

However, we may test our experimental condition by using groups of subjects. For example, we could randomly select two groups of subjects from some population. The groups would then differ only randomly from each other in the extra-experimental conditions to which the individuals of the population had been subjected. If we now impose our experimental manipulation on one group (the experimental group) and not the other (the control group), then we will see whether the experimental condition has an effect over and above the random extra-experimental differences between the groups occasioned by the random selection of the subjects.

Many ways for conducting such research have been designed by statisticians, so there are experimental designs of this type to suit various types of research needs. When our ability to lessen the effects of extra-experimental conditions is poor, or in a case where it is uneconomical to do so, we can use group designs with good effect. Most of the principles of learning have been explored in detail in this way. Thus, the development of these methods was and is quite important to the science. This methodology has allowed laboratory simplification that would have been difficult to obtain in other ways—and because of this has enabled the discovery of basic, analytic, principles.

The use of group research methods has been criticized by Skinner and his associates on the basis that the effect of the experimental condition is measured by the *average* of the responses of the subjects in the experimental group versus the average of the control group subjects. That is, it has been said that an average is a fiction in the sense that no one subject may have responded in the manner the average indicates. The same average may be obtained in a group all of whom are slightly affected by the experimental condition, as well as in a group of subjects part of whom are greatly affected in one direction and part of whom are affected to a lesser extent in the other direction.

Such occurrences could conceivably arise. The empirical fact is, however, that the use of groups of subjects and statistical analyses have proved effective. Most of the major principles of learning have been found through the use of this type of methodology and have not been contradicted by findings of other methodologies. There are many circumstances when group methods are the only ones available, the most economical, necessary in the sense already described, and so on.

Moreover, group research methods can be considered in terms of replication of experimental findings—which is actually at the heart of the problem of observational reliability. Other things equal, one observation of the relationship between two events is not as strong as when the relationship has been shown a second time. In general, we may say that we are never absolutely sure that our experimental condition will affect each and every possible case in the predicted manner—because it is impossible for us to test each and every possible case. However, after we have obtained data upon a representative number of individuals our confidence becomes so high that it approaches certainty. This type of reliability and generality is gained by increasing the number of times we observe the experimental manipulation and its effect upon the behavior, and this ultimately involves groups of subjects, whether or not they have been run in groups, and whether or not statistical evaluations are involved.

While recognizing the contribution of group research and statistical designs to psychological experimentation, it must be suggested that for many purposes this research method is inadequate, incomplete, or not maximally effective. Several examples will be given where short-term group research methods are not maximally appropriate and where other types of research methods would provide a more suitable methodology. Take, for example, the case where there is an analysis of a behavior in terms of basic principles but where the behavior is very complex and requires a very long period for its acquisition. This was the case with some of the repertoires that have been described. In such cases it is impossible to study the behavior in a short period of time. To adequately study the behavior the research must be of long duration. However, where a great deal of time and expense is spent with a single subject, it may be impractical or impossible to deal with groups of subjects—at least in the beginning stages of the research.

Furthermore, in cases where long-term research is necessary, the behavior involved is likely to be quite complex, involving many different stimulus manipulations and many different kinds of response. Thus, in training a child to a complex repertoire like reading or number concept learning the stimuli presented are variegated as are the responses. These may not lend themselves to unitary description and quantitative (and statistical) analysis.

In addition, in the innovational stages of research it may be too costly in time and money, and too inflexible, to set up a group study for every procedure or principle that is to be assessed. Before one can conduct a formal experiment involving groups in a new area of study, it may be necessary to work out procedures and analyses for the conduct of the study. Each of the major points of innovation of the research reported herein involved innovational research to work out procedures and theoretical analyses—which because of these developments could be tested later in group studies. Yet we have not had materials by which to train our students to do this type of research, nor have we had a philosophy to justify doing or publishing this type of research, although it may be of crucial importance in the development of novel research projects.

The major point of these examples, however, is to indicate that restriction to the one research methodology of group research and statistical analysis is restrictive in terms of the types of problems we can work with. Other methods can be used to get the types of observations we need, and in a reliable manner. For example, reliable observations may be made upon single subjects, when the experimental condition is very powerful and when its systematic variation produces clear-cut results. A moment may be given to mentioning this type of research method.

Single-Subject Research Methods

Single subjects may be used under certain circumstances while producing reliable observations, and this can be done in a manner in which an experimental condition is varied and studied. Skinner and associates (Ferster and Skinner, 1957; Sidman, 1960) have by example and in statement outlined the techniques involved in conducting this type of research with animals—in contrast to group methods of research and statistical analyses.

Derivations may be made from this methodology for use in research with humans—as has been demonstrated in some of the studies that have been reported. Thus, experiments were conducted in which one subject was presented with two experimental conditions and rates of response under the two conditions were obtained. The study of many basic principles with humans may be conducted using an operant conditioning methodology and single-subject research designs. However, the methods of research with single subjects and operant conditioning technology do not fulfill our needs for work with the complex behaviors of humans. Like the short-term group methods, the types of responses that have been dealt with using these methods have been simple responses that are repeated many times. Thus, it is possible to record each response on a cumulative recorder with no further specification of the response. When dealing with complex repertoires, however, the stimuli and responses are variegated and operant conditioning recording methods are not appropriate. There are other requirements of such research which will be discussed further on.

It may also be added that in single-subject research we still require the reliability and generality that is obtained by using many subjects, and that ultimately we wish to replicate our findings on the one subject with additional subjects. Thus, the logic of the group methods may be considered to hold generally. The converse is also true, however. We want also to be sure that the principles we discover in group research will pertain to the individual subject. It is only in that way that we know that we have a basic principle and experimental control that permit extrapolation to the individual organism. This is especially true in the realm of human behavior where ultimately one will be interested in treating the behavior of individuals.

Long-Term Group Research Methods

In the study of complex human behavioral repertoires short-term studies simply do not get samples of the behaviors in which one is interested. What, one may ask, about the possibility of conducting long-term group studies? This adaptation of group research and statistical analysis to long-term training experiments has been made, especially in the field of educational and clinical research.

Typically, one teaching or clinical method will be applied to one group of subjects and another method to another group of subjects. Both groups will be given some type of achievement test, for example, to measure the degree of learning. The two groups will be compared using some statistical analysis to evaluate the possibility that the experimental conditions have produced an effect over that expected by chance. For example, two different types of reading training materials might be compared in this manner. Many times such studies have involved very large numbers of children.

While this method of research may be very useful in terms of comparing two sets of training materials, or of one training procedure to no training at all, it is not an analytical method. That is, the observations made upon the children are not detailed. Typically, when comparing two training methods, the children will only be "observed" one time. That is, the two groups will be treated differently and after a semester of training the average level of skill attained will be measured and compared.

From this type of data a specific and detailed analysis of the learning involved could not be made. One method could be better than the other during one portion of the training program, but not as good during other portions. Thus, even though one method may come out with an overall better result, the data do not give specific information concerning the method. On the basis of such research it is thus not possible to make progressive improvement in a set of training materials. Furthermore, since the research is nonanalytic and does not specify the nature of the specific stimuli presented to the subject, nor the subject's response to the stimulus, this method cannot be used to discover or test basic principles.

Nonexperimental Longitudinal Research Methods

In the fields of child psychology and educational psychology there has been large scale employment of what has been called the longitudinal method of research. In this method the behavior of the child is observed in and of itself. Most of this research is nonexperimental in the sense that no conditions are manipulated (even in a naturalistic way) to see what the effect will be on the behavior of the subject.

Much of this research usually involves repeated observations of children over a period of time. Or, as a variant, groups of children at different age levels may be observed. Then a systematic description will be made of the behavioral changes that occur in the child. These changes in development of behavior may be stated in terms of time; that children of a certain age typically evidence certain types of behavior, and so on.

The products of this type of research are very useful. On the basis of the descriptions of typical child behavior over different ages, a particular child's behavior can be judged in terms of advancement or retardation. Using systematic longitudinal data, these judgments can be made objective and more soundly based than judgments of the parent or professional who has only personal and unsystematic observations.

In addition to what is typically thought of as exemplifying this type of longitudinal research, there are other fields that use essentially the same method. For example, the field of intelligence testing may be seen as a formalized variant of the method, although the single child may be observed only once. That is, observations of the behavior of children of various ages are made in standard stimulus conditions (test items). The responses to the various items are summed as though they were equivalent to yield a quantitative score. On the basis of the description of the results of groups of children, a quantitative judgment may be made of the relative standing of a particular child.

Another, more recently developed, application of the longitudinal method of research has occurred in the field of psycholinguistics in the study of the language development of the child. That is, a number of individuals have begun applying the framework of structural linguistics to the systematic observation of children's speech. These studies may consist of the straightforward observation of a single child over a long period of time, or of groups of children at various age levels. The observation may be undifferentiated in terms of providing different standard stimulus conditions, or the child may be given certain materials which will elicit certain types of speech in children who have the repertoire. This research may be expected to give us a more detailed and objective description of language development under usual conditions than is now available.

The productivity of this longitudinal approach should be recognized, but also, its limitations should not be ignored. In being nonexperimental, that is, in not manipulating conditions to see their effect upon the development of behavior, the approach cannot be explanatory. It is one thing to observe and describe an event, but it is another thing to know the conditions that give rise to the event, and to be able to manipulate conditions to produce the event in the manner we desire. Thus, longitudinal research that depends solely upon observations of behavior cannot be expected to yield elementary principles by which we can state how behavior comes about, or to yield procedures for doing something about the behavior.

Furthermore, the longitudinal methods as used in the field of developmental psychology can tell us only what skills children develop under the usual conditions of everyday life. We should not conclude that this indicates in any way what cognitive, emotional, or sensory-motor skills children would be capable of acquiring if subjected to optimal learning conditions. We have traditionally thought that observations of children's behavioral development reflected biological maturational processes. When we realize that what is actually reflected is the nature of the learning conditions to which the child is subjected, we also realize that observations of children's behavioral development is strictly relative and not absolute. The descriptions of child development that have been made and the stages of development hypothesized are relative to the training customs of our society.

An example will prove useful here. Piaget has made many valuable observations of the manner in which children's cognitive skills develop. However, he has made the usual mistake of assuming the behavioral development was due in large part to internal maturational development—and thus that rate and form of cognitive development is fixed.

> A child of 5 or 6 may readily be taught by his parents to name the numbers from 1 to 10. If ten stones are laid in a row, he can count them correctly. But if the stones are rearranged in a more complex pattern or piled up, he can no longer count them . . . [H]e has not yet grasped the essential idea of number (1953, p. 75).

However, the results of the experimental-longitudinal research with children far younger than 5 or 6, children of 2, 3, and 4 years of age, showed that these and other functional cognitive repertoires could be developed under appropriate learning conditions. Moreover, this could be done with children classified as maturationally retarded. Thus, developmental norms obtained with traditional longitudinal methods will require revision as the conditions of learning are altered.

In any event, it must be concluded that longitudinal observations of behavioral development cannot provide us with an explanation of development; that is, knowledge of the principles by which children acquire their behavior. Moreover, traditional longitudinal observations cannot yield knowledge of the specific conditions that produce behavior we desire and prevent undesirable behavior, nor do the observations indicate what children at any particular age *could* develop (under maximal learning conditions), only what they develop under the unsystematic training conditions of everyday life.

Experimental-Longitudinal Research Methods

There is no question that it is important to establish the elementary laws of learning in well controlled laboratory conditions, using the group and single-subject experimental methods that have been briefly described. Moreover, it is important to make detailed observations of human behavior, and also to relate these observations to age in the longitudinal methods summarized. A problem, however, has existed in devising methods for investigating complex human behavior which is only acquired over long periods of time and which involves variegated stimuli and variegated responses—and do this in an experimental manner. It is clear that we have had one or the other—experimental studies have been limited to simple behaviors, at least when dealing with behavior in an analytic manner. And longitudinal studies have for the most part been nonexperimental in terms of manipulating causative conditions. We need new methods of research to combine both the experimental manipulation of independent variables, while at the same time analytically studying the specific effects of complex variables on the complex behavior of the individual over a long period of time.

In the latter stages of the study of language learning reported herein, an approach called an experimental-longitudinal method was used. The method appeared to produce reliable data in the sense that it was possible to replicate the findings, and to produce general statements in the sense that the findings could be extended to different types of subjects and different types of repertoires. It would seem productive to briefly describe some of the general rationale underlying this method.

It may first be noted that it is understandable that the long-term study of complex human behavior has not been conducted, because of the great difficulty involved. From a very practical standpoint, group studies are precluded—since the experimental time involved would be exorbitant. Thus, one is forced to deal only with one subject, or at most a very few. In view of this, one may ask how it is possible to insure that the conditions we have manipulated have been the real determinant of the change in behavior—that is, how can reliability of the findings be obtained? In short-term experimental methods the behavior of the experimentally-treated group is statistically compared to the behavior of a control group. In the single-subject research the behavior of the subject in the experimental period is compared to his behavior in the control period (without the experimental condition). Neither of these methods is available when working with one subject over an extended period of time on a behavior that is important to the subject's adjustment.

Moreover, how can generality be obtained from working with one human subject? Although a particular experimental condition may produce a behavior in one subject, one might ask whether we can expect to be able to generalize the finding to other subjects. There are several points that require discussion in the context of these questions.

First, it should be remembered that the traditional experimental methods we presently have were developed for the *discovery* of principles in a state of knowledge in which the basic principles of behavior were unknown or were in doubt. At this point, the point of discovery, a principle found in one study, for the first time, does not instill us with a great deal of confidence. To increase the weight of our finding we must be rigorous in excluding any other possible determinant. Without that rigor the finding would not merit publication. Even then, we will not be content that the novel principle found in one study is reliable until we have replications which increase our confidence.

When we begin a study with a well verified principle, however, we face different circumstances, at least to some extent. We require less evidence before we conclude that our results constitute a verification of the principle than we would if the study involved the discovery of a principle. When a principle has been verified so many times that it may be said to be true, we no longer see the study as a test of the principle plus a test of the specific conditions involved in the study, but only as a test of the specific conditions. If we fail to get the expected results, as a matter of fact, we are more likely to conclude that there were elements in the specific experiment that were awry.

Thus, a long-term study with a single subject that begins with an explicit analysis of the behavior in terms of well established basic principles, with the stimulus materials derived from the analysis, merits greater confidence than one that rests on a less firm basis. More evidence is required for the latter.

It should also be indicated that there are (or should be) varying standards with respect to the control of extra-experimental variables that might affect the behavior which we study. It may be suggested that the control of the effect of extra-experimental variables need not always be as formal as a control group as used in short-term group experimental methods, or as a control condition as used in single-subject experimental methods. Again, the requirements for controls against extra-experimental effects depend upon the state of our knowledge—and discovery stages of research are different than the stage when we have a good deal of knowledge of the variables which will and will not affect the behavior.

For example, in previously discussing the stimulus value of speech, the author cited an experimental-naturalistic study in which a cat was trained to respond to a verbal stimulus. It was possible to do this with one animal, and to draw conclusions from the results, because other information was available indicating that cats do not ordinarily respond to a verbal stimulus in the manner described. It is known, for example, that this behavior does not develop through physiological maturation. Thus, there was an implicit control group in this experimental-naturalistic study—the control group was formed by observations of the behavior of other untrained cats, and our general knowledge. The same is true of training a preschooler to a number concept repertoire, or to writing, or reading. Our previous evidence tells us that unless the child is given special training he will not develop these repertoires in his usual home life. Again, there is an informal or implicit control group.

Furthermore, the subject's past performance can also serve as an informal control condition—in a manner that is analogous to the variation of experimental and control conditions used in single-subject research methods. Thus, in the study with the juvenile delinquent the child's preceding 8½ years of school were considered as a control period which occurred prior to the institution of the experimental condition of 4½ months of special training. It was also suggested that the methods of subjecting the same subject to two different conditions could be extended to more complex behaviors. Thus, two different methods of reading training could be given to the same subject and the effects studied over a long period. Or, as another example, conditions of reinforcement could be varied within a long term experimental-longitudinal training procedure.

It must be concluded that as useful and important as our standards of experimentation have been and are, we have to know when they require modification. Rigidity in techniques is an obstacle. This stems from being concerned with specifics rather than with general principles of methodology. What we must take from our experimental methods are principles, the general logic which has been developed in experimental psychology. We must be prepared to adapt the principles to the requirements of the problem area.

This by no means need take us away from the fundamental principles of the experimental method. In any case where the research does not produce reliable and general results, it can be abandoned. It is suggested, however, that we can now begin long-term research on complex human behavioral repertoires—within the context of an experimental method. Our principles and experimental logic, and our general knowledge of man, are so developed that we are ready to innovate to new behaviors, new subjects, and new areas of study. Moreover, we have in our hands heavyweight conditions that when manipulated produce strong effects so they override other extra-experimental conditions. It would be mistaken not to realize this and not have this realization affect our methods of research and the subject matter of our research. The preceding experimental-naturalistic and experimental-longitudinal studies, it may be suggested, indicated the possibilities for developing new research areas and new research methods, while obtaining replicable and general results. This is not the place for a full discussion of methodology. However a few more points concerning the experimental-longitudinal method are appropriate.

The first topic, which will be elaborated in a later section, concerns the importance of theoretical analysis of the behavior as the basis for experimental-longitudinal research on human behavior. Part of one's confidence in the research findings depends upon the reliability of the principles utilized and in the ability to derive the stimulus materials and experimental procedures from the analysis. The analysis must be specific and detailed. This means that the stimuli involved in the training and the responses produced must be explicit. It is this type of analysis that makes it possible to derive the stimulus materials for the training and to observe the responses made by the subjects. In addition, as will be indicated later, the analysis in terms of basic principles is what gives the research its theoretical significance.

Moreover, it must be possible in the research to record the various stimuli that are presented to the subject as well as the subject's responses. When this is done well the study has all the objectivity of the laboratory—it is possible to specify what has happened to the subject in the research and what the resulting behavior was. It is this which will make it possible to see the action of the principles involved in the analysis and to assess in detail the experimental treatments.

It should be stated that when the experimental conditions have been stipulated in terms of basic principles, when the extra-experimental conditions have been reasonably well controlled, and when the experimental conditions and the subject's responses can be recorded, the results meet all the requirements of the data of natural science. The raw, untreated, data fulfill these requirements, even without sophisticated ways of analysis. However, it may be suggested that when such raw data have been gathered, ways of organizing and evaluating it may be studied. The problems that arise in the recording and evaluation of this type of data are presently unique. In most basic research in psychology, for example, the stimulus is simple and the response is simple. In studying complex human behavior, however, many different stimuli will be used and many different responses will ensue. The ways of organizing and evaluating the data represent new challenges for the methodologist. However, it cannot be said that the data do not have the objective character of an experimental science.

These several considerations—theoretical analysis, stipulation of the stimuli and responses upon the basis of the analysis, and detailed recording of the stimuli and responses—are all involved in producing reliable data. That is, when these objectives have been attained, a primary standard of experimentation can be met, the requirement of replication. Based upon explicit analysis, derivation of materials and procedures, and recording of stimuli, studies can be conducted in which the research conditions are repeated. Whether or not the data can be quantified must be considered to be secondary to this requirement for the objectivity, public nature, and replicability of research. It is interesting to note that with number concept learning, writing acquisition, and reading acquisition (both with original and remedial learning) the procedures were first worked out and tested with a single subject. In every case, however, the results were closely replicated with additional subjects.

This discussion is by no means offered as a complete presentation of the methodological questions involved in doing long-term research on complex human repertoires. Nor has it been suggested that the experimental-longitudinal method as discussed represents a finished research methodology. The discussion is intended, however, as a step to open for consideration the development of research methods that will bring us into contact with the problems that face the student of complex human behavior and the professional who deals with human behavior. Experimental design has, for the most part, meant the study of group research methods and statistical methods of analysis. And publication in journals is ordinarily dependent upon the use of such methods. It must be suggested, however, that these methods are restrictive and do not allow us to treat many of the major topics of interest in psychology. Moreover, our research skills, experimental logic, and theoretical advancement have brought us to the point where we are prepared to develop methods which will allow us to deal with these topics of interest. This demands that we use what is relevant from our backgrounds and innovate what is necessary within that general methodology—and this is the primary suggestion of the preceding and following discussion.

A RESEARCH STRATEGY FOR THE EXTENSION
OF LEARNING PRINCIPLES TO COMPLEX
HUMAN BEHAVIOR

A major tenet of the integrated-functional learning approach is that the stage has been reached where the basic principles of learning and the general methods of experimental psychology are ready for extension and application to the study and treatment of complex human behavior and the problems of behavior on a general front. Our major conditioning principles are well validated, we have much skill in experimentation with human behavior, it is possible to analyze complex behaviors in explicit stimulus-response terms. Furthermore, there are many studies that demonstrate the relevance of the principles in studies of various types of human behavior (see Staats, 1964a). However, most of the effort has been in extending the principles of learning to relatively simple samples of human behavior. In addition to these demonstrations we must on a wider scale have investigators begin to deal with a particular complex human repertoire in systematic theoretical and experimental analyses.

This approach involves selecting different significant behaviors and proceeding in long-term analyses of the behaviors in extended research programs. It may be suggested that this process will involve several steps: (1) selection of and theoretical analysis of the behavior, (2) demonstrational studies testing the major principles in the analysis, (3) long-term studies of the actual repertoires, (4) replication, generalization, and application studies that extend the previous findings. A few words will be said about each of these aspects of the strategy.

Selection and Analysis of A Repertoire

There is a marked tendency, even among researchers who are oriented along learning lines, when investigating some aspect of complex human behavior, to utilize the theory already existent in that area of study— in contrast to following a pure behavioral approach. Thus, as one example, Dollard and Miller (1950) utilized the concepts of psychoanalysis to a large extent in analyzing personality and psychotherapy, rather than making a pure learning analysis. The same is true in other areas. As previously mentioned, learning people who have experimented with concept formation or problem solving, as other examples, have tended to use previous categorizations of behavior as well as the traditional experimental tasks based upon those categorizations rather than to use samples of actual human behaviors. Somehow the abstract term *concept formation*, for example, seems more fundamental or basic, less applied, than a term like reading or counting. However, there is nothing more basic about the study of an artificial sample of problem solving, concept formation, perception, or what have you, in comparison to actual repertoires of cognitive learning. In either case what makes the study basic is the extent to which basic principles are involved in the theoretical or experimental investigations. The use of precise and well controlled experimental methods in conjunction with "faculty psychology" concepts —which is actually the combination many studies in academic experimental psychology employ—constitutes an unproductive strategy which produces findings that are not basic and not applied. That is, such studies are not derived from or related to basic principles and are thus not basic, and yet the findings have no extension to problems of human behavior and thus cannot be applied. It is time that we expect studies of complex human behavior to demonstrate one or the other characteristic, or both.

In an earlier chapter it was suggested that psychology in general has followed what may be called a "category-underlying process approach" rather than a "representative behavior sample and S–R analysis approach." This notion may be elaborated a little in indicating the first step in the latter research strategy.

The primary suggestion is that much of the research in psychology today is inadequate in its inception. That is, most present day research deals with experimental tasks (behaviors) that are trivial. This is done because it is assumed that it is the mental process underlying the task that is important. Thus, *any* task will reflect the workings of that process. The researcher feels that *any* particular problem task taps the internal problem-solving ability as well as any other problem, that copying a diagonal taps the process involved in copying nature in fine art (Olson, 1967), that *any* task of identifying categories of stimulus items constitutes a case of concept formation, that *any* change of behavior through language typifies communication, and so on.

If, on the other hand, one does not accept the assumption involved—that of an implicit determining process for every behavioral category—then the experimental task becomes all important as a representative of some universe of actual behaviors. Then we are not satisfied with just any task—selection of the task is a central part of the research. It is suggested that we must in any case specify a universe of significant human behavior and select for study a representative sample of the universe. We must dispense with our idealized conceptions of human behavior and the artificial experimental tasks we construct on the basis of the conceptions. Before discussing a more appropriate research strategy, several examples will be given of the errors that the "category-underlying process strategy" produces.

First, the categorization approach leads one to treat as different behaviors that are actually the same. The same behaviors were discussed herein under the names of communication, meaning, perception, attitudes, motivation, and so on. Yet use of one label ordinarily restricts interest in the study to investigators working within that particular category. Studies done under one label are not related to those done under another.

In addition, many times behaviors are discussed as though they were the same, although different learning principles are involved in each case. Using communication as the example again, it was shown that classical conditioning and instrumental conditioning principles were involved in communication acts—as well as various S–R mechanisms. Categorization schemes that suggest a unitary process narrow the scope of our considerations. For this reason it is necessary to promulgate a "pluralistic" approach to many areas of human behavior.

Furthermore, our classificatory system and its related assumption of underlying, unitary, psychological processes has led us astray in another direction. Because it is felt that the *underlying* process is *primary*, studies which utilize this research strategy are considered basic and general. On the other hand, studies that pointedly attempt to study the behavior itself —even when the behaviors are more significant—are considered as applied and of far lesser value. If it was not because of the error in strategy, there would be no reason to consider a relatively trivial experimental task, such as sorting a deck of cards (to categorize stimuli), as generally typical of concept formation while relegating the learning of letter reading or initial number learning to a less "basic" role—in a direct reversal of reality. The opinion (based on the categorization approach) that dealing with actual human behavior is unscientific is entirely unfounded. The study should be considered to be basic to the extent that we investigate or employ basic principles and methods. In the present view there are three levels of basic study in the field of learning—those that deal directly with the higher-order conditioning principles, those that deal with the derived S–R mechanisms, or those that employ these principles in the study of human behavior. All relate to the basic theoretical structure. When the concern is with human behavior, in the third level of study, the closer the sample of behavior is to an actual human behavior the greater the basic value of the study.

At any rate, it has already been suggested that psychology is ready to deal with samples of actual human behavior using the methods and principles of the basic science. It is felt that more psychologists must begin their research efforts by looking to actual human behaviors for samples they wish to investigate, rather than looking to the categories of the past and the limitations of the presently used experimental tasks that enjoy popularity. (See Staats, 1967d, for a more complete discussion.)

The question may arise concerning how one selects a behavior to study. This could be done in various ways, depending upon the repertoire involved. For example, the psychologist interested in cognitive behavior could commence with the types of specifications of cognitive repertoires that the child must acquire in reading, or arithmetic, mathematics and so on—as these are found in children's school books. Or, in the area of language, linguists have made careful, precise, and detailed observations of certain aspects of language behavior. In the area of clinical psychology, books on psychopathology contain many straightforward descriptions of abnormal behaviors, for example, the distortions in language which the schizophrenic displays. Books in sociology, social psychology, anthropology, and so on, also include descriptions of repertoires important to human adjustment. Longitudinal studies many times yield descriptions of important human behaviors, as well as the manner in which the behaviors change.

The investigator could also begin his study by becoming interested in a behavior that he has observed in the naturalistic circumstance, even though no one else has described it in a general manner. In any event, in many cases, it would be expected that the investigator would need to make first hand observations of the repertoire in the naturalistic situation, be it the clinical, educational, or other institution. Ultimately, however, it is necessary to make close contact with the behavior so that the behavior may be stipulated in detail.

This is not a simple injunction to investigate complex behavioral samples—if that was the case the work would not have a relationship to the basic science. The strategy is to start with observations of a behavior but then to make a specific, detailed, theoretical analysis of the behavior in terms of learning principles and S–R mechanisms. To do this the various stimuli acting upon the behavior (as well as the responses they affect) must be specified.

The controlling stimuli may be produced by the individual's own behavior, or by someone else's behavior, such as language, motor, or emotional behaviors. The stimuli may be environmental or social stimuli. The stimuli involved may be also of various sorts. They may include conditioned stimuli, discriminative stimuli, or conditioned reinforcers, as examples. Although the stimuli may have immediate controlling value in the situation, it is likely that a long course of training was involved in which the stimuli acquired their controlling properties. Thus, we have to look to the training circumstances and consider what the principles were that were involved.

When this type of analysis has been completed it constitutes a theory of that particular complex repertoire. Such an analysis may be considered to be productive as a theory from which experimental hypotheses may be drawn, which is an important aspect of the power of the approach. It should be remembered, however, that the research which stems from an analysis of human behavior in terms of basic principles has theoretical significance, regardless of what behavior is dealt with. That is, research on reading, for example, would ordinarily be considered to be applied research. However, when the experimental hypotheses are drawn from a set of basic principles, and the methods of research are drawn from experimental methodology, then the study has great significance for the basic science, even though it may also have social utility.

Demonstrational Study

When a theoretical analysis of a complex human behavior has been made, the next step in the long-term study is to derive an experimental hypothesis from the analysis that is susceptible to empirical test. The author commenced the study of word meaning with the classical conditioning analysis. If word meaning is a classically conditioned response, however, then pairing a word with a ^{uc}S should condition a response to the word. This empirical hypothesis was derived from the learning analysis of word meaning.

The author conducted the first demonstrational study with a cat and then with additional animal subjects. Although the studies were in this case not formal enough to be published independently, they can be used to illustrate the importance of the demonstrational study. The purpose of the demonstrational study is to test the main basic principle involved in the analysis in the context of the behavior of interest. When the principle is supported in the context of the behavior, this may be considered to some extent to support the whole analysis of the behavior.

In demonstrational studies, various of the experimental methods could be useful. Group designs and statistical analyses or single-subject designs might be most effective. It should be indicated that in addition to the value of the demonstrational study to the science in opening up a new field to experimentation, the individual investigator in conducting the study will learn a great deal about the behavior involved and the subject population selected for the study. This knowledge is the basis for advancing to further studies of the repertoire.

Extensions and Replications of Demonstrational Studies

The research may be expected to advance in two ways. When a principle has been validated in the context of a new behavior, this suggests that other related principles in the theory will also be relevant to the behavior. This expectation will give impetus to research which tests this possibility. Thus, as an example, after demonstrating that reading acquisition involves the principle of instrumental discrimination learning, further experiments were conducted on corollary principles like those of the schedule of reinforcement. In general, these extensions will also produce additional information about the repertoire itself, and also provide necessary replication studies. (It cannot be overemphasized that replication studies conducted with additional subjects is fundamental to experimental-longitudinal research.)

In addition to research of this type, studies should be conducted to obtain better and better samples of the repertoire to analyze these samples in terms of the basic principles, and to devise better ways of experimentally studying such samples. Many times research ends with the demonstrational study. The investigator (or other investigators) moves on to the study of another behavior, contents himself with studying other principles in the context of the same behavior, and so on. It is worthwhile to indicate, however, that completion of the theoretical-experimental task involves movement along the dimension of dealing with samples of the behavior that are more and more like the actual behaviors that occur in life. Theoretical extrapolations and implications are not enough. *We cannot consider that the principles involved in a study actually apply to problem solving or reasoning, for example, or any cognitive skill until the principles and methods can be extended to a representative sample of the repertoires involved.* Again, each additional study may constitute a replication.

Although short-term studies may have been used in the first demonstrational studies, if the behavior is complex and requires long-term training the conduct of additional studies may involve the development of experimental-longitudinal methods of research. We have to distinguish the modification of what are actually relatively simple behaviors, or classes of behavior, from the modification of more complex behaviors. It is stimulating to us, and a momentous step, to extinguish temper tantrums, or shape walking versus crawling, or shape going to bed at night without a fuss, the cooperative interaction of children, the restoration of speech in a mute but formerly vocal schizophrenic, the extinction of phobic responses, and other cases that have been reported in the literature. But we have to realize what the nature of this progress in learning extension is, and the task that lies ahead as well. These are impressive demonstrations of the relevance and applicability of learning principles to the treatment of behavior problems. However, we cannot expect to restore the word scramble of the schizophrenic to high-level communication and good language behavior in reasoning through a short-term procedure. Most of the important, complex, repertoires such as the original acquisition of the basic behavioral repertoire, speech, reading, the development of a full repertoire of social behaviors, work behaviors, and so-called mental retardation, are acquired or are not acquired only over a period of many years. We must expect that it would take years to change or institute these behaviors even under good training procedures. Nevertheless, we must begin the study of such complex human behaviors, as well as more simple ones. But we must expect the task to be as difficult as the discovery of the basic principles of learning. Although it would be expected on the basis of available findings that the principles of learning hold from rat to man, many of the repertoires to be acquired by man are fantastically complex and this complexity requires study in and of itself.

Applications to Actual Problems

As has been stated, when the principles of a field of study are relevant to problems of the world, then one way of verifying the principles is in the extent to which the principles contribute solutions to those problems.

Following this view, when we have chosen a complex behavior for analysis, then one of the means of assessing the analysis is in the ability to use it and our research procedures to consider some of the problems of that type of behavior.

Thus, when we make a theoretical analysis of language, this is only part of the task. Another part is the conduct of studies to verify the analysis in laboratory type research. In addition, however, an important part of the task is to take the knowledge we have gained and to begin the solution of problems involving that behavior. (In each case replication with additional subjects is central to the method.)

For these reasons the author sees a central aspect of the psychology of learning to involve taking a significant aspect of human behavior and treating it theoretically and experimentally to the point where actual applications are made. It will also be this type of endeavor that will breach the schism between academic-experimental psychology versus professional-applied psychology. When the professional psychologist uses the theory and procedures of basic psychology, the work of each will contribute to the interests of the other. There are many, many complex human repertoires that must be systematically studied to the point where applications are made. The approach has the two-fold possibility of contributing to the solution of human problems as well as contributing to the science of psychology and the other social and behavioral sciences. It should be stated that the study of human behavior using learning principles and methods, when all potentialities are employed, contains all of the constituents of a classical natural science, a topic about which a few words should be said in concluding the present outline.

THE INTEGRATED-FUNCTIONAL LEARNING APPROACH AS A CLASSIC THEORY

In advanced stages of a science higher-order (more general, abstract, or more basic) statements may be made concerning the complex inter-relationships of lower-level empirical laws (or principles). Thus, a simple, elegant, set of theoretical statements can be developed that will account for a number of different observations or empirical laws—in fact hypotheses may be derived from the theoretical statements that suggest empirical laws not yet discovered. This process of scientific theory construction has been succinctly summarized by Spence.

> The physicist is able to isolate, experimentally, elementary situations, i.e., situations in which there are a limited number of variables, and thus finds

it possible to infer or discover descriptive, lower-order laws. Theory comes into play for the physicist when he attempts to formulate more abstract principles which will bring these low-order laws into relationship with one another. Examples of such comprehensive theories are Newton's principle of gravitation and the kinetic theory of gases. The former provided a theoretical integration of such laws as Kepler's concerning planetary motions, Galileo's law of falling bodies, laws of the tides and so on. The kinetic theory has served to integrate the various laws relating certain properties of gases to other experimental variables. (1944, pp. 47–48)

When such an advanced stage of a science is reached the theoretical body may instill much confidence by being well verified observationally. And it may allow one to predict diverse happenings as well as to control those happenings. Much of the advancement in the science may then come in further developments in these theoretical, or higher-level, statements—in reorganizations of these statements that better incorporate the various empirical laws and observations. The spectacular results of such reorganizations in being better able to account for past observations, and in suggesting new ones, and in solving various problems hitherto unsolved elevates these theoretical activities of science to a lofty perch and tends to make less lofty-seeming the original observations and empirical laws upon which the higher-level theoretical statements were based. Some philosophers of science have thus given precedence to "rational" or theoretical elements in science rather than to the empirical elements and have considered the sciences that have attained this advanced stage as the model for all sciences.

Psychological theory in the field of learning, which has served as the model for theory construction in psychology, has attempted to follow this example from classic theory in the physical sciences. In doing this the original theorists in psychology *considered the laboratory established empirical principles of learning as the lower-order laws.* This had a crucial effect on theory-construction in the field. The task of constructing a theory was seen as the search for a set of more abstract statements, higher-order laws, from which the empirical principles of learning could be derived. The early theorists in psychology accepted this approach, and it was stated formally by such psychologists as Hull and Spence.

However, this approach to theory construction in the field of learning has not led to success. It spawned a number of antagonistic theories, and research that had no relevance except to the parent theories which later lost their importance and their adherents. This orientation to theory construction in learning was in its general sense unsuccessful and, except for those interested in mathematical models, no longer inspires much enthusiasm. It is interesting to note that even Spence indicated in 1960 that this approach had not yet reached that stage of development where there was a set of interrelated higher-order theoretical statements that constituted a general theory.

It may be suggested, however, that use of the model of theory taken from the physical sciences is not in error, although it was misapplied by the early learning theorists. That is, the physical science model of theory can be applied to psychology to produce a classic theory of human behavior—but in a different way than has been seen by theorists in learning.

To see the usefulness of the physical science model of theory it is necessary to accept the empirical laws of learning in a *new role*. These empirical laws of learning are not the lower-order laws in the theory, to be accounted for by other more abstract statements. *The principles of learning* (although not complete) *are themselves the higher-order laws, from which the lower-order laws are to be derived.* The task is not one of developing a theory to account for the laws of learning. The task is to elaborate and employ the laws of learning as the higher-order laws to establish a theory of man's behavior; that is, to account for the empirical observations and principles of man's behavior that we see in the various parts of psychology as well as the other social and behavioral sciences. This suggestion constitutes a change that has many implications for basic and applied psychology, and for their relationship as well. It has the same implications for the social and behavioral sciences.

The type of theory which is being proposed herein has three major constituents; (1) the higher-order (basic) laws of learning, their derived interrelationships, and their corollaries, (2) the second-order S–R mechanisms which are or can be derived from the higher-order laws of learning, and (3) the lower-order laws and hypotheses that refer to specific types of human behaviors which are or can be derived from the two preceding types of higher-order statements. A brief description of these three constituents of the theory will help illustrate the conceptualization.

The formulation of the set of learning principles that is to compose the higher-order laws of the theory is not a simple task and is crucial to the endeavor. As has been described, the field of learning has involved various approaches each with its separate terminology, as well as a welter of experimental studies using a multitude of experimental methods and the various terminologies. The task at this level of the theory construction is to sift the products of the area of learning to select those laws that are parsimonious, internally consistent, and yet comprehensive enough to perform the necessary functions when elaborated and extended to the relevant empirical events of human behavior. This means cutting across previous interpretations and various research methods and research procedures to examine learning principles as they may play a part as the basic laws in a theory. Some of these higher-order laws may be abstracted from previous experimental and theoretical findings and will only require restatement within the framework of the theory. It may be expected, however, as was demonstrated herein, that some of these higher-order laws will not have been recognized yet—since the *goals* of the theory construction task will also give indications concerning what is to be sought. Thus, for example, it was previously stated that a discriminative stimulus will pass its control over a response to any new stimulus with which it is paired. This is not a basic principle that has been stated or explicitly studied in the laboratory, it emerges from applying the set of learning principles to aspects of man's language behavior. Many other such examples were discussed. At any rate, part of the theoretical and experimental task at this level of the theory construction task is to discover and derive all of the laws that will be required.

In addition to this, of course, the laws must be stated in a form that stimulates theoretical derivation of laws not yet observed, and especially derivation of the interrelationships of the basic principles that are not readily seen in the laboratory. In this task, terminological developments are necessary, as was suggested in proposing the notational system which was used to integrate the various learning principles and show their interrelationships. Theoretical endeavors at this level may also be expected to reveal new discoveries. Thus, as examples, it was clarifying and had many implications to consider (1) that when a neutral stimulus is paired with an unconditioned stimulus which is also a reinforcing stimulus the neutral stimulus will become a conditioned stimulus and also a conditioned reinforcing stimulus or (2) that reinforcement value and discriminative stimulus value are directly related in human behavior so that increase in the former increases the latter, and so on. The author (see Staats, 1964*a*, 1966; Staats and Staats, 1963) has formulated a set of higher-order learning laws, and in a less comprehensive but more advanced manner has elaborated the account herein using the improved terminological convention. These may only be considered to be tentative, however. Much of the task lies ahead. It may be expected that reformulations at this level of the theory will be very significant in its development.

As has already been stated, single S–R processes will not account for complex human behavior. However, S–R processes may be formed into complex constellations that will account for the infinite variety and flexibility of human behavior. For learning principles to constitute a theory of human behavior it is necessary to indicate how these complex S–R mechanisms can be derived from the higher-order laws of learning.

It is suggested that this is an essential part of theory construction in creating a learning theory of human behavior. This task also includes empirical verification in laboratory circumstances of the manner in which these complex S–R mechanisms may be learned by the individual. Many experiments in the areas of concept formation, reasoning, problem-solving, communication, perception, memory, motivation, verbal mediation, serial and paired associate learning, and so on, may be seen as examples of studies demonstrating the formation and (or) the functioning of such complex mechanisms. A more systematic, conscious, effort to explore the various types of complex S–R mechanisms might be expected to add significantly to the present findings. Moreover, it is important to recognize the relationship of the second-order S–R mechanisms to the higher-order laws of learning. Self-conscious recognition of the role of the S–R mechanisms in the theory will lead to more systematic exploration of the type of S–R mechanisms that can be derived from the higher-order principles, and research will be begun with this type of theoretical derivation as the foundation.

The last constituent in the theoretical endeavor involves extending the higher-order laws, or the second-order laws (the complex S–R mechanisms), to actual human behaviors. In doing this the abstract S–R statements in the two types of higher-order laws must be empirically defined in terms of the stimuli impinging upon the human, including motivational stimuli and the stimuli of one's own behavior, and so on, as well as the responses produced by the experiential processes. The preceding discussions in the present chapter have indicated some of the general aspects concerned with the task of analyzing human behavior in both theory and experiment in terms of learning principles.

The present book exemplifies these three aspects of the theory construction task. In the book the theory has been extended to the consideration of certain aspects of language learning and cognitive behaviors. It may be suggested, however, that it is possible to derive lower-order analyses from the theory of human learning that are important to various areas of psychology and to the other social and behavioral sciences. By means of the learning approach it is possible to integrate diverse areas of psychology, diverse experimental methods and findings, and diverse concepts, into one theoretical structure. A major aspect of theoretical psychology must be devoted to this type of theory construction. Moreover, this activity should not be limited to areas of psychology but must also be extended to the various social and behavioral sciences—which has and will continue to be a primary focus of the author's work (see also Staats, 1964a, 1966, in press, b; Staats and Staats, 1963). The aim of the present approach is to produce a unified, comprehensive, theory or conception of human behavior based upon a natural science approach and experimental principles and methods. It is suggested that progress in achieving this goal raises the study of man's behavior to the status and theoretical advancement shown in the physical sciences—that is, which makes the psychological conception a theory in the classical sense.

To the investigator interested in functional human behavior, it is the last level of the theory construction task that is of focal interest. The two more basic levels of the theory are of primary interest to the more basic researcher and theorist. It is true that the man who deals with the higher-order principles of a theory many times is dealing with the most generally significant matters—for the more fundamental the principle the more general it is in the sense that more problems are effected by derivations from the principle. It is also true, however, that a scientific principle or theory also derives its significance in ways other than in demonstration in the basic laboratory. One must ask, thus, is the principle or theory of narrow scope restricted to the animal lab, for example? If so it is of interest, but of limited interest. Or is the principle one that has great generality, applying to many human behaviors, and valuable in the sense of contributing to the solution of important problems involving those behaviors? Does the principle pertain to many organisms, many stimulus situations, and to man himself, for a wide variety of complex behaviors in complex situations? If so the principle is very basic and very general and very significant—and if as one of a set of such principles it is possible to understand and deal with human behavior generally in areas important to the various social and behavioral sciences, then the principle is part of a great conception. Thus, it is in this third area of development that the theory has its great social significance—and progress in this area is one of the three integral parts of the theory construction task.

It is the author's contention that an integrated learning theory composed of heavy-weight principles of instrumental and classical conditioning and their interrelationships, the complex S—R mechanisms that these principles can produce, and the findings, concepts, and methods of the various areas of experimentation in psychology and the other areas of the study of man form such a conception of human behavior. This conception, it is suggested, is potentially capable of dealing with behavior of even the most complex kind: individual, group, and societal.

A necessary part of establishing this conception of human behavior is the repeated verification of this theory or conception in the context of important complex human behaviors. A major aim of the present book has been to demonstrate the feasibility of doing this. This effort can only be considered a beginning, even in the areas under study. It may be suggested, however, that enough progress has been made to indicate that a very prominent part of psychology, contributing to the science itself and to other social and behavioral sciences, but also to human welfare and progress, should be in similar efforts in the study of additional aspects and problems of human behavior.

References

Allport, F. H. *Social Psychology.* Boston: Houghton Mifflin, 1924.

Ayllon, T., and J. L. Michael. The psychiatric nurse as a behavioral engineer. *J. exp. anal. Behav.,* 1959, **2,** 323–334.

Azrin, N. H. Time-out from positive reinforcement. *Science,* 1961, **133,** 382–383.

Ball, R. S. *Reinforcement conditioning of verbal behavior by verbal and nonverbal stimuli in a situation resembling a clinical interview.* Unpublished doctoral dissertation, Indiana Univer., 1952

Bandura, A. *Social learning through imitation.* In M. R. Jones (Ed.), *Nebraska symposium on motivation.* Lincoln: University of Nebraska Press, 1962.

Bandura, A., D. Ross, and S. Ross. A comparative test of the status envy, social power, and the secondary reinforcement theories of identification learning *J. abnorm. Soc. Psychol.,* 1963, **67,** 527–534.

Bandura, A., and R. H. Walters. *Social Learning and Personality Development.* New York: Holt, Rinehart and Winston, Inc., 1963.

Berko, J. The child's learning of English morphology. *Word,* 1958, **14,** 150–177.

Berlyne, D. E. The arousal and satiation of perceptual curiosity in the rat. *J. comp. physiol. Psychol.,* 1955, **48,** 238–246.

Bever, T. G., J. A. Fodor, and W. Weksel. On the acquisition of syntax: a critique of "contextual generalization." *Psychol. Rev.,* 1965, **72,** 467–482.

Bigge, M. L., and M. P. Hunt. *Psychological foundations of education.* New York: Harper & Row, 1962.

Birge, J. S. *Verbal responses in transfer.* Unpublished doctoral dissertation, Yale University, New Haven, 1941.

Bloomfield, L., and C. L. Barnhart. *Let's read: A linguistic approach.* Detroit: Wayne State University Press, 1961.

585

Bousfield, W. A., B. H. Cohen, and G. A. Whitmarsh. Verbal generalization: a theoretical rationale and an experimental technique. *Tech. Rep., No. 23*, Contract No. Nohr—631(00) between the Office of Naval Research and the University of Connecticut, 1958.

Bousfield, W. A., B. H. Cohen, G. A. Whitmarsh, and W. D. Kincaid. The Connecticut free associational norms. *Tech. Rep. No. 35*, under Contract Nohr—631 (00) between Office of Naval Research and the University of Connecticut, 1961.

Brogden, W. J. Sensory pre-conditioning. *J. exp. Psychol.*, 1939, **25**, 323–332.

Brogden, W. J. Sensory pre-conditioning of human subjects. *J. exp. Psychol.*, 1947, **37**, 527–540.

Brown, R. W. *Words and things.* New York: Free Press, 1958.

Brown, R. W., and J. Berko. Word association and the acquisition of grammar. *Child Developm.*, 1960, **31**, 1–14.

Brown, R., and C. Fraser. The acquisition of syntax. Paper delivered at the Second ONR-New York University Conference on Verbal Learning, June 1961, Dobbs Ferry, New York.

Brown, R., and E. H. Lenneberg. A study in language and cognition. *J. abnorm. soc. Psychol.*, 1954, **49**, 454–462.

Butler, R. A., and H. M. Alexander. Daily patterns of visual exploration behavior in the monkey. *J. comp. physiol. Psychol.*, 1955, **48**, 247–249.

Carter, H. D. Over- and underachievement in reading. *Calif. J. educ. Res.*, 1964, **15**, 175–183.

Chomsky, N. Verbal behavior (a review of Skinner's book). *Language*, 1959, **35**, 26–58.

Cofer, C. N., and J. P. Foley. Mediated generalization and the interpretation of verbal behavior: I. Prolegomena. *Psychol. Rev.*, 1942, **49**, 513–540.

Cohen, B. H. Role of awareness in meaning established by classical conditioning. *J. exp. Psychol.*, 1964, **67**, 372–378.

Cohen, D. J., H. I. Kalish, J. R. Thurston, and E. Cohen. Experimental manipulation of verbal behavior. *J. exp. Psychol.*, 1954, **47**, 106–110.

Das, J. P., and P. C. Nanda. Mediated transfer of attitudes. *J. abnorm. soc. Psychol.*, 1963, **66**, 12–16.

Deese, J. On the prediction of occurrence of particular verbal intrusions in immediate recall. *J. exp. Psychol.*, 1959, **58**, 17–22.

Di Vesta, F. J., and G. O. Bernheim. Some semantic relations among word-associates: A replication. *J. gen. Psychol.*, 1967, **76**, 101–105.

Di Vesta, F. J., and D. O. Stover. The semantic mediation of evaluative meaning, *J. exp. Psychol.*, 1962, **64**, 467–475.

Dollard, J., and N. Miller. *Personality and psychotherapy.* New York. McGraw-Hill, 1950.

Dostálek, C. Formation of a temporary connection in man between two "indifferent" stimuli of equal intensity, with different time intervals between commencements of both stimuli. *Physiol. Bohemoslov.,* 1959, **8,** 47–54.

Downing, J. A. *The i.t.a. reading experiment.* London: Evans Bros. Limited, 1964.

Edwards, A. L. *Experimental design in psychological research.* New York: Holt, Rinehart and Winston, Inc., 1960.

Ellis, N. R., C. D. Barnett, and M. W. Pryer. Operant behavior in mental defectives: exploratory studies. *J. exp. anal. Behav.,* 1960, **1,** 63–69.

Ellson, D. Hallucinations produced by sensory conditioning. *J. exp. Psychol.,* 1941, **28,** 1–20.

Ervin, S. M. Grammar and classification. Paper delivered at the American Psychological Association Symposium: "Language and the child's formation of concepts." New York, 1957.

Eysenck, H. J. *Behaviour therapy and the neuroses.* New York: Pergamon, 1960.

Ferster, C. B. Intermittent reinforcement of matching to sample in the pigeon. *J. exp. anal. Behav.,* 1960, **3,** 259–272.

Ferster, C. B., and B. F. Skinner. *Schedules of reinforcement.* New York: Appleton, 1957.

Finley, J. R., and A. W. Staats. Evaluative meaning words as reinforcing stimuli. *J. verb. Learning verb. Behav.,* 1967, **6,** 193–197.

Fodor, J. A. Could meaning be an r_m? *J. verb. Learning verb. Behav.,* 1965, **4,** 73–81.

Forehand, G. A. Epilogue: Constructs and strategies for problem-solving research. In B. Kleinmuntz (Ed.), *Problem solving.* New York: Wiley, 1966.

Fowler, W. Cognitive learning in infancy and early childhood. *Psychol. Bull.,* 1962, **59,** 116–152.

Goldman, L. The Kwakiutl Indians of Vancouver Island. In M. Mead (Ed.), *Cooperation and competition among primitive peoples.* New York: McGraw-Hill, 1937.

Grant, P. A., and L. M. Schipper. The acquisition and extinction of conditioned eyelid responses as a function of the percentage of fixed-ratio random reinforcement. *J. exp. Psychol.,* 1952, **43,** 313–320.

Green, B. F. Introduction: Current trends in problem solving. In B. Kleinmuntz (Ed.), *Problem solving.* New York: Wiley, 1966.

Greenspoon, J. The effect of verbal and nonverbal stimuli on the frequency of members of two verbal response classes. Unpublished doctoral dissertation, University of Indiana, 1950.

Harlow, H. F., N. C. Blazek, and G. E. McClearn. Manipulatory motivation in the infant rhesus monkey. *J. comp. physiol. Psychol.*, 1956, **49**, 444–448.

Harris, F. R., M. K. Johnston, C. S. Kelley, and M. M. Wolf. Effects of positive social reinforcement on regressed crawling of a nursery school child. *J. ed. Psychol.*, 1964, **55**, 35–41.

Heber, R. F. Motor task performance of high-grade mentally retarded males as a function of the magnitude of incentive. *Amer. J. ment. Defic.*, 1959, **63**, 667–671.

Herrick, R. M., J. L. Myers, and A. L. Korotkin. Changes in S^D and S rates during development of an operant discrimination. *J. comp. physiol. Psychol.*, 1959, **52**, 359–364.

Herrnstein, R. J., and J. V. Brady. Interaction among components of a multiple schedule. *J. exp. anal. Behav.*, 1958, **1**, 293–301.

Hobbs, N. Helping disturbed children: Psychological and sociological strategies. *Amer. Psychologist*, 1966, **21**, 1105–1115.

Hogan, B. *Ben Hogan's five lessons of the modern fundamentals of golf.* New York: Barnes, 1957.

Holland, J. G. Human vigilance. *Science*, 1958, **128**, 61–67.

House, B. J., and D. Zeaman. Visual discrimination learning and intelligence in defectives of low mental age. *Amer. J. ment. Defic.*, 1960, **65**, 51–58.

Hull, C. L. Quantitative aspects of the evolution of concepts. *Psychol. Monogr.*, 1920, No. 123.

Hull, C. L. Knowledge and purpose as habit mechanisms. *Psychol. Rev.*, 1930, **37**, 511–525.

Hull, C. L. The concept of the habit-family hierachy and maze learning. *Psychol. Rev.*, 1934a, **41**, 33–54.

Hull, C. L. The concept of the habit-family hierachy and maze learning: Part II. *Psychol. Rev.*, 1934b, **41**, 134–152.

Hull, C. L. *Principles of behavior.* New York: Appleton, 1943.

Irwin, O. C. Infant speech: Development of vowel sounds. *J. speech hearing Disorders*, 1948, **13**, 31–34.

Irwin, O. C. Speech development in the young child: 2. Some factors related to the speech development of the infant and young child. *J. speech hearing Disorders*, 1952, **17**, 269–279.

Jenkins, J. J. , and D. S. Palermo. Mediation processes and the aquisition of linguistic structure. In the *Acquisition of Language, Monograph of the Society for Research in Child Development*, 1964, **29**, No. 1.

Jenkins, J. J., and W. A. Russell. Annual technical report: Basic studies on individual and group behavior. Contract No. N8 our—66216 between the Office of Naval Reseach and the University of Minnesota, 1956.

Kagan, J. Personality and the learning process. *Daedulus*, 1965, **94**, 558–559.

Kapustink, O. P. (The interrelation between direct conditioned stimuli and their verbal symbols). Trudy Laboratorii Fiziologii Vysshey Nervnoy Deyatel'-nosti Rebyonka pri Leningradskom Pedagogicheskom Institute Gertzena, 1930, **2**, 11–22. (Cf. *Psychol. Abstracts*, 1934, **8**, 18. No. 153.)

Keller, F. S., and W. N. Schoenfeld. *Principles of psychology*. New York: Appleton, 1950.

Kendler, H. H., and M. F. D'Amato. A comparison of reversal shifts and nonreversal shifts in human concept formation behavior. *J. exp. Psychol.*, 1955, **49**, 165–174.

Kendler, H. H., and A. D. Karasik. Concept formation as a function of competition between response produced cues. *J. exp. Psychol.*, 1958, **55**, 278–283.

Kendler, H. H., and M. S. Mayzner. Reversal and nonreversal shifts in card-sorting tests with two or four sorting categories. *J. exp. Psychol.*, 1956, **51**, 244–248.

Kendler, H. H., and P. Vineberg. The acquisition of compound concepts as a function of previous training. *J. exp. Psychol.* 1954, **48**, 252–258.

Kent, G. H., and A. J. Rosanoff. A study of association in insanity. *Amer. J. Insanity*, 1910, **67**, 37–96.

Kleinmuntz, B. (Ed.). *Problem Solving*. New York: Wiley, 1966.

Krasner, L. Studies of the conditioning of verbal behavior. *Psychol. Bull.*, 1958, **55**, 148–170.

Lacey, O. L., and P. S. Siegel. An analysis of the unit of measurement of the galvanic skin response. *J. exp. Psychol.*, 1949, **39**, 122–127.

Laffal, J., L. D. Lenkoski, and L. Ameen. "Opposite speech" in a schizophrenic patient. *J. abnorm. soc. Psychol.*, 1956, **52**, 409–413.

Lenneberg, F. H. The natural history of language. In F. Smith and G. A. Miller (Eds.), *The genesis of language*. New York: M.I.T. Press, 1966.

Leuba, C. Images as conditioned sensations. *J. exp. Psychol.* 1940, **26**, 345–351.

Lindquist, E. F. *Design and analysis of experiments in psychology and education*. Boston: Houghton Mifflin, 1953.

Long, E. R., J. T. Hammack, F. May, and B. J. Campbell. Intermittent reinforcement of operant behavior in children. *J. exp. anal. Behav.*, 1958, **1**, 315–339.

Lorge, I., and R. L. Thorndike. *Lorge-Thorndike Intelligence Tests.* Boston: Houghton Mifflin, 1954.

Lott, B. E., and A. J. Lott. The formation of positive attitudes toward group members. *J. abnorm. soc. Psychol.*, 1960, **61**, 297–300.

Lovaas, O. I. Effect of exposure to symbolic aggression on aggressive behavior. *Child Developm.*, 1961, **32**, 37–44.

Maccoby, E. E., and P. K. Gibbs. Methods of child-rearing in two social classes. In W. E. Martin and C. B. Stendler (Eds.), *Readings in child development.* New York: Harcourt, 1954.

Maltzman, I. Thinking: From a behavioristic point of view. *Psychol. Rev.*, 1955, **62**, 275–286.

Maltzman, I., P. C. Raskin, J. Gould, and O. Johnson. Individual differences in the orienting reflex and semantic conditioning and generalization under different UCS intensities. Paper delivered at the Western Psychological Association meetings in Honolulu, 1965.

McNeil, D. The capacity for grammatical development in children. In D. I. Slobin (Ed.), *The ontogenesis of grammar.* New York: Academic Press, in press.

Mednick, M. T. Mediated generalization and the incubation effect as a function of manifest anxiety. *J. abnorm. soc. Psychol.*, 1957, **55**, 315–321.

Metropolitan Readiness Tests. New York: Harcourt, 1948.

Miller, G. A. Some preliminaries to psychologinuistics. *Amer. Psychologist,* 1965, **20**, 15–20.

Miller, N. E., and J. Dollard. *Social learning and imitation.* New Haven: Yale University Press, 1941.

Mowrer, O. H. *Learning theory and personality dynamics.* New York: Ronald, 1950.

Mowrer, O. H. The psychologist looks at language. *Amer. Psychologist,* 1954, **9**, 660–694.

Mowrer, O. H. *Learning theory and behavior.* New York: Wiley, 1960*a*.

Mowrer, O. H. *Learning theory and the symbolic processes.* New York: Wiley, 1960*b*.

Murray, A. A. *Explorations in personality.* New York: Oxford Univer. Press, 1938.

Noble, C. E. An analysis of meaning. *Psychol. Rev.*, 1952, **59**, 421–430.

Olson, D. R. From perceiving to performing the diagonal. Paper presented at the 1967 meeting of the American Psychological Association, Washington, D. C.

Orlando, R., and S. W. Bijou. Single and multiple schedules of reinforcement in developmentally retarded children. *J. exp. anal. Behav.*, 1960, **3**, 339–348.

Osgood, C. E. *Method and theory in experimental psychology.* New York: Oxford University Press, 1953.

Osgood, C. E. A behavioristic analysis of perception and language as cognitive phenomena. In *Contemporary approaches to cognition.* Cambridge, Mass.: Harvard University Press, 1957.

Osgood, C. E., and G. J. Suci. Factor analysis of meaning. *J. exp. Psychol.,* 1955, **50,** 325–338.

Osgood, C. E., G. J. Suci, and P. H. Tannenbaum. *The measurement of meaning.* Urbana, Ill.: University of Illinois. Press, 1957.

Paivio, A. Generalization of verbally conditioned meaning from symbol to referent. *Canad. J. Psychol.,* 1964, **18,** 146–155.

Patterson, G. R. Prediction of victimization from an instrumental conditioning procedure. *J. cons. Psychol.,* 1967, **31,** 147–152.

Phillips, L. W. Mediated verbal similarity as a determinant of the generalization of a conditioned GSR. *J. exp. Psychol.,* 1958, **55,** 56–62.

Piaget, J. How children learn mathematical concepts. *Scientif. Amer.,* 1953, **189,** 74–79.

Pollio, H. R. Word association as a function of conditioned meaning. *J. exp. Psychol.,* 1963, **66,** 454–460.

Pollio, H. R. Some semantic relations among word-associates. *Amer. J. Psychol.,* 1964, **77,** 249–256.

Razran, G. H. Stimulus generalization of conditioned responses. *Psychol. Bull.,* 1949, **46,** 337–365.

Reynolds, G. S. An analysis of interactions in a multiple schedule. *J. exp. anal. Behav.,* 1961*a,* **4,** 107–117.

Reynolds, G. S. Relativity of a response rate and reinforcement frequency in a multiple schedule. *J. exp. anal. Behav.,* 1961*b,* **4,** 179–184.

Rheingold, H. L., J. L. Gewirtz, and H. W. Ross. Social conditioning of vocalizations in the infant. *J. comp. physiol. Psychol.,* 1959, **52,** 68–73.

Rosen, B. C. The achievement syndrome. A psychocultural dimension of social stratification. *Amer. sociol. Rev.,* 1956, **21,** 205–211.

Ross, L. E. The decremental effects of partial reinforcement during acquisition of the conditioned eyelid response. *J. exp. Psychol.,* 1959, **57,** 78–82.

Russell, W. A., and J. J. Jenkins. The complete Minnesota norms for responses to 100 words from the Kent-Rosanoff word association test. *Tech. Rep. No. 11.* Contract No. N8 onr-66216 between the office of Naval Research and University of Minnesota, 1954.

Russell, W. A., and L. H. Storms. Implicit verbal chaining in paired associate learning. *J. exp. Psychol.,* 1955, **49,** 287–293.

Salzinger, K. Experimental manipulation of verbal behavior: A review. *J. gen. Psychol.,* 1959, **61,** 65–94.

Salzinger, K. S., K. Salzinger, S. Portnoy, J. Eckman, P. N. Bacon, M. Dentsch, and J. Zubin. Operant conditioning of continuous speech in children. *Child Develpm.*, 1962, 33, 683–695.

Samuels, S. J. The effect of experimentally learned word associations on the acquisition of reading responses. *J. ed. Psychol.*, 1966, 57, 159–163.

Schutz, R. E., and H. Naumoff. An application of Mowrer's sentence conditioning paradigms in developing evaluative meaning. *J. verb. Learning verb. Behav.*, 1963, 1, 459–462.

Shute, W. G., W. W. Shirk, and G. F. Porter. *Plane and solid geometry.* New York: American Book, 1960.

Sidman, M. *Tactics of scientific research.* New York: Basic Books, 1960.

Sidman, M. Operant techniques. In A. J. Bachrach (Ed.), *Experimental foundation of clinical psychology.* New York: Basic Books, 1962.

Skinner, B. F. *The behavior of organisms.* New York: Appleton, 1938.

Skinner, B. F. *Science and human behavior.* New York: Macmillan, 1953.

Skinner, B. F. *Verbal behavior.* New York: Appleton, 1957.

Skinner, B. F. Teaching machines. *Scientif. Amer.*, 1961, 205, 90–102.

Soffieti, J. P. Why children fail to read: A linguistic analysis. *Harvard educ. Rev.*, 1955, 25, 63–84.

Spence, K. W. The nature of theory construction in contemporary psychology. *Psychol. Rev.*, 1944, 51, 47–68.

Spence, K. W. *Behavior theory and learning.* Englewood Cliffs, N.J.: Prentice-Hall, 1960.

Staats, A. W. *A behavioristic study of verbal and instrumental response hierarchies and their relationship to human problem solving.* Unpublished doctoral dissertation, University of California, Los Angeles, 1955.

Staats, A. W. Learning theory and "opposite speech." *J. abnorm. soc. Psychol.*, 1957a, 55, 268–269.

Staats, A. W. Verbal and instrumental response hierarchies and their relationship to problem-solving. *Amer. J. Psychol.*, 1957b, 70, 442–446.

Staats, A. W. Meaning and word associations: separate processes. *Tech. Rep. No. 12*, Contract Onr 2305(02) between the Office of Naval Research and Arizona State University, 1959.

Staats, A. W. Verbal habit-families, concepts, and the operant conditioning of word classes. *Psychol. Rev.* 1961, 68, 190–204.

Staats, A. W. Comments on Professor Russell's paper. In C. N. Cofer and B. S. Musgrane (Eds.), *Verbal behavior and learning.* New York: McGraw-Hill, 1963.

Staats, A. W. *Human Learning.* New York: Holt, Rinehart and Winston, Inc., 1964a.

Staats, A. W. A case in and strategy for the extension of learning principles to problems of human behavior. In A. W. Staats (Ed.), *Human learning*. New York: Holt, Rinehart and Winston, Inc., 1964*b*.

Staats, A. W. Operant learning principles and communication. In A. W. Staats (Ed.), *Human learning*. New York: Holt, Rinehart and Winston, Inc., 1964*c*.

Staats, A. W. Conditioned stimuli, conditioned reinforcers, and word meaning. In A. W. Staats (Ed.), *Human learning*. New York: Holt, Rinehart and Winston, Inc., 1964*d*.

Staats, A. W. An integrated-functional learning approach to complex human behavior. *Tech. Rep. No. 28*, Contact Nonr-2794(02) between the office of Naval Research and Arizona State University, 1965.

Staats, A. W. An integrated-functional learning approach to complex human behavior. In B. Kleinmuntz (Ed.), *Problem solving: Research method, and theory*. New York: Wiley, 1966.

Staats, A. W. Emotions and images in language: A learning analysis of their acquisition and function. In K. Salzinger and S. Salzinger (Eds.), *Research in verbal behavior*. New York: Academic Press, 1967*a*.

Staats, A. W. Integrated-functional learning theory and clinical psychology: I. Human motivation and the conditioning therapies. In mimeo, 1967*b*.

Staats, A. W. Outline of an integrated learning theory of attitude formation and function. In M. Fishbein (Ed.), *Readings in attitude theory and measurement*. New York: Wiley, 1967*c*.

Staats, A. W. Categories and underlying processes, or representative samples and S–R analyses: Opposing strategies. Paper presented at the annual meetings of the American Psychological Association, Washington, D. C., 1967*d*.

Staats, A. W. Integrated-functional learning theory and language development. In D. I. Slobin (Ed.), *The ontogenesis of grammar: Facts and theories*. New York: Academic Press, in press, *a*.

Staats, A. W. Principles of the reinforcer (attitudinal) system: An integrated-functional learning conception of human motivation. In A. G. Greenwald, T. C. Brock, and T. M. Ostrom (Eds.), *Attitude change theory and research*. New York: Academic Press, in press *b*.

Staats, A. W., and W. H. Butterfield. Treatment of nonreading in a culturally deprived juvenile delinquent: An application of reinforcement principles. *Child Develpm.*, 1965, **4**, 925–942.

Staats, A. W., J. R. Finley, K. A. Minke, and M. M. Wolf. Reinforcement variables in the control of unit reading responses. *J. exp. anal. Behav.*, 1964*a*, **7**, 139–149.

Staats, A. W., J. R. Finley, J. G. Osborne, W. D. Quinn, and K. A. Minke.

The use of chain schedules in the study of reinforcement variables in a reading task. *Tech. Rep. No. 25*, between the Office of Naval Research and Arizona State University, 1963.

Staats, A. W., K. A. Minke, J. R. Finley, M. M. Wolf, and L. O. Brooks. A reinforcer system and experimental procedure for the laboratory study of reading acquisition. *Child Develpm.*, 1964b, **35**, 209–231.

Staats, A. W., K. A. Minke, W. Goodwin, and J. Landeen. Cognitive behavior modification: "Motivated Learning" reading treatment with subprofessional therapy-technicians. *Behav. Res. Therapy*, 1967, in press.

Staats, A. W., and C. K. Staats. Attitudes established by classical conditioning. *J. abnorm. soc. Psychol.*, 1958, **57**, 37–40.

Staats, A. W., and C. K. Staats. Effect of number of trials on the language conditioning of meaning. *J. gen. Psychol.*, 1959a, **61**, 211–223.

Staats, A. W., and C. K. Staats. Meaning and *m:* Correlated but separate. *Psychol. Rev.*, 1959b, **66**, 136–144.

Staats, A. W., and C. K. Staats. *Complex human behavior*. New York: Holt, Rinehart and Winston, Inc., 1963.

Staats, A. W., C. K. Staats, and H. L. Crawford. First-order conditioning of meaning and the parallel conditioning of a GSR. *J. gen. Psychol.*, 1962, **67**, 159–167.

Staats, A. W., C. K. Staats, and J. R. Finley. Operant conditioning of serially ordered verbal responses. *J. gen. Psychol.*, 1966, **74**, 145–155.

Staats, A. W., C. K. Staats, and W. G. Heard. Language conditioning of meaning to meaning using a semantic generalization paradigm. *J. exp. Psychol.*, 1959a, **57**, 187–192.

Staats, A. W., C. K. Staats, J. R. Finley, and K. A. Minke. Meaning established by classical conditioning controlling associates to the ^{uc}S. *J. gen. Psychol.*, 1963, **69**, 247–252.

Staats, A. W., C. K. Staats, and W. G. Heard. Denotative meaning established by classical conditioning. *Tech. Rep. No. 13* Contract Nonr-2794(02) between the office of Naval Research and Arizona State University, 1959.

Staats, A. W., C. K. Staats, W. G. Heard, and L. P. Nims. Replication report: Meaning established by classical conditioning. *J. exp. Psychol.*, 1959, **57**, 64.

Staats, A. W., C. K. Staats, R. E. Schutz, and M. M. Wolf. The conditioning of textual responses using "extrinsic" reinforcers. *J. exp. anal. Behav.*, 1962, **5**, 33–40.

Staats, C. K., and A. W. Staats. Meaning established by classical conditioning. *J. exp. Psychol.*, 1957, **54**, 74–80.

Staats, C. K., and A. W. Staats. Attitude development and ratio of reinforcement. *Sociometry,* 1960, **23**, 338–350.

Stevens, S. S. *Handbook of experimental psychology.* New York: Wiley, 1951.

Terman, L. M., and M. A. Merrill. *Measuring intelligence.* Boston: Houghton Mifflin, 1937.

Thorndike, E. L., and I. Lorge. *The teacher's word book of 30,000 words.* New York: Teachers College, Columbia University, 1944.

Triandis, H. C., and C. E. Osgood. A comparative factoral analysis of semantic structures in monolingual Greek and American college students. *J. abnorm. soc. Psychol.,* 1958, **57**, 187–196.

Underwood, B., and J. Richardson. Some verbal materials for the study of concept formation. *Psychol. Bull.,* 1956, **53**, 84–95.

Verplanck, W. S. The control of the content of conversation: reinforcement of statements of opinion. *J. abnorm. soc. Psychol.* 1955, **51**, 668–676.

Watson, J. B. *Behaviorism.* Chicago: University of Chicago Press, 1924.

Watson, J. B., and R. Rayner. Conditioned emotional reactions. *J. exp. Psychol.,* 1920, **3**, 1–14.

Webster's Seventh New Collegiate Dictionary. Springfield, Mass.: G. & C. Merriam Co., 1965.

Weinreich, U. Travels through semantic space. *Word,* 1958, **14**, 346–366.

Weisberg, P. Social and nonsocial conditioning of infant vocalizations. *Child Develpm.,* 1963, **34**, 377–388.

White, A. D. *A history of the warfare of science with theology in Christendom,* 1899 (1955 Ed.), New York: Braziller.

Whorf, B. L. *Language, thought, and reality.* J. B. Carroll (Ed.), New York: Wiley, 1956.

Wickes, T. A., Jr. Examiner influence in a testing situation. *J. consult. Psychol.,* 1956, **20**, 23–26.

Wilson, W. C., and W. S. Verplanck. Some observations on the reinforcement of verbal operants. *Amer. J. Psychol.,* 1956, **69**, 448–451.

Witryal, S. L., and W. F. Fischer. Scaling children's incentives by the method of paired comparisons. *Psychol. Rep.,* 1960, **7**, 471–474.

Woodrow, H., and R. Lowell. Children's association frequency tests. *Psychol. Monogr.,* 1916, **22**, No. 5.

Young, D. R., and W. A. Bousfield. Recall of connotative meaning. *Psychol. Rep.,* 1959, **5**, 319–320.

Zimmerman, D. W. Durable secondary reinforcement: Method and theory. *Psychol. Rev.* 1957, **64**, 373–383.

NAME INDEX

A

Alexander, H. M., 521, 586
Allport, F. H., 80, 585
Ameen, L., 352, 589
Ayllon, T., 352, 585
Azrin, N. H., 452, 465, 473, 585

B

Ball, R. S., 145, 585
Bandura, A., 426, 442, 450, 451, 585
Barnhart, C. L., 314, 493, 585
Berko, J., 160, 162, 163, 585, 586
Berlyne, D. E., 585
Bever, T. G., 154, 156, 168, 585
Bigge, M. L., 390, 585
Bijou, S. W., 237, 590
Birge, J. S., 187, 585
Blazek, N. C., 588
Bloomfield, L., 311, 314, 493, 585
Bousfield, W. A., 83, 181, 512, 586, 595
Brady, J. V., 240, 588
Brogden, W. J., 42, 586
Brooks, L. O., 239, 594
Brown, R. W., 143, 160, 161, 162, 163, 164, 167, 187, 586
Butler, R. A., 521, 586
Butterfield, William H., 351, 362, 364, 365, 368, 369, 376, 593

C

Campbell, B. J., 589
Carter, H. D., 453, 586
Chomsky, N., 5, 71, 154, 156, 586
Cofer, C. N., 47, 586
Cohen, B. H., 31, 586
Cohen, D. J., 353, 586
Cohen, E., 586
Crawford, Hugh L., 17n, 594

D

D'Amato, M. F., 138, 589
Das, J. P., 31, 586
Deese, J., 83, 586
Di Vesta, F. J., 31, 182, 439, 586
Dollard, J., 59, 349, 353, 354, 426, 442, 572, 587, 590
Dostálek, C., 142, 587
Downing, J. A., 289, 475, 477, 486, 489, 490, 587

E

Edwards, A. L., 116, 587
Ellson, D., 42, 48, 587
Ervin, S. M., 164, 587
Eysenck, H. J., 109, 587

F

Fernald, Grace, 350, 526
Ferster, C. B., 54, 236, 442, 562, 587
Finley, J. R., 112n, 226, 226n, 230, 232, 233, 234, 235, 239, 594
Fischer, W. F., 117, 595
Fodor, J. A., 157, 585, 587
Foley, J. P., 47, 586
Forehand, G. A., 178, 587
Fowler, W., 388, 587
Fraser, C., 160, 161, 164, 167, 586

G

Gewirtz, J. L., 591
Gibbs, P. K., 453, 462, 590
Goldman, L., 453, 587
Goodwin, W., 351, 375, 594
Green, B. F., 178, 587
Greenspoon, J., 353, 587

H

Hammack, J. T., 589

SUBJECT INDEX

A

Abnormal behavior, 350, 351–352, 354
  clinical treatment of, 546–548
  and reinforcer system, 434–435
Achievement, 452–453
Advertising, as conditioning, 39
Alphabet learning, 280–282, 284, 285–286, 308, 316, 317, 474–476, 485–495
"Animal" concept, 139–144
Arithmetic (*see* Number concepts; Numbers)
Attention, 394–395, 408–422
  conditioning control on, 410–414
  cross-modal control of, 414–420
  and discrimination, 421–422
  and imitational repertoire, 426–427
  verbal stimulus control of, 414–420
Attitudes, classical conditioning of, 32–34
Attitudinal word meanings, function of, 107–118
Autistic children, 547

B

Behavior (*see* Abnormal behavior; Cognitive behavior; Human behavior; Motor behavior)
Behavior modification, in the clinic, 546–548
  instructional-technicians used in, 374–379
  learning theory and, 346–379
  in nonreading delinquent, 355–374
  and "opposite speech" syndrome, 352–355
  in the schools, 548–556
  social reinforcement in, 351–352, 353–354
Behavioral repertoire, acquired in the home, 544–546
  attentional, 394–395, 408–422

imitational, 425–427, 441–451
intelligence as, 388–391
language as, 397–407
and memory, 405–407
parents as trainers of, 466–469
and reading acquisition, 509–511
stimulus control of, 446–451

C

Child learning apparatus, 323–325, 341–344
Classical conditioning, of attitude, 32–34
  communication developed by, 120
  of denotative meaning, 41–50
  of emotional word meaning, 13–40
  experimental - naturalistic research in, 14–15
  first-order, 11, 13–22, 91
  higher-order, 23–31, 34–40, 91–92, 94
  interaction of, with instrumental conditioning, 93–95, 106–118
  principle of, 12–13
  and reinforcement system, 432–433
  second-order, 23
  of sensory response, 41–50
  third-order, 23–24
  of word meaning, 13–40, 134
Cognitive behavior, in arithmetic, 202–215, 298–301
  experimental-longitudinal study of, 264–346
  innovational experiments in, 267–305
  in number concept learning, 202–215, 298–301, 325–328
  in preschool children, 262–263, 321–346
  and punishment, 345–346
  in reading, 218, 219–263, 280–293, 309, 316–317, 333–334
  reinforcement of, 269–274